TROUBLE BOYS
THE TRUE STORY OF
THE REPLACEMENTS

BOB MEHR

DA CAPO PRESS
A MEMBER OF THE PERSEUS BOOKS GROUP

Designed by Jack Lenzo
Set in ten point Janson by The Perseus Books Group

Library of Congress Cataloging-in-Publication Data

Mehr, Bob.
  Trouble boys : the true story of the Replacements / Bob Mehr.
    pages cm
  Includes bibliographical references and index.
   ISBN 978-0-306-81879-0 (hardcover : alk. paper) -- ISBN 978-0-306-82203-2 (e-book : alk. paper) 1. Replacements (Musical group) 2. Rock musicians--United States--Biography. I. Title.

  ML421.R47M43 2015
  782.42166092'2--dc23
  [B]

                              2015026791

First Da Capo Press edition 2016

Published by Da Capo Press
A Member of the Perseus Books Group
www.dacapopress.com

Da Capo Press books are available at special discounts for bulk purchases in the U.S. by corporations, institutions, and other organizations. For more information, please contact the Special Markets Department at the Perseus Books Group, 2300 Chestnut Street, Suite 200, Philadelphia, PA 19103, or call (800) 810–4145, ext. 5000, or e-mail special.markets@perseusbooks.com.

10 9 8 7 6 5 4 3

For Bob and Joey Stinson

CONTENTS

PART III: DREAMS AND GAMES

PART IV: THE LAST

Mates.

We controlled rage with humor, struck the wrong chords 1st to acquaint ourselves with disaster, to ease the inevitability of our next return. Our next assault.

Baring all, as an offsetting pose then . . . HIT, SCREAM, JUMP, CRASH as one.

Quicksilver morons. We love it, so we stop. Why? Because soon we won't and this way it won't hurt as much.

Afraid? Terrified. Out numbered. Retreat? "They'll kill us" never enters our mind.

We load and on 4 we charge laughing. The enemy babble: "I don't believe my eyes"; "What the fuck?"; "This is a trick."

Bang we land in their trench: "Gotta light?" *Hey, what do you guys think you're doing?*

"See ya!"

They aim at our backs as we fall over each other. The bullets always missed.

 **PAUL WESTERBERG,**
LETTER TO AUTHOR, 2012

INTRODUCTION

The family made sure his sleeves were rolled up so everyone could see the tattoos.

He'd gotten them as a kid, after being locked up in the cursed halls of the Red Wing State Training School. His left arm said LUV HER—for Kim, his first girlfriend, who'd broken his heart. On his right arm was a mystery: his initials, with three arrows shooting in different directions. He never told anyone what the arrows symbolized, though friends would tease him that they represented the three things he cared about most in life: music, beer, and drugs.

For several days, local newspapers had reported the basic facts: Bob Stinson, former "lunatic guitarist" of the Replacements, found dead in his Uptown apartment. He'd founded the group, then been fired from it in 1986, when he couldn't "curb his out-of-control lifestyle." A couple of stories hinted at his troubled background: broken home, in and out of juvenile institutions, long-standing addiction problems, recent diagnosis as bipolar.

A syringe had been discovered near where he lay in his apartment. Given his history, everyone assumed he'd expired from an overdose, or even committed suicide. Later, the coroner's final report would contradict the initial suspicions—not an OD but organ failure. Just thirty-five, Bob Stinson died of natural causes, his body and heart simply worn out. He'd gone to sleep and never awoke.

"When he died, he had a turntable in front of him, a bunch of records . . . a Yes record might've been playing, I think," said his brother, Replacements bassist Tommy Stinson. "That's the way he would want to go. He'd put a hunk of vinyl on and sit and listen and study. He was probably going, 'Fucking A—this is *great*.'"

The tone of the subsequent outpouring—memorials and obituaries in *Rolling Stone* and *SPIN*, the *New York Times* and the *Los Angeles Times*—was revealing. Nine years after Bob's firing, and four since the group's breakup, the

Replacements were suddenly spoken of in reverential terms. They had become "legends" without ever really becoming stars, an epitaph as unlikely as their beginnings.

They had come together as the children of war veterans and alcoholics, from families steeped in mental illness and abuse, products of Midwestern recalcitrance and repression. "That held the bond in a peculiar way," said front man Paul Westerberg. "We hit it off in ways that normal guys don't. We understood each other."

Back when they got their first little flush of fame, Westerberg would say, as a cockeyed boast, that they were losers, that there wasn't a high school diploma or a driver's license among them. They'd never had any clear-eyed ambition or direction. They got as far as they did only because they hungered: for attention, for love, for sanction, for volume, for chaos.

The band's music filled the funeral chapel that day, an insolent soundtrack for a send-off. Bob's mother, Anita Stinson, had asked Peter Jesperson—the man who'd discovered the group and been their closest ally—to make a tape of their early albums. He felt funny about a song like "Fuck School" blaring in a mortuary, but you don't deny a grieving family's request.

One by one, the surviving Replacements arrived: Paul, Tommy, drummer Chris Mars, and guitarist Slim Dunlap. This was the reunion none of them had wanted and all of them had feared. And there was Bob, still the center of attention, lying in his casket. When Westerberg walked in, "Johnny's Gonna Die" was playing. It hit him square in the face.

Johnny always takes more than he needs
Knows a couple chords, knows a couple leads

He'd written those lines about the doomed ex–New York Dolls guitarist Johnny Thunders after seeing him looking wasted and sounding brilliant at a concert back in 1980.

And everybody tells me that Johnny is hot
Johnny needs somethin', what he ain't got

"Bob picked up guitar, learned how to play a few rock songs, and then just beat the shit out of the thing for all the frustrations in his life," noted Westerberg. "He was a lot like Thunders. In his hands the guitar didn't scream; it cried for help, practically. We used to say Johnny made a guitar sound like an animal in pain. Bob had that too."

Two hundred or so mourners filled the pews. Bob's acoustic guitar leaned against the casket. In a quiet corner the Replacements gathered with Jesperson. The air was heavy for a moment. The group had fired Peter, then Bob, then Chris, and they'd sniped at one another in the press and in song lyrics. All of that was forgotten now.

"They say death brings you together," said Mars. "I hadn't seen Tommy for a long time, and I hadn't really seen Paul for a long time. We were talkin', shootin' the shit for a bit. But it was bathed in this sad, sad thing." Mars had done an etching for the cover of the memorial program: a Stratocaster with wings.

Bob's mother had asked Jesperson to deliver the eulogy, but Peter demurred—he didn't think he could get through it. The duty went to local musician–turned–rock writer Jim Walsh, who'd known the group since its early days. He spoke of Stinson's great appetite for life and noted how un-Bob-like the occasion felt: "He would've laughed at us in our suits today, the pomp and circumstance. He would've wanted to know where the beer was." Babes in Toyland drummer Lori Barbero, one of Bob's close friends, sobbed through a reading of the Lord's Prayer. Afterwards, people stood up and told "Bob stories," among them the young musicians he'd worked with after the Replacements.

Ray Reigstad had played with Bob for five years in Static Taxi, the band that had given Stinson new life after the heartbreak of his Replacements exit. ("That was like his new family," said Barbero. "They were all like brothers, and they treated him really wonderfully. It covered up the sore spot.") "It was the only time I was ever laughing and crying at the same time in my life," said Reigstad. Mike Leonard, who shared an apartment and a group, the Bleeding Hearts, with Bob for several years before his passing, recalled, "It was such a rock-and-roll funeral. Every musician that knew him was there paying their respects."

Anita Stinson sat stoically through it all. She'd been gripped by terror when she got the call about Bob a few nights earlier. "Then that passed. I don't think I got sad until, I bet, a month after the funeral . . . before the sadness and missing Bobby really hit me," she said. As she accepted condolences and sympathy, heard and felt the stories' emotion, a peculiar pride seized her: "As hard as Bobby had it, he did amazing things. He was loved by a lot of people."

Bob's sister Lonnie would remember "sadness, because you'd always hoped for more for him," she said. "And guilt, especially because of the way we were raised, what happened to us as kids, and feeling like I could've made a difference, or changed him somehow. And yet . . . there was relief that maybe his torture is over."

"The one thing I know when he died, and that was pretty immediate, was that he was safer," said Tommy. "He had a hard fucking time. He had a hard existence, just trying to be a human."

Up front, near the casket, was Bob's ex-wife Carleen and their six-year-old son, Joey. Bob's only child was a quadriplegic with cerebral palsy, unable to walk or talk. "But Joe was always very receptive to Bob, and he loved taking Joe around," said Carleen. "When Joe saw his dad at the funeral, he just reached out for his hand like he always did. He squeezed that great big hand of his. And when he didn't squeeze back, he knew his dad was gone."

A few rows behind, Paul Westerberg hung his head and wiped away tears. "I went downstairs for a cigarette, 'cause I couldn't bear it," he said. Westerberg had been vilified when Bob had been fired from the band; the pall was espe-cially heavy now.

As he stood smoking, a couple girls who'd known Bob in his final days approached him. "They made a point to come down and talk to me. They said, 'Bob loved you. Whenever he asked you for anything, he said you always gave it to him.' For those girls to seek me out and tell me that . . . I was like, 'Let the world think I'm a villain as long as I know what Bob thought and felt.'

"I knew we didn't hate each other. We were close and I loved him. He was Tommy's brother, but he was my brother too. And when he died, it all made us feel that much more vulnerable."

As the service concluded, Paul called to Carleen. He leaned in and whis-pered to her in a broken voice: "We were just kids. We didn't know shit. We were . . . just kids."

PART I   Jail, Death, or Janitor

[We were] miscreants who had no other choice, had no other road out. We were one of the few, the chosen, you know? It's either this or . . . jail, death, or janitor.

PAUL WESTERBERG

CHAPTER 1

Bob Stinson had dangerous bloodlines. His mother, Anita, came from Excelsior, Minnesota, a dozen miles outside of Minneapolis on Lake Minnetonka. Her father, Ernest Martin Hafner, was the first mystery in the family. "All I know is he left home when he was fifteen and started riding the rails," said Anita.

Hafner spent time in the Navy and then settled near Lake Minnetonka, where he met his wife, Virginia Lebens, born 1919 in Shakopee. Her family was Dutch and Polish, and big drinkers. "I have a family genealogy that traces to the 1840s or something," said Anita. "And every single relation was a drunk."

Virginia Lebens also battled mental health issues, problems that would intensify among later generations of the family. Two of Bob Stinson's cousins would commit suicide by hanging, one at the age of ten, the other at seventeen.

Ernest and Virginia had seven kids. Anita was the second oldest, born April 3, 1942, following big brother Tom and ahead of Mary, Eugene, Rosie, and twins Ronnie and Rita. Ernest was superintendent of the Water and Sewer Department of Excelsior; despite his fancy title, the Hafners led a modest existence. "Dad tried to feed seven of us on his little salary," said Anita. "We weren't poor, but it wasn't easy, I'm sure."

Anita was a fourteen-year-old eighth-grader when she met Neil Stinson at a dance. Some fifty years after the fact, she had difficulty recalling their initial spark: "Beats the bejeebers out of me. Can't help you there."

Granite-jawed, black eyes, dark crew cut, Neil wasn't bad-looking—the strong, silent type. He was an introverted high school dropout; he was also functionally illiterate.

Neil's family history was no less complicated than the Hafners'. Born in 1939 and raised in Mound, Minnesota, Neil was the fifth child of ten. His father disappeared early; his mother was such a severe alcoholic that the state eventually took her children away. Some were adopted, and some were put in foster care; those who were of age, or close, were left to fend for themselves.

After running away from foster homes a couple times, Neil moved in with his older sister Ruthie. Her husband, a roofer, taught him the trade, and Neil Stinson remained a roofer the rest of his life. His only other interests were hunting, fishing, and drinking.

Neil and Anita started going steady. "I was still in Catholic school then—I used to skip catechism class on Monday nights to meet him," she said. In the spring of 1959, she got pregnant. "My family being Catholic, they didn't talk about s-e-x. I hardly knew what was going on." She quit Minnetonka High and accepted Neil's shotgun marriage proposal.

On December 17, 1959, she went into labor. Since neither Excelsior nor Mound had a hospital, the baby was delivered one town over in Waconia. "Neil drove me there, then he left and got drunk with my brother for three days," said Anita. "The only thing I remember is they put a mask on my face and when I woke up it was three days later and I had a kid. Then they tell you, 'Now you have to nurse him.' I was like, 'What are you talking about?'"

Her firstborn son, Robert Neil Stinson, had blond hair, blue eyes, and a sweet disposition. "Bob was a prince, just a prince," said Anita. A couple months later, Anita was pregnant again. In November 1960, she gave birth to a daughter, Lonnie. "Because we were so close in age, me and Bobby were almost like twins," said Lonnie. "We were real close growing up."

Not yet eighteen, Anita struggled to care for her young ones. "I was a child, trying to raise two children. It was overwhelming," she said. What little social life she had revolved around drinking. "My parents took Bobby and Lonnie and said, 'It's time you got drunk.' So that's what I did. I was drunk for two days. That was the culture." Over time Anita, too, became an alcoholic.

Despite the children, their marriage was soon failing. Neil was a heavy drinker and tightfisted. He was also emotionally distant, particularly toward his son. When Bob was three, Anita said, "Neil was outside working on his car and Bobby went to be around him. Neil literally picked him up by the britches and ran him back into the house and told me: 'Take care of this kid.' I thought, *That's your son too.* There was no feeling there. Poor Bobby, it started young with him, when he was first rejected. I don't know why that scene sticks in my mind so much, but it does. It's still difficult. When I saw the way that was going, how Neil was, it just led me to think: *I gotta get out of this mess.*"

The couple separated in 1963. Anita got a job waitressing at Skippers Café in Excelsior. "Neil wouldn't give me any money for child support," she said. "We went to court over that. Being a roofer, he was making fairly good money. The judge asked him what he did with it. He said: 'I pay for groceries and rent, and I pay for my drinking and it's gone.'"

Anita looked west for an escape route. "My brother Tom had been in the Marines, stationed in San Diego, and he just raved about the place. It sounded like there was opportunity there. And I wanted to travel. I wanted to see new things." It was a major leap of faith: other than a few trips to Minneapolis, Anita had barely been out of her hometown.

"Leaving was an act of salvation and desperation," said Lonnie. "She didn't want to continue to live in a family of major dysfunction. Deep inside of her was that little piece of healthy rebellion. Her saying, 'I'm not going to live this unhappy, suppressed life that you tell me I'm supposed to.'"

In December 1964, Anita forged Neil's signature on his tax return check, went to the Super Value in Excelsior—where the clerks knew her—and cashed it. She had fifty bucks, two little kids, and three train tickets. They hopped aboard the *Twin Star Rocket* and headed for the Golden State.

* * *

When he finally noticed his wife and kids had disappeared without a word, Neil Stinson made some cursory efforts to locate them. "I think he called my mom's brother Tom to get ahold of us," said Lonnie. "I don't know that he ever found out where we were." Neil wouldn't bother much more than that—in fact, he would not communicate with his two children for another decade. Anita never filed for divorce; technically, they remained married.

In San Diego, Anita and the kids settled into a little cottage near the ocean. First she was a receptionist for a rug cleaners; then she saw an ad for a job at Lyman's Pizza & Bar, on C Street in downtown San Diego, a popular hangout for Navy and Marine men from the nearby ports and bases.

"I was a go-go dancer," said Anita. "We'd dance to a jukebox. I guess it would be comparable to Hooters nowadays. I wore go-go boots and a bikini. It was fun." It certainly beat slinging hash at Skippers Café in Excelsior.

Pert and pretty, Anita was popular among Lyman's clientele. "At Christmas, the whole side of the bar was filled with toys for my kids [that] the sailors had brought." Among them was a Kenner Close 'N Play record player that Bob claimed.

Life in San Diego was idyllic. "We'd go to the beach, catching starfish off the rocks, trapping crabs," said Lonnie. "Bobby loved the water."

Sun and sand, freedom and excitement—the move west had delivered Anita's dream of finding a better future for herself and her family. But she would soon give up the liberated lifestyle, only to settle down again.

* * *

Everyone at Lyman's knew him as Nick, the bartender. He was a shade under six feet, with jet-black hair and Gallic features. "He looked like a total Frenchman," Anita Stinson would recall of the man she spent much of the next decade with.

His full given name was Neely Horton Griffin. His people had been among the early Irish and French settlers of Glascock County, Georgia, in the mid-1800s. His forefathers fought on the Confederate side during the Civil War, but could do little to stop William Sherman's Union forces from scything through their home county. After the war, the Griffins remained in the area, farming the land for a couple more generations, until the Great Depression hit.

Born February 13, 1932, Nick moved to Cloud Lake, Florida, as a child, living there until he was nineteen, then joining the Marines during the Korean conflict. He trained at Parris Island and Camp Lejeune, but never made it overseas. Instead, he ended up at Camp Matthews outside San Diego, serving barely seven months before being discharged in 1952. He stayed in San Diego and eventually landed at Lyman's.

Griffin also had a musical streak. "He did play drums, but not professionally," Anita recalled. "He putzed around with them, I don't know where, but he had played."

Ten years older than Anita, Nick had been married twice and had three children from the first relationship. His boys, Billy and Alan, were grown, though another daughter, Linda, was still around in the midsixties, when he and Anita met. They were involved casually, then more seriously, and she and her children moved in with him. "I was raised in that era where there had to be a man in your life or you couldn't do anything," she said. "You couldn't even write a check—that's not a joke. You couldn't go into a bank and open your own account."

Griffin didn't care for Anita's kids, Bob in particular. Nick worked nights, slept and relaxed during the day, and didn't want a six-year-old boy tearing around his home. "Bob was always told he couldn't come in the house," said Lonnie. "So he'd go out and wander the beach or the canyons nearby."

The record player he'd gotten for Christmas offered a whole other world to explore. "He would save his money and buy these little 45 records of the Beatles," said Lonnie. "Bobby and I would wander downtown and go to record stores."

It didn't take long for Anita to realize that she'd made a mistake: Nick was a drunk and a degenerate gambler whose moods swung with the betting results. The affair might have ended early on, except in the winter of 1966 she got pregnant.

Their son, Thomas Eugene, was born on October 6, 1966. Anita named him after her two brothers, but because of her marital status, the boy was given the Stinson last name.

Tommy Stinson would inherit his father Nick's features—round-tipped nose, triangular jaw—but got his mother's coloring and bright personality. "As a baby, he was a joy," said Anita. "He had charisma from early on. You could tell from the look in his eye when he was little, he was full of spit and vinegar."

★ ★ ★

Buried in the archives of the Minnesota Juvenile Court is a thick case file on Bob Stinson from the early 1970s. In the section focusing on his early life, there's a one-paragraph description that sums up his decade living with Nick Griffin:

During the ten years that Mrs. Stinson lived with her boyfriend, Nick, Bobby was subjected to both physical and mental abuse at Nick's hands. . . . Nick was an irascible man who singled Bobby out for abuse. She estimates he beat Bobby with a belt approximately once a month. Bobby was the family scapegoat. His sister, Lonnie, was a family favorite. Bobby must have felt like an outsider in his own family and he freely admits that he hated Nick. It was probably during these years that he retreated into fantasy. According to his mother he never had any really close friends, which seems to indicate that distrust was an early component of his personality structure.

What the report didn't reveal was that for much of those ten years Nick Griffin was also abusing both Bob and Lonnie in far more serious ways.

"It was physical and sexual and verbal for both of us," said Lonnie. "With me, it was more the sexual and Bobby more the verbal. But all of it, for sure: I caught him [molesting] Bobby when we were real young. But I only caught him once. So I don't know how long or how extensive it was."

Both children kept silent, largely out of fear—that they wouldn't be believed, that they were the ones doing wrong.

At the time Anita was totally unaware; it went on while she was away at work. "You look back and you go, 'God, how could I have not known?'" said Anita. "You feel like you failed."

Griffin, who died in 1989, was possibly a serial child molester. Though he was never charged with any sex crimes, the Los Angeles County sheriff once held Griffin for a weekend in 1967 for loitering suspiciously near a grade school. "When he got back, he told me straight out that he'd been in jail because 'they thought I was watching kids in the schoolyard,'" recalled Anita. "Why the heck didn't that mean anything to me?"

Griffin's sexual abuse of the children started when Bob was only seven. "I know exactly in my mind the first time," said Anita. "I had been at work the night before and Nick was off. It had to have happened then, because the next day he was different. He wasn't Bobby anymore.

"That night we were having dinner, and Bobby couldn't eat. Then he started throwing up. He ended up throwing up all over the place. Lonnie and I took him to the doctor. He was throwing up nothing but bile. He had no fever, nothing. The doctor could not find a thing wrong with him."

Compounding the physical trauma was Griffin's belittling of Bob, in private and in front of the family. "Bobby never felt like he was worth anything because Nick always told him he wasn't," said Lonnie. "He grew up, even into his twenties and thirties, believing that. What hurts the most is what he did to my relationship with Bobby. We were tight until Nick came along. I was kept in the house, and Bobby was forced outside. That's the part of my life that I hate the most, what he did to us. And I know my mom: she'll probably take that to her grave."

Beyond their frequent verbal arguments, Nick was sometimes physically abusive toward Anita as well. She tried to end their relationship several times. "She'd leave him and she'd go back to him, leave him and go back to him," said Lonnie. "I think she knew in her heart it wasn't the right thing, but she didn't know how to not be there."

* * *

In 1969, Nick Griffin's mother died. He decided to move back to Florida and pledged to make a fresh start there with Anita and the kids. Eventually he got a job bartending at the Ramada Inn. Anita started working for Howard Johnson's on Okeechobee Road. They got an apartment on M Street in West Palm Beach.

Initially, things were stable, relatively speaking. The couple had a daughter, Lisa—whom Nick favored most—in 1971. "Lisa was the only child that I ever saw him be even a touch nurturing with," said Anita. Not so Bobby and Lonnie, who were reaching adolescence. "We tried not to have friends, we didn't want to bring them home because of Nick," said Lonnie. "I was in the house taking care of Tommy or Lisa, and Bobby was outside most of the time."

Nick began taking fewer bartending shifts and tried to earn his living instead as a gambler betting on greyhounds at the Palm Beach Kennel Club. Only in his early forties, he'd already developed emphysema because of heavy smoking. He was prone to dark rages, or worse.

Anita had become the family's main breadwinner. She served as a hostess for PGA Tour events as well as the fairly lucrative Howard Johnson's gig. "I made big tips, sometimes a hundred bucks a night—which was amazing back then," she said. Anita began socking the money away, eventually saving enough for down payments on a new car and a three-bedroom trailer home—but the banks wouldn't guarantee her loans, so everything was put in Nick's name.

Despite this new stability, Bob had started ditching classes in sixth grade and ran away for short periods of time. Once, he broke into a house and vandalized it. None of it came to the attention of the juvenile authorities.

Bob also developed into a bit of a shut-in, holing up in his room to avoid his drunken stepfather and to listen to and play music—first the Beatles and the Jackson 5, then the era's wilder rock artists he'd developed an adolescent affection for, in particular the albino blues guitarist Johnny Winter. Bob badgered his mother to buy him a guitar for Christmas; the instrument quickly became an obsession. "It was nothing for him to sit and plunk away at his guitar for eight, nine hours," said Lonnie. "That was his escape."

From there Bob found his way to prog rock and the band Yes, whose guitarist Steve Howe became his musical idol. The band's top 20 hit from 1972, "Roundabout," featuring Howe's furious electric runs and atonal soloing, would exert a profound influence on Bob's playing. He put together a couple of bands with neighborhood kids, staging some shows at the clubhouse of the trailer court. "Bob was only twelve or thirteen," said Lonnie, "but because he had such a passion, he would find people around him who would play."

In November 1973, Anita's father died. Ernest Hafner had left his wife and family not long after Anita had bolted for California. He spent a decade living and drinking in Colorado, then succumbed to cirrhosis.

"When Daddy died, it just dawned on me: 'What's left of my family is in Minnesota,'" said Anita. Her mother, Virginia, had relocated to Minneapolis. Their relationship was strained, but things with Nick had so deteriorated that Anita was considering every escape route.

An attorney informed Anita that her common-law relationship with Nick wouldn't be recognized by the state. She would have to battle for everything she wanted in court. But she was ready to cut her losses.

As Nick grew drunker and more belligerent than usual over the 1973 holiday season he raised his hand to Anita again. "I'd already told him, 'If you ever touch me again, I'm gone.'"

This time she meant it. Anita bought a couple of sea trunks and waited until she knew Nick would be gone for the night. Then she threw everything she could fit into them, gathered her four children, and fled to the Greyhound station.

"I had this one train with a little battery pack. That was my favorite toy," said Tommy. "It was so tight getting out of there that I couldn't bring that. And it was a thing I could've put in my pocket. It was like: 'We gotta go *now*.'" Bob was even more upset: "My mom made him leave his fucking guitar," said Tommy.

Bob and Lonnie, thankfully, would never see Nick Griffin again. But the damage he'd caused would not disappear. "My sister, she grew up and worked through all the shit my father did to her," said Tommy. "But my brother . . . he was such a broken kid at such a young age. He never really got past it."

CHAPTER 2

Paul Harold Westerberg was a child of the 1950s, just barely. The second son of Harold Robert Westerberg and Mary Louise Philipp, he hit the sheets on December 31, 1959, though he wasn't due for a few more days. "My ma always told me that she flipped a mattress that day to hurry up the process—so I would make it there in time to be a tax deduction," said Paul. Years later, in the song "Bastards of Young," he'd write: "Income tax deduction / One hell of a function."

His father Hal was born in 1918, the oldest of Robert Westerberg and Margaret Harris's six boys, and spent his first year in South Dakota before the family resettled in Minneapolis. "I don't remember a whole lot of him talking about his youth," said Paul of his father. "We've got a picture of him when he was four. Then it's pretty much blank until he hits the service."

Hal's passion was golf; he was a zero handicap as an amateur and played in regional tournaments. "He had illusions that he would be a professional golfer," said Paul. "That was his love and what he wanted to pursue." But after college came World War II, and Hal never got a chance to fulfill his dream.

The war deeply affected the Westerberg family: Hal's younger brother Billy was killed at Iwo Jima in the spring of 1944, and Hal fought in the Normandy Invasion that June. "He got off the boat and there was thousands of guys blown to bits," said Paul. "They had to walk through all the carcasses. It probably wrecked every guy who saw that for the rest of their lives."

After a few scotches, Hal would let slip that his particular duty had been to walk among the corpses of the fallen soldiers, collecting dog tags and personal items and prying wedding rings off bloated fingers to send to their wives and families back home. But otherwise, he didn't speak about the war. Hal was tight-lipped, period: "He was never a great communicator via words," said his son. "It was always a twinkle of the eye, or a roll of the eyes. He's a very smart guy. He's just quiet."

So were the Westerbergs generally. Primarily of Swedish and Finnish ancestry, with some Scotch and English blood added later, they became farmers and railroad workers in America. What showbiz there was came from Paul's mother, Mary Louise Philipp, who was German and Prussian on one side, Austrian on the other, and Catholic going back many generations.

Her brothers were musicians: Paul Philipp was a part-time trombonist (and full-time bus driver), and Bob Philipp was a pianist, first with his own band and then as a lounge entertainer working in downtown Minneapolis. Mary Lou also played a little piano: "I knew every word to every song that ever came out in my day," she said.

After his discharge, Hal returned to Minneapolis and worked at a department store. Nearly thirty, he was ruggedly handsome with dark hair and piercing eyes. He spied Mary Lou at the Minnesota State Fair in 1948, where her brother was playing a gig. "I had wanted to go to a baseball game, but my mother said, 'For once in your life you're going with your family,'" recalled Mary Lou. She was a ravishing twenty-four-year-old with warm features and a knowing smile, and Hal asked her to dance. They married later that year. A year after that, in 1949, she gave birth to Anne, the first of their five children; Julie followed in 1951, then Philipp in 1954. Paul and Mary came five and then eight years later.

Hal spent the bulk of his life in the auto business, mainly working for Warren Cadillac in Golden Valley. But he was inherently cynical about the business world, something he bred into Paul. "He'd come home and tell me, 'There's larceny in every salesman's heart.' Things like that stuck with me." So did the dealer-demo Cadillac Hal drove, which, Paul recalled, "always had a sticker in the window: FOR SALE."

Paul's first years were spent at 3734 Pleasant Avenue, kitty-corner from the Church of the Incarnation, where Hal and Mary Lou had been married. It was known as the Cathedral in the Pines, a working-class, Catholic, heavily Irish South Minneapolis neighborhood where the Westerbergs were surrounded by Patricks, Gallaghers, and Malarkeys. The house was within eyesight of the Catholic school that Paul attended until he was a teenager.

One of Westerberg's childhood friends was a roughneck named Scotty Williams. Williams came from a "wild-ass family of nine boys, who'd all served in the Marines," he recalled. Scotty was Paul's bad-boy buddy, his corrupting influence from an early age. "Me and Scotty smoked our first cigarettes in kindergarten, used an old Marine helmet for an ashtray," he said. "Nobody over at his house gave a shit."

A number of neighborhood kids played music, including Kevin Patrick, a gifted drummer who'd later join the Prince-affiliated band Mazarati. One of Paul's schoolmates was Jimmy Mars, whose little brother Chris played drums too. "Chris was a couple years younger, which at that age is an eternity," said Paul. "I didn't really know him, but I was always aware of him."

In 1965 the Westerbergs moved nearby to 4126 Garfield Avenue—a stately four-bedroom, three-level, prairie-style home with a wrought-iron fence. "My dad couldn't really afford it," said Paul. "But people would see the car and the house and go, 'Aha, your dad's rich.' I used to be embarrassed by that."

Mary Lou had instigated the move—her younger sister Peggy had married well, to a man rumored, only half-jokingly, to be mob-connected. (This same "uncle" later gave Paul amps and PAs from various nightclubs he was involved in.) "There was pressure for my dad," recalled Paul. "I think my mom was always pressing him, 'cause her younger sister had this and had that. So he tried to keep up, got a bigger house. When really all he wanted was to play golf and drink beer."

In the late '60s, Hal became head salesman at Anoka's Main Motors—only to return to Warren (later renamed Anderson) Cadillac within a few years. "They demoted him to, like, floor salesman," said Paul. "Then the seventies hit, with the oil and gas shortage, and he's stuck pushing these big cars. That's when times got a little funky."

Hal had already lost a chunk of money chasing his golf dreams when his daughter Julie went to work selling investment property in Arizona—an operation fronted by singer Pat Boone—and he decided to invest. "Basically my dad bought a fucking hunk of desert," Paul said. "He got hornswoggled." By the early seventies, Mary Lou was forced to get a job at a bank while Paul was in high school—"Probably to pay for my Catholic school education, which I'd end up throwing down the drain."

The Westerbergs and Philipps had always been big boozing families: "My cousins, my aunts, uncles, whichever side of the family," said Paul, "whenever they got together, they'd break out the liquor." For Hal, though, it was more than a social lubricant: "Like a junkie who needs it just to get straight," said Paul, "he'd have a couple quick belts when he got home. And then would drink until he'd go to sleep. But then every morning he was fairly chipper and ready to go."

Hal's problem was spoken of fairly openly. "My mom would say that on a regular basis: 'Such is life with an alcoholic,'" said Paul. "Not that she was teetotal by any means, but she could function without it." There was no violence in the house (apart from once when Hal disciplined Paul for "bugging my sister . . . he knocked me down and felt bad right away"), but his parents' moods and emotions vacillated. "My dad was depressed. My mother was anxious," said Paul. "A swell combination there."

When Paul was thirteen, one of his older sisters dared him to drink a glass of vodka. As he absorbed the drink's effects, his world changed. "What I felt was immediate release from all anxiety," he said. "I'd found the elixir of life that makes you calm and fearless. I think that's the alcoholic trigger. I started at thirteen, and I kept it up. It was in our genes."

* * *

From a young age, Paul Westerberg had a mind that seemed to work differently.

"It probably has to do with all the blows I took to the head," he would say, only half-joking.

When he was twenty months old, his sister Anne accidentally whacked him in the noggin with a baseball bat: "Just as my right cerebral cortex was forming," he said. At nine, swinging on a rope in a junkyard, he fell and cut the left side of his head badly; he was left with a permanently pointy Spock-like ear. "That probably impaired my hearing too—as well as knocking all the math, language, and reasoning out of me."

In school he sometimes had trouble making sense of words. "I don't know if you'd classify it as dyslexia," he said. "But even now, if you wake me up in the morning and have me read something, I turn some of the letters backwards. It forced another part of my brain to grow stronger."

Much of the memorable inverted imagery in Westerberg's songs would come from a real place in his mind. "I really do think the opposite of what I'm told. If [someone says,] 'White sheet rain,' I think, *Black blanket sun*. Musically too, I think the opposite of what makes sense sometimes." Schoolwork became a constant struggle. "I had to work really hard just to be an average student."

What came naturally was music. Paul never took formal lessons, but he could fiddle with the piano in the house, and his mother would lullaby him with "Hello Mary Lou" and "Come On-a My House." "I thought my mom wrote those," he said.

The proximity to his musician uncles also stoked his interest. "We'd go to my Uncle Bob's at Christmas, and he would play the piano. When it really got good was when the other uncle, Paul, would come over and crack out his trombone and they'd actually play jazz," he said. "That was pretty exciting to hear in somebody's living room."

The Beatles arrived when Paul was five, especially for his older sisters, who watched *Ed Sullivan* with their friends. "They're all squealing, 'Oh, Paul's so cute!' It definitely perked me up. Whatever they would've looked at—if it'd been Tab Hunter—I probably would have dug that. Fortunately, it was the Beatles and the Rolling Stones." His older brother Phil hipped him to folk and blues music. Inevitably, Bob Dylan had a formative impact; early on, Westerberg wrote "a vague rip of 'Mr. Tambourine Man,' called 'Mr. Tonic Guy' or 'Mr. Tonic Man.'"

Westerberg also absorbed early-seventies AM pop radio, putting a pair of transistor radios to his ears in bed each night. His friend Tommy Byrne's stepfather owned a bowling alley and would hand over discarded jukebox 45s. "It was pop music, bubblegum," he recalled, "whatever was a hit in 1970–71": "Here Comes That Rainy Day Feeling Again" by the Fortunes, "Temptation Eyes" by the Grass Roots, the Jackson 5's "I'll Be There," the Partridge Family's "I Think I Love You," even silly novelties like Daddy Dewdrop's "Chick-A-Boom (Don't Ya Jes' Love It)."

He bought his first real records in 1972, picking up *Seventh Sojourn* by the Moody Blues, mostly to impress his sisters. He also got *Never a Dull Moment*, the fourth solo LP by Rod Stewart, the laddish, raspy-throated singer for the Faces. Paul would stare at the unusual album cover—Stewart looking bored and deflated, sitting in an armchair—and wear the record out, absorbing its raw, beautiful folk songs and loose-limbed rock numbers. Later, for a couple of days before a session, Paul would shout at the top of his lungs to get Stewart's huskiness into his voice.

He also fell for the glam rock coming from the United Kingdom circa 1972. "I was a Slade fan all the way. That was, for that one year, year and a half, my favorite thing," he said. "Parents thought it was asinine. I thought it was exciting."

Paul was a small kid—and his mother had enrolled him in school earlier than normal—but still played baseball through eighth grade, though the glasses he was prescribed at age nine made it hard to see the ball. "I was always pretty fast. My reflexes were very good. But I was mostly a tenacious benchwarmer. By the time I was ten, I was absorbed in listening to rock-and-roll and trying to get a guitar for years until I got one." He'd initially wanted to play drums. "My mother's words of wisdom were: 'Some musicians can get one girl, but remember: a guitar player always has his pick.' How right she was."

He bought his first guitar, a cheap Harmony Sovereign acoustic, off his sister when he was twelve, for $10: "Mowed the lawn about ten times to get it. The neck had gotten so bowed I couldn't even play a chord. But that was very good. It was almost like exercising with weights on your leg."

Westerberg wasn't a natural performer. "If I sang, I'd do it from underneath the table," he said. "One time, I played a little song for my mom and dad on the guitar, something that I told them I wrote for them, for their anniversary. They looked really embarrassed. That was the last time I ever did that." Mostly, he devoted himself almost secretly to the instrument. "My plan was to learn the thing and pull it out one day and wow them."

* * *

By the early seventies, Phil Westerberg had become something of a tearaway, often in trouble with the law. "He was the total black sheep of the family—in jail about five times," said Paul. "He didn't really do anything bad. He did stupid things. He definitely ran with some criminal dopes. One time he came home with the bullet holes in his car, all beat up."

During this period, Paul said, he and his younger sister, Mary, "went under the radar. That was 'the great distraction' for my parents. I saw my mom go from happy, when I was young, to very hand-wringing in my early teens. I used to get that 'don't turn out like your brother' shit. I heard that more often than I think was necessary."

He also heard the music Phil sometimes made. "My brother had friends who were musicians, and I used to hang when they would come home drunk late at night and I would sit and watch them," he said. "I was taught some shit from a few of his buddies—they were into everything from Zeppelin to bluegrass. So I got a crash course on everything from mandolins to guitar solos."

Paul would spend years practicing undisturbed. "The guitar became my companion."

CHAPTER 3

In January of 1974, Anita Stinson and her children arrived from Florida with little more than the clothes on their backs to a freezing Minnesota winter. "I remember how devastated me and Bobby were," said Lonnie Stinson. "We were sad to leave our friends so suddenly. It was so cold. We didn't have clothes for that. And we didn't have money to buy clothes." They headed to the house of Anita's mother, Virginia, where the kids were given generation-old hand-me-downs, supplemented with items from Goodwill.

Showing a resilience that would mark his character going forward, seven-year-old Tommy adapted best. "The first thing I remember was waking up for school and walking outside and there was snow up to my shoulders," he said. "I'd never even seen snow. I remember embracing it." The move, said Anita, "was the most traumatic for Bobby. As difficult as the situation in Florida was, that's where his friends were."

They'd barely been in Minneapolis a couple weeks when Bob, then fifteen, tried to run away back to Florida, hitchhiking all the way to the Iowa border before the cops picked him up. Anita's brother Gene retrieved him. Years later, in counseling, Bob would admit murderous impulses toward Nick; it's possible he'd gone to seek revenge.

For the first time in a decade, Bob and Lonnie visited their father, Neil Stinson. It went awkwardly: Neil was still cold and uncommunicative toward his only son. "When they left, Neil gave Lonnie a hug and kiss good-bye," said Anita. "Bobby wanted a hug and kiss. Neil wanted no part of it. Bobby didn't go back to see him."

Bob enrolled in ninth grade at Folwell Junior High and quickly began skipping class, attending forty-one days and missing forty-eight during his first semester. His grades had been average in Florida. In Minneapolis they plummeted: Fs across the board, except for music, where he earned a D. The only bright spot during this period was Kim Jensen, one of Lonnie's friends—a pretty redhead Bob began dating. She liked the fact that he could play guitar.

After a few months at her mother's house, Anita rented the upper half of a duplex on Eighteenth Avenue. Bob set up shop in the attic, blasting his stereo and hanging black-light posters. He got a part-time job cooking at Pizza Shack on Lake Street and began to frequent the nearby Suneson Music Center. The owner, Roger Suneson, hosted weekend picking parties and numbered big-name country stars—Merle Haggard, Charley Pride, Dave Dudley—among his clientele. Suneson's musical bent is probably the reason Bob began playing a Fender Telecaster, a model popular with country players, and he soon amassed several other guitars.

When Bob wasn't playing in his attic, he'd cruise around Uptown Minneapolis exploring, much as he'd walked the canyons and beaches of California and Florida. The Stinsons' place was near railroad tracks that he'd walk along while ditching school, alone with his thoughts.

Adult supervision was scarce: Anita worked as a waitress at the Uptown Bar on Hennepin Avenue, a beer joint–cum–private dancer club owned by pharmacist-businessman Frank Toonen. "As a waitress, you would have to dance with the customers," said Anita. "It floored me. I said, 'I'm not dancing with that drunk.' They said: 'That's part of your job.'"

After finishing her day shifts, she'd stay on and drink through happy hour. She began seeing an engineer and fellow drinker named Doug McLean. "Doug was mean," recalled Lonnie. "He was not as harmful as Nick, but he was a jerk. We'd be home alone. It was almost like we had our own apartment."

Anita and Doug quickly got serious, and she finally decided to file for divorce from Neil Stinson in order to marry McLean. This did not sit well with her oldest son. "Bob's impression of any man was going to be negative," said Anita.

Later, Bob would tell a social worker that he "gets so angry at Mr. McLean that he would like to beat him up with a baseball bat." Such threats carried a real weight: Bob may have been a child emotionally, but he'd quickly grown into a strapping five-foot-nine and 160 pounds.

His behavior was becoming disturbing. In the summer of 1974, he got angry at Lonnie and a group of friends and shut himself in his room. The kids wanted him to come out, but he didn't want to face them, so he jumped out of the second-floor window to escape. Another time he jumped off a railroad bridge onto a moving train. He avoided serious injury both times.

Early that September, Kim broke up with Bob. He was devastated at losing the one good thing to happen to him in Minneapolis. "He didn't have the coping skills to get through that grieving and pain," said Lonnie.

There is some suggestion in Bob's welfare report that he may have tried to commit suicide during this period and was hospitalized as a result. Those portions are largely redacted; neither Anita nor Lonnie recalled any specific incident. What is clear, however, is that Bob was cutting himself with a razor, "playing tic-tac-toe on his arms."

In October, he began to turn violent toward his siblings. He hit Tommy and chased him around the house with a butcher knife. Bob insisted he was only "playing around." He also threatened Lonnie and tore up her yearbook, then tried to set fire to the bathroom. Anita told Bob's assigned social worker that he "showed no emotion except anger" and never cried. The welfare report noted that Bob had also smashed all of his guitars: "[He] takes his anger out on himself as well as others."

Something needed to be done. On October 15, Anita took him to the St. Joseph's Boys' Home, dropping him off there with no real explanation. Bob thought he was being punished for skipping school. It would later transpire that the decision was largely Doug McLean's. "If you were my kid, I would have done this a long time ago," he told Bob on the drive to the home. In fact, McLean had contacted a caseworker he knew there personally.

Bob was left at St. Joseph's for a week with no contact with his family. Scared and confused, he was assigned to a welfare agent from Hennepin County's family counseling service named Margarette Appleby.

She contacted the family, and after some back and forth, Anita finally agreed to bring Bob home. Appleby conducted counseling sessions with him and his mother, and things seemed to improve for a time. But after a few months the erratic behavior came back.

In February 1975, Bob got into a fight with Tommy and threatened to burn the house down. Around that time, Doug McLean moved in—he and Anita would marry in April—and promptly got into a physical altercation with Bob, throwing him against a wall. Bob ran away for several days.

"Mr. McLean has a fiery temper of his own, says Bobby hasn't given him a chance and Bobby baits him," noted Appleby in her case log. McLean told Appleby: "The only way you can trust [Bob] is to hold a gun on him twenty-four hours a day." He wanted Bob sent away permanently, committed to the St. Cloud Children's Home, a teen mental health facility run by the Catholic Charities, until he was eighteen, then to enlist him in the military.

Finally, Lonnie was compelled to tell Anita the real reason her brother had become so out of control and antagonistic. In front of Appleby, Bob's fourteen-year-old sister revealed to her mother everything Nick Griffin had done—the years of sexual, physical, and mental abuse.

Anita was dumbfounded. "For me, at that age I needed to know she believed me, and the way she responded told me she didn't," Lonnie said. "She was in shock. But I took it as she didn't believe me."

"I think I believed her," said Anita. "But I was like 'Why did you wait to tell me until now?'" Anita had been a victim of Nick's abuse herself, but Lonnie's revelations were beyond anything she'd ever considered. Suddenly, all the disconnected clues made sense.

Margarette Appleby asked Anita if the family wanted to prosecute Nick. "I remember that social worker saying, 'We have a statute of limitations of seven years, so you'll have to make a decision,'" said Lonnie.

Still reeling from the revelations, the last thing Anita wanted to do was be forced to go back to Florida, or have her kids ever face Nick in court. "I didn't want my children to ever see him again," she said. Nick Griffin's name would never be uttered in the Stinson house again, except at the end of a stream of damnations and curses.

* * *

For Bob, living under the same roof as Doug McLean seemed untenable. The next few months saw more calm broken by spasms of anger and violence between Bob and McLean or his siblings, followed by more self-destructive behavior. At Appleby's urging, Bob was finally examined by a psychiatrist named Dr. Joel Finkelstein. The specific findings of his examination are unknown, but he did recommend that Bob be placed in a residential treatment center.

In the spring of 1975, Bob was sent to the St. Cloud Children's Home. Anita resisted, but McLean on one side and Appleby on the other were pushing. "That was the last thing he needed, in my opinion, to be separated from the family," said Anita.

St. Cloud was an unsecured facility, and Bob ran away four times in just a couple months, hitchhiking across the state for days at a time. He'd also started drinking for the first time and was beginning to steal: shoplifting food from a grocery store, breaking into his grandmother Virginia's house and taking cash. Then he'd turn himself in to the Minneapolis police.

After another escape in May, the cops returned him to St. Cloud. Supervisors noted that he was still drunk when he arrived. He was assigned to the facility's substance abuse treatment center—but ran away again. Eight days later, Bob turned up back at his family's house. His mother and Appleby took him to the Juvenile Center in Minneapolis, where he faced a series of "absenting" charges, and a detention hearing was held.

Bob was sent to the Eastern Region Reception Center for Boys, where for the next few weeks he was observed and given a series of mental and behavioral evaluations. He showed average to below-grade ability in standardized reading and math tests and unwillingness to do his work. It was noted that Bob spent most of his time at the center disengaged, reading rock magazines. Asked about his goals, Bob said he planned to finish high school, but not to attend college: "His only vocational preference is to become a singer and make money."

After several weeks, it was determined that he was "incorrigible." A report recommended he be remanded to the State of Minnesota Commissioner of Corrections. Barring some dramatic change, he'd be in the state's custody until he was twenty-one.

His next stop was Red Wing.

* * *

The State Training School at Red Wing had a notorious reputation as the San Quentin of "juvenile prisons." Built in 1889, it was a foreboding, castlelike complex on the outskirts of the city of Red Wing, off Highway 61, an hour southeast of Minneapolis. For nearly a century it had been the place where Minnesotan kids guilty of any crime short of murder were sent.

By the time Bob Stinson arrived in the summer of 1975, Red Wing was no longer the draconian penal colony of legend. Beginning in the late sixties, the school's programs were dramatically modernized, reflecting a more progressive approach to rehabilitating young men. It housed some 500 boys in a series of cottages spread across several hundred acres.

Bob was settled into Red Wing's Harvard Cottage. Though it was a secured facility, he had no trouble finding his way out, running away again at the end of July, after just two weeks, then again in September. Both times he was caught and returned within a few hours. On his third attempt in October, he disappeared for eight days before being brought back in.

Bob actually told his counselors that he craved the structure that Red Wing provided. What he was escaping was the peer-based rehabilitation program in which he had been placed.

A pioneer in treating troubled youth, Harry Vorrath had created the Positive Peer Culture (PPC) program and implemented it in New Jersey, Kentucky, and Washington, DC, with considerable success. He was brought to Red Wing following a 1968 incident: over a hundred kids staged a mass runaway. PPC, Vorrath wrote in 1974, was "designed to 'turn around' a negative youth subculture and mobilize the power of the peer group in a productive manner . . . in group sessions and day-to-day activities." Unlike most traditional treatment approaches, PPC did "not ask whether a person wants to receive help but whether he'd be willing to give help. As the person gives and becomes of value to others he increases his own feelings of worthiness and builds a positive self-concept."

But Vorrath's "positive caring behavior" system did not serve Bob well. "When discussing things he often grimaces or displays a nervous sort of smile, and this frequently leads to confrontations with his peers as they think he is laughing at them when he is not," ran a report on Stinson from the summer of 1975. Rather than be a helpful force among his peers, Bob was more inclined to play the clown: "Bob will act foolish and get others to act foolish as well in an attempt to be accepted," noted his group leader Michael Kilen.

What disturbed Bob most was having to his discuss his problems with the other boys: "He has only reluctantly told the life story and even then has made his difficulties appear relatively inconsequential." Instead, he'd disappear into his room and obsessively practice guitar, deconstructing the playing on Johnny Winter's *Saints & Sinners* or Yes's *Fragile* with single-minded focus.

In recent decades, doctors and researchers have found that music therapy and its unique features can help emotionally disturbed children, particularly the survivors of sexual abuse. For Bob, those Johnny Winter and Yes licks were an essential self-therapy. The Red Wing counselors simply saw music as a distraction.

Twelve months in, it was clear to his counselors that Bob was making no appreciable progress at Red Wing. Nor was he ready to go back to his family. Instead, the authorities tried to place him in a Minneapolis group home where he might get more individualized attention.

To celebrate his release, Bob and several other boys gave themselves home-made tattoos. "Me and three other guys sat with a bottle of Indian ink and a sewing needle," said Bob, who tattooed LUV HER—an homage to his ex, Kim Jensen—on his left forearm, and his initials, B.S., along with a trio of mysterious arrows, on his right.

In May 1976, Bob was formally granted parole from Red Wing and committed to Freeport West, on Twenty-Seventh Avenue in southeast Minneapolis. He was enrolled at the Portland Transitional School to ease his move back to high school. Bob also began one-on-one counseling sessions. More and more, his case file would acknowledge the guitar as a possible path to a more stable future.

"It has been suggested that Bob's ability or potential ability be evaluated so that he can be encouraged or discouraged appropriately," one progress report guardedly noted. "If he had some potential and maintains the interest, it would seem reasonable to arrange guitar lessons."

★　★　★

Robert Flemal first laid eyes on Bob Stinson as he stood on the flat roof of the Freeport West house, wailing on guitar, eyes closed. *That guy plays pretty good,* thought Flemal. *I hope he ends up being my roommate, so he can show me how to play.*

Born in Michigan and raised in Bob's hometown of Mound, Minnesota, Flemal had been a teenage truant and thief. "I got caught stealing a car," he said. "My dad just said he was gonna let the state deal with me. So I ended up in Red Wing." Late in the summer of 1976, Flemal was paroled to Freeport West. He and Bob would room together. "I felt there was a reason we were put together," said Flemal. "We both needed music to keep us sane. Bob was like a twin brother. Our birthdays were only a few days apart."

Stinson and Flemal were among a dozen kids living at Freeport, which required its residents to attend school, get jobs, and take part in loosely structured group activities. For a time, Bob and Robert both attended Marshall University High School. Flemal graduated; Bob dropped out. In the fall of 1976, Stinson got a dishwashing gig at Mama Rosa's, an Italian joint in Dinkytown near the University of Minnesota, and Flemal was soon working there too. "We started saving our money and spending it on musical instruments," said Flemal.

Together they'd haggle deals at Suneson's. "We could put down a hundred bucks on a seven-hundred-dollar guitar and [Roger Suneson] let us take it home," said Flemal, who picked out a Gibson SG. "Before long we were playing up a storm."

Bob would teach Flemal the rudiments and show him tricks. "He would take the needle and set it down on a record and learn a couple licks," said Flemal. "And take it back and set it down again and learn more. He was really dedicated."

Freeport was supposed to be a chemical-free group home, but, said Flemal, "we took acid, smoked pot, tripped on LSD. I remember getting some angel dust. I took a couple hits and it laid me out. Bob did it and he liked it. There was nothing he didn't like, I don't think."

Flemal also recalled that Bob drank secretly and heavily. "There [were] mornings I couldn't believe he was drinking first thing. I was like, 'It's way too early for that crap.'" Bob was busted several times at Freeport and forced to quit his job at Mama Rosa's as punishment. He eventually got back on track and returned to the restaurant full-time.

Flemal and Stinson decided to start a band together. "None of us had any religion in our lives. Music was our religion," said Flemal. Determined to get back home, Bob focused on convincing Freeport West's counselors that he was ready for release. Part of that meant a rapprochement with his family. He began counseling sessions with his mother.

There were dark, difficult moments together as Bob and his mother discussed the years of abuse at Nick Griffin's hands. "During one of the counseling sessions at Freeport House, I asked Bobby, 'How did you feel?'" recalled Anita. Bob replied, she said, "If I'd had a gun, I'd have blown his head off."

Anita's marriage to Doug McLean had been short-lived—another controlling alcoholic who lost his job and then lost the plot. With McLean gone, Anita agreed to take Bob back. "He seemed to be more independent," said Anita. "He wanted to be part of the family, but only to a point."

Bob asked his mother to let Flemal live with them. Flemal didn't want to return to his own family in Mound. "I saw nothing to gain living back home and living under my dad's rules," he said. "I just wanted to have my hair long, play music, and nobody tell me what to do. And Anita, she was willing to take me in."

Bob was paroled from Freeport in the summer of 1977 and quickly proved he'd changed. "Bob's mother is thrilled because Bob is getting along fine at home with the family and fitting in very well," noted Minnesota Department of Corrections agent J. Robinson.

That December, Robinson recommended a satisfactory discharge for Bob on his eighteenth birthday. "Bob has . . . not simply 'not been caught' or made superficial changes. His changes appear to be deep and integrated into his personality so are more likely to last."

Robert Neil Stinson's final juvenile report—case number 20937-A—also mentioned his new band. "He is still heavy into his music, has a group formed and hopes to perform when he feels good enough," wrote Robinson. "Others say he is good enough already."

CHAPTER 4

The Academy of the Holy Angels in Richfield, a first-tier suburb just south of South Minneapolis, had been an all-girls school for most of its first century. Founded in 1877 as an institution of learning for fledgling nuns, it became a private day school in 1931. It began admitting boys in 1972. Paul Westerberg was a member of the second class that included males. "I was a little hesitant to go 'cause it had been all-girls," he said. "But that also meant there was gonna be a lot of chicks there."

Most of the students were from Richfield, a solidly working- and middle-class area. Though none of his classmates' families owned lake homes like the "cake eaters" of fancier enclaves like Edina, Westerberg still felt slightly disconnected from them. He was a city kid and they were suburbanites, even though the distinction was a matter of a couple miles.

Other than the standard Catholic school uniform—white shirts and brown slacks, no exceptions—Holy Angels offered a fairly liberal environment. The staff was mostly laypeople; there were just a handful of nuns left, and the only priest was the principal. When Westerberg arrived, the school had gone to a modular scheduling system that gave students long, leisurely gaps between classes on an open campus.

Holy Angels also accepted troubled kids from other schools, mostly alcohol and drug offenders. "They sent these users from the inner city to come hang out with us, thinking us good Catholic kids would rub off on them," said Westerberg. "But they rubbed off on us." Pot was easy to find, and students regularly toked up on the campus's fringes.

Despite its laxity, Westerberg chafed at Holy Angels. His grades, good through junior high, fell dramatically. "I literally went from getting As in ninth grade to Bs in tenth, to Cs, Ds, and Fs by eleventh grade," he said. "It was the worst four years of my life." Westerberg's academic struggles were partly due to worsening eyesight. "By the time I was fourteen, I couldn't see the blackboard. And I didn't want to wear my glasses." It was also the chief reason he chose not to learn to drive: "I knew I'd be the first one to ram a car into a tree."

Paul was convinced music was his destiny. "I learned about rock-and-roll secondhand through magazines," he said. "I was weaned on critics. I read every issue of *Creem, Rolling Stone, Crawdaddy!*—I never saw bands until I was [playing] in one."

As a freshman, Westerberg won a radio call-in contest. "For the prize, you had a choice: they'd give you some albums or a couple hours of free recording time, and play your song on the air." Westerberg chose the latter, taking the bus to a small downtown studio with his guitar. "I recorded an acoustic song, an instrumental that I made up. I put a little harmonica on top and a little mandolin, which I didn't really know how to play, but I was very good at Brian Jonesing shit." A week later the song made its debut on the station. "I listened with my sister and my mom and Diane Martini, the girl next door. Of course, they never played my thing again."

The Harmony Sovereign acoustic that Paul bought off his sister had outlived its usefulness by the time he was fifteen. One day in his brother's attic bedroom, Westerberg had a fit and smashed it—the first guitar he destroyed.

Though he'd learned to play in a folksy style, Paul jumped to an electric guitar—a used black Stratocaster he played through a battered forty-watt Carvin amplifier.

"I used to play really loud," he said. "One day the woman down the block left a bunch of instructional books on the doorstep, rang the bell, and ran off. It was sort of a hint." Paul took it: "I read enough and learned enough, about jazz even. I wanted to learn all that shit and then forget it and do my own thing."

Though he was relatively small—a wiry five-foot-seven—Paul's hands were perfectly suited for the instrument: he had long, thick fingers with unusually large fingertips. His deficiencies, however, would define his playing style: he had congenitally malformed pinkies that curved dramatically toward his fourth fingers, a condition known as clinodactyly. "I was born that way, though for years I thought my brother had broken them: 'Look what Phil did to me!'"

Westerberg's real limitation was his elbows. The ulnar nerves in both arms had been problematic from a young age and hampered his fretting flexibility. "Every time I bend my arm it hurts. So I had to find a guitar style where I didn't have to move around so much," he said. What he found was "more open-tuning stuff, where I wouldn't have to change the fingers."

Westerberg was a natural rhythm guitarist, with an unrelenting right hand. He copped his chunky playing style studying Keith Richards and Mick Taylor on records and in the 1973 concert film *Ladies and Gentlemen: The Rolling Stones.* "I went and saw that a bunch of times when it came out," he recalled.

But he would ultimately stake his claim playing lead. "Alvin Lee [of Ten Years After] was a big influence. But to my ear, [Duane] Allman was the best. He had the feel that no other white guitarist had. It all came from Duane's tone—every note sounded good. I think that's where I learned, even if I couldn't play flashy, at least make the handful of notes you play have a pleasing sound or texture to them. I spent the next few years learning to be a hot-shit player . . . until I realized that was nowhere."

* * *

Like Westerberg, John Zika was the fourth child of five, and a strain of depression ran through his Czech-Irish family. Unlike Paul, Zika was an exceptional athlete, starring in baseball, football, and hockey; he was already being scouted in eighth grade. Popular and charismatic, he wasn't the usual jock type. "He had a cerebral, artistic side," said his friend and Holy Angels classmate Ben Welter, who recalled of Zika's hockey playing, "On the ice, John worked out his demons in a way that no one else did. He would typically get in drop-the-gloves fights."

In high school, Zika underwent a fairly dramatic change after Welter's older brother, Vincent, committed suicide during John's freshman year. By sophomore year, Zika had quit sports entirely. "He was more into writing music, writing poetry, and reading," said Welter. At Holy Angels, Zika was suspended when he got caught with pot in his locker; soon after, said Welter, "he told his Spanish teacher . . . to fuck off, and walked out. Everyone was talking about it."

Westerberg only knew Zika by reputation, but was in awe. "He was like James Dean. He stuck out by a country mile from the rest of the kids. In the early seventies, we're walking around in our platforms and bell-bottoms and he had straight leg jeans, plaid shirts, and a rope for a belt. I looked up to him."

What really caught Westerberg's attention was Zika's infamous performance at Holy Angels' annual talent contest: instead of presenting a little magic act or a polite folk number, Zika and another student named Braun performed an electric version of the old blues number "Rolling and Tumblin'." "In the middle of the song, Braun put the guitar between two chairs, jumped up in the air, and smashed it, and John took his harp and threw it into the crowd," said Westerberg. "Then he whips out another guitar and John whips out another harp and they keep playing. That was the most anti-authoritarian thing I'd ever seen in my life. He instantly became a legend among us outcasts."

Not long after, Zika sought out Westerberg. "I remember the day he spoke to me. I was leaving school going for the bus," he said. "The bus was starting to leave, and Zika appeared, came up behind me, and said, 'Let's catch this motherfucker.' And I immediately started to run next to him. That was how we started running together."

Zika was a blues purist — hated Led Zeppelin, loved Chess Records. He tried to press Paul into playing as a duo at the Artist's Quarter, a South Minneapolis jazz club. "He fancied himself a man of the road. I was scared shitless: 'Go play for people in a real bar? No way.'"

The two fell in with Holy Angels' other would-be musicians, including drummer Dave Zilka, smoking weed near the giant oak trees on the campus's periphery. Zilka was relatively chatty, while Westerberg and Zika would bond over their mutual disaffection from the world. "What drew Paul to John was that they were the same antisocial, introspective type of personality. They struck a chord there," said Zilka. "But unlike Paul, John ended up having some demons that he couldn't deal with."

Usually in the company of Dave Zilka, and sometimes John Zika, Paul began playing after school in ad hoc formations at people's houses in South Minneapolis and Richfield, or for parties with the parents away. Often they would end up at the home of Holy Angels freshman Jeff Johnson, a guitarist. "Mainly 'cause my parents didn't care if we smoked cigarettes," said Johnson.

Bassist Bruno Pellagalli would round out the quartet, but they never found a lead singer. "Teenagers are notoriously terrified of singing," said Johnson. Occasionally, Zika sat in on harmonica. The material was typical: Stones, Faces, Chuck Berry. Westerberg had picked up on Django Reinhardt through his brother and would bring his records to rehearsal. "We weren't strictly a rock-and-roll band," said Johnson.

Despite being relatively quiet, Westerberg turned heads with his playing. "He had developed his own style by seventeen," said Johnson. "The soloing, the leads—he wasn't trying to sound like Eric Clapton or Duane Allman, or even Ronnie Wood. He was playing what he heard in his own mind."

In late 1975, Zilka landed them a real show at a roadhouse in rural Ramsey—Westerberg's first ever "professional" gig. The pay was free beer, plus a bonus of amphetamines. "We called 'em sod farmers, the people who lived out there," said Zilka. "This place we played was rough. We got up onstage and started playing Stones tunes, and they didn't like it very much. It was pretty comical."

Westerberg and his pals spent their weekends playing music or hopping the fence of Lakewood Cemetery, a burial ground for Minneapolis's rich and famous. "We'd smoke dope and sit by the big huge monuments," said Westerberg. "I used to try to think of band names by looking at the gravestones."

Paul was a romantic. "I liked girls from day one. I had crushes from first grade on." Though he was a fairly cute adolescent, puberty had turned him awkward and bulbous-featured. "He just had a hard time communicating with girls," said Zilka. Instead, Westerberg and his buddies took drugs and went to rock shows. His first real concert, on February 14, 1975, was "The St. Valentine's Day Massacre," which teamed bluesman James Cotton with rock headliner Johnny Winter at the Metropolitan Sports Center.

"That was my baptism," said Westerberg. "Cotton played that big sixty-four-reed harp, and this was back in the days of 'Let's blow their heads off with the PA.' Man, to hear a harp that loud, that skillfully played, that just went right to my gut. It was almost a letdown when Johnny Winter came on later."

At a Foghat show in 1976 at the Civic Center, Paul bought some PCP-laced marijuana in the parking lot. "It frightens me now how foolishly we took stuff," he said. "God only knows what it was." (The incident would inspire his song "I Bought a Headache.")

Paul's most visceral concert experience was Rod Stewart and the Faces at the Minneapolis Auditorium in November 1975. The Brit-rockers were a wild and wooly bunch: they cranked their amps, drank heavily—even had a bar and bartender onstage—and played a heavy percentage of cover songs. "No other redoubtable band gets that close—physically or spiritually—to its audience and lets the crowd get that close to it," wrote *Minneapolis Star* critic Jon Bream of the concert.

"When they came on, we charged right up to the stage," recalled Westerberg. "The excitement and the fun of the Faces . . . it was almost sexual. Virgins that we were, it was the closest thing to sex we'd experienced. In no time flat, I had a chick bouncing up and down on my shoulders."

Unbeknownst to anyone at the time, it was the band's final show: Ron Wood joined the Rolling Stones, and Rod Stewart decided to pursue his solo career full-time. But, for Westerberg, seeing the Faces was the start of formulating a concrete vision of his own future: "It was the most fun I'd had doing anything, being that close to a real rock-and-roll band that was so fucking deafeningly loud."

* * *

In 1976 Westerberg crossed paths with another aspiring guitarist named Jef Jodell, a sharp, opinionated Richfield High student who glimpsed him playing a keg party. "The place was pretty packed: eighty or a hundred people in this suburban basement," said Jodell. "Paul and these guys played instrumental versions of, like, 'Freebird.' I felt like we could be this brilliant guitar team." Over the next few years, they'd often jam in Westerberg's parents' basement. "His mom was very tolerant of us playing," said Jodell. "Once or twice she even brought us down cookies. But it was very clear, there was going to be no band stuff in the house when the old man was around."

They eventually formed a semiregular band, with Jodell's older brother Jack singing, bassists John Stegner and Paul Bolin, and drummer Wade Whipps. There was no consistent name—everything from Rain to Cunning Stunts. Their final gig was played as Neighborhood Threat, from a song on Iggy Pop's *The Idiot*.

Their handful of shows, mostly in 1977, took place in basements and at backyard parties. They played lots of early Beatles numbers. "You haven't lived until you've heard Paul Westerberg play 'All My Loving,'" said Jodell. "It makes those speed metal guys look like amateurs. Paul could spit that out like you wouldn't believe."

Sometimes onstage they would slip in one of Jack Jodell's prog-oriented originals. Later on, they performed a number Westerberg had written called

"Tarnished." It was a spindly, picky instrumental that owed a debt to Wishbone Ash's "Blowin' Free."

Mostly they played a grab bag of classic rock covers—Cream, Jethro Tull, Rush, Led Zeppelin, Aerosmith—but also more elaborate numbers like Al Stewart's "Apple Cider Reconstitution." "We bit off a lot of material we had no business trying," said Jodell. "We tried to concentrate on roots rock, but the bass player and drummer and my brother kept going towards that [prog-rock] stuff."

For the better part of four years, Westerberg had been trying to perfect his skills on the guitar, to inject a level of precision into his playing. He figured that kind of dedication would lead him somewhere special. Instead, he found himself playing Al Stewart songs in a basement in Richfield. "Paul was growing frustrated," said Jodell. "His thinking was: 'I would rather be good at something simple than so-so at something complex.'"

* * *

Westerberg recalled his Holy Angels schoolmate and sometime bandmate Paul Bolin as the proverbial rock snob. "In his bedroom he had issues of the *NME* and *Creem* stacked floor to ceiling, an insane stereo system, and the best weed," he said.

Bolin lived with his divorced mother in Richfield. "My mom was gone a lot, so I pretty much did whatever I wanted," said Bolin. "I had disposable income to buy albums, so I admit that I was something of a gospel-spreader in my crowd for new music."

Bolin shopped at the city's best record store, Oar Folkjokeopus, in South Minneapolis. Though he was mostly a fan of progressive rock bands like Yes, Bolin had been reading the fevered coverage of the United Kingdom's burgeoning punk rock movement. Oar Folk's manager, Peter Jesperson, urged Bolin to preorder the first Sex Pistols single, which Oar Folk was having shipped from England in late 1976.

Not long after, Westerberg and some friends were over at Bolin's house when he played them the Sex Pistols' "Anarchy in the UK."

"I shat myself," recalled Westerberg on hearing the band for the first time. "I thought: *This is my music.* The drumming, you could tell, was not Fancy Dan–type shit. It struck me right in the heart. The song was barely over before I'd gone home and cut my hair off and smashed my records. I'd already heard the Ramones. But hearing Lydon's voice made me think, *Forget these guitar solos I've been trying to play. I'm gonna lead a fucking band. Real rock-and-roll is not complicated.*"

Paul explored the Damned and the other English punks, then worked back to their American antecedents, particularly the New York Dolls. Johnny Thunders's guttersnipe guitar and David Johansen's gravelly yowl provided another touchstone. "I was supposed to graduate high school in '77, the spring of that year. [Punk] made me think, *Fuck this school shit. Fuck everything.*"

Though he was only a couple of months away from a diploma, Westerberg stopped going to class. The elders at Holy Angels gave him opportunities to get his degree. "But by then I'd already made up my mind. It was also the rebellion factor: 'Fuck 'em. I'm gonna stop before the finish line and not cross it.'"

Toward the end of his school days, Westerberg's English teacher took him aside and offered a bit of advice. "He said, 'Do what you know how to do.' Hell, why didn't you tell me that four years ago? What I really know how to do is play a G chord with the hammer on and the hammer off. I'm gonna do that."

* * *

Westerberg started seeing a lot less of John Zika in 1977. Zika had transferred to Richfield High briefly, before moving on to a vocational tech school to get his GED. He began working as a janitor, then as a cab driver, and would busk in downtown Minneapolis. Sometimes he and Westerberg played together near the Mississippi River.

The mythos of the Big River drew Zika in even further. He began working as a deckhand on a river barge. Though he dreamed of walking in the footsteps of the itinerant blues and jazz musicians he admired, it wasn't quite that romantic. "He'd be on the barge a month or two at a time," said his older sister, Mary Rose Zika. "In some ways it was probably the worst thing he could've done because you're alone with your thoughts."

By the fall of 1977, Zika's thoughts had increasingly turned to suicide. He'd just had a breakup, and his moods had grown darker. "My parents tried to get him to see somebody and get on medication," said Mary Rose. "But he was not willing to do it."

Zika was back in Minneapolis that Thanksgiving. Staying with his family for the holidays, he seemed unusually happy. "I didn't realize that he had sunk that low at all," said his younger sister, Maggie.

Sometime on Thursday, December 1, John walked into his parents' basement. A few hours later, his older brother Mike came home and discovered his body. "He blew his brains out on his mother's carpet," Westerberg would recall, haltingly, many years later.

Gill Brothers Chapel in Richfield was packed with his friends and classmates, all of them dazed. Given the nature of Zika's death, his passing was "shrouded in mystery," said Paul. He thought about reaching out to Zika's sister Maggie, to his family, but he couldn't bring himself to attend the funeral. Instead, Paul brooded about the hints that were there with Zika. "He'd play me Paul Butterfield's 'I Got a Mind to Give Up Living.' He used to say it was his favorite song," said Westerberg. "He'd make comments about 'this shitty life.' But we were moody teenagers; we all had a bit of that."

Thoughts of suicide were not unknown to Westerberg. In 1975, as a confused, neglected fifteen-year-old, he had tried to overdose. "My sister was a nurse's aide and had a closet full of sample narcotics. One afternoon I took a whole shitload," he recalled. "I think my mom came home from work and I was lying on the bed unconscious. I remember seeing quadruple at nine o'clock at night, sitting at the kitchen table, with my dad shoving a banana in my face, saying, 'Eat this, goddamn it.'

"The whole thing was probably the typical fears of adolescence: 'Am I gay? Am I retarded? Do I fit in? What do I do, where do I go next?' I don't think I was really trying to kill myself. But John was . . . different."

A couple weeks prior to Zika's suicide, he'd played Westerberg Bruce Springsteen's *Born to Run*, then gave him his copy. "It was his way of saying, 'If you're gonna play this rock-and-roll shit, it's at *least* gotta be as good as this,'" said Westerberg. "To this day, around the holidays, I'll listen to 'Jungleland' and I can't help but think of him."

In life, Zika had been Westerberg's idol. In death, he would become his guiding spirit, the rock-and-roll ghost who would haunt his psyche. "When Zika killed himself, that was a big part of what changed me," said Westerberg. "I believe that I took it as a passing of the torch.

"From then on, when in doubt, in my mind, musically, or whatever, I would think: *What would John have done?* My attitude changed too; I became a little more of a 'fuck you' type. It's the classic thing: after he died, I took on a bit of his personality."

CHAPTER 5

Tommy Stinson was just seven when his big brother disappeared into the state juvenile system. "He was completely out of the picture," said Tommy. "I don't even remember going and visiting him. Which is dark."

Apart from some vicious spankings, Tommy had been spared the worst of Nick Griffin's cruelty. But the facts would mark Tommy nevertheless—with survivor's guilt, on the one hand, and a sense of his own indestructibility, on the other.

By the time Tommy was ten, he was the man of the house. Anita was bartending days at the Uptown, then drinking afterward. "Most of the time I would come home half in the bag," she admitted. Lonnie was left to watch over Tommy and baby sister Lisa between high school classes and shifts at Arby's.

Since the family's midnight escape from Florida, Tommy's childhood had been an unsettled blur. "By the time I was twelve years old, I'd lived in twelve different school districts and gone to twelve different goddamn schools," he said. The constant turmoil took its toll on his education. "They held me back in fifth grade. They said it was because I was too young to go into the next grade. But the reality was, I was too stupid. No one wanted to come out and say, 'You're not smart enough.'"

Constantly being the new kid gave Tommy a peculiar strength: always precocious, he became cocky and quick to joke, laugh, accept a dare, or break a rule. To his family, however, he still seemed an innocent. He was his grandmother Virginia's favorite; she'd take him on weekends and single him out for presents at Christmas: "She gave everyone else a five-dollar check. But me, she went and found gifts for."

When the Stinsons moved to Thirty-Sixth and Bryant, Tommy became fast friends with Curtis Olson, a hyperactive neighbor. Each delivered newspapers, but they soon found more exciting, illegal uses of their time. Initially, it was kid stuff: vandalism, throwing rocks through windows. Then they shoplifted slot cars from Target. Tommy was pinched twice for theft before turning eleven. Both times he was slapped on the wrist and sent home by juvenile court.

Tommy and Curtis moved on to stealing bikes. One rainy night when he didn't come home, Anita hysterically "called every police station, every hospital in town. And then here he comes walking in the door, looking up at me like nothing has happened. Of course, he'd been sitting in his friend's garage tearing up bicycles that they'd stolen. I didn't have a clue."

Finally, Tommy and Curtis went on a spree at a nearby elementary school: "[We] took about ten bikes and stashed them." Then they made their way into a church and stole a microphone. Finally, they returned to the school. "We had the audacity to walk across their playground at recess with wrenches sticking out of our back pockets." A custodian began asking questions: "He dragged us into the office and we got arrested."

Waiting outside the juvenile courtroom with his mother and grandmother, the judge tried to scare Tommy straight: "The way you're headed right now," he told him, "I will send you to a place out west, in Colorado, and I won't let you come back until you're twenty-one." At that, Anita and Virginia burst into tears. "I felt like the worst person on the planet," said Tommy. The judge decided to give him another chance. Still, he needed something in his life that would keep him occupied, off the criminal path. "Right after that," he said, "is when Bob came home."

* * *

When Bob Stinson and Robert Flemal settled into Bryant Avenue in the fall of 1977, they set up guitars, amps, and recording equipment in their second-story bedroom.

Like his brother, Tommy had always been fascinated by music. For years he kept a little transistor radio by his bed and would fall asleep to the sound of the local oldies station. He'd briefly taken up baritone sax in the grade school band and even learned to read a little music. He had a good ear for things, a natural sense of swing and rhythm (perhaps passed down from his drummer father).

Music would become the bond between the Stinson brothers—though there was a distance between them initially. It seemed like a lifetime since the two had been under the same roof, and Tommy regarded Bob almost as a stranger at first: "Absolutely," he said, "I didn't really know him."

Bob was aware of Tommy's brushes with the law and took it upon himself to keep tabs. Tommy had stopped stealing, but he was aimless. Then one afternoon in the spring of 1978, the eleven-year-old was in Bob's bedroom, looking at some of his brother's equipment. He opened a case under the bed and found an old Sears Silvertone bass. He'd just set the instrument on his lap when Bob walked in. "Hey, you wanna learn how to play that?" Bob asked, and then showed him a few rudimentary blues figures.

"I was like, 'Nah, this sucks. This is hurting my fingers,'" said Tommy. "Just getting my hands wrapped around the neck was hard enough. But he kept coaxing me. He was determined."

Teaching Tommy how to play, Bob used both the carrot and the stick. "He started by offering to buy me a candy bar here or a Coke there to practice," said Tommy. "Then I'd want to quit and he'd get pissed and would throw shit at me. I'd cry and say, 'I'm telling Mom.' So I upped the ante: 'I want two Cokes and two candy bars.' Then it got more painful and he'd get mad and throw a whole speaker cabinet at me."

"When he was showing Tommy how to play bass, Bob would just punch him: 'Get it right!'" said Flemal. "I was kinda shocked."

The first four songs Tommy learned encapsulated Bob's tastes perfectly: Peter Frampton's "Show Me the Way," Johnny Winter's version of "Boney Maronie," Rick Derringer's "Rock and Roll, Hootchie Koo," and Yes's "Roundabout." Bob was desperate to start a band. "He was insistent: 'I need a bass player *today*, man,'" said Tommy. "Plus, I came a lot cheaper than most bass players."

As Anita observed, there was another reason he pressed Tommy to learn. "Bobby basically grabbed him by the scruff of his neck and was saying to Tommy, 'You're going to do this because you're not going to end up like I did.'"

"I was going down that road," said Tommy. "Before my brother taught me how to play bass, they wanted to send me away to a boys' reform school. Next thing would've been grand theft auto, then . . . murder, fucking rob a grocery store or whatever. I was just a total hoodlum at a very young age, so he saved me from that."

Within a couple of months, Tommy became proficient on the bass. "I was amazed," said Flemal. "I was always kind of tone-deaf. But Tommy and Bob had natural ability. They could hear something once and just pick it up." Tommy added, "I played a lot. My mom knew I was hanging out, smoking weed, but she figured, 'You know what? He can smoke weed as long as he doesn't go to jail.' It was a trade-off."

* * *

Tommy's partner in crime, Curtis Olson, had an older sister, Andrea, or Andi—sixteen, a well-built blonde with big glasses and a free spirit. Her stepfather taught band, and she'd learned violin, French horn, and bass by her teens and was even hosting a radio show on the local community station KFAI. Like Bob, she'd attended Marshall University High for a time, then went to Southeast Free School her senior year. "I bounced around a lot," she said.

Walking home, Andi would sometimes hear a band playing on Bryant Avenue. Then she went with Curtis to meet the Stinsons. "The first thing Bob asked me was, 'Do you have any weed?'" she recalled, with a laugh. They were like-minded and soon became a couple. "He was a real trip. Like nobody I ever met."

After school each day, Olson would hang out at the Stinsons'. "It was a zoo over there, with four kids from six to twenty running around. Anita took in strays too—I ended up living there for a little while myself." She'd watch the band rehearse. "I think Bob was partially deaf already from jamming so close to the amp. He used to crank it up so loud, the dishes would rattle right off the shelves."

The band shook the house so much, the kitchen trash can tipped over. Bob would empty the bin before they played. "It was like a daily ritual," said Olson. "If he didn't take the trash out before he started jamming, it would fall over. Then Anita would see the mess and yell: 'Bobby!'"

The band didn't yet have a name, but they were already notorious on the block. In summer, Bob, Tommy, and Robert would hang out on the flat roof of the house with their instruments, amps pointed out the windows, and blast the neighborhood . . . "until the cops would show up and tell 'em to finally shut it down," Olson said.

Eventually, they were invited to play a couple of local backyard parties and beer busts. "They didn't even have a drummer yet," said Olson. "Flemal was not very good. He thought the band was just for getting chicks."

Even when Bob and Andi hung out alone, his mind was on music. They'd go to Suneson's to look at guitars or walk around Lake Harriet talking about riffs and records. "Back then, all he would do was drink a little beer, smoke a little weed," said Olson. "He didn't have any money for hard drugs; he wasn't even into hard liquor. He didn't like the taste of it. He didn't talk to me much about his past. But I knew he'd been in treatment. And I knew he wanted to never go back."

Their relationship ran hot and cold over the next couple years. "I found out that he'd slept with one of my girlfriends. He was kind of a slut. But back in those days, everybody was. People were just a little more free with themselves."

Olson would eventually move out west to California with her parents, leaving Bob and Minnesota behind—but not before making a very important introduction. "I knew the band needed a drummer," said Olson. "I told Bob, 'Have I got a drummer for you.'"

CHAPTER 6

The Mars family was a big, lively brood of native Minnesotans. Patriarch Leroy Linus Mars was born in 1906, his wife Constance Mary Evans fourteen years later. Both were World War II veterans: Leroy in the Navy, Constance in the Waves, the all-female branch of the Naval Reserve.

Starting in 1948, the couple had seven children: Mary, Joseph, Kevin, John, Rita, James, and the youngest, Christopher Edward, born April, 26 1961.

Leroy Mars was a high school dropout; before and after the war, he was a self-employed painter. Though blue-collar, he was distantly related to Franklin Clarence Mars, founder of the Mars candy company and one of the wealthiest men in America. "I wrote them once, and I think they sent me ten boxes of M&Ms," recalled Chris Mars. "That was the extent of the riches."

The Mars family lived at Thirty-Seventh and Garfield, near where the Westerbergs had settled, and Chris's older brother Jim was in Paul's class at Catholic school. The Church of the Incarnation loomed large for the Mars family, as it did for the Westerbergs; Constance sang in the choir.

Much of Chris's childhood—and later life too—was dominated by his oldest brother Joe. "He'd crack us all up," said Mars. "He would be there to help if he could with anything you might be doing. He cared about fitness and lifted weights. He was the best fisherman of any of us."

But in the midsixties, during his teens, Joe began exhibiting signs of severe schizophrenia. Doctors diagnosed him with a "nervous breakdown" and sent him to the St. Cloud Mental Hospital. "I was around five or six," said Chris, "and didn't know what was happening."

Joe spent stretches in various institutions throughout Mars's childhood and adolescence. "I remember visiting him in the hospital," he said. "It frightened me."

His brother's problems "stigmatized him amongst his friends and, sadly, even within our family to a certain extent," said Chris. "It was never fully talked about or understood; we would try to reach out and comfort him when he went through these periods, though we were not equipped with the proper tools to fully understand his schizophrenia—that word wasn't even used until much later."

Chris's personality turned inward. "I remember suffering from some periodic bouts of depression as early as third grade," he said. "If I look back, it does coincide with the beginning of my brother's troubles." There was also an abiding worry as he grew up that "it could happen to you as well."

From earliest childhood, Chris channeled those fears into visual art. Chris would explore the family's *World Book Encyclopedia* set ("Since I could barely hold a pencil"), looking for the letter P. "I would repeatedly go to the 'Paintings' section and study them. I would notice how light and atmosphere would play off of water and various textured surfaces in nature; how clouds and trees grew and formed; how thunderstorms would suddenly alter and blacken out the day."

The tree-lined streets and funky back alleys of Mars's neighborhood also captured his troubled young mind. "In summer, running around at night, there would be glowing and smoldering trash barrels up and down alleyways. I loved Halloween and the colors of fall. I would try to put it to paper from memory."

Mars's artistic gift was clear from the start. "As a little shit, I actually won a couple of prizes from the local newspaper for my drawings of turkeys and football players," he said. Once, at school, he was sent to the principal's office: "I was trying to figure out what bad thing I did that I'd forgotten. When I got there, I was praised for some drawings."

Music came to mean just as much. Down the block from his house lived a family rock band, the Churchills. "They'd draw the police every summer and disrupt the neighborhood," he recalled. Listening to them bash out "In-A-Gadda-Da-Vida," he'd notice the drummer was the loudest.

At ten, Mars got a Snoopy "toy" drum set from Sears. "The rims were held on by springs. I was real careful, but by the end of the summer I beat the hell out of it." He replaced it with "another Sears model—but this had a real snare."

The Who at the St. Paul Civic Center was Mars's first concert, in 1976. "I was right behind [Keith] Moon," said Mars. He thought they sounded terrible, but didn't care: "It was a show." Though he never abandoned visual art, music came to the fore in his teens. "There's an immediate reaction you can get from music that you can't get from art," said Mars, who picked up the guitar as well. "He would get interested in something and go full bore," said his brother Jim. "That's all you'd hear about for a while."

Outwardly genial but inwardly alienated, Mars managed a couple years at the Catholic high school, DeLaSalle, before transferring to Central, eventually dropping out in eleventh grade. His experiences with his brother Joe had given him a sense of solidarity with people who were marginalized.

Though he gave off an innocent vibe, Mars wasn't immune to trouble. He liked to drink and zip around the neighborhood on his motorbike. "I was in a motorcycle accident about the time I was drinking more heavily," he recalled. "I spent a week in the hospital. I fractured my skull. The sac around my brain had a rip in it, and there was spinal fluid coming out of my nose. So it was a pretty traumatic experience for me."

One day, while at work bagging groceries, Mars saw a magazine with a picture of the Sex Pistols on the cover. *What the hell is this?* he thought. Turned out, his older brother Jim had already bought the Pistols' album. "So I wore it out," he said. "It was something to identify to separate myself from my peers. And maybe try and get into something different. And that's kinda how I got into music."

Mars would jam in basements, with ad hoc groups in his teens, occasionally encountering Westerberg through his older brother. Paul had been impressed with his playing during a keg party thrown by their mutual friend Scotty Williams, and again a couple years later when Chris took over a kit belonging to Paul's friend Kevin Patrick: "He was like a little Keith Moon," Westerberg said. "In the back of my mind, I thought whatever band I was going to be in, it'd be good to have Chris in it."

* * *

Bob Stinson's group had tried out a couple drummers, but nobody wanted to play with them again. Then Andi Olson mentioned her next-door neighbor, Chris Mars. "My bedroom faced his bedroom," said Olson. "I thought it might be better for my sleeping if I could get him to move his drum set over to Bob's house." She knocked on Mars's door, and the next day Mars dragged his kit to the house on Bryant.

Instantly, Chris and Bob connected. Like Mars's brother Joe, Bob Stinson was a big sweet lug hiding some deeper damage. Chris was equally intrigued by the eleven-year-old on bass: "Bob would strap a bass on [Tommy] and force him to play against his will," said Mars.

Mars immediately impressed Flemal; the drummer had a well-coiffed shag haircut and peach-fuzz mustache. "He was kind of a handsome young man," said Flemal. "I always thought of him as really intelligent too. After he left that first day, Bob said, 'What do you think of him?' I said, 'He's in.' I didn't hesitate."

They began rehearsing several hours a night. Though the house was set back from the more heavily trafficked corner of Thirty-Sixth and Bryant, they could still be heard for blocks in every direction. "The cops would tell us to turn down at nine, and shut it down after ten," said Flemal. Sometimes they'd keep playing past the curfew, prompting another police visit: "'We told you before that you need to turn it down before ten—but you guys are getting better all the time.'"

The group's covers paid little heed to the originals. "We did 'Rock and Roll, Hoochie Koo' and 'Roundabout' at a hundred miles per hour," said Flemal. "We weren't trying to be a punk band, it was just natural." The covers were played instrumentally: "There was no way you could really sing over what we were playing." Eventually they began to include originals that Chris Mars had written, such as his Aerosmith pastiche "Dogged in the Alley." "I think he [was] the only one brave enough to actually write something," said Tommy.

The band needed a name, and Bob seized on Dogbreath, after asking everyone to come up with "the most disgusting thing you guys can think of." Mars painted a gold Dogbreath logo on his kick drum, as well as a pot leaf on the back of Tommy's Silvertone bass. By late 1978, Dogbreath was performing at keggers for friends and Bob's Mama Rosa's coworkers.

All of eleven years old, Tommy was now playing parties, smoking weed, and, crucially, getting female attention. "It was a self-esteem thing," he said. "There wasn't a lot of [women] there, but they were all going, 'Oh, look at how cute he is!' That was pretty rad." He added: "For the first time, as opposed to just sucking at everything and getting nothing from life except hate and failure, suddenly I'm getting positive reinforcement from something I'm doing. We all were."

★　★　★

Paul Westerberg spent much of 1978 and 1979 searching. "When John [Zika] killed himself . . . I drifted for a couple years," said Westerberg. "I was jumping from group to group. It was my job to find this perfect band out there somewhere, and if they're not out there, dammit, I'm gonna create 'em."

Though he'd avoided getting a diploma, Westerberg spent a lot of time self-educating. "Once school was out, I could wear my glasses till my heart was content. So I'd go to the public library every day." If he wanted to be a songwriter, he figured he'd have to study. "I forced myself to read literature, even if I didn't enjoy it, as a mental exercise: 'I have to work this muscle a bit.'"

He read up on show business history, from "P. T. Barnum to Sinatra," he said. He also digested every rock magazine and book he could get his hands on; he was a particular fan of the irreverent humor of *Creem* writer Rick Johnson.

Westerberg had little money to spend on records, so much of his listening and learning came from the library as well. He made odd finds there: instructional jazz LPs; an old folk record by Glenn Yarbrough; *Fog on the Tyne* by English rock band Lindisfarne. Sometimes he'd sell his used LPs to local record store Oar Folkjokeopus and buy new ones with the money. He also liked that he could scavenge discarded cigarettes from the store's ashtray to smoke later. "They had the longest butts at Oar Folk," he said.

Eventually, Westerberg's father began to ask, "When you gonna get a goddamn job?" Paul had decided to keep his serious musical ambitions even from his mother: "I'd heard my brother say, 'I'm gonna play my music.' My mom's response was: 'Well, are you gonna take lessons? Are you gonna join the union?' So I knew not to say that." To appease his parents, he began looking for work.

By the late 1970s, the US economy was stagnating, prior to the major early 1980s recession. In Minnesota, the disparity between the haves and have-nots was growing wider. High-wage workers were making 3.1 times more on average than their low-wage counterparts. As a high school dropout with no trade or skills, Westerberg was firmly in the latter camp.

He went to the local labor pool and got assigned to a steel mill in St. Paul, loading scrap metal. On his first day, Westerberg leaned too close to the compacter. Someone shouted for him to get back. Just then, a piece of scrap-metal debris flew at his face, narrowly missing his eye but leaving a permanent scar.

After a stint "at the Munsingwear factory downtown, pushing around carts of wet fabric," Westerberg started working at the Control Data Corporation's headquarters as a janitor—in Bloomington, a soulless suburb south of Richfield that Westerberg came to detest. The gig meant having to maneuver around "skilled" workers soldering computer parts. He remembered cleaning under the work stool of a woman who, offended by his scruffy presence, fixed Westerberg with a disdainful stare.

"That was the last straw for me. It hit home: 'You're just a peon putting a circuit into a thing. You're no better than me.' I thought, *I'll be damned if I'm going to be doing this in a year.*"

Soon as he had enough money for a new guitar and amp, he was done with dead-end day jobs. He was going to play music for the rest of his life. Most of all, he was determined that no one would ever look at him that way again.

* * *

Westerberg had reconnected with his childhood friend Tom Byrne, a singer who was still attending Holy Angels.

Byrne would front Westerberg's new trio—bassist Tom Billiete and drummer John Holler, and occasionally Kevin Patrick. They played first as the Mollitive Nerves, then as Oat, with a repertoire of deeper cuts by Cream, Peter Green's Fleetwood Mac, Cheap Trick, and the Ramones.

Westerberg also introduced a couple songs of his own. "'Lookin' for Ya,'" he said, "was just a George Thorogood rip," but the lyrics were sharper than usual for a beginner: "Half a mile from the liquor store / It's five to eight, I could use some more." Another tune was a nod to Phil Westerberg titled "My Brother's in Jail." They played at keggers, as well as a dance at the school where Byrne's mother taught. "Tom's mom wanted us to play dance music," said Westerberg. "We may have done 'Le Freak' by Chic. That's when I went out and smoked a cigarette."

Byrne and Westerberg also played an open mic at a tap bar called the 38th Parallel. "Some guy approached us afterwards and wanted to manage us. We were all like '*Oooh,*'" said Westerberg. "My brother told me, 'He's probably gonna try to steal your equipment.'"

As Oat struggled along, Westerberg landed a gig with Marsden Maintenance, working an evening janitor gig in a downtown building that included the office of US Senator David Durenberger. "That was the best of the crappy jobs," he said. "I'd turn on all the radios to the same station, eat the doughnuts left over at the office, and sing along."

He would sometimes write out the band's set lists on Durenberger's stationery: "There'd be songs like 'We're Gonna Get Drunk Tonight,' and at the top it would say, 'From the desk of US Senator. . . .'" More importantly, the job provided him with enough cash to pick up a red Gibson ES-335 and a new Marshall cabinet.

Westerberg still hadn't found musicians with the same fire or passion as the Sex Pistols. The closest he'd come was seeing the Doggs, an early group of South Minneapolis punks playing a house party. They had spiked haircuts, loads of attitude, and acted like a marauding gang. "It was the aggression that got me," said Westerberg. "It keyed in my mind that this is where the shit's going."

Westerberg was becoming aware of the local punk and new wave scene developing at the new downtown club Jay's Longhorn, which was booking shows by Blondie, Talking Heads, and Elvis Costello, along with local acts like the Suicide Commandos and the Suburbs. Paul would occasionally see bands and drink at the Longhorn's beer bust nights (until 1986, the drinking age in Minnesota was nineteen), usually with his friend Steve Skibbe, a fellow janitor getting his own band, the Dads, off the ground.

Westerberg realized that he should be leading a band himself. "It came little by little. The Mollitive Nerves played a lot of Ramones songs, and I started singing on that stuff. But it wasn't like I opened my mouth and thought, *Here's gold.*"

That fall, Westerberg's "connected" uncle gifted him with a PA system. "It was like 'Paulie's making music? I got some amps and shit here, I'll have some guys bring it over.'" In November he got together again with Jeff Johnson and Dave Zilka to play at his house. Johnson arrived with a TEAC cassette player and a couple of microphones. When he walked into the basement, Johnson saw Westerberg's new PA system and microphone setup. "I thought, *What's this?*" he said. "That was the first time I'd heard him sing."

The recording—the earliest document of Westerberg singing—is a mishmash of material: covers of the Who ("Long Live Rock"), Ten Years After ("Choo Choo Mama"), the Doors ("Roadhouse Blues"), even the Knack's current hit "My Sharona." "To us it was a joke, but it was fun," said Johnson. Even in that loose atmosphere, Johnson saw that Westerberg was becoming a more serious musician.

In January 1980, Johnson and Westerberg got together again. "It was the last time I played with Paul," said Johnson. More and more, Westerberg was performing punk songs: the Ramones' "Cretin Hop," the Only Ones' "Another Girl, Another Planet."

Westerberg had also concluded that he wouldn't get anywhere with his old friends. "I would keep missing practices and stuff," said Tom Byrne. "Paul had a vision. He was extremely driven."

"I'd had it with playing with guys who were half-assed into it," said West-erberg. "I did that probably from age fourteen to nineteen. Five years of play-ing with guys in garages, basements, cover bands, parties, keggers. I'd already fucked around with guys who really didn't want to go for it. All these dudes were eventually gonna go off to college or go become accountants. And it took me a long time to find guys who had no other fucking options in life. I needed desperation. 'Cause that's where I was coming from."

During a cigarette break, Paul told his friends, "I just met these guys—this weird guitar player, his kid brother, and a drummer I kinda know." There was a determination to what he said next: "We're putting a band together."

CHAPTER 7

Paul Westerberg often walked back home from his job at Marsden Mainte-nance. On the days when he didn't have bus fare—and sometimes even if he did—he would hoof the thirty-plus blocks from downtown to his house in South Minneapolis, taking Bryant Avenue all the way. "I was thinking of trying to build up my lung power," said Westerberg. "I'd read that Sinatra had swum laps. I always got good ideas when I walked too."

In the early fall of 1979, Westerberg was half a mile from his house when he caught a torrid wailing in the distance and followed it to 3628 Bryant Ave-nue. It sounded like Yes's "Roundabout," but really fast and screaming.

"What got to me was the sheer volume and the wild thunder," said West-erberg. "That was a major attraction: the balls of a band to play that goddamn loud. I mean, you'd hear bands around occasionally. But this was different. It was like 'Holy fuck—what *is* this?'" He would pass the house a few more times that fall. "I think I heard them once or twice more, and then I finally decided to take a look down in the basement." Westerberg skulked around the left side of the house. He knelt down near a little basement window surrounded by shrubs. He tried but couldn't get a good look at who was making the noise. Yet that sound—that volume, that thunder—stayed with him.

Had Westerberg been able to see inside he would've glimpsed an evolving version of Dogbreath. After a year of practicing and playing the odd keg party, Bob Stinson was trying to take things in a more serious direction. He brought in a couple different singers to sit in. Among them was Stuart Cummins, an older hippie type with an unnaturally high-pitched voice, who would some-times join them.

Meanwhile, Robert Flemal's membership was becoming an issue. That fall he caught a nasty case of hepatitis A—it had broken out among Mama Rosa's kitchen staff. "We all had to get shots—the whole family," said Anita Stinson. "Bob was so scared: 'I can't go in there, Mom, that needle will go right through my arm!'"

Flemal's illness forced him to move back to his parents' house in Mound to recuperate, where he stayed several weeks. Dogbreath kept on playing without him. "It didn't take long," said Flemal. "Spend a couple weeks away from a band, they're thinking you're not too into it."

* * *

Westerberg's and Mars's mutual friend Scott Williams had urged them to play together all fall, so in late November 1979, Chris invited Paul over. Williams drove him to the Bryant house, which Westerberg immediately recognized: "We pull up and I'm thinking, *This is the joint!*" he said. "I walked in very casual, though. I didn't say, 'Hey, I've been listening to you guys in the bushes.'"

On this night, Dogbreath was upstairs and in the middle of a Ted Nugent song when Paul said hello to Chris. He recognized Bob too—the "stoned, weird-looking guy" he'd sometimes see riding the Bryant Avenue bus. Introductions made, Westerberg pulled a present out from behind his ear. "He gave me a joint from his brother," recalled Bob. "He goes, 'Smoke this!'"

The two chatted between puffs. They'd been born just a couple weeks apart. "And whatever chemical imbalance we both shared, we bonded on that level too," said Westerberg. Bob was also impressed with the fact that Paul had played for money: "Pitiful as it was, I had actually been paid a couple bucks."

As they talked, Westerberg realized he'd heard a bassist on his way up the stairs, but didn't see one in the room.

"Where's your bass player, man?" asked Westerberg.

"He's right there," said Bob, pointing behind him. Westerberg wheeled around and saw a little towheaded kid sitting on a chair, obscured by an amp cabinet.

If Paul Westerberg ever experienced anything like love at first sight in his life, it was the moment he laid eyes on Tommy Stinson.

"What's up," said Tommy, in a chipper squeak. His voice hadn't even broken yet.

"He's my little brother," said Bob. "He's twelve. He's real good."

Westerberg looked at the boy with the bowl haircut, blue hoodie, and Sears bass and broke out in a grin. "He just looked like . . . a *star*," he said. "That's what I saw: a twelve-year-old who sounded like a little girl and played like a motherfucker. And I thought, *This kid is a fucking star.*"

Robert Flemal was still in Mound that night. Singer Stuart Cummins was absent. "It was just the Stinson brothers and Chris," said Westerberg. He listened to them play for a while in close quarters, and it only confirmed what he'd heard in the bushes. "They were very fast and very loud and very close to the excitement that I felt seeing the Faces, or seeing the Doggs," said Westerberg. "And I thought, *Hmmm, this might be my ticket right here.*"

At that point, Westerberg was neither a singer nor a songwriter—he was a guitar player. It wasn't quite clear how he would fit in with Dogbreath. On the verge of regaining his health, Flemal had plans on moving back into the house and resuming his role as the group's other guitarist.

Even so, Bob's interest was piqued by Paul. The feeling was most definitely mutual. "I knew that they had the raw power that I'd been looking for," said Westerberg, "and that they might just be gullible enough to fall for me giving a little leadership."

* * *

When they got together again, the band was back in the basement. Along with his guitar and amp, Westerberg also brought over a handful of records: Johnny Thunders & the Heartbreakers' *Live at Max's Kansas City*; Dave Edmunds's *Tracks on Wax 4*; the Buzzcocks' *Singles Going Steady*; the New York Dolls' eponymous debut. "Basically I said to them, 'Let's take all this shit and kinda copy it,'" said Westerberg.

"When Paul joined, I know he brought a direction that we didn't have," Chris Mars said. "We did have this reckless abandon that he was also looking for in a band. It was the right combination."

"I just figured, if I'm gonna make anything happen, it's gotta be my way," said Westerberg. "It was like: 'Wake up! You guys are great if you do this. If you keep playing Ted Nugent, you're not going anywhere.'"

After working up the Heartbreakers' "I Wanna Be Loved" and "All By Myself," Westerberg went to the bathroom. He walked up the stairs and heard the others whispering: "'This is friggin' punk rock!' . . . like I was trying to slip them angel dust or something," said Westerberg. "Those were fighting words to them." Though Mars knew the Sex Pistols, for the Stinson brothers "punk was way off our radar," said Tommy.

"It was so cool," said Westerberg. "They hated punk bands. But they were playing like the MC5 or something. They had some type of punk energy they had no idea they possessed."

Westerberg plied the Stinsons with the Pistols and Ramones until they came around. Bob was unsold until he heard the Damned's 1979 LP *Machine Gun Etiquette* and the high-wire playing of Captain Sensible. ("Captain Sensible! I ripped him off good," said Bob.) "They went hook, line, and sinker once they got into it," said Westerberg.

Early on, though, Westerberg had doubts about Dogbreath's lead guitarist. "I wanted to get rid of Bob from day one," he would admit. He even talked to Chris privately about starting another band without Bob. "I wanted to steal Chris, but he wouldn't go. I wanted to steal Tommy, too. But Chris was like, 'It's Bob's band and Tommy's his little brother. We can't do that.'"

Bob and Paul were immediately suspicious of each other's tastes. "He had an awful record collection. He thought mine was awful too," said Westerberg—particularly Paul's affection for Jackson Browne and Joni Mitchell. Westerberg couldn't stand Bob's bad metal records (e.g., Angel).

They bonded over having inadvertently shared a first show—Johnny Winter in 1975. "That was the common uncool factor," said Westerberg. Both had a passion for screaming glam and AM radio pop from the early seventies, as well as a more recent rockabilly rediscovery phase.

What brought Westerberg fully to Bob's side was his recklessness. Unlike everyone else Paul had played with, Bob approached the guitar with total freedom. "He had fast fingers: they weren't always well guided, but they were fast," noted Tommy. But he was also fearless and forceful, qualities Westerberg intuitively prized: "He had the confidence not to go, 'Oh, shucks, I fucked up there.' If he fucked up, he would fuck up with majesty."

Paul's and Bob's loose guitar weave became an essential part of the band's sound. "When I listen back, I'm astonished at how they played off of each other," said Tommy. "They really worked off each other rhythmically—even though Paul didn't listen to Yes and shit like that."

Besides covers, they learned a couple of Westerberg's holdovers from previous bands. "Lookin' for Ya" was given new muscle and speed. Though Keith Moon had been his first idol, Mars's playing was closer to the Sex Pistols' Paul Cook—rigorous snare work and simple, minimal fills, plus his own left-field flourishes. "He had a very unorthodox way of playing the kick drum pattern," said Tommy. "It wasn't always four on the floor, but it wasn't a typical pop beat either."

Nor was Mars's physical stance: he sat up high behind the kit and almost leaned down into the drums. ("I can control my foot pedal, go faster, that way," he said.) It wasn't an ideal position to play from, but it made it feel as though he was constantly bearing down on the beat.

Westerberg's unusual chording style and untutored musical mind could be vexing. "It's always been hard to follow me by looking at my hands, because I'm not always making a real chord. You need to have an ear to follow me, and Tommy had that. He would understand you could play notes that weren't necessarily the root." Tommy became the de facto musical director for the band before he hit puberty. "For the next ten years I'd be asking Tommy, 'What chord does that start with?'"

The band spent the winter woodshedding—"Four or five times a week at first," said Tommy. "We played loud in the basement, out-louding one another," said Westerberg. "Bob never turned it down, and Tommy was as loud as anyone, so you had to fight to be heard."

During one weeknight rehearsal, as they tore through a version of Dave Edmunds's "Trouble Boys," they took the song's twanging rhythm and gave it a screaming thrust. "There's trouble boys all around me," howled Westerberg as he and Bob traded lead and rhythm back and forth, while Chris and Tommy battered away at the beat.

When the last note rang out and the song was over, there was silence. Looking at one another, they realized, as Paul would recall, "that we had fallen in together."

* * *

Paul Westerberg's effort to mold Dogbreath into his dream combo was still going to require some work. To put himself in a position to be the undisputed rhythm guitarist, singer, and leader, he'd have to clear a path and get rid of a few obstacles, starting with Robert Flemal.

When Flemal returned to the Stinsons' after his illness, he immediately sensed a difference. "I remember the first couple times Paul came over, I felt like there was an invader in the basement," he said. "I didn't even know some of the songs they were playing. All of a sudden they started sounding more punk rock."

With three guitarists fighting for space, it was a mess. "[Flemal] would be hanging around and it would just get cacophonous," said Westerberg. "He was the hardest to oust because he kinda lived there and was tight with Bob. But he wasn't any good. It was not like a battle of the guitarists or anything."

Flemal realized his place in the band had been usurped, and his attentions wandered. He soon met his future wife and gave up on Dogbreath. "It's either the girl or the band," Bob told Robert. "The band is going places and you're not keeping up." Flemal said: "I never spoke to Bob again after that."

Although Westerberg had been singing in rehearsal, Bob felt they needed a "real" vocalist. Stuart Cummins continued dropping by periodically. "Chris would give me a ride home on his motorcycle, and I'd say, 'Man, that fucking singer has gotta go; fire his ass,'" said Westerberg. "And Chris was like, 'Yeah, I know what you mean.'"

They soon dispatched Cummins, and Westerberg brought in his old Oat singer Tom Byrne to audition. Bob, in particular, liked Byrne. "I then did what I had to do," said Westerberg, who told Dogbreath that Byrne didn't care for the band. Then he told Byrne that the band didn't really want him.

"He told me, 'We've decided to keep it a four-piece'—meaning I was out," recalled Byrne. (In later years, even at the peak of the band's success, Bob Stinson would still bemoan the fact that Byrne hadn't become their singer.)

Having kicked around with him in various lineups over the years, Byrne felt Westerberg had finally found the right group: one powerful enough and malleable enough to fulfill his vision. "Their name was Dogbreath, you know?" said Byrne. "They had no real direction. But they were good. From the cradle they were good musicians, they could play well. Paul just took them and pushed it and molded it a certain way, and that created a magic."

The band had been playing for a couple months with people coming in and out. Then one day they looked up and Flemal was a memory, Cummins was gone, and Byrne was no more. Finally, it was just the four of them—Paul, Tommy, Bob, and Chris—and that's how it would stay.

The last thing that needed to be changed was the name. "At first I wanted to call us the Substitutes, after the Who song," said Westerberg. "À la the tradition of the Rolling Stones—let's take a great song and name ourselves after that." For whatever reason, the Substitutes didn't fly with the others.

Westerberg grabbed a dictionary and tried to find something else that would fit. He got halfway through the letter "I" and stopped on a word that caught his eye. He scanned its various meanings: *"An obstruction . . . a hindrance . . . an obstacle . . . a physical or psychological problem."* Perfect. They would become the Impediments.

CHAPTER 8

The Stinson family had found some stability on Thirty-Sixth and Bryant. But in early 1980, the property owners decided to move back in, forcing the Stinsons to pick up stakes again.

Gary Bowman was a regular at the Uptown and heard Anita was looking for a place and didn't have a lot of money. His family owned a two-story frame house on Twenty-Second and Bryant that he could rent to her at a discount. She warned him that her boys had a band and that it could get noisy. Bowman assured her the place was big: six bedrooms, four-thousand-plus square feet—it had actually once been a rooming house. The band could practice in the large unfinished basement. Bowman didn't mention that the basement was also where his father had committed suicide.

Down a rickety staircase, the basement was a cramped brick-and-concrete bunker dominated by a giant octopus furnace and surrounded by exposed piping. "The guy had hung himself from the pipes, and the boys played right next to that," said Anita, who noted that the house was haunted. "You definitely heard things at night. But [the ghost] was friendly. He enjoyed us being there." Despite sharing space with the undead, 2215 Bryant Avenue South would become the band's headquarters.

"Maybe being a little hipper than [my] older parents, she figured, 'Well, if they're going to do this stuff, at least they're under my roof,'" said Westerberg. "We wouldn't have gotten off the ground but for Anita allowing us to play in the basement. And she had to fuckin' put up with that noise."

Though Dogbreath had started out as a weed-centric band, the fuel for the Impediments soon became alcohol. Westerberg wasn't drinking when he joined; in fact, he'd been toting a bottle of grapefruit juice when he met them. "I was on one of my first spells on the wagon," he said. "I was determined to grab the bull by the horns a little bit as far as finding a band to play with. Before that, it felt like a band just was something to do in between partying."

Having been a drug guinea pig through adolescence—taking double hits of whatever his friends dared him to—Westerberg's reaction to pot had become distorted. "If I drank beer and smoked weed, I would get a weird LSD-type high. So I stopped."

Chris Mars had stopped smoking pot too. Booze offered a better buzz for the kind of fast, raucous, rowdy music they were making anyway. They drank cheap domestic brew: Mickey's Big Mouths from the Hums liquor store around the corner, with occasional bottles of Arriba: "One of those Thunderbird–Mad Dog 20/20–Ripple lighter fluid wines," said Westerberg.

Though the band's drinking would come to define and even consume them in later years, in the beginning it was a perfect lubricant for the long hours of practice and their burgeoning friendship. "That was the glue that held us—ol' Jack Daniels," said Mars. Westerberg noted: "They weren't heavy fall-down drunks when I met them. None of us were. We learned to be that together."

* * *

Early on, Chris Mars passed along a tape of his tunes to Westerberg. "One of the songs, I believe, was called 'Down in the Basement,'" Westerberg said. "There were two or three other things. They had a lot of stops and starts and chord changes." Paul rebelled at learning them: "It's no different than playing 'Aqualung' or the Allman Brothers. I said, 'Fuck this. Why don't I just write my own?'"

Westerberg's immersion in punk and garage rock had slowly liberated him from his mind-set as a guitar geek. His years reading music magazines heavily informed the type of songs he would write. "I started to get a sense of what critics think is cool," said Westerberg. "I was very hip to what they'd liked about the New York Dolls. The Dolls' songs were classic rock-and-roll because they had beginnings, middles, and ends."

Westerberg wasn't sure he could really come up with anything truly original, but a Ritchie Blackmore quote in *Guitar Player* magazine—"You're either a genius or a clever thief"—provided a spark. "I thought, *Okay, I'm no genius*, so I went and ripped off a bunch of Johnny Thunders songs and rewrote them. If Johnny can make two chords for 'All by Myself,' I'll just change the key and call it something else."

There would be other influences too: "The Who, the Raspberries, the Sex Pistols, the rockabilly revival, and all the '70s pop radio shit I used to love," said Westerberg. "It was all mashed in there."

Westerberg wrote in his parents' basement in the daytime. By summer he'd amassed nearly thirty tunes. "It was out of necessity. I figured if we're going to have to play an hour set, as fast as we play, we'll need thirty songs."

"Paul's songs were together, rockin' numbers," said Bob. "He basically came with all the words and maybe the bridge, and he'd stumble onto something, and I'd throw something in, and he'd say, 'That's it, that's it!'"

"It was bubblegum garage music sung by a guy who couldn't sing," said Westerberg, "and they sort of harnessed that with their loud rock chops and made it better."

The leitmotif of Westerberg's first songs was searching: looking for girls, drugs, jobs, rides. Others were written as tacit rejections: of school, authority figures, any kind of community ideal. "I can't write happy songs, so I write about the things that make me the most frustrated," Westerberg said.

His greatest frustration was women. He'd always been consumed by romantic crushes on unapproachable figures. "Try Me" was about a curvaceous waitress he'd admired from afar; "Customer" was inspired by the clerk who sold him cigarettes. "Near my house, there was SuperAmerica, a gas station," he said. "There was a cute girl who worked behind the counter who never had time for anything. There was always a line of five truck drivers, and you'd have to get your thing and go."

He also mined the band itself. Bob Stinson's history of juvenile delinquency, Tommy's snotty adolescent antics, and the mad dashes clinging to the back of Chris Mars's motorcycle were the basis for some of his most memorable numbers. "I figured if I'm gonna sing these tunes, it's gotta be something they can relate to," said Westerberg. "If I wasn't specifically writing about them, I would use something they said, their terminology or a phrase, to sew the whole thing together."

The band would become his muse, characters for him to play with in song, and ultimately a kind of myth to promulgate. "I could tell you right now that those things wouldn't have gotten written without them. It's taken me years to realize what they facilitated," he said. "It was the four of us; it was an attitude that made those songs."

★ ★ ★

That spring, Jef Jodell asked Westerberg to fill in on guitar with his new band, Resistor, for an opening slot at the Longhorn. He was secretly trying to bring Paul back into his band. "I figured, if the Impediments don't work out, then we'll be back on track," said Jodell. Westerberg agreed—the Longhorn was the hip venue in town, the center of Minneapolis's burgeoning new wave scene, and he hoped to make a connection there and get a show down the line. He also knew Jodell had some decent equipment and wanted him to record the Impediments' new songs.

As they practiced Jodell noticed a change in Westerberg. "He'd increasingly take the attitude of 'fuck it,'" said Jodell. "He'd come over to our rehearsal spot and take a cigarette and throw it in your beer. Then he'd drink the beer with the cigarette in it and say, 'Head or gut—what's the difference?' It was his way of stealing your drink."

In early March, Resistor played a Longhorn Wednesday Tiger Night beer bust. A suburban muso outfit like Resistor clearly didn't fit in. Westerberg hung back, out of the spotlight. "I knew what they were doing was fucking corny as hell," said Westerberg. "I clung to the amp with my back to the audience, and Jef said something like, 'Come on, step out with me,' so we could do back-to-back Wishbone Ash guitar solos. I was thoroughly embarrassed."

Afterward, a guy from the audience approached Westerberg. "I like your attitude," he said. "Lose these fuckers."

If Westerberg had any question about throwing his lot in with the scruffier Stinson brothers and Chris Mars instead of the more polished Richfield contingent, that night erased his doubts for good. "Playing with Chris and Tommy and Bob, I felt more comfortable," said Westerberg. "They were street-smart and were willing to take a chance and a dare. There was a feeling like, yeah, these guys are troublemakers and fuck-ups. But I can stand with these guys and I'm not going to be afraid."

★ ★ ★

To record the Impediments, Jef Jodell borrowed his brother's reel-to-reel tape machine, got a proper PA from his bass player, and scrounged up a mixing board and microphones. The Stinson basement was too cramped, so they found a private residence—possibly Chris Mars's place (memories differ on this point).

They worked longest on "Try Me," the band's most commercial-sounding song, as well as "Lookin' for Ya" and some others. "She's Firm" and "Looks Like My Old Girl," remained instrumentals or had barely audible scratch vocals. They tracked the songs with Paul, Tommy, and Chris playing live. "Bob overdubbed his guitar," said Jodell, "because Paul didn't believe we could get rhythm tracks clean the first time through with him playing."

Vocally, Westerberg had not yet settled on the Johnny Rotten–inspired ranting that would mark the band's first releases, but sang in a vaguely bluesy manner. Unsure of his voice, he insisted on using a heavily flanged vocal effect on "Try Me." Jodell mixed the songs down and gave two copies to Westerberg. Paul in turn entered "Try Me" and "Lookin' for Ya" in a local talent contest.

The *Songwriter* LP was a collaboration between Minneapolis indie label Twin/Tone Records, rock station KQRS, and monthly music magazine *Trax*. In the late sixties, KQRS had been a groundbreaking FM outlet, but by 1980 it was a tired album-rock warhorse. Teaming with Twin/Tone and *Trax* was the station's attempt to up its cachet among the new wave.

This record's 12 songs were selected from more than 760 entries. A panel of judges evaluated over 38 hours of tapes. Among the acts chosen were the Twin/Tone-affiliated Fingerprints and the Pistons, the power-poppers Twin City Terrors, the Prince-connected duo Chris Moon and John Rivers, and the punk outfit Phil and the Blanks.

One of the many bands that would be passed over for the compilation was the Impediments. Paul Westerberg got a polite but firm (and form) rejection letter from Twin/Tone a few weeks after sending in their songs.

* * *

M innesota, the Land of 10,000 Lakes, was also the land of 10,000 rehab centers. The pioneering clinic Hazelden, which opened in the late 1940s, originally treated alcoholic priests before gearing itself to the professional classes. Hazelden would spawn a new, gentler, more all-encompassing approach to battling addiction known as the "Minnesota Model." By the early 1970s, an influx of federal funds created a rehab boom in the state, with treatment programs popping up all over.

The members of the Dads, the new band of Paul Westerberg's friends Mike Lasley and Steve Skibbe, had almost all been through the teen rehab system. "It was a big industry here," said Lasley. "Any kid who got in trouble remotely related to drugs got sent to treatment."

In April 1980, the younger brother of Dads singer Shawn Micheau was marking his six-month sobriety anniversary, so his mother let him have a party on the grounds of the family farm in Burchville. The Dads invited the Impediments to open. It was a small show—a smattering of friends and acquaintances attended—with the Dads performing outside atop a hay wagon and the Impediments set up in front of an old barn. "It was very cold," said Skibbe. "There were not very many people there."

The Dads had hooked into a small circuit of venues catering to sober teens. "Whenever these chemical-free clubs would open up, we'd hear about them and try to get some work there," said Lasley. One such venue was a teen rehab center in St. Paul called Team House.

The head counselor was Mike Burns, himself a recovering addict. Burns had begun putting on regular weekend concerts at Team House, which was located in the old Assumption Church School. Soon other area treatment programs would bus in groups of newly sober kids for the shows. "It was not unusual to have two hundred, three hundred people at these dances any given night," said Burns. "People came from AA clubs, some people came just because they'd heard about it. It was open to people from the neighborhood as well. But it was policed with the same requirements: No drug or alcohol use on the premises. If someone showed up stoned or high they were asked to leave. This is a chemical-free group of people. We can't have anybody drinking or blowing grass."

On a Saturday in early April, the Impediments were booked as the evening's entertainment. It would mark the band's first public concert.

Kevin Bowe—who would eventually join the Dads as a guitarist—attended the show; he was an eighteen-year-old resident of another treatment center called Shanti House. "It was the most surreal thing," he said. "Here's a bunch of sixteen- to twenty-two-year-old idiots that are crawling out of their skin—because you're spending the first week of your life not stoned all the time. Imagine how great a band had to be to get my attention under those circumstances."

Bowe called watching the Impediments "the weirdest musical experience of my life. They weren't exactly good, but I just loved them. And I couldn't figure out what I liked about them so much, but I knew they were the best band I'd ever seen. They were totally exciting."

The Impediments had steeled their nerves for their first public performance by getting good and drunk. "We were all insecure people at that time," said Mars. "That was a way for us to release our inhibitions and go a little bit more wild onstage." They mostly played covers: Heartbreakers, Slade, Kinks. The audience was scandalized when they noticed that the back of Tommy's bass had a big pot leaf painted on it. "Which, at a sober dance, was kind of indicative of things to come with the group," said Bowe.

The Impediments had been scheduled to play two short sets, but they were caught drinking in the parking lot during the break. A buzz went through the crowd: "Everyone was like, '*Ooh, ooh*,'" said Bowe. Word soon got back to Mike Burns. "At these dances I was the big Kahuna," said Burns. "I was judge, jury, and executioner." Burns brought the guillotine down swiftly. He booted them off the stage, out of the building, and swore he'd have them blackballed: "The Impediments," he told them, "will never play in this town again!"

* * *

A few days later, Westerberg got a call from Jef Jodell. Resistor had landed a monthly gig at the Paradise Ballroom in Waconia, forty miles west of Minneapolis. Would the Impediments open? Westerberg agreed, with one caveat. "We can't be the Impediments," he said. "We've already ruined that name for good. We're gonna be the Replacements." After Mike Burns's threat, the band decided to change their name, just to be safe. As Chris Mars would later note, becoming the Replacements "seemed to . . . accurately [describe] our collective 'secondary' social esteem."

Since none of them could drive, some friends of Chris's helped them get to Waconia. The Paradise Ballroom was big, with a capacity of one thousand. Resistor's gig was a Saturday night special: for three bucks' admission, you got to drink free beer for an hour.

Maybe 150 people were scattered about the venue, getting wasted, when the Replacements went on. Half the crowd was Resistor fans from Richfield, the other half locals. Westerberg remembered playing to "eighty drunk cowboys who were sitting back with their bottles of whiskey and not knowing what to think of us."

They opened with Slade's "My Town." It was chaos onstage: "We counted off the first number and probably each started a different song," recalled Westerberg. "I remember Bob being airborne—jumping around and shit. And Tommy was scared shitless. Jodell came up and said, 'Ya gotta turn down,' and then all of a sudden the power went out and we were done."

Though Westerberg recalled that the band "got about thirty-five seconds in" before being "booed off the stage," the Replacements actually played a handful of songs. But the audience was grousing by the middle of the first number.

Jodell was in the back of the room, mixing sound and taping the gig, when the ballroom's owner ran over. "You gotta get these guys off the stage," the old duffer told him. "I've just had this table of four come up and tell me this is the worst band they've ever heard and they want their twelve dollars back so they can go out for pizza instead."

Jodell tried to argue, biding for time, but eventually was forced to go up and relay the message to Westerberg. "I told him, 'We're gonna have to pull ya,'" said Jodell. "I think he spit on the floor or something. He was pissed."

Being booted only reinforced the group's defiant, contrarian impulses. "We were well aware that if we get onstage and every time we're pissing people off to where they can't stand to even see us or hear us, we must be doing something pretty outrageous," said Westerberg, who wrote a "weapon song" he could pull out the next time they faced a hostile crowd, called "Shutup."

Playing sober dances and ballroom gigs in the sticks was a road to nowhere. Somehow the Replacements needed to play Minneapolis proper, at a place like the Longhorn, where their music would be appreciated and their behavior tolerated. But they had no idea how to get their foot in the door of the club. Fortunately for the band, fate intervened.

"There was a lost link, this guy we only knew as Denny," said Westerberg. "We were rehearsing one day at the Stinson house, and this guy and his friend stopped in. They heard us playing from outside, they were decked out in sort of punk military gear. And this Denny character said, 'You guys are fucking good.' He was probably the first person who had told us anything positive—all we'd heard was 'Turn that down' or 'You suck!'"

The mysterious Denny said something else too. He told them they should make a tape and take it to this guy, a local mover and shaker. He was a deejay at the Longhorn and helped book the club some. He happened to manage the nearby record store, Oar Folkjokeopus. His name was Peter.

CHAPTER 9

Peter Jesperson never liked going to church. When he was a boy—around seven or eight years old—it annoyed him mostly because it interfered with watching *Bowery Boys* reruns on Sunday mornings. He loved the Bowery Boys, a motley crew of tough-talking city kids who seemed to court trouble constantly.

A few years later, another gang of working-class wiseguys captured his imagination: the Beatles. By then, Jesperson didn't need church at all; he'd found another religion in rock-and-roll. Whatever room he had in his heart for faith, for belief, he devoted to music—discovering, consuming, and collecting it with a rhapsodic passion.

Peter Louis Jesperson was born February 11, 1954, in St. Paul, Minnesota. A brown-haired boy with green eyes and a bony countenance, he was the second son of Chester "Chet" Jesperson and Carolyn Fosnes. His elder brother Alan was almost seven years his senior, and Peter's arrival had come as a bit of a surprise to the family.

Growing up in the western Minneapolis suburb of Minnetonka, Jesperson and his brother enjoyed a bucolic childhood. "We had five acres," he said, "a pasture surrounding the house, a stream and a woods, and lots of horses, dogs, cats." Inside their home, it was a less idyllic atmosphere.

Jesperson's mother, a former executive secretary who'd become a homemaker after having kids, was a fragile woman with myriad problems. Carolyn's father had died when she was two, her mother when she was six. She'd spent her childhood bouncing around between different relatives. "She grew up feeling like 'I don't belong, like I'm not wanted,'" recalled her youngest son. "She was, I would say, a little unbalanced as a result. She had some mental issues. Some drinking issues. She had some depression too."

Carolyn's problems impacted Jesperson's early childhood. One of the most haunting memories of his mother came when he was six years old. "She'd been drinking and took some kind of medication and came into my room and just collapsed at the foot of my bed. We had to call an ambulance that pulled up on the lawn and carried her out," he recalled. "I was aware of my mother being difficult, because of her mental state and her drinking and the pressure that it put on my dad. I really thought they could divorce at a certain point." Carolyn would improve after spending time in a mental institution in Prescott, Wisconsin. "They helped her get better, and things were fairly normal after that. I mean, things were always a little dodgy, especially when she drank too much. But she ultimately came out the other end."

Life in the Jesperson house was one of deep inquisitiveness and intellect. His father, a salesman for Curtis Circulation Company, which distributed the *Saturday Evening Post*, among other publications, had a genius-level IQ. Both his parents were lifetime bridge masters and voracious readers. Neither, however, was particularly musical. "When stereo sound came in," said Jesperson, "my mom actually said, 'Oh, I don't like to be surrounded by music'—she just liked the one speaker over in the corner."

Jesperson, on the other hand, loved the feeling of being enveloped in sound. His earliest musical memories, as a tot, were hearing Elvis singles—"Hound Dog," "Wear My Ring Around Your Neck." Thanks to his older brother Alan—who would go on to become an accomplished bluegrass picker—he also got swept up in the early '60s folk boom: the music of the Kingston Trio; Peter, Paul and Mary; and Minnesota's native son, Bob Dylan, whose 1963 album, *The Freewheelin' Bob Dylan*, was a particular favorite. From the first, Jesperson was a passionate advocate for the artists he liked. "Even as a kid, I defended Dylan's singing voice," he said. "I thought those who criticized him weren't listening."

★ ★ ★

I n early February 1964, just a couple of days before his tenth birthday, Jesperson's life changed for good. He'd heard of the Beatles—the Liverpool foursome then descending on America amid a wave of unprecedented anticipation—and dug their first singles on the radio. That Sunday night, as the band made its historic appearance on *The Ed Sullivan Show*, his family was eating dinner with the television on in the background. When the Beatles came on and the screaming began, Jesperson rose from his chair, almost in a trance.

"Peter Louis Jesperson!" scolded his mother as he pressed right up to the glass of the family's Zenith, lost in the sound and vision of the four figures in front of him.

"Seeing the Beatles, it was such a fundamental, profound thing that happened to me," said Jesperson. "It felt like destiny, like this was my music. As people, they were funny and irreverent too. I fell so hard, so fast, for them."

The next day he went to Record Lane at the nearby Knollwood Mall and bought a copy of *Meet the Beatles*. "This was the first time I felt like 'I *need* to have this record.' I remember putting it on my dresser and, before I fell asleep each night, looking at the album cover. I just couldn't stop staring at it."

That rush of discovery, the sweet, almost narcotic quality of losing himself in a new band or record, was a feeling Jesperson would become addicted to. He began to devour the music of the British Invasion: the Beatles and Stones, the Kinks, Yardbirds, and the Who. He loved American bands too, such as Paul Revere and the Raiders, the Cryan' Shames, and the Left Banke. He also adored local Twin Cities favorites like the Castaways and the Jesters, who were featured on the *Big Hits of Mid-America* compilations put out by the Minneapolis-based label SOMA.

As a kid, Jesperson delighted in turning his family and friends on to his latest finds, playing deejay on his little portable turntable as he recited liner notes and recording details from memory. By the time Jesperson hit his teens, it was obvious he didn't care about girls or sports or anything but music. His mother would admonish him: "You've taken something that was intended to be a hobby and you've blown it all out of proportion."

Though Jesperson took drum lessons and had a solid sense of time, he felt he'd never be able to play an instrument "like the people I held in such high esteem." Instead, he began hanging out with some junior high friends who had a garage group called The Gross Reality. Jesperson referred to himself as a "Band Aide": he helped carry their equipment and suggested material for them to cover. They mostly played dances at country clubs or school functions, and Jesperson would be at the gigs, fussing over their performance, a pint-sized aesthete consumed with the minutest details. He fancied being a rock-and-roll impresario, like Beatles patron Brian Epstein or Rolling Stones producer-manager Andrew Loog Oldham. "They seemed like pals with the band," said Jesperson, "like they hung out and were really hands-on, an extension of the groups."

By the time Jesperson reached Hopkins-Lindbergh High, he'd started growing his hair long and was going to concerts and getting into drugs—pot, then psychedelics. Somewhat ironically, given what lay in store in his life, it was years before Jesperson ever took a drink. "We didn't like drinking, me and my friends," he said. "We were part of that generation that was into mind-expanding drugs, and drinking was something the older generation did. But another part of the reason I didn't like it is that I saw my mom and what it did to her. To me, drinking and getting drunk was just an ugly thing."

After getting his heart broken by a girl his senior year, Jesperson's behavior became more bellicose: he refused to have his picture taken for the yearbook, finished his classes through independent study, and skipped the formal graduation ceremony altogether.

In the summer of '72, his father's publishing company began doing a trial run selling *New Musical Express* (*NME*) out of the United Kingdom. Jesperson landed a gig hustling copies to all the newsstands and record stores in the Twin Cities, earning a nickel for each issue he distributed. ("My first real job in music," he recalled.)

The *NME* experiment didn't fly and ended after just a few months. But one of the record stores on Jesperson's route—located in South Minneapolis—was a place called North Country Music, owned by Wayne Clayman. In early 1973, Clayman sold the business to Vern Sanden. A gruff family man who'd worked as an air traffic controller, Sanden seemed an unlikely figure to buy a record store. But he was a passionate rock-and-roll fan, who took the titles of two favorite records—*Oar* by Skip Spence and *Folkjokeopus* by Roy Harper—and renamed the store Oar Folkjokeopus.

"Everyone thought he was crazy," said Jesperson. "All the adjacent businesses—the hardware store across the street and furniture store next door—figured, 'Oh, this place will be gone in a month or two.'" But Oar Folk, located at Twenty-Sixth and Lyndale, flourished thanks to a dedicated clientele of record collectors, music freaks, and heads like Jesperson, who was a fixture at the store. One afternoon he was browsing the used LPs when Sanden approached him. "Vern could be such an intimidating guy. I remember thinking he didn't like me. When he came up, I honestly thought he was going to say, 'Get out of my store!'" Instead, he offered Jesperson a job.

Jesperson started work there in April 1973 and also attended a broadcasting school called the Brown Institute, in the hopes of becoming a late-night radio deejay. He realized that ambition soon after graduating, landing a graveyard slot on KFMX, a "gold record only" station in town. Jesperson chafed, however, against its limited playlist. He broke format once, spinning John Lennon's version of "Stand by Me" without permission, and nearly got fired for it. He finally quit the station in 1975, blowing off his shift to go see a Bruce Springsteen show at the Guthrie Theater. By then, Sanden had offered Jesperson a full-time gig to manage Oar Folk.

With his fussy, fastidious nature—down to the crisp white dress shirts he wore, buttoned all the way to the top—Jesperson didn't so much manage Oar Folk as curate it, gradually building it into the best record store in the region. When the UK punk explosion hit in 1977, Jesperson began express airfreighting the latest singles from England directly to the store. The day the Sex Pistols' debut arrived, there was a line out Oar Folk's door of customers waiting for the UPS truck. Soon the shop was hosting in-store appearances by the likes of Ian Hunter and Mick Ronson and David Johansen; the Ramones, Dead Boys, and Talking Heads all became regular visitors as well. Customers began coming from far and wide—Chicago, Milwaukee, even Canada—as Oar Folk became known as "The Rock 'n' Roll Head Quarters for the Upper Midwest."

* * *

By the midseventies, record stores in the Twin Cities—not just Oar Folk but the Wax Museum and Electric Fetus, among others—were the only real oases of rock-and-roll culture. Minneapolis had flourished as a music town for much of the sixties, with a strong folk and blues community, a post-Beatles garage band boom, and a colorful psychedelic scene. But that golden era came to a crashing halt in the early seventies as professional cover bands came to dominate the local music landscape.

As Tim Holmes would write in a historical survey of the city for *Trouser Press:* "By the end of the [1960s], a band's worth was measured by how precisely it could replicate the hits of Britain and the Coasts and a certain daffy originality got lost in the struggle towards Serious Musicianship. The local band scene became, not untypically, the province of human jukeboxes. Most anybody with real talent split town in order to be heard."

Among the only people left playing original music were wispy folk singers and white blues bands on the West Bank. The quietly thriving African American R&B/funk scene in Minneapolis was confined to a relatively segregated area on the north side of the city and was invisible to the public at large—at least until the emergence of Prince in 1978.

The lack of original live music was compounded by the abysmal state of radio at that time. The city's big FM rock station, KQRS, was long deteriorated from any sense of its free-form, underground roots and was playing the worst kind of '70s AOR (album-oriented rock) schlock. In general, the Twin Cities was among the most conservative radio markets in the country. When local band Lipps Inc. scored a number-one *Billboard* hit with its disco number "Funkytown" in 1980, there wasn't even a station in Minneapolis that would play it.

The first stirrings of change came in the summer of 1974, when the New York Dolls made an appearance at the Minneapolis State Fair, playing the Teen Stage, in support of their Mercury Records debut. The band was late getting to the show, stuck in traffic, as the crowd—which included many future players in the local punk and indie rock scene—waited eagerly. When the Dolls finally arrived onstage, singer David Johansen took to the microphone, looked out over the fair—still very much a rural, farm-based event—and chided, in his gravelly Long Island accent, "What I really want to know is: *who won da pie-eatin' contest?*"

The Dolls' state fair performance was instructive: they played short, sharp songs that heralded a return to the simpler 1950s roots of rock-and-roll. The impact was felt by local bands like Thumbs Up—a group, fronted by white soul shouter Curt Almsted, aka Curtiss A, and featuring guitarist Bob Dunlap, that would transform from a covers act to playing original material. A handful of other bands, including the early Rolling Stones–influenced outfit Flamingo, and the *Nuggets*-digging garage crew the Hypstrz, soon emerged with the same back-to-basics sensibility.

While all that was happening in the city, Minneapolis punk was being birthed in Peter Jesperson's home suburb of Minnetonka. That's where two boyhood friends, singer-guitarist Chris Osgood and drummer Dave Ahl, launched the Suicide Commandos. "Dave and I both hated everything we heard on the radio, and we knew we wanted to form a new kind of band," said Osgood. "We listened a lot to Gene Vincent and Eddie Cochran, that's what we were thinking."

The second bass player they auditioned, Steve Almaas, joined in the summer of '75, and the group was off and running. Though the term had not yet come into vogue, the Commandos were a "punk" band—playing a batch of fast, reductive originals, much like the Ramones, who were developing a similar sound in New York City.

While the Commandos had a definitive musical identity, they had nowhere to play. In the fall of '75, Oar Folk employee Andy Schwartz convened a meeting in his apartment to address the situation. He gathered together the Commandos and other frustrated acts, including Flamingo and Curtiss A, and pitched a plan. "It was my thought that we got all these places that are exclusively booking cover bands, but we got other bars in this town, some of which have no music or used to have live bands in the '60s," said Schwartz. "What if we just approached them or canvassed them and said, 'Let us play for the door'?"

The Commandos beat the pavement and got a foothold playing shows at the Blitz Bar, located in the basement of The Roaring Twenties, a strip club in downtown Minneapolis. Beyond finding venues to play, the bigger goal was to will a new rock scene into existence. "We even wrote a little manifesto," said Osgood, "that we wanted to change the center of gravity of the local scene from the West Bank and the blues to Twenty-Sixth and Lyndale and rock-and-roll."

★　★　★

In 1976 the Commandos put out their first two singles. The recordings were engineered by a brainy twenty-four-year-old studio owner named Paul Stark.

The son of a successful hardware wholesaler from Minneapolis, Paul David Stark was born into a fairly conservative family with a legacy of black sheep artists. He attended the prestigious Blake School, alongside future *Saturday Night Live* writer-producers Al Franken and Tom Davis. A financially adroit youth, as a freshman in college Stark ended up buying a house in Dinkytown at 606 Thirteenth Avenue Southeast. He rented the upstairs bedrooms to some friends to cover his mortgage and turned the first floor into a recording studio, called P. David Productions. He cut a number of odd projects there—from a piano-playing Catholic priest to pre-fame new age musician Yanni—before hooking up with the Commandos.

By 1977, Stark and Osgood both saw the obvious need for a new independent rock label in Minneapolis. "The indie labels of the sixties had come and gone, and there weren't any other real companies operating at the time," said Stark. He and Osgood decided to start a record company with Charley Hallman, a sportswriter and sometime rock critic for the *St. Paul Dispatch*. Hallman had championed the Suicide Commandos and could supply the needed seed money for the label.

Stark figured he'd handle the business and recording side, and Osgood would serve as the label's talent scout and A&R (artists and repertoire) man. But by then, the Commandos, having made a splash at CBGB's in New York, had signed a major-label deal with Polygram's punk imprint, Blank Records. Osgood bowed out of Stark's venture, but not before recommending Oar Folkjokeopus manager Peter Jesperson as his replacement.

Despite having diametrically opposed personalities—Jesperson was passionate and excitable, while Stark was measured in the extreme—something clicked between them. "Paul was a very unique individual, very smart," said Jesperson. "He liked rock, but knew about classical music. I found that all very interesting."

Stark, Jesperson, and Hallman began meeting weekly over drinks at the CC Club to hatch plans for the label, which Jesperson suggested naming Twin/Tone. They drew up a list of local artists they wanted to work with. Twin/Tone would feature Curtiss A as its flagship act. "Curt was the main reason I wanted to get involved in doing a label," said Jesperson, who'd been watching Almsted tear up the Tempo Bar and other local venues for several years. Fingerprints—who included two of Jesperson's childhood friends, drummer Kevin Glynn and guitarist Mike Owens, along with singer Mark Throne and bassist Steve Fjelstad—would also join the roster. Glynn and Owens also moved their recording gear into Stark's Dinkytown digs, launching Blackberry Way, which would become Twin/Tone's in-house studio.

In hopes of finding a new band to round out the roster, Twin/Tone threw an audition party at Blackberry Way in January 1978. Half a dozen groups turned up and played, including the one they signed: the Suburbs. The Suburbs were a juxtaposition of high musicianship (in the case of the gifted pianist Chan Poling), appealing amateurism (most of the rest of the band were still learning their instruments), and art-school conceptualism (they wore monochromatic suits and played in front of a postmodernist stage backdrop designed by guitarist Bruce Allen).

"I didn't come from blues and rock," said Poling. "I liked the packaging of rock. I liked Bowie and Roxy Music. I liked everything about the showmanship of it. I dug the idea of having a band logo and dressing a certain way. That was a big part of it, as much as the music." Early on, the Suburbs fit into the punk/new wave mold largely on the strength of front man Beej Chaney's manic stage presence and a clutch of minimalist, minute-long tunes like "Chemistry Set" ("I'm into chemistry and that's about it.")

Twin/Tone would formally launch in April 1978, with EPs from Curtiss A's group the Spooks, Fingerprints, and the Suburbs. Despite a manufacturing snafu—Allen had designed the jackets too big for the printer's template, so everyone had to chip in and hand-fold and glue several thousand sleeves—the records themselves were a surprise success. They were all well reviewed—written up in *Trouser Press*, the *New York Rocker*, and the UK's *New Musical Express*—and sold through their initial pressing. Emboldened by their first slate of releases, which included a couple more singles from Fingerprints and the Jets, Twin/Tone decided to put together a snapshot of the growing local scene. They went to Amos Heilicher of SOMA Records and got his blessing to produce a spiritual sequel to the label's *Big Hits of Mid-America* compilations. Featuring a dozen tracks from the Suicide Commandos, the Suburbs, Curtiss A, the Pistons, and the Hypstrz, among others, *Big Hits of Mid-America: Volume III*, released in early 1979, cemented Twin/Tone's place as the leading rock label in town. "We used to joke that Twin/Tone was really forced into existence," said Jesperson. "There were so many groups, someone had to record them. We figured it might as well be us."

* * *

The late '70s rock-and-roll renaissance in Minneapolis got a further boost in the summer of 1977 with the opening of a nightclub called Jay's Longhorn. Jay Berine had been a drag racer in North Minneapolis, and he parlayed a successful speed shop business into a piece of a downtown disco called Scottie's on Seventh. His partners there eventually pushed him out of the business, and Berine was determined to open a new venue. He found the ideal spot at Hennepin Avenue and Fifth Street, a restaurant called the Longhorn. It'd once been part of the Nino's Steakhouse chain and had a bit of an unsavory reputation; a restaurant manager was stabbed there over a gambling debt in front of a roomful of customers.

Opening its doors on June 1, 1977, with a show by the local group Flamingo, the Longhorn followed soon after with its first national act, booking New York rocker Mink DeVille. The drinking age in Minnesota was still nineteen ("Not that we checked IDs very well," said Berine), and the hunger for live, original music was massive. "The day we opened there were twenty people, and they told twenty other people, and another twenty after that. The Longhorn went from zero to monstrous in a matter of weeks, not months," said Berine. "Kids from the University of Minnesota, hipsters from South Minneapolis, it seemed like everyone was in a band or knew a band in those days. I don't want to say we created the scene, but the scene certainly found us."

Promoters soon began funneling big touring punk and new wave acts—Iggy Pop, Elvis Costello, the Police, Blondie, Talking Heads—into the club. The Longhorn's legal capacity was 350, though they might sell as many as 700 tickets to a concert and let another 100 people sneak in. Before long, Berine and his booker, Al Wodkte, were putting on local and national shows seven nights a week.

"The Longhorn was where you could sit and look up Debbie Harry's skirt, hang out with David Byrne, and have a drink with David Johansen," said Chan Poling of the Suburbs, who quickly became one of the top draws at the club. "I remember Bruce Springsteen coming down to the Longhorn and me and Hugo [Klaers] and the Boss drinking beer together. The Longhorn was totally the place that tapped into that whole world."

Borrowing an idea from his time at Scottie's, Berine hired local deejays to spin in between band breaks. Peter Jesperson began playing records at the

Longhorn practically every night and became something of an attraction himself. "Peter was fantastic," said fellow deejay Kevin Cole. "He had an interesting way to put things together where you might hear the Sex Pistols and Donna Summer back to back . . . or he'd be playing Elvis Presley and then the Only Ones, just a great mix." Jesperson also started consulting with the Longhorn on which artists were selling well at Oar Folk, who they should bring to the club, and which local acts were worth booking.

Over its first two years, the Longhorn's reputation soared, but its finances struggled. "We had tremendous overhead, and everyone was stealing," said Berine, who almost sold the club eight months in, before taking on some outside investment.

Berine's reign at the Longhorn would ultimately end in his arrest. With the club's public profile growing, he became a target for authorities. "Everybody was doing cocaine and Quaaludes in those days," said Berine, who sometimes paid bands in powder. "It was huge fun, but I was dumb enough to think I was invisible." In 1979 he was busted at home, with a couple thousand counterfeit Quaaludes, as part of a sting operation. Taking a plea deal, he was sentenced to a year in Sandstone Federal Penitentiary. Berine reluctantly handed over control of the club to his cousin, Hartley Frank.

An outsized character and a professional caterer by trade, the 300-pound Frank worked all the high-class weddings and big concerts in the Twin Cities. He drove a Lincoln Continental with suicide doors and a license plate that read: Rock 1. Frank had repellent manners and hygiene, as well as insatiable appetites: each day he typically devoured a dozen chocolate Cokes—each thick with Hershey's syrup. Frank was gay and a notorious chicken hawk, hitting on every young attractive customer and band member who passed through the club, and he was usually seen at the bar with a new boy sitting on his lap each week.

Though he came up with a range of gimmicky promotional ideas—including staging "new band" beer bust bills called "Tiger Nights"—and gave away free tacos and spaghetti to drum up business, Frank was ill suited to run the club. He had no organizational skills and was bad-tempered. He fought with customers, promoters, and artists alike—at one point he nearly got into a physical altercation with Talking Heads' diminutive bassist Tina Weymouth—and generally had a menacing air about him. "Hartley looked like Jabba the Hut and acted like the head of an illicit organization," said Poling.

With the help of liquor store owner Zelmer Shrell, Frank would buy out Berine's interests in the club in 1980. He eventually changed the name to Zoogie's, before turning it into a full-on gay bar and then running it into the ground in 1982. (Frank would die of complications from AIDS in 1983.)

By then, the Longhorn would be supplanted by another downtown venue called Sam's. Located at the corner of First Avenue and Seventh Street, in the former Greyhound Bus station, it went through a couple of incarnations in the '70s. It had started the decade as a hip rock club called The Depot—hosting concerts by Gram Parsons, the Mothers of Invention, the Faces, and Procol

Harum—before becoming part of a national disco franchise based out of Cincinnati called Uncle Sam's.

In 1979 the Uncle Sam's chain decided to cut ties with its Minneapolis location, leaving the club deeply in debt. The owners wanted to close, but a group of employees, led by manager Steve McClellan, offered to take a cut in pay in order to keep the venue going. McClellan had already begun booking some national acts into Uncle Sam's—amid the usual disco dance nights and mud wrestling promotions—but saw an opportunity to do more. In addition to its 1,500-capacity main room, Sam's—as it would be called before changing its name to First Avenue—converted an adjacent side storage space into a 250-capacity club called the 7th St Entry. Opened in March 1980, the intimate room became a haven for local bands. McClellan, by his own admission, was still learning about booking: "I didn't know metal from jazz, but I knew which people to go to, to help figure that out," he said. One of his key contacts in helping shape the clubs' calendars early on was Peter Jesperson, with whom he'd become close friends.

The emergence of Sam's and the 7th St Entry was yet another confirmation that a golden age of Twin Cities music was at hand. "People started moving from Kansas and the Dakotas and Wisconsin to come to Minneapolis," said music critic P. D. Larson. "Every time you'd turn around there was another new band, more shows, and everyone was releasing records. There was this headstrong momentum. You didn't have time to worry about your place in the cosmos 'cause there was always another exciting gig coming up."

* * *

The new wave scene in Minneapolis crested in September 1979, with "Marathon '80: A New-No-Now Festival." The brainchild of Tim Carr—a rock writer and programmer at the Walker Art Center—the two-day concert event was held at the University of Minnesota Fieldhouse. Carr and Jesperson lived across the hall from one another at the Modesto Apartments, and the two would stay up late, hashing out bands and ideas for the festival. M-80, as it came to be known, would feature performances by Devo (performing as DOVE, The Band of Love), James Chance and the Contortions, the Fleshtones, and the dB's, as well as much of the Twin/Tone roster, including Curtiss A, Fingerprints, and the Suburbs.

Arguably the first alternative music festival ever held, M-80 proved to be a watershed. In a few short years, Minneapolis had gone from a tertiary market and musical backwater to a city that was on the leading edge of rock-and-roll.

In the middle of all this action—linking the record store, the label, the clubs, and the festival—was Peter Jesperson. In the fall of 1979, he was the subject of a flattering profile piece in the *Minneapolis Star* by pop critic Jon Bream. "Jesperson is not a disc jockey on a far-reaching radio station or a columnist for a big-circulation newspaper," wrote Bream. "Yet he is the most important rock music tastemaker in the Twin Cities." The story, which included a big photo of Jesperson sitting in his apartment at the Modesto surrounded by piles of records, confirmed his status as "the gatekeeper to the hip crowd, the guru of the underground, the godfather of the rock cognoscenti," and someone whose support could make a local band.

Jesperson had seen plenty of good groups and singers. It was his nature to be enthusiastic and encouraging of anyone with promise. But he'd yet to find the thing he was most looking for—that one extraordinary band that felt like the discovery of a lifetime.

* * *

For the first six months of their career, the Replacements—née the Impediments—had led a schizophrenic existence. They'd met by charmed happenstance and quickly created an alchemical magic as a band. But their subsequent efforts to perform and garner public attention had been disastrous, to put it mildly.

By the late spring of 1980, they'd done two proper gigs—and been booted from one for their behavior and practically booed off stage for their playing at the other. They'd made a demo recording that had been simultaneously rejected by both the hip label and the not-so-hip rock station in Minneapolis.

The Replacements had zero prospects, but they were undeterred. "Bob and I at least understood that this was the only road up and out," said Paul Westerberg. "We had no skill: he was a cook, I was a janitor, and it was like, 'We make it out in rock-and-roll or we die trying.'"

They decided to push ahead with another recording.

The origin of this second Replacements demo would be the subject of some later debate. Westerberg's Richfield pal Jef Jodell would insist that the recording was, in fact, from a live tape he made of the band's truncated Paradise Ballroom set that April. Others, including Tommy Stinson, would recall the demo as having been self-recorded by the band in the basement of the Bryant Avenue house. "My brother had a reel-to-reel TEAC, two-track, with two microphones in the room," said Tommy. "I think that's what we used to cut those songs."

Whatever the actual genesis, by early May the Replacements had recorded four new Westerberg compositions: "Raised in the City," "Shutup," "Don't Turn Me Down," and "Shape Up."

The difference between the band's first and second demos was dramatic. Westerberg's initial songs—"She's Firm" and "We Ain't Got No Class" among them—were unsure and overcomplicated, stuffed with too many ideas, words, and changes. A couple were old holdovers, written before he'd even met the band, and the rest were penned before he'd developed a full sense of their strengths.

With the new batch of material, he pared down the arrangements and sharpened his lyrical focus. Compact and driving, the songs took advantage of Chris's battering beats, Tommy's kinetic rhythm, and Bob's bullish riffs.

Westerberg also abandoned his efforts to warble in a conventional manner—letting the naturally raw, raspy quality of his voice come to the fore.

The first demo had been cut in a clean, controlled atmosphere and tracked as a three-piece, with Bob overdubbing his parts later. The new songs were captured live, with the four of them working in close quarters, with sound ricocheting all around and the band playing as though their very lives and futures depended on it. They very well might have.

Heeding the advice of the mysterious Denny—the punk-attired passerby who'd dropped in on the band during a basement rehearsal—Westerberg decided to hit up Peter Jesperson. Unaware of Jesperson's role with Twin/Tone, the Replacements' sole intention was to solicit a gig at the Longhorn.

* * *

In the second week of May, Westerberg purloined a used Maxell C-90 tape from his older sister Anne, dubbed the Replacements' tracks over her Santana record, and got ready to try the band's luck again. With the cassette in his jacket pocket, he walked the dozen or so blocks from his house and through the doors of Oar Folk.

Jesperson was easily identifiable from Westerberg's previous visits to the store. "I knew Pete as the guy at the counter, and thought him, frankly, rather snooty," said Westerberg.

Clutching the tape, he hesitated for a time, waiting for the right moment to make his approach. "I'd gone in there with the thing in my clammy palm, afraid to give it to him," he said. "I would think, *I'll go over now*, and then another cool guy would show up and I'd think, *No, I can't.*"

He finally worked up the nerve and handed the tape to Jesperson. "I remember him accepting it, but not graciously," said Westerberg, who wrote down his first name and the number to his parents' house on a scrap of paper. "I was very quick to get out of there."

Jesperson didn't listen to the tape right away. In fact, Westerberg had to call a couple of times to follow up before he did. "I apologized and told him I'd listen and get back to him," said Jesperson. After a couple weeks, and with other Longhorn and Twin/Tone submission tapes piling up, Jesperson began feeling guilty. One afternoon he took a shoebox of demos into the back office at Oar Folk. He started going through them, popping the tapes into a little tabletop boombox, while doing paperwork for the store.

Typically, he'd listen to a couple of songs before rendering a verdict and moving on. "I was playing one cassette after another. I remember having the feeling that there were a lot of bands that sounded like the Stooges," said Jesperson. "Not a bad thing to sound like, but it was odd. I'd gone through maybe six or seven of them already. Then I picked up the tape Paul had given me."

Jesperson looked at the cassette quizzically. It had something crossed off and the Replacements' name written in, along with the titles. "It cracked me up," Jesperson remembered, "because not only was there no case for it, but on the flip side, in very girly cursive, it said: 'Santana—*Moonflower*.'"

He popped it in, hit play, and resumed his work. Upon hearing the jolting, distorted guitar riff that kicked off the opening track—which Westerberg had written out as "Raze the City"—Jesperson's ears perked up.

"It was the fierceness, I guess," he said. "It was a crappy recording, but, man, it was such a rush from the first notes."

He listened intently until he heard Westerberg howl the start of the second verse: "Got a little honey, nice tight rear / She gets rubber in all four gears."

Jesperson wheeled toward the boombox, stopped the tape, and rewound it. He listened again and felt a familiar excitement. It was the same instant, overwhelming sense of discovery he'd experienced as a boy seeing the Beatles on *Ed Sullivan*. "If I've ever had a magic moment in my life," Jesperson would say, "it was right then, listening to that tape."

He went through the rest of the songs, bowled over by the ferocity of the singer, the keening power of the guitars, the inherent swing in the rhythm—this was no paint-by-numbers punk band—and the guttersnipe lyricism. It sounded to him like some magic merger of the ring-a-ling teen anthems of Chuck Berry and the aggrieved snarl of the Sex Pistols.

By his own admission, Jesperson "went completely nuts" over the tape. He immediately called several friends, including his girlfriend, Linda Hultquist, and best buddy, Steve Klemz, raving about it. "I said, 'You've gotta check out this tape. Either I've lost my mind or this is the best thing I've heard in years. . . .' They came down and corroborated my excitement."

Musician Danny Amis happened to be in the store that day, and Jesperson ushered him into the back to hear the demo. "We both mistakenly commented—"'Well, the Replacements isn't a good name,'" said Amis. "But 'Shutup'—I remember hearing that and going, 'This is better than the stuff coming out of New York.' Peter was so excited, you could tell immediately he wanted to sign them to Twin/Tone."

The following afternoon, a now-frustrated Westerberg decided to stop by Oar Folk to see if Jesperson had finally gotten around to their demo. He stepped a few feet into the store when he heard the Replacements' tape blasting. Worried what Jesperson's reaction was going to be, he practically ran out.

Westerberg walked around for a while nervously before finally heading home. He'd just settled down to dinner when the phone rang. "I started to take a bite of a hamburger," he said, "and there was Pete calling."

After dispensing with the pleasantries—Jesperson explained his role with the Longhorn, as well as his position at Twin/Tone—he matter-of-factly asked Westerberg: "So, were you thinking of doing an album or just a single?"

There was a long silence.

"You mean, you think this shit's worth recording?" replied a disbelieving Westerberg. "I was just trying to get a gig opening for someone."

Jesperson told him he still had to play the tape for his partners at the label, but that he was serious about signing the band. "I was on cloud nine," said Westerberg. "This was just to put in a good word with him as deejay at the club that he might let us open for another band some night. The fact that he called wanting to make a record? It was like, 'Whoa, are you kidding?'"

Before he hung up, Jesperson also told Westerberg he wanted to see the band the next time they played, hopefully as soon as possible.

* * *

Suddenly, Westerberg needed to scare up a gig. He again turned to his Marsden Maintenance coworker Steve Skibbe, whose group, the Dads, had made connections on the sober-house circuit.

Skibbe would help the Replacements line up a show with the Dads in early June at a venue in Southeast Minneapolis called the Bataclan. Located on Twenty-Sixth Street and Chicago Avenue, the Bataclan had started out as a church, then become the Pillsbury Theatre. The owner, Mike Foreman—a prominent player in the city's musical theater scene—had recently gone through his own alcohol treatment. Inspired by the experience, he decided to turn the venue into a chemical-free meeting and performance space.

Almost immediately, plans for the Replacements' crucial showcase hit a snag. A few days before the gig, Tommy Stinson was in an accident that nearly ended his bass playing career. "My brother and I got stoned and were climbing trees in the back of our yard," recalled Tommy. The branch Tommy was standing on snapped, and he fell onto a picket fence below, landing right on his armpit. "I severed the muscle. It was horrible," he said. "Luckily, it didn't get the nerves. But I had to go to the hospital and get stitches. I was in a sling for a while."

Not wanting to miss their chance, Chris, Bob, and Paul showed up at the Bataclan to play the gig as a three-piece. To calm their jangled nerves, they'd started drinking beforehand. Chris had also smuggled some booze into the venue via his drum bag. As he set up his kit, Paul and Bob found the basement of the Bataclan and began ramping up for the show. "I think we were down there doing some [speed]," said Westerberg.

Upstairs, Foreman caught Mars drinking. Furious at the violation of his sober sanctuary, Foreman told him to pack up and get out. It felt like a replay of the band's first gig at Team House.

Jesperson arrived for the show a few minutes later. As he approached the Bataclan's entrance, he saw a black-haired kid sitting on the steps, head hanging down and looking dejected.

"Oh, hey . . . you must be Peter," said a bleary-eyed Mars, looking up. "I'm Chris, the drummer. We just got kicked out; we ain't gonna play."

Before Jesperson could respond, Westerberg and Stinson spilled out of the front door. "By the time we came upstairs," said Westerberg, "Chris had already been ejected from the premises, literally tossed out on his ass and down the stairs, as Pete shows up to view the band for the first time."

It appeared they'd squandered their opportunity to impress the Twin/Tone boss. "They'd gotten the guy from the label to come see them and figured they'd blown it," said Jesperson. "They all felt really bad, they were embarrassed. But it didn't faze me at all. I hate to say it, but I thought it was kind of funny—a halfway house for chemical dependency [*sic*], and they get caught with chemicals. It cracked me up at the time."

Jesperson consoled the band, told them he'd use his pull to get them a gig at the Longhorn as soon as he could.

In the meantime, he continued playing the Replacements demo at the store, touting the group to everyone who came in. "He had a very specific idea for them already, before he even knew what was happening himself," said Oar Folk employee Terry Katzman. "In his mind, I think he knew it was something special—or that it could be." It wasn't long before Paul, Chris, and the Stinson brothers began dropping by Oar Folk regularly. "At first, I remember Pete thinking my name was Paul Mars," chuckled Westerberg. "I remember him being disappointed that my name was Westerberg, because he thought 'Paul Mars' sounded more like a star."

Meeting Tommy—still just thirteen and radiating youthful charisma—and hearing Bob's stories about his reform school raising fascinated Jesperson. He thought Chris seemed unusually thoughtful and grounded, a much-needed anchor for the Stinsons, while Westerberg had a canny wiseguy air about him, like he always knew more than he let on.

There was a bit of Jesperson's beloved Bowery Boys in their scrappy manner; one could see Paul as the band's pugnacious leader Leo Gorcey, with Bob taking on Huntz Hall's role as the group's resident oddball.

These South Minneapolis kids—and they all seemed very young, even though Jesperson was just a few years older—were the perfect rock-and-roll characters. They might not have hewed precisely to Beatle-esque archetypes—the cute one, the smart one, etc.—but they were charming and funny and irreverent, with an immediately evident rebellious streak.

CHAPTER 10

I t would take a few weeks to crack the Longhorn's crowded calendar, but Peter Jesperson was finally able to secure the Replacements a gig at the club. They would appear on one of the venue's multi-band beer bust "Tiger Night" bills. Their coming out would take place on Wednesday, July 2, 1980, opening for the Dads.

The night of the show roughly forty people were spread around throughout the bar. Many of them had already been hyped on the group by Jesperson, who'd been playing their demo nonstop at Oar Folkjokeopus.

"We went from playing it in the back to playing it in the store," said Oar Folk's Terry Katzman. "We all got on the bandwagon; it was hard not to with Peter driving it—'cause he was very passionate. It wasn't any question of if you were going to show up, it was mandatory. And we were all obviously as excited as he was to see what they were like in the flesh."

The Replacements ambled onto the stage silently and counted off their first number—a new song called "Careless"—with a Westerberg scream. "Irresponsibility's my closest friend, forget my duty, obligation," he spat as Bob Stinson volleyed taut riffs back at him. "Tell me about the fuckin' ordinance, tell me that we're insubordinate."

They played eighteen tunes in a fast thirty-five minutes, racing through the songs because of their nerves. The set list consisted of the strongest originals they'd mustered to date, plus some old '60s garage nuggets (Syndicate of Sound, the Kinks) and punk deep cuts by 999 and the Ramones. The Johnny Thunders influence was pronounced: they also played three Heartbreakers covers (as well as "Get Off the Phone," a Westerberg original that took its title from a Thunders song of the same name).

"It certainly wasn't professional, but they had this reckless abandon," said Jesperson. "You could see they were a traditional rock-and-roll band. It certainly had its punk elements, but at its roots it was very Stones-y, very Chuck Berry. And it was every bit as good [as] I thought it would be."

Immediately, as each song ended, Jesperson would begin to clap hard and fast. Over the next several years, his rapid, encouraging applause would become a familiar sound at Replacements shows. "We'd play one of these gigs with ten people, and then we'd hear from the back of the room . . . [*clap-clap-clap-clap*]," said Westerberg. "We knew Pete's clap. And bless him for trying to get the crowd going, but we found it pretty comical."

Watching alongside Jesperson, Terry Katzman was also bowled over by the Replacements' rough-hewn charms. "They impressed me with their haphazardness and brilliance rolled together. It was all one package," he said. "There was this really focused thing to their sound, but there was this other part of them that was caterwauling and a lot of that was Bob."

Bob Stinson's unorthodox musicianship stood out as he wailed away, playing wild, dexterous solos while grinning broadly. Meanwhile, Chris Mars—mouth open, baring his teeth and breathing hard—lurched into his drum kit, as Tommy Stinson rapped eighth notes furiously, bouncing up and down like a kid who'd had too many bowls of Sugar Smacks during a Saturday morning cartoon binge.

Center stage, Westerberg—eyes pressed shut, singing up into the mic—cut an oddly compelling figure as a front man. "Paul had this presence," said Mike Hoeger, a writer for the *Minnesota Daily*, who caught the show. "He set up a lot of things that first night that carried on. The way he jerked up his left shoulder, twisted and craned his neck up to the mic, and gargled out the words like a coyote; the way he shouldered his guitar and slung it around like a giant fish, a nuisance; and the way he stumbled into his own bandmates as if they didn't exist. Or how he'd miss the cue to get back on the vocals. When you watched the Replacements play, they were loose, all just kind of laughing. Almost like 'We really can't believe we're here performing in front of people.'"

The band's relative youth—with Tommy pulling the median age down to sixteen—gave them an element of novelty. "They set up a mic for Tommy," recalled Hoeger, "not because he would sing, but because in between songs, during a lull, he would walk up and say something like, 'Kiss my ass!' or 'Fuck You!' He was so young that it was still amusing to hear himself curse over a PA. But anybody who came to scoff at Tommy for being young, once they heard him, they knew it wasn't a joke. The kid could play."

It was that combination of naïveté and deception—as Nabokov might have said—that made the band so compelling. "The Replacements' energy was a beautiful thing—as crazy as it was, there was an innocence to it," said Longhorn waitress and future Babes in Toyland founder Lori Barbero. She had gone to high school in New York City and hung out on the fringes of the CBGB scene, palling around with Johnny Thunders. "To me, the Replacements had the same rawness the Heartbreakers and the New York rock bands had, but they were so much younger."

Unlike their big-city brethren, however, the Replacements didn't look punk—there was no leather, Mohawks, or safety pins. Nor did they favor the emerging new wave fashions: skinny ties, cool suits, and sharp-angled coifs. Instead, they had desperately unstylish haircuts, wore Dickies work pants, and dressed in hand-me-down Pendletons and torn softball shirts. They took the stage in dirty sneakers, or what one wag described accurately—after glimpsing Westerberg's footwear—as "cheap janitor shoes." "They didn't look like any other band then," said Katzman. "They looked like they all just came off their jobs, or came in from the bar next door."

The Replacements didn't feel a need to dress up or don costumes (at least at that point). "We just wanted to be what we were," said Westerberg. "Those early pictures of us wearing like baseball jerseys and running shoes and stuff . . . we had no pretense that we needed to look like the Ramones. We were hip to that. We knew the Ramones looked like the Ramones, and we loved them, but we had to be sort of individual if we were gonna get anywhere."

Another area in which the Replacements were decidedly unlike the Ramones was in the pacing of their show. They didn't blitz through their sets, but rather played a song, paused and mumbled among themselves, then tuned their guitars for a while. (Endless between-song tunings were common during the band's first few months.) There was almost a feeling you were watching a rehearsal. "But once they started to play," said Hoeger, "it was a terrific noise that they produced."

Where other groups evinced a certain artfulness or tried to present an idealized vision of themselves, the Replacements were all rough edges and struggle. That was part of the attraction: watching them, you couldn't help but root for the band.

"In the beginning our 'show' had more to do with how hard it was to play that shit," said Tommy Stinson. "It wasn't like we were putting on this great show because we knew how to pose and look cool. We were playing physically. There was no way not to bend and grind and move around because you had to, just to play it. That was the show: look at these four guys fuckin' grind it out."

* * *

When the Replacements returned to the Longhorn in mid-July, they played a similar set but without the first-night nerves. "Thank you and all that shit," said Westerberg to a smattering of applause after their opening song, before noting, "We get more people in the basement than this."

The show was another high-velocity mix of well-chosen covers and a growing selection of originals that ended with a new Little Richard–style burner called "Oh Baby."

"I think that's all we dare," said a breathless Westerberg, before the band was summoned for an encore by the hooting audience, led by an emphatic Jesperson.

"Ain't we professionable?" cracked Westerberg as the Replacements lit into a fiery version of "Trouble Boys" to end the night.

Over the next few months, as the Replacements began to take their act to other clubs—including the newly opened 7th St Entry, Duffy's, and the Cabooze—they added more original material and sharpened their attack with each show.

"Maybe it was purely playing venues that were meant for bands, and that was more exciting than some of these goofier gigs we'd done before," said Tommy Stinson. "All I remember is when people started showing up to actually see us, it meant something different. And I'm sure it wasn't lost on Chris, Bob, and Paul that something was starting to build. After we started playing out, there was no turning back."

Though they sometimes drank beer to excess and occasionally did speed before gigs, there was nothing particularly unhinged about the band's performances during this initial period. Though they could be sloppy, the drunken disaster sets of lore were still years off. "We were not drunk. If anything, we did take amphetamines, at least I did, I was a sucker for that shit from day one," said Westerberg. "But it took us a while to get into liquor and make it more of a boozy thing."

If the Replacements had any negative reputation early on it was mostly for being loud. They were constantly battling soundmen and were sometimes given the cane by club owners for their obscene stage volume. Terry Katzman, who was working sound at the Entry, soon began engineering the band's shows. "Peter sorta drafted me into the nightmare world of mixing those guys. He was very fussy about Paul's vocals and wanted to make sure they were riding nicely on top in the mix. But it was hard," said Katzman. "You'd do a sound check with the band, and then the second they went on they'd just fan [all the levels] up. So, consequently, everything I'd done was out the window."

After the Replacements' second or third gig, longtime Curtiss A guitarist Bob Dunlap approached Westerberg and complimented him, told him he sounded like a young Eddie Cochran. (Westerberg acted annoyed, but then went out and bought a Cochran album the next day.)

Dunlap had known Bob Stinson a bit. He'd seen Stinson trudging through the snow of Uptown while driving his cab, given him a ride, and befriended him. "He would come and see the Curt band and heckle us," recalled Dunlap. "But Bob was a fun guy. He would always put a smile on your face."

Dunlap was taken aback by the wild energy and sound of Stinson's fledgling combo. "The Replacements right off the bat . . . it was like, 'What the hell? Where did this come from?'" said Dunlap. "What could they have been listening to, to have churned that out? But Paul was always like that. He could take all these ideas and put them together in a way you hadn't thought of."

Lou Santacroce, who'd migrated from upstate New York to the Twin Cities, was another musician who flipped for the Replacements. "The first song I saw them do was 'More Cigarettes.' I heard Paul sing: 'I don't watch the TV / I watch the clock,' and I thought, *Okay, this guy's got something*," he said. "I'd been listening to other Minneapolis bands. I'd heard the Suburbs, and Curtiss A, and I was knocked out. I didn't think there was going to ever be anything better than Curtiss A. But when I heard the Replacements, that was it—it was like I'd been waiting to hear that all my life." Newly divorced and at loose ends in his life, Santacroce immediately threw his lot in with the band, volunteering to become their first roadie.

Westerberg and the band may have been amassing a gang of admirers, but the acclaim for the Replacements was not universal. Some of the more established figures in the Minneapolis scene were dubious. "With a name like the Replacements, it dawned on us that they were there to replace us," said Chris Osgood of the Suicide Commandos, whose band had broken up a few months earlier.

While they weren't quite seen as "Jesperson's Folly," there were plenty of people, Osgood among them, who were vexed by his enthusiasm for the Replacements. "They were pretty ragged at first, a garage band—or a basement band. And there was a broad range of opinion because they were so ragged. I didn't have the vision that Peter had about where the band could go," admitted Osgood. "I immediately liked Tommy and Chris just as people. Paul never said too much to me one way or the other. And Bob sort of menaced me. He would walk around and always remind me that he was a better guitar player than I was. That being said, he was a sweet guy."

If there was any direct competition to the Replacements, it was the other group of youthful up-and-comers on Twin/Tone, the Suburbs. "One day Peter said to me, 'Oh, I got this demo tape'—like Paul was this rec room savant that he'd discovered," said Suburbs leader Chan Poling. "And Paul was a great, great songwriter. And the band, they were awesome. You hate to overuse that word, but they were really something to see."

Because of their differences—the Suburbs dressed up, played art rock, and had conceptual leanings—there was a natural inclination to pit the two groups against each other. "They were city kids as opposed to us, being from the 'burbs, so there was a sense of that. But it wasn't that much of a different aesthetic otherwise," said Poling. "There was a lot of alcohol and punk credos shared between us." The Replacements would spend much of their first year opening shows for the more established Suburbs—usually to Westerberg's chagrin, who perceived their fan base as less than welcoming.

The Suburbs were secure enough that the Replacements didn't pose an immediate threat. But Jesperson's embrace of the band left more than a few other local groups smarting. "Prior to the Replacements, there were a couple of bands, including us, who were in the mix for Peter and Twin/Tone," said Steve Skibbe of the Dads. "But he saw them and that was it—literally love at first sight. There was no question in his mind that this was the gig he was looking for. He was just totally consumed by the Replacements and getting them to be the greatest rock-and-roll band since the Rolling Stones."

"We felt the backlash from all the other groups and all the other wannabes," said Westerberg, "because we were being courted by the crown prince of pop or something."

One particularly disgruntled figure was Bob Mould, singer-guitarist of Hüsker Dü. The demo for the fledgling St. Paul hardcore trio—which also featured drummer Grant Hart and bassist Greg Norton—had been turned down by Twin/Tone just a few months earlier. One night at the Longhorn, as the Replacements finished their set, Mould found Jesperson at the bar. "Well, Peter," Mould said peevishly, "I guess now that you're involved, the red carpet's just going to roll out for these guys."

"I was probably annoyed at him," said Mould. "Like 'What about our demos? What about our tape?' But it was one of the best things that could've happened at the time. There's nothing like being spurned by the cutest label in town to make you really suck it up and do it on your own terms. That's pretty much what happened. We ended up starting our own label, pressed up a single, and started touring until we found sympathetic ears outside of Minneapolis." Twin/Tone's rejection of the Hüskers and its support of the Replacements would fundamentally determine the paths of both bands, as well as color a friendship and competition between them that would grow intense over the next few years.

As in any other scene, if the Replacements met with resentment in some quarters in Minneapolis, it was because there was a hierarchy, a pecking order. "There was a sense of 'Who are these young guys coming in? They're gonna have to pay their dues,'" said Terry Katzman.

The Replacements were neither patient nor respectful about such formalities. The way Westerberg figured it, he'd been kicking around for five years paying his dues on the kegger circuit; the way Bob saw it, he'd been paying them his whole life. "They try to tell me that I should learn / They told me it's best I wait my turn," Westerberg would sing in "Shiftless When Idle." "I can't wait forever / I can't wait that long." Or as he offered more bluntly during an early interview: "Where was it written, where was it said, that you had to play in a bar for eight years before you made a record?"

But the Twin Cities indie rock world was an especially insular community. To many of its denizens, the Replacements seemed to have simply materialized, fully formed, out of thin air. "They did come out of nowhere," said Katzman. "In that sense, they were total outsiders."

It was a notion—like so much else that was established in that first year—that would come to define the Replacements moving forward. They were outsiders among their peers in Minneapolis and would remain so later on as they rose in the national ranks and eventually joined the major-label world. "The way things rolled out, we were always outsiders," said Westerberg, "even among the other outsiders."

* * *

After a couple of shows, Peter Jesperson was chomping at the bit to sign and record the Replacements. Twin/Tone's Charley Hallman supported the move—though, as time would go on, he would become more of a silent partner in the company. It was really the label's other principal, Paul Stark, who needed convincing. Stark didn't want to commit to doing an LP with the band, cautioning Jesperson that they should test the waters with a single first.

If Stark was dubious about the Replacements' readiness, they erased any doubts as they confidently blasted through more than a dozen songs during a demo/audition session for him at Blackberry Way on July 21. "I remember [Stark] sitting there with his poker face," said Jesperson, "before finally cracking a smile and saying, 'You're right, we're talking an album here.'"

From the first, Stark's relationship with the Replacements was a complex proposition. Perhaps this was inevitable: compared to Jesperson's wholehearted support, the enthusiasm of anyone else for the band was certainly going to seem tepid.

With the Suburbs, Stark had served as the band's supporter, adviser, and friend. "With the Replacements, I had to take the other role," he said. "I was the bad cop, the principal at the school that the kids were always trying to cheat. They were always trying to do something to go against the rules—that's the way their nature was."

Though he was only twenty-eight, Stark seemed far older. His detached, deliberate manner—described as "Spocklike" by many—was an easy subject for ridicule. The Suburbs had nicknamed him "Fish Finder" after he'd once told them he enjoyed taking a boat out on the lakes armed with a sonar device because he could more easily "find fish" that way. Stark's rock-and-roll bona fides were always a question mark as well. Curtiss A recalled recording with him and asking for a maraca sound like "Jumpin' Jack Flash." Stark was vexed: "What exactly is a 'Jumpin' Jack Flash'?"

Almost immediately, Stark mistrusted Westerberg—a "manipulator from the word go," in his opinion. "I wrote Paul off the second time I ever met him," said Stark. "This guy will not be a friend of mine. I wouldn't want to trust him with anything I cared about, wouldn't want my daughter going out with him." Even still, Stark conceded, "he's probably a genius and can probably sell some records."

The antipathy was mutual. Westerberg—who likely had some clinical degree of oppositional defiant disorder—tended to view anyone in a position of authority or power with extreme hostility. It also didn't help their relationship that Stark was a forward-thinking tech-head, while Westerberg was a die-hard Luddite, even in his late teens. It was also clear to Westerberg that, despite Jesperson's equal piece of Twin/Tone, it was Stark who ultimately controlled the company purse strings and, as a result, its key decisions. Their mutual suspicion would prove a major stumbling block when it came time for the Replacements to sign a formal contract the following year. "I decided early on the Replacements were going to be Peter's deal," said Stark. "It's best if he's the one in between the band and the label. Because I was destined to make decisions that they weren't going to like."

Still, Stark was intuitive. He'd immediately grasped the fact—well before the starry-eyed Jesperson—that the Replacements were going to be a handful, professionally and personally.

"I thought they were so dysfunctional that it should be amplified, that it should almost be encouraged," said Stark. "Peter had the opposite view; he wanted to mold them into a little bit more of a polished band. I felt that if you reined them in, what would you have? You'd have a mediocre band at best, with a good songwriter, who wouldn't amount to anything. I thought the only chance the band had was to amplify the dysfunction . . . though they would go far beyond my imagination in being dysfunctional."

★ ★ ★

Thanks in large part to Peter Jesperson's sponsorship, the Replacements began getting immediate interest from local writers and critics. The band's timing was fortuitous, as the Twin Cities press corps was exploding.

By 1980, the region boasted four daily newspapers (the *Minneapolis Star*, the *Tribune*, the *St. Paul Dispatch*, and the *Pioneer Press*), two alternative papers (*Sweet Potato* and the *Twin Cities Reader*), and a college paper (the University of Minnesota's *Minnesota Daily*). The overall circulation of these publications was massive, and their arts section alums included key critics such as Jon Bream, Tim Carr, and Debby Miller.

At the daily *Star*, pop critic Bream had the inside scoop on the Twin Cities' brightest new light, Warner Bros.–signed R&B singer Prince, because he was close with Prince's manager, Owen Husney. But the coverage of the burgeoning indie rock scene in town was led by the alternative press. Marty Keller was a *Minnesota Daily* alum who'd become music editor of the newly founded monthly-cum-biweekly *Sweet Potato* in 1979. Keller started giving significant ink to the new wave of bands, including the Replacements.

"The first time I heard their name was from [freelance writer] P. D. Larson. He'd been played their tape by Peter, who said they were best thing he'd ever heard," said Keller. "But Peter was the biggest music fan in the world, he's got a million 'best things' he's ever heard. So I kinda took it in stride."

Still, Keller assigned Larson the job of following the band around and writing a story on them, which would land on *Sweet Potato*'s cover the following February. "It was the first, or one of the first, local music covers *Sweet Potato* did," recalled Larson. "The idea was to find somebody, a band that's up and coming, and write about them as they developed. The Suburbs and Curtiss A had been going for a while, so the Replacements were an obvious choice."

With their aesthetic, the Replacements were ideally suited to become a darling of the critics—an identity they would maintain throughout their career. "There was a certain un-prepossession about them," said the Suicide Commandos' Chris Osgood. "They didn't seem to be posturing. That's why I think Paul resonated so much with some of the local rock writers. And also because he was writing about feelings, fundamentally."

The first published piece on the Replacements, a one-page feature that ran in the local music monthly *Trax*, would appear in August 1980, barely three weeks after their Longhorn debut. "Four white punks out of South Minneapolis who play music their lead vocalist Paul Westerberg calls 'dirt'," wrote author Christopher Farrell, who, in somewhat purple prose, would capture the band in its embryonic glory:

> The brothers Stinson, Tom on bass, Bob on guitar, are Laurel and Hardy in contrast. Bob the taller and heavier by far while Tom, whose real age is guarded in confidentiality, is nonstop leap-and-jump. . . . Tom plays wise kid, walks up to the mike in between songs snarls one-worders: "Rowdy?"
>
> Chris Mars drums loud, fast and hard, the back against which the rest of the band play foreground. Lead vocalist Paul Westerberg points his jaw at the ceiling, his attitude in the lights, so poised for a new kid, his voice beguiling by strength and native purity unsullied by bad habits.
>
> It's still too early to tell how all of this will work itself out, but the talent is unmistakably there in the raw, as everyone in the room senses . . . they're just getting into the good. Destiny is the stranger.

A couple of months later, Mike Hoeger published a piece on the Replacements in the *Minnesota Daily*. (It was actually a three-part profile of new bands that included the Dads and Ben Day Dots.) Hoeger noted how the Replacements charged into their sets "with the urgency of an escaped convict" and observed Tommy's preshow habit of walking around wearing five-pound weights around his ankles as a warm-up in order to be able to leap higher during the set.

Hoeger also chronicled the band's formation, recounting how Westerberg had strategically edged out the group's other members to become their front man. "He joined us and just sort of took over," noted Chris Mars. Though it remained buried in the background for the next decade, Mars would never quite forget the fact that he himself, prior to Westerberg's arrival, had been the band's chief songwriter and creative force.

When Hoeger asked about their career aspirations, Westerberg articulated a prescient vision of the Replacements' future: "We'd like to become famous without being professional," he said. "Maybe like a giant cult."

"There's a Norwegian word that a lot of Minnesotans know: Jantelagen," said Hoeger. "It pretty much means, 'don't brag' or 'don't have big aspirations.' That whole Minnesota thing of being humble, I think that's really reflected in Paul, his whole self-deprecating humor and attitude. But at the same time, you knew deep down that he thought the Replacements could rock out better than anybody else, that they were something special."

Hoeger asked Westerberg to write out the lyrics to a couple of the songs he wanted to quote in his piece: "Shutup" and "Careless."

"What was funny was that he signed them and misspelled his own name— he wrote 'Paul Westeberg,' without the *r*. And he misspelled a couple other words, real easy words," said Hoeger. "So I wondered: is he drunk or high, or was he just kinda doing that on purpose to mess with me a little bit?

"I came to realize later Paul was much smarter than he ever let on. He claimed that he didn't read reviews or books, and played up the fact that he didn't graduate from high school. He liked to make you think he was a bit of a bumpkin. But it was obvious he had a drive, an ambitious drive, early on. Even the story he told about kicking out the Replacements' other lead singers. There was a sense of his own modest destiny that the other band members just didn't have."

* * *

In his *Trax* feature on the band, Christopher Farrell noted that the Replacements seemed "to be writing a new song every day, the amount of material they have assembled in just four months is a bit staggering."

The running joke for a time was that Paul Westerberg wrote songs more often than other people went to the bathroom. From the beginning of 1980 to the fall of that year, he penned roughly fifty songs—a fairly impressive number considering he'd only written a couple tunes prior to meeting the Stinson brothers and Chris Mars.

This prolific output was the result, Westerberg would observe much later, of a prolonged manic phase. "My mania tends to come quicker and leave faster now, but at this time, I was around . . . twenty-one, [and] it came out of five years playing in basement groups that were going nowhere, and realizing that I had to grab this by the horns."

Westerberg would generally come up with rough ideas, then jam away in his parents' basement or sometimes make rudimentary recordings on his brother Phil's boombox. He'd seize on a name or hook line that spurred him on. "I like stuff that isn't vague, where it says it all in the title," he said, noting the "action titles" of songs like "Kick Your Door Down" and "We'll Get Drunk."

Thematically, he drew on what he knew firsthand: his teenage attempts at getting high, hitching rides, picking up girls, and finding thrills, while facing the bleak future of a dropout-janitor. Writing with a lyrical economy and mordant wit, it was as if Westerberg, critic David Ayers observed, "set out to pants every tyrannical force of Midwestern-American Catholic middle class adolescence: boredom/desire, ambition/sloth, isolation/inebriation, rejection, reproach and sheer terror."

The abundance of new material also came from Westerberg's uncanny ability to absorb sounds and records he heard and synthesize them into new riffs, melodies, and songs. Ever since he picked up the guitar, Westerberg had been a musical sponge. "He could hear the new Vibrators record and be able to play 'Sweet Sweet Heart' after listening to it just once," recalled his sometime playing partner Steve Skibbe. "He had that kind of natural thing, so it didn't come as a surprise to me that he could turn that talent into cranking out quality songs."

Lou Santacroce remembered one occasion that summer when Westerberg came into Oar Folk with enough money to buy just one record. "He had to decide between some pop record and the new LP by the Damned," said Santacroce. "A few days later he came up with this new song that sounded like the Damned, and he said, 'Well, that would've come out a lot different if I'd bought the other album.'"

Crucially, during this period, Westerberg also dialed back his musicality in order to better serve the group. "Paul made himself fit into the Replacements, both writing and playing in the early days, 'cause he always had all of the chops that he ever displayed when he was sixteen," said Skibbe. "He could play pretty much anything you wanted and play it well."

Westerberg decided that the musical technique he'd picked up during years of self-study had no place in the Replacements' world. "It was the catharsis of knowing all these chords and runs and riffs that I'd worked on and sat and learned, and suddenly I was freed from that," he said. "You don't need that. You just need a brutal rhythm and something they can sing along to. And it was like 'Whew.' All that shit got shoved in the closet."

Mostly, Westerberg knew he had to deliver the kind of material the band would respond to. "He had to write something that we would play," said Tommy Stinson. "That was the part that was key, I can tell you."

The rest of the Replacements would listen and rehearse Westerberg's new songs, then pass judgment. Some would make it into the live sets for a period. But numerous tunes—little-heard gems like "Excuse Me" and "Looks Like My Old Girl" or fun throwaway show fillers like "Off Your Pants" and "Mistake"—were eventually winnowed out and forgotten. For every three or four songs Westerberg presented to the band, one or two might stick; the others would be discarded—and still others were never even considered. "I bet you there's a lot of stuff that we didn't even get to hear," said Tommy, "that he's still got in his basement."

Despite their age and outward appearance, the Stinsons and Mars were a fairly sophisticated, innately musical bunch. "We actually played a little bit too well for our own good at first," said Westerberg. From a strategic standpoint—to promulgate a "loser" mythos, which would come to serve as both shield and sword—Westerberg decided it would be more to their benefit to play up their "inability" as musicians.

It was a subject that became fodder for songs, as in the self-effacing verse of "Shutup" where a spastic Westerberg confesses that "Tommy's too young / Bob, he's too drunk / I can only shout one note / Chris needs a watch to keep time. . . . "

On "I Hate Music"—"it's got too many notes," as Westerberg would declaim—the notion was further explored via a violently chugging stop-start rhythm. The concept and music came together spontaneously during a rehearsal in the basement.

"One of the standing jokes in the band is that we're not musicians, and we're sorta proud of that in that we don't wanna be," said Westerberg. "It's like, we can try to play music and try to play it tight, but we just don't have any fun. One day Chris said, 'I hate fuckin' music,' . . . and Tommy went *dadadada* on the bass, and we all came in, and it was done in five minutes." (The song would be one of two on their debut LP, along with the similarly ferocious "Rattlesnake," that would be co-credited as a band composition.)

The song also included the lyric "I hate my father; one day I won't." Among a batch of songs brimming with teen angst, ennui, and petulance, it was a jarringly insightful, unusually mature observation.

Hal Westerberg had never been particularly thrilled about his son's musical ambitions. But whatever adolescent fear and loathing Paul had once held toward his father was long gone. "I disliked him more when I was thirteen or fourteen," he said. "By the time I was nineteen, I actually sorta dug him." As Paul pursued his rock-and-roll fantasy, he could empathize with Hal's frustrations about his own dashed dreams as a younger man. "And he sorta got what I was doing too," said Westerberg, "and why it was important to me."

* * *

Beyond his band and family, Westerberg was finding inspiration for songs wherever he looked.

At the end of July, ex–New York Doll and Heartbreaker Johnny Thunders came to Minneapolis to play with his new band Gang War, a short-lived team-up with Wayne Kramer. The former MC5 guitarist, who'd done a spell in federal prison on a drug trafficking charge, was trying to keep straight, but playing with Thunders undid those plans. Hitting the road, Gang War soon became a drug-fueled carnival. "The tours became utter nightmares," recalled Kramer. "If Johnny wasn't sick with too much drugs, he was sick from not enough drugs."

Gang War was scheduled for a pair of shows: one at the 7th St Entry, and then a concert the following night in First Avenue's main room. Westerberg and the Replacements desperately wanted to open, but were beat out for the gig by Hüsker Dü and Bob Mould. "I had such a personal investment with Thunders, one of my guitar heroes, I think I went to Steve McClellan and pleaded my case," said Mould. "I must've made a good case."

Mould became Thunders's "de facto babysitter" during his stay in Minneapolis. The task proved a major undertaking as Thunders became dope-sick, moaning that Kramer had stolen his supply of heroin.

Thunders ordered Mould to fetch him some Dilaudid, or painkillers, anything to get him straight. Eventually, someone scored enough cocaine that Thunders was able to make it onstage for the main-room show.

Out in the crowd, Westerberg and Chris Mars stood waiting for Thunders eagerly. "Kramer came out and said, 'Guess who's not ready?'" recalled Westerberg. "Then Johnny finally appeared, strung out, wearing leather pants. The moment he walked on . . . I saw it."

The look on Thunders's face—imperious and desperate all at once—struck Westerberg: "He was frightening and beautiful and mean at the same time," he said. "Like a child."

Physically struggling through the show, while battling an audience hurling brickbats, Thunders had been rendered a prisoner of his own addictions and cult infamy. "When Johnny was playing, it looked like he was walking dead," recalled Westerberg. "It was pitiful, like watching a guy in a cage."

That image of Thunders lingered with him. The following morning Westerberg sat at home with his guitar, rejiggered the chords to the Heartbreakers' "Chinese Rocks," and turned out a haunting ballad, a requiem called "Johnny's Gonna Die":

> *Everybody stares and everybody hoots*
> *Johnny always needs more than he shoots . . .*
> *And New York City I guess it's cool when it's dark*
> *There's one sure way Johnny you can leave your mark*
> *Johnny's gonna die . . .*

It was, as Jesperson noted, a "pivotal song"—the first slower, ballad-style number Westerberg had written. And as it romanticized and crucified Thunders all at once, the song also evinced the Janusian quality that would later mark his best work.

Predicting the passing of a still-living punk icon and massive personal influence was a bold act—Westerberg was ceremonially killing his idol, though, typically, his own view of the song was more jaundiced.

"Half the people who hear it know he's gonna die," said Westerberg at the time, "and the rest won't know who we're talking about."

* * *

Although coming up with material was relatively easy, recording the Replacements' first album was a drawn-out affair—the product, unlike most slam-bang indie productions of the day, of many months of work and several passes at multiple locations.

After the initial Blackberry Way sessions in July, Jesperson felt that the band had been a bit reserved, even uncomfortable, in the studio environment. "It was clean, almost like a hospital," said Bob Stinson. "The atmosphere was really clean. That's what probably made us nervous." To put them more at ease, Jesperson decided to try capturing them playing in a club.

In September, Paul Stark brought Twin/Tone's new twenty-four-track mobile recording unit to the Longhorn, and then again the following month to Sam's, where the band did a pair of faux concerts during the day. They went through their repertoire a couple of times, hoping to capture the lightning of their live show. But playing to an empty room felt even more bizarre. The recorded results were predictably uninspiring, so in November the band returned to Blackberry Way to make the album in earnest.

By then, it was also apparent that Stark and the Replacements were a bad fit ("Those personalities clearly didn't work," said Jesperson), so Blackberry Way house engineer Steve Fjelstad was charged with the task of recording the group. A musician himself—having played in numerous bands, including Fingerprints—Fjelstad was an easygoing "Minnesota nice" character. He was smart enough not to tinker with the band's methods or moods; instead, he adjusted to their idiosyncrasies and simply captured the results.

The Replacements sessions mostly took place at nights, not just because Tommy was in school during the day, but because of volume. Basically a house studio in the heart of Dinkytown, Blackberry was located across the street from a church that emptied out after dark. It was also surrounded on both sides by other residences—most of which, fortunately, were rentals occupied by University of Minnesota students, who didn't mind the noise. And there was a lot of noise.

"Tommy had his [Ampeg B15] stack in a room that wasn't soundproofed," said Fjelstad. "I remember going outside to listen as he was playing and just cringing—'Jesus, this is loud.'"

"We used to joke that Tommy didn't pick his amps based on how good they sounded," said Jesperson, "but how big and loud they were so he could torture everyone."

In an effort to put the band at ease, Fjelstad had them set up as they did live. "We tried to have everyone play together at the same time, to feel like they were onstage," he said. "The whole band could see each other, and we got some kind of headphone mix going. And we let them play loud; that was part of their sound. I never had anyone turn down in the studio. That would've been defeating the purpose."

Fjelstad also knew to always have the tape rolling: "A lot of times the first thing they did was the best," he said. Often, before counting off a song, the band would get distracted. Once, Fjelstad gently reminded them, in his nasal honk, that money was being wasted.

"Uhhh, guys, tape's rollin' . . . "

"*So what?*" Westerberg replied dismissively. (The exchange, along with several others, was preserved on the album and became a crucial part of the record's snotty ambience.)

"There was not a lot of drinking going on—relatively speaking, anyway," Fjelstad said. "But musically, there was something magic happening with them. Something definitely that was not there with other bands." Part of that was Tommy Stinson, whose rapid maturation on bass added a new element of dynamism to the songs. "For a little kid, he turned into a very good musician very fast," noted Westerberg.

Tommy would dismiss his early style as "me just playing eighth notes" (though as the band's later producer Jim Dickinson observed, "No one on earth played eighth notes quite like Tommy Stinson"). The younger Stinson's nimble fretwork and animated runs highlighted tracks like "Oh Baby" and "Love You Til Friday."

Typically, the Replacements cut fast, knocking out songs after a couple of passes. A track like "Kick Your Door Down" was done in one take, with no overdubs. "Some took longer, depended really on how much alcohol we had in our blood," said Chris Mars. "There's some that you have to get a certain force [behind]. It's hard to get that raw sound on a tape."

Often, their errors turned out to be gems, as on the album take of "Customer." "The lead was a mistake," noted Bob Stinson of his spiraling, madcap guitar break. "That's why we kept it."

"To me, the soul of rock-and-roll is mistakes. Mistakes and making them work for you," Westerberg would note. "In general, music that's flawless is usually uninspired."

Their collective power as a unit—which seemed to grow exponentially during the late months of 1980—was a mystery even to themselves. They'd finish cutting a track and marvel at some peak they'd reached, never sure of the path they'd taken to get there. "We'd just kinda . . . listen back," said Mars, "and say, 'Hey, that was great—*how did we do that?*'"

Another element of the Replacements' character was their inability to replicate performances. "Those songs, they'd change like every time we'd do them," recalled Mars. Each version of a song would move, swing, and take flight differently—most of which was down to Westerberg. He would tweak guitar parts on the fly or simply alter his energy—and the feel of the track—along with it.

Mostly, Westerberg was fond of changing or ad-libbing intros and lyrics. Kicking off an unused take of "Careless," he paid homage to the New York Dolls' homage to the Shangri-Las: "When I say I'm in debt," Westerberg drawled, "you best believe I'm in debt—D-E-T."

In one unreleased version of "Johnny's Gonna Die," he improvised lines—"Everybody says, Johnny looks fine / This time, Johnny, take one more line"—while on another he ended the song by screaming "*Good riddance!*" An outtake of "Love You Til Friday" showed Westerberg's Catholic roots: "Girls are a pain in my ass / when they don't go to mass. . . . "

On "Raised in the City," he did away with the line that first drew Jesperson's attention—"Got a little honey, nice tight rear"—replacing it with the more prosaic "Raised in the city, raised on beer." These changes were partly the result of boredom—Westerberg had little patience for repeating himself—and partly out of an unwillingness to commit to any one version as the definitive lyric or take. "Our patience, our attention spans, were so short," said Westerberg. "I mean, Steve Fjelstad was lightning fast compared to Paul Stark. But even the thought of doing a song twice, three times—whaddya fucking mean? We didn't understand the recording process. I didn't anyway."

* * *

Another element underlying the sessions was a quiet creative frisson between Paul and Bob as to how melodies, solos, and arrangements should go. The musical tug-of-war that was so effective between them onstage could get sticky in the studio.

"If Paul didn't get what he wanted out of his melody, he'd either show Bob how to play it or he'd just do it himself and Bob would pick it up," said Tommy Stinson. "Then they would argue over the solos. Again, if it wasn't happening, then Paul would start playing it.

"They had a little battle of the wills early on over that stuff. That's what him and Bob fought about and bumped heads on. It should be more like this, or more like that. It should go this way, it should go faster. Should you play the solo or I play the solo? Or, fuck you, you play the solo."

These minor arguments masked a more crucial, though unacknowledged, conflict over control of the band. Since its inception, Dogbreath had been Bob's baby. He'd been the one who'd decided to bring Westerberg into the fold in the first place. Within a few months, as they morphed into the Impediments and then the Replacements, Westerberg—who'd elbowed his way to the front as singer over Stuart Cummins and Tom Byrne and then as songwriter over Chris Mars—also became the group's de facto leader, taking over the role from Bob.

As Paul Stark would observe, even by the band's first demo session back in July, "Westerberg had already won [that battle]. But Bob always thought he was the leader. He had to. It was an element to his ego."

By early December, the band had tracked a big chunk of the material, but they continued to record as Westerberg kept coming up with more songs, including the spritely standout "I'm in Trouble." On the eighth of that month, they were rehearsing some of this new material in the Stinson basement when John Lennon was murdered outside his apartment in New York City. "By the time we got done practicing, we'd heard about it," said Westerberg.

Peter Jesperson was shattered by the news and proceeded to drink his grief away. "I think it was less of a shock to us right then, just because we had to keep up the punk rock facade," said Westerberg. "I remember someone spray-painted 'RINGO'S NEXT!' in the dressing room downstairs at the Entry. It was that sort of attitude."

* * *

A few days later, the Replacements played their first show outside of the Twin Cities, borrowing Paul Stark's van and traveling to Duluth to open a concert for the Suburbs at the Saints Roller Rink.

Chris Mars would remember the strange atmosphere of the venue. "There were a lot of young people, and they were just skating around, and we figured they wouldn't pay much attention to us," said Mars. "As soon as we got up onstage, they kind of all just turned and rushed up to the front and totally surprised us. And from then on, we just kinda went nuts. They helped us, they just pushed our adrenaline up a couple notches."

Toward the end of the set, during a scorching version of "Rattlesnake," Westerberg jerked his guitar violently toward his body. As he did, the neck snapped off and the momentum caused him to cut himself in the head with the broken, jagged piece. As blood spilled down his face from his temple, "it was this very dramatic rock-and-roll moment onstage," said Jesperson, who was at the back near the soundboard.

By the time Jesperson made his way through the crowd of skaters and up to the stage to check on Westerberg, the band was rumbling through "I Hate Music." Toward the end of the song, a bloodied, frustrated Westerberg peeled off his Gibson ES-335 and began hammering it into the stage. "These kids were just like, 'Oh my God,'" recalled Jesperson. "It was stuff like you read about seeing the Who or something." Westerberg smashed his guitar, sang the last verse, and then walked off, leaving behind a stunned crowd.

The incident in Duluth revealed Westerberg as an impulsive, compelling stage performer. As shy and retiring as he could be in real life, the few feet of elevation on the floorboards changed him, as did the security of having a gang of brothers to fall back on. Duluth and various other early concerts made him aware that there was a power that could be wielded from that perch, an ability to create moments that could make a band's reputation.

"I knew that we had to make them remember us somehow," said Westerberg. "If we played on a Tuesday night, on Wednesday afternoon you don't see your friend and say, 'Man, did you hear the Replacements last night?' It's like, 'Did you *see* the Replacements?!' It became a visual thing more and more.

"I felt like, let's have good songs on the record, and then make the shows more of a shambles or a performance art thing. Me and Chris were in cahoots pretty good on that. I think what the Stinsons had was something we didn't have: a kind of brute force and outrageousness. But Chris and I had a little better knowledge of theater and art and the idea of having a crowd and being able to manipulate them."

From reading biographies of P. T. Barnum, Westerberg recalled the grand showman's words: "Clowns are the pegs on which the circus is hung." Over the course of their career onstage, the Replacements would happily play the role of jesters and buffoons, but their concerts were also a high-wire act as well as a geek show.

On one level, it was theater, pure performance—but it was real too. The band was constitutionally unable to put on a conventional act. If they were bored, they sounded bored; if they were drunk, the sets careened; if they were angry, their playing seethed; if they felt ornery, the show might devolve into one long piss-take, a joke on the crowd. That kind of calculated authenticity—in all its paradoxical glory—would be the Replacements' methodology moving forward.

"We were a new breed of entertainer," Westerberg would claim later. "It was show business, but we took it to a different level. We were the first ones to really sorta say: 'Take it like we make it. Take us as we are. This is it.'"

CHAPTER 11

As the Replacements recorded and played into the winter of 1981, Peter Jesperson's role with the band continued to grow. In addition to being their label owner, A&R man, and coproducer, he would become their manager as well.

It started with him driving the band to gigs—none of them had a car or even a license. He'd help them set up gear before the show and then settle up with the club owners after it was over. The relationship was ultimately formalized—at least as formalized as anything ever got with the Replacements—following an argument with the Longhorn's Hartley Frank, who was trying to bully the band into taking a last-minute gig at the club.

Frank was generally lousy at managing the Longhorn's calendar and was constantly scrambling to fill in dates, trying to strong-arm bands into playing poorly promoted and sparsely attended weeknight shows. "He'd done that with a couple other groups already," recalled Jesperson. "When I saw him starting to do that to the Replacements, I stepped in." He and Frank got into a heated debate at the Longhorn's bar about the haphazard booking. Frank whisked Jesperson and the band outside to continue the conversation away from the other patrons. In front of the club, along the Fifth Street plaza, Frank and Jesperson squared off as the four Replacements took a seat on a bench.

"Look," Frank complained to the band, "I'm trying to give you guys an opportunity here. Do I have to talk to Peter every time I want to book you now?"

Westerberg looked at Jesperson wonderingly. They'd never discussed the possibility of him managing the band before. But after a moment's pause, they exchanged nods.

"Yeah," Westerberg said, turning to Frank. "You do need to talk to him."

And with that, the Replacements became Jesperson's charges. "The fact that he was gonna manage the band was secondary to us," said Westerberg. "It was like, 'You talk to the fat guy at the club and we'll be over here drinking.'"

At the same time, it seemed almost inevitable that Jesperson would take on a managerial role. "I don't know if he had visions of being our Brian Epstein, but it certainly fit," said Westerberg. "Given his love for the Beatles, I think he'd thoroughly digested the Epstein myth. He's the record store guy, and here's this little group that he's the first person in the world to love."

Over the years Westerberg could be parsimonious when assessing Jesperson's importance to the group. "It depends on how generous I feel for him at the moment," he told an interviewer in 2008. "If it wasn't for Pete, I believe we would have found someone else, which would have gotten us out of the [basement]."

But those close to the band agree that they simply wouldn't have gotten far without Jesperson's particular combination of patience, diligence, and faith. "The Replacements were the proverbial 'couldn't organize a two-car funeral' type band," said writer P. D. Larson. "They couldn't even get across Lake Street without help. Their logistical baseline was nonexistent. It was one of those fortuitous things that they had a Peter Jesperson. I don't think I'm exaggerating to say he did a miraculous job. People inside and outside the group can bad-mouth him all they want, for whatever reason, but that band probably wouldn't have made it to 1981 without him."

"There's plenty of great talent that languishes with no Peter Jespersons," noted Lou Santacroce. "He wasn't just someone to sign them or manage them . . . he was someone to believe in them."

In warmer moments, Westerberg would acknowledge that Jesperson's patronage was crucial. "Look, I love him, to this day even. In a way, he gets under my skin and always did," said Westerberg. "But he's enthusiastic. And when for the first time in your life someone is enthusiastic about you . . . well, we lapped it up like little puppies and believed what he told us. He was the best thing in the world for us, because he was so positive and over-the-top."

The relationship with Jesperson in those first few years would prove particularly important in forming Westerberg as an artist and a person. For one thing, Jesperson's involvement was reassuring to Westerberg's parents. "They felt I was taking okay care of their son," said Jesperson. "I had the impression he'd hung around with some lowlifes, so I looked pretty good in comparison." It was enough that Hal and Mary Lou Westerberg quit pestering Paul about getting a job and allowed him to leave his short-lived janitorial career behind to focus fully on writing songs and making music.

Moreover, the friendship that would develop with Jesperson was different from anything Westerberg had experienced with his siblings, high school buddies, or neighborhood pals. At heart, Westerberg was a sensitive intellectual who craved a kind of male intimacy—even if his whole mien argued against it. "Paul was a real thoughtful person who did not want you to know he was a real thoughtful person," said Santacroce. "Like that was betraying some kind of vulnerability."

Through his sheer enthusiasm, Jesperson managed to bring Westerberg away from his solitary, cloistered self. They would spend hours talking, smoking through shared packs of True cigarettes. "Even though he was generally a loner, there was a period where we were really tight," said Jesperson, "where I probably was the best friend he had."

Westerberg grew close enough to Jesperson that he began giving him cassettes of songs he'd been demoing on his boom box at home since the summer of '80. These were not Replacements' tunes or even rock numbers at all, but wholly different musical expressions which came as part of his first big writing burst. There was the rueful ballad "You're Getting Married," the Springsteen-esque narrative experiment "It's Hard to Wave in Handcuffs," and the autobiographical janitor's blues of "Bad Worker" ("I'll give you minimum effort for minimum wage").

"Ripping off punk and rockabilly stuff was exciting and fun," said Westerberg, "but then I sat down and thought, like 'God, could I actually write something that had some words that meant something, where I bared my soul?' And so I started writing stuff like that. That started the confessional aspect to [my] writing."

Rather than erase these songs out of uncertainty or embarrassment, as was his inclination, Westerberg would instead walk to the Modesto at all hours, ring the buzzer—he had his own special code: long-short, long-short—shove a tape of fresh tunes into Jesperson's hands, then leave without a word.

"This was obviously not something the band was going to play, but I was realizing that shit had a place in my life," said Westerberg. "Even if it's just putting it on a cassette and playing it for Pete and then being satisfied with that. I knew he had at least the heart to be able to listen to something like that and accept it for what it was."

Jesperson would prize these recordings, playing them in secret for a cadre of special friends and selected journalists. Though they clearly wouldn't fit the Replacements—even their existence was mostly kept from the rest of the band—he pushed Westerberg to keep working along those lines. It was a crucial encouragement that would lead him from being a sharp-tongued rocker to developing into a songwriter of depth and range.

"It wasn't like I could do no wrong in Peter's eyes," said Westerberg. "He didn't like everything I did. I would bring him a song, and he'd say, 'Nah.' But I did feel a need to go, 'Okay, here's someone I can try and impress.' Later on it was like, 'I'll write for critics,' or, 'I'll write for a record company guy,' or whoever. But in the beginning it was just Pete."

✶ ✶ ✶

Over that first year the rest of the band would form their own individual and collective bonds with Jesperson. The five of them grew into an odd little family unit, and their lives centered around Twenty-Sixth Street and Lyndale Avenue.

On a typical day, the band members would variously hang out at Oar Folk, rifling through records or sitting near the little heater by the window and reading magazines. In the afternoons, after Tommy got out of class, they'd adjourn to the Stinson house to rehearse. Usually, they'd follow up with drinks and palaver at the CC Club, the local tavern kitty-corner from the Oar Folk that became their unofficial headquarters. Although Tommy wasn't allowed in at first, by age fifteen he was a regular—usually found playing video games in the corner of the bar—despite still being several years under the legal age.

At night they'd end up walking over to Jesperson's apartment—which was well stocked with music, rock books, and booze. "It was a place for us to hang out and drink beer and spin records—I mean, Pete was a record store unto himself," said Westerberg, who would go through Jesperson's massive collection of singles, fixating on finds like Mission of Burma's "Academy Fight Song" and Prince's "When You Were Mine."

"The musical education for all of us came from right there," said Tommy Stinson. "Peter turned us all on to shitloads of stuff. Even stuff that he knew each of us would like separately. He would hip Paul on to certain things, and then I would get turned on to things he thought I'd like."

Tommy gravitated toward smart, quirky pop groups like Squeeze as well as more outré artists such as Captain Beefheart. (He used to do a funny, fairly spot-on impression of Beefheart singing "Ashtray Heart.") Jesperson also spoon-fed Tommy the kind of culture that he'd never experienced before, taking him to see Werner Herzog films and old Greta Garbo revivals at the Uptown Theater.

Bob Stinson, too, would hungrily consume the volumes in Jesperson's rock library, pore over his prog albums, and banter with him, often teasingly, about the relative merits of his beloved Beatles. Jesperson managed to turn Bob back on to the band. "I started listening to them again," said Bob, who'd hook up his record player to a phalanx of guitar amps, toke up, then crank *Revolver*, hearing it with new ears.

For Chris Mars, Jesperson's apartment was like manna. It was filled with comics of the recent sci-fi film *Alien* and books by its imaginative artist, H. R. Giger (who would exert a profound influence on Mars's later paintings). Chris, like the other Replacements, would also come to treasure the records of NRBQ, who, with their lyrical cheek and rootsy eclecticism, were everyone's idea of the perfect bar band.

Then there were the acts that Jesperson passed along like prized heirlooms—among them, a group of cult artists and bands unfairly consigned to the margins of history. He would play them the collected works of doomed Memphis power-pop band Big Star, who would become a Replacements favorite. He would also trumpet the work of star-crossed English rocker Terry Reid, spinning songs off his 1969 self-titled LP, including the halting breakup ballad "Mayfly."

As Jesperson's apartment filled with the sound of Reid's soaring vibrato, the Replacements sat silently marveling in discovery. The notion that someone as gifted as Reid should toil in relative obscurity was daunting—particularly as they pondered their own promise and prospects.

★ ★ ★

n March, the band wrapped up their debut album at Blackberry Way. With Bob working at Mama Rosa's, Tommy in school, and Chris off doing his art, it was left to Westerberg, Jesperson, and Fjelstad to finalize the album. (The three would share coproduction credit on the LP.)

It was a collective effort to get the record's mix just right. "We didn't have automation at Blackberry," recalled Fjelstad. "So Paul would have his hands on the faders, Pete would have his hands on them—everyone had a little bit of hands on." After playing back the finished LP, Fjelstad shrugged his shoulders and offered a sufficiently heartening verdict: "Well, if nothing else, it's *louder* than the Ramones' first record."

Fully ensconced in his multi-hyphenate role with the band by early '81, Jesperson took charge of several big picture decisions. He persuaded the Replacements to launch their career in classic fashion: releasing a 7" picture sleeve single with a non-LP b-side. He chose "I'm in Trouble" as the lead track somewhat to the band's surprise, as Westerberg thought his vocals were a bit flat.

Late in the mixing stage, Paul was messing with a country-styled barroom narrative titled "If Only You Were Lonely," a cheeky look at a man on the make, redolent of Rod Stewart's "Every Picture Tells A Story." "He called me to his house and played the first verse on a demo he'd recorded, then the rest of what he had on his brother's acoustic," said Jesperson. Westerberg, feeling protective of the band, was reluctant to record a solo song. But Jesperson convinced him it was a perfect b-side for the single. "He finished the song in the van on the way over to cut it at Blackberry Way. I was driving and he was scribbling furiously and crossing out things. He was so earnest."

With the full-length, Jesperson had originally wanted to include twenty-two tracks—"because the first Wire album [*Pink Flag*] has twenty-one songs on it, and I think they should one-up 'em," he said at the time. Ultimately, the decision was made to scale back the LP. Though not necessarily by design, they ended up cutting a batch of Westerberg's more orthodox rockabilly/rock-and-roll rave-ups (such as "Get on the Stick" and "Oh Baby") because the performances, they felt, were lacking. That left the album with eighteen songs—nine to a side—and a nearly thirty-seven-minute running time.

The band also decided to ditch the working title they'd been using, "Not Suitable for Airplay," in favor of something better at playing up their adolescent spirit.

For a time, Jesperson had sought to tag the band as avatars of "low-class rock"—a description that graced a number of gig flyers during the period. "We were always looking for a new angle," said Westerberg, "'cause we weren't really punk rock, and we didn't fit in with what was considered the rock-and-roll of the time." Eventually, Westerberg came up with the snappier term "power trash." (Jesperson would include a helpful note to retailers on the LP's cover to "File Under Power Trash.")

With its inherent allusions to the New York Dolls classic "Trash"—as well as Bob Stinson's Dogbreath-era rehearsal chore of emptying his mother's kitchen bin—it would inspire them to name the album *Sorry Ma, Forgot to Take Out the Trash.*

Westerberg also penned a set of liner notes—heavily influenced by *Creem* magazine's resident rock critic/comedian Rick Johnson—that perfectly conveyed the Replacements' brand of humor and general self-disregard as effectively as the songs themselves. Assessing their performance on "Careless," he wrote: "Don't worry, we're thinking about taking lessons." Of "Hanging Downtown" he observed, "We wanted to put car horns over the mistake, but none of us own a car," while noting that "Kick Your Door Down" was a "1st take—written 20 mins after we recorded it." Elsewhere, he complimented Bob's lead on "Customer" as being "hotter than a urinary infection," while "Otto" was "proof that Chris Mars is one of the best drummers we could find at the time." In what would become one of his running themes, Westerberg played up their inherent laziness, cracking that "More Cigarettes" "could have come close to rockabilly if we had taken the time" and confessing, on "Don't Ask Why," to stealing "a mess of these words from a guy who's never gonna listen to this record" (referring to B. B. King, whose "You Done Lost Your Good Thing Now" he'd pilfered lyrics from).

The record's dynamic cover image—a shot of a leaping Tommy and a mic-throttling Paul—was captured during a gig at the 7th St Entry by Greg Helgeson. The design came courtesy of Bruce Allen of the Suburbs, who gave the sleeve a cut-and-paste aesthetic—ripping up the photo, adding a beaming blue–hot pink color scheme and hand-scrawled lettering—that owed much to the work of the Sex Pistols' graphics maven Jamie Reid.

By the spring, the single and album were complete—though they'd have to wait several months for it to come out so that Twin/Tone could line up multiple releases in order to save money on pressing and promo costs.

That April the group was in high spirits, partying late at the Modesto as Jesperson spun his favorite R&B tunes. He grabbed an old Atlantic Records compilation and played "Sweet Soul Music" by Otis Redding protégé Arthur Conley.

"Chrissake—that shit is *too* good. I ain't ever gonna be able to sing like that, Pete," muttered Westerberg. "Why don't you play me something white and talentless instead?"

Jesperson just happened to have a fresh test pressing of "I'm in Trouble" sitting next to the turntable. In a flash, he put it on and dropped the needle as everyone fell about laughing.

PART II   A Band for Our Time

We started to leave home and go play other places . . . and people started to show up. Once that happened it was like "Game on." We're not like a little basement band, just guys in the neighborhood, anymore. We're something else. We may not have been great, but we were fuckin' special.

TOMMY STINSON

CHAPTER 12

In September 1981, *Sorry Ma, Forgot to Take Out the Trash* finally saw the light of day. Twin/Tone released the Replacements' debut album in concert with the Pistons' *Flight 581* and the Suburbs' *Credit in Heaven*.

Thanks to Peter Jesperson, the Twin Cities music press had been in the tank for the Replacements from the start. What came as a surprise was the response the band got from several influential national voices. In *New York Rocker*, critic Phil Davis singled out the group. "[Their] subject—Midwestern angst—hasn't been better rendered by any punk band," he wrote. "The endless car rides to nowhere, Stop-N-Go Snacks, familial pressures, drug induced escapism—they all have psychic consequences. Confronting the internalized damages through simple external summations is the group's forte."

The *Village Voice*'s eminence, Robert Christgau—the self-appointed "Dean of American Rock Critics"—graded *Sorry Ma* a B-plus in his "Consumer Guide." He hailed the Replacements as "a not quite hardcore Twin Cities quartet who sound like the Heartbreakers might have if they'd started young and never seen Union Square: noisy, disgruntled, lovable." Even the legendary Lester Bangs, in what would prove to be the last dispatch before his death, gave a positive nod to *Sorry Ma* in the *Voice*.

The plaudits were gratifying to the group, but also a much-needed means of promotion, as commercial radio—particularly in Minneapolis—was closed off to bands like the Replacements. Program director Doug Podell, of Minneapolis rock powerhouse KQRS, noted in print that fall that the band was "just too hard for us."

Twin/Tone tried other ways of promoting the group. With his filmmaking background, Paul Stark decided to set up a professional multi-camera concert shoot at the 7th St Entry for the label's roster, as well as several other local bands. The Replacements played well enough, though their footage was deemed unusable because they were out of tune for so much of the set.

Ironically, given their later much-publicized stance against making videos, the Replacements would actually attempt to film a clip for their first single, "I'm in Trouble," in 1981. MTV had premiered that August, and though Jesperson didn't have cable, local clubs like First Avenue were airing the network on big screens in between bands. "There was this burgeoning thing with music videos happening," said Jesperson. "I thought, *Maybe this is something we should tap into.*"

Jesperson contacted his friend John Brister, a Minneapolis filmmaker he'd known since the '70s: "He was one of the early people interested in making videos, and he wanted a guinea pig," said Jesperson. Brister shot footage of the band walking in Loring Park and spray-painting REPLACEMENTS STINK on the brick wall outside Oar Folk. Another narrative segment saw Westerberg wearing pajamas and lying in bed, as if waking from a dream.

After a while, the band began to lose interest—Bob kept missing shoots to work shifts at Mama Rosa's—and Twin/Tone rejected Brister's request for funds to complete the project. The whole thing went away—much to the band's relief.

"It just got so dumb," complained Westerberg of the video a few years later. "I hate to think it'll surface one of these days." He needn't have worried. The footage was tossed after Brister—who went on to an award-winning career as an animator—died from AIDS in 1989.

* * *

Throughout the first half of their career, money was tight for the Replacements. The band members all lived at home, and none of them except Bob—who kept his line cook job—worked. They subsisted on the gig money they made in those first couple of years—anywhere from $50 to $300 a show, split four ways, minus expenses. Occasionally the band would supplement its earnings with contributions from the audience, beseeching crowds to "throw money." "You would not believe how much people would whip out and throw onstage," recalled Lori Barbero. "Those boys fighting over the money onstage was hysterical. I remember one show at Duffy's their pockets were bulges, they couldn't fit any more [change] into their pants."

Despite the struggles of those early lean years, "we were very content," said Westerberg. "I remember me and Chris cashing in his food stamps to buy cigarettes. We had a pack of smokes, and we were gonna go down the basement and jam with the Stinsons. Pretty soon some girls would show up, and we were happy as shit."

Once the group gained some local renown, the women quickly found them. "That was the faucet we could never turn on where, suddenly, the handle flew off," said Westerberg. Female attention had always been a major motivation for playing in a band in the first place. "Girls were 50 percent of the reason," he said. "And we wanted to do something worthy that we could be proud of—but that was about it. It wasn't like we were out to change the world, or become wealthy. Having read every rock biography, I knew it starts raining women long before you're famous and rich . . . and you might not ever get famous or rich."

Though Westerberg had kicked around for years in little combos before the Replacements, those efforts hadn't generated any interest from the opposite sex. "I'm told that women are attracted to confidence and power, and none of those early bands had that. Even if the Replacements lacked confidence, we didn't let it show. We were just down your throat." It was this gaggle of early female fans who took to calling the band the 'Mats—short for Placemats, Westerberg's drunken colloquialism for Replacements.

Among these women was Paul's first girlfriend—Lucinda Teasley, a fellow high school dropout and a musician from Duluth. She'd seen him playing the Longhorn in late 1980 and made doe-eyes at him from the audience; they started going out soon after. Since Westerberg had no money, driver's license, or apartment of his own, their dates had to be creative. "We might meet at Lakewood Cemetery at midnight and walk around together—mind you, we had to break in," said Teasley. "Another time we were sitting on the couch writing romantic letters back and forth to one another—as though he were an inmate on the inside and I was his girl on the outside waiting for him to get out. We were using our middle names, Harry and Janie. Those are things that he thought to do."

They'd been together six or seven months and Teasley wanted the relationship to become more serious. But having gotten his first taste of flesh, Westerberg began a lifelong pattern of romantic indiscretions. Several of *Sorry Ma*'s songs were colored by what he saw as Teasley's attempts to tame him ("I'm in Trouble," "Love You Til Friday") and guilt over his own licentiousness ("Rattlesnake"). "At one point," recalled Teasley, "he said, 'I'm just a rat-rat-*rattlesnake*'—as a way to excuse his behavior."

Bob made his own strides with the opposite sex ("He was so strange that girls that would succumb to Bob's advances were strange too," noted Jesperson), while it would be years before the ever-shy Chris got a girlfriend. Tommy, however, had become the subject of much female fascination in the local scene.

"There was a group of girls, older women, who were enamored with him and God knows what else, because he was a cute little boy," recalled Westerberg. One local musician, a guitarist in an instrumental combo, decided she was going to deflower Tommy. "There was a big competition for that honor," said Lou Santacroce.

It was another girl, several years Tommy's senior, who ended up being his first. She was riding with Tommy and the band after a show. Dropping her off at home, he followed her in and shut the door behind him. "When everybody realized what was happening, you could've heard a pin drop," said Jesperson. "Then the whole van erupted. Like, 'Well, there he goes. Good luck, son!'" Recalled Tommy: "The girl I was with was eighteen. I was thirteen. That's a little young, even by today's standards. It probably caused a lot of weird growing-up shit right away."

Tommy's first serious relationship started in 1982, with the woman who would eventually become his wife, Daune Elizabeth Earle. Born in 1959 and a native of New York, Earle had moved to southern Minnesota when her father, a Birdseye executive, was transferred there. She arrived in the Twin Cities in the late '70s to attend college and became a regular at the Longhorn and Oar Folk, where she first encountered Tommy. "I didn't know who he was at the time," said Earle. "There was a little alcove in the store, and he would be sitting there watching soap operas—*All My Children*—that Peter had taped. That was their thing."

One day after leaving the store, Earle realized Tommy was trailing behind, following her home. She ignored him, but they met up again at a party a few nights later: "I'm Tommy Stinson," he said, introducing himself formally. "I'm in the Replacements."

Despite a seven-year age difference, they dated for the next nine months, before splitting up. They would reunite a few years later. "Tommy was everybody's little darling and a jackass at the same time," chuckled Earle. "He was this charmed, cocky kid. But I always saw something more in him."

* * *

Tommy Stinson's early teens were a strangely schizophrenic time. At nights he would play with the Replacements, carry on with older women, and exist in a totally adult world. Then, in the morning, he'd have to go back to school.

His closest friend during these years was a baby-faced kid named David Roth, whom he'd met at Anwatin Middle School. Though they lived in the same neighborhood, they grew up in different worlds. "I'm from like middle-class intellectual Jews; my father was an English professor," said Roth, "and Tommy's from this lower-class, working-class background. But we liked the same things: first it was candy and movies, then girls and pot. So we started hanging out."

Roth had spent a year in England in 1979 during his father's teaching sabbatical and came back to Minneapolis as an earring-wearing punk rocker. He began publishing his own fanzine (*Power for Living*) and underground comic (*Ferret Comix*) and became a fixture in the local music scene. "I was embraced almost like a mascot. Grant from Hüsker Dü, the guys from Rifle Sport, they thought it was real cute that I was this little punk rock kid," he said. "I was thirteen, but looked about nine. I couldn't get into bars, but I would go to after-hours parties." Roth tagged along with the Replacements, sneaking into clubs with them by carrying gear. "You could tell Tommy was very enamored of Paul," he said. "Paul would say things, and Tommy would repeat them. Little jokes or in-jokes. Paul had this cool factor, and you wanted to impress him."

Over time Tommy would establish his own visual identity in the band, donning creepers and styling his hair—at one point he dyed a streak of shocking white in it, prompting Westerberg to nickname him "Skunk." At West High School, Roth and Stinson stood out and were forced to steer clear of a gang of aggressive jocks looking to beat up punks and queers. "The football players from West, we called them the Disco Rumblers," said Roth, "'cause they listened to disco and they liked to rumble. It was like the jocks against the freaks. They'd spit on me and Tommy as we walked through the hall."

Even in his own neighborhood, Tommy had to move carefully in order to dodge a couple of hulking bullies who didn't like his look. Sometimes Tommy would hang out with Suburbs road manager Casey Macpherson, who had an apartment nearby. "Tommy would ask me to walk him home," said Macpherson. "'Cause there was always guys who wanted to thump him."

Inside the clubs, Tommy had mostly managed to avoid any trouble. But after a couple of incidents—including one where Wendy O. Williams of the Plasmatics chased him around Zoogie's for throwing a cigarette at her—Jesperson decided they needed some legal protection. In February 1982, Anita Stinson signed a notarized agreement making Jesperson her son's legal guardian while he was performing and traveling "as a member of the musical group—The Replacements." It wasn't quite a Faustian pact, but in Tommy's mind his fate had been sealed.

"We were talking about what his future plans were once," recalled Rifle Sport singer Chris Johnson. "I was like, 'You can't play in the Replacements forever.' And Tommy was like, 'Oh yah, I'm gonna. By the time I'm twenty-five, if this is all over, you'll find me playing at a Holiday Inn somewhere.' He was saying that at fourteen, fifteen years old—that was it, he'd decided. I'm not doing anything else but music."

Bob had put the bass in his hand to save him from a life of crime, but opened up a new world of possibilities in the process. "That was a very fortunate accident. If that had not been the case, he might not have discovered what a brilliant musician he was," said local critic Dave Ayers. "And Tommy was—he could've played with Miles Davis if he'd been in the right place at the right time. He's just really gifted. But he was also a kid—he was bratty, he was gonna try to get on your nerves. This is someone who'd been onstage since he was twelve years old. He never had a normal adolescence because of that."

Westerberg would recall his own teen years—how nervous and uncertain he'd been—and marvel at how confidently Tommy carried himself. "Being in the 'Mats must've been like being a child circus performer or something," he said. "If you weren't strong enough, that would really screw you up."

★ ★ ★

The Replacements' post–*Sorry Ma* period would be most defined by their relationship and friction with a fellow Twin Cities band—Hüsker Dü.

The Hüskers came together in early 1979, when New York native Bob Mould—a student at Macalester College in St. Paul—hooked up with a pair of local record store clerks in drummer-vocalist Grant Hart and his friend, bassist Greg Norton. A strident punk power trio, the Hüskers were the senior outfit, having formed almost a year before the Replacements came along.

"They may have started first, but we were soon vying for the same opening slots," recalled Paul Westerberg. "The big one being for Johnny Thunders [and Gang War]. They got it and we didn't. The other one was Black Flag; we weaseled them out of that. There was competition from the get-go—for gigs, for attention. Whenever we played together, it was a friendly competition, but competition nonetheless. We wanted to see them fail. We wanted them to be the second-best band in the city."

Though Bob Mould was not without ego when it came to Hüsker Dü's status in the local scene, he embraced the creative push-and-pull with the Replacements. "It was about who's going to play louder, who's going to play faster, who's going to play the better shows, who's going to make the better records," said Mould. "Historically, that's what drives the business: bands jockeying and competing and trying to top one another. We all have these messages and ideas. It's about who tells a better story, who's going to get more ears to listen to the story."

Their dialogue would play out onstage and on record. *Sorry Ma* had included a song about band life called "Something to Dü" ("Amphetamine sweat, girls you bet / Beats workin' too"), which featured a winking coda referencing their rivals ("Something to Hüsker . . . break the mould!"). The Hüskers would nod back in the 'Mats' direction by pilfering some of their riffs for the drinking song "First of the Last Calls" ("Hundred, hundred, hundred bottles on the wall / You wonder if you can drink them all").

Though they shared some musical influences—namely, Johnny Thunders, John Lydon, and the Ramones—when it came to conducting their careers, the two bands had little in common. As a point of pride as well as necessity, the Hüskers were the quintessential self-sufficient, do-it-yourself outfit. "The three of us, we learned every aspect of the business that we could," said Mould. "We felt like we had to. That was what we did with our lives."

The Replacements, meanwhile, couldn't be bothered. They were totally, unapologetically dependent on others. As one observer put it, "The Replacements were never DIY; they wanted someone to carry their gear for them."

"When we looked to the Replacements, there was a little bit of a feeling of like, 'Those guys don't even know what's happening to them,'" said Mould. "Peter Jesperson does everything for them."

In 1981, the Hüskers started their own label, Reflex Records—with a loan from Hart's mother's credit union and the assistance of Oar Folk's Terry Katzman—as a direct reaction to being rejected by Jesperson and Twin/Tone. In the process, Reflex would also help release records by Minneapolis compatriots like Rifle Sport and Man Sized Action and put together local scene compilations like *Barefoot & Pregnant* (to which the Replacements contributed a cover of Motörhead's "Ace of Spades").

Mould was a big believer in the concept of community, the theory that rising tides lift all boats. "We helped out other bands in the scene, at least our scene. We were trying to raise everybody up," he said. "The Replacements hardly did anything like that. It's not a knock on them, it's just a huge differ-ence between us." (There were other notable contrasts between the groups: Mould and Hart were both gay, a fact known in the Twin Cities but not widely elsewhere. Asked to elaborate on the main difference between the Hüskers and the 'Mats, Tommy Stinson once told a journalist, smirking: "We like girls.")

Despite Hüsker Dü's professional vigilance and communal instincts, they would ultimately be done in by one of their own. After a couple of years touring and building a reputation out west, the group signed with SST, the California indie label run by Black Flag guitarist Greg Ginn. In the end, the Hüskers would spend the next thirty years fighting Ginn over royalties—their album masters held hostage by someone they'd thought was a brother-in-arms.

* * *

Having established themselves early on in the hardcore-dominated Chicago scene, the Hüskers starting taking the Replacements to the Windy City as a support act in late 1981. "There was a period there in the beginning where we actually tried to fit into that world," said Tommy Stinson. "It wasn't always com-fortable." Mould felt that some more dogmatic audiences viewed the 'Mats "as a rock-and-roll band . . . trying to be hardcore. Maybe the overlords of the existing hardcore scene saw them as poseurs. But those people didn't know shit anyways."

From the start, Westerberg scoffed at the narrow orthodoxy of the era's hardcore scene. "[They] didn't see us as a punk band, but we embodied more of what a punk was than they did," he said. "That was the weird little rub. Lenny Kaye's *Nuggets* helped open up a broader picture of what's punk and what's not punk. I mean, the Stones were punks when they started."

Westerberg was also dubious of the po-faced herd mentality that quickly overtook American hardcore audiences in the early '80s. "They used to all show up in the same uniform," he recalled. "And it became political and it became serious and it became deathly. . . . It was not the way we wanted to go."

He resisted the genre's ideological aspects, the hectoring anti-Reagan polemics that were de rigueur at the time. Westerberg was an avowed cynic when it came to politics, particularly politics mixed up with rock-and-roll. "There's nothing that bores me more than a hardcore band that says, 'Reagan sucks,'" he said. "That's about as overused and easy and silly as 'Let's make love tonight, baby.' I mean, yeah, Reagan sucks—so?"

Still, the months spent playing the Midwest hardcore circuit in Hüsker Dü's shadow would have an impact on the Replacements' sound. For a time they tried to keep up with the Hüskers' penchant for speed—both their tempos and their use of amphetamines. Westerberg even began writing a batch of his own sloganeering songs, like "Fuck School," "God Damn Job," and "Stuck in the Middle," though these were seen by some as satire more than a genuine embrace. "When Paul wrote 'hardcore' songs, it felt like he was basically send-ing up the genre," said Katzman.

"You could tell Westerberg was doing things for the upstart nature of it," said David Roth. "I think he was maybe pissed at how popular Hüsker Dü was in a certain circle. Minneapolis was going pretty hardcore at that point—the whole Midwest was."

During this 1982–83 period—with the release of the albums *Land Speed Record* and *Everything Falls Apart*—Hüsker Dü would dramatically ratchet up its presentation. "It was an acceleration of consistency," said Mould. "We kept building on top of the good stuff instead of letting it crumble. I had a high expectation of what Hüsker Dü was going to be every single night." As Hüsker Dü transformed into a kind of towering hardcore monolith, the Replacements went the other way: they became loose, louche, and unpredictable, and all the more so as their alcohol intake increased. "Over time it seemed like their drinking became part of their presentation," noted Mould.

A buzzed Westerberg would look out over the teeming testosterone-driven crowds slam-dancing into one another and weigh his options. Instead of giving these people what they wanted—sharp, nonstop aggression—he'd go the opposite way: trying songs that the band hadn't rehearsed, calling for incongruous pop covers, or simply slowing their well-honed material down to a frustrating dirge. "Paul enjoyed playing his mood basically," said Katzman. "Playing sloppy didn't bother him. That's something the Hüskers wouldn't have done. If they had some new song or a cover that wasn't ready, they wouldn't play it in the set. Where Paul would say, 'Let's give it a whirl. If we screw it up, so what? I don't care what these people think.'"

Over time these types of performances would evolve into what became known as the Replacements' "pussy set"—a weapon of mass frustration that would be wielded against unfriendly audiences, hardcore or otherwise, that the band encountered.

Though the Hüsker Dü–Replacements rivalry would largely peter out by 1983—the point at which each band was big enough to headline the Twin Cities on its own—the public continued the debate over who were the kings of the scene.

"There were distinct factions in town. You were either a 'Mats person or a Hüskers person," said local critic P. D. Larson. "There would be very heated arguments at parties over the keg—'Fuck you.' 'No, fuck you.' 'They're better.' 'No, they're better.' In the end, it was totally junior high playground stuff."

* * *

The most significant development to come out of the Replacements' hardcore phase was the rush recording of the band's second record.

The impetus for the album came in mid-January '82, when the 'Mats borrowed the Suburbs' van and drove to Chicago. Opening for Hüsker Dü at O'Bannion's, the band premiered a new song called "Kids Don't Follow."

Westerberg would remember penning it as a rejoinder to U2's dogged anthem of devotion "I Will Follow" ("If you walk away, walk away / I walk away, walk away—I will follow"). He'd seen the fledgling Irish band perform in April 1981 at Sam's, where they actually played the song twice in their set.

Ever the reactive writer, Westerberg noted that "if I hear something I like, I steal it, and if I hear something I don't like, I write about that." While he dug the clarion quality of "I Will Follow," he balked at what he considered its unrealistic message. The kids he knew weren't going blindly forth, their faith steadfast, their belief unwavering in the face of adversity.

Propelled by Bob Stinson's keening, hurtling riffs, Westerberg's response took the form of a howling dissent: "Kids won't listen / What you're sayin' / Kids ain't workin' / Kids ain't playin'" (though it was decidedly hardcore, the song would namecheck the 'Mats' bar band favorites, NRBQ, in the opening verses: "Who says worry? / Who says tolerate? / Who says NRBQ?").

Driving back home through Wisconsin after the O'Bannion's show, the band popped in a boombox recording they'd made of the gig. Upon hearing "Kids Don't Follow," Jesperson had a revelation. "I thought: *We have to record this, we have to make another record right away.*" At the time, *Sorry Ma* was only four months old. Twin/Tone hadn't gotten a chance to recoup on the project yet. Selling Paul Stark and Charley Hallman on the idea of paying for another Replacements record so soon was going to be a challenge.

Jesperson met with his label partners at the Lincoln Del and laid out his case. He told them "Kids Don't Follow" was an important song, a potential game-changer for the band and the label, and insisted they had to get it on tape. Driving all this was his awareness of Westerberg's proclivity to quickly grow bored with certain songs after a while and toss them aside.

Jesperson told them the band had a handful of other new tracks to record as well, though he conceded there probably wasn't enough grade-A material for a full album. They could do a mini-LP, an EP—whatever—but they had to put "Kids" out into the world right away. "Listen," pleaded Jesperson, "we'll do it cheap—we'll cut the whole thing in one day. I'll fucking hand-stamp jackets if I have to."

That was enough to sway the cost-conscious Stark, who was rarely able to resist Jesperson's infectious enthusiasm. "Okay, okay—I'll pay for the recording, and I'll buy blank jackets for you to stamp," said Stark. "That's the deal."

★ ★ ★

Lost in the excitement surrounding Westerberg's new song was the fact that the Replacements and Twin/Tone had never drawn up a contract. With sessions for a second record suddenly in the offing, the issue came to a head.

In hindsight it seems strange that it had taken so long to make their relationship formal, but at the time Twin/Tone was still a fairly loose operation. The label had handshake agreements with most of its artists—though Paul Stark would make a point of getting the Suburbs' signatures down on paper before they departed for major label Mercury in 1983.

Starting with Tommy's guardianship agreement, Peter Jesperson had begun efforts to put the band's affairs in some kind of order. In early '82, he helped Westerberg establish a publishing company, NAH Music. The name, noted Paul, was a pessimistic acronym: Nothing Always Happens.

Representing both the band and Twin/Tone, Jesperson often had difficulty determining where his loyalties lay. "During the whole phase of making the first record, the band and the label were all for one, one for all," he said. "But when Paul Stark had to put his foot down about a few things, Westerberg got a little hot about that and it became a little issue."

Westerberg had waited restlessly for six months after *Sorry Ma* was completed for the label to have the funds to release the album. Once it was out, he was itching to get the band on the road nationally. But the reality—despite all the good reviews for their debut—was that there was little demand for them outside the region. Beyond that, they had no van and no money to buy one, or any other means, to tour. Westerberg felt that Twin/Tone should be giving them support. But the label simply didn't have the funds to fully bankroll the Replacements' ambitions. Stark's refusal to "pony up," as Westerberg put it, created a further tension. "Paul needed to hate me," said Stark, "in terms of seeing me as the guy who never gave him money for an extra beer or to buy the new van or whatever it was he wanted."

In the first week of March, in this somewhat strained atmosphere, Twin/Tone decided to draw up a deal memo for the Replacements. The terms were fairly standard, if not particularly favorable, for an indie label contract at the time. The proposed agreement granted Twin/Tone "full, exclusive, and perpetual rights" to the band's albums for which they would pay "a royalty of twenty percent . . . from sales of your product which we manufacture and sell" and "fifty percent on sales of your product in cases where we lease your tapes and art work to another company." It was an album-by-album contract, though technically it required the band to give at least a one-record notice before leaving the company and forced them to pay back any outstanding advances.

Jesperson had found a young Minneapolis entertainment lawyer, Dan Satorious, to help set up Westerberg's publishing company. Satorious also began representing the band in their contract talks with Twin/Tone. "We went round and round with several drafts and eventually came up with something to which Dan said, 'Okay, this will do,'" recalled Stark. "So we typed it up and sent it to the band to sign."

But the band—effectively Westerberg—rejected the contract. "I don't think it was the agreement he didn't like," said Stark. "He just didn't want to sign, period."

Westerberg's version of events was slightly different than Stark's. He would recall that Satorious "told me not to sign. Stark was saying, 'Oh, come on . . . he doesn't know what he's talking about. It's a standard form. Just sign it.'" Stark's insistence immediately made him suspicious. "We met a couple times, and the lawyer says don't sign it. So I just rested on that and never signed it."

While Satorious had advised Westerberg against signing the first draft of the contract, after making changes to the deal, he was satisfied with the new terms. Westerberg simply ignored his later recommendation, held fast to Satorious's original advice, and refused to put his signature down.

At the same time, the band also balked at signing a management deal with Jesperson. It was a complicated ten-year agreement—with an out if they signed with a major label—that would effectively pay Jesperson between 12.5 percent and 15 percent of their gross income to serve as their adviser, manager, and producer.

Again, Westerberg wouldn't sign. "Suddenly, the band was in a feisty mood," said Jesperson. "It was like, 'Do we push the issue or just move on?'"

While Jesperson was satisfied to let the management deal drop—the band would go on to honor his commission terms anyway—Stark hunkered down. "I just said, 'Well, this band's not going to see any money from us until they sign a contract,'" said Stark. "'We'll pay for the records . . . we'll give them tour support once we can, but if they expect anything beyond that, they're not going to see anything.'"

Of course, as it stood, there was nothing to see; the Replacements were already in debt to the label and would grow more so with each album. It would take several more years—and not until they were well away from Twin/Tone—before their records would actually recoup and royalties come due.

By then, the lack of a contract would become a major point of contention. The band's fight with Stark became a pitched battle that would rage for years, playing out in lawyers' offices and district court and eventually reaching the bottom of the Mississippi River.

* * *

Even with the contract matter unsettled, on March 13 the Replacements returned to Blackberry Way to record. They'd booked the session under a fake name, the Amps. Blackberry had a public calendar on the wall, and to avoid being nagged by public questions about what they were doing and when the album would be out, the band elected to work in secret.

The Replacements set up for a daylong session that would result in a record Westerberg pointedly wanted to title *Too Poor to Tour*—though the eight-song effort would ultimately be called *Stink*, subtitled *"Kids Don't Follow" Plus Seven*.

In contrast to *Sorry Ma*'s prolonged gestation, *Stink* was, by necessity, a quickie affair. Reuniting with engineer Steve Fjelstad—who also got coproduction credit along with Peter Jesperson—the band was focused, having sharpened up the songs onstage in the weeks preceding the session.

Much of *Stink* was filled with reductive punk numbers: "I couldn't write hardcore worth a shit," admitted Westerberg, "but I certainly tried to sound as tough as I could." There was a pothead diss ("Dope Smokin Moron"), a life-in-the-Midwest lament ("Stuck in the Middle": "I got a headful of dreams, I got a pocket full of nothing"), and a brilliantly inane response to his father's one-time admonition to find work ("God Damn Job"). "I knew it was very stupid, but I thought that's okay . . . we can get mileage out of this," Westerberg said. "There's certain kinds of songs that absolutely require being innocent or dumb, and you play up to that sometimes."

Where the opening track "Kids" was a response to U2, the album's book-end, "Gimme Noise," served as a rebuke of the Suburbs. The Chan Poling–led outfit had undergone a dramatic stylistic change over the previous year, ditching its arty, elemental punk rock in favor of what he called "underground disco music" with the single "Music for Boys" and their *Credit in Heaven* LP. "It was a decision to make this insistent kind of music that could move people, and make them dance," said Poling. "Going for the dance floor was onerous to [Westerberg], and he let me know that."

"I can't figure out Music for Boys. . . . Don't gimme that noise," wailed Westerberg. "I'll give you my jacket, if you gimme your glamour. / Gimme that racket / Gimme that clamor." It was a song rife with not-so-subtle jabs at the Suburbs' new direction. "That kind of hurt my feelings," admitted Poling.

"I was jealous of them, certainly," said Westerberg. "But I could say a ton of nice stuff about the Suburbs. They tolerated us when they didn't have to. They let us open and knock over their amps. We couldn't outplay them, and they had a thousand people cheering and girls throwing underwear. It was like, 'What are we gonna do? We'll be louder and ruder.' That's what that was about."

The distorted blues shuffle "White and Lazy" harkened back to Westerberg's earliest roots. "I used to listen to Sonny Boy and Little Walter for years and years, then I heard the Sex Pistols and everything changed, but I still had that blues shit in me." Having learned to play harp from an instructional manual by Minneapolis bluesman Tony Glover, Westerberg gamely blew through another self-deprecating account of his own indolence—before breaking into a mock-hardcore chant: "*White! Lazy! Ashamed of nothing!*" "That was probably as political as Paul ever got," chided Tommy Stinson.

The album's real outlier—and a truer indication of where Westerberg's musical ambitions were heading—was the lovelorn warning "Go," which sounded more like an early mood piece by Blue Oyster Cult than anything by Black Flag.

Overall, the record was the most democratic of the 'Mats' career: half its songs were four-way band cowrites, and given the fast, hard, riff-heavy nature of the material, *Stink* served as a showcase for Bob Stinson's lacerating guitar work.

* * *

Having finished tracking on a Saturday, the plan was to do the mixing on Sunday. But unlike *Sorry Ma*, the whole band showed up for the mix and little work got done. "Fjelstad finally had to kick them out," said Jesperson.

"Paul couldn't be serious when the rest of the band was around. He would be like, 'Let's do something stupid to the guitar effect on this one.' It just became a *Monkees* episode."

However, one inspired touch did get added to "Kids Don't Follow" during the mix. In late January, the Replacements had played downtown's Harmony Building, a rent-party for visual artist Don Holzschuh, opening for the Warheads and L7–3. It was a massive multi-keg affair attended by an array of local scenesters and underage kids. The Replacements' noise levels drew a visit and warning from the local constabulary. Not long after they'd finished their set, Minneapolis's finest decided to end the fun entirely.

As he watched a uniformed officer take the microphone to disperse the crowd, Replacements' soundman Terry Katzman pressed record on his tape player. *"This is the Minneapolis Police . . . the party is o-ver,"* he announced, to a collection of groans and boos. Hiding back by the soundboard, a group of kids, including future Soul Asylum singer Dave Pirner, were cursing out the cops. "We were yelling as loud as we could, 'cause they couldn't figure out who was saying it," recalled Pirner, who claimed to have delivered the moment's distinctive "Hey, fuck you, *maaaan*!" Katzman's recording of the incident would lead off the 'Mats new record, serving as an atmospheric intro to "Kids."

Final work on the record was completed, sans Replacements, a few days later. As promised, Paul Stark delivered several thousand blank record jackets. The band and various friends spent a couple Grain Belt-fueled evenings hand stamping the covers (often with distinctive, drunken results).

Catching the public by surprise, just as the 'Mats had intended, the record was released in June to glowing reviews. In *Sweet Potato*, music editor Marty Keller—who'd been somewhat on the fence about the band—raved that "[*Stink*] has everything" and pointed to "Kids Don't Follow" as "Westerberg's 'My Generation.'" "It's his best work to date and may rank with some of the best songs to come out of the land of 10,000 guitars." Even Hüsker Dü's Bob Mould was impressed: "I think the sound and fury of the band was at its most focused on *Stink*," he said. "'Kids Don't Follow' was a true anthem."

Robert Christgau of the *Village Voice* weighed in again, giving the record an "A plus" and calling it "a fierce funny cataclysmic slab of summer vinyl . . . better than the young marauders' memorable debut LP." The record would also place at number eight in his year-end "Pazz and Jop" ballot.

Despite the praise, in later years Westerberg would look back on *Stink* as the Replacements' record that "rang falsest of them all."

"That was our first mistake. Our first stumble. Trying to play up to what we thought was going to keep us in sync with what was going on. . . . That was us trying to stand with Black Flag and the Effigies and saying, 'Yeah, we can do this too.' . . . 'Cause right off we did not feel like we fit in the scene as a 'punk' band. We were sorta acting like a punk band."

"[*Stink*] was about as close as it was going to get," noted Tommy Stinson. "It wasn't in the cards for us to be hardcore. It wasn't like we could suddenly be that all the time. The inability of us ever being any one thing all the time was pretty evident early on."

With *Sorry Ma* and *Stink*, the 'Mats had firmly established a musical identity, but Westerberg sensed it was time to try something different. "After the first rush of being loud and snotty, we realized the next thing is to keep moving," he said. "They can hit you with a bottle if you stand still."

CHAPTER 13

As was so often the case, the Replacements' career fortunes got a crucial boost from a true believer. Raised near Minneapolis's Lake Harriet, Tom Carlson had been a scrappy wrestler and football player at Southwest High. Burdened by a heavy depressive streak (mental illness and suicide would leave a tragic mark on his family), in the late 1970s Carlson became a fan of confrontational Brit-punk bands like the Sex Pistols and Wire. In 1981 he was working night security at the Walker Art Center and checking out gigs at the Longhorn, where he saw the Replacements and felt an immediate connection.

After the show, an excited Carlson approached Peter Jesperson to tell him he loved the band and would do anything to help them. Carlson had a car and started shuttling the 'Mats to and from gigs, joining their retinue as a volunteer roadie (just as Lou Santacroce was leaving the fold to focus on his singer-songwriter career). Later, while riding his bike around Lake Street, Carlson was hit by a motorist and ended up with a hefty insurance settlement. He used $6,000 of the money to buy the Replacements their first vehicle—a rough-looking but otherwise well-functioning former electrical company van.

Thanks to Carlson—variously nicknamed Carton or Huck—making regular weekend road trips was finally a viable proposition. For much of 1982 the band solidified itself playing venues across the upper Midwest: the Atwood Student Center in St. Cloud, the St. Croix Boom Company in Stillwater, the Showcase in Duluth, and the Revolution in Sioux Falls, South Dakota.

The college town of Madison, Wisconsin, would prove the group's first real stronghold outside the Twin Cities as they became a top draw at spots like Merlyn's, G.S. Vig's, Club de Wash, and Headliner's. The band would make the five-hour trek from Minneapolis, drinking heartily along the way. They'd pull up hammered and fill up on what was—to them anyway—an exotic delicacy, gyros (which Westerberg refused to pronounce correctly, insisting on calling them "jai-rohs," like a stereotypical Midwestern bohunk). Then the debauchery began.

In Madison the crowds were rowdy, the after-parties were good, and the drugs were even better. "That was like our Hamburg," said Peter Jesperson, referring to the down-and-dirty German city where the early Beatles came into their own. "Madison was that place for the 'Mats; it was a big deal in the development of the band.

"The whole thing of being in a band is like putting on a mask, it gives you license to do things you wouldn't normally do, especially when you're away from home," Jesperson would later note. On the road and in close quarters, the Replacements' personalities became exaggerated: the sometimes petulant Tommy became "The Brat," penny-pinching Chris became "The Chince," Bob, ever in his cups, was dubbed "The Drunk," while moody, churlish Paul was "The Louse."

* * *

Tagging along with the Replacements as opener on a number of these regional dates was a fledgling group called Loud Fast Rules. The band was led by Dave Pirner, a South Minneapolis Catholic school refugee who was a year ahead of Tommy Stinson at West High. Pirner had started playing music as a kid, taking up trumpet ("It was the loudest instrument and had the fewest buttons") before switching over to saxophone. When punk happened, he learned to play guitar and drums. One day Pirner showed up at high school hockey practice with a Ramones "Gabba Gabba Hey!" button on. "And I got the shit beat out of me," he said. "The hockey players did not want punk rock to infiltrate their sport. So I walked away from that." Instead, Pirner went on to front a short-lived band called the Shitz, which made a couple of appearances at the Longhorn.

The Shitz—whose standout song was a rowdy cover of Simon and Garfunkel's "The Sounds of Silence"—had impressed Dan Murphy and Karl Mueller. Murphy was a Marshall High grad and guitarist who'd been playing in a group called At Last. Mueller was a bassist who'd spent a little time in England and come back looking like Sid Vicious. They were both working as carryout boys at the Lund's grocery store on Lake Street. "I would go over to Lund's and take a weed break with them," recalled Pirner. "That's how I got tight with those guys."

They formed Loud Fast Rules in the summer of 1981, initially with Pirner on drums, before Pat Morley took over the kit and the band changed its name to Soul Asylum. Their early performances evinced the same raw, youthful dynamism as the Replacements' first gigs.

The 'Mats would go on to adopt Soul Asylum as a kind of baby brother band. "I was quite intimidated being around Westerberg, 'cause he'd written all these great songs," said Murphy. "It seemed pretty heavy that he would come to our shows and be into us."

Westerberg struck Murphy as strangely ill suited to the spotlight. "I don't think he played himself as an outcast, I think he was an outcast. He could be charming when he had a few drinks in him. But he was really shy." Onstage, Pirner was far more at ease, a whirling dervish who relished performing. "Pirner was trying to be sexy," said his friend and West classmate David Roth. "Westerberg was trying to be working-class angry. Pirner was trying to get the chicks. It didn't seem like Westerberg was trying to do that."

The Replacements' patronage helped Soul Asylum secure a deal with Twin/Tone the following year, after a standout gig in Madison that wowed Peter Jesperson. Eventually, though, a sense of competition came between them. Soul Asylum stopped opening shows for the 'Mats, though the two camps remained friends.

Writer David Ayers, who went on to manage Soul Asylum, reckoned that Westerberg was uncomfortable with the contrasts between himself and Pirner. "Something that always informed Paul's sensibility was his inwardness. He was fundamentally uncomfortable with people looking at him," said Ayers. "And he recognized that Pirner kinda liked it—and I'm not sure Paul liked that."

★ ★ ★

As the Replacements developed a habit of living and playing hard during their first sojourns, the effects were often damaging—particularly for Westerberg, who was smoking, speeding, and blowing out his voice regularly.

Riding home one night following a gig at the St. Croix Boom Company, he began having a physical freak-out. Jesperson was driving and Chris Mars was riding shotgun, when they heard Westerberg hyperventilating, then retching and writhing around in the backseat. "I thought he was having some kind of heart attack or something—dying basically," recalled Jesperson. "So I just floored it . . . and was driving really crazy into the city, running red lights to get to a hospital."

A panicked Jesperson had a knot in his stomach, fearing the worst. Just then, he felt Westerberg's hand reach up and grab his shoulder.

"Pete . . . Pete," Westerberg croaked.

"Yes, Paul, what is it?" Jesperson replied breathlessly.

"If I die . . . don't let Bob sing," cracked Westerberg, before slumping back.

The comedy continued as Jesperson pulled up to what he thought was Hennepin County General's emergency entrance but turned out to be an adjacent office building instead. "We carried Paul out of the car, and it was the wrong door," he said. "And then we had to carry him back into the car." By the time they reached the bay of the emergency room and medics whisked him away, Jesperson was almost as ashen as Westerberg: "I really thought one of the greatest artists I've ever known is gonna die on my watch."

It would transpire that Westerberg was having an adverse reaction to some potent pharmaceutical amphetamine someone had given him at the club that night. "The doctor wanted to know if I'd been [freebasing]," said Westerberg, who was given a sedative to normalize his heart rate. He was also diagnosed with pleurisy—a painful inflammation of the membrane surrounding the lungs. "It was probably that I was straining, trying to sing like Lemmy from Motörhead," he said. The doctor suggested he slather his chest with Ben-Gay before he sang—which he did for the next few years, giving the Replacements' dressing rooms a distinctive preshow aroma.

The following morning, semi-recovered, Westerberg began writing a frantic blues ramble recounting the incident ("I don't wanna die before my time . . . I've already used eight of my lives") called "Take Me Down to the Hospital."

* * *

Though it wouldn't become fodder for any song, a few months later Bob Stinson nearly bought it in even more dramatic fashion during a trip to Kansas. The Replacements had become small stars in the college town of Lawrence, where the University of Kansas radio station, KJHK, had been playing *Sorry Ma* endlessly (largely thanks to the station's Blake Gumprecht, a 'Mats champion who would eventually go to work for Twin/Tone).

That May the band was booked to play a pair of sets at the Off the Wall Hall in Lawrence for $350. It would prove to be their biggest payday to that point, as well as their farthest gig away from the Twin Cities.

Arriving at the venue, which had been converted from an old airplane hangar, the band started sound-checking. Bob, who was playing through a ratty rig—a rundown head and an old Sears Teisco amp—stepped to the foot of the stage. With one hand around the neck of his Gibson Firebird, he went to adjust the microphone when something went horribly wrong. A massive jolt hit his body, electrocuting him. The surge caused him to spasm and lock up. Unable to let go of the mic, he then began shaking uncontrollably—snapping the neck of the guitar in two places.

Chris Mars had his head down, adjusting his drums, when "I heard a stuttering moan coming from Bob. The shock was so great that he couldn't even yell." As Bob collapsed to his knees, Mars leapt from behind the drum kit, spread eagle, knocking over his cymbal stands. "I grabbed Bob by the shoulders and tried to yank him away, and I got a jolt that felt like I'd put my hand into an electrical socket," said Mars. "It was one of the most frightening things I have ever witnessed." He was finally able to roll Bob on his back as the club's soundman, realizing what was happening, cut the power. "Chris probably saved his life," said Jesperson.

Dazed but living, Bob laughed off the incident, a surge of adrenaline carrying him through the aftermath. But later, during a preshow dinner, Tommy Stinson would remember sitting across from his brother, "and we locked eyes . . . and we both started crying. It was super surreal that it had happened. After everything had calmed down, that's when it hit us just how scary it was."

When the band returned to Minneapolis, Bob went to get his guitar fixed at the Knut Koupee Music Store. There he encountered the Suicide Commandos' Chris Osgood, who gasped when he saw Stinson. "The whites of his eyes were red, blood red," recalled Osgood. "He showed me his left hand, and he had six burn marks where the strings had singed into his skin. I remember thinking, *This would've killed anybody but Bob.* A normal human being would've been fried on the spot. But Bob managed to take it because he was such an ox."

Added Mars: "Whenever the band was onstage or around the amps or PA gear, you can bet your life we were pretty damn cautious from then on . . . for at least a week."

★ ★ ★

I n the spring of '82, the Replacements opened a gig in Madison for UK punks the Damned. Seeing the band's flamboyantly styled guitarist and resident character Captain Sensible would exert a profound influence on Bob Stinson.

The Damned leader took a shine to Bob, who was wearing some unfashionable jeans his mother had bought him and a scoop-neck Mama Rosa's shirt. The Captain offered him a bit of showbiz advice. "Bloody hell, mate—you need to lose the fuckin' flares," he told Bob. "If anyone's gonna notice you up there, you need to look and act the part."

Bob would heed those words and come into his own as an outré performer and onstage personality. "When I saw [Captain Sensible] playing naked or in his underwear, he wasn't scared," said Bob. "If he didn't like the sound check, he'd just whip it out and piss on the monitor." Bob began to take the stage in wild outfits: a detective's trenchcoat, a ballerina tutu, a woman's house dress, or occasionally in the buff. "He started to find his own act, his own image, and then really lived that up," said Westerberg. "That's where he started to get his own fans and his own following."

Between his scorching leads and comic attire, Bob became the key element of the band's spectacle. "To me, Bob was the best part of the Replacements, the funniest part," said Tommy's pal David Roth. "When he'd grab Westerberg's mic stand during 'Rattlesnake' and everyone would get pissed at him, he didn't care . . . he was fucking goofy. But he gave the Replacements this brutal energy too."

"He was so much the 'X factor' of the live show," noted Dave Ayers. "Tommy was always exciting, and Chris was totally dependable. But that snowflake quality of the shows usually came down to Paul and Bob." The two might tussle onstage, wrestling and booting each other, either out of joy or frustration. "We have fun when we play good, and when we have a bad night and we fight, that keeps it real," noted Westerberg at the time. "If Bob plays shitty and the crowd isn't gonna let him know, I'm sure as hell gonna. That's the immediate way, to kick him. That's what we all understand. That's part of the deal."

When he wasn't donning outrageous garb and playing the guitar, Bob was an altogether different person. "There was this whole other side to him that had nothing to do with the stage Bob; there was nothing loud or attention-grabbing about his personality," said Ayers. "There was a kind-hearted, quiet guy underneath the oaf in the dress."

Bob's deep fascination with Yes guitarist Steve Howe continued unabated into the '80s, even as the Replacements went pseudo-hardcore. Even in the 'Mats context, Bob would continue to cop Howe's lovely, lilting neoclassical riffs and put a jet engine on them. Howe's new supergroup, Asia, had released its debut that March. When the band played Minneapolis, Jesperson got a giddy Stinson backstage to meet his idol. "Steve Howe is pretty much the antithesis of punk," said David Ayers. "But that showed Bob wasn't just a slash-and-burn guitar player. He was really unique in what he played and how he saw things."

Westerberg would famously acknowledge Bob's sometimes confounding duality, claiming: "I don't know if he's the stupidest genius or the smartest idiot I've ever known."

* * *

Ever since his release from the group home, Bob drank consistently, if not chronically, as a way of numbing the pain of his childhood. As the band developed so, too, did Paul's and Chris's tendency to abuse alcohol. (Teenage Tommy had yet to start imbibing.) Drinking had always been part of the Replacements' methodology, a way of shedding their nerves and shyness and getting up onstage—but it would eventually come to define them as well.

The 'Mats' growing reputation in this regard was divisive within the Twin Cities. During a live KFAI radio interview, deejay David McGowan took Westerberg to task for the band's turn toward wasted performances.

"Don't take this wrong," said McGowan, "but I don't have as much fun seeing you guys live as I used to, and I think it's 'cause you're too damn drunk."

"Then again," countered Westerberg, "there are nights we were so drunk we couldn't recognize each other and we played good too."

"Well, I'm tired of seeing wrestling matches onstage."

"We're tired of playing sometimes."

In a sense, the band's drinking and dissolute behavior had been wrapped up in the mythology of their songs from the very beginning. "The songs were about what we were. It was never a pose," said Westerberg. "It may have come suspiciously close when we got attention for being fuck-ups. Where we thought: *This works, people come to see this.* I think then we accentuated it, and maybe even stretched the limits of what we actually were. Let's get even drunker."

"A certain segment of fans, they latched on to that," said Kevin Bowe of the sober rockers the Dads. "Like, 'Boy, these guys are drunk all the time, I wish I could do that, but I can't because I have a job,' or, 'I'm in school.' The Replacements got to be the poster boys for who they wanted to be. And none of that had to do with music." It was a by-product of the Midwest's hard-drinking culture. Said Bowe: "You think Minneapolis is bad, you oughta go to Duluth. You think Duluth is bad, hop over to Superior, Wisconsin."

True Replacements fans—not the ones coming to live vicariously through them or to find sanction for their own behavior—were a different breed.

"When we started, we were mixed-up kids, and we wrote about it," said Westerberg. "It's funny that the people who related to it the most weren't fucked-up kids, though. Our fans have always been, dare I say, a little more intelligent than the band was labeled as. I always thought that ironic."

Replacements partisans were, on the whole, literate, dark-humored, and a bit confused about their place in the world. They weren't the go-getters or yuppie types, but they weren't hopeless wastrels either. They were, Tommy Stinson would note, "more like us than they fuckin' knew. They didn't really fit anywhere. They probably didn't aspire to a whole lot, but also didn't aspire to doing nothing either. That's the kind of fan we probably appealed to most: the people that were in that gray area. Just like us."

* * *

In June 1982, as *Stink* was being released, there was a sudden focus on Westerberg's work as a writer. "What the Replacements were known for mostly was being loud and fast and drunk," said David Ayers. "There hadn't been a whole lot of attention paid to what the guy really had to say." Ayers would pen a cover story for the *Minnesota Daily* on the band's creative engine.

"Paul Westerberg is likable. Even onstage during his worst, shrug shouldered, grumbling, half-drunks he's magnetic and a little disarming," wrote Ayers.

> He's also polite, thoughtful, and inquisitive. It's not that he's got a trumped-up, angry stage persona; he's still sorting himself out. He takes great pains to be honest, even if that means contradicting himself at times as he does in his conversation and in his music. In his words, "sometimes my mind goes a hundred different ways at once." He wasn't speaking on the topic at the time, but that's a pretty fair description of a young man trying to come to grips with his own raw genius.

The article would reveal that the B-side "If Only You Were Lonely" was merely the tip of the iceberg when it came to Westerberg's solo material. While Ayers was privy to Westerberg's "secret" stash of songs—Jesperson had played them for him—"the public knowledge of that stuff was non-existent up to that point." Ayers raised the possibility that Westerberg would use the material to make a solo record. "'Sometimes I think that's right around the corner, sometimes I think it won't be for five years,' said Westerberg. 'I'm uncomfortable about it causing tension with the band right now, because if I were to do that I can honestly say it would not be the Replacements, and that would be weird. To do it solo . . . I'd feel vulnerable. Now if somebody throws a bottle at least I've got three guys with me.'"

A few months later, however, Westerberg would play his first solo acoustic show, opening for former Jefferson Airplane/Hot Tuna guitarist Jorma Kaukonen at First Avenue. The seven-song set saw Westerberg strip down some

'Mats material and fidget nervously onstage. "I've never been so scared in my life as when I did that," he would recall. "You're so naked up there . . . no noise to hide behind. No one dancing. They're just standing there staring at you." (It would be his last solo appearance for two decades.)

Westerberg was still giving Jesperson new home recordings all through the *Stink* era, including revelatory pieces like the fragile acoustic experiment "Hold Me in Suspension." "He called me up and said, 'I just recorded this song, and I sing it all in falsetto, and I want you to hear it—but I've got to get it out of the house right now or I'm going to erase it.' It was like he'd done something and freaked himself out." Sometimes Paul would deliver a cassette cued up to a certain spot and tell Jesperson not to listen to anything else. "I honored that for a while, but when he didn't ask for the tape back, I got curious. Thought maybe he doesn't mind me exploring what else is on here," said Jesperson, who found other songs hidden on the tapes, like the fingerpicked beauty "You're Pretty When You're Rude."

Very little of this material, if any, was ever presented to the Replacements. "A lot of the reason why Paul didn't bring in certain things was because he knew either all of us or definitely Bob wasn't going to be into it," said Tommy. "The dynamic was that if we weren't all into it, it would just go away. And I'm sure there were times where that stung."

"I'm a little edgy about bringing songs now because each guy has his own tastes," noted Paul at the time. "If it doesn't rock enough, Bob will scoff at it, and if it isn't catchy enough, Chris won't like it, and if it isn't modern enough, Tommy won't like it."

During a gig in Duluth that summer, a tipsy Westerberg pulled Jesperson aside. "I just came up with the best lyric I've ever written," he told him. "I can live without your touch / If I can die within your reach." The delicately poetic "Within Your Reach" would be another "signpost song" for Jesperson, heralding a further evolution in Westerberg's work. But he began to worry that Paul's best material was going undocumented and would be lost. So, in July, Jesperson called Steve Fjelstad at Blackberry Way to book a solo session for Westerberg— without telling him. When he finally laid out the offer to Paul, there was a long, nervous pause. "Fuck yeah," said Westerberg finally. "Let's do it." But he was desperate to keep it secret from the band.

On the evening of the session, Westerberg met Jesperson at Oar Folk to head down to the studio. Just as they were about to leave, Chris Mars turned up unexpectedly. Mars took one look at Westerberg and his guitar case and figured something was up. They took Chris into their confidence and all headed down to Blackberry Way together. There Westerberg cut a trio of tracks: a version of Big Star's "September Gurls" that he made Fjelstad erase immediately; a rough sketch called "Warning Sound" (which would eventually mutate into "We're Comin' Out"), and an exquisite take of "Within Your Reach."

Westerberg thought the song needed some percussion. Fjelstad suggested they try using a Dr. Rhythm drum machine that was sitting in the studio. It was exactly the sound Westerberg was looking for, but Mars convinced him he could add a live drum track and jumped on a kit that was set up on the floor. He made a few unsuccessful passes at the track—unable to replicate the rigid mechanical beat that Westerberg had in mind. "I remember Chris actually getting teary-eyed," said Jesperson. "Like, 'I suck. I'm not good. I can't do what you're asking me.' I don't think I'd experienced it, before or again, where Chris got that emotional. It was pretty shocking. He was sitting there feeling like, 'I've been replaced by a machine.'"

It was a watershed moment in Westerberg's and Mars's musical relationship. From then on, it would always linger in the back of Paul's mind that Chris had his limitations as a drummer; that he might not be able to deliver as needed on some of his songs. "I'd done things to make everybody happy. There was some things that I wanted and if it made somebody unhappy . . . well, in that particular case I chose to do it," said Westerberg. "For every 'Within Your Reach' that got recorded, there was five or six that I squelched or erased because I didn't want to spoil the party."

* * *

The Replacements formally began work on their third album in October 1982. Rather than return to Blackberry Way and its limited eight-track setup, Twin/Tone's Paul Stark engineered the project, using his twenty-four-track mobile unit. "I hadn't worked with them since the demo a couple years earlier," said Stark, who along with Jesperson would coproduce a series of three- to four-day sessions in a pair of suburban warehouse spaces through the winter.

The 'Mats had actually gotten a head start on the record, cutting a few songs that summer at Blackberry—mostly a selection of *Stink*-centric holdovers like "Junior's Got a Gun" and "Ain't No Crime," which wouldn't appear on the LP. Only one of the tracks from this batch, "Run It," would make the final sequence.

It was breakneck rocker based on a true story: That spring Westerberg and Mars had been out drinking at Bob Mould's house. They left together, riding Chris's motorcycle, with Paul on back. As they sped through the streets of South Minneapolis, a police squad car drove up alongside and tried to pull them over. Instead of stopping, a suddenly wild-eyed Mars told the cops to "come and get me, you old fuckers!" and took off.

The police gave chase as Mars fled down an alley with a shocked Westerberg clinging on for dear life. He tried cutting through someone's front yard but clipped a hedge, which sent Westerberg flying off. The cops descended on Paul, who innocently claimed he'd only been hitchhiking and had clearly been picked up by a madman. "I'm not sure they believed me, but they were mostly after Chris," he said. They soon caught up to Mars and arrested him. Later that night, Jesperson got a call from Westerberg: "Chris is in jail—what are we gonna do?" Peter chuckled; Westerberg made it sound as though they should try to bust him out of the joint. Mars's family would ultimately post his bail.

The resulting song—a manic Bob Stinson–led blitz with Westerberg recounting the harrowing ride ("Lyndale . . . Garfield . . . red light, red light . . . run it!")—would prove to be the final gasp of the band's hardcore phase.

"It had been like a year or six months of touring and doing the *Stink* thing, and the last thing I wanted to do was really bash out another one like that," said Westerberg. Being a student of the Beatles and the Stones, he understood that the best bands underwent massive changes from year to year, from album to album. "I didn't think we were on their level, but I knew . . . if we just stood still and played the one thing, we'd be gone as fast as the Youth Brigade." Mars was in agreement. "He was the first one who didn't want to play fast—at that Hüsker Dü tempo—anymore," said Westerberg. "He wanted to slow it down a little, and I was more than happy to oblige. It was impossible to sing that shit anyway; it was ripping my throat raw."

Westerberg felt that the 'Mats' new record should move in a different direction—several of them, in fact. Cutting at a warehouse in Roseville, they began to work up a series of genre exercises. There was the electro-pop of "Within Your Reach," which Westerberg abetted with some synth flourishes; the surf-rock instrumental "Buck Hill" (which name-checked a local ski slope), the moody soundscape "Willpower," influenced by the Psychedelic Furs' "Sister Europe," and the bluesy desperation of "Take Me Down to the Hospital." "Mr. Whirly" nicked the Beatles' "Strawberry Fields" and "Oh! Darling" for its intro and Chubby Checker's "The Twist" for its melody, while "Lovelines" saw the band recycle the boogie groove of their old nugget "Lookin' for Ya" as Paul improvised lyrics, reading from the personal ads of alt-weekly *City Pages* ("Wednesday, October thirteenth, nineteen eighty-two, volume four, number seventy-nine . . . ").

The record had a free-flowing quality, a reflection of the band's listening habits. "Every time we'd get in the van we heard all kinds of music and liked a lot of different shit," said Westerberg. "We got cocky and thought: 'Why can't we play a little cocktail jazz, or a little blues or some folk?' We always used to fool around with that stuff in the basement anyway."

The model was a group like NRBQ—"bands that would go from this to that, bands that had a sense of variety," said Westerberg. "We wanted to do that. It was like, 'Okay, that'll be the "fuck you" for this record.'"

The album's emotional anchors were a pair of Westerberg's best outsider anthems: "Color Me Impressed" ("Everybody at your party, they don't look depressed") and "Heyday" ("Times ain't tough, they're tedious"). These were pop songs, but ones connected to the band's power trash aesthetic. "You could hear me more or less trying to find my voice, or trying to find out where I fit in," said Westerberg, who saw the album as "a way of trying to fuse what I had been listening to growing up into what was happening at the time."

As they worked through January of '83, the band would indulge in other musical experiments, cutting the odd, electronic-sounding "Shoot Me, Kill Me" and the mood-piece instrumental "Sea Hunt." Though the songs wouldn't make the final cut, it was part of a process of finding the right dozen tracks for the record. "There was less concern of trying to make an album that was all fast rock-and-roll songs," said Westerberg. "The record was going to be whatever turned out best on tape."

Early on, the 'Mats decided to call the album *Hootenanny*—a joking reference to folk boom–era jam sessions. Twin/Tone's Charley Hallman had actually found a 1963 Crestview Records sampler with the same title. The 'Mats would change some of the text, but otherwise nicked the package—its design, liner notes, etc.—wholesale. "We figured, 'Let's use this old stupid folk record and put our name on it,'" said Westerberg. "We just pissed our pants laughing. When it came to those kinds of decisions, if it made us laugh hard enough, then it was right."

* * *

While most of *Hootenanny*'s tracks were cut live as a group, the band would overdub vocals and lead guitar. The latter proved a particular challenge. "The major consideration was how drunk Bob was going to be when he came to the sessions and how much you could get out of him before he got too drunk to work," said Stark. "With Bob, we only had about twenty or thirty minutes to record every night."

Bob was aware of his issues with the bottle. That summer he'd voluntarily gone on the wagon, and the band's shows had benefited. But he soon resumed drinking and alienating the others with his behavior onstage and off. "Even before *Hootenanny*, his shenanigans were becoming overbearing," said Tommy, who sounded out Soul Asylum's Dan Murphy about possibly replacing his brother. "He did have a talk with me at the Entry one time, saying they might be looking for someone else in the band," recalled Murphy. "They were having some problems with Bob. I remember him saying, 'This might be the last show you see with my brother playing guitar.'"

During the Roseville sessions, things also reached an uncomfortable impasse over the band's material. Though Westerberg had mostly kept his solo songs separate from the 'Mats, "Within Your Reach" had already been earmarked for the LP. He also wanted the band to work up a new ballad called "You're Getting Married." But Bob wasn't having it. Jesperson would recall the guitarist essentially throwing the recording: "Bob was not trying, or sabotaging it to some degree because he didn't like the song. He was playing wrong notes, turning his back." (Years later Bob would deny the charges: "They said I kept them off 'cause I didn't like them? Shucks, I can play anything, you know?")

Finally putting his foot down, Bob halted the recording of "You're Getting Married" and told Westerberg flatly, "That ain't the Replacements . . . save it for your solo record, Paul." Bob got his way; the song would not appear on the album.

It was clear that creative battle lines were being drawn. And given Westerberg's growth and predominance as a writer, it was a fight that Bob was bound to lose. "I don't know if there was a moment where he thought, *This is no longer my band*," said Westerberg. "Because when we played the loud, fast shit, it was his band. But I felt like I can only do so much of that. I have to do this [ballad] crap too."

The issue would fester, coming to a head gradually over the next few years. But for the time being, Bob remained, for better or worse, the band's undeniable force. "I remember one night he knocked me and Tommy's heads together," laughed Westerberg. "We were arguing about something and Bob just smacked us together, like the Three Stooges. We both fell like bowling pins. He would still take charge in the end."

* * *

Much as there might have been frustration with Bob, the real animosity during the session was directed at the ever-enigmatic Paul Stark. The band was pissed off about having to record in some freezing suburban warehouse, and they took it out on him nightly. They would typically show up late, drop off their gear, and then run to the nearby Holiday Inn bar, leaving a waiting Stark seething.

Sitting in the mobile unit, Stark couldn't see the band as they recorded. "So we bent over backwards to play jokes on him," said Westerberg. "That record was more attitude than music, I think."

At one point while working on "Willpower," Westerberg was arguing over the talkback mic with Stark, saying his vocals should be buried in reverb. Not wanting to mar the actual recording, Stark rejected the idea out of hand—he told him they could add the effect during mixing—pissing Westerberg off.

After the exchange, Westerberg motioned to the others to switch instruments: Paul went to the drums, Bob got the bass, and Tommy and Chris the guitars. "What's the next song?" Stark asked, rolling tape.

"'Hootenanny' in E," said Westerberg as they improvised a title track, a blues shuffle that consisted of little more than him bleating the phrase, "*It's a hootenanny*," over and over again. "They just made that up on the spot, as a way to flip the bird to Stark," said Jesperson, who was in the room. "It was so funny to watch it go down—they played with such determination. I remember Chris doing the lead—him thinking, *Whoa, that wasn't too bad*, surprising himself." The band was trying to stifle their laughter during the take. "Stark didn't even know it was a joke," said Westerberg. "He took it seriously."

When the track was over, Stark's voice came through the talkback. "Uh, okay," he said, sounding confused about what he'd just heard. "Do you want to try that again or come in and listen to it?"

"Nope," said Westerberg. "That's it: first song, side one."

* * *

As the sessions wrapped up, everyone was optimistic that *Hootenanny* might represent some kind of breakthrough for the band. Even though they had assimilated a number of styles, Westerberg would remark that it was "the first album that sounds just like us."

Before the record went to mix, Westerberg stopped by Jesperson's apartment to show him a new song he'd just finished. "It's kind of like 'The Ballad of the Replacements,'" he told Jesperson. Titled "Treatment Bound," it was a woozy chronicle of the band's misadventures "from Duluth to Madison."

> *We're getting no place*
> *Fast as we can*
> *Get a nose full*
> *From our so-called friends*
> *We're getting nowhere quick as we know how*
> *We whirl from town to town*
> *Treatment bound*

Westerberg's original idea was to play the song for the band in the Stinsons' basement and have Jesperson record the performance and their reactions. It was an interesting idea—high concept in a way—but it didn't work out sonically.

Instead, the whole band took a stab at cutting it as a country ramble. The live-in-the-basement version—replete with flubbed chords and rolling beer bottle sounds—would fittingly fall apart at the end, as Westerberg's lyrics seemed to ask the question on all their minds: "We're gettin' nowhere, what will we do now?"

CHAPTER 14

By early 1983, it was time to take on the coasts. There was one obvious issue, however: Tommy was still a sophomore at West High School. The band's first few years, being managed around his schedule, had been limited to weekend regional runs and weeknight shows in the Twin Cities. "There was times I would come to school pretty beat up," said Tommy, "because I'd played the night before."

The 'Mats had firm offers to play New York and Boston, with a longer spring tour of the East Coast shaping up. Jesperson and the band gathered for a meeting at the Stinson house. Peter expected a broad discussion about accommodating Tommy's school obligations.

Instead, he recalled, "Paul looked Tommy square in the eye and said, 'Quit school or we get a new bass player,'" recalled Jesperson. "It was blunt and funny, in a Westerbergian sort of way. Tommy was like, 'Whoa—okay, I guess I'm quitting school.' He was startled and sort of laughed about it. I remember being surprised that Paul was so direct about it."

Westerberg vociferously denied Jesperson's version of events. "I think that's bullshit. I don't believe that I would have told a ninth-grader [sic] he's got to quit school," said Westerberg. "If he got a little nudge from somebody, I would bet it was more from Bob."

But Tommy didn't need to be pushed by anyone else. "I wasn't good at school anyway," he said. "There was no point in it anymore. I presented it to my mom, and that was the end of it. She figured, 'Well, he hasn't been going to jail, he's making a little money—I'll sign off.' She made my brother try and look out for me—which didn't really happen all that much. Peter was the one that had to look out for me."

* * *

F rank Riley was a rare breed: an agent who specialized in the unglamorous world of club and college booking. "Frank was one of the few agents who would actually go to the venues he booked," said First Avenue's Steve McClellan. "You seldom had the big mainstream agents show up at the clubs they placed their shows. The clubs were what big agents gave their trainees."

After working with the dB's agent-manager Bob Singerman, Riley launched his own New York–based independent company, Venture Bookings Ltd. He would help nurture the American indie rock circuit—a loose network of nightclubs, punk halls, and college campus gigs—that coalesced in the early eighties. Venture's roster included the Dream Syndicate, the Feelies, Green on Red, and Violent Femmes, among others.

In the spring of 1983, Riley cold-called Jesperson at Oar Folk and told him he'd be willing to represent the Replacements nationally, sight unseen. "Suddenly we had an agent," said Jesperson. "We were headlining or being put into good packages. We felt empowered by it."

"I used every bit of my resources, smarts, and what little experience I had at the time on their behalf," Riley said. It was a thankless job—one that grew more thankless over time.

Before heading east, the Replacements added a key member to their ragtag road crew. A dark-haired, puckish twenty-four-year-old, Bill Sullivan had been raised in the first-tier Minneapolis suburb of St. Louis Park. "My dad was a very strict Catholic," Sullivan said. "The first time he let me out of the house to a record store by myself I came home with [Alice Cooper's] *Love It to Death*. For a Catholic guy who thought I was going to be a priest, he was not very happy."

Sullivan, who worked night security at the Walker Art Center and was a childhood friend and roommate of Replacements roadie Tom Carlson, had caught the band early on at the Longhorn. After a while, Sullivan and the band began socializing at the bar. "We'd get together at the CC Club and try and scam free drinks off the waitresses." He and Westerberg in particular were foils; both had a mordant wit as well as a penchant for wild behavior after a few libations. (Westerberg would dub Sullivan Father O'Ruckus.)

Sullivan went on the Replacements' "Eastern Whirl" tour unpaid. "After the first week they felt bad and started paying me [a few bucks] a day." Sullivan would become the band's dutiful court jester and caretaker. "My main job turned out to be stage security," he said. "I became the barrier between the band and an irate audience."

"There were times where he would come back from going out to eat and he'd bring me back a hamburger, 'cause he knew I hadn't eaten in two days," said Westerberg. "Bill always knew when we *needed* something, as opposed to just wanted something."

* * *

After a short, solid set opening for the Circle Jerks in Milwaukee on April 8, the band played Detroit's City Club the following night—challenging the soundman and the few fans there with their volume, something they'd do the entire tour. "Back then they didn't even have good equipment, but they would pin everything to the wall," said Sullivan.

After the first song at City Club, Jesperson went to the stage and whispered to Westerberg about adjusting the volume. "He had a glass of scotch on the floor by his mic stand, and he kicked it so it splattered in my face," Jesperson said. "Then he turned his amp up and went into the next song." The soundman stormed off in anger; a wet, furious Jesperson dutifully tried to man the board. "They totally cleared the room. When they were done, I said, 'Fuck this.'" Jesperson walked to a nearby bar and ordered a double.

Offstage, but especially on, Paul could be rash and indifferent to people's feelings. Part of it was a rebellious front-man act—but the cloak of the band also gave him free rein to indulge his more callous impulses.

The next morning the band awoke to find someone had siphoned all the gas out of their van. Despite the rough start to the trip, they glimpsed New York City just before dawn, checking into a cheap motel in Jersey City. Jesperson registered four and snuck in seven.

Enticed by their first vision of the Big Apple, Peter, Tommy, and Bob decided to take a PATH train into the city. As the others explored, Westerberg stayed back at the motel. Rather than try to fit into New York, he decided, the Replacements were going to stick out.

"We accentuated the fact that we were bohunks. We knew that we didn't fit in, and we went to the extreme to get in their face. Like, 'Hey, wheyre's the Eym-pire Stay-ate Billdin'?' We were determined to be as Midwestern as possible."

* * *

New York Rocker was founded in 1976 by Alan Betrock and later purchased by former Oar Folkjokeopus employee Andy Schwartz. It was one of the first national outlets to cover the Replacements: the February 1982 issue ran a glowing review of Sorry Ma.

Later, managing editor Michael Hill received a spec feature story about the band by Minneapolis writer Tony Lonetree. "It really intrigued me," said Hill of the piece. "It made them sound like backwoods bluesmen some anthropologist had stumbled across on a field trip." But that fall the Rocker would fold before the story could run.

Shortly after Hill lost his job, he and onetime Rocker contributor Ira Kaplan (who later founded Yo La Tengo) began booking a weekly showcase at Greenwich Village's Folk City called "Music for Dozens"—three bands for three bucks, every Wednesday. It would help launch a number of emerging underground acts: the Minutemen, Violent Femmes, Sonic Youth.

The band Hill was most eager to bring to Folk City was the Replacements. They would make their New York debut on April 13, headlining a bill with Boston's Del Fuegos (also playing New York City for the first time) and locals the Del-Lords—"Whom everyone was afraid of, 'cause they thought they looked like bikers," recalled Hill.

With multiple New York–area appearances that week, Westerberg and Carlson crashed at a friend's apartment in the city, while Jesperson and the Stinsons took over the Hoboken, New Jersey, flat Kaplan shared with his girlfriend, Georgia Hubley. "I can recall Bob being sacked out in a sleeping bag in the middle of the afternoon—every afternoon—and we'd step over him," said Hill. "Tommy left quite an impression with his hairspray in the bathroom."

The Replacements kicked off the Folk City show with a "Hayday" that practically stripped the paint from the walls. The woman running sound at the club told Jesperson he needed to get the band to turn it down. "That's not in my job description," he said, still shaken after Detroit. She bolted, and Jesperson once again tried to salvage things at the board. The band blasted through nearly thirty songs off their first two albums and the still-unreleased *Hootenanny*. The covers-heavy closing section yielded inspired versions of tunes by the Grass Roots, the Clash, and Lloyd Price. They ended with a rumbling take on Motörhead's "Ace of Spades" that blew out the club's feeble PA. "The owners of Folk City were not happy," recalled Hill.

While Jesperson remembered the show as a bit of a nonstarter due to the sound issues, others were bowled over. Glenn Morrow, the former *New York Rocker* editor and front man for Hoboken post-punks the Individuals, pressed against the stage, utterly transfixed. "Normally you can dismiss someone: 'Ah, they're a bar band,' or, 'It's generic punk,' or, 'They're art damaged.' But the Replacements were this other life force beyond easy pigeonholing," said Morrow.

For jaded Manhattan, these Midwesterners were exotic. "The weirdest thing was that they weren't really on anybody's radar," said Morrow. "It was a total Jon Landau–Springsteen moment for me: 'This is the future of rock-and-roll.'"

The band's second gig in town took place a few nights later at the chic Danceteria on Twenty-First Street. "It was a velvet rope–type club," said Jesperson. "They had multiple floors with dance rooms everywhere. It was an eye-opening place. I remember walking through and seeing people having sex in the stairways, doing cocaine out in the open. We were like 'Wow, *really?*'"

Milwaukee folk-punks the Violent Femmes opened the show, and the Replacements didn't take the stage until well after 2:00 AM. "It was so late by the time they got on," said Jesperson, "that the band had gotten drunk and already sobered up. So they played really well."

The following night, the Replacements were paired with hometown rivals/ friends Hüsker Dü at punk club the Great Gildersleeves. It was a significant enough event that both the *St. Paul Pioneer Press* and the *Minnesota Daily* dispatched stringers to cover the show. "There was a little competitiveness there between the bands," said *Daily* writer Mike Hoeger. "Kind of like, 'Who can rock the best tonight?'"

Musically speaking, the evening was a draw—though, as Hoeger's piece noted, the contrasts between the Replacements and Hüsker Dü remained as stark as ever:

"The Hüskers drink coffee before their gigs, always stick to their song list (they have little choice, their set is like an avalanche), and are always emotionally and physically fatigued after a show," he wrote.

> The Replacements . . . play don't-stand-in-my-way rock 'n' roll. Westerberg sings and Westerberg thinks and the other three disagree with him. Jesperson makes out their song list, which they never follow. Their set is a series of sprints, of starts and stops. Once in a full moon, they maintain a sprint just for kicks, or so it seems, and on that night there is no better band in America. And, they drink beer before their gigs.

Also attending was a group of writers from *Rolling Stone* and the *Village Voice*. The *Voice*'s music chief, Robert Christgau—who'd written favorably about the Replacements' first two albums—had already seen them play at First Avenue the year before. He seemed less impressed with their Gildersleeves set, but intrigued by Twin/Tone. "How does Jesperson do it, anyway?" Christgau asked Hoeger. "Where does he get the money? Do any of his bands make a living?"

In New York, Jesperson had been sent a test pressing of *Hootenanny* to approve for manufacturing. During the Gildersleeves show, Westerberg and Jesperson were up in the club's booth, talking to deejay Jack Rabid, who edited *The Big Takeover* 'zine. Paul wondered if he wanted to play a cut off of the LP advance. "How about you play the first song," Westerberg said to Rabid, grinning. "You can never go wrong with that, right?" Jesperson winced.

Rabid faded from an Effigies track into "Hootenanny in E." The hardcore crowd below started booing, then hurling bottles.

* * *

The Replacements bounced between hit-and-miss gigs in Philadelphia, Albany, Bridgeport, and Hoboken. In Boston, however, they would be passionately embraced from the first by a core of rabid fans.

The Rathskeller, or Rat, was a dingy 300-capacity club in Kenmore Square near Boston University. Julie Farman became the booker after putting together a successful show with the Dream Syndicate. "The owner, Jimmy Harold, was like, 'You know what you're doing,'" said Farman, one of many locals who became close friends with the 'Mats.

Another was Lilli Dennison, who began as a waitress at the club in 1979 and went on to manage the Del Fuegos, led by Concord, New Hampshire, brothers Dan and Warren Zanes. Like Anita Stinson, the Zaneses' mother was young, single, and working-class. There wasn't much money around, but she imbued her sons with a sense of possibility and achievement. The Zanes boys won scholarships to the prestigious Phillips Academy in Andover, the prep school of various Kennedys and Bushes, before rock lured them away. With drummer Brent "Woody" Giessmann and bassist Tom Lloyd, the Del Fuegos signed to LA's Slash Records, the start of a tricky journey through the music business that mirrored the Replacements' precarious path. (The two groups would ultimately come to share roadies, managers, a booking agent, and a record company.)

"I had gotten the *Sorry Ma* record, and it incorporated everything I loved," said Dennison. "Then we met the band, and they were all so witty and sarcastic. The Del Fuegos and Replacements sort of fell in love." So did the Rat's audience. "I remember me and Doug Simmons, who was music editor at the *Boston Phoenix*, banging on the heating unit next to the stage in excitement," said Dennison. "Everyone was blown away."

The Replacements would make Boston a second home, often flopping there for days at a time between East Coast gigs. "All across town there was girls and drugs and drinking," said Dennison. "It was full tilt."

"They got lost in a few strange bedrooms that I also got lost in," said Warren Zanes. "Sometimes it'd be like, 'Whose shit is that on the nightstand? Oh, the Replacements are in town.'" At one point Farman had to kick Tommy out of her place because, she said, "he was fifteen or sixteen, and I couldn't deal with him bringing all these girls in every night."

Julie Panebianco, who wrote music features for the *Phoenix*, hit it off immediately with Westerberg, remaining one of his closest confidantes. "The Replacements had all the stuff that was cool about rock music: the excitement and glamour. But you—the audience—were part of the show too," said Panebianco. "That was the twist."

The tour wrapped up the next night at Worcester's Xit Club. "There was like eight people there, and they fucked around the whole night," said Farman. "Didn't play a single Replacements song; played Glen Campbell covers. But it was every bit as good as the night before."

The release of *Hootenanny* in late April 1983 was the Replacements' career pivot. Its sprawling, messy scope fundamentally shifted both public perception of the band and the band's own sense of itself. The *Minneapolis Star-Tribune*'s critic Jon Bream called it the band's "version of the Clash's *Sandinista!*—an unexpected exploration in eclecticism." *Playboy* hailed it as "wailing Midwestern garage punk meets humorous thirties folk," concluding, perversely, that it was "so terrible, it's great." The *Village Voice*'s Christgau approved: "This young band has a loose, freewheeling craziness that remains miraculously unaffected after three records. They'll try anything."

CHAPTER 15

The path to the Replacements' West Coast audience came partly from the high-profile patronage of Los Angeles band X. Formed in 1977 by singer-songwriters Exene Cervenka and John Doe, grinning guitarist Billy Zoom, and drummer D. J. Bonebrake, X was a poetically inclined outfit with a rootsy streak who'd made a successful jump to major label Elektra after two indie releases on Slash.

The two bands met up in Madison, Wisconsin, where the Replacements opened for X at Merlyn's. "At the end of the night we gave them a case of beer and they were forever our friends," recalled Doe, laughing. X offered the Replacements the opening spot on a two-week Midwest tour. "They were good, and it wasn't the same thing as us," said Doe. "We felt we could give them some exposure."

Already, Westerberg was writing and performing the evolutionary material that would make up their fourth album—songs like "I Will Dare" and "Sixteen Blue." "It was obviously the beginning of an arc," said Doe. "They felt like they could do something significant." Cervenka would take in the Replacements' sets from the front, scolding unmoving crowd members and dragging people to the foot of the stage to watch.

X also laid the groundwork for the Replacements' first West Coast tour, twelve dates starting in late November '83. Another influential LA fan was Chris Morris, the music critic for the alt-weekly *Los Angeles Reader*, who'd first heard them during a house party at Doe and Cervenka's place. "I became a typical Replacements fan in that it was a love affair," said Morris. "You fell madly in love with them, as people and as musicians."

Morris, who would become a critic at *Billboard* a few years later, was one of the writers who forged a lasting connection with the band. "In that period I was getting fucked up a lot," he said, "and those guys liked getting fucked up too."

Like a lot of Southern Californians, Morris bemoaned the way punk had gone hardcore by 1983. "All the kids from Orange County and the South Bay invaded the town and fucked shit up and made it very difficult to go to a punk rock show with any comfort," said Morris. "The Replacements were like a tonic when they first appeared because they were Midwestern guys. The axes were ground in their songs."

Hootenanny made it clear that the Replacements weren't predictable punks. "Maybe it's the rock critic's disease of always wanting to be surprised," Morris said. "But with the Replacements, you weren't ever sure if a thick steak or a hand grenade was going to appear on your plate. That was intensely exciting."

"In their LA debut at the [Club] Lingerie on Saturday the group drew a weirdly eclectic audience that seemed unsure what to make of this band of outsiders," wrote the *Los Angeles Times*'s Kristine McKenna. Mooning over Westerberg in print ("A rail-thin wraith with cheekbones Bowie would kill for"), McKenna was amused by the strange makeup of the band: "Lead guitarist Bob Stinson was performing in his underwear," while "drummer Chris Mars looked as though he should be enrolled at Yale." High school dropout Mars turned up for the next gig in a hand-lettered T-shirt: YAIL UNIVERSITY.

Months of national touring had only sharpened the Replacements' instincts. When they hit the stage, they'd make immediate and critical adjustments to whatever environment they were in, whatever kind of audience they found themselves playing to. "Their attitude in a live situation was very fine-tuned," said Morris. "They'd pick up on hostility, they'd pick up on boredom, and they'd serve shit back to people. I never saw a band that was so locked in to what was right in front of them."

After celebrating Thanksgiving Day at John and Exene's house, the Replacements highlighted their LA run with a show at Hollywood's Cathay De Grade, a former Chinese restaurant with an upstairs bar and a dingy subterranean performance room whose ceiling tiles were stained and falling out. The 'Mats fronted a bill headlined by the venue's house band, Top Jimmy & the Rhythm Pigs, and the Fullerton punk outfit Social Distortion.

"Social Distortion brought in the typical hardcore audience," said Morris. "All these dressed up OC punk shit-heads. This was anathema to the Replacements. These were people they felt didn't walk it like they talked it." Tommy Stinson walked onstage, took one look at the crew of cartoonish Mohawks jostling with each other, and droned sarcastically into the mic: "Wow . . . *punk rockers.*"

Westerberg decided to "pull a hootenanny." Starting off with the bluesy shuffle of "White and Lazy," the band proceeded to work their way through every ballad and country tune in their repertoire. By the time Westerberg went into full hillbilly mode—delivering a cornball version of Hank Williams's "Hey, Good Lookin'"—the punk contingent at the foot of the stage was nearly apoplectic. Tommy Stinson admiringly recalled Westerberg doubling down with the audience: "I couldn't have been more proud."

* * *

I f anyone in the underground could challenge the Replacements as the American rock underground's most buzzed-about band in 1983, it was Athens, Georgia, combo R.E.M.—enigmatic singer and lyricist Michael Stipe, guitarist Peter Buck, bassist Mike Mills, and drummer Bill Berry.

Like the 'Mats, the members of R.E.M. had met in 1979 and played their earliest shows in 1980. Their first single, the cryptic call to arms "Radio Free Europe," was released by the tiny indie Hib-Tone in the summer of 1981. R.E.M. first played Minneapolis on a frigid Thanksgiving night that year, appearing at First Avenue for a small but enthusiastic crowd.

During the visit, Buck, the group's resident record hound, got a copy of *Sorry Ma.* "About four months later, I finally listened to it and thought it was great," said Buck. "Every town had one or two bands like us. None of us were really punk rockers, but we were inspired by punk to do something and ended up using the language of the music we grew up with."

When Peter Jesperson met Buck at the Entry, a close friendship began, and he would champion the band to his Oar Folk customers. The band would return several times over the next couple of years; the Replacements opened R.E.M.'s outdoor show at St. Paul's Navy Island in May 1983.

In R.E.M., said Buck, "we all listened to the same music, ate the same food, and did the same things. But the Replacements were four completely different characters. From Paul being really taciturn to Tommy really acting out, Chris being very genial to Bob being . . . well, Bob. It was like, 'What are these guys doing in a band together?'"

Quickly, R.E.M. zoomed past the Replacements professionally. They'd become proud flag-bearers for the burgeoning Amerindie movement, turning down major label RCA and signing with Miles Copeland's indie IRS Records. An unusually democratic band, R.E.M. made a point of sharing songwriting credits and royalties equally.

R.E.M. went out of its way to praise the Replacements. Buck would note, in an essay for *Rock* magazine, that the 'Mats had "all the energy and excitement of rock 'n' roll and none of the self-consciousness that has crept in over the last decade." In an issue of *Matter*, Berry called *Hootenanny* "one of the greatest records of all time."

Though Westerberg liked R.E.M. personally and guardedly admired their music, there was a certain friction between the two bands, particularly their front men. "Stipe was definitely more of an intellectual than myself, so I'd play the guttersnipe to his more cultured hoo-ha," Westerberg said.

In July, the Replacements opened an R.E.M. tour through the Midwest and East Coast. Though they weren't booed outright, it was clear that the 'Mats' roughneck charms simply weren't suited to the more genteel sensibilities of R.E.M. audiences. "The way Westerberg works, as soon as he knows he's not well received, then he has to pull something," said Jesperson. "The shows would get weird as soon as any sort of animosity or negativity was perceived."

With the Replacements around, Mills, Berry, and especially Buck drank, partied, and raised more hell than usual. "Everyone was really drunk all the time," Buck said. "All I remember is chairs being smashed and people wrestling. I have a feeling R.E.M was a little more in control than the Replacements. Just marginally."

Sixteen-year-old Tommy was often frustrated with how the band's drinking would affect their performances, particularly on the R.E.M. tour. "He wanted to move up and get going with it," said Bill Sullivan. But his innocence slipped away after R.E.M. headlined Bogart's in Cincinnati on July 7.

The 'Mats weren't even supposed to be on the bill. After some fussing, the venue's manager relented and allowed the Replacements on first. "But he said, 'They're not on our contract, we don't have to pay them anything—we'll just give them free beer instead,'" recalled Bogart's publicist Brian Baker. "A legendarily horrible mistake."

A predictably dreadful set ensued. "At some point fairly early on, Paul and Bob started pouring the beers into R.E.M.'s stage monitors," said Baker. "Of course, R.E.M's sound guy was furious. He was like, 'I'm going to kill every fucking one of them.'"

Tommy had had enough. He ripped off his bass, threw it down on the stage, and stalked off angrily—ready to quit the Replacements there and then. Arguing with Jesperson in the club's production office, he tried to get Anita Stinson to wire him money for a flight home. After a little while, Jesperson managed to calm him down.

Bogart's would be Tommy's last stand. "What ended up happening after that is I went to the other side: I started drinking," Tommy said. "That's where the turn happened."

Alcohol served many functions in the Replacements. For Chris, drinking was a form of rock-and-roll socialization, a way to fit in. Bob's consumption inched toward hardcore addiction. Westerberg largely used alcohol to self-medicate, to manage his moods—but also to work up the nerve to go onstage.

With booze, as with everything else, Westerberg's whole mien emphasized a gang mentality: "We might look like fools, but at least we'll all look like fools together," he would say. While it wasn't the same clear-cut choice as quitting school, Tommy was essentially faced with a decision: either leave the band or join the party.

It didn't happen overnight, but within a few weeks of the Bogart's incident, certainly within a few months, Tommy Stinson was chugging vodka like a pro. "He was an Absolut guy," said Jesperson. "He had class the moment he started drinking; he wasn't going for any low-shelf stuff."

"For a while there I was able to corral them a bit, because I was young and full of it and ready to conquer the earth and had to remind them of that," said Tommy. "But once I started drinking, there was no conquering of the earth. There was no conquering of the block. Just the curbside."

* * *

That summer, R.E.M. had a busy schedule—including a handful of stadium shows opening for the Police—and were between tour managers. After a gig in Madison, Buck asked Jesperson if he'd be willing to come out with them for a couple of months.

Jesperson figured the opportunity would only benefit the Replacements. "I thought it would be great for me to work with another band that was further along, to see a different side of the business," he said. He asked the 'Mats, Westerberg in particular, for their blessing. "Everybody was saying, 'Hey, this is good, you'll meet more people and learn stuff,'" said Jesperson. "The Replacements were supportive—at least that's what I thought the general attitude was."

"Peter didn't take that job just to learn the business," said Jesperson's friend Casey Macpherson. "R.E.M. was a big thing at the time, and as he was wont to do, he worshiped them, much as he did in the Replacements, but in a different way." Jesperson quit Oar Folk after ten years to devote himself full-time to the music business.

Jesperson began the July tour with the Replacements. He would then switch to R.E.M.'s van when the two bands played the Paradise Theater in Boston. On the way out to the first gig, the 'Mats made a pit stop at a favorite roadside bar in Wisconsin. As they sat drinking, Jesperson made a joke.

A stone-faced Westerberg blindsided him. "Don't you understand, Peter?" he said coldly. "You're not one of *us* anymore."

It quickly became clear that his decision to take the R.E.M. gig was not sitting so well with the Replacements. "It was like I was a traitor all of a sudden," said Jesperson. "It was really weird. But, with all due respect to Paul, he could turn on you. I'd seen it happen to other people, and I thought I was immune to it."

Jesperson's decision would foster a lingering, unspoken resentment among the 'Mats toward R.E.M. "For him to just up and leave us for a prettier girl—it was never the same after that, really," said Westerberg. Macpherson adds, "There was a certain part of Peter that didn't realize the strength of that emotional dependency those guys had on him."

With Jesperson's departure, roadies Tom Carlson and Bill Sullivan were in charge of the Replacements' fortunes that summer. "God love Bill and Huck, but I mean, that might've damaged our career a little bit too," said Westerberg. "There was nobody responsible at all walking into these clubs or handling things." Tommy called this configuration "a party on wheels": "Sometimes we'd pull up drunk for sound check. I think we made it to most of the gigs anyway."

Once, they didn't even do that—at least Tommy didn't. In New York City, he'd gone off with some young friends and spent the night at a YMCA. The next morning he dialed the place where the rest of the band was staying to tell them to come pick him up. "I call and there's no answer," said Stinson.

"Apparently, someone had kicked the phone cord out of the wall. I finally call my mom, pissed off: 'You gotta find somebody to help me out. I don't know where they went.'"

"We waited for him," said Westerberg. "We couldn't find him."

"Then they got tired of waiting, so they ditched me and went to Boston for the next gig," said Tommy. "Thanks, dudes."

Tommy finally got a hold of Lilli Dennison in Boston. "He'd been calling my house all day. There was, like, a hundred messages," said Dennison. "'Hey, it's Tommy, I used to be in the Replacements—but not anymore!'" The band played the Rat with Del Fuegos bassist Tom Lloyd filling in, before doubling back to New York City.

Meanwhile, Tommy was stranded, broke, and hungry in Manhattan. He spent the day wandering around Central Park, feeling very much like a vulnerable child.

"I ended up hanging out with this painter guy who had his wares up. I could tell he was gay. He wasn't hitting on me so much, just being real friendly," recalled Stinson. "He offered to buy me a hot dog. It got to be kind of weird, though, like he might've thought I was making up my part of the story."

Later Tommy met a pretty teenage girl in the park. When he told her his story, she admonished him: "You need to go home to Minneapolis. You need to go back to school." Stinson dismissed her: "It's all over for me."

Beyond his role as Tommy's guardian, Jesperson's diplomatic skills were sorely missed during the tour—particularly when the band debuted at Washington, DC's 9:30 Club. The headliners, New Orleans pop-punks the Red Rockers, had canceled at the last minute. The club slashed the admission to a buck for the Replacements. Some forty people milled about the club as the band played Bachman-Turner Overdrive covers at shattering volume.

"They were drunk and fucking around, being contemptuous of the Red Rockers fans who'd stuck around to see them," said DC rocker Tommy Keene, who was being courted by Twin/Tone at the time and who attended the show. "The club owner was this artsy-fartsy woman who didn't like rock-and-roll. She was getting really annoyed as they basically drove out most of the audience."

Through Carlson, the owner demanded that the 'Mats get offstage. "Gotta quit—club owner is pissed off as shit," said Westerberg into the mic, repeating what he'd been told verbatim. They kept playing until the PA was cut off on them midsong. "The shenanigans were constant when Peter was gone," said Tommy.

Meanwhile, Jesperson enjoyed the relative calm of working with R.E.M. "There was a great camaraderie, and people were helpful to one another," said Jesperson. Since he spent most nights after the shows doing paperwork and accounting, however, he had to admit that it wasn't nearly as fun as being out with the 'Mats. "Honestly, I was never going to be the person shouting at the guy in the box office about ticket counts," said Jesperson. "And that's kinda what they needed." Later, Buck's girlfriend told Jesperson that he was simply "too nice a guy" for the job.

CHAPTER 16

The Replacements' fourth album brought a rapprochement between Westerberg and Jesperson. "We might've been closer in that period than we were before or after," said Jesperson. "He knew he was entering some important phase of his writing. We had a big connection on that stuff. We were nose-to-nose talking about that record, really bonding."

"I was writing a lot of the songs on acoustic and taking them to the band and playing them electrically," Westerberg said. "In the back of my mind, for that album, I was thinking *Beggars Banquet*."

The band reunited with engineer Steve Fjelstad at Blackberry Way; the Dinkytown studio had boosted its operation since the Replacements last recorded there, from sixteen to twenty-four tracks. Sessions began on August 27, just as Jesperson wrapped up the final R.E.M. date.

He flew back to Minneapolis with a couple of Peter Buck's guitars. Buck himself followed a day later and was a presence for the first week of recording. "Me being there was really just kind of an excuse to run around at the clubs at night," Buck recalled.

Buck figured prominently on the album's first and most famous song, "I Will Dare." A chiming pop number, Westerberg had written it that February, just as *Hootenanny* was being mastered. "I got a call from Paul saying, 'I've just finished the best song I've ever written. We need to record it now,'" recalled Jesperson. "But the record was already done, so we couldn't do it."

Not long after, during a 'Mats show at Goofy's Upper Deck, Jesperson heard the song for the first time. "It was so instantly catchy," he said. "The joke was, 'Oh my God, we're going to be rich! He's written *the* song.'"

Like "Kids Don't Follow," "I Will Dare" was another song influenced by the anthemism of U2. "That might have been another answer to 'I Will Follow,'" said Westerberg. "Part of it has to do with the band: we'll dare to flop, we'll dare to do anything. 'I Will Dare' was a good slogan for a Replacements single. On the other hand, it was a kind of love song: 'Ditch the creep and I'll meet you later. I don't care, I will dare.'"

The song's element of illicit romance was rooted in Westerberg's reality. "I think Paul had some dalliances with girls that he probably shouldn't have at that time," noted one of the band's confidantes.

Paul, Tommy, and Chris laid the rhythm track as a trio, but there were tuning problems. "We tend to thrash around in the studio like we do onstage, and things go haywire," noted Westerberg. After getting the basic take down, Westerberg borrowed Buck's twelve-string electric Rickenbacker to add to the song's jangle, while the bouncy riff that threaded the tune was Bob Stinson's invention.

In the control room, Buck watched in amazement as Bob played through the tracks. "Bob knew all the songs, but he referred to them as 'that one song,' or 'that other song,' or 'that other fucking song.' He didn't know the titles of anything. No matter how many times they played the song, it was a brand-new song for Bob."

Bob's frustrated attempts at a solo led to Buck's famous cameo on "I Will Dare." "I was just sitting there, and Bob said something like, 'I can't play a solo on this fucking thing.' Those weren't his chords," recalled Buck. "And Paul goes, 'Hey, Peter, you do it.'" Buck delivered a spindly sixties folk-rock figure, à la the Lovin' Spoonful's Zal Yanovsky. "That's exactly who I was thinking of when I did it," said Buck. "It only took a minute."

Buck and Westerberg hung out a few evenings, getting drunk and putting on pancake makeup and eye shadow and playing out their mutual Marc Bolan/Peter Perrett fantasies. They ended up invading the First Avenue ladies' room, later nearly getting into a fight at White Castle with some Northeast Minneapolis toughs who objected to their "faggy" appearance.

For a while that autumn, Westerberg donned kohl makeup before he went onstage. Leaving his parents' for a gig one night, he walked past his father all dolled up. "Who does he think he is, Big George?" asked Hal Westerberg, referring to Culture Club's Boy George.

Westerberg's flirtations with femininity would result in the album's most delicate composition, the piano ballad "Androgynous." "A girl said it to us," said Westerberg. "I didn't know what the word meant." After looking it up, he wrote the song on his parents' piano.

It was a rare Westerberg third-person narrative, about a gender-bending couple named Dick and Jane: "Now something meets boy / And something meets girl / They both look the same, they're overjoyed in this world."

"Sixteen Blue" was inspired by Tommy Stinson. Westerberg had witnessed how he'd been forced to grow up way faster than most kids, yet still faced the typical adolescent issues and doubts: "Your age is the hardest age, everything drags and drags / You're looking funny, you ain't laughin', are you?"

"Hearing it the first time they did it, at a sound check in Boston, I thought, *Jesus, he's written a song about Tommy*," said Jesperson. "Tommy was kind of the mascot of the band, and Paul had written about him in songs before. But this wasn't just some goofy thing. This was serious and tender."

It was also a song addressed to Paul's younger self. "Drive yourself right up the wall / No one hears and no one calls." The ennui and loneliness of Westerberg's teenage years were still vivid in his mind.

* * *

That winter, between sessions, Paul fell for a girl in Ann Arbor, Michigan, and would court her long-distance. Sometimes he'd call to sweet-talk her and get her answering machine instead. "I'm not a modern person," said Westerberg. "Technology irritates me." He transformed that frustration into "Answering Machine": "How do you say I miss you / To an answering machine?"

Cut solo with himself on guitar and percussion, Westerberg considered it among his best songs: "There was real passion, and there was a real person on the other end, and that made it all come to life." At the song's conclusion, amid a wall of noise and effects, he would shout out Michigan's 313 area code; he also threw out a couple others, including New York City's 212, to cover his bases with a few other girls, just in case.

"Unsatisfied" may have been inspired by Westerberg's developing interest in palmistry. Every palm reader he saw told him that the lines of his hand meant he was doomed to be unhappy forever. The song—keening folk-rock in the style of Rod Stewart's early solo work—was a testament to the band's seat-of-the-pants approach. Westerberg barely had any lyrics, save for the "I'm so unsatisfied" hook, and improvised as he sang.

Bob Stinson hadn't even heard the song before cutting it. "We ran through it one time. Then [Bob] came in and played along for about half of it. Steve rolled the tape, and that was it," said Westerberg. "That one was really nice because there was no time to think. He played real well on that—reserved, but with emotion."

Bob disagreed: "If we'd put another five minutes' worth of time into it, it would have sounded fifty times better," he complained.

Part of the song's charm was its off-the-cuff quality, coupled with the intensity of Westerberg's vocal delivery. Still, to its author, "Unsatisfied" is "one of the most overrated, half-assed, half-baked songs. It doesn't have nothing but one line." Perhaps it cut too close to the bone. "It's about as melancholy as we want to get," he said, "and [still] be alive."

* * *

This album would offer significantly less opportunity than usual for Bob Stinson to go wild. "The material was changing," said Jesperson. "It was the beginning of the landscape changing and Bob not wanting to change with it to some degree." Though he contributed key parts to "Sixteen Blue" and "Unsatisfied," Bob wasn't involved on "Androgynous" or "Answering Machine."

In the past, Westerberg's solo songs had been anomalies, but fans' and critics' favorable reaction to "Within Your Reach" encouraged him to continue in this vein of bruised romanticism that would become his signature. "By then, he felt like, 'Fuck it, I'm not going to be worried anymore. If Bob doesn't like these songs, it's his problem, not mine,'" said Jesperson.

They were buoyed by group-written rockers, composed in rehearsal or on the studio floor, that showcased Bob's animated fretwork and the band's irreverent, often insider humor.

"We're Comin' Out" was a throwback to the fast and furious songs of *Stink*. Originally titled "Warning Sound," it was another potent bit of self-mythologizing as they portrayed themselves as a gang of rock-and-roll marauders. Its hard-brake tempo change, false ending, and rapid-fire finale were conceived spontaneously in the studio.

"We were supposed to stop, and I guess somebody didn't stop, so we said, 'Take it down to hell after the lead'—we weren't sure what to do," said Westerberg. "You can hear me yell, 'C!' and everybody ended back on the C chord. It was a lucky guess. Then Chris started slowing it down. He was thinking, *Aw, fuck this, let's end it.* Then we picked it back up. Later we overdubbed the piano and finger snaps."

The snotty-riffed "Favorite Thing" had already been road-tested; in the studio, Bob gave it a memorable, drawled-out guitar opening. "Bob started on the wrong note so he bent it [up] to make it fit," recalled Westerberg.

They'd also been messing with a chanted chorus called "Rico Gets a Haircut," after the band's nickname for Mars. Eventually, Westerberg found the opening sample—a singsongy, spoken "Tommy gets his tonsils out!"—on his little sister's children's record. From there he formulated a narrative about a ne'er-do-well surgeon who tears out kids' swollen glands between rounds of golf.

"Gary's Got a Boner" was a funny throwaway founded on an odd Westerberg peeve. "He'd say, 'Have you ever known anyone named Gary who was smart?'" said Jesperson. "For a while all dumb people were 'Garys.'" They cadged the song's riff from Ted Nugent's "Cat Scratch Fever," earning the Motor City Madman a tongue-in-cheek cowriting credit. Accordingly, the track's appeal rested on Bob Stinson's searing, uninhibited guitar work.

The mostly instrumental "Seen Your Video" had once been called "Adult": "You look like an adult / Walk like an adult / Who taught you that?" But Westerberg hadn't come up with verses, so the song was recast as a defiant rejoinder to the growing behemoth of MTV ("Seen your video / It's phony rock-and-roll").

Westerberg had become outspoken in his disdain for the music videos the channel played. "I think it takes the danger out of rock and makes it false and silly," he said, relieved that the Replacements' own embarrassing clip from 1980 had never been completed. "I don't want our band to have anything to do with it." It was a stance he and the band maintained, with some difficulty, for years to come.

The 'Mats also cut some early '70s covers: the Grass Roots' "Temptation Eyes," T. Rex's "20th Century Boy," the DeFranco Family's "Heartbeat (It's a Lovebeat)," and Kiss's slow-burn rocker "Black Diamond." "The hip song to put on the record would be T. Rex—the curveball would be Kiss," said Jesperson. "We decided it was cooler to put on the 'uncool' song."

"Black Diamond" was Kiss's ham-handed story-song about a tough prostitute on the prowl. "That was, in 1974, dangerous, exciting rock-and-roll for us," said Westerberg. "I was ashamed to admit it at that time, but now I'm smart enough to know that that stupid music was the thing that got me going."

Between tours, work on the album carried into January and February. Westerberg tacked a twelve-string acoustic intro and keening lap slide onto "Unsatisfied" and added a memorable mandolin part to "I Will Dare"; Mars overdubbed maracas and tambourine to several tracks, and Tommy added background vocals, notably on "Black Diamond." While Westerberg's plonky piano playing had sufficed for a couple of tracks, the Suburbs' Chan Poling gave a more refined quality to "Sixteen Blue." The band even built sand blocks, from chunks of wood found in Blackberry Way's basement, to add to the shuffling mood of "Androgynous."

Mixing dragged through March. "It's tough trying to make four out-of-tune guitars sound good," noted Westerberg. He, Jesperson, and Fjelstad took production credit; it was easily the best-sounding record they'd made, and it mixed material that captured the 'Mats' smart and stupid sensibilities in one perfect package. "That was the most complete record we made," said Westerberg.

The band marked the album's completion that spring at the Coffman Memorial Union on the University of Minnesota campus—a benefit for a relative of a student who was getting a heart transplant. But the heart proved to be the wrong size. The gig was put on hold until another suitable organ could be found.

A few weeks later, the 'Mats finally had their moment. "It was really exciting that they were playing a big room full of kids at the university," said Jesperson. "It's like, 'Wow, we're really making progress here.' I just remember the band looking so cool . . . and Paul strapping on the guitar as he's getting himself situated."

Just before the 'Mats slammed into a *Let It Be*–heavy set that began with a fitting cover of "Heartbeat (It's a Lovebeat)," Westerberg paused at the microphone: "Let's just hope the fucker fits this time—'cause we ain't coming back."

* * *

That spring the band was en route to a gig in Madison when inspiration struck. "We were riding around . . . kicking around silly [album] names and we thought, 'The next song that comes on the radio, we'll name it after that,'" said Westerberg.

Just then, the sound of plaintive piano chords and Paul McCartney's voice filtered through the speakers: "When I find myself in times of trouble . . . "

It was fate: *Let It Be* would be the title of the Replacements new album. "We peed our pants [laughing], and Peter is at the wheel, silent as hell, thinking, 'They're not going to do this,'" said Westerberg. "We did it pretty much to piss him off and pretty much to show the world, in a Ramones kind of way, how dumb-smart we were. . . . Just to figure how many feathers we can ruffle."

Twin/Tone had recently hired the local music writer—and sometimes caustic 'Mats critic—Dave Ayers to help around the office, and he was the one who would coordinate the cover. At first, the band wanted to keep the cheeky Beatles theme going. Photographer Greg Helgeson was dispatched to the Stinson house and made some pictures of the Replacements crossing Bryant Avenue, single file. "We went through an entire shoot of us walking across the street, à la the *Abbey Road* cover," recalled Westerberg.

Another of the band's key visual chroniclers, Daniel Corrigan, was responsible for *Let It Be*'s iconic image. Corrigan had been shooting photos for the *Minnesota Daily*, including several previous Replacements sessions. The gig that brought him to the Stinsons' house in the spring of 1984 paid $250. It was a second attempt, after a shoot in an elevator didn't work out.

For some months, Corrigan had been exploring a series of conceptual setups he called "danger shoots"—taking bands and putting them in precarious positions. "Getting the Replacements anywhere was always an incredible hassle," noted Corrigan, so instead of traveling somewhere for the shoot, he suggested they climb onto the second-story roof of the Stinson house.

The band made their way out of Lonnie Stinson's bedroom window—where her softball trophies were prominently displayed—and onto the dirty white-tiled landing. For a while, they teetered on the edge, goofing off, beers in hand.

At one point, the Stinson family dog was brought out, and they posed fake-kicking it, with Mars jokingly grabbing the terrier as though he was going to hurl him off. Corrigan stood on a van parked on Bryant and snapped away; then he joined them upstairs.

Crouched in the far left corner of the roof, Corrigan took a couple of shots of the band sitting down together with a wider lens, then moved closer and fired off a dozen more. This would yield *Let It Be*'s final cover.

Given a cyan-toned treatment by sleeve designer Bruce Allen, the photo captured something ineffable about the band, the four of them clad in denim and sneakers: Westerberg aloof, looking away from the camera; Tommy sleepily cool, wiping his eyes; Bob craning his neck curiously; Mars peering guardedly into the lens.

Corrigan's image—bootlegged, imitated, paid homage to for the next thirty years—would be subject to numerous theories and readings. One critic suggested the "roof on which they're perched seems the refuge of a heart-on-his-sleeve would-be romantic who escapes out his bedroom window to peer up at the stars on lonely nights."

"I don't know what to say about all that," Corrigan chuckled. "It's just those guys on the roof and me trying to line up some angle so that it's visually pleasing."

* * *

Having quit school, Tommy Stinson was always the antsiest when the Replacements were idle. For a time he played drums with John Freeman's punk band, Irenic Regime. He also had a steady girlfriend, Mary Beth Gordon; five years older than him, she'd moved to Minneapolis from Chicago after high school.

Mary Beth and Tommy enjoyed a scuffling rock-and-roll existence together, kicking around Uptown Minneapolis. "You'd ride around on the 4 bus, and then head back to your little punk-rock ghetto with sixty cents in your pocket and hopefully you could afford Taco Bell on the corner," said Gordon.

Bob, the only Replacement who maintained a regular job—still cooking at Mama Rosa's and the West Bank Valli Pizza and Pub—retreated into his own odd world at home. "He didn't hang with the pack, he was a bit of a loner," said Peter Jesperson. "Bob had his strange habits. Like, it'd be time to go sit on the bench by the railroad tracks. He would have these things that would call him away."

That summer some of Chris Mars's self-described "fantasy type" artwork was showcased at the Minneapolis Underground Art Fair. Another selection of drawings, "Hillbilly Soup," was later displayed at the Norwest Bank. Over the next few years, Mars began to spend the downtime between tours—and even on tour—sketching and painting. "The calling to draw and to paint really started to creep up," he said.

Westerberg's distractions were mostly women. On the road, he had the proverbial "girl in every port." His fleeting rock-and-roll relationships were both an entertainment and something more, particularly for a naturally sensitive character who clung to a certain masculine ideal in public. "I had relationships with guys, and the band was the ultimate one, but my relationships with women were more relaxed and easy," he said.

In early 1984, Westerberg's life underwent a serious change with the arrival of Lori Bizer. Nine months older than Westerberg, Bizer was born and mostly raised in suburban Detroit, the youngest of five children, and only daughter. Bizer's mother worked as an administrative assistant and her father as a graphic artist in the advertising business.

As they had for Westerberg, mental health issues cast a shadow across Bizer's childhood. "My dad was not an alcoholic, but he was bipolar," said Bizer. "He would be hospitalized [off and on] for many years. There were shock treatments. His issues were hidden from us for a long time."

Bizer had long been obsessed with rock-and-roll, with many touchstones handed down from her older brothers, two of whom would become professional musicians. "It was Hendrix and Zeppelin, and the stuff that was going on in Detroit at the Grande Ballroom and that you'd read about in *Creem* magazine," said Bizer.

In high school, Bizer helped launch a little radio station that broadcast across campus: "I played Sparks records at lunchtime for students in the cafeteria." After two years of community college, she enrolled at the University of Michigan in Ann Arbor in 1979. There she served as a deejay on student-run WCBN and got a job at Schoolkids Records, a pro-Replacements Midwest indie chain. "When *Hootenanny* came out, I really latched on there," said Bizer.

She first saw them in late 1983 at the Heidelberg in Ann Arbor; the performance, she said, was "wild, magical, spirited." Westerberg approached her while she was deejaying in the club after their set.

"He brought me a record to play—a Chairmen of the Board single that he'd bought that day," she said. "He handed me the side with 'Everything's Tuesday' on it. So I played that, but he'd intended me to play the [A-side] 'Give Me Just a Little More Time.' That's how we got to talking." Bizer was dating someone else then, but by the Replacements' next trip to town in January 1984, she was single and things quickly heated up between her and Westerberg.

For Westerberg, the attraction was obvious: Bizer was a stunning, statuesque redhead, with a turned-up nose and down-to-earth grace. "Lori was the first girl he went with who was more his match . . . than just a girl to sleep with or hang around with," said Jesperson.

Westerberg spent the spring writing and calling Bizer (hence "Answering Machine"). On a couple of occasions, he zipped up to Michigan to visit her between tours, using free tickets from his sister Julie, a Northwest Airlines flight attendant. In February, Bizer came to Minneapolis. Hal and Mary Lou Westerberg embraced her immediately. "They were like my second family," she said. "Took me in like I was their daughter, they were so welcoming."

It was an eye-opening trip. "It was my birthday, and it was odd because the Replacements were playing a show at Regina High," Bizer said. "It felt weird spending my twenty-fifth birthday at a high school. I tried to keep up with Paul drinking that night. And I think I threw up in the bushes at his parents' house. That's the last time I ever had whiskey. The lesson learned was, do not try to keep up with Paul Westerberg . . . ever."

By May, Bizer decided to move to Minneapolis. She got a job with CD manufacturer East Side Digital, then at the Northern Lights record shop, before she was hired by Twin/Tone. She settled into a basement efficiency apartment, just south of Loring Park, where she and Westerberg became domestic, after a fashion: "He would come over after I got off work and then stay until the next day, then go back to his parents' house and do whatever—write songs, I guess. I made dinner; I cooked all the time. Occasionally we'd go out. Mostly, we'd watch TV or read."

Things were fairly blissful, except when it came to music. Bizer was into finding new records and bands, but Westerberg was largely uninterested in her discoveries. (The Young Fresh Fellows, the Jacobites, and oldie favorite Ricky Nelson were exceptions.) "He said he didn't want to be influenced by anything," said Bizer. "It might've been his insecurities in hearing somebody else that was good. I should've realized how stubborn he was at that point."

The relationship with Bizer also marked a division between Westerberg's personal life and the Replacements. She never really got to know the other band members well and hung out with them only a few times after shows or, on rare occasions, on the road. "By that point, I don't know that he liked hanging out with them," said Bizer. "He spent enough time with them when he toured that he wanted to be off when he was home."

Bizer wasn't sure how far the Replacements would go or last. She knew Westerberg wrote great songs. "But would the band be the vehicle for that? Not necessarily," she said. "I don't know if that was his end-all either. I'm not sure he thought it was."

* * *

By mid-1984, Twin/Tone was in significant transition. After years working out of the basement of Paul Stark's home in Bryn Mawr, the operation would move to Twenty-Sixth Street and Nicollet Avenue in South Minneapolis. The complex of offices—parts of which would later be occupied by Hüsker Dü and the Minnesota Music Academy—also included a suite of label-owned studio rooms run by Steve Fjelstad, who broke off from Blackberry Way that summer.

The previous year Twin/Tone's biggest cash cow, the Suburbs, had signed with Mercury Records. The Replacements were expected to follow suit. Stark and Jesperson had always viewed Twin/Tone essentially as a farm team for the major labels. "Frankly, we didn't have enough money to take bands to the next level," said Stark. "And our back catalog wouldn't have been worth a lot if they didn't go further—so it was a win-win for both sides."

While EMI and Columbia had expressed cautionary interest in the Replacements, the band's behavior concerned Stark. Still, he strenuously avoided advising Jesperson or involving himself in Replacements affairs. "I only put up with the Replacements because of Peter," said Stark.

"I don't think Paul Stark really got it," said Blake Gumprecht, who handled Twin/Tone's marketing. "He understood Peter's enthusiasm for the band . . . but would Stark ever really put on a Replacements record for fun? I seriously doubt it."

By 1984, the group subsisted on small salaries Jesperson cobbled together from gig proceeds. Westerberg, in particular, would rail about not having enough money (specifically Twin/Tone not giving him enough) but go out of his way to burn through what he had.

"There was a number of times we'd be in Madison, on our last date before going home from a tour, and Westerberg would be like, 'Shit, we got three guitars left'—then he'd go out there and smash them," said Jesperson. "That happened more than once. Not even onstage always." About this time, Westerberg took to slapping a giant FIREWOOD sticker on his guitar. "We'd had enough for salaries for the next month—now that's gone. And we have to get new guitars too."

Still, with Gumprecht on board full-time, the label spent much of the spring and summer of 1984 setting up *Let It Be*, creating a foundation none of the band's previous projects had received. "Twin/Tone didn't know how to work records," said Gumprecht. "My job from the get-go was to establish an aggressive campaign—putting together radio station lists and reviewer lists."

Part of *Let It Be*'s advantage was its unusual amount of lead time: originally planned for a late spring release, the album was pushed to October. The delays actually caused the band to cancel a summer West Coast tour. "The wait for *Let It Be* was a long one, but for all the right reasons," said Dave Ayers. "Still, the band was pretty miserable waiting for it to come out. I remember Tommy, in particular, being really depressed."

The LP's release was preceded by the September single "I Will Dare," a major college-radio hit. The album hit number one on 55 campus stations across North America, from Berkeley to Brunswick, and made the top 10 of 161. "I Will Dare" also gained a toehold at some more adventurous commercial stations, like Chicago's WXRT and Long Island's WLIR.

This success only served to highlight a rather uncomfortable fact: the Replacements had yet to sign a contract with Twin/Tone. In the run-up to *Let It Be*, Stark again pushed to formalize the deal, though the band never did so.

CHAPTER 17

Between their first national outing in the spring of '83 and the end of the *Let It Be* tour two years later, the Replacements would play some 200-plus shows in forty states, crisscrossing the country half a dozen times. "None of us had ever really traveled before we got on the road," said Paul Westerberg. "We went from not having seen the world to suddenly getting more of it than we could digest."

The band's first vehicle—the Chevy van financed by Tom Carlson— quickly wore out. They replaced it with a beat-up Ford Econoline that they dubbed Otis, after the drunk on *The Andy Griffith Show*. It didn't take long for the 'Mats to turn it into a second home, ripping out its seats and staining the interior with beer, trash, and urine. (The band was constantly pissing out of the step down to the side door, which came to be called "the trough.") Its walls were soon marked with all manner of lewd graffiti and inside jokes. Westerberg insisted that an image of the van's guts adorn the back cover of *Let It Be*: "To give people a sense of what life with us was like," he said.

It might've been grungy and gross, but it was all theirs. "When we got in Otis, it was our sanctuary as well as our jail cell," said Tommy Stinson. "There was constant chaos: anything you could imagine with four guys stuck in a van, driving across the country with copious amounts of booze and whatever else we could find; all together, loving and annoying each other at the same time."

After a year of battling house soundmen, the band finally hired their own engineer in early '84. Bill Mack was a nineteen-year-old South Minneapolis kid with a background in theatrical light and sound. He'd been trained by Minnesota Singers' Theatre founder Mike Foreman—the same Foreman who'd booted the Replacements from the Bataclan in 1980. (An adolescent Mack was actually supposed to run sound for the gig.)

Impressing Jesperson with his work mixing the band at Duffy's, Mack got a call to go on the road. "I was a brat. I cried and whined about everything," said Mack. "But one of the reasons they put up with me is because I didn't drink, so I could drive." Joining a road crew that also included Carlson and Bill

Sullivan, his initial impressions of the band were that "Bob was insane; Tommy was going to be a serious rock star, no matter what happened; Chris was an average blue-collar working guy with an interesting imagination; and Paul was an old man stuck in a young man's body. Peter was the den mother/wrangler/psychologist trying to keep it all together."

As Mack would discover, life on the road with the Replacements brought its own strange habits and superstitions. One of the band's more peculiar touring talismans was a pair of "magic slacks": a set of gaudy white-and-blue-striped hip-hugger flares that each of them would take turns wearing. Among other things, the slacks were doled out as a punishment if someone had gotten too wasted during the previous night's gig. "You could either wear them proudly or in disgrace—or both," said Tommy. "Proudly in disgrace was the more common way to wear them."

The Replacements traveled to a constantly cranked soundtrack. Sometimes the van radio would be working; if not, a boombox would be blaring, with Westerberg generally manning the controls. "He was always spinning the dial; he was a real knob twister," said Jesperson. "Especially at night; he didn't lay down and go to sleep like other people did." The 'Mats listened to mix tapes that Jesperson made, while certain records—by NRBQ, Big Star, and Robyn Hitchcock—were universally liked. Westerberg would fixate on other albums—like Jerry Lee Lewis's *Live at the Star Club*, repeating it so often that everyone was soon sick of The Killer. "We actually had to physically stop him from playing that after a while," said Jesperson.

Then there were the times when someone would pop in a tape of the DC hardcore band Bad Brains, which was a cue for the 'Mats to start going crazy. "People would be leaping around, having wrestling matches," said Jesperson. "There was times when I was driving and the van would be shaking, nearly tipping . . . you could feel it lift off two tires. It still strikes terror into my heart hearing the Bad Brains."

Driving a mosh pit on wheels was just one of many occupational hazards Jesperson endured working with the Replacements. If he zoomed past a highway patrol car in a speed trap, that was an invitation for the band to douse him in beer; if he'd picked up some valuable LP along the way, Tommy might toss it out the window. On one occasion, he smelled smoke and turned to find that the band had started a newspaper bonfire in the back of the van. He tried to put it out and nearly caught his pants on fire.

Usually, the bad behavior took the form of a competition between Tommy and Paul. "Paul would break something, and Tommy would laugh," said Jesperson. "Then Tommy would try and outdo Paul and break something bigger."

As much as he encouraged the free-for-all atmosphere, Westerberg could be dogmatic when it came to his view of proper rock-and-roll deportment on the road. His famous admonishment was: "We're on tour; we're not tourists." "He'd get really mad if you ever did anything practical," said Jesperson. "The first trip out east, Chris and I went to a museum, and he was furious."

During those financially lean early touring years, the entire band—save for the always stout Bob—would transform into rail-thin figures. "There were times when we were living on $5 per diems," said Jesperson. On the occasions when they did eat, Mars usually insisted on stopping at International House of Pancakes, while Westerberg—whether it was morning, noon, or night—would subsist mostly on clam chowder. Meanwhile, Bob almost never dined with the rest of the band. "One of his nicknames was Bob 'To Go' Stinson," said Jesperson. "'Cause we'd all be eating and Bob would get his to go and save it for later."

At night they would typically rent one cheap motel room that all of eight of them would cram into, unless anyone got lucky. "If you caught on with a girl, you might have a decent place to sleep," said Tommy. Anything was generally preferable to snuggling up next to Bob. "I don't think I ever saw him take a shower, and he usually slept with his shoes on," said Mack. "I recall him in bed, clothes or no clothes, it didn't matter; his Converse All-Stars would be sticking out of the covers."

Tommy and Paul would usually let the roadies have the beds, while they took to the floor. Chris would hole up in the closet most of the time, to avoid being stepped on when someone stumbled to the bathroom in the dark to piss. "Bad as it was, we didn't care," said Westerberg. "We were living the dream. It was camaraderie to the extreme."

Late at night, long after the din of the amps and the clatter of the club had faded and everyone was drifting off or passing out, there would finally be a rare moment of silence. Mars would turn over in his closet and make like a salty John-Boy Walton. "Well," he would say, "good night, fuckers."

* * *

Though Westerberg quipped that the Replacements actually spilled more than they drank, their considerable level of consumption was becoming very real. Soundman Bill Mack recalled an occasion when Westerberg and Mars sat face to face, downing two dozen tequila poppers between them just before a gig. "Who can take ten, twelve shots of tequila and stand up, much less play a show?" said Mack. "Somehow they could shrug it off and play. Then they'd feel it the next day. But that's what van rides are for: recovery time."

By 1984, there were more substances around too. The band had graduated from cheap speed—ramping up with a few white crosses before a hardcore gig—to regularly indulging in cocaine. After a while it became an official expense; the ever-meticulous Jesperson would note their drug buys in his checkbook ledger, listing the purchases as "Bat Food" or "REF," for Replacements Entertainment Fund.

The biggest effect that coke had was that it allowed the Replacements to drink even more. "There was a time where we'd get drunk twice a day," said Westerberg. "We would be hammered by the afternoon, then probably take something to wake us up, and then start up again before the show and go till the wee hours."

Backstage, preshow drinking sessions would come to serve as referendums on how the gig would go. "'Let's let 'em down'—that was another battle cry after a while," said Westerberg. "It was like, 'Do we rule tonight, or do we let 'em down?'"

The public perception was that the Replacements' performances, particularly the train-wreck gigs, were the by-product of their consumption. But that wasn't always the case. "There would be some nights where we couldn't be that drunk onstage because we were hungover—there was no possible way we could get drunk," said Chris Mars. "There would be some times where we wouldn't be in sync. Paul would be really drunk and the rest of us would be sorta sober. Or I'd be drunk and everyone else would be sober. It became this 'Who's gonna screw up tonight?' sort of thing. Then some nights we'd all be in the same boat, which was disastrous.

"But there was such a buzz about the band that people liked that part of it too; it became a sideshow. We were this band that could really rock and do really good, but on the other hand we were this circus act too."

*   *   *

Fans and the press were beginning to lap up these displays, embracing the Replacements' aesthetic and spinning their legend.

"One of the great mysteries of popular music is why so many bands that play very well are so bad, while some bands that play quite poorly manage to be undeniably great," noted the *Washington Post*. "This Minneapolis quartet plays as though neatness didn't count, with shuffles that seem more like stumbles and rave-ups that verge on mere raving. Yet everything fits, even the wrong notes, because the Replacements are careful not to let the details of proper playing get in the way of their real business: rock and roll."

"They're misfits, but they're not misfits in any of the predictable rock musician ways," suggested New York's *Newsday*. "They're not peroxide punks, or heavy-metal Hell's Angels, or philistine folkies. Instead, they're inspired dilettantes who play whatever they feel like." Even The Gray Lady would offer validation. "The Replacements refuse to take themselves too seriously," ran a review in the *New York Times*. "They've found the vital balance of yearning and rudeness, humor and defiance, melody and noise that makes brilliant rock and roll."

For Mike Bosley, a 7th St Entry soundman who went on the road with the 'Mats for a spell in '84, the Replacements never seemed in possession of what made them so compelling. "Whether the show was going to be good or bad was almost left up to fate," said Bosley. "Their collective energy was a living breathing thing that they didn't have control over. Maybe sometimes they wished they could control it. But having that kind of control would've taken away the magic."

As their fame as a live act began to spread, the 'Mats started noticing groups of fans turning up repeatedly, coming to multiple gigs on every tour. "When the same ten people in front started showing up," said Westerberg, "we really felt like we had to throw them curveballs." He could be especially creative in this regard—like a show in Canada when he came onstage as Alfalfa from the Little Rascals, wearing fake freckles and suspenders, and sang the set in a cracking pubescent voice.

Frequently, the entertainment came in simply erasing the divisions between the band, the crew, and the crowd. Sometimes it meant letting the audience members get onstage and play or, more often, allowing roadie Bill Sullivan to take over vocals. A natural ham, Sullivan would enthusiastically warble "If I Only Had a Brain" from *The Wizard of Oz* and deliver Alice Cooper covers. (In between tours the other Replacements would sometimes back Sullivan in a Cooper tribute band called Spyder Byte, as well as dress up and play in the drag outfit Jefferson's Cock.)

Generally, the tenor of the Replacements' performances were a direct reflection of the crowd. "We would go out there, and if the audience was tepid or hostile, we would go with that: 'Let's see how hostile this can get,'" said Westerberg. "If they were behind us from the word go, we would give them what they wanted."

That fall, Minneapolis musician John Freeman ran into the Replacements in Arizona while visiting family and hitched a ride back to the Twin Cities with the band. Catching a number of shows in the Southwest, Freeman marveled at how subtly the band shifted its presentation. "They would react to each situation a little differently," said Freeman. "In Phoenix and Austin, they really went for it. In Houston, they didn't give a damn, played country stuff for a whole set."

By the time the band reached Oklahoma City for the last date of the tour, they were burned out and ready to blow the gig off entirely. They arrived at The Bowery—a former church turned gay disco turned indie rock venue—and were greeted by an enthusiastic staff. The club's deejay, Ross Shoemaker, had borrowed a tape recorder to capture the concert. "I told Paul before the show I was gonna be recording them," recalled Shoemaker. "He said, '*Why?* We suck.'"

By showtime there were only thirty or so scattered souls in the cavernous 1,200-capacity venue. "Paul started by asking them to pull up their tables and chairs closer to the stage," recalled Freeman. "He screamed at me, 'Go get them some beer.' I grabbed a twelve-pack and started passing them out to the front row." After a few attempts at playing their own material, the band shifted into an evening of covers that moved between the Carter Family and Mötley Crüe, Lynyrd Skynyrd and U2. "It was amazing how they would pull these things out of their hat," said Freeman.

Unbeknownst to Shoemaker, toward the end of the set soundman Bill Mack had gone up to the deejay booth and snatched the tape from his recorder. The band listened to the concert all the way home, laughing. They would release the twenty-three-song set a few months later as an "official bootleg," fittingly titled *The Shit Hits the Fans.*

* * *

With Paul, Tommy, and Bob generating most of the chaos, Chris Mars came across as the sensible, somewhat diffident figure in the band. In a way, he seemed oddly miscast to keep the beat for such a collection of torrid troublemakers. "I remember once, after the Replacements played Al's Bar in LA, Chris was sitting reading a book," recalled Gun Club guitarist Ward Dotson. "Everyone else was out there trying to score drugs or get laid or whatever, and he was reading a book backstage. I thought that was pretty unusual."

That sort of behavior led Mars to be labeled the "quiet one" in the 'Mats. "It's easy to be the quiet one when you got a buncha loudmouths out front," said Westerberg. "But Chris did his share of hooting and hollering."

On occasion, Mars was given to fits of strangely theatrical behavior. This usually coincided with the appearance of his outré alter ego, "Pappy the Clown." The first time Pappy appeared was during a gig at a punk club in Virginia Beach. "We did a sound check, and then Chris came back for the show made up like a clown, with no explanation," recalled Westerberg. "And he wouldn't say a word. It was all mime. It kinda startled us. We all thought this is pretty much genius . . . but weird as hell."

"It was . . . God . . . it was funny," said Tommy Stinson. "It was pretty disturbing at first too, because it was so out of the blue."

Taking their cue from Mars—who'd developed a serious distaste for herd mentality punk crowds—the band delivered its "pussy set," slowing all the songs to a crawl, playing country covers, and generally doing everything it could to antagonize the hardcore audience. The proud Southern punks took this as a serious act of disrespect. "I remember one guy saying, 'Y'all wouldn't pull this shit in New York,'" said Westerberg. "And I was thinking *Oh yes we would.* We were equal opportunity offenders, north or south of the Mason-Dixon Line."

Over the years, Mars's evil twin would pop up periodically to cause trouble. "I think by the second time Pappy came out, it was like, '*Oh, no,*'" said Westerberg. "The first time it was quizzical and exciting; the next time it was kind of like, 'Well, somebody's gonna get hit with a bottle tonight.'" He sometimes wondered if Pappy was a manifestation of some deeper disturbance in Mars. "How much of that was the schizophrenia that runs in his family? I don't know."

Even out of greasepaint, Mars would occasionally tie one on and lead the band's bad behavior. Those times were often the worst collective displays; if Chris was out of control, then the others felt totally free to run wild.

During the latter stages of the *Let It Be* tour, the band was booked for a gig at the Coffeehouse on the campus of the University of California at Davis, in central California. The school's entertainment liaison brought Jesperson to a place called the Oak Room, which would be serving as the band's dressing quarters. It was a beautifully appointed, wood-paneled conference room, with a long table, chairs, and big-pane windows looking out on to the campus. A lavish deli tray and an unusually generous supply of liquor had been laid out.

His head immediately filling with visions of the havoc the 'Mats would wreak on the room, a nervous Jesperson actually asked for lesser accommodations. "Um, I'm not sure this is going to work," he told the liaison. "Can you show me something in concrete?"

The college didn't have anywhere else to put them, so Jesperson tried his best to head off trouble: "You guys," he told the band, "let's try and be careful in here."

"Yeah, we'll take care of this place," said Mars, grabbing a bucket full of ice and beer and hurling it against the wall. Glass and suds splattered everywhere. "It was like, *Oh my God*," said Jesperson, his worst fears immediately realized. "I don't remember a whole bunch else after that."

"We kinda went nuts," admitted Tommy. "We totally ripped the fucking room to bits. We had no idea the aftermath of that was going to be as bad as it was."

After a soused, subpar gig, the band packed its gear and hurried away before anyone in an official capacity realized the shape they'd the room left in.

The next day, with a gig in nearby Fresno looming, Jesperson sheepishly checked in with booking agent Frank Riley in New York.

"What the hell happened in Davis?" asked Riley.

The college had flipped out when they saw the damage—estimated at a couple thousand dollars, and several times what the band's fee was. "They've got a warrant out for your arrest!" Riley told him.

The Replacements played the gig in Fresno, bracing for a police raid, while Jesperson—whose name was on the contract at Davis—spent the evening hiding out from the cops, who never showed.

* * *

While Chris Mars's occasional flights of madness were regarded with amusement, Bob Stinson's behavior was becoming a cause for consternation.

Donning dresses or diapers, performing in the buff, or seizing the mic to sing the '60s wrestling novelty "The Crusher," he'd become the band's crazy, comic attraction. While his onstage displays helped boost the 'Mats' live legend, there was occasionally annoyance about his over-the-top antics. "[A] sore spot with Paul was that a lot of fans really liked me," Bob would claim in later years.

On one level, Westerberg and the others couldn't help but admire his sheer bravado. "When Bob was in the band, there was always that element of 'I dare ya' in the mix," said Tommy Stinson. "We dared him to play naked; he played naked. We dared him to rub Ben Gay on his balls and play naked; he played naked with Ben Gay on his balls, and fucking hated it. He'd get drunk and he would open himself up to 'I dare ya.'"

"It's great to see someone who's not afraid to play the fool," Westerberg noted at the time. "Till the day he dies Bob won't take himself seriously."

"But the drinking did get bad with him," said Jesperson. "He wouldn't remember stuff; there would be blackouts. That got a little scary. We started calling him Mr. Hyde because he was really a different person then."

The more they were on the road, the more Bob would retreat into his own world. Even apart from the gang, he had no difficulty finding trouble. "And if he couldn't find it, he'd make it," said Westerberg. "He needed a certain amount of excitement, some daring, to keep him from being bored. But the people who liked that sideshow aspect, they weren't the best for him." As Tommy would note, "By *Let It Be*, it was painfully obvious that Bob was going down that road more than he was being involved with the songs and the music."

Bob's behavior presaged a fundamental shift in the group as Tommy and Paul began to form their own tight kinship. In the beginning, Paul was naturally more connected with Bob. They were the same age and had the same goals in mind, while Tommy was just a little kid. "Shit, he was twelve, thirteen—he was a novelty," said Westerberg. "Pete looked out for him. And then this little gaggle of young ladies took him under their wing."

But by 1984 Paul and Tommy—brought together in part by drink—were socializing and scheming with one another, even starting to look and dress alike. "I felt that it was right that we sort of fell into step finally," said Westerberg.

"Me and Paul would hang out together, more as friends, rather than just being in a band together," said Tommy. "Also, I knew there was something happening with him musically that I was into. I was impressed. I thought he was great. I thought he was the greatest fucking songwriter."

"At a certain point, with Bob being so weird and so unmanageable, Tommy started siding with Paul a little bit," said Jesperson. "Tommy was smart enough to realize what he had in Paul, in terms of a partner, in terms of a chance to achieve something musically. And certainly there was a lot of love between them at that time."

CHAPTER 18

Nineteen eighty-four would prove a watershed year for Twin Cities music. In July, Hüsker Dü released their double-LP opus *Zen Arcade* to much acclaim. Also that summer, Prince and the Revolution issued the soundtrack to the movie *Purple Rain.* The album would go on to sell 14 million copies, and the film would become one of the top box office hits of the year. Shot on location at First Avenue, *Purple Rain* would turn Steve McClellan's club into a tourist attraction as out-of-towners and looky-loos from the 'burbs began turning up, hoping to get a glimpse of Prince.

"When Prince was popular, it was a great way to meet girls," said 'Mats roadie and sometime First Avenue employee Bill Sullivan. "You just told them, 'Sure, I know Prince. He hangs around all the time. He comes over to my house and does bong hits.'"

Although seemingly polar opposites, Prince's and the Replacements' sense of showmanship had a common root. "We experienced the same weather and a lot of the same things growing up," said Paul Westerberg. "Minneapolis audiences are mighty reserved, and learning to command an audience in a place where people are notorious for being quiet will either make you a wallflower, quiet artist, or it will make you really boisterous, aggressive, or flamboyant, which is what it did for both of us. I really think a lot of his flamboyance came from the suppression of the place that we live. It's a cold place to live in more ways than one."

The 'Mats genuinely admired Prince. On one occasion, Tommy Stinson was watching Prince perform from the wings at First Avenue while standing next to Ric Ocasek of the Cars, who were also at their pop chart zenith that year. After the Purple One peeled off a breathtaking Hendrix-like solo, then danced his way across the stage and into a leg split, Tommy slapped Ocasek on the back hard, pointed at Prince, and said, with a measure of Minneapolis pride, *"Let's see ya top that, buddy!"*

Prince was rumored to have lurked in the shadows at some of the Replacements' shows at First Avenue, but it was in the bathroom of a club in St. Paul where Westerberg finally ran into him.

"Oh, hey," said Westerberg, seeing the dolled-up singer standing next to him at the urinal. "What's up, man?"

Prince turned and responded in cryptic fashion: "Life."

* * *

While Prince grabbed most of the big headlines in '84, the Replacements' year was filled with important press. That spring the *Minneapolis Star and Tribune*'s music critic, Jon Bream, wrote a story on the band that appeared on the front page of the arts section. Featuring a photo of Westerberg at the piano, the piece offered validation to his parents.

"They were relieved that maybe I'd found my niche," said Westerberg. "Of course, my ma tried to take credit. In her mind, the musical pedigree came from her side of the family. But the tenacity to carry on through boos and bottles being thrown, that was my dad." Hal Westerberg rarely offered any comment on his son's career, though secretly he took great pride in his achievements. "My mom, as moms do, would clip the newspaper story out and put it on the fridge. But the old man was very cool about it. The most he ever said—one time, after reading some article where I'd been cursing—was, 'Why don't you clean up some of these "fucks" and "shits"?'"

That fall, the band also got its first mention in *Rolling Stone* when former Minneapolis writer Debby Miller penned a four-star review of *Let It Be* for the magazine—which ran ahead of a similarly lavish four-star review of Hüsker Dü's *Zen Arcade*. Ultimately, the Replacements' record would become one of 1984's most acclaimed. It would place fourth in the *Village Voice*'s annual Pazz and Jop critic's poll, behind only Bruce Springsteen, Prince, and Los Lobos (and ahead of the Hüskers and R.E.M.)

The Replacements' cozy relationships with the Minneapolis rock critic community would extend to national writers as well. The band was instinctively drawn to critics who shared their background: those who drank heartily, joked readily, and came from the Midwest. *Creem* magazine co-editors and Michigan natives Bill Holdship and John Kordosh became running buddies, as did former Chicagoan and *LA Reader* and *Billboard* writer Chris Morris. The 'Mats' golden status among this fraternity was inevitable. In his songs, Westerberg was articulating a particular kind of male adolescent frustration. Rock writers—mostly male, attitudinally adolescent, and often frustrated—ate it up. Still, Westerberg was wary of what that kind of adoration could mean. "Being the critic's band," he remarked in early '84, "is the curse of death."

Beyond a cadre of critics, the deeper impact of the Replacements and *Let It Be* would be felt by those who would come to define the next generation of alternative rock music. "You have to wonder—the Frank Blacks, the Kurt Cobains of the world—how many of them were anonymously out there in the crowds in the '80s seeing the 'Mats come through town," said Twin Cities writer P. D. Larson. "You wonder how many people were sitting there and saw them and it spoke to them in a way to start a band."

For Black, aka Charles Thompson—who would found the Pixies in 1986— *Let It Be* "totally liberated things. It made you feel comfortable doing some of the things they were doing," said Black. "You got the impression when you were listening to the album that they understood punk music, but they weren't all hung up on it. They're just fine doing a cover of a Kiss song; they're just fine doing a ballad. They weren't all caught up in it's gotta be straight-edge, it's gotta be punk, it's gotta be hardcore, it's gotta be indie rock. It's like, whatever, man. It's just gotta be cool.

"Most bands, especially back then, didn't have that much swagger. They were so uptight about proving their point and their passion that it could get precious in its own way. Whereas, like, Dean Martin had swagger; the Rolling Stones had swagger . . . the Replacements had swagger."

In Oklahoma, Wayne Coyne, a fast-food franchise employee and leader of the fledgling psych-rock band the Flaming Lips, also found inspiration in the Replacements. "They played the music we liked: it was punk rock, but it was classic rock, and it was loud and kind of fucked-up," said Coyne. "They were better musicians than we were at the time, but we saw something in them, and we were like, 'Yeah! Look, they're getting away with it. We could do that.' We didn't care that they might've only been playing to nine people in some club in Norman."

Even for established musicians, like veteran Los Angeles guitarist Ward Dotson, the 'Mats had a life-altering effect. Dotson had been a member of the punk-blues band the Gun Club with Jeffrey Lee Pierce. But he'd grown disenchanted with the band's Gothier direction and what he saw as its fashionista fan base. Quitting the group, he eventually formed the Pontiac Brothers, a rough-and-ready rock outfit that owed a major debt to the 'Mats. "Looking back, it's like, 'God, could we have been more influenced by the Replacements?'" said Dotson. "It's laughable. But I could have picked a worse band."

The Pontiac Brothers would open a series of shows for the Replacements during the *Let It Be* tour, and Dotson and Westerberg—united by a love of Slade and early '70s bubblegum music—would become fast friends. Though Westerberg took pride in his skills as a writer, Dotson knew he was uncomfortable with the attention his work was starting to garner. "A total conversation killer with Paul was to start complimenting him on his songwriting, or talking about how much you love this song or that song . . . just conversation over," said Dotson. "He didn't know how to deal with it."

At the time, Westerberg was reluctant to focus on the writerly aspect of the 'Mats' music. "I remember not wanting to play 'Sixteen Blue' and 'Answering Machine,' because it wasn't part of the MO of the live band," he said. "I always felt that we can have that stuff on record and the show is more of a performance.

But it eventually became clear that a lot of the people were coming to hear this slower song, or that ballad, and not 'We're Coming Out.'"

With *Let It Be*, people were paying ever closer attention to Paul Westerberg's words. "It was a mixed blessing when I started to attract fanatics who would read something into a song that maybe wasn't there, or maybe someone who would read exactly what's there," he admitted. Still, Westerberg never took the power of his songs, his ability to connect with listeners, for granted. "People always come up and say, 'You wrote this just for me,'" he noted. "And I say, 'Yeah, I did. I don't know you, but I knew you were out there.'"

★ ★ ★

Within a few months of its release, *Let It Be* was selling briskly—nearly 11,000 copies and trending upward. In comparison, by the end of '84, *Sorry Ma* had sold only 6,000, *Stink* 4,000, and *Hootenanny* 8,000 in total. Given their success, the band, especially Westerberg, felt they'd earned the right to complain about Twin/Tone's minuscule tour support and question what the label was doing to advance their careers. "He was frustrated," said Peter Jesperson, who was constantly having to balance his loyalties to the band and the label. "Paul felt like, 'We're barely scraping by, and we need the label to give us more money.' There just wasn't that kind of money available. When I explained that, he would take it as me not siding with the band."

The solution to everyone's problems—the band's, Jesperson's, and Twin/Tone's—was obvious: have the Replacements sign with a major label. But that brought its own set of complications, compounded by the stigma of indie rock politics and the band's own uncertainties.

In 1984 only a handful of groups had made the transition from the American/indie underground into the major-label mainstream world. Rising young A&R man Steve Ralbovsky had signed the indie-roots bands Jason and the Scorchers and the Del-Lords to EMI America on modest deals, with both groups being slowly cultivated via EP releases and touring. The highest-profile move had been undertaken by the Los Angeles paisley underground outfit Dream Syndicate, who'd signed with the boutique major label A&M Records. They hired Blue Oyster Cult/Dictators/Clash veteran Sandy Pearlman to produce and spent a quarter of a million dollars over five months in three studios recording their label debut, *Medicine Show*. Released in the summer of '84, the album was hardly a commercial-sounding effort, but it vexed underground purists who looked at the circumstantial evidence—major label, name producer, big budget—and lobbed lazy accusations of "sellout" and catcalls of "corporate rock."

Within the underground, there remained a deep suspicion about any band who dared try to cross the major-label Rubicon. When it came to the Replacements, those misgivings were voiced most loudly by Steve Albini.

The leader of the Chicago post-hardcore band Big Black and a noted recording engineer, Albini had deep connections to the Minneapolis hardcore scene. He was also a professional gadfly, punk rock moralist, and sometime music critic writing for the Chicago-based magazine *Matter* (generally a bastion of Replacements love, as the group was frequently fawned over in print by editor Liz Phillip and writers like Julie Panebianco).

Albini had been dubious about some of the lighter aspects of *Hootenanny*—particularly tracks like "Within Your Reach." When *Let It Be*—filled with a further assortment of pop songs and ballads—was released, he seized on the album as a total betrayal, one that he laid at Westerberg's feet. Albini concluded his review of the record for *Matter* with the line: "I used to love these guys; now I hate this guy."

"I do remember hating that record," said Albini. "When a band made the transition from being a punk band to being an R.E.M.-type band, that was the point where you could write them off—'cause they were never going back. There's no way that a band that aspires to being a credible pop/rock FM radio band is ever going to make a snotty, smelly, messy punk rock record again. It's never happened in history. It's basically an indication of the kind of people they always were. And you feel a little bit foolish for having been duped."

After Albini further badmouthed the 'Mats in a *Forced Exposure* piece—in which he actually wished Westerberg dead—the Replacements front man finally rose to the bait. "[Albini's] in show business, and that's the point everybody misses," said Westerberg. "Of course if you told him that he would probably fall on the floor and vomit and kick the wall out."

In truth, Albini's broadsides showed just how little anyone, even their supposed indie contemporaries, understood the Replacements. The 'Mats never claimed to be punk or hardcore, never operated in DIY fashion, and certainly didn't conduct themselves in a carefully considered manner that suggested they aspired to become like R.E.M.

The dustup with Albini underscored the larger point: no one—maybe not even the band itself—really knew what the Replacements were, or what they were capable of becoming. Would the group continue as an adolescent lark until they simply burned out? Would they become small-time lifers grinding it out on the club circuit? Or were they going to aim for something bigger?

In all his time hanging with the Replacements, R.E.M.'s Peter Buck said the band never once discussed making the jump to the major labels. "It wasn't ever even a topic. I just assumed that they would stay with Peter and Twin/ Tone forever," said Buck. Although R.E.M.'s label, IRS Records, was distributed by a major, they were in much the same situation as the Replacements. "We had minor league promotion. There was no money. We had two great [promo] guys, but they didn't have a penny. We tried to get a tour poster done once—like 300 posters for 150 bucks—and the record company didn't have enough money to do it."

Like the Replacements, R.E.M. found itself at a career crossroads at the end of 1984. "Even in my band there was some doubt—are we gonna get bigger or are we going to step back from it?" said Buck. "My feeling was, this is a once-in-a-lifetime opportunity. I'd feel stupid if I threw it away. It was a deci-sion, though, and it took a lot of talking and thinking through. There was an understanding where the four of us in R.E.M. said: 'This is how we're going to do it from here on out.' I don't know that the Replacements ever had that talk. I'm not even sure how much Paul wanted it. Everyone wants it a little bit. If you get up onstage even once, you must want it to a certain degree. Then it's just a matter of finding out where your lines are."

* * *

For the Del Fuegos, the lines began to move quickly. After signing with Warner-distributed indie Slash for their debut *The Longest Day*, the band moved over to Warner Bros. Records proper for its second LP, *Boston, Mass.* The band's producer, Mitchell Froom, sanded off their rougher edges, and the label gave them a visual makeover. When they came back to Boston after a spell polishing up in LA, Bill Sullivan joked that they'd gone to "John Cougar Summercamp."

The Fuegos then fired their manager, Lilli Dennison, to sign with the label-endorsed firm of High Noon. Fatefully, the band also joined several other up-and-coming groups—including the Long Ryders and dB's—and signed on for a promotional deal with Miller Beer's Rock Network at the end of 1984. The pact meant a much-needed injection of tour support money and a merch line. It also meant appearing in a Miller television commercial.

"Rock-and-roll is folk music," grinned singer Dan Zanes in the ad's kicker. "It's music for folks."

The reaction to the Del Fuegos' Miller spot—which debuted during the Live Aid telecast and aired on *Monday Night Football* and all over MTV—was damning. They would be attacked by their peers (the Young Fresh Fellows lam-pooned them with the song "Beer Money") and the rock critic establishment alike. Short-term, the Miller deal improved the Fuegos' life on the road and got them on the mainstream radar, boosting their sales and draw. "The problem was the clown population increased," said Warren Zanes. "Suddenly, we've got guys who wouldn't know the Gun Club, X, and the Blasters from a hole in their heads going crazy for us. At the end of the day, you have to wonder, what made them love us? A beer commercial? It's not the best way to cultivate a thinking, listening audience."

* * *

Paul Westerberg was somewhat oblivious to the industry buzz building around the Replacements in the wake of *Let It Be*. "I remember a writer coming up to me saying, 'Do you know where you're at right now? Do you know what's happening?' And I remember thinking like, 'No—what?'" said Wester-berg. "At the time we were exploding we weren't seeing it or acknowledging it. Our reaction was to dismiss it, like, 'Yeah, yeah—don't forget to spit on us when we're in the gutter next year.'"

"We bought into that whole 'lovable loser' thing," noted Tommy Stinson. "And it wasn't good for us."

Westerberg had serious qualms about the prospect of signing a major-label deal. He was worried about what would happen to the band and how they would be perceived. "He definitely wanted to be a success," said his girlfriend, Lori Bizer. "But he didn't want to sell out, he wanted to keep his rebelliousness intact, he didn't want to kowtow to The Man. He didn't want to have his music be used for a commercial, he didn't want to make any videos. He didn't want to do the things you would actually have to do to get to that point."

His reluctance to play the game was spurred by a collection of fears: of success, but mostly, of failure. It would become the dominant theme of the latter half of the Replacements' career—Westerberg was more inclined to sabotage himself than risk rejection. "There's a certain amount of admitting failure before I will actually say, 'I might be defeated,'" said Tommy. "Paul definitely had that. Paul felt more comfortable going, 'I can't live up to that,' than actually trying to live up to that. And me? I was just following my leader, dude.

"The weirdest part of that period was feeling like, on one hand, 'Wow, we're actually getting somewhere.' And on the other hand, as things were getting more positive, we were acting more negative. You couldn't help but feed off Paul's dissatisfaction with certain things—'cause he wore it on his sleeve. But I think he had problems that were bigger than him. That were bigger than all of us, that we didn't even know about."

The mental health issues in the Replacements camp had already begun to crop up. That fall longtime crew member Tom Carlson quit his job with the band, following what had been, in retrospect, the first signs of a mental break. Carlson would eventually fall into a spiral of schizophrenia. (He died prematurely from a heart condition at the age of fifty-three in 2011.) Bob Stinson's difficulties, the residue of his traumatic childhood, were on the verge of becoming a major issue as well. In the meantime, entering his midtwenties, Westerberg was starting to feel a black cloud settle over his own mind. "I remember Paul saying to me, 'It's like World War III in my brain all the time,'" recalled Jesperson.

Alcohol, which had fueled their public spectacle, also served as both a salve and a mask. "There was a lot of medicating happening and not really knowing what we were medicating for," said Tommy. "Paul is the first one to tell you today, 'I have a problem with depression.' He didn't know what that was then."

At the point where he should've been most triumphant, Westerberg was feeling anything but. "I never think of him as being happy," said the Rat booker Julie Farman. "Or grateful to be where he was. I never think of him any way other than depressed . . . no, not depressed, but sad. And internal." Former Fuegos manager Lilli Dennison would sometimes play sob sister to Westerberg. "He was a pretty confused guy, I think," said Dennison. "I just remember our talks being about unhappiness, about his dissatisfaction in general. It was like the Peggy Lee song: 'Is that all there is?'"

Yet, despite all of Westerberg's fears and uncertainties, it seemed like the band was being pulled inexorably toward a major-label career, toward some grand destiny. "We'd like to take it as far as possible, to say we did it, to see what it's like," he told an interviewer that fall. "Why the fuck not?"

CHAPTER 19

Twin/Tone's Dave Ayers was a native of Stillwater, a hamlet outside the Twin Cities—population 10,000—best known for its state penitentiary. So was a rising young music business lawyer named George Regis; a few years older than Ayers, his Stillwater High reputation was well known. "He had moved to New York," said Ayers, "and I knew him well enough to call him up and make some introductions—which I did for both the Replacements and Hüsker Dü."

The oldest of five, Regis grew up in a Catholic household filled with music and alcohol. His father had played trombone on the Midwest jazz circuit. When he became the band director at Stillwater High, he brought a drinking problem with him. "My mother told me that he would hide a vodka bottle in his desk drawer when he was teaching," said Regis. "He had a violent temper. I had a recurring nightmare, owing to him blowing up at me when he was drunk."

In the early sixties, the elder Regis went to rehab at Hazelden, then still in its infancy. "After that, he never relapsed. He worked through it," said Regis, whose father would go on to have an illustrious career as one of the nation's top school band directors.

After attending the University of Minnesota, Regis moved to New York in 1979. Within a few years, he was working for a shooting star of the music biz, attorney Owen Epstein of the firm Levine, Thall and Epstein, whose clients included U2 and Pat Benatar. Epstein was a wild child with plenty of the era's bad habits, including a serious cocaine problem. Regis would later help him into rehab; Epstein would die of a brain tumor, not long after getting sober, in 1988.

Between his father and his boss, Regis was well suited to deal with the Replacements' chemically fueled chaos: "It certainly wasn't unknown to me." He'd seen the band around late 1982, after Ayers and Jesperson raved about them, and immediately hit it off with Westerberg—no mean feat in itself. "I knew quickly that they were deathly afraid of success. And that they wanted to be in a situation where they couldn't get pinned down or forced to do anything they didn't want to do."

With Regis's help, the Replacements began feeling out labels as early as the fall of 1983. During the band's first West Coast tour that October, they met with Bob Biggs, head of Los Angeles–based Slash Records. The label was technically an indie, but had distribution and development ties with Warner Bros.

John Doe and Exene Cervenka of X had been talking up the 'Mats to Biggs. "I remember trying to go to the meeting with just Paul and I, and Tommy insisting on coming," recalled Jesperson. The younger Stinson then "looked at Biggs and said, 'Okay, how much money are you gonna give us?' It was like, 'Tommy, come on.'"

Soon after, Columbia Records junior A&R woman Joanna Spock Dean began pursuing the band. Dean had worked for Miles Copeland's management firm and at IRS and Faulty Records. "I'd go backstage to say hello," said Dean. "Peter was cool, Tommy was bratty, Chris didn't talk too much, and Bob was crazy. And I was like every other female—madly in love with Paul Westerberg."

Dean flew to see the Replacements that September at Joe's Star Lounge in Ann Arbor. On the plane ride out, she realized a couple of representatives from A&M were on the same flight, for the same reason. The 'Mats couldn't quite fathom these big labels flying out to "bumfuck" Midwestern cities to sweet-talk them. "I met these two guys in Michigan and didn't believe they worked for a label," said Westerberg. "They were wearing tennis shoes and said they were from A&M records. So I grabbed one of them and said, 'Fuck you! Where's the coke?'"

Columbia would become a more serious suitor with the arrival of New York–based Steve Ralbovsky. In the eighties, Columbia was a behemoth, home to Bruce Springsteen, Cyndi Lauper, Toto, and Loverboy, among other blockbuster acts. Hired there in 1984, Ralbovsky immediately signed British power pop band the Outfield, gave a development deal to a nineteen-year-old Matthew Sweet (on R.E.M.'s recommendation), and brought Russell Simmons and Rick Rubin's fledgling hip-hop label, Def Jam, to the company.

Ralbovsky convinced Columbia A&R head Mickey Eichner that the 'Mats were worth bringing aboard, pitching them as low-cost and low-effort. "I didn't have to do a whole lot of lobbying at the company." He knew it would take some persuading, but the band was more than a little intrigued. "In those days, if you were on an independent label, there was a ceiling," Ralbovsky said. "They were kicking the tires as far as their opportunities went."

* * *

No A&R man had the in with the Replacements that Michael Hill had—he'd booked their first New York show and established a friendship that predated his career working for Warner Bros.

Born in 1954 in Newark, and raised in Orange, New Jersey, Hill was, unusually, the only child in a lower-middle-class Irish-Italian Catholic family. His father's struggle with depression and drinking forced the young Hill to become a calming, mediating influence in his home, an ability that "would eventually come in handy" working with the Replacements.

Hill attended Fordham in New York, largely so he could go see concerts at the Fillmore East. Soon he was writing music criticism for the Jersey-based *Aquarian Weekly*. He worked for AT&T before *New York Rocker*, which folded in 1982, and his byline appeared in *Rolling Stone* and the *Village Voice* while he co-booked "Music for Dozens" at Folk City.

In the spring of 1982, Hill attended *Voice* music critic Robert Christgau's fortieth birthday party and met Karin Berg, an old friend of Christgau's. An influential and much revered A&R woman, Berg had signed Television and the Cars to Elektra before becoming head of East Coast A&R for Warner Bros. "We started chatting about bands, and she complimented me on my writing," said Hill.

In the late summer of 1983, Berg hired Hill as an A&R man—he had to turn down Christgau's offer to become the *Voice*'s music editor to take the job. With his smiling eyes and olive complexion, Hill was an attractive figure—a well-read, unaffected intellectual whose easy confidence in the showbiz world belied his blue-collar beginnings.

Upon landing at Warner Bros., Hill's immediate priority was to sign the Replacements. "What convinced me was hearing *Hootenanny*, hearing 'Within Your Reach,' as well as the stuff that Peter would carry around," said Hill. (Jesperson would play his well-guarded cassette tapes of Westerberg's unreleased solo songs, like "You're Getting Married," for select intimates like Hill.) "I loved the band, but I loved that other side of Paul especially—that wonderful, sensitive singer-songwriter guy who seems so improbably expressive."

The Replacements appreciated him in turn. "Michael was a lot like us," said Westerberg—meaning, young and from the underground, and also Catholic, working-class, and steeped in similar familial dysfunction. "I came prepackaged to cope with them," Hill said.

In October 1983, Hill brought several top Warner staff—including Berg and department head Michael Ostin—to see the Replacements at Club Lingerie in Hollywood. "Karin got mad at me, because she said I was jumping around too much during the show," said Hill. "'You're not here as a fan. You're here as the record label.'"

But the band didn't take it seriously. That fall, prior to a CBGB show, Hill casually mentioned to Westerberg that he liked the Rolling Stones' "Start Me Up." During the show, Paul called to Bob for the riff, then started singing: "Start me up . . . you want a flop?" he howled. "I'll take you places . . . you never want to go to." Afterward he wheedled into the mike, calling out to Hill: "Do we get a record deal yet? Come on, *pleeeeeze?*"

CHAPTER 20

Much ink had been spilled over the Replacements already, but no single article would be as essential in crystallizing their legend as a *Village Voice* cover story from December 1984.

The author was twenty-five-year-old RJ Smith, a Detroit native who'd attended the University of Michigan, where he wrote for the school paper and was a classmate of Lori Bizer. He spent a year at a daily paper in Buffalo, then headed to New York, where he hooked on at the *Voice*. He quickly proved to be one of the paper's most incisive music critics and feature writers.

The paper's editor, Robert Christgau, had been following the 'Mats for several years. In 1982 he'd given a lecture in Minneapolis and been taken to see the band at First Avenue. During the set, Paul Westerberg grimly announced that Chuck Berry had just died, before playing "Maybellene" in tribute. A panicked Christgau scurried to a pay phone before he realized he was being put on.

Smith had fallen hard for the *Stink* EP and was there for the band's New York debut at Folk City. "Anybody with a brain or a taste for adventure could tell from watching an 'average' Replacements show that this would be a fun group to follow on the road." Smith penned a lively review of *Hootenanny* for the *Voice* in late '83: "They end up acting fucked up about being fucked up—metafuckedupitude—and grabbing at anything that might serve as a buoy. The result is a solid sensibility, shows capable of spontaneous combustion, and a new album that passes like a warm beer shit."

With *Let It Be* out that fall, Christgau pressed Smith into an in-depth feature on the band, the Twin/Tone label, the Minneapolis scene, and the burgeoning indie rock culture in America. Smith embedded himself with the 'Mats for a week. "That notion of bands traveling in a van from town to town, with an address book that had the names of club owners and record store guys and people with couches you could sleep on, was still new," said Smith. "This network had sprouted up simultaneously across the country."

In September, Smith met the band in Ohio and rode with them through the Midwest, into Canada, and back. The band had set up for sound check at Stache's in Columbus, and Jesperson and Westerberg were waiting for Smith to arrive at the club. "When the door opened and RJ walked in, it was like, 'That's the guy.' He kinda reeked of rock critic—he had the glasses and just looked the part," said Jesperson.

Just as Smith strode over and put out his hand to introduce himself, Westerberg stood up and announced: "Well, I gotta take me a warm beer shit," quoting Smith's line back to him. "Everybody cracked up," said Jesperson.

"People got comfortable with RJ," said Jesperson. "He got into the spirit of things and had a few drinks with us and got a little silly." In turn, Smith openly scribbled in his notebook for the next few days. His observations added up to a remarkably raw, sometimes unflattering, but essentially accurate portrait of a band that was flying high and living low.

"They were showing me and saying things they probably shouldn't have," said Smith. "I mean, if you're going to do cocaine next to me and then fall asleep—which Paul did and which I was very impressed by—then that's fair game. Though I left that one out of the story."

Chris Mars had sworn off the sauce for this particular tour. "Chris seemed a little fragile, the most wary of what I was doing and the least outgoing," said Smith. "He showed me some of his drawings. He was more observer than participant in a lot of things."

Smith found Bob Stinson elusive but likable. Mostly it was Paul and Tommy Stinson doing the carrying on. The bassist exhibited his brattiest and most hedonistic tendencies, partly for Smith's benefit. "When I'm impressed or in awe or appalled, people can read it on my face pretty quickly," said Smith. "I think he had a good time showing me what he was capable of."

Smith's interaction with Westerberg was more personal—yet another writer who felt a deeper connection with him. "Paul was at this incredible moment where he was unguarded about his yearnings and his vulnerabilities, certainly a lot less protective of himself than he became later on," Smith said. "He had the gambler's instinct to take a shot that might be good for their career."

The story also showed precisely how *un*-DIY the Replacements were, how reliant on Jesperson. "He was willing to do all kinds of stuff that was *way* outside the usual résumé description," Smith said. "I could tell: 'Oh boy, this is not going to end well.' He loved them too much."

Smith was also able to see the cracks forming between Bob and the band, as when Bob complained to Paul about Jesperson: "I just don't know why he's here." Westerberg replied: "Because he liked us when nobody else did."

Reading the exchange surprised Jesperson. "It was odd. The only way that Bob resented my presence was that maybe I was one of the guys he saw giving Paul too much credit, and allowing Paul to take over the reins. Where in Bob's mind he still saw himself as the leader. There [was] some resentment building there."

Though the story, "The Replacements: A Band for Our Time," landed them on the cover of the *Village Voice*, the group was dismayed by the piece. "Everyone sorta groused about it," said Jesperson. "It painted us like a bunch of drunks that weren't going to go anywhere." Tommy Stinson would later allow that Smith "probably captured everything pretty accurately, which is really what bugged us." While the article caused a major stir in music biz circles, "it was the worst-selling issue of the *Voice* that year," noted Smith, "as the paper's editor reminded me repeatedly." A few days after the issue came out, Smith was walking through the East Village when a vehicle pulled alongside him threateningly. Just then a cackling Paul Westerberg popped his head out of the window before it sped off: "Hey, RJ. Get a job, ya bum!"

* * *

The Replacements booked a secret gig—as Gary and the Boners—at CBGB's December 9, in advance of their "proper" New York City show at Irving Plaza five days later. The *Village Voice* hype helped to turn it into a label showcase. Owen Epstein and George Regis lined up executives from Columbia, Warner, Chrysalis, A&M, and other labels to see the band Sunday night on the Bowery.

Jesperson knew this was the big opportunity of the band's career, and he feared it: "As soon as you let them know there were important people in the audience, it was a good bet that they were going to pull something really ridiculous." Sure enough, the band spent two hours sticking out their tongues at the New York A&R community. "It was a drunken lollapalooza," said Regis. "It was absolutely fucked up."

The show began with a snippet of "You're a Mean One, Mr. Grinch," then turned the early "Lookin' for Ya" into an underwater boogie jam. Next came the West Bank blues of "Never Been to College," the four of them making a racket like gears meshing. It only got weirder. The audience was soon shouting lines from the *Voice* story: "Do the 'pussy set'!" "Play your 'goofy covers'!" They obliged, delivering a light-fingered "Color Me Impressed" before zigzagging randomly from Dolly Parton's "Jolene" to Led Zeppelin's "Misty Mountain Hop."

The most focused moment came when roadie Bill Sullivan sang Elvis Presley's "Do the Clam." When they actually got all the way through U2s "I Will Follow" without falling apart, Tommy almost sounded shocked: "Hey, we did one!" he said. The show featured forty-three songs and snippets, including maybe half a dozen by the Replacements, most of those mangled. "This is our last, *last* fucking performance ever," croaked Westerberg.

Near set's end, Kiss bassist Gene Simmons sauntered in. Jesperson was at the soundboard: "They had a talkback system at CBGB where you could communicate from the booth into the monitors." He alerted Westerberg to the God of Thunder's presence, and the band went right into "Black Diamond." "Simmons was looking all around like 'How did they know I was here?'"

recalled Jesperson. The 'Mats' "suck ass version" quickly chased Simmons from the venue. The band followed up with an X-rated version of the "Ballad of Jed Clampett," then whistled their way through the theme from *The Andy Griffith Show* before finally leaving the stage.

The crowd's exodus had begun earlier. "About halfway through, all of these senior executives from these various labels, one by one start to leave," said Regis. On their way out, they stopped to shake Epstein's hand and pat Regis on the back, offering condolences. "They were commiserating with me. It felt like I was at a funeral."

Watching the band self-destruct at CBGB's, it occurred to Regis that the Irving Plaza concert a few days later was likely to be spectacular. "I was already aware of that propensity in them," he said. "And it made me want to see the next show."

* * *

At least one person loved the Replacements' CBGB set: Alex Chilton. The erstwhile Big Star leader was no stranger to desultory performances or ruinous displays of self-sabotage. He'd recently emerged from several years in "hiding," during which he'd moved to New Orleans, quit drinking and music, and worked as a dishwasher. In the fall of 1984, Chilton began to play shows again, reemerging as a quasi-legendary figure to a generation of bands who saw him as an alt-rock forerunner.

Chilton and the 'Mats shared a booking agent in Frank Riley. The band hoped to tour with Chilton, but the economics hadn't worked out. Instead, they invited him to open the CBGB gig—he was living temporarily in New York. "We were in awe of his set, and then he went into the audience and watched the Replacements," said Jesperson. "That was a huge deal."

When the 'Mats went through their routine, Chilton had a grin plastered on his face. After the show, both Jesperson and Chilton were waiting to get paid by CBGB owner Hilly Kristal. Jesperson offered to buy breakfast the next morning. Chilton accepted.

Getting ready to leave the Iroquois Hotel, Jesperson stopped by Westerberg's room to remind him of the day's interview schedule. Still sleepy and hungover, Westerberg asked where Peter was going. When he found out, Paul shot out of bed, threw on his clothes, and tagged along.

Paul did not impress easily, but he was very impressed with Alex Chilton. They taxied to the Gem Spa newsstand on Second Avenue and St. Mark's Place. "He was standing by a trash can with a bag full of matches," said Westerberg. "He was playing a game . . . pretending, 'I'm Alex the Weirdo.' I sucked up to it, and played the role."

Over an Indian buffet lunch, Westerberg and Chilton circled around one another with a guarded curiosity. "His aura is different than the average person's," Westerberg said. "He could be from another planet."

At one point, Westerberg got up to go to the bathroom and Chilton leaned over to Jesperson. "Man, I gotta tell you I thought they were great last night," he said. "I'd love to work in the studio with them someday." Once Jesperson was sure he was serious, he practically ran to a phone booth to call Steve Fjelstad back in Minneapolis to book a week of studio time in early January.

Meanwhile, everyone else in the Replacements' camp was feeling various degrees of panic about the performance the night before. Dave Ayers waited in Minneapolis for news of the show. "The next morning the phone didn't ring. I finally called George like, 'So?' And he said, after the longest pause, 'Dave . . . *they were awful.*' My heart sank."

A process was establishing itself. When it came to choosing a label, manager, booking agent, or producer, the Replacements would behave in horrible, offensive, alarming ways, and whoever survived was typically who they'd work with. "That's Westerberg," noted Regis, "in all of his [professional] relationships."

* * *

Seymour Stein was in bad shape. It was a Friday night in mid-December, and the Sire Records head was making the rounds of music-biz holiday parties, getting progressively more wasted. By his final stop, the annual MTV bash, Stein was, in the words of Aerosmith's Steven Tyler, "gakked to the nines." There he ran into his lawyer, Owen Epstein, who immediately steered Stein away from the party and out of the building.

"Owen saved my life," said Stein. "I could've died that night from excess. He said, 'Look, I'm going to Irving Plaza to see the Replacements, and you're coming with me.'" Epstein plied Stein with coffee and told him the 'Mats truly belonged on Sire.

Stein had heard about the Replacements, most of it bad. "Hilly Kristal hated them . . . and Hilly hated no one," said Stein. "I'd never seen him be this down on a band. He said, 'I couldn't even distinguish the music.'"

His interest piqued, Stein had the band's records delivered to his office. He was impressed with what he heard, but what he would see that night would surpass anything on vinyl. Irving Plaza was one of the best gigs anyone—including Jesperson—ever remembered the 'Mats doing. "They really went for the throat that night," said Jesperson.

"Whatever state I was in, I knew they were fabulous," said Stein. As the band worked up songs by Bill Haley, the Beach Boys, and Vanity Fare, Stein began scribbling down other cover ideas. When Stein met the group backstage afterwards, he greeted them excitedly as bits of paper spilled out of his pockets. "We partied, we sang old songs together," said Stein of their post-show soiree.

Even before the evening was over, a relieved Regis pointed to Stein and whispered to Jesperson: "He says he's going to have you guys signed before you even get home from this trip."

CHAPTER 21

Born Seymour Steinbigle in April 1942, he was raised in Brooklyn's Benson-hurst section, the youngest child in a heavily religious, lower-middle-class Jewish family. Weaned on Big Band music, then discovering the earliest R&B and rock-and-roll records being spun on New York radio, Stein became consumed. "I was a fan in the truest sense of the word. I was a fanatic," said Stein. "Growing up, I wasn't good at sports. I hated school. All I cared about was music." As a twelve-year-old, he began visiting the *Billboard* offices to study bound volumes of back issues and learn the history of the music business. "After my first year, Tom Noonan, the chart editor . . . offered me a job," said Stein. "I thought I was just paying him back for accommodating me. They actually gave me a check. I ran home and told my mother, '*I can't believe it! I should be paying them!*'"

In high school, Stein spent summers in Cincinnati apprenticing under King Records owner Syd Nathan, whose biggest star was James Brown. Stein eventually would work for King full-time, learning every aspect of the business at the company's one-stop operation. Back in New York, he became an assistant to record man George Goldner in 1963, then in 1966 broke off with producer-writer Richard Gottehrer. Their label's moniker scrambled the first two letters of their first names—SE and RI—to get Sire.

Each put up $10,000 in seed money. Stein's funds had come from Beatle-mania's 1964 height, when Capitol Records in Canada sold a selection of Beatles singles not available in the United States. Stein had spirited a mass of the records out of the country, then offloaded them to US wholesalers, making a small fortune in a week. "The statute of limitations has passed," said Stein. "But that's where my share of the money came from."

Sire's early roster was a hodgepodge, mostly licensed from Europe: Climax Blues Band, Renaissance, Barclay James Harvest, Peter Green's Fleetwood Mac, Focus. Gottehrer left the label just as Stein turned his attention to New York's nascent punk scene to sign CBGB acts the Ramones, Talking Heads, and

Dead Boys. He also coined the phrase "new wave" to sell them to consumers leery of the term "punk."

During its first decade, Sire had been distributed by various companies, including London Records and ABC. In 1977 Warner Bros. would come on as distributor; a year later they bought a 50 percent stake in the label. Two years after that, they would purchase Sire outright. Stein remained the label's president and was also made a Warner VP. Sire moved into a corporate office complex on East Fifty-Fourth Street, and its publicity, sales, and promotion were taken over by Warner.

The Sire/Warner union was successful, if occasionally fraught. Stein could be excessive in his personal behavior and demanding and difficult when it came to business. He was a collector: of artwork, of antiques, and especially of bands. His perceived profligacy was a source of irritation to Warner Bros.'s head, Mo Ostin, and other executives at the company. "There was always the idea that Seymour was signing too many things, spending too much money," said Warner A&R man Michael Hill. "Seymour has voracious appetites, and if he wanted something, he could be very petulant if he didn't get it. But at the end of the day, everyone knew he would deliver the goods. He was the key to so much for that company."

By the early '80s, Stein was constantly globetrotting, picking up cutting-edge bands from all over. He spent much of his time in Britain, using the country's hip indie label entrepreneurs—Geoff Travis at Rough Trade, Daniel Miller at Mute, Martin Mills at Beggars Banquet—as a kind of unofficial A&R staff. Stein would sign the UK groups the Undertones, Pretenders, Madness, Echo and the Bunnymen, the Smiths, the Cult, Depeche Mode, Soft Cell, Modern English, and Aztec Camera. His forward-looking vision would pay off in a big way when he signed Madonna, a New York dance club ingénue, in 1983 and watched her explode into a pop culture phenomenon.

By bringing these artists into the Warner Bros. fold, Stein helped raise the company's hip quotient. Warner was a Burbank, California–based company, a fact reflected in a roster loaded with West Coast boomer acts. While it was an artist-friendly haven, Warner wasn't especially attuned to what was happening in the underground scenes of New York and London, much less in marginal Middle American cities like Minneapolis.

Michael Hill had been trying to convince Warner Bros. to sign the Replacements for the better part of a year. None of his A&R superiors were sold on the band. Karin Berg felt the group would be better served maturing and making another album on Twin/Tone. "She didn't think it was time yet for them—they were so raw," said Hill. "She felt, these guys really need to show they can be professional musicians."

Stein had no such qualms. He came swooping in after the Irving Plaza performance, ready to offer a deal, convinced they were his next great discovery. "Seymour was always willing to be the first one there when he saw the potential," said Hill. "There were visceral things that appealed to him about the Replacements."

To Stein, the 'Mats had the benefit of great songs, as well as the perfect rock-and-roll tandem in Paul Westerberg and Tommy Stinson. "It was like when the Smiths were brought to my attention," said Stein. "I signed them instantly because of the combination of Morrissey and Johnny Marr. Most bands are lucky to have one superstar, and this band has two superstars. That's really the way I felt about the Replacements." (Tommy's good looks and raffish manner held particular appeal to Stein, who had an affinity for handsome young men. "Lord knows I flirted enough with Seymour to where I thought it would help our career," cracked Tommy.)

Quickly, Michael Hill became part of the package to entice the 'Mats to Sire, with the idea that he would serve as their A&R man. "It put me in a slightly odd position," said Hill, whose boss, Karin Berg, had a long-standing rivalry with Stein. "But in the end it was a win-win for me because I was gonna be with the band I wanted."

To the Replacements, Stein was unlike any label exec they'd met: he was loud and wild and raged right along with them. "There would be lots of drunken dinners with the Replacements, and Seymour can drink with the best of them," said Sire staffer Sandy Alouette. Westerberg gravitated toward outré, larger-than-life figures. "And Seymour certainly was that," he said. "I always got a kick out of him." At the same time he was a little suspicious: Stein's impetuous interest in signing the band seemed too good to be true. "Maybe he wanted a tax write-off," said Westerberg.

In addition to Stein, the setup at Sire was especially attractive. It offered the cool factor of a boutique label associated with the paragons of punk, but also had the money and muscle of the Warner machine behind it. Plus, as Westerberg would note, Sire had "the best-looking chicks." "The girls in the office, we were all in our twenties, and we all had crushes on the Replacements," said Alouette. "Paul and Tommy could charm the socks off of anyone, including Seymour. They were a little wayward—these outsiders who were trying to fit in by not fitting in. But their charisma kinda pardoned all their sins."

Seymour Stein was ready to waltz this charismatic band of outsiders through the doors of Warner Bros.

★ ★ ★

The year 1985 began with Alex Chilton arriving in Minneapolis to cut tracks with the Replacements—a trio of new Westerberg tunes inspired by his romantic and road experiences: "Nowhere Is My Home," "Left of the Dial," and "Can't Hardly Wait."

Chilton was not a producer per se, though he'd helmed several rollicking records for horror-punks the Cramps, among others. "The rumor was that when he'd produced them he'd ordered a case of beer and moved the faders with his feet," said Westerberg. "We thought, '*Yeah*—this will be right up our alley.' But it was nothing like that. He was sort of adult about it."

Chilton had put his own drinking problems behind him a few years earlier. "Alex was very in tune to how antsy we were," said Westerberg. "I remember him saying, 'If you're going to take some cocaine, don't take it yet. Wait until we set up the mics.' Of course, me and Bob were raring to go."

It was the 'Mats first time at Nicollet Studios. Built as a vaudeville theater in 1914, it became a movie house until 1955, when legendary engineer Bruce Swedien, who'd worked with everyone from Nat King Cole to Michael Jackson, transformed it into one of Minnesota's first commercial studios. A couple of years later a group that included Amos Heilicher, head of SOMA Records, purchased it. In the 1960s, the renamed Kay-Bank Studios turned out several major hits, including Dave Dudley's "Six Days on the Road," the Trashmen's "Surfin' Bird," and the Castaways' "Liar Liar." It changed hands several times before Twin/Tone took over in late 1984.

Twin/Tone's house engineer Steve Fjelstad left Blackberry Way to run things. Fjelstad found one drawback: "It was haunted," he said. "A piano player for the vaudeville theater had died there. You could hear loud booming noises at odd hours of the night—it freaked me out a few times."

The Replacements spent parts of four days in the studio with Chilton and Fjelstad, kicking off with "Can't Hardly Wait." Westerberg had cut a ghostly template of the song—backed by Chris Mars's light snare work and cooing harmonies—in Nicollet's echo chamber/projection booth, but the band couldn't hear the headphone playback over their instruments. They recorded a rumbling rock version instead, which wasn't quite what Westerberg had envisioned.

On "Left of the Dial," Paul's romanticized ode to college radio, Chilton added his high harmony to Westerberg's voice and cemented the song's yearning coda. "He really took great care in working that up," said Jesperson.

For the first time on a session, Bob Stinson didn't have a natural place in the songs. The band was almost working around him on the acoustic "Can't Hardly Wait" and the finessed atmosphere of "Left of the Dial." "Nowhere Is My Home," however, charged along riding Stinson's coruscating riff, propelling Paul's impressionistic ode to the band's gypsy existence in vans and bars.

Chilton stayed at Jesperson's apartment at the Modesto, rolling joints, listening to records, and sleeping on the couch. It was a chance to bask in Chilton's mesmerizingly inscrutable presence. "Alex . . . he scares me in a way, but he's real," said Westerberg. "He's weird."

"Real weird," added Chris Mars.

"He was just a normal guy, like the rest of us," said Bob Stinson—a remark that may have been the best indication of how peculiar Chilton truly was.

Chilton was unusually effusive about the tracks they'd cut, playing the mixes over and over. At the end of the week, he played a solo show opening for the Replacements at the Uptown. Tommy sat in on bass, and Alex introduced him as "Miles . . . Miles Off."

Later that month, Twin/Tone released *The Shit Hits the Fans*—the official "bootleg" of the 'Mats' performance at the Bowery in Oklahoma City the previous fall. Its limited cassette-only release was intended as a farewell of sorts to Twin/Tone, since the band would be on a major label soon.

* * *

S ire Records was making headway in contract talks with George Regis, but the Replacements' attorney encouraged Columbia A&R man Steve Ralbovsky to continue pursuing the band. (If nothing else, Regis wanted a bit of leverage in his negotiations.)

Ralbovsky headed out to Minneapolis in January to court the group, but was fighting an uphill battle. For a start, Columbia was only willing to offer a one-record deal, as opposed to Sire, which was guaranteeing two (with further options for six). Pitted against the historically hip Sire, Columbia—whose rock roster was led by the likes of Loverboy and Judas Priest—simply paled in comparison. Ralbovsky returned to New York crestfallen. Soon after, Regis informed him that the 'Mats had agreed to terms with Sire.

The Replacements' contract called for an all-in budget—covering recording costs and band advance—of $125,000 for the first album, then double for the second. But the band's concerns had more to do with control than money.

"It was more about 'Don't tell me what to record, don't tell me who to do it with, don't tell me what's on the record,'" said attorney George Regis. "Warners was an artist-friendly home, so I didn't have to pull teeth to get that right." He did make a crucial amendment: in the section that read, "The artist will seriously pursue its career," he crossed out the word "seriously."

Reviewing the nearly sixty-page contract with the band in Minneapolis, Regis recalled, "Bob would poke me: 'George, am I gonna get this?' 'Am I gonna get that?' I can't tell you that he asked me about fair use in the copyright law or anything." Westerberg adds: "We were terribly naive. To us it was a foreign language, these business deals."

Still, Westerberg was sharp enough to make sure he wasn't giving away any of his publishing. "Even while subscribing to the band's ethos of nihilism," said Regis, "he had one ear cocked at things that meant something to him."

Though Westerberg was still leery of signing contracts, with Sire there was no way around it. As a hedge, Westerberg and Mars signed each other's names to the contract. "In our own fucked-up way, we thought that would be our out if we ever had to go to court," said Westerberg. "We could swear to God that we never actually signed our names on the contract." Following a long fall on the road, the band was heavily in debt, so they saw very little money up front. "After paying off our lawyers, friends, the paternity suits, the abortions . . . we should end up with about a thousand bucks a piece," cracked Westerberg.

They played a run of West Coast shows in April just as the paperwork was finalized. They dubbed it "Hawaii by Bus," though they were still using a van. Their Hollywood Palace stop doubled as a showcase for Warner Bros.'s Burbank brass. News of the signing was front and center of a *USA Today* profile on the Replacements that month. ("We're not going to be able to jump into this and immediately become a well-oiled machine," observed Westerberg.)

At the Palace the band appeared in matching baby-blue pajama tops and white chinos—and began a covers onslaught, from Hank Williams Jr.'s "All My Rowdy Friends Are Coming Over Tonight" to X's "More Fun in the New World." At one point, someone requested "We Are the World," the all-star anti-hunger ballad released a few weeks earlier. "We got our own version," said Westerberg, as the band worked up a short original. "This is called 'Let 'Em Starve.'"

The show ended in a perfect ball of confusion as Palace officials tried to hustle them off the stage in order to start the club's dance party night. The band ignored the warnings and went into a ferocious version of "Gary's Got a Boner" instead—at which point the venue brought the curtain down on the 'Mats midsong. The band kept playing until the power was shut off amid a hail of boos. Then Bob pulled Chris offstage and into the audience on top of a group of perplexed spectators and label employees.

Warner staffer Kevin Laffey filed an official interoffice report on the gig: "Dangerous band to see 'blind.' Some preparation necessary for the faint hearted, but will leave an impression nonetheless," he wrote. "Those that find them abrasive live at least will find them genuine. I don't know, however, how long the charm of their drunken devil-may-care personae will last."

The Palace performance was part welcome, part warning to their new label benefactors: Sire and Warner Bros. were officially in the Replacements business.

CHAPTER 22

In the spring of 1985, Bob Stinson met the woman who would become his most serious love and ultimately his wife. Carleen Krietler was born in Los Angeles in 1962, the middle child in a family of three. Her parents were from the Midwest—her father was a doctor, her mother a nurse. "Every time I coughed or sneezed I got poked or got a pill shoved down my throat," said Krietler. "I developed a phobia towards medical practices."

Despite her parents' zeal, she grew up sickly: "I had a mystery illness from age ten. My gall bladder was ready to explode. I was forming and passing gallstones for seven years. It kept happening, no one could figure out what was wrong."

While in high school, Krietler's parents moved back to their native Nebraska. After a couple of years in junior college, she enrolled at the University of Nebraska at Lincoln, where she declared an art major and began playing in bands. Her professionally minded father cut her off financially, so she put herself through school as a waitress.

In August 1984, Krietler's home was invaded, and she was held at knifepoint for several hours. "It was a life-changing ordeal," she said. She developed post-traumatic stress disorder. "I had a hard time sleeping, a hard time feeling secure." Looking for a fresh start, she decided to move to Minneapolis at the end the year. There, she fell in with the band Go Great Guns and started dating its guitarist, Mark "Earth" Lauer.

On Easter Sunday, she and Lauer had a fight and broke up. She was sitting in the corner of the Uptown Bar, sobbing and getting drunk, when Lauer's bandmate Tom Cook told her someone wanted to meet her. "Bob was sitting in the booth all by himself, trying to act suave," said Krietler. "He introduced himself; he said he was a cook, and that he thought I was real pretty. He noticed I'd been crying and wanted to know what was going on."

They left the bar and spent the night walking and talking around the lakes in Uptown, and Krietler began to feel safe for the first time in ages. "We ended up in his room around the time sun [was] coming up," she recalled. They soon began dating, doing "Bob things," like sneaking six-packs into movies and exploring the railroad tracks. "He knew everything there was about trains," said Krietler. "He'd call them 'choo-choos' in a kiddie voice."

They'd been hanging out together several weeks before Krietler found out that Bob was in a band on the verge of signing to a major label. He finally invited her to a Replacements show: "My boyfriend's playing and everybody likes him. He was on pins and needles waiting for me to get there. When he saw me, he stopped playing and parted the crowd for me to come down front."

Krietler introduced Bob to Ray Reigstad and John Reipas, teenage musicians who'd just moved to the Twin Cities from northern Minnesota. The three immediately hit it off and began hanging out. They found that Stinson could be incredibly childlike. Once, on the way to the Uptown, "We cut through an alley behind Lagoon and Hennepin," said Reigstad. "Bob kicked in a garage window and yelled, 'Run!'—this is a twenty-five-year-old man."

Bob and Carleen moved into an apartment at Twenty-Eighth and Dupont. Though he was reluctant to share, she began to understand his personal history, and how all that ugliness had been transmuted into an obsession with music. "He didn't hear music as songs; he heard it as parts chained together," said Krietler. "He understood and analyzed music in a microcosmic way." However, she added, "he didn't allow Replacements music in the house."

That spring Bob's band-rehearsal attendance was sporadic at best. "He felt he was in the back of the boat, when he was used to being the captain," said Krietler. Paul, Tommy, and Chris spent the period developing a new chemistry together. "The four-piece had gotten lost, because Bob was so out there. But when the three of us were rehearsing the songs," said Tommy, "there was a power behind it that was still intact." There were no screaming arguments at first, just a building tension. "They would just make little snaps at each other: 'You gonna be there or not?'" said Reigstad.

Signing to Warner Bros. seemed to make little difference. Bob insisted on keeping his job as a cook at Mama Rosa's. "The sense I got was that Bob wanted to stay playing the Entry forever," said Reigstad. "To him, being in Uptown was heaven. He didn't really aspire to anything beyond that."

* * *

Although everyone liked the Alex Chilton-produced demos, he wasn't seriously considered for the Replacements' Sire debut. To the industry, his dissolute seventies reputation lingered; even Karin Berg, a close friend and champion of Chilton, didn't support his candidacy.

The options quickly narrowed to one: Tommy Erdelyi, founder, former drummer, and longtime producer for the Ramones. He was born Tamás Erdélyi in Budapest, Hungary, in 1949, and his parents, both professional photographers, were among the only relatives to survive the Nazi purge. "Most of my family was murdered in the Holocaust," said Erdelyi. The family moved to the United States in 1956, after the Soviet invasion of Hungary, eventually settling in Forest Hills, Queens.

In the late sixties, Erdelyi interned at New York's Record Plant recording studio, assisting on Jimi Hendrix's *Band of Gypsies*. After seeing the New York Dolls, Tommy formed the glam-trash outfit Butch, then set up a showcase/ rehearsal space called Performance in Manhattan. In 1974 he formed the Ramones with his high school buddy John Cummings, a tough, working-class Irish guitarist who brought in a couple of other talented misfits from the neighborhood: Douglas "Dee Dee" Colvin and drummer-then-singer Jeffrey "Joey" Hyman.

Starting out as their manager-mentor, Erdelyi would become the band's drummer, cowriter and producer, helping shape the Ramones' epochal early albums for Sire and defining punk rock in the process. Though he continued to produce the group, he quit playing with the Ramones in 1977 amid the increasingly contentious personal atmosphere of the band.

After making three early '80s albums apart, the band reunited with Erdelyi for 1984's *Too Tough to Die*. In the interim, Erdelyi worked for another New York City studio, the Power Station. "I was scouting talent for them," said Erdelyi. "I was involved with all kinds of odds and ends, working on a solo career as well."

Erdelyi had actually sought out the Replacements on his own a few months earlier, introducing himself after December's CBGB show. "The *Village Voice* article got me excited," recalled Erdelyi. "I saw Tommy Stinson after the show, walked up to him, and told him who I was. He was kind of startled." Sire suggested Erdelyi fly to Minneapolis for a two-day session at Nicollet for a couple new Westerberg songs, "Kiss Me on the Bus" and "Little Mascara," and to break the ice generally.

At the end of March, Westerberg and Jesperson picked Erdelyi up at the airport. "We got on right away," said Erdelyi. "There was a certain chemistry there. I think I understood them." The Replacements blasted through the material a couple of times, doing their best Ramones impression. "The songs were done very quickly, very raw and punk," said Erdelyi.

Bob Stinson's imprint was heavy on "Kiss Me on the Bus," which he turned into a showcase for his breakneck riffing and power chords. He had a harder time with "Little Mascara," a still-developing vignette of domestic strife. On the take, Stinson seems uncertain, playing a couple of ill-fitting solos that threaten to fall apart.

Back in New York, Michael Hill played the two new tracks to Seymour Stein at Lenox Hill Hospital, where he was recovering from a heart procedure. He agreed that Erdelyi should produce and that the band would be well served staying in the Twin Cities, recording at Nicollet with their longtime engineer Steve Fjelstad assisting. "To preserve some sense of continuity," said Hill, "and keep the band comfortable. As much as that was ever going to be possible."

CHAPTER 23

On June 2, the eve of the first session for the Replacements' major-label debut, Tommy Erdelyi and the Replacements were hanging out at Peter Jesperson's apartment when Paul Westerberg announced to Jesperson, in front of everyone, "Hey, Pete, we don't want you in the studio while we're making this record."

Jesperson had been an integral part of each of their albums to that point. He'd just mapped out the next six weeks of his life, thinking he'd be at Nicollet working with the band again. Jesperson had no illusions: he knew that Michael Hill was handling A&R now and that Erdelyi was there to produce, but he still thought of his presence as indispensable. So did Erdelyi and Hill—they'd come to rely heavily on his counsel.

Shocked, Jesperson sputtered out: "Why?" Only Chris Mars spoke: "I might be inclined to be more spontaneous and do something different if you weren't there," he said, framing the decision in creative terms.

Looking back, both Paul and Tommy admit that the move was belated payback for Jesperson leaving them to tour-manage R.E.M. nearly two years earlier. "It still stung," said Tommy. Jesperson would inevitably have to be around the sessions to a degree: someone had to dole out per diems and drive the band and Erdelyi around. But he was not welcome during recording.

Jesperson wasn't the only one missing. Bob Stinson was little more than a spectral presence at Nicollet—he spent his days working at Mama Rosa's, which left Erdelyi somewhat bemused. "It was an absurd, avant-garde situation," said Erdelyi. "Here's a guy who's very important to the band, working as a cook while we're recording."

The two demo sessions had cemented Bob's belief that his voice wasn't being heard anymore. "I could never sit in a bar with Paul and talk," said Bob. He also felt betrayed by Mars, whom he said "acted like a session man." When he wasn't at work, Bob was with Carleen and his new pals, Ray Reigstad and John Reipas—and when not with them, he was somewhere getting drunk or high.

As Westerberg noted, there was never any direct confrontation between them. "Bob may have said, when I wasn't around, 'This is my band, what the fuck does Paul think he's doing?' I'd been in fifteen bands before the 'Mats and finally found the right thing. So I was determined to take it the way I wanted."

Tommy tacitly sided with Westerberg. "I knew we were stepping up," he said. "It felt like Paul had taken it up a level with his songs. Maybe in an unconscious way, we were starting to move on without [Bob]."

Before the Sire deal, said Westerberg, "We wouldn't have played, we would've waited for [Bob]." Now they carried on regardless. "To me, a lot of this was just ingredients to make a soufflé or bake a cake—including the problems and the troubles and the turmoil," said Erdelyi. "I was accepting it for what it was."

* * *

Paul, Tommy, and Chris spent the first week of the session cutting rhythm tracks live in the studio's expansive main room. "There was some baffling around the drums, and we separated the amps," said Erdelyi, "but the band was playing right next to each other, they had strong eye contact." By the mid-'80s, recording trends had moved away from live tracking to cutting parts individually, but the 'Mats had never been separated in the studio.

Unlike the high-velocity "Kiss Me on the Bus" recorded with Erdelyi in March, the new rhythm tracks had a more measured feel—Westerberg wanted slower tempos. "I thought, 'Okay, great,'" said Erdelyi. "I didn't want to make a full-out punk record with them; that had already been done."

Erdelyi helped Westerberg rein in the pace. "Chris always preferred playing things faster than I did," said Westerberg. "I was always going for a [Rolling Stones] 'Tumbling Dice' feel, and that was not in his canon. But having Tommy Erdelyi being a drummer producing helped. Chris would be outvoted."

Westerberg was less impressed with the sounds the producer was getting. "After about a week, Tommy [Stinson] and I sort of talked to each other on the side and said, 'Well, I guess it was Ed Stasium that we really wanted,'" said Westerberg, referring to the Ramones' engineer.

Part of the problem was the band's gear: "I think I had a blown speaker, two blown speakers, in my amp, and those were the ones that were miked for the entire record," said Westerberg. The bass on the album—or lack thereof—was also an issue. Tommy Stinson had decided to record using his somewhat thin-sounding Rickenbacker. "I would've preferred a [Fender] Precision," said Erdelyi. "It would've been more of a solid bottom."

Apart from the technical aspects, the album represented a new process for the 'Mats. "This was about the time that I came in with some songs and said, 'Here's how they go,'" said Westerberg. Structurally, several of them —"Left of the Dial," "Bastards of Young," "Little Mascara"—were modeled after his favorite early Who records, beginning with two bars of guitar. "I followed that formula for a long time, where I would start with the guitar and the band would crash in, and then there would be a part somewhere in the song where we'd break down a little bit and then really rave it up."

Westerberg wrote several of the songs "a week before the album was recorded," giving it a loose improvisational quality, including the LP opener, "Hold My Life." "Yeah, because that one doesn't have any lyrics," laughed Westerberg. "That's the perfect example: there's no damn words to it. We were going for a feeling, and the [hook] line 'Hold my life, 'cause I just might lose it' was all I needed to say."

Erdelyi liked the almost indecipherable way Westerberg delivered the verses of "Hold My Life": "To me, that added anxiety to the song." "I'll Buy" was slightly more crafted ("It had some seventh chords in it," said Westerberg), with a hint of Broadway, but again, the lyric was largely made up on the spot. Westerberg's pleurisy-ravaged rasp was in full effect here. "Paul had that kind of warm distortion in his voice that I really enjoyed," said Erdelyi.

The album's biggest joke was an inside one: "Waitress in the Sky" was a winking nod to Westerberg's sister Julie, a career flight attendant. Set to a jaunty rhythm lifted from Johnny Rivers's "Mountain of Love" and T. Rex's "Hot Love," Westerberg came on like every stewardess's loutish nightmare passenger: "Sanitation expert and a maintenance engineer / Garbage man, a janitor and you, my dear. . . . You ain't nothing but a waitress in the sky."

As Westerberg recalled, "I was playing the character of the creep who demands to be treated like a king. I'd heard all the stories from my sister about how [passengers] would yell at the flight attendants and how then they'd 'accidentally' spill something on them."

The biggest revelation of the new material was how Westerberg dropped the punk rock mask of the 'Mats' infancy to showcase his tender ballads and wistful pop songs. "Kiss Me on the Bus" was touched by both seventies AM Gold and a heavy dose of Big Star.

Like the Chilton-penned "Thirteen," it was a chronicle of adolescent longing recalled by a man a decade removed from the experience. Westerberg was still capable of conjuring teen years filled with unrequited romances. "Fine, don't say 'Hi,' then," Westerberg sneers, before playing a biting little solo—a nick of Keith Richards on "Heart of Stone"—that yields to the gentle sound of sleigh bells.

"Little Mascara" was an altogether new kind of Westerberg number: a fictionalized character study. There was no model for the distressed protagonist shedding tears and Maybelline. "It's me trying to write a short story and put it to music," said Westerberg. "I went through a phase where I read all of Tennessee Williams and Flannery O'Connor, a lot of great Southern tragic people."

In the midst of the session, as comic relief, roadie Bill Sullivan came in and tracked a rendition of the Soft Boys' post-punk protest "I Wanna Destroy You." Meanwhile, Tommy Stinson sang an original he'd written called "Havin' Fun." It was a melancholic rocker in the mold of Westerberg's songs from the period;

in fact, Paul liked it enough that he cut a version himself. Though it would have fit the album, the track was ultimately left off.

In the van the previous fall, the band had taken to passing around a communal Walkman. On one ride, Westerberg handed his headphones to Jesperson to check out a particularly moving Frank Sinatra song. Later that day, Jesperson responded with a live bootleg of Neil Young playing an old Buffalo Springfield gem.

Musically, the new "Swingin Party" drew on Sinatra's version of Rodgers and Hart's standard "Where or When" and the Springfield's "Flying on the Ground Is Wrong"—with traces as well of Frank and Nancy Sinatra's "Somethin' Stupid" and early-sixties popster Brian Hyland's "The Joker Went Wild." "If you steal from everything," noted Westerberg, "nobody can put a finger on you."

The song's oscillating rhythms and quavering guitars provided a perfect backdrop for the lyrics. "One of the reasons we used to drink so much is that it was scary going up onstage. That's one of the things 'Swingin Party' is all about," said Westerberg. "The funny thing is, people think you must have all this confidence to get up onstage."

For the first time, these kinds of songs were coming more naturally and more fully formed to Westerberg than the rockers. They allowed him to express a vulnerability he didn't reveal in his life: "I could hide behind a character and then shed myself of it. I used to mine my deepest feelings and use that for the songs and then keep my relationships light. As light as I could, anyway."

* * *

Westerberg's finest and most heartfelt anthem, "Left of the Dial," celebrated the esprit de corps of the eighties American indie rock scene and was a tribute to the tiny-watt college stations populating the far end of the FM radio band—many of whose number let the Replacements crash after shows at campuses. "That's where all our airplay came from," said Westerberg. "We ended up going to college in an odd kind of way."

"Left of the Dial" was a "hidden love song" as well—a chronicle of Westerberg's infatuation with Lynn Blakey, singer-guitarist for North Carolina's Let's Active. They'd met when the bands shared a bill at San Francisco's I-Beam in the fall of 1983. "He followed me around and bummed cigarettes off me," recalled Blakey. The following night, after a show in Berkeley, the two spent hours walking in the rain. They would exchange calls and letters as Blakey moved to Athens, Georgia, where she joined Michael Stipe's sister Lynda in the band Oh-OK. "I figured the only way I'd hear her voice was with her band on the radio . . . on a college station," said Westerberg. "And one night we were passing through a town somewhere, and she was doing an interview on the radio. I heard her voice for the first time in six months for about a minute. Then the station faded out." The moment provided the song's denouement: "If I don't see ya, in a long, long while / I'll try to find you / Left of the dial."

The version on the fifth 'Mats album was actually a holdover from the Alex Chilton January demos. Chilton received a special thank-you on the LP, but not an official production credit.

The album's other epic was a howl of youthful uncertainty and alienation called "Bastards of Young." Set against a clarion guitar riff, the lyrics were loaded with multiple layers of personal meaning. "Income tax deduction, one hell of a function" pointed to both Westerberg's fear that the 'Mats' career could end up as no more than a corporate write-off and his induced New Year's Eve birth as a tax break for his parents. (Lyrically it was one of the few numbers from this period that Westerberg truly labored over, sharpening the verses over a couple of drafts, though its often misheard chorus—"Wait on the sons of no one, bastards of young"—remained unchanged.)

The song was a residue of Westerberg's Catholic upbringing, with lyrical allusions to the gospel of Matthew, ruminations on the love of family versus the approval of strangers, and a cynical take on the slippery slope of earthly ambition:

> God, what a mess
> On the ladder of success
> When you take one step, and miss the whole first rung
> Dreams unfulfilled, graduate unskilled
> It beats picking cotton and waiting to be forgotten

Paul's younger sister, Mary, provided a spark for the lyrics. At eighteen, she'd left Minneapolis to pursue an acting career in the Big Apple. "To me, a part of that song is about my sister who felt the need . . . to be something by going somewhere else," said Westerberg.

"It is sort of the Replacements feeling the same way . . . not knowing where we fit. It's our way of reaching a hand out and saying, 'We are right along with you. We are just as confused.'"

* * *

As the band worked, Bob Stinson would occasionally turn up at Nicollet, usually with Carleen in tow. "He'd come in every couple of days, listen back to what we'd done, make a funny face, and walk out," said Westerberg.

Finally, after two and a half weeks, Bob cut his parts in a messy state. "He's coming in and he's all fucked up," recalled Tommy Stinson. "We're wasting time because he's dragging the tracks down, either 'cause he didn't like them or he was drunk. That was an uncomfortable set of circumstances altogether."

"I'd send out for drugs while we were in the studio," admitted Bob in a 1990 interview, "and then I'd lie down in front of an amp, behind a partition so they couldn't see me, and then just fall on the floor and play. That's what you hear on *Tim*."

They tried to cut "Can't Hardly Wait," but Westerberg was unhappy. The song everyone figured was the "hit" wouldn't even make the album. "The ones that didn't come easily, Paul didn't have a lot of patience for trying to figure out," said Tommy Stinson. "Our whole career, that was the way a lot of songs came and went."

More upsetting than Bob's nonparticipation was his playing—he'd try to force solos into songs they didn't fit, like "Swingin Party." "Bob's whole thing mirrored Brian Jones frighteningly," said Westerberg, who was reminded of the Rolling Stones' founding guitarist who spent his final days in the band asking Mick Jagger what he could play. "I don't know," replied Jagger coldly. "What can you play?"

To mitigate things Westerberg dashed off a couple of Bob-ready rockers. "Lay It Down Clown" was based on R.E.M. guitarist Peter Buck, who had an affinity for speed. Buck often carried a knife with which to chop his stash ("Got a big switchblade") and had famously twitchy leg moves onstage ("The only exercise you ever get is the shakes"). "That was basically what we used to say to Pete Buck," said Westerberg. "'If you got that shit, lay it down, clown.'"

The band also worked up "Dose of Thunder," a boys-on-the-prowl number ("Looking for the eight ball . . . Only want a little, you need a ton") credited to Paul, Tommy, and Chris and inspired by both Slade's stomping numbers and Minneapolis's stormy summer season. "I was always a fan of big loud thunderstorms and threatening weather and wove that in there too," said Westerberg. In fact, one day while working, a tornado siren went off, spooking the Queens-bred Erdelyi. "I didn't know about tornados," he said, "other than growing up watching *The Wizard of Oz*."

After his first attempt, Bob Stinson returned to the studio a few days later in better shape and did all of his overdubs. "He seemed very paranoid at the time, I'm not sure why," said Erdelyi, "'cause I don't know the internal politics." Erdelyi let Bob run wild and edited the best bits into the record.

But the guitarist's contributions felt like afterthoughts; Westerberg often replayed the lead parts. When people asked Bob how the new album was coming along, he would snap uncharacteristically: "How the fuck would I know? I'm not on it."

* * *

Michael Hill visited Nicollet a couple of times and was sent tapes of the Replacements' progress, but otherwise he was careful not to crowd the band at work. Still, his touch would be felt in crucial ways. Hill suggested they splice in the ending from an earlier version of "Bastards of Young," with Westerberg shouting, "Take it, it's yours," repeatedly as Mars battered away wildly. Erdelyi agreed, and the song gained its memorably climactic coda.

Hill's greatest contribution, however, was pushing for what became the album closer and emotional anchor, "Here Comes a Regular." A sad paean to the drinker's life, it had been inspired by "hanging out at the CC Club, the fact that we'd go there every day with nothing to do," said Westerberg.

It was also created under the influence of *Jacobites*, the melancholy classic by UK duo Nikki Sudden and Dave Kusworth. "I sat down and wrote 'Here Comes a Regular' with the purpose of writing a song that was sadder than . . . their record," said Westerberg. He caught what Peter Buck called the band's "Midwestern fatalism": "It was always like, 'What are you going to do?'" said Buck. "'Well, let's go to the CC and get drunk.'"

At one point Westerberg casually let Hill know about a "solo song" in his back pocket. He hadn't mentioned it to anyone else. "['Regular'] wasn't one where I immediately thought like, 'Oh great, there's a good backbeat for Chris, and Tommy's gonna dig this, and there's a part for Bob's big lead guitar,'" said Westerberg. "It sort of felt like, 'God, here's another I don't know if the band can play on.'"

His hesitation also had something to do with the subject matter—"Here Comes a Regular" wasn't cheeky and exultant, like "Treatment Bound," but was about the drudgery of drinking, the ennui of alcoholism, the dead end of a bar life where everyone knows your name.

"I was painfully self-aware of that," said Westerberg. "Maybe that's why I was hesitant about the song. We'd always said, 'We're a bunch of drunken fucking losers.' That was the joke. But to put it in serious terms wasn't something I was ready for."

Hill felt otherwise and told Jesperson about the song. Having been welcomed back to the fold for the final bits of recording, Peter put Westerberg on the spot. "He almost wished I hadn't brought it up, but the cat was out of the bag," said Jesperson. "I said, 'Well, this record could really use something like that.'" Westerberg relented. Playing and singing live, he pulled up a pair of choir baffles—fifteen-foot dividers used to separate vocalists—and hid behind them. No one in the control room could see him, and Jesperson shut the lights to near-total darkness.

Sitting on his stool, reflecting in the dim light of the barroom, the song's narrator looks back at the friends, love, and chances that have slipped away: "Opportunity knocks once, then the door slams shut." The song was filled with glimpses of the drinkers Westerberg had known, both distantly and well. "There's a little of my father in there," he said. "There's a little bit of Bob in there too." Erdelyi, Fjelstad, and Jesperson sat blinking back tears during the take. "It was breathtaking," said Jesperson.

Even Bob Stinson couldn't deny Westerberg this one. "I have to give him credit [on] 'Here Comes a Regular,'" said Bob, who tried but fell short of a fitting part for it. "I was in that mood but couldn't pull it out of me."

* * *

On July 2, after nearly a month of recording and overdubs, Erdelyi hunkered down at Nicollet to mix the album with Steve Fjelstad. It worked very differently than on past 'Mats records. "Erdelyi was much more in control of mixing—not like before where everyone had their hands on stuff," said Fjelstad.

The Replacements weren't entirely pleased when they heard his first batch of mixes. Westerberg was far more likely to grumble privately than say something directly. But Tommy Stinson didn't hesitate. "At that time I was just starting to get into a place where I was growing into a young man, where I would speak up and would have things to say about shit," said Stinson. "I remember saying, 'Can you turn the bass up? I can't really hear it.'"

Later, both Paul and Tommy would claim that the reason for the album's tinny sound was Erdelyi's failing hearing. "Tommy Erdelyi had ear problems," said Tommy Stinson. "He listened to a lot of it and, frankly, mixed a lot of it in headphones, quietly. That's the fact." Erdelyi steadfastly refuted these claims. "There's no hearing problems. As far as mixing, I would check things with headphones sometimes. That's all."

Whatever the reason, all quarters grumbled about the sound after the fact. "There was no agreement whatsoever," said Bob Stinson. "I mean, me and Paul had some real good licks and every one of them got taken out. . . . [Erdelyi] doesn't know how to mix the leads."

Westerberg was more sanguine—it wasn't the worst thing to release a rougher-sounding record than people were expecting. "Had we done something more polished, maybe it would've pissed off a bunch of people," he said. Even so, there were a few comically dogmatic critics who cried "sellout" over the album, which, frankly, was far less "produced" than *Let It Be.*

While Warner Bros. and Sire had been largely hands-off with the band so far, Michael Hill was hearing the more disturbing scuttlebutt regarding Bob's behavior. He also felt that Paul's songwriting leaps on "Swingin Party" and "Here Comes a Regular" were important developments. "I was less worried about Bob's presence in general, aesthetically," said Hill. "Though I was becoming concerned about his behavior."

The album wrapped early on July 19 with the band at Nicollet. "We finished the final mix at like two or three in the morning," said Fjelstad, who was actually set to be married the following afternoon. "Paul brought beer and stuff and said, 'Here's your stag party.'" In the drunken glow of the evening, there was finally a sense of excitement about what they'd achieved. "That album, to me, is one of my favorites," said Tommy Stinson. "It represented a lot more of what we were about, and what we could be."

At five AM, the phone rang. It was Fjelstad's bride-to-be. "Where the hell are you? Do you remember you're getting married today?"

CHAPTER 24

Though Bob Stinson had changed much about his life in 1985—developing a new social circle outside of the band, becoming increasingly attached to Carleen—during the Replacements' ascent the guitarist's mental health remained largely unaddressed. It was not until the final months of his life that he would be given a proper diagnosis of bipolar disorder.

Given his personal history and the anecdotal evidence, it's likely that Bob's specific condition was schizoaffective disorder, an illness that has features of both schizophrenia and bipolar disorder. Many studies indicate a direct link between the condition and severe childhood trauma or abuse.

The condition typically results in severe changes in mood and some of the psychotic symptoms of schizophrenia, including hallucinations, delusions, and disorganized thinking. (Sufferers are also known to shy away from most social situations.) The most severe periods can be broken up by stretches when the person shows improvement or sometimes no symptoms at all. One-third of people with schizoaffective disorder typically begin to develop the most acute symptoms in their midtwenties.

In the summer of his twenty-fifth year, Bob would begin to show the most serious signs of his condition yet.

Though they'd only been dating for a few months, that August Bob and Carleen got engaged. "We were sitting up in First Avenue in the middle of the afternoon, at the back bar," recalled Krietler. "We could see across the street, and there was a jewelry store. He looked out the window and said, 'Let's walk over there.'"

Bob got an advance from the band and bought her a little gold band. A few days later, he came home with the ring and proposed, in his own way. "He didn't get down on one knee. But we both knew what it meant. Bob did a lot of talking with his eyes," said Krietler. "I was scared to death, because I'd never been in love like that before. But I totally loved him, he totally loved me."

But Bob's relationships largely ran on fear—fear of losing, fear of betrayal. As a result, he was always suspicious, even without reason. "He never trusted the girls he dated because he didn't know how—which was kind of sad," said Bob's sister Lonnie. "It made him become obsessive."

"Carleen was not flirtatious," said Ray Reigstad. "But Bob would think, 'You're hitting on that guy,' or, 'You're letting that guy hit on you,' and it just drove him crazy. He was very, very insecure."

That summer Bob took Carleen to a house party concert above an antique store on Lyndale. As he watched her go to the kitchen for beer, he took another man's casual remark to Carleen ("The guy in line in front of me turned around and said, 'This is a really good band,' or something," she said) as a kiss. Bob suddenly become enraged and, without warning, ran and punched Carleen. "Bob saw things that weren't there and it would flip him out."

Suddenly realizing what he'd done, Bob panicked and ran out. A group of guys from the party took off after him, but he eluded them and made it back home. When Carleen returned to their apartment, she found Bob pacing the floor, beside himself. "He was so apologetic. Bob had snapped back into his body and realized what had happened. He wasn't drunk. It was a mental snap."

Still confused and scared, Carleen decided to call the police. "I told him, 'This is not good. I'm calling the cops, because this is never gonna happen again. If you wanna be with me, you have to take some steps to make sure this never happens again.'"

Stinson was arrested by the Minneapolis Police Department, booked, and held in jail overnight. He was arraigned for assault the following day. Bob's family—his mother Anita, brother Tommy, and sister Lonnie—all came to court to support him.

The presiding judge was whipping through cases on his docket and was about to release Bob with a small fine and probation. He asked if anyone had anything to add before he handed down a sentence. Tommy spoke up immediately, but quickly deferred to Carleen, who explained the situation with Bob's substance abuse, mental health issues, and the family's fears about it all.

The judge considered their pleas and ruled that, as part of his sentence, Bob would have to attend a court-ordered in-patient treatment program. He was recommended for the Chemical Dependency Therapy Program at St. Mary's Rehabilitation Center in downtown Minneapolis.

At first it seemed like a saving grace. St. Mary's was a highly regarded center with a national reputation. Bob was committed to a month-long program with limited outside contact. After the first three weeks, patients were supposed to engage in educational and therapeutic sessions with "concerned persons": relatives, lovers, friends, roommates. This relatively new form of "family therapy" was designed to bring about a more long-lasting recovery among addicts.

The rest of the band knew Bob was in rehab, but not the specifics. "I didn't know it was a court-ordered thing. I didn't know about the [incident] with Carleen," said Westerberg. "They didn't want me to know that. And I guess it was none of my business. I don't know if I would've felt differently if I'd known [going to rehab] was something that he had to do. It wasn't real clear at the time. I must've been in my own fog."

After ten years, Bob was back inside another institution. One time he fled after he wasn't able to reach Carleen for their daily call. "I didn't get to the phone in time, so he escaped the treatment center to come check on me," she said. On another occasion, Bob bailed to go buy drugs. "What I remember hearing is that he cut out of the place to go score, like, an eight-ball or some-thing," said Westerberg (though another source claimed that Krietler had actu-ally sneaked drugs to Bob at St. Mary's).

Bob's refusal to get straight was aggravating to the band, which was under-writing the costs of his rehab stay. "It just didn't click for Bob. He wasn't ready for it," said Tommy. "The one thing about alcoholics and drug addicts is that they have to know it's time and be willing to go. And he wasn't at that place."

Eventually Bob made his way through the detox portion of the program and into the counseling stage. Krietler suddenly became aware of the depths of his problems. "I had never experienced addiction like that," she said. "I got a glimpse into the horror of what it was in the family sessions. They tell you that 95 percent of people who are addicts die from their disease."

* * *

Slated to hit stores on October 14, the Replacements kicked around a few silly titles for their major-label debut—*Whistler's Mammy, Van Gogh's Ear, Let It Bleed* (to keep the theme going)—before settling on the rather obtuse *Tim*. "It started off as an inside joke. I can't even remember what the reference was to," said Tommy Stinson. "Calling a record *Tim*—after a bunch of drinks, it was funny. The next day it wasn't so funny. But if you had more drinks, it became funny again."

To up the album's class factor, Warner Bros. hired Robert Longo, a down-town New York art star of the '80s, to do the cover, in hopes of getting him to direct a video as well. Longo flew to Minneapolis to hang out with the Replace-ments for a couple of days. "I needed to know who they were before I did it," he said. "I was trying to make a voodoo object. I was trying to make it something more personal." They helped Longo research by bringing him to "that fucking bar they went to"—the CC Club—and getting him "blind drunk. And I had been sober for a long time."

One night Longo was hanging out with Westerberg, who confided his misgivings about the Warner deal. "I had the feeling [Paul] was really worried about Bob. One of the reasons he didn't want the band to have a lot of suc-cess was because he was afraid of what Bob would do, what would happen to him." Longo advised him, "Stop taking the weight of the world on your shoul-ders." Westerberg recalled "getting fairly emotional with him. I might've even sobbed, or cried; I remember embracing him and shit."

Longo conjured a strange mixed-media tableau for *Tim*'s cover. The bottom portion depicted the foreboding corridor of an Orwellian building that seemed to stand in for the music business. The top section featured a series of charcoal drawings of the band members, based on Longo's photos of them. Mars and Westerberg appear to be blinded by some overpowering light; Tommy stands with his back turned, head bowed. The three of them are dominated by the giant upside-down image of Bob Stinson's face, inspired by a shot of Martin Sheen in *Apocalypse Now*, which registers as an ominous peering force—all bathed in hot pink.

"It's very much about him," said Longo. "Bob was obviously kind of this weird presence holding the band down, holding the band back."

★ ★ ★

In the third week of October the night sky in downtown Minneapolis was lit up by a curious sight: a flashing Bat Signal.

It was Paul Westerberg's idea of a joke. To mark the release of *Tim*, the Replacements had decided to do something special. Rather than play a show in the main room at First Avenue, they elected to do a five-night stand at the 7th St Entry, one of them for an all-ages audience. "Paul's demands were that he wanted [a Batman] klieg light out for the gigs and free [soda] pop for the kids," said Jesperson. "That was Paul's idea of driving a hard bargain."

Several Warner/Sire execs flew out for the shows, squeezing into the cramped, overheated atmosphere of a more-than-oversold Entry. "All the people from New York came in," said 'Mats roadie Bill Sullivan. "We made sure they were as uncomfortable as they could be."

The Replacements had hired a new soundman, Monty Lee Wilkes of Duluth, in time for the stand. At the Entry, he watched as Seymour Stein desperately tried to escape the crush of the crowd. "I remember Seymour looking terrified," said Wilkes. "It was packed in there. I've possibly never seen anything quite so packed."

Onstage, Bob Stinson was grinning at the spectacle. He'd spent the weeks after his release from St. Mary's doing his best to maintain his sobriety. "We went through family counseling and agreed to not have alcohol in the house or around him in support of his program," said Carleen Krietler. "Things were pretty good for a while. The old Bob came back, the happy-go-lucky Bob."

That rejuvenated spirit manifested in the Replacements' Entry shows, the bulk of which were remarkable for their sheer power. On their home turf, in their favorite venue, the band burned. They started with a Tuesday afternoon all-ages set. The *Minnesota Daily* noted that the band was "playing hard (that's typical) and straight (that's not), and sounding tighter than anyone could remember."

There were still occasional flashes of the tension festering within the band. First Avenue deejay Kevin Cole recalled one less than playful exchange between Paul and Bob: "They began a song, and Paul pulled down Stinson's dress or pants or whatever he was wearing. They got into a fistfight onstage. Amps were falling down. It seemed like the fury of built-up frustration. That was just stunning to see."

Bill Sullivan decided to mark the final Entry show with a celebratory flourish. "I took a case of champagne out of the . . . cooler and brought it onstage and [passed it into] the whole crowd," said Sullivan. "There was champagne everywhere. It was fun."

Despite the bubbly, the gig was the week's worst. Playing four nights in a row made the band bored, then cranky, and they began messing with the crowd and with each other. Things reached an awkward point when the champagne bottles were passed around among the band. Bob demurred, not wanting to drink.

Standing just a few feet from the stage, Carleen Krietler recalled what happened next: "Paul took a bottle of champagne, and he pointed it right at Bob and popped the cork at Bob as he was playing his lead. The cork hit him, I think in the eye or the temple. As he's popping it, Paul said, 'Either take a drink, motherfucker, or get off my stage.' That's what I heard."

Others there that night would recall Westerberg's words—though Tommy Stinson was not among them. "If it happened onstage, I was on the other side and I didn't hear it," he said. "Or I've conveniently forgotten. Which is probably better."

After the cork hit Bob, he dove into Paul and they tussled for a moment. As Krietler would recount, Bob then reluctantly drank from the bottle. Other more dramatic versions of the story—some of which Bob himself would later relate to friends—had him chugging the whole thing with tears streaming down his face.

Carleen would famously tell her version to *SPIN* in 1993 in a harrowing and controversial portrait of Bob's post-'Mats life. The tale would be repeated in the Replacements chapter of Michael Azerrad's 2001 indie rock history *Our Band Could Be Your Life*—and told and retold in dozens of stories and articles since.

The problem is that Carleen's original *SPIN* recounting was wrong in both conceit and chronology. She drew a straight line between the champagne incident and Bob's exit from the band, depicting Westerberg's offhanded jibe as a serious ultimatum; she claimed that Bob was fired from the group just two weeks later. In fact, nearly another year—ten months of other issues, problems, and conflicts—would pass before Bob Stinson was booted from the band.

The champagne incident has bedeviled Westerberg for more than twenty years. "Yeah—he came out of his treatment, and I poured the liquor down his throat," said Westerberg, dismissing the notion and the story entirely. "Everyone who knew Bob knew he was on a bad track from early on. The man would've self-destructed had he been a cook, if he'd never picked up a guitar."

Even now, Westerberg genuinely doesn't believe the Entry incident happened, certainly not in the way it's been portrayed. He could often be careless and cutting in what he said and did, especially when he was drunk and onstage. But the suggestion that he somehow did irreparable harm to Bob devastates him. "For everything that ever happened, or would happen between us," said Westerberg, "I still fucking loved the guy."

* * *

Whatever actually transpired, Bob was affected by it, at least according to Krietler. "He came home that night in tears," she recalled. "He was doing his best to keep the band moving and that show moving forward. He felt like everyone was trying to bring him down into clown mode."

A couple weeks later, the Replacements left home, to tour in support of *Tim*. For Bob, this meant an end to his brief sobriety. On the road, he soon plunged back into booze and other substances with a recidivist's glee.

Between the drink, the drugs, and his escalating mental health issues, Carleen was noticing distressing changes in Bob during the breaks between tours. She'd begun to push him to consider whether the band was a good thing for him anymore. "I asked him, 'Is this relationship healthy, is being in the group healthy for you?' I don't know if he wanted to answer that honestly."

For Carleen the answer came later that fall when she arrived home and found Bob collapsed in the closet, with a belt wrapped around his throat. It had been a clumsy suicide attempt. The closet beam couldn't support his weight. Even if it had, the distance of the drop could never have killed him. It was like so much else with Bob: a wounded child's cry for attention.

It had been a long time since Bob had felt so desperate, probably not since his teen years. Back then, too, he'd made a couple of halfhearted suicide attempts—jumping out of second-story windows and the like.

This time he shrugged the whole thing off and returned to the road.

CHAPTER 25

Just as the Replacements released *Tim*, Warner Bros. A&R woman, Karin Berg, signed Hüsker Dü to the label.

Hüsker Dü was the beginning of a wave of "alternative" American rock bands that Warner would sign over the next few years: Faith No More (via a partnership with Slash Records), Jane's Addiction, and Throwing Muses among them. "It was an experiment," said Larry Butler, Warner's vice president of artist relations. "Let's not let this get by us. Let's not get too comfy with Fleetwood Mac and Van Halen."

But within the company there was a certain level of disconnect. Out at the label's Burbank headquarters, it was still all about ZZ Top and Eric Clapton. "This was the pre–alt rock era. So either you were a big FM pop/rock artist or you were not," said Michael Hill.

Most alternative acts were given modest expectations. Hüsker Dü was never expected to become the next Tom Petty. The Replacements' songwriting and personal charm lent itself to a push. But, said Tommy Stinson, "most of the people at Warner Bros. were like, 'What the fuck are these guys doing? And when are they gonna stop?'"

Seymour Stein should have been the person to take the Replacements into the heart of Warner Bros., but he was often as full of paranoia and pique as Westerberg. "Seymour wasn't terribly realistic as to what was radio-friendly and what wasn't," said Sire's Sandy Alouette. "If something didn't connect at radio, Seymour would often assume that Sire's getting shafted." And in 1985 radio was not ready for the Replacements. "The sad reality was that radio was looking at an image," said Butler. "It was, 'This is that alternative band, and we don't play alternative bands.'"

In a way, the Replacements were guinea pigs for the way alternative music would be developed, promoted, and sold at Warner Bros. "The alternative format was still kind of like playschool for most executives," said label executive Steven Baker. "It didn't mean big sales, it wasn't powerful enough. So Warner

Brothers, being the groovy company it was, allowed people to play around in that world." Baker soon moved from A&R into product management, essentially to look after the new cutting-edge signings at the label. He would handle those duties for the Replacements and become one of the band's key West Coast allies.

"Warner Brothers was a fabulous machine that could sell millions of Fleetwood Mac records," said Adam Sommers, vice president of Warner's creative services department. "When it came to bands like the Ramones, Richard Hell and the Voidoids, even Talking Heads, there wasn't any understanding of how to market these bands."

Warner's explosive eighties success—with ZZ Top, Prince, and Madonna all peaking at once—further marginalized smaller acts. "The WEA guys are overwhelmed," said Sommers. "They're focused on selling their hits, because they make their commissions that way. And Seymour was saying there needed to be a specialized group of people who could make sure these other records wouldn't fall between the cracks."

In 1984 Sommers put together an "alternative marketing department." It was an anomaly within the company—a young, female-dominated division that started with Mary Hyde and Cathy Lincoln and later included Jo Lenardi and Julie Panebianco. Both Lenardi and Panebianco had been friends with the 'Mats for years, and all knew the burgeoning indie/alternative world unlike anyone else at Warner Bros.

The alt-marketing department ran wild contests and promotions, hosted listening parties, interfaced with independent retailers, and advanced tours. They worked grassroots retail and avoided Warner groupthink. "Eighty percent of the people that worked at the label just didn't get what we were doing at all," said Jo Lenardi. "They couldn't understand it, didn't think it mattered. They were dinosaurs in our eyes."

These alt-marketing "girls" were the Replacements' closest conduits to the label for the first couple of years. "Even then, we still found ways to make a mess," said Tommy Stinson. As much as he and Paul were beginning to see the promise of a career, they seemed incapable of accepting the compromises of one. "We were not smart enough to know how to play that game, or didn't want to play the game because we thought it was beneath us," said Tommy.

Sommers, like many at the label, saw the band's rebel stance as naive, if not hypocritical: "Once you sign with Warner Brothers, you're in the game. You're not indie renegades." But that conflict was acute within the Replacements and played out in their conduct and the way they performed. "Anybody who saw them on a good night drank the Kool-Aid," said Warner's sales vice president Charlie Springer. "I think maybe the problem was that some people rarely saw them on a good night. There were regional sales people who *never* saw them on a good night."

* * *

After nearly three years touring the country, the Replacements' reputation guaranteed some kind of chaos wherever they went. "Sometimes we would come into a venue and people would be terrified off the bat," said soundman Monty Lee Wilkes. "It depended on what had happened the last time."

In addition to Peter Jesperson and Bill Sullivan, the band's traveling retinue now included Wilkes and their old friend Casey Macpherson. Macpherson had just come from tour-managing the Suburbs and would soon leave to do the same job for Hüsker Dü. With the 'Mats, he served as monitor man—despite the fact that he had no experience or qualifications for the job. Each show, like a running comedy, Westerberg would become frustrated with the monitor mix and fire Macpherson from the stage. "Then at the end of the night he'd come very sheepishly, apologize, and rehire me," said Macpherson.

The *Tim* tour provided more and better targets for mischief. "There were bigger PAs and more expensive microphones to break, and nicer wedges to pour drinks into," said Wilkes, laughing.

At the board, Wilkes began to understand that, contrary to popular belief, the band's alcohol intake wasn't always the reason for their more unhinged performances. "I've seen them so drunk they could hardly walk and go out and just amaze. And I've seen them where everything looked like it was going pretty good and, God knows what, but something happened between the dressing room and the stage, and it turned."

Heading into Oklahoma, Texas, and Tennessee, there would be plenty of those turns. Something about the South brought it out in the band; their history in the region would be checkered with riotous gigs, audience battles and arrests. "When certain bands came down south to play, there was a radical-ness to the shows in the region," said Wayne Coyne of Oklahoma's Flaming Lips. "The Replacements shows in the area were always like that too."

In Nashville the 'Mats shared a bill at Rooster's with their buddies Agitpop. "Tommy wore a green plastic cowboy hat and made some snide comments that really pissed the crowd off," recalled Agitpop's John DeVries. The next night the two bands played together at the Antenna Club in Memphis. "That show was kind of a downer. There wasn't a lot of people there," said DeVries.

"We were gonna meet at Graceland the next morning to visit Elvis. Everybody was hungover." Apparently Westerberg had no desire to linger at the King's backyard grave. "I think him and Tommy found a bar across the street that was selling Budweisers at ten-thirty in the morning, while the rest of us went," said DeVries.

In Norman, Oklahoma, the band had been booked to play the Subterranean, run by Wayne Coyne's girlfriend, out in the middle of a dry county. She brought in booze for the band, with a warning to keep the alcohol confined to the dressing room.

Just before showtime, Tommy was swinging on a back door leading to the alley, when a cop car happened by and spotted him. "They made some comment, and he lipped off to them, and they got out and said, 'Young man, come over here,'" recalled Jesperson.

"So they pull me out and go, 'Can you walk a straight line?'" recalled Tommy. "Fuck, probably not. I'm getting ready to go onstage here and I'm having a drink. I guess I was underage down there. They threw me in the fucking clink." Stinson was charged with public intoxication.

Now missing their bass player, the band was forced to take the stage as a trio. "Everybody was worried about Tommy, but the show must go on," said Wilkes. Someone whispered to Westerberg that Wilkes could play bass. "Now, I can barely bang out a crappy punk rock song," said Wilkes. "But they start calling me from the stage."

Jesperson came over to the sound booth and told him to head up.

"I'm not doing it," insisted a mortified Wilkes.

Peter sighed wearily: "Monty, you've got nothing to do with this," he said. "You're going up there, and if you don't, they'll leave the stage and they'll come back here and they will physically drag you up there. So save yourself and everybody a lot of trouble and just go do it."

Bill Sullivan was throwing punters back into the pit, all of them angling to get up and play bass, as Wilkes walked up and strapped on Tommy's Rickenbacker. The band started banging out the easiest thing it could think of: Cream's "Sunshine of Your Love." In the spirit of the moment, Macpherson got up to sing. But after a few half-baked covers the crowd grew restless.

Paul surveyed the scene and leaned over to Wilkes. "They're getting ugly. We need to give them what they want," said Westerberg, who called for "I Will Dare."

"My blood ran cold," said Wilkes. "I didn't have the slightest idea how to play that."

Up to that point, Bob had been helping Wilkes, facing him and playing well-defined power chords so he could follow along. When Westerberg started up "I Will Dare," Bob looked at Wilkes, laughed, and turned away. He was on his own.

"I don't think we made it to the chorus before it fell apart and people started pelting us with all kinds of shit," said Wilkes. "I saw Chris split first. Then I said, 'I'm out.' That was the end. There was nothing else we could do." The band actually came back and soldiered on, with Westerberg grabbing the bass and letting a few audience members play before the whole enterprise finally collapsed.

They got Tommy out of jail around three in the morning. Wayne Coyne drove Jesperson down to the police station in his Volkswagen Bug. By this point, Peter had knocked back quite a few himself, and he was acting a little cocky toward the night sergeant as he arranged Tommy's release. The cop on the desk sniffed at him: "Hey, pal, I can smell liquor on your breath—you wanna join your little buddy in there?"

Jesperson quieted down, paid the $50 fine, and sprung Tommy. He made sure to save the receipt for tax purposes.

In the world of the Replacements, bail had become another business expense.

* * *

The rising action of the tour reached its climax a few nights later in Houston, where the 'Mats played the Lawndale Art Annex.

It was an unusual venue for the band—a couple of miles from the University of Houston campus, it was basically an old warehouse the school used for more highbrow art events. The gig's promoter, Tom Bunch, had been booking hardcore and punk shows in the city for several years, working with Black Flag and the Dead Kennedys (he would go on to manage the Butthole Surfers) without any problems.

The Replacements had sold some 600 tickets in advance to a mix of punk scenesters and college kids. The latter demographic was making up a more noticeable chunk of the band's audience. "Hey, Greeks! If you like Springsteen, R.E.M. or U2, you'll love the Replacements!" ran a show ad in one student newspaper that autumn.

There was also an increasingly large contingent of rubberneckers. "The audience no longer exclusively consisted of people who 'got it,'" said Wilkes. "I could see it looking around every night. There were the people that had come solely to see the car crash. You'd overhear them in the can: 'I hope they're not too drunk tonight.' 'Oh man, that's the *only* way to see them.' These were the kind of people who would've tried to beat up the band at a party two years earlier."

The Lawndale Annex gig also reunited the Replacements with Alex Chilton, who'd come up from New Orleans to play a couple of shows with the band. Perhaps Chilton's presence played a part—Westerberg was always looking to impress him—but that night Paul almost singlehandedly started a riot. "For years I claimed Alex had spiked my drink backstage and put some sort of hallucinogen in it," said Westerberg, "because my behavior was so off the map."

From the start, Jesperson sensed it was going to be one of *those* shows. Early on the *Tim* tour, he'd tried harder to dole out the booze in increments, and not too far in advance. "I'd have to lie to them all the time about that: 'We can only get a twelve-pack now.' I was trying to ration it out as best I could."

In Houston, Chilton asked Jesperson for a lift back to his hotel and to wait while he got ready, then took his time shaving and getting dressed. Meanwhile, the band got its hands on the rest of the liquor: "A bottle of whiskey, a bottle of vodka, two cases of Bud, one of Heineken, and one bottle of red wine," recalled Bunch. When he went into check on them a little later, "every bottle was empty. Completely bone dry. I thought, *This is going to be interesting*." When

Jesperson finally returned, he walked into the dressing room to find the band had "actually embedded bottles of Heineken into the drywall. Not only was the liquor gone, but I was required to get them more."

Outside, fans did double takes: Paul and Tommy and a couple of local women "were sitting out front of the venue, in the gravel parking lot, in a kiddie pool, with no water in it, completely fucking drunk," said Bunch. Meanwhile, Chilton's set was being marred by some hecklers. "So Paul and Tommy dragged the kiddie pool out into the middle of the people who were being assholes, just to mess with them," recalled Wilkes.

The 'Mats began. As a local alt-weekly reported: "To say 'degenerate' implies that the Replacements started out in control." Drinking Jack Daniels from the bottle, Paul stumbled back into the amps, and then fell into Chris Mars's drum kit. "I was legless when we went on and couldn't play at all," said Westerberg. "We finally tried 'Johnny B. Goode,' thinking that might come easy, but I couldn't finish a song."

After about thirty minutes of this ineptitude, Westerberg knew what had to be done: "It became plain that we could suck or we could incite a riot and get this thing over with," he said. The audience's ire was already obvious, as they booed and shouted at Westerberg. "People were fucking pissed off that they'd paid eight bucks to see this," said Bunch. "Then they started throwing stuff at him." The band promptly picked up the half-full beer cans aimed their way and drank the remains.

Westerberg got on the mic and offered the audience their money back. He grabbed his wallet, fished out a few dollar bills and threw them into the crowd. At that point, a line of disgruntled patrons formed at the box office looking for their refunds—"whereupon the doorman spirited the cash box to safety," as the *Houston Chronicle* noted.

Once things began to devolve, much of the crowd—which included the Velvet Underground's Sterling Morrison, whom Bunch had invited to the show—fled in fear. "Half the audience bolted when it got weird, 'cause they thought it was going to get violent," said Bunch. "The other half stayed to the bitter end to see the debacle."

The older couple who ran the Annex quickly called campus police. It took them only a few minutes to arrive, and they were followed closely by a group of City of Houston police officers. By then, however, things had gotten even uglier:

"You *suuuuck!*"

"Go back to Minneapolis, you Yankee pieces of shit!"

At that, Westerberg went into his wrestling heel routine, laying it on thick.

"You guys are a buncha fucking ignorant rednecks. If you come up north to Minneapolis, this is what we call *music*," he said mockingly. "This is actually considered quality music north of the Mason-Dixon Line. You fuckers wouldn't know good music if it hit you in the head."

"That really, really pissed the audience off," said Bunch. "Calling Texans a bunch of ignorant hicks? Those were fighting words."

Sure enough, a group of shit-kickers down front lunged at Westerberg's legs, trying to pull him down. "I remember getting a cowboy boot right up the spine, right up the ass," said Westerberg. "A guy literally kicked my ass back up on the stage."

When the cops showed up, they immediately ordered Wilkes to shut off the PA. "But they were the kind of band that was so loud you could turn the PA off and not notice any difference," Wilkes said.

Attempting to bring it to a close, the police were forced to go onstage and physically take the instruments from the band. Jesperson watched as one of Houston's finest snatched Westerberg's guitar from around his neck. "I'd seen a lot of stuff with the Replacements, but I'd never seen that happen," he said.

Westerberg continued jawing and tussling with the crowd. It appeared he was about to be pulled into a sea of angry Texans when the police intervened. "Five cops tried to keep thirty or forty people from beating up the band," said Bunch. "The cops were throwing people off the stage, throwing them by their arms and hair and trying to keep them from pummeling those guys."

The 'Mats made a hasty exit stage left; Westerberg figured they'd arrest him for inciting the whole mess. "I do remember," he said, "someone shoving me under the table in the dressing room behind a tablecloth, hiding me from the police."

The band managed to escape without being locked up. Bunch, meanwhile, was billed several thousand dollars for the police services and the venue damages to the Annex. "They never did another musical event there," he said.

After the show, Westerberg, still seriously wasted, realized he needed to call his girlfriend Lori Bizer back home to check in. Jesperson stopped at a pay phone and marveled as Paul chatted casually with Bizer.

"I was close enough to overhear, and he was talking totally normal. 'Hi, honey, how you doing?' He was acting as if nothing had happened."

"Paul's thing was performance art," said Agitpop's John DeVries. "I was never once under the impression that it was some dumb guy who was drunk, stumbling through all this. He knew exactly what was up, always."

CHAPTER 26

S ince 1980, Peter Jesperson had been the 'Mats' band manager, road manager, driver, babysitter, and best friend. But moving to Sire/Warner Bros. meant he was now expected to interface with label executives, schmooze with industry players, and plan business moves. Jesperson was a music lover, not a mogul in training, and the job had outgrown his particular skill set.

No one was more aware of it than Jesperson himself, especially after a fall strategy session at Warner Bros. in New York with lawyer George Regis. "I remember thinking, *This is not my world*," said Jesperson, who wanted to bring in outside management to handle the band's industry concerns. "I'd remain their personal manager," he said.

Despite their acclaim, the Replacements were a tough sell. "It was the thought that these people are genuinely out of control," said Jesperson. When they tried to engage Ramones and Talking Heads manager Gary Kurfirst, "he did not want the trouble," said Regis.

Veteran Mike Lembo of Mike's Artist Management, whose roster included the Church and NRBQ, had a typically troubling encounter when he met the band in Minneapolis. "They were all so drunk they could barely sit and have a conversation," recalled Lembo. "I was really angry. I knew they had a reputation as drunks, but this was about business. If this is something they're doing for fun, I'm not amused. And if this is how they're going to treat their career, I'm not amused either."

* * *

T here was only one serious candidate: High Noon Management, the fledgling New York City–based company founded by Russ Rieger, then twenty-six, and Gary Hobbib, then thirty-one. They were an almost comic contrast in style, personality, and manner.

Born on Long Island, the feisty Rieger was the youngest of three children in an upwardly mobile, middle-class Jewish family. He was a student at Levittown's Island Trees High School in 1975 when the campus became a First Amendment battleground: The local board of education had removed a number of books from the school's library in the middle of night. Rieger was one of five students who stepped forward to sue. The Supreme Court decided 5–4 in favor of the students—a landmark censorship ruling. Rieger saw the power in making a grand gesture, and it would guide his thinking going forward. He attended the University of Albany, where he majored in political science and, more decisively, became besotted with Bruce Springsteen and the Clash. After working as the music director of the college radio station and promoting campus concerts, he decided to pursue a music-biz career.

The oldest of four kids in a Lebanese-Italian family, Gary Hobbib grew up lower-middle-class in Plainfield, New Jersey, where his father worked as a quality control manager at a factory. Gary attended college at the University of New Hampshire, where in the early seventies he booked shows on campus. "I did Aerosmith and they drew forty-five hundred people to the field house; the band trashed the dressing room," Hobbib recalled.

Quiet, brainy, and methodical, Hobbib earned bachelor's degrees in both math and psychology. "Had I known I was going to manage the Replacements, I would've gone for the PhD in psych," he said. He moved to Boston and became a booking agent there, meeting Rieger in 1981. They got to know each other the following year working for Side One, a New York–based music marketing and management company.

Hobbib was tanned, with jet-black hair, a monochrome wardrobe, and a muted manner. Rieger was fair-skinned with flowing blond hair and lots of chutzpah. He was also a kind of rock-and-roll chameleon. "Whoever was popular, Russ would come in and dress that way," said Hobbib. "One day he'd come in dressed like Prince, the next day he'd come in dressed like Springsteen."

Improbably, they became fast friends. "I was very intense, talked very fast," said Rieger. "Gary was much more laid-back, very thoughtful. It was a yin-yang thing." Added Hobbib, "Russ had a mouth, I didn't. In this industry, if you have a mouth, nobody trusts you if that's all you have. But if you don't have a mouth, you don't get anything done."

In early 1984, they launched High Noon out of Hobbib's apartment with two acts: South African band Juluka, on Warner Bros., and the Wanted, rockers from Allentown, Pennsylvania. Then they landed the Del Fuegos just as that group was transitioning from Slash to Warner Bros. proper.

High Noon didn't become aware of the Replacements until late 1984. "I thought, 'How the fuck is this band on the cover of the [*Village*] *Voice?*'" recalled Hobbib. "I saw they'd come up from the bottom, from the street. That was appealing to me." At Michael Hill's office the following summer, the managers heard an advance of the *Tim* closer "Here Comes a Regular." "It gave me chills," said Rieger. "Who are these guys and how can we work with them?" he demanded.

It helped, said Sire's Sandy Alouette, that "Seymour [Stein] had a good relationship with them. They knew how to work Seymour and work the building." Not that Warner Bros. expected a hit out of the box. "Warner Brothers was like a bunch of music-loving entrepreneurs working in their own little fiefdoms," said Hobbib. "It was a laid-back kind of company."

* * *

Rieger and Hobbib headed out to Minneapolis in October for their first band meeting. Predictably, the 'Mats auditioned High Noon with a marathon twelve-hour bar hop.

"We got there at two in the afternoon, met them at the CC Club, and basically went to every bar in Minneapolis until three or four in the morning," recalled Rieger. He and Hobbib had been warned about what they might face, and so they'd fortified themselves. "Gary and I both drank a lot of milk beforehand to make sure we were going to be okay."

Conversation was strained at first, but after a few rounds had been ordered, everyone loosened up. "Paul and Tommy were the only ones you could talk to. Chris didn't really talk that much. And Bob was just out there," said Rieger. "But they were fun. They had a lot of life in them, and it was genuine."

At one point they all piled into a rental car to hit the next bar. Hobbib was behind the wheel when Tommy Stinson suddenly leapt from the backseat and covered his eyes. "If you can guess who this is, you get us as clients," said Stinson, as the car swerved wildly across Hennepin Avenue. "Then I think one of them opened the door and was trying to throw the other one out," recalled Hobbib. "It was antics, all antics."

At the CC Club, Westerberg punched up "If Only You Were Lonely" on the jukebox. "He was trying to trick me, saying, 'Forget us—you should manage *this* band,'" said Rieger. "He was trying to see if I knew the song or not, which I don't think I did."

Westerberg laid out his ideal manager—a cracked vision gleaned from years of mythmaking rock bios and magazine stories. Paul wanted a combination of Andy Warhol and Malcolm McLaren—someone both artistic patron and merchant of chaos. "I remember him yelling over the music, telling me he wanted to be represented by a shoe magnate," said Rieger, "who would just give them money to do whatever they wanted. Probably everything we ever should have known about the Replacements we learned that night."

Already, Rieger was wary of the culture of "enabling" he saw around the band. "The fans, the press, some of the people at the label even, reveled in their drinking and their shows being like a car crash," he said. "People lived vicariously through them and egged them on."

Initially, Rieger and Hobbib had little inkling of the growing issues surrounding Bob Stinson or his fractured relationship with the rest of the band. Nor did High Noon grasp the depths of Westerberg's innate aversion to authority. "We knew they were dysfunctional and big drinkers, but not enough to give us second thoughts," said Rieger.

For their part, Rieger and Hobbib were smart, fun, and said all the right things. The 'Mats were even willing to overlook the fact that Hobbib's first name was the dreaded "Gary." Wisely, High Noon also voiced support for Jesperson's continued involvement. "We wanted Peter. We wanted that stability," said Rieger.

While his commission would drop from 15 to 10 percent, Jesperson's redefined role as part of the 'Mats management would never really be made clear. High Noon saw him as a road manager as well as a kind of band buffer. "We were never thinking of co-managing," said Rieger. "We thought of him as part of the old team in a lot of ways."

In late November, Jesperson called to tell High Noon they'd passed the audition. Rieger could barely control his excitement, screaming into the phone and across the room at Hobbib: *"Gary, we got the fucking Replacements!"* as hoots of excitement broke out. It was the last time they would ever feel such unadulterated joy about the band again.

CHAPTER 27

They weren't going to light the tree for hours, but Rockefeller Center was already jammed. It was the morning of December 9, 1985, and the whole area around New York City's Forty-Ninth Street was teeming with tourists anticipating the annual holiday ritual.

Making his way through a crowd of Christmas carolers and promenaders, Lorne Michaels hurried past the pageantry and into the lobby of NBC Studios without looking up. The creator and producer of *Saturday Night Live*, Michaels had no time for holiday cheer; he was too busy worrying about saving his beloved show.

Having helped shift the comedic and cultural zeitgeist with his original group of "Not Ready for Prime Time Players," Michaels left *SNL* following its first glorious five-year run in 1980. The program had continued—first, briefly and near-disastrously, under producer Jean Doumanian, then with the steadier guidance of network pro Dick Ebersol. Though Ebersol's *SNL* had showcased a stable of stars like Eddie Murphy and Billy Crystal, by 1985 its ratings were nearly half of Michaels's final season.

Michaels's own golden boy status had been severely damaged the previous year when his prime-time NBC program, *The New Show*, was canceled midseason. "I had won big and now I was losing," recalled Michaels. With NBC's president, Brandon Tartikoff, threatening to cancel *Saturday Night Live*, Michaels felt duty-bound to return and try to revive its fortunes.

The show's eleventh season team included a mix of first-generation *SNL* writers and producers, hot young actors (Anthony Michael Hall, Robert Downey Jr.), veteran performers (Academy Award nominee Randy Quaid), and rising stand-ups (Dennis Miller, Damon Wayans). The opener had featured Sire Records supernova Madonna as host and musical guest. The premiere was a ratings winner, but a critical loser: "This was comedy the way Hiroshima was comedy," jibed a reviewer. By December, ratings were plummeting again, and NBC was hinting at canceling the show once and for all. "Everyone was on pins and needles, every week," said *Saturday Night Live* music booker Michele Galfas.

On *The New Show*, Galfas had booked adventurous acts like ex–New York Doll David Johansen, performance artist Laurie Anderson, and post-punks the Pretenders. That continued on *SNL*, where she brought in Dream Academy and the Cult (on one episode), Simple Minds, Queen Ida & the Bon Temps Zydeco Band, Sade, Sheila E., and Mr. Mister.

Michaels, by his own admission, was not up on things musically. "I had to ask who Mr. Mister was," Michaels recalled. "It turns out they have this number-one song." The Replacements had something just as valuable: the endorsement of one of Michaels's close friends, Warner Bros. chairman Mo Ostin.

★ ★ ★

I n mid-December, the Replacements wrapped up a month-long tour with two triumphant nights at Hollywood's Roxy. The year-end accolades for *Tim* were starting to pour in: it would place second in the *Village Voice*'s "Pazz and Jop" poll, just behind Sire labelmates Talking Heads. But the praise had done little for the album's commercial prospects: *Tim* had stalled at a modest 30,000 copies after three months, failing to crack the *Billboard* top 200. The label needed something to kick-start sales.

In California, Westerberg and Jesperson were summoned to Burbank to meet with Warner creative director Jeff Ayeroff. The company had been pushing the 'Mats on the video issue. Ayeroff wanted to change their hard-line stance against making a video. Silver-haired and hulking, Ayeroff exuded a sort of Zen-hipster arrogance. He'd already overseen video campaigns for the Police's *Synchronicity* and Madonna's *Like a Virgin*.

"I don't wanna hear about the fact that you don't want to make a video," Ayeroff said. "I want to talk about the video that you *will* eventually make."

"Tell you what," said Westerberg, without missing a beat, "you get us on *Hee-Haw* and I'll lip-synch to 'Waitress in the Sky.'"

At this, Jesperson burst out laughing. Ayeroff wasn't amused. Nevertheless, a serious conversation began about Warner Bros. getting the band on television. "The compromise was that we'd do live TV if they could swing it—thinking that they couldn't," said Westerberg. "Me and my big mouth."

First, Ayeroff sent a letter to Galfas touting the group. Then the 'Mats' product manager, Steven Baker, and Warner A&R head Lenny Waronker pressed Mo Ostin to put in a call to Lorne Michaels. "Mo was the one who got them on *Saturday Night Live*, because he had such a strong relationship with Lorne," said Waronker. "There was an understanding how important they could be for the company."

Based on Warner Bros.'s faith, Galfas put the 'Mats on a shortlist of acts for the show—without having seen the band play live. "That," said Galfas, "may have been a mistake."

* * *

Early in 1986, after a couple of years apart, Tommy Stinson suddenly rekindled his romance with former girlfriend Daune Earle. Awkwardly, he was still dating Mary Beth Gordon, and Earle was living with Pete Conway, bassist of the hardcore band Rifle Sport. "Tommy came up to me at First Avenue," said Earle. "It was New Year's Eve, and my boyfriend was playing. Tommy said: 'I'm still in love with you.' I told him, 'You're drunk, go away.'" Early the next morning Earle's phone rang. "I'm not drunk now," Stinson told her.

This only added to Tommy's local rep as a lothario. "He was quite hated around town, because he was such a cocky kid," said Earle. "But I saw something in Tommy that a lot of people didn't see. At his core, I knew he was a really good person." The couple were soon living together, but the day Earle moved into his apartment, Tommy hit the road. "It seemed like the band was just gone all the time," she said.

Bob Stinson's domestic situation was no less complicated. Following his assault arrest, his rehab stint, and the halfhearted suicide attempt, he'd toned down his drinking and drugging to appease his fiancée. But after a fall and winter on the road, he'd fully returned to his old habits.

"He'd get up at the crack of dawn and I'd hear him go into the kitchen and pop a can of beer," said Carleen Krietler. "A beer for breakfast, a six-pack by lunch, a case by midnight, and he'd get up the next day and do it again, and again. He couldn't go fishing, go to the movies, couldn't go anywhere, unless we picked up a six-pack on the way. I thought it was just beer—but I later found he was hiding whiskey in his sock drawer."

As Bob's drinking escalated, his involvement with the band became even more strained. The Replacements had effectively recorded *Tim* as a trio. Now Tommy, Paul, and Chris were rehearsing without Bob on a regular basis.

The Replacements, Bob in tow, did return to the stage on January 11 at Chicago's Cabaret Metro. The one-off gig was a tune-up for an East Coast tour scheduled to commence later in the month.

When the group arrived back home from Chicago, they got word that a last-minute slot had opened up on *Saturday Night Live*. The Pointer Sisters, scheduled for that week's show, had to cancel.

The band was going to make their national television debut, fittingly, as replacements.

* * *

In early January, NBC chairman Grant Tinker was asked for his assessment of *Saturday Night Live*. "It's a hard job to keep a show like that fresh and alive. . . . I'd like to give it the benefit of the doubt," said Tinker ominously, "for a little while."

Harry Dean Stanton would host the January 18 edition of *SNL*. One of the more offbeat choices in the program's history, the fifty-nine-year-old character actor was enjoying a late-career surge thanks to hip directors like Wim Wenders and John Hughes. The episode would also feature controversial stand-up comic Sam Kinison as a special guest, as well as the Replacements—a potential powder keg of a lineup.

The 'Mats arrived in New York on Wednesday and did a run-through at NBC's studio 8H Thursday morning. It was clear from the outset that this was not the "wild and crazy" *SNL* of the seventies. "They'd stocked the dressing room with breakfast stuff—fruits and juices," recalled Peter Jesperson. "Bob wanted beer. And the people at *SNL* were really, really appalled by this. I had to go down and find a store in Rockefeller Plaza and get a six-pack."

"They didn't like us too much down there," Bob Stinson would recall. "They pretty much ignored us, thinking we would probably crumble—when, in fact, it was quite the opposite."

The show's uncertain status was palpable even to outsiders. "We could feel that the show wasn't funny and wasn't popular at the time," said Jesperson. As it turned out, a number of NBC affiliates had already committed to preempting *Saturday Night Live* that week in order to air a syndicated cerebral palsy telethon. (The episode was shown on late-night tape delay in numerous markets, including the band's hometown of Minneapolis.)

Newly minted Replacements co-manager Russ Rieger turned up to the rehearsal with his poodle coif, leather pants, and snakeskin boots. "Okay, guys, you know what camera blocking is?" he asked the band. "That's where you've gotta stand in the spot they tell you." Jesperson winced. "That was the worst kind of thing you could say to the Replacements," he said. "It was the first time I started to wonder if picking [High Noon] was such a good idea."

Oddly, the 'Mats toyed with performing "Answering Machine" on the show. Warner Bros. was understandably miffed that the group would use the *SNL* spot they'd lobbied for to play a Twin/Tone number. Finally, the band settled on "Bastards of Young" and *Tim*'s putative single, "Kiss Me on the Bus."

During rehearsal, Westerberg recalled *SNL*'s soundman working on a crossword puzzle. He'd occasionally glance at the decibel meter, then yell at the band to turn it down. "They told us the scream at the beginning of 'Bastards of Young' wouldn't come across on TV," said Paul.

The 'Mats' lawyers and label benefactors showed up Saturday to wish them luck. The band members' significant others had flown out for the occasion; even Twin/Tone's Paul Stark made the trip. Coincidentally, Stark had attended prep school in Minnesota with *SNL* writer-producers Tom Davis and Al Franken, and he spent time catching up with them on set.

By that evening the band's reputation as a handful was clear to everyone on the show's staff. None of the Replacements realized they'd be trapped on the eighteenth-floor set from sound check till showtime. When Warner Bros. publicist Mary Melia arrived to look in on them, Tommy, Paul, and Chris were on a dressing room couch, watching uncomfortably as Bob paced like a caged animal. "He was out of his mind to leave," said Melia. "Bob was scary."

To soothe the band's nerves, soundman Monty Lee Wilkes smuggled some alcohol into the studio in a little road case. As the 'Mats began to dip in, the show's host said hello. When "Harry Dean stuck his head in, we asked him to have a snort," recalled Westerberg. "He slammed the door behind him and proceeded to gulp."

Word began to circulate that the host was getting drunk mere hours before the live show. Panic ensued until a production assistant dragged Stanton out of the band's dressing room.

Sufficiently lubricated, the 'Mats' dress rehearsal set went off smoothly. Bob had wowed everyone by donning a striped lady's unitard that Julie Panebianco and Lori Bizer had picked up for him the day before. The only hitch occurred during "Bastards of Young"—Bob was late coming in on the solo. Westerberg would make sure he didn't miss his cue during the live broadcast.

*　*　*

Episode seven of *SNL*'s new season was yet another dog: weak commercial spoofs, a one-joke send-up of *Miami Vice* set in Cleveland, a hackneyed Western gunfighter skit. Stanton was still wearing his frontier finery when he introduced the band just after midnight.

As the group blasted the opening notes of "Bastards," the cameras practically recoiled at the volume. Following the dress rehearsal, the 'Mats had secretly turned up their amps; it took a few seconds for the engineers to turn the sound down.

Mars, looking pale and antic in denim overalls, bared his teeth as he played; Tommy bounced around vigorously, ignoring any notion of camera blocking, and was mostly out of frame; Bob hunkered down to wrestle manfully with his guitar, a comic counterpoint to his flowing, feminine outfit.

Westerberg performed in a state of drunken insouciance. Several times during the song he walked away from the mic in the middle of a verse and casually strolled around the stage as if they were jamming in Ma Stinson's basement and not to a television audience of eight million. "We just pretended we weren't on camera," he recalled.

As the solo break approached, Westerberg shouted toward Bob, just off-mic: "Come on, fucker." The epithet, delivered as he turned his head, slipped past the censors. "It wasn't really something I planned," he said. "It was more me saying to Bob, 'Let's give it to 'em with everything we got.'"

Quickly, however, the show's producers realized that an obscenity had gone out live on the air. Producer Al Franken, standing in front of the band and gripping a clipboard, began to frown. Westerberg gave him an exaggerated vaudeville wink.

After Mars bashed out the climactic machine-gun coda, "Bastards" careened to a halt. Tommy and Paul bowed comically. Bob followed with a backward somersault, revealing a tear in the seat of his outfit—his bare ass flashed briefly on-screen. The crowd, packed with 'Mats partisans, cheered wildly. Most people in the studio audience had missed Westerberg's obscenity. But Lorne Michaels hadn't.

SNL had a troubled history with the F-word. In 1981 cast member Charles Rocket had said it during a *Dallas* spoof; the slip led to Rocket's firing and loads of bad press for the program. "The whole deal with the network, in my mind, is that we operate on a level of trust," said Michaels. "We have live air." The producer was already on edge about *SNL*'s precarious position with NBC. Any kind of controversy, especially now, could be a fatal blow to the show.

Jubilation followed the 'Mats to the dressing room. Everyone agreed they'd delivered a momentous performance. Rieger and Hobbib were busy shaking hands and slapping backs when there was a knock at the door. "An assistant told me, 'Lorne Michaels wants to see you in the hall,'" said Rieger. "I'm thinking he wants to congratulate us."

Instead, Michaels stormed up and began to berate Rieger loudly: "How dare you do this? Do you know what you just did to this show? Your band will never perform on television again!"

Rieger was genuinely perplexed as to the cause of Michaels's anger. "Finally, I figured out that Paul had said 'fuck' on the air," said Rieger. "I immediately started apologizing. Michaels wouldn't hear of it. Since we were a new band and young, and a favor for Warner Bros., he could unleash. And he did." Mid-tirade, Michaels caught a glimpse of the dressing room—the band had "redecorated" it. "He saw that and reamed them a new asshole," said Hobbib. "It was horrible."

Michaels's fit cast a pall over the band, but there was still another song to do. After Kinison's stand-up set and several more sketches—including one called "Barroom Drunk"—the 'Mats went back out to play "Kiss Me on the Bus." Perhaps a bit unnerved, the band botched the count-off and had to start the song twice. They quickly recovered, though, and played a gleeful, grooving version.

They were quite a sight too: during the break, Paul, Tommy, and Chris had all changed clothes with one another. "I was in the bathroom getting high," said Bob. "I had no idea those three had switched clothes, I didn't even know until I saw the playback."

During the guitar solo, Michaels and the network censors held their collective breaths as Tommy sauntered toward Westerberg's microphone. Grinning, he sarcastically whined, "Darn it!" The performance ended with Bob shouting, "Thank you!" and hurling his Les Paul behind his head—the guitar crashed in a heap of feedback. "Rock-and-roll doesn't always make for great television," said Westerberg. "But we were trying to do whatever possible to make sure that was a memorable evening."

The 'Mats returned to the stage for the end-of-show good-night. Aside from Bob, mugging behind cast member Joan Cusack, the rest of the band joked among themselves on the fringes, departing before the credits finished.

Afterwards, band and entourage headed to the post-show wrap party at Café Luxembourg. When Michaels saw Rieger, he summoned him over to his table. "He proceeded to dress me down a second time in front of a bunch of people. I looked at him like, 'Are you getting great pleasure out of this?' But there was nothing I could do. All I could think about was him calling Mo Ostin."

Michaels may have been running hot, but the rest of the cast was decidedly cold. "We were ignored by everybody," said Michael Hill. As Bob Stinson put it: "They put their noses up at us, and we spit up their nose hole."

* * *

Bob Stinson returned to the Berkshire Hotel and, in a chemical-fueled rage, proceeded to tear up his room, breaking a door, smashing a window, and shattering a pair of phones. He then got into a violent argument with Krietler, who emerged the following day visibly battered. "She came out all bruised up," recalled Tommy. "It was troubling how much they fought. It was really dark and fucked-up."

Westerberg had been shielded from Bob's previous assault incident and the extent of his mental and emotional troubles. But now everyone—including the label—was becoming aware just how deep his problems ran.

On Monday, when Michaels got the $1,100 bill for the hotel damages, he hit the roof again. He was threatening to ban not just the 'Mats but *any* Warner Bros. act from appearing on *SNL*. In one night, the Replacements had managed to destroy a decade of cozy relations between the show and the label. "After that, we had to start over with half the executives at [Warner Bros.]," said Gary Hobbib.

"I didn't get it," said Steven Baker. "I saw the performance and thought the Replacements were great." Eventually, the hotel damages were paid for, the label issued apologies, and Michaels was soothed. "He was willing to let it go because of Mo," said Baker.

A couple of weeks later, Baker was invited to dinner with Ostin and Michaels at the Ivy Restaurant in Los Angeles. *SNL* cast members Jon Lovitz and A. Whitney Brown joined them. When they found out about Baker's role in the Replacements' booking, the table began to tear into him. "They were being jerks," said Baker. "I remember saying to them, 'If John Belushi was on the show, he probably would've been up there playing with the Replacements.' They had no sense of humor about it."

A couple months later, NBC's brass decided to cancel *Saturday Night Live*; only a last-minute reprieve gave Michaels another year to right the ship. *SNL* would soon return to ratings glory and cultural prominence.

The Replacements wouldn't appear on American television for another three years.

CHAPTER 28

For all the hand-wringing and teeth-gnashing, the Replacements' *SNL* performance actually had a positive effect: a week later, *Tim* finally cracked the *Billboard* top 200 after four months, at number 192. It spent seven more weeks in the chart's lower reaches, doubling sales to roughly 75,000. Still, the Lorne Michaels dustup effectively ruled out live TV as a viable promotional tool for the band.

The same month the *Star-Tribune*, the band's hometown newspaper, reported that the *SNL* appearance had persuaded Warner Bros. to consider "a satellite broadcast of a half-hour 'Mats concert to several cities around the country." This was pure PR hype: the label was instead upping pressure for a video.

Then Jeff Ayeroff had another idea: what if they made a video in which the band didn't appear? "It gave them plausible deniability," said Ayeroff. "They could go: 'Oh, the record company did that, we didn't do that.'" Several fellow Warner alternative acts, like the Smiths and New Order, had made videos in which they didn't perform or appear. For the 'Mats, Ayeroff proposed something radical: a mostly static black-and-white shot of a stereo speaker blasting the band's song.

"The premise was, you're in a college kid's dorm room with a cinder-block bookstand and a stereo. The guy would be smoking a cigarette, listening to the song, and we'd show the speaker rumbling," recalled Ayeroff. "The original idea was that he drops the cigarette and the carpet catches on fire. We couldn't get that cleared by MTV. But it was making lemonade out of lemons."

That March, Westerberg told a reporter: "We've been able to resist making a video until now. But then, the video we're making no one will ever want to watch again."

★ ★ ★

At the end of March, Bob Stinson and Carleen Krietler tied the knot at Blaisdell Manor, a Georgian-style mansion in South Minneapolis. The cards sent out by the bride's family read: "On the dawn of a dream come true . . ."

But Krietler's doctor father was anything but thrilled—and this was before he'd found out about Stinson's assault arrest and the couple's violent relationship. "My family thought he was marrying me for my inheritance, and his family thought I was marrying him because he was in the Replacements," said Krietler. "We didn't have a lot of support from anyone."

Though the other 'Mats attended the ceremony, Bob's young pals Ray Reigstad and John Reipas were his best men. Most of the people at the wedding didn't know who they were. "If anyone asks," Bob told them, "I'm just gonna tell them you guys are my fishing buddies from Florida."

It was a formal affair with a few dozen guests watching as a justice of the peace presided over the nuptials. When Bob was asked if he took Carleen as his bride, he replied innocently, "Sure." The justice snapped, telling him to follow instructions. Bob shrugged and said: "O-kay . . . I do." After a quick Las Vegas honeymoon, the band resumed touring the Midwest and East Coast in early April.

* * *

Peter Jesperson was now merely part of a chorus instead of the only one with the Replacements' ear. He responded to his diminished status by ratcheting up his drinking and drug abuse. "Maybe there was a point where I was drowning my sorrows," said Jesperson.

This was risky behavior for a band road manager: "There were a couple [of] situations where I did the settlement after the show, and the promoter knew I was several sheets to the wind." In Oklahoma City the previous fall, Westerberg had found Jesperson passed out in the hallway instead of settling accounts with the venue. "It wasn't about the money," said Westerberg. "I was thinking to myself: *How long has this been going on, where the 'responsible adult' is one of us?*"

The next day Westerberg offered Jesperson a gentle warning. "If you're not careful, this could be a problem." Jesperson got the message: "Basically, 'Your job's in jeopardy if it keeps up,'" he recalled. But the 'Mats were becoming habitually destructive, and impossible for Jesperson to deal with.

In advance of the *Tim* tour, Jesperson wanted to rent a vehicle with a commode. "They were drinking so much they'd have to stop to go to the bathroom constantly," he said. But no one in the Twin Cities was interested in renting an RV or Winnebago to a rock band. Jesperson found a sympathetic dealer in Elk River, Minnesota, named Rollie Stevenson. "He said, 'Peter, I'm tired of rock bands being treated like second-class citizens. I'll rent to you,'" said Jesperson. "Famous last words."

The band's new mini-RV had couches in front, a kitchenette, a bathroom, and a lounge in the back. It wouldn't last long.

A week into the tour, following a gig at Toronto's Concert Hall, Jesperson was already dreading getting the band back across the border. "Our rallying cry was always 'Drunk for customs!'" recalled Westerberg. Jesperson decided to leave the sozzled 'Mats in Bill Sullivan's hands and hopped into the equipment van with Monty Lee Wilkes ahead of them to deal with customs.

They got to the Bond Court Hotel in downtown Cleveland earlier than expected. Jesperson had just enjoyed a nice shower and hot meal when he stopped at the front desk to see if the band had checked in. Just then, a set of keys went flying over his shoulder and landed on the desk in front of him. He turned and saw a haggard Sullivan standing there, covered in white paint. "You go park that thing," Sullivan told him. "I'm never getting in it again."

Tommy and Paul were in the corner of the hotel lobby, averting their eyes like guilty children. "You park it," Jesperson told Sullivan wanly. "I'll deal with it tomorrow."

Jesperson's mouth was agape as he surveyed the damage in the morning. In Toronto the band had stolen a couple of cans of paint backstage and turned the inside of the RV into a Jackson Pollock canvas. "They'd broken every window except the front windshield. Bob had been in the passenger seat and was about to give that a heave-ho too when somebody came to their senses and stopped him," said Jesperson.

The toilet was ripped out and tossed through the back door while speeding down the highway. Cabinets and fixtures were yanked out of the walls. All that was left were broken boards and lumber piled up in the back lounge.

There was another week of dates left. "We actually had to finish the trip like that, driving around with all these broken windows. It was cold and, at times, rainy," said Jesperson. "They struggled to find a clean dry place to sit, and they'd get ornery. The toilet was gone, so they just went to this heap of debris in the back and took a leak on that. Bob took a dump back there once. It was miserable driving that thing back. The moods were terrible at that point."

Jesperson would eventually concoct a story for the RV's owner about over-zealous fans partying and causing most of the damage. The bill: $10,000, a major chunk of the tour's proceeds. It made Jesperson appear ineffectual to High Noon. Later, he would wonder aloud, "Maybe they were trying to make it so bad that I would quit."

* * *

Touring only exacerbated Bob Stinson's distance from the other Replacements. He'd started to bail on sound checks, disappearing for hours to do drugs, then showing up late for sets. "It's difficult to play in a band like the Replacements when all of a sudden you've got a stranger in the band," Westerberg said. "We'd only see him onstage, really. He just drifted away from us."

At a Washington, DC, show, a fight broke out at the foot of the stage, and roadie Bill Sullivan got pulled into the mix. "Tommy and I dropped our instruments and dove into the crowd immediately to help, and Bob just stood there laughing," said Westerberg. "In my head, I thought, *God, I always figured he was with us fists-a-flying, no matter what.* We could've used his muscle, and he didn't join in. And we got our asses kicked."

Paul and Tommy had lightly fantasized about getting another guitarist over the years. Now those conversations were becoming more realistic. It was difficult to conceive of the Replacements without Bob, but things had become seriously problematic. The situation was further complicated by family ties and shifting loyalties: a deepening fraternity between Tommy and Paul was slowly supplanting the Stinson brothers' bond.

"Paul and I, we started to think, 'Wow, we might have a chance here to do something,'" said Tommy. Paul had pushed a broom just long enough to afford his guitar and amp. Tommy had lasted all of a day washing dishes. Now, being a musician—a *rock star*—was within reach.

Bob's perspective couldn't have been more different. The amount of road-work required to support *Tim* had finally forced him to quit Mama Rosa's. Between tours, he started working with an old friend, guitarist Bob Dunlap, in a cleaning crew tidying up local clubs during the day. The band had earlier joked about it, scrawling on flyers: "Bob Stinson (who wants to be a janitor anyway)." But Bob had no hang-ups about manual labor, and he clearly wasn't suited for a music career.

To Dunlap, Bob admitted that part of him had never wanted to play any-place bigger than the Entry; he had never wanted to leave Minneapolis and preferred being a big fish in a small pond. Those feelings only increased when he fell in love with Carleen, and then again as more and more people he didn't know—whose names he couldn't remember, and who only seemed interested in Paul and Tommy—came into the band's camp.

* * *

There was another element at play regarding the band's ownership. "There was always a very strange force within Bob to defeat Paul, to prove that Paul wasn't any good, to somehow kick him out of the band," said Dunlap.

Six years after the fact, Bob was still mad that Westerberg had schemed to get singer Tom Byrne out of the group. Ward Dotson of the band's onetime tourmates the Pontiac Brothers once had cornered Bob to ask about the 'Mats' history and was surprised by this lingering animus. "I'm like, 'Are you aware that you're in a band with the greatest songwriter of the eighties?'" said Dotson. "Bob couldn't even see that. He was like, 'Nah, that other guy was a real good singer, and this asshole . . . maneuvered him out.'"

At one time, Bob could make a show of rejecting Westerberg's softer mate-rial. But *Tim* shattered that illusion. Now a whole machine catering to Wester-berg acknowledged Bob only as part of the band's sideshow, and it hurt being condescended to or ignored.

The only power Bob had left was to act out, to get fucked up, to derail per-formances—a sad replay of his teenage days at Red Wing: *Bob will act foolish and try to get others to act foolish in an attempt to be accepted.*

Yet Bob wasn't that much worse off than his bandmates. "They were all doing the same thing," said Anita Stinson. "He was no more abusive than any-body else." Even Westerberg agreed. "The farce of it all: Bob going through treatment as though we're some little angels who were clean and sober. We were as dirty as anyone. But at least we were holding it together to do what we had to do to keep the thing moving."

"The band was only two steps behind Bob," said Russ Rieger. "On a human level, how could they kick him out? His reaction would've been, 'Why me? What about you?'"

★ ★ ★

Early 1986 delivered a wake-up call for Warner Bros. "Particularly after *Sat-urday Night Live*, [Bob's] behavior at the hotel was really disturbing," said Michael Hill. "He was the wild card in that mix—even though Paul was the one who said the F-word on television."

High Noon, still relatively new to the band, was powerless to intercede. "We felt this is something internal, something the four of you have to deal with," said Gary Hobbib. "But they couldn't. It was all passive-aggressive behavior between them."

"We're not the kind of guys who sit around expressing our feelings," West-erberg would later admit, likening it to "Henry Fonda syndrome. You know, he couldn't tell his children he loved them, and it was the same with us. We couldn't talk. We couldn't communicate."

The watershed moment came with an appearance at the Michigan Theater in Ann Arbor on April 5. Once again, Bob was late. "That was the only show that the guy said, 'Get out there, we can't wait any longer,'" recalled Westerberg.

The three-piece band went on and announced they were auditioning for a new lead guitarist. They grabbed someone from the opening band the Sky-scrapers for a couple of numbers. Meanwhile, Jesperson finally found Bob hold-ing court in a bar a few blocks away. Bob had to fight his way past bouncers who didn't believe he had any business onstage. He raised his arms in triumph as the crowd cheered. "You should be booing him," Westerberg scolded.

"A tempestuous reunion followed," observed a reviewer for the *University of Michigan Daily*, "in which every member of the band got drenched with beer." Eventually, they settled down and locked in. When they were together and on, they still had a remarkable power. But those moments when all four charged together as one were becoming rare.

The show devolved into chaos. Tommy and Paul left the stage, still playing their instruments, as Bob elbowed his way to the mic to sing a highly ironic cover: "Takin' Care of Business."

★ · ★ · ★

Peter Jesperson's 1986 datebook, filled with the Replacements' gigs and commitments, ended abruptly in the final week of April. He was clearly no longer suited for road managing. Apart from his drinking, he was not dispassionate enough to crack the whip—however much that was even possible—with the 'Mats.

After six years with the band as its benefactor, champion, and guiding light, Jesperson was on his way out. In a sense, he'd made his position expendable by bringing in High Noon. Worse, his behavior made him vulnerable; he'd gotten careless and reckless at the wrong time. "Everybody thought the band partied too hard, and it didn't look good for me to be doing it too," he said.

On April 23, Peter was back in Minneapolis. The Replacements' first European tour was upcoming, and he'd been sorting out passports and permits. He was heading out to buy a present for Anita Stinson—she was getting married that weekend to her fiancé Tom Kurth—when Westerberg called and told him they were having a band meeting at the Uptown.

"Why don't you have the meeting without me, and just fill me in later," Jesperson told him.

"No, Pete," said Westerberg. "I really think you gotta be present for this one."

When he showed up at the bar, it was just Paul and Tommy there.

"One thing I remember was Tommy, he was smirking a little bit before Paul dropped the bomb," said Jesperson. "He was sitting there like, 'I know something you don't know.' We were so tight, had been such close friends. I harbored a really deep resentment towards him after that."

After dispensing with the small talk over drinks, Westerberg broke the news: "I'm really unhappy with the way things are. And when I'm pissed off I wanna start swinging, and I don't want you to be in the way catching any punches." Jesperson said, "It was a fairly humane way to put it."

Jesperson's dismissal would mark the start of a pattern: whenever Westerberg grew frustrated, he'd start pointing fingers. "In a nutshell, 'Things are going bad. Let's fire somebody, and maybe that will fix that,'" Chris Mars said. Mars, who didn't endorse the firing, had refused to come in protest. Bob, meanwhile, was lost in his own world.

As the news sank in Jesperson froze. "It was like being kicked out of a club you'd helped start," he said. "I felt humiliated, and I wasn't going to humiliate myself further by begging or pleading for my job. At that point, I was like, 'I guess this is done.'"

In the end, the decision to fire Peter was not High Noon's but the 'Mats'—specifically, Westerberg's. "Paul didn't even call to tell us he was doing it," said Rieger. Westerberg did confide the decision to George Regis. "They had outgrown Peter's abilities," said Regis. "Peter's an enormous part of it; he's the fifth Replacement. But at that point in time, things had moved on."

It might have been a purely professional decision, but it couldn't have felt more personal to Jesperson. "Peter was too much in love with them and had become too protective," said Twin/Tone's Dave Ayers. "That's something that Paul was initially attracted to, and ultimately repelled by."

After Paul and Tommy left, Uptown waitress Victoria Norvell asked Jesperson if he wanted another drink, telling him, "You look like your dog just died." He went home to a quart of Johnnie Walker Red and an uncertain future. "I drank myself into unconsciousness," he said—the start of a five-year free fall.

CHAPTER 29

Warner Bros.'s director of video, Randy Skinner, had been tasked with bringing Jeff Ayeroff's proposed "speaker" clip to life. She had joined the label in August 1984 and was part of a team churning out over 200 videos a year by 1986. The Replacements' project, filmed in LA, was modestly budgeted for one day at $10,000. Skinner hired a young director of photography named Bill Pope (who would become a major video director and cinematographer, most notably on the *Matrix* films) and shot at her apartment on Orange Drive, near Hancock Park.

For the set, they brought in a funky old couch and used Skinner's milk crate, turntable, and speakers. They also added a dog walking around, for some homey atmosphere. The "professional movie dog" demanded a $500-a-day wage. "That was the most expensive thing," said Skinner.

They also needed a human being—the camera was to slowly pull back from a speaker close-up to show a partial view of someone sitting on a couch listening to the music, smoking a cigarette, and tapping a foot. Though they were both on set, neither Westerberg nor Stinson was willing, even with their back to the camera. In the end, set production designer Robert Fox took the part, though Westerberg did allow his pack of cigarettes to appear.

Pope shot several variations of the video in color; the images were dialed to black-and-white in postproduction. The various versions would be synched with different songs from *Tim*. In the main "Bastards of Young" clip, Fox smokes, fidgets on the couch, and eventually kicks the speaker before walking out of the apartment. The video for "Left of the Dial" is similar, minus the dramatic exit. For "Hold My Life," the video begins with Fox flipping through a stack of LPs, tossing out several, until he comes to a copy of *Tim*.

The throbbing movement of the exposed subwoofer was actually the result of the Replacements LP. "We really cranked up the volume," said Skinner. Soon the entire building was rattling with the 'Mats' music. "It drove my landlord crazy."

Though the video for "Bastards" would air only a handful of times later that summer on MTV's alternative music program *120 Minutes*, it was the subject of much industry talk. "It may not be the best rock video ever made," offered the *Los Angeles Times*, "but it's certainly the *ultimate* rock video." Steven Baker noted, "It added to [the Replacements'] mystique. That began their weird relationship with MTV."

* * *

In mid-May, the Replacements headed to Europe for the first time, to play fourteen dates in three weeks. None of them had been overseas before. "Shit—to us, Madison, Wisconsin, was still exotic," said Westerberg.

The 'Mats got a late start in the international market. None of their Twin/Tone albums were available in Europe until early 1986, when the UK label Glass Records issued a compilation that included the unreleased Alex Chilton–produced "Nowhere Is My Home." Westerberg wanted to call the record *England Schmengland*; it went out as *Boink!!* instead. With the stateside noise over *Let It Be* and *Tim*, the UK music press was growing curious, and the weekly papers *Sounds* and *New Musical Express* both dispatched reporters to America that winter.

Mat Snow's *NME* feature, "Hits from the Sticks," gave the 'Mats their biggest exposure in the United Kingdom. Snow followed the band up the coast of California for several days on tour. "If you can show me a more rootin' tootin' new musical combo burning the boards anywhere on the planet right now, I'll kiss your arse," he wrote.

Westerberg was keen to play up the band's high school–dropout history. "I'm a borderline illiterate," he told the paper. Snow wrote: "But Paul Westerberg is far from stupid. He is, however, of that breed almost entirely extinct (in Britain, at least) outside the heavy metal fortress: Paul Westerberg is a solid-gold easy-action through and through rocker."

The United Kingdom was in a strident political mood in 1986. Seven years under Margaret Thatcher had yielded a golden era of protest music. The previous fall a collective of British performers—including Billy Bragg and Paul Weller—had formed a group called Red Wedge to try to actively unseat Thatcher and the country's Conservative Party.

In the midst of this, Westerberg saw an opportunity to grab some attention and wind up the *NME* audience by espousing his views on the separation of rock and politics:

> Reagan? I like him. A President, to me, should look good. I like the fact that he dyes his hair and wears make-up. Seriously! He's not supposed to have a brain, he's just supposed to look good an' shit. I'd rather have an actor as President than a politician.

When the band, Monty Lee Wilkes, and Bill Sullivan landed at Gatwick Airport on May 14, they were met by British tour manager Andy Proudfoot, a twenty-four-year-old veteran of tours with American bands like Green on Red and the Rain Parade.

"The specific thing that was communicated to me was that they had a bit of a reputation for destroying things," said Proudfoot. "There was an episode where they'd had an RV and virtually gutted it." Proudfoot wasn't scared off, but he did err on the side of caution. Instead of renting a nice vehicle, he got an old box truck—basically a stripped-out panel van with windows cut into it and a separate cab for the driver.

One thing that had not been exaggerated to him was the extent of the band's drinking. "It was more full-on than any band I'd worked with," said Proudfoot. "The Replacements would drink large amounts *all the time*. The tour became a bit of a marathon."

The tour began and ended in London, where audiences were sufficiently enthusiastic about, if mildly suspicious of, this gang of boorish Yanks. So they opened the first show at Dingwall's with a roaring, goading cover of "The Marines' Hymn": "From the halls of Montezuma to the shores of Tripoli . . . "

A few weeks earlier, the United States had bombed Libya in response to its role in several terrorist attacks against American interests. US planes had taken off from British airbases, and there were fears that the United Kingdom would be subject to terrorist reprisals because of its involvement in the raids. Westerberg was only too happy to give them his Ugly American shtick. "We came over as the secret weapon," Westerberg told the crowd. "We're here to save you—don't ya know?"

They broke out all the old tricks for the new audience: swapping instruments, wrestling one another onstage, jumping on and wrecking Chris Mars's (rented) drum kit. "Probably a lot of people were shocked by them," said Proudfoot.

Further into the country, attendance began to wane. "The best and worst show was in Leeds—some workingman's club," recalled Wilkes. "The PA system consisted of a Bose hi-fi speaker on each side of the stage and the very first mixing board manufactured by Soundcraft, which had no EQ. I have never seen that band play with such fury as they did that night. It was so kick-ass—one song after the other, just tight and powerful. It's very possibly the best show I ever saw them play, and hardly anyone was there, maybe twenty people."

The venues got better outside the United Kingdom. "Holland was pretty mad for American bands," said Proudfoot. "The Dutch shows we did were great." But generally speaking, the 'Mats had no idea what to expect city to city, country to country, and their performances, accordingly, were just as unpredictable. "It was a complete box of chocolates," said Proudfoot. "You never quite knew what you were going to get."

Only one thing remained consistent: the band's strange, ritualistic activities. "They had such short attention spans, they got bored incredibly quickly," recalled Proudfoot. "They'd take the food from the dressing room and smear it all over the windows of the van. I remember thinking it was really funny, until I realized I was going to have to clean it off."

One night before a gig in the north of England, Proudfoot heard a series of explosions coming from the dressing room. Standing alone at the far end, Tommy was methodically winding up and then pitching a case of beer cans at the wall, where they'd burst across the room. Tommy seemed somewhat confused by Proudfoot's concern. "I'm getting ready for the show," he explained innocently.

Gary Hobbib popped over to check on the tour. Traveling with the band in close quarters for the first time, he became aware of the depths of their drinking. "They'd show up for a two PM sound check, and they didn't go on until eleven at night. That's eight, nine hours of drinking. Paul would be on the floor, just pouring bottles on top of himself."

The band made some radio and TV appearances in Europe, playing a short set on VPRO, the Netherlands national station. They were also booked on *The Old Grey Whistle Test*, the BBC's venerable live music showcase. "We get there at eight in the morning, and we'd come from France," said Westerberg. Bill Sullivan bribed someone at the BBC for a fifth of Scotch and watched as the band jumped on it—"Like flies on shit," Mars recalled.

Lubrication notwithstanding, their British television debut was no repeat of *Saturday Night Live*. Using the gear of Elvis Costello and the Attractions, also guests on the show, the 'Mats got through "Kiss Me on the Bus" without any complaints about language or volume.

* * *

P roudfoot had been briefed at the outset about Bob Stinson—his behavior, his drug habit, his growing proclivity for getting his hands on some gig cash and disappearing until well past showtime. "I'd had a lesson from Russ and Gary about not letting Bob collect money from the promoter under any circumstance," said Proudfoot. "But he turned out to be one of the more respectful guys."

Bob's great European-tour expense was all the phone calls to his new bride. The charges were astronomical; one all-night call cost $1,700. While he didn't reveal much to Carleen, she could sense he was becoming troubled and fearful. "I found out later he was basically on the verge of a mental breakdown," said Krietler.

There were flashes of strange behavior in Europe. Bob was a milk drinker in the morning, to salve the previous night's boozing. In Holland the cartons came with a tricky, unfamiliar design that he couldn't open. He got so worked up about the mechanics of the container that he flew into a massive rage and threw it against the dashboard of the van—a disturbing glimpse of his state of mind.

About six dates into the tour, in Genoa, Italy, Bob disappeared for the first time. Genoa was a port town; you could find lots of trouble without even trying very hard. With the set time upon them, Bob had yet to show. "Bill Sullivan and I were standing at the main door of the club, looking up and down the street, wondering, 'Where is he?'" said Proudfoot.

Suddenly, they could make out Bob's figure at the end of the long, winding avenue. Looking closer, they saw that he was being chased by a small mob: "Eight angry Italians, two brandishing knives," recalled Proudfoot. "He barreled through the doors, and club security stopped this gang who were after him. The guys eventually went away. I never found out what the story was."

"He must've scored that night," said Westerberg. "Because I remember he was horseshit when he tried to play. He actually fell off the stage."

Bob would remain lost in his own world. "He'd show up for a gig an hour late," said Krietler. "That was no longer acceptable. There's three band members playing 'Scooby Doo, Where Are You?' and Bob is on the phone across town calling me long-distance to find out where the venue is."

"I don't think he was trying to be malicious," said Krietler. "I think it was his last cry for attention. I don't think that in his wildest dreams he ever suspected they were gonna cut him out of the picture."

* * *

Europe was the first time the Replacements ever felt like they'd gone backwards in their career. "We were used to packing clubs in the States," said Tommy Stinson. "Over there, there wasn't anyone there at most of the shows. It turned us off to the place." They spent the latter half of the tour grousing about the continent. "I believe Sullivan had the best quote about the place: 'The toilet paper's like cardboard, and the money falls apart in your hands,' which was pretty much true," said Westerberg.

"We were a bunch of young twerps, spoiled Americans," said Wilkes. "'What do you mean the phone doesn't work the same way?' 'Haven't you people ever heard of ice?' 'What do you mean we can't get dinner at two in the morning? Where's the Perkins, for God's sake? Isn't there a Denny's around here?'"

Though Mars snuck out to visit the Louvre in Paris (only to find it was closed), the band kept to their scheduled clubs and hotels, maintaining Westerberg's old dictate: "We're on tour, we're not tourists." At one point the band did a gig on the southern coast of Spain, just a few miles from North Africa, across the Straits of Gibraltar. "It's weird to think we were that close to Africa and we didn't know or didn't care," said Westerberg.

Another night in Italy, the band found itself loose inside the ancient walls of Perugia following a show. It was a magnificent old Etruscan city, founded sometime in the sixth century BC and later part of the Roman Empire. "It was such a beautiful and fascinating place," said Proudfoot, who had to laugh as he watched the Replacements drunkenly wandering through its cobblestone streets, searching in vain for a Denny's.

CHAPTER 30

At the end of May, the Replacements were included in *Rolling Stone*'s first annual "Hot Issue." Alongside 1986's other rising talents (actress Laura Dern, director James Cameron, boxer Mike Tyson), the 'Mats were named the year's "Hot Band," an accolade accompanied by a multi-page interview with Westerberg by David Fricke. "On one side, I wish I was famous; I couldn't stand for someone else to be famous and not us," confessed Paul.

The months of touring behind *Tim*, the press piling up, and word of mouth about their live show had created an unmistakable excitement about the band by summer's start—just in time for another East Coast and Southern tour in mid-June. High Noon brought Andy Proudfoot over from England to watch them on the road. "They hadn't been able to find a victim for the US," he said. "Their reputation preceded them."

On June 17, Proudfoot was running late picking up the band at Boston's Logan Airport. "I went into the terminal, and I didn't have to look very far—I just went to the bar. Bob had on a summer print dress with boots. Paul and Tommy had blue-and-white-striped trousers and massive braces, and their hair was tousled out. They looked like clowns, basically." As he led them through the airport, Proudfoot recalled seeing "people's jaws drop open; kids were pointing."

At the Living Room in Providence for the first gig, Bob picked up where he'd left off in Europe and pulled a runner. "I hadn't done my speech before with the owner, about not giving him money," said Proudfoot. "They gave him two hundred bucks out of the fee." Though Bob went off for several hours, he returned in time for the show.

Being on familiar turf renewed the band's confidence. The Living Room and Boston's Channel the following night were riotous affairs. "The band looked more comfortable onstage than in Europe," said Proudfoot. "They had more of a swagger about them."

On Long Island, the band made an appearance at a local record store for several hundred enthusiastic fans. Westerberg noticed a large cardboard display of the band Sire had sent. He, Tommy, and Chris were on one side; Bob was on the other side, alone. The portion with Bob could be cut off completely without affecting the display—a telling sign of how the label had come to view the band.

The Replacements reached Manhattan for two sold-out nights at the Ritz on June 20 and 21. The gigs would be their biggest ever in New York City, and the excitement and nerves were palpable. Warner staffer Julie Panebianco was backstage, trying to calm Westerberg, who was eager to get the show started.

"I said, 'You can't go on now, nobody goes on early in New York—the guest list line is a block long,'" said Panebianco. "The lightbulb went off in his head: *You mean I get to fuck over all these people?*"

The 'Mats took the stage *that minute.* Patrons were still stacked at the ticket windows. Once the band started, recalled Panebianco, "people were screaming at each other to get in. It was hysterically funny."

The second night was even more memorable. To open the set Bob Stinson asked the crowd for drugs. Standing with a large contingent of Warner staff attending the show, manager Russ Rieger blushed with embarrassment.

The real mayhem ensued once the music started. Jon Pareles of the *New York Times* noted that, "with the band's first song, the area near the stage of the Ritz became a slam-dancing pit where people happily flailed and collided; every few minutes, someone would be heaved up to the stage, usually to somersault back into the crowd and continue dancing."

In the middle of one song, Westerberg decided he'd try a little stage diving and leapt into the audience spread-eagle. "Suddenly the sea of people parted and, *Whaam!*" he recalled. "It was pretty damn embarrassing. I jumped off the stage—and nobody caught me."

On the ground, somebody stomped on Westerberg's left hand with a combat boot. Immediately he felt a sharp pain in his middle finger. Paul soldiered through a few more songs. Later in the set, when the band members switched instruments and he took over the drum kit, he "hit a rim shot and finished the job on the finger."

Tim cover artist Robert Longo squired Paul to the emergency room. The finger wasn't broken, but it was hurt badly enough that the band canceled the remaining nine shows, mostly in the South.

That afternoon Paul visited Sire's offices to meet with Seymour Stein. He'd taken a handful of pills to kill the throbbing pain in his hand. Westerberg was in the midst of a conversation with Stein when they kicked in. He slowly slid out of his chair and passed out under Seymour's desk.

"Paul, there's things about me you don't know," said Stein impishly. "You definitely don't want to be in that position." Westerberg was carried out of the office.

He did manage an upright conversation with Stein later. The Sire head was one of the few record company figures Westerberg liked and respected—as much for his personal flamboyance as for his musical acumen. "Seymour was living a pretty wild life back then too," said Sire assistant Sandy Alouette. "There was this notion of 'We can relate to this guy.'"

Stein had been aware of Bob's issues for some time. It was nothing to him, of course. He'd endured the Ramones' bickering, the Dead Boys' insolence, the Pretenders' heroin problems. "I thought they were all a little crazy. But there's degrees of crazy," said Stein. "When the Replacements' issues first started, I said, 'You guys gotta try and work it out; there's two brothers here.' I tried to let nature take its course."

Now Stein sensed the issue could no longer be avoided. Moreover, he'd come to realize that Sire actually had a valuable commodity on its hands. He felt that if the Replacements could come up with the right song, they could be massive.

Stein had no relationship with Bob to speak of. (Backstage in New York during the *Tim* tour, Bob had approached Karin Berg and asked: "Are you Seymour?") Neither did Michael Hill, nor High Noon, now solely in charge of guiding the band's career. "We never discussed Bob to the way that Bob should've been discussed," said Gary Hobbib. "It wasn't about, 'He's hurting himself, and because he's hurting himself, he's going to pull us down with him.' And that should've been the conversation. We didn't handle that one right."

As Stein and Westerberg talked it became clear that the Replacements' future might hinge on whether Bob remained in the band. In time Westerberg would be said to have fired Bob Stinson owing to label dictates. But that was an oversimplification. "Paul came to me—I didn't go to him," said Stein. "I do remember saying to him, 'I regard you and Tommy as "the band." To me, the songs are everything, and you're the songwriter.' But I certainly didn't instigate anything."

"There was a little more emphasis on 'He's wrecking it for you guys—and the band is going to pay for it,'" said Westerberg, who didn't feel Stein had issued him an ultimatum but rather had offered reassurance about Sire's support of the band, whatever they decided to do. Westerberg left New York thinking that Bob would be all right, that the band would figure out things on their own.

* * *

Bob Stinson was relieved to return to Minneapolis earlier than planned in June, but he'd come back to a bad situation. He and Carleen had settled into a brownstone on Franklin and Dupont. They'd had to leave their previous place after it'd been broken into. But they were burglarized again at the new house. Bob couldn't even keep a guitar at home. He was feeling beset from all sides.

His schizoaffective disorder would flare in these times of crisis. July was marked by all the symptoms of manic and major depressive episodes. Carleen recalled him being "upset and crying. He'd just sob. And not eat." In the past, these spells had been marked by outbursts of violence against others—or himself.

This was the lingering damage of his childhood and the transgressions of Nick Griffin. "He never had the counseling to learn how to deal with that and go forward—if that's even possible for that level of abuse that he sustained at Tommy's dad's hands," said Krietler. "He'd tell you it was no big deal. . . . [But] once something triggered those memories, he would go on an emotional roller coaster."

This time, said Carleen, "I think it was a direct response to the [band's] attitude that 'Bob is the problem.'" She wanted him to quit the group: "I said, 'This isn't healthy. If this is causing you so much anxiety, why can't you just get in another band?' That didn't seem like an option to him."

His friends grew worried at what they saw that summer. "Bob was coming unglued," recalled Bob Dunlap, who tried to counsel him. "I wasn't worried about him getting kicked out of the band; I was worried what being in the band was doing to Bob."

One afternoon in July, Carleen arrived home, opened the door, and stepped into a puddle. She looked and saw water coming into the living room from the bathroom. Throwing the door open, she found Bob lying unconscious in an overflowing tub. He'd swallowed a bottle of Carleen's prescription muscle relaxers (for her back), turned on the hot water, gotten into the tub, and waited to die.

Panicked, Carleen called an ambulance. Bob was rushed to Hennepin County Medical Center, where his stomach was pumped. Anita came down as her son was put under a seventy-two-hour psychiatric hold. Unlike his suicide attempt the previous fall—which had seemed more like a cry for attention—those around Bob were convinced that this was a serious attempt to end his life.

Tommy and the Replacements were not made aware of the overdose attempt. Bob didn't want them to know. "It felt like a big deal at the time," said Ray Reigstad of the incident. "Of course, later on, Bob just laughed the whole thing off."

* * *

After a month at home, Westerberg's finger healed and he got restless. Rather than stay idle, the 'Mats wanted to demo some new songs—they'd already previewed a few on tour. Warner Bros. booked several days for the band (under a pseudonym) at their old Dinkytown haunt, Blackberry Way.

The prospect of going into the studio—the most direct reminder of his loss of standing in the band—only seemed to unnerve Bob further. "I think it drove him nuts a little bit," said Tommy. "He just didn't fit into any of the new material." Westerberg argued that Bob had simply refused to evolve with the band: "Slice the pie twenty ways: Bob wanted to rock harder. Bob wanted more metal music. Bob liked fast power chords, he liked to take long big solos. We started to craft the songs . . . [and] it left less space for him to be Bob the Maniac."

In early August, Tommy called his brother several times to rehearse for the session. Bob refused to answer. "If you offered him the phone, he'd smash it," said Krietler. "He probably broke ten phones in a two-week period."

Come session time, Bob showed up, albeit grudgingly. With Blackberry Way's Mike Owens and Michael McKern engineering, the four-piece Replacements cut template versions of "Valentine" and "Red Red Wine." Bob left after the first day and didn't return. The remaining trio completed six songs over the remaining days, including a pair of new thorny rockers, "PO Box (Empty as Your Heart)" and "Time Is Killing Us," plus "Bundle Up," a winter-themed reworking of Hank Mizell's 1958 rockabilly novelty "Jungle Rock." Tommy even recorded several solo numbers, with McKern playing drums.

The whole session, however, became an afterthought. Westerberg knew Seymour Stein was right: "[Bob] didn't show up, and that was the last straw," he recalled. Something needed to be done. So Westerberg decided *he* would quit the Replacements.

He met Tommy and Chris at the Uptown. Anita Stinson was behind the bar serving drinks. "I said, 'I'm gonna quit the band. I can't do this with Bob anymore,'" said Westerberg. "And they said, very sweetly, 'Well, who's going to play bass with you?' 'Who's going to play drums?' I thought, 'Well, do you guys wanna?'

"I was ready to say fuck it: fuck Sire, fuck the Replacements. And Tommy and Chris wanted to stick with it. So then it became, 'What are we going to do about Bob?'"

It was the conversation they'd all dreaded.

Mars didn't want to fire Bob. Given his own brother's mental health issues, he understood there was something deeper going on. He also knew that the band's professional problems were bigger than any one person. "But I did not have a whole lot of say," said Mars.

The decision came down to Tommy Stinson. "None of us *wanted* to get rid of Bob. We all were against it," said Tommy. "But there was a fact there: we couldn't keep going the way we were."

Tommy knew that, if he wavered, the 'Mats would end there and then. But what about Bob? For all his fuck-ups, all his problems, he was still family—the one who'd put the bass in his hands and given him this life to begin with. Tommy was being forced to make an impossible choice.

After a long silence, he spoke up: "Well," he sighed, "I guess we gotta fire my brother."

That evening Paul steeled himself and called Bob. This time Bob answered the phone. "I don't know what the hell I said," Westerberg commented later. "We never talked on the phone, ever. Our communication usually didn't go beyond 'Look at her ass,' or 'Are ya holdin'?'"

"So when I called him . . . he knew. He's immediately like, 'Don't fucking tell me that you're . . .' And I'm going, 'Man, it's not working. What we're doing now, you're not shining anyway. We're playing acoustic guitars and shit like that.'"

"Yeah," said Bob, meekly. "I guess I'm not happy doing this anymore."

"Then we both got sad," recalled Westerberg. "I thought, 'Well, fuck, we can keep trying.' And then I thought, 'No, I wanna quit the whole thing.' And then he sort of acquiesced. He accepted it. But I think he was sad. He was sad as hell that it was over."

* * *

Though news of Bob's dismissal was kept from the public for several weeks, privately the fallout was immediate.

Anita Stinson hadn't taken sides. "I don't know the conflicts between him and Tommy over that, because Tommy and Bobby at home were not Tommy and Bobby in the band," she said. Like Carleen, Anita felt that Bob's life might actually be improved if he was out of the band.

Anita's mother, Virginia, was furious. "She never forgave me," said Tommy. "'How could you fire your brother?' Shit, well, this is my life *too*."

"Tommy was pretty logical, even at that age," said Daune Earle. "But it was still horrible. He was really depressed, because it fell on him. Even though Paul made the decision and they all backed it, even Anita backed it, he still had to look him in the eyes."

"I can't sit here twenty-five years later and give you an emotional portal to look into it and go, 'Whoa, that's what that was like.' There's no way," said Tommy. "You can't put into words how that affects people, and how you move on from that." Though the two brothers would see each other at family functions and make nice in later years, the hurt and estrangement lingered, unresolved, until the very end of Bob's life.

With the deed now done, "there was concern all around: do these guys really know what they're doing?" said Rieger. "It left a massive hole. There was uncertainty on how to proceed."

Bob's ouster would fundamentally alter the delicate dynamics of the group. "Things were never the same for me after Bob left," said Mars. "When he was gone, I felt that emptiness from behind the drums." As Mars moved away, Paul and Tommy grew closer. "We figured: now we're in this thing together come hell or high water," said Tommy. "And from that point on, it was mostly hell and mostly high water."

Bob and sister Lonnie, with their parents Neil and Anita Stinson in Minnesota, 1961. The couple's marriage would not be happy or long-lived.

A new life in California: Lonnie, Bob, and Anita with baby Tommy.

Bob, age 7, at the start of his troubles.

Tommy rockin' the cradle: "He was full of spit and vinegar." **(Courtesy of Anita Stinson)**

Harold "Hal" Westerberg in Paris at the end of World War II.

Bastard of Young: Paul, making faces with his mother, Mary Lou Westerberg, 1963. **(Courtesy of Paul Westerberg)**

Tommy and Lisa Stinson with Bob upon his return home after years in the state juvenile system. **(Courtesy of Lonnie Stinson)**

Paul's high school friend and mentor John Zika, who would commit suicide in 1977. "After he died," said Westerberg, "I took on a bit of his personality." **(Courtesy the Zika Family)**

Paul Westerberg's 1975 yearbook photo from the Academy of Holy Angels. **(Author collection)**

A teenaged Mars on the drums. "He was like a little Keith Moon," recalled Westerberg. **(Author collection)**

Chris Mars, as a student at DeLaSalle High School, 1976. **(Author collection)**

Mars, manning the kit for Dogbreath, 1978. **(Photo by Andrea Olson Lorimer)**

Bob Stinson, fresh out of group home and intent on getting his band off the ground. **(Photo by Andrea Olson Lorimer)**

Tommy Stinson: "A twelve-year-old [who] played like a motherfucker." **(Photo by Andrea Olson Lorimer)**

Chris Mars' hand-drawn Dogbreath kick drum.
(Photo by Andrea Olson Lorimer)

Longhorn deejay, Oar
Folkjokeopus manager and
Twin/Tone Records co-founder
Peter Jesperson at his South
Minneapolis apartment, 1979.
**(Photograph from the Minneapolis
Star and Tribune News Negative
Collection; courtesy of the Minne-
sota Historical Society.)**

The Replacements demo
tape that Paul Westerberg
gave to Jesperson. **(Photo by
Kevin Scanlon)**

The fledgling Replacements, messing around in the Stinson basement.

The band, still finding their act and spots on stage, at Duffy's, 1980.
(Courtesy Twin/Tone Records)

The band's first publicity photo shoots, taken at the Walker Art Center.
(Photos by Greg Helgeson)

Paul and Tommy on stage at the 7th St Entry in 1981; the image would serve
as the cover of the band's debut album, *Sorry Ma, Forgot to Take Out the Trash*.
(Photo by Greg Helgeson)

Tommy, aka "Skunk."
(Photo by Steve Linsenmayer)

The brothers
Stinson, taking
flight in Madison.
(Photo by Steve
Linsenmayer)

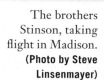

Chris Mars bears
down on the beat.
(Photo by Steve
Linsenmayer)

Paul and Bob messing around. **(Photo by Steve Linsenmayer)**

Switching up instruments for a "hootenanny." **(Photo by Steve Linsenmayer)**

The 'Mats make it to the Big Apple on their April '83 "Eastern Whirl."
(Photo by Jason Sands)

Playing the Rat in Boston. **(Photo by Wayne Viens)**

Peter Buck and Westerberg, dolled up and drinking around the sessions for *Let It Be*. **(Courtesy of Lynn Blakey)**

Bob and Paul conferring post-show at the Rat. **(Photo by Wayne Viens)**

The bootleg
Beatles: the
Replacements
do their version
of *Abbey Road*,
walking across
Bryant Avenue.
**(Photo by Greg
Helgeson)**

An outtake
from the *Let
It Be* rooftop
photo session.
**(Photo by Dan-
iel Corrigan)**

Clowning around at the University of Minnesota's Coffman Memorial Union, 1984. **(Photo by Daniel Corrigan)**

Bob and Paul on stage during the December 1984 "Gary & the Boners" gig at CBGBs. The concert was supposed to have been the band's major label showcase—instead, it turned into a "drunken lollapalooza." **(Photo by Lisan Seroty Lima)**

A wild ride: Inside the 'Mats' beat-up tour van. "Once we got in there," said Tommy, "it was our sanctuary, as well as our jail cell." **(Photos by Just Loomis)**

PART III   Dreams and Games

The goal became simplistic and unrealistic, which was to have a hit. And that's where we died. We weren't made of the stuff that makes popular music.

PAUL WESTERBERG

CHAPTER 31

High Noon was eager to get the Replacements back into the studio for the next album before they changed their minds about staying together. "I hoped that making a record would be a rallying point—to prove that Bob Stinson did not define the band," said Russ Rieger. "I wanted to make it an us-versus-them situation; I wanted to add to the chip on their shoulders."

He appealed to Westerberg to prove to one and all that it was his band creatively, and he urged Tommy to step into the rock star role he was destined for. "They wanted to do that," said Rieger. "If there wasn't an ambition somewhere in them, they would've fallen apart right then."

But a couple of things needed to be sorted out. First, the band decided to record as a three-piece. Finding a new guitarist wasn't going to be easy; besides, replacing Bob so soon felt strange. Westerberg would handle all guitars for the time being.

The other challenge was picking a producer. Reuniting with Tommy Erdelyi was quickly dismissed. "What I hated about 'alternative' records at the time was how incredibly thin they all sounded," said Russ Rieger. "You couldn't get them on the radio; you couldn't put them next to Van Halen. My fight was always to make the band's records sound competitive."

Even before the *Tim* tour had wrapped, Paul and Tommy began meeting with producers. The day of the "Bastards of Young" video shoot in Los Angeles, Warner Bros.'s Steven Baker arranged for the band to hook up with Dave Jerden, a top-notch engineer who'd worked with Talking Heads and Herbie Hancock and went on to produce career-making albums for Jane's Addiction and Social Distortion.

At the El Coyote restaurant post-shoot with the drunken 'Mats, "it turned into this ice-throwing contest," said Jerden. "I couldn't even talk to them." Jerden was on the wagon and didn't partake. "Paul and Tommy look at each other and are like, 'If you can't drink with us, you can't produce us.' And that was it," said Baker. It would be a mere preview.

* * *

Finding a producer who could meet the Replacements' very particular standards was more difficult than it may have seemed. Big-time producers wanted to spend a lot of money and do things their own way. The 'Mats' entire budget was a relatively modest $150,000—and the band wasn't going to repeat takes endlessly, play to click tracks, or work banker's hours. The band needed someone flexible, not technique-driven, and someone who'd be willing to charm, distract, and cajole them into making a record.

Warner Bros.'s A&R man Michael Hill mooted a large number of candidates. Among them: Sandy Pearlman (the Clash, Dictators), Jack Douglas (Cheap Trick, New York Dolls), Don Gehman (John Mellencamp), Chris Thomas (Roxy Music, Pretenders, the Sex Pistols), a much-diminished Jimmy Miller (the Rolling Stones' golden period between *Beggars Banquet* and *Exile on Main Street*), Mike Chapman (Blondie, the Knack,), and Seymour Stein's former Sire partner, Richard Gottehrer (the Go-Gos, Marshall Crenshaw). Obvious "name" indie candidates like Mitch Easter and Don Dixon were rejected out of hand. "The Replacements didn't want to use the producers that R.E.M. had used," said Hill. Glyn Johns, who'd worked with the Stones, the Who, and the Faces, among others, was considered seriously. But he commanded an exorbitant fee that would've eaten up more than half the 'Mats' recording budget.

Part of the problem in selecting someone to supervise the 'Mats' fourth album was that the band didn't quite grasp what a producer *did*. "It was all a big question mark to us," said Stinson. "We didn't know what we were supposed to be looking for."

As the Replacements talked with various candidates, they were by turns insulting ("Boy, you made a lot of shit records"), self-deprecating ("Why do you wanna produce a bunch a losers like us?"), or simply rude—talking among themselves or yawning exaggeratedly while the producers spoke. "The Replacements were completely disrespectful and obnoxious to each guy that came in. Anything you could think to tweak someone, they were doing it," said Rieger. "They had an animal instinct. In some ways, that's a good quality to have. But they didn't use it well. They wielded it like a baseball bat."

When Seth Justman, the keyboardist of the J. Geils Band, came to meet with them, it took only minutes before the 'Mats ran him out of the room. Finally, Rieger had had enough.

"You're not just immature," he unloaded. "You're scared shitless. You're scared of trying. You're so afraid of failure that you won't do anything but shoot yourself in the foot."

Tirade over, Rieger thought he'd crossed a line. The band was shocked silent; he figured he might be fired on the spot. Instead, the Replacements broke into grins and began laughing and patting him on the back. "They made jokes about it: 'Look at this young pup yelling at us and giving us our comeuppance.'

Instead of me getting canned, it got me closer to them. It was the first time I acted older than them, like I had some gravitas. They made jokes about it for days after—'Oooh, we're afraid of Russ. We're afraid.'"

That personal breakthrough did nothing, however, to improve the band's behavior. Later that afternoon, the meetings moved over to the label's offices, by which time the three 'Mats were more than well lubricated. Now it was Michael Hill's turn to be appalled.

The band locked themselves into Sire's conference room. With several producers scheduled to visit, Hill would slip records by the prospective candidates under the door for the band to listen to. The 'Mats would break the LPs and slip the shattered pieces back to him.

Inside, the band rummaged through several storage closets and found a stack of red credit card carbons and began smearing the ink on their faces and the walls. Soon they were blasting songs and rattling around Seymour Stein's vintage Wurlitzer jukebox. A horrified Stein began yelling at Hill: "My jukebox! This is your fault! Get them out of there now!" "Oh God, it was so embarrassing," recalled Hill. "I was never a hugely prideful person about that stuff, so I didn't take it personally, but it was exasperating. 'Guys, please don't fuck with me like this.'"

The band paused in time to meet with Scott Litt, a former Power Station engineer who'd produced the dB's and had gone top 10 the previous summer with Katrina and the Waves' "Walking on Sunshine."

As Litt walked into the room, the band—their faces inked up to look like tribal war paint—gang-tackled him onto the floor. "It was like *Lord of the Flies* in the conference room," recalled Litt. "I was kind of ready for it, since their reputation preceded them. What am I gonna say to them looking like that? 'I have a new way to make a record with you'?"

The Replacements weren't interested in meeting with a young up-and-comer like Litt and turned him down. A few months later, he began working on R.E.M.'s breakthrough, *Document*.

By the end of that long, fraught day, even the typically restrained Hill ran out of patience. "After they came out, I closed my door and said, 'I'm locking myself in my office and I'm not coming out. I've had it.'"

"Part of all our behavior was an act," said Westerberg. "But when Bob was gone, we *were* scared. It was just the three of us then, and we were trying to do every kind of weird, wild thing to distract ourselves from that."

"They would piss everyone off," noted Rieger. "But there was a lot of respect for them as artists. If they were an ordinary band, they would've been dropped. But it was the brilliance of Paul's writing, and the humanity that would come out of him, and the magic of the group, that would keep everyone believing . . . even when you wanted to kill them."

CHAPTER 32

B orn in 1941, Jim Dickinson was the only child of a hard-drinking salesman dad and music teacher mom. He was born in Arkansas, and his father's job for the Diamond Match Company took the family to Hollywood and then Chicago for several years. In 1949 they resettled in the South, in Memphis.

"I really hated Memphis at first," he said. "But the music played a big hand in capturing me." Accompanying his dad to work, he would encounter aging relics like Will Shade's Memphis Jug Band—street buskers since the 1920s—and cross paths with Howlin' Wolf. He'd soon play boogie-woogie piano and lead one of Memphis's earliest high school rock-and-roll bands.

Dickinson figured his playing career had peaked with a 1959 gig backing Bo Diddley. He headed to college the following year, largely to avoid the draft, and landed at Baylor University in Waco, Texas. There he studied drama and volunteered for government-sponsored LSD experiments. Dickinson would be dosed and then asked to compete in standard physical and psychological tests against a group of chimpanzees. He also worked on a novel, *The Search for Blind Lemon*. He left Waco, however, after a couple of semesters.

Dickinson eventually earned a history degree from Memphis State University. As a member of the New Beale Street Sheiks, he recorded a growling jug band number, "You Do It All the Time," then sang on the Jesters' garage-rock nugget "Cadillac Man"—the last great gasp from the original Sun Records. He became a session player at Chips Moman's American Studios and began his production career at John Fry's Ardent Studios; a satellite for the soul label Stax Records, Ardent eventually became the hub for Alex Chilton and Chris Bell's band, Big Star.

In 1969 Dickinson helped the Rolling Stones record at Muscle Shoals Studios in Alabama, adding plaintive piano notes to the band's ballad "Wild Horses." (He lucked into the assignment because the Stones' keyboardist, Ian Stewart, refused to play minor chords.) Dickinson would become Keith Richards's sometime running buddy and confidant.

As the seventies dawned, Dickinson formed the Dixie Flyers, a crew of Memphis players who became the house band for Atlantic Records at Criteria Studios in Miami for a couple of years. Dickinson also released his first—and for three decades, only—solo record, the cult classic *Dixie Fried*.

Dickinson's production discography ranged wide and deep: Ry Cooder's *Into the Purple Valley* and *Boomer's Story* (with Warner Bros. exec Lenny Waronker), among others; Big Star's desultory *Third*; and later the brilliant chaos of Chilton's *Like Flies on Sherbert*. In the early eighties, Dickinson worked with a series of up-and-coming American rock bands: Nashville's Jason & the Scorchers, Austin's True Believers, and LA's Green on Red.

Dickinson didn't fit the image of a sharpie record producer. Paunchy and grizzled, with a calculated backwoods air, he'd impart axioms that flew in the face of industry-think: "Hits are in baseball, singles pick each other up in bars, and your royalty lives in a castle in Europe." He refused to work on Saturdays, when he always watched professional wrestling on television. A gifted raconteur, musical philosopher, and cultural historian, he brought an existential approach to production, not to mention a practical one: "Pure and simple, a producer's an actor. You've gotta be indirect, create a diversion, *trick* the artist into giving something he doesn't wanna give," he said.

In late '86 his old friend Seymour Stein called Dickinson, who was sent a copy of the Replacements' Blackberry Way demos. Dickinson began talking with Michael Hill. "He understood the sensitivity and insecurity of an artist— he almost romanticized it to an extent," said Hill. Dickinson endeared himself to High Noon by espousing a grand sonic vision for the album: "Like a big boombox blasting," he told them. "That's exactly what we wanted," said Rieger.

Crucially, when it came to the band, Dickinson opted for the soft sell. After meeting with "guys who would walk in and say: 'You . . . need a hit, so you're gonna do what I say and rehearse more, and I'm gonna make you a hit,'" said Westerberg, the man from Memphis was a relief. "When we gave the demos to Dickinson, he liked it as it was."

* * *

With Peter's and Bob's firings still heavy in the air, it was a good time to get out of Minneapolis for a while. The Replacements landed in Memphis on November 4, 1986—the day the Republicans would lose control of both the Senate and the House of Representatives for the first time since Reagan's election.

Jim Dickinson's burly, bearded production assistant Jim Lancaster met the band at the airport. Lancaster—quickly nicknamed "Vito" by the 'Mats, for his Memphis Mafia–style air—was a musician and songwriter who would serve as the 'Mats' driver, minder, and occasional background singer. He immediately noticed that Chris Mars had arrived in Dixie with a suitcase decorated with a caricature of Jed Clampett. "I knew right away these were some irreverent kids," he said.

He took the band directly to Ardent, to set up their gear and meet Dickinson. "It was like when I met the Stones," said Dickinson. "When they come into the room, another presence comes with them. You know how when the Stones come together, all their personalities change? The same thing happens with the Replacements."

At the time Memphis had a draconian election day law prohibiting the sale of alcohol until the polls closed. The band made do with a cocktail of NyQuil and Vivarin as they cut a warm-up blues jam dubbed "Election Day," with Westerberg howling, "I don't care who gets e-lec-ted," over a keening slide guitar.

Next morning the band and Dickinson had breakfast at Paulette's, a nearby crepe joint. It was their first opportunity to discuss the recording in depth. Westerberg was drinking screwdrivers and throwing down gauntlets. "Paul's going, 'So, you recorded Big Star—*so fucking what?*'" said Tommy Stinson. "Just being a cocky asshole. It was like, 'Yeah, we hired you because you did all that—but what are you going to do for *me?*'"

Westerberg finally eyed the producer defiantly and told him: "I'm not gonna give you a hundred percent, 'cause you don't deserve it."

"I've heard black artists espouse that notion before," said Dickinson, "but I'd never heard a white artist say that."

For Dickinson, there was a glint of recognition: his father, Big Jim, had been a similarly confrontational alcoholic. Instead of rising to Paul's bait, Dickinson wisely took a step back. "When you're making a punk record, you can't do it without punks," he said. "I pretty much let 'em do what they wanted to do."

There was more to this hands-off approach than met the eye. When recording was at an impasse, Dickinson would strategically disappear. "I'd leave the room for ten or fifteen minutes, and they would, without talking to each other, solve the problem," said Dickinson.

Though he didn't drink, because of severe stomach problems, Dickinson would roll fat joints and tell stories. "He talked more than any person we'd ever met. And I don't think he repeated himself," said Westerberg. "In a way, it helped us relax and forget about what we were doing, 'cause he would have a million and one stories about everyone from Otis Redding to the Rolling Stones to Elvis. Then he'd say: 'Shall we try one?' It was a good way of taking our mind off what we were there to do."

The band had set up in Ardent's smaller studio B, which was typically used for overdubs and mixing. Mars's drums were placed in the main tracking area, while Stinson played in the control room; Westerberg was sent to a neighboring five-by-seven concrete sound lock known as "the dungeon." It was, Dickinson noted accurately, the first time the Replacements had ever truly been separated in a recording studio. "I couldn't see them at all when we were cutting our rhythm tracks," said Westerberg, who was initially dubious of the setup.

Despite his old-school reputation, Dickinson staunchly advocated new methods and technology. "As primitive as I am, I consider myself a primitive *modernist,*" he said. Ardent had recently purchased a cutting-edge $360,000 Solid State Logic SL 6000E console and a $150,000 Mitsubishi X-850 thirty-two-track digital tape machine, which immediately became Dickinson's preferred recording setup. "I embraced digital as soon as I discovered it because it enabled me to record sounds that up to that point had been unrecordable," said Dickinson. He would then jerry-rig Ardent's state-of-the-art gear with a mix of ancient preamps and limiters, like an old Ampex eight-track tape deck, a sixties Fairchild compressor, and a nasty-looking Gates Level Devil, originally used for radio broadcasting.

Turning knobs was Ardent's engineer Joe Hardy, himself something of a tech wizard. Hardy had made his reputation working with the Fairlight, one of the very first digital samplers, which allowed everything—drums, vocals, guitars—to be copied, tuned and timed, and moved around in proto cut-and-paste fashion. Dickinson was enamored of the endless possibilities the Fairlight offered, and it would play a significant role on the Replacements' album.

The comically cantankerous Hardy sparred with the 'Mats immediately. "Occasionally you would get annoyed if one of them would sidle up next to you while you were trying to do something fairly complex," said Hardy, "and they'd be rambling drunkenly at you."

"Hardy put me in my place early on," said Westerberg. "I said something like, 'Jesus, how many fucking records have you made?' He turns around and goes, *'About a thousand!* How many have you made?' I went, 'Okay. Carry on.' I knew when I was full of shit."

The Ardent crew immediately focused on Chris Mars's drums. Mars was a ferocious snare player, but worked his kick drum inconsistently. "I started talking to him about his kick drum pattern—and he did not know what I was talking about," said Dickinson.

To help him focus, the engineers took a big barrel-shaped container of Green Sweep—a chemical powder used to clean Ardent's floors—emptied it, cut off the ends, and fastened it to Mars's kick, creating a four-foot-long extension on the drum. "It didn't do much to change the sound, but it centered his brain on this huge fucking kick drum in front of him," said Hardy. The device worked: within two or three days, said Dickinson, Mars "was playing his kick drum like Ringo."

Dickinson could sense the 'Mats' anxiety as they adjusted to Bob Stinson's absence and found their way in a new configuration. "Just the three of us," said Westerberg, "scared out of our wits."

Somewhere around the third day everything fell into place. The Blackberry Way demos hadn't hinted at a direction, but as they played through a stomping power pop instrumental that would become "Valentine" at Ardent, a new sound took shape. Instead of playing like three guys waiting for their fourth to show up, Paul, Tommy, and Chris locked in as a trio.

The results were promising. They recorded an exciting, if still evolving, version of "Red Red Wine"; the bittersweet fuzz-pop nugget "Kick It In"; a charming goof called "Beer for Breakfast"; and a few other similarly raucous numbers. Westerberg was being cagey and hadn't shown Dickinson his best material yet, such as the dark rumination "The Ledge" and the Who-styled "Nevermind."

At the end of the week, Michael Hill and Russ Rieger arrived in Memphis, desperately hoping for good news. At playback, the new tracks leapt out of the speakers. Dickinson had won them over. And the Replacements had decided to carry on as a band. "Tommy told me later . . . that they'd really come to Memphis to break up," said Dickinson. "They'd had it planned that they were going to theatrically combust."

CHAPTER 33

Jim Dickinson never let the truth get in the way of a good story, and the making of *Pleased to Meet Me* would become wrapped in the producer's tall tales. "In a way, that was the best thing Dickinson ever did for us," noted Paul Westerberg. "He helped build the legend."

Though he may have exaggerated the band's excesses, conjured nefarious record company plots out of thin air, and embellished the album's technical manipulations, Dickinson would fundamentally portray the recording as a transformative journey for the Replacements. In that respect at least, he couldn't have been more truthful.

The Replacements made three separate Memphis recording trips between November and January, working eight- to ten-day stretches. "Westerberg would do it for as long as he could put up with it, and then when he'd start to feel a compromise, he'd leave," said Dickinson.

Following the precipitous fall of Stax Records in 1975, the Memphis music scene had all but collapsed. The community was still psychically scarred from the assassination of Martin Luther King, Beale Street was lifeless, Sun Studio was boarded up, and the Stax building was empty and crumbling. Tommy Stinson described the city in late 1986 as "this weird ghost town where rock-and-roll had come from."

But Ardent Studios was flourishing again in the early eighties. It was situated in Midtown, once a thriving nightlife epicenter that, by the time the 'Mats arrived, was home to the indie rock venue the Antenna Club and little else.

Flopping at a nearby Holiday Inn, the band would start work around noon and begin drinking soon after. "After Bob left, it got worse," said Chris Mars. Added Westerberg: "The three of us were now drinking for four."

Soon Dickinson could chart the arc of their inebriation and get the best results accordingly. "Every day they were like a sine wave," he said. "They wouldn't be drunk enough early on in the day to get anything. Then they'd be good and drunk, and it would be great. And then they'd be too drunk, and they'd get useless."

The band's formal album sessions kicked off in mid-November with a new engineer, John Hampton. (Joe Hardy, called to other duties, would return to complete the record's mix.) Hampton had worked extensively with Alex Chilton. He began the session by tracking the band's call-and-response rocker "I Don't Know," a thrusting State of the 'Mats Address: "One foot in the door; the other one in the gutter / The sweet smell that you adore, I think I'd rather smother." Improvising a litany of questions as verses, Westerberg threw in a cheeky dig at Hampton: "Who's behind the board? They tell me he's a dope."

"IOU" was more band biography, Westerberg eager to cancel out old relationships: "I want it in writing / I owe you nothing." The song appeared to be directed at Peter Jesperson and Bob Stinson, but Westerberg said the literal inspiration came from an encounter with Iggy Pop: "I was on the bus with him after a show, and somebody asked for his autograph. He wrote, 'IOU NOTHING.' I thought it was the coolest thing in the world."

Like most of the harder rocking tracks, "IOU" and "I Don't Know" were nailed after just a couple of attempts. As a producer, Dickinson was always wary of losing the essence over multiple takes. The 'Mats' short attention spans also played a part. "They couldn't conceivably play the same song four or five times in a row, because they would get bored," said Dickinson. "So I would pick three or four songs, and we'd cut them like a set."

The band labored a bit more to nail "Red, Red Wine." Ironically, Westerberg's roaring ode had been written and demo-ed sober in his parents' basement. "I had the tape recorder on my mother's ironing board," he recalled. In Memphis, he topped off the track's bridge with a larynx-shredding scream—though he had to fight Dickinson to keep it on the record. Dickinson's wife, Mary Lindsey, insisted it remain.

The serrated scuzz metal chords of "Shooting Dirty Pool" provided the perfect backing for Westerberg's riposte to all the club owners and promoters they'd ever encountered. The song was sparked by an incident with Randy "Now" Ellis. A mailman by day and punk rock promoter by night, Ellis had staged a number of Replacements shows at City Gardens in Trenton, New Jersey. But after a disastrous August 1985 concert, Ellis called up the local college radio station and badmouthed the 'Mats, who heard the interview while driving. Westerberg had the van pull over to a pay phone, and he called up the station. He got in a heated conversation with Ellis on the air, which ended with Westerberg telling him to "blow it out your fuckin' ass."

To give the song's bar fight narrative some aural atmosphere, Dickinson recorded Westerberg smashing a beer bottle in the dungeon. Two Michelobs later, they had their sound effect. "It smelled like beer in there for a long time," said John Hampton.

The Replacements would leave another, more lasting mark on the studio. One afternoon Westerberg was inside the control room of studio B, swigging from a large jug of Gallo wine. "He took a gulp, and it came back up through his nose, and he caught it in his hands," said Dickinson, who claimed Westerberg stared at his upchuck for a moment, then casually tossed it into the air.

Weeks later, Ardent owner John Fry noticed the stain. "I'm not complaining, Jim," he told Dickinson, "but I'm just curious: how *did* they get the vomit on the ceiling?"

* * *

Though it was a dank little hole, Westerberg quickly made a home for himself in the dungeon cutting his parts. It was where Alex Chilton had set up for the moodier tracks on Big Star's *Third*. Ardent's engineers were quickly forced to pad the side walls with mattresses for fear that Westerberg would bang his head on the concrete while thrashing around.

Of more pressing concern, however, were Westerberg's lungs—his pleurisy began to flare up again during the sessions. On one occasion, trying to summon the strength to cut a vocal on "Shooting Dirty Pool," Westerberg stripped to the waist, slathered his chest with Ben-Gay, and howled until hoarse. "Spit and spew would come out of him," said Jim Lancaster. "When that session was done, that little closet was nasty."

The loud, fast tracks the 'Mats were capturing were arguably more ferocious than anything they'd done since *Stink*. Admittedly, the band was aided by some performance-enhancing drugs. Lancaster had visited a quack doctor out in the sticks who supplied him with copious amounts of speed. "That kept them awake and allowed them to drink more," he recalled. "The Replacements would take anything, anytime."

When the pills ran out, the band would spike their drinks with a natural liquid speed from China called Rocket Fuel. "It's good stuff," said Westerberg. "You come down real quick. After a half-hour, you have a headache and your stomach aches."

Outside of the studio, the 'Mats soaked up plenty of local color. Lancaster became their cultural tour guide. "These guys were from Minneapolis—to us they might as well have been from the fuckin' Netherlands," he said. Inside Lancaster's ever-present black satchel, he kept sundry drugs as well as cassettes of rare Southern R&B and country music. "I would play them shit you couldn't hear anywhere else: Eddie Hinton, Bill Brandon, various black singers from Jackson, Mississippi, like Tommy Tate."

Lancaster would take the band to the blues burger bar Huey's and the famed Peabody Hotel to hear the Fred Ford and Honeymoon Garner Trio. Wherever they went, the Replacements attracted attention, a magnet for women and odd characters. "I would have to try and keep them out of trouble," said Lancaster. "But they had a pretty good idea of where the arrest line was."

On one late-night excursion, Westerberg, Stinson, and a handful of groupies wound up at an after-hours club in the predominantly black section of North Memphis. Downing glass after glass of a strange blue liqueur, Westerberg noticed they were surrounded by a group of serious-looking characters, guns dangling as they leaned over and shot pool.

"We're sitting there with these girls, and one of them rips her shirt off to get our attention," said Westerberg. "And these dudes all around, packing heat, are staring at us and this bare-chested young woman. Me and Tommy just look at each other and laugh. We were too wasted to even perk up. *Shit . . .* we coulda got killed every day we were down there."

* * *

After seven years of letting Bob Stinson take the lead, in Memphis Westerberg "was a little anxious about being the sole guitar player and having to carry it all by himself," said John Hampton. "But he was so well medicated it was probably okay."

Westerberg tracked much of the record with a couple of Les Pauls, including his gnarled old gunmetal Junior and a black '57 "fretless wonder." Dickinson eventually sent the band to nearby Pyramid Guitars, where they picked out several new instruments on Warner's dime. Westerberg came back with a "see-through" Plexiglas Dan Armstrong—originally made famous by Keith Richards—that he'd feature on a number of solos.

Westerberg struck up a friendship with Pyramid's owner Rick Raburn. "He would come by shit-faced early in the day," recalled Raburn. "One time my wife and little daughter were there, and he was real embarrassed by it. He told me, 'When I'm home, I'm nothing like this. We only get like this to record and play.'"

For Dickinson, the biggest challenge was that Westerberg was constitutionally unable to repeat anything, frequently inverting his rhythm guitar parts. "Westerberg got mad at me for this, although later he copped to it in public: he's obviously dyslexic," said Dickinson. "He would play rhythm parts backwards, literally: the V chord for the IV chord, and the IV for the V."

Dickinson would piece together complete tracks out of the parts using the Fairlight sampler, and he'd do the same with Westerberg's lyrics. The singer wasn't yet in the habit of writing down complete lyrics and would sometimes dump out bits of paper, napkins, and matchbooks from the night before with verses scrawled on them. Once on the mic, he would usually deliver lyrics off the cuff, changing the words wholesale each time. "I realized he was throwing away [good] lines," said Dickinson. "So I kept them all, and I put together several of the songs in a computer."

Westerberg was nonplused about the sonic manipulations. "I knew they were sampling some of [the] drums, and I knew they were cutting my guitar and looping it. But I also knew enough about pop music—hell, the Byrds didn't play on a bunch of their best records. Whatever. We're still a rock-and-roll band."

* * *

The Memphis sessions were liberating for Westerberg. "When we started, 'art' was a word he wouldn't let me use," said Dickinson. "By the end of the session, he was calling himself an 'artist.'"

"It's been hard for me to do," Westerberg would admit shortly after the session, "but I've come to grips with the fact that I'm an artist. For years I pretended I wasn't. I pretended I was a punk, I pretended I was a rocker, and a drunk, and a hoodlum. I'm not a hoodlum. I'm a fucking artist. And now I can deal with that."

Though only a couple of delicate numbers made it onto the finished album, Westerberg cut half a dozen ballads in Memphis, songs he would have never considered if Bob Stinson had still been in the band. Rather than the teenage ardor of "Within Your Reach" or the youthful angst of "Unsatisfied," numbers like "Run for the Country," "Learn How to Fail," and "Birthday Gal" were about adult issues: grown-up love, the regrets that come with age, the difficulties of trying to mature in an adolescent rock-and-roll world.

That December, during a holiday break from recording, Westerberg decided to propose to Lori Bizer. "We were talking about what we were going to do for Christmas gifts," recalled Bizer. "And for me, it turned out to be a ring."

The language of Westerberg's lyrics was also evolving, as glimpsed on "Valentine," which borrowed its conceit from Joni Mitchell's "A Case of You": "If you were a pill I'd take a handful at my will / And I'd knock you back with something sweet and strong." He would abandon the song as unfinished, but when Warner Bros. requested another track to fill out the album's running time, Westerberg simply added a long solo and repeated the chorus in lieu of a final verse.

The simplest and most affecting number was the Twin Cities observational "Skyway"—written, ironically, in Memphis—about unrequited love, through a protagonist watching the object of his affection moving along the elevated walkways connecting frigid downtown Minneapolis. "It's generally the people who are shoppers or who work," said Westerberg. "I don't go up to the skyways. I sit down there and watch the people walk by." Still gun-shy about his softer material, Westerberg arrived at Ardent early one morning, while Tommy and Chris were still sleeping, to cut "Skyway" in private. (Mars's gentle rhythm and Dickinson's vibes were added later.)

The album's biggest departure was the cocktail jazz nocturne "Nightclub Jitters," which Westerberg wrote on his way to pick up smokes at a Super-America. In Minneapolis, Westerberg rarely ventured to bars or clubs anymore; he was tired of superficial relationships ("It don't matter much if we keep in touch") and felt disconnected from the crowd as he got older. "Sometimes someone . . . wants to come spit a drink in your face or pick a fight with you or something," he said.

Westerberg was uneasy about the song. "Paul said, 'Well, if we're going to cut this song, we're gonna have to get real musicians'—as if they weren't," said Dickinson, who'd brought in an old Yamaha electric piano and an odd electronic stand-up bass. "I left the room for fifteen minutes, and when I came back, Paul was playing the piano and Tommy was over in the corner playing the bass. We cut it in one take."

The song also offered Dickinson an opportunity to bring in the first of several guest players. Over the years the producer would try to portray the use of outside musicians as a Warner dictate; in truth, those choices were Dickinson's. He began by enlisting Edward "Prince Gabe" Kirby for "Nightclub Jitters," guessing correctly that the band would be charmed by the colorful Memphis horn legend, a Beale Street fixture since the 1930s and an almost vaudevillian character the 'Mats fell for instantly.

After Kirby completed his smoky, woozy sax solo, the band—listening in the control room—broke into spontaneous applause. Dickinson caught the moment on the talkback mic and added it to the end of the track. Just weeks later, Kirby collapsed at his home and died at age fifty-seven, after a longtime battle with high blood pressure and asthma. "We heard he died fucking a whore," recalled Stinson. "That's the way we wanted to go out. If you gotta go, you wanna go out onstage or fucking." Chris Mars's drawing of a sad-eyed sax man inside of the finished LP served as memoriam to Kirby.

* * *

At first Tommy and Jim Dickinson butted heads. Stinson tended to police those he felt were messing with the band's integrity. "I talk to people pretty much as I see it, and Tommy does pretty much the same thing," said Dickinson.

During one early argument, Dickinson dismissed Stinson, whom he felt wasn't being serious about the work.

"You don't think I'm serious?" asked Stinson. "I fired my fuckin' brother. *That's* how serious I am about this band."

From then on, the producer viewed Stinson differently. "I really let him produce that record whenever I didn't know what to do. His instincts were so sharp."

Their relationship grew beyond the sessions, taking on profound significance for each man over the years. "Tommy Stinson may be my favorite musician I've ever worked with," Dickinson would claim. "People say Keith Richards is the living embodiment of rock-and-roll? I'm sorry, but I know Keith, and it's Tommy."

"There was a kind of father-figure aspect to their relationship," noted Warner Bros.'s Michael Hill. "I don't think Paul needed that, but Tommy did."

Crucially, Dickinson would encourage Stinson's songwriting as well. In the midst of the session, the producer told Westerberg to take a day off from the studio in order for Stinson to cut his own material.

Stinson's writing was still in its infancy. He'd attempted one original, "Havin' Fun," during the *Tim* sessions, and he'd demo-ed several more at Blackberry Way over the summer. Inevitably, his songs were heavily influenced by Paul Westerberg. "Paul was always encouraging of me writing," said Stinson. For his part, Westerberg always felt awkward about Stinson's tunes. "[It] was a little painful, because he sounded so much like me," he said. "It was a little like listening to your own voice for the first time."

Stinson, playing most of the instruments, cut two tracks in Memphis: the full force rave-up "Trouble on the Way" and a gentle song dedicated to Daune Earle, "Try to Make This Your Home." Though rough and unpolished, Stinson's musicality and sheer exuberance shone through. "Without question the best things we cut . . . were Tommy's two solo songs and they're the only things that have never come out," said Dickinson. Stinson disagrees: "As I listen back, I can't sing; they're not great songs."

Stinson wasn't the only one: Chris Mars also wrote and sang an amusing, if slight, original called "All He Wants to Do Is Fish." Mars's deadpan delivery on the Sons of the Pioneers' Western loper "Cool Water" also wound up as a *Pleased to Meet Me* B-side—the first non-Westerberg lead vocal on a 'Mats release.

* * *

The music industry lived and breathed singles, so the Replacements needed some commercial songs, an issue High Noon's Russ Rieger pressed Westerberg on throughout the sessions. The manager saw the unfinished, mostly instrumental "Nevermind" as having the most potential. "In my mind that was an AOR single," said Rieger, who urged Westerberg to craft a populist set of lyrics to the song.

The lyrics to "Nevermind" would become a serious bone of contention. Rieger would regularly call the band in Memphis, pleading with Westerberg to make it a hit. "He'd say no . . . repeatedly. He'd start chanting it, actually: '*No, no, no, no, no, no!*'—then he'd hang up," recalled Rieger.

Rieger was crestfallen when he heard the finished track. "All over but the shouting . . . just a waste of time . . . nevermind." "That was my 'fuck you,'" said Rieger, "I always believed that." But the lyrics were also colored by Paul's uncertainty about his impending marriage ("I'm not as ready as I'll ever be . . . You oughta say if you're not sure"). Mostly, though, Westerberg admitted, "That's basically a song to Bob."

The months after the split had been awkward around Minneapolis. Neither Paul nor Tommy had seen Bob, and both feared the guilt that would accompany their first meeting since his firing. In a way, "Nevermind" recounted the breakdown of the band. As Westerberg recalled, "The line 'The words I thought I brought, I left behind' is the kind of thing where you intend on saying something to someone, apologizing, and then you get together and you're speechless, you don't know what to say. So, you know, *never mind.*"

The other track with rock radio potential, at least musically, was "The Ledge." Westerberg had cribbed the riff from "Highway Song," the 1979 hit from the Southern rockers Blackfoot, building it into a darkly melodious minor-key burner. Lyrically, it was rather knottier. Inspired by the deathly reckoning in Hank Williams's "Long Gone Lonesome Blues," Westerberg had been toying with the idea of a defiant suicide song for some time. Back in 1980, he'd come up with a number called "D-E-A-D"; the song's kicker line was: "You'll be sorry when I'm dead."

"The Ledge" would contain an undeniable element of autobiography—a whisper of Westerberg's own teenage overdose attempt and the suicide of his friend John Zika. Sitting home on a rainy afternoon in the fall of 1986, he wrote "The Ledge" in forty-five minutes, from the perspective of a jumper looking down at a gathering crowd below: "I'm the boy they can't ignore / For the first time in my life, I'm sure."

In the studio, the band vested the song with a perfect combination of nervous energy and fatalistic drive. "They reached beyond themselves on that one," said John Hampton. Cut in a single take, everything was done live, even Westerberg's haunted vocals, which ended with the song's protagonist hurtling to his death. "When he finally jumps off—it sounds like he's actually jumping off the ledge," said Hampton of the recording. "It was like, 'What did we just go through? Did we just go through a suicide?' It felt like we had."

When the take was over, a drained Westerberg collapsed on the control room couch and asked Dickinson: "I don't have to do that again, do I?"

★ ★ ★

The figure casting the longest shadow over the Memphis sessions, in more ways than one, was Alex Chilton, whose connection to Dickinson had been the initial lure for coming to Ardent. The producer made a point of using many of the same microphones he'd utilized to record Big Star's *Third*.

The band hadn't seen Chilton since the infamous Houston concert riot a year earlier. Chilton would occasionally turn up at Ardent, usually barefoot. "We caught a couple funny glances from him when he heard like 'Shooting Dirty Pool,'" recalled Westerberg. "He rolled his eyes to the ceiling and walked out."

Westerberg had been messing with a song titled "George from Outer Space"—loosely inspired by a 'Mats road pal named George Lewis—before reworking it into an homage called "Alex Chilton." When Westerberg first met Chilton backstage at CBGB in December 1984, he'd fumbled for an icebreaker: "I'm in love with that one song of yours—*what's that song?*" (He was thinking of Big Star's "Watch the Sunrise.") For the Memphis sessions, Westerberg had turned it into a lyrical hook ("I'm in love / With that song") and developed a chord sequence that "reminded me of a singsongy pop kind of thing [like] Big Star."

Westerberg worried that a song about Chilton was too on the nose. But Mars and Stinson pushed him to complete it; in return, he gave them each a cowriting credit. "If there's a sense of 'Oh God, what if this is looked on as being stupid or weird?'—that's usually a tip-off that it's worth doing," he said. "Those are generally the best songs, and I had that feeling about 'Alex

Chilton.'" The lyric represented a hopeful projection on Westerberg's part as well: in a world where "children by the million" clamored for Alex Chilton, surely they'd beg for the Replacements too.

The timing was perfect. The Bangles had just covered Big Star's "September Gurls" on their multi-platinum *Different Light*, and R.E.M. and other young acts were regularly name-checking the group in interviews. "There was more than a grain," said Westerberg of lines like "I never travel far / Without a little Big Star," "that I thought it would appear hip. But a lot of it was genuine. We did absolutely live with those Big Star tapes for years, so it sunk in there."

Ironically, Chilton never listened to the song in Memphis. "We made sure to turn 'Alex Chilton' off every time he came in," said Westerberg, "because I didn't want him to take it the wrong way." It wasn't until the following spring, when he opened some concert dates for the 'Mats, that Chilton finally heard it for the first time.

"I couldn't really make out the words," Chilton recalled. "Then I heard the record and couldn't make out the words there either." Still, he would allow that it was "a pretty good song" and a boost for his reputation. "I feel like a great legendary outlaw, like John Wesley Harding or something," he would say.

Originally, the idea had been for Chilton to play lead guitar on the track. Instead, he played on "Can't Hardly Wait."

It was the song that wouldn't die. Since writing "Can't Hardly Wait" shortly after the *Let It Be* sessions, Westerberg and the band had tried recording it myriad ways. A live version had appeared on *The Shit Hits the Fans*; they'd cut both acoustic and electric versions with Chilton producing in early '85, then re-recorded it for *Tim*. "We had played it so many times that we were tired of it," Westerberg said.

Michael Hill urged them to take one last shot in Memphis. After a couple of unenthusiastic early passes at a straight eighth-note pace, they returned to it after a particularly grueling night out. "I was hungover," Westerberg said. "So we started off with the quiet guitar, and everything fell in from there."

Fittingly, it was a Memphis-style interpretation, with everyone, even Mars, laying back on the groove. Westerberg rewrote the final verse in bed at the Holiday Inn. To punctuate its dramatic stops and starts, Dickinson spiked the song with a couple of big moments of digital silence just before Westerberg's pleading choruses.

The more prominent contributions would come from a pair of the city's most famous sidemen: tenor saxophonist Andrew Love of the Memphis Horns and Ben Cauley, trumpeter for the Bar-Kays and the lone survivor of the Otis Redding plane crash. Westerberg didn't object to using horns, but he was initially concerned they might be too jarring. To ensure plausible denial, he and Stinson left Memphis the day before the horns were actually cut.

With the band gone, Dickinson took further liberties: he hired classical violinist Max Huls from the Memphis State University music department to add strings—a nod to Dan Penn's pop-soul productions with Chilton's Box

Tops. Westerberg would blanch at the string additions and later disavow them to the press, mostly to defuse backlash from their more orthodox fans. "It's like the Replacements trying to sound like 1968," he said, "in [our] own feeble way."

* * *

The Replacements might have been recording at a $10,000-a-week studio, but after seven years, they were still scraping by. "We're making welfare money," Westerberg told a reporter at the time. "Seven hundred and fifty dollars a month . . . [and] all the beer you can drink."

Westerberg had long resigned himself to penury. "I remember I was having a tuna fish sandwich in some restaurant in Memphis," he said, "when Vito [Jim Lancaster] kinda exploded at me: 'You think your fucking manager up in New York City is having a tuna sandwich right now? You think those guys up there are living like you are?' That was the first time it came in those terms: *Those guys up there*."

As sessions continued into 1987, the record's paradoxical character—Dickinson's high-fidelity recording of a low-fidelity sound—came clear. Mars's drums had been given new prominence. "[The] drums don't just sound like they're being hit, but like they're flying apart, *exploding*," said Dickinson. That propulsion was balanced as Dickinson filled the spaces with bits of weirdness: "I'm doing stuff like taking the echo and syncopating it, creating a kind of groove with nothing but an effects loop," he noted.

For all its electronic manipulation, *Pleased to Meet Me* was highlighted by a number of very human mistakes. Tommy cackling during takes, Paul fumbling to find his microphone in the dungeon, Chris knocking his cymbal off its stand and sending it crashing onto the floor—Dickinson studded the tracks with such moments.

By mid-January, basic recording was complete, and the 'Mats went back to Minneapolis with a batch of John Hampton's rough mixes. The band was under the impression that the final mix wouldn't be radically different, but Dickinson had other ideas.

With Joe Hardy back on board, the producer spent another three weeks in the studio mixing; Hampton returned again for final tweaks. Dickinson layered organ and piano overdubs, crediting himself as East Memphis Slim. He created the clattering opening of "I Don't Know" with a drum sample and ran Westerberg's guitar through a Leslie speaker to conjure the quavering feel on "Nevermind." He also made tons of tiny embellishments via the Fairlight.

Westerberg didn't fight the postproduction changes. "We really didn't fucking care," he said. "They were spending a lot of money, and Jim was determined to give the company the product of the day." It would be the last time the 'Mats were ever so accommodating in the studio. "I think they learned a lot about how to make a record watching me," noted Dickinson, "and took it out on the next couple of producers."

CHAPTER 34

The Replacements still hadn't replaced Bob Stinson, and the band was deluged with correspondence from guitarists angling for the gig. "[They] were, for the most part, pretty bad," said Westerberg. "All of them were big Replacements fans and were trying to fill Bob's shoes, and that's not at all what we wanted."

High Noon, meanwhile, was making a more serious effort to push the band to hire, in Gary Hobbib's words, "a guitar-slinger." What High Noon really wanted was another Tommy Stinson: someone young, with an attractive look and personality, who could also play.

The most intriguing candidate was Texas phenom Charlie Sexton. Already a burgeoning solo star, having hit the charts the previous year with an aggressively marketed debut for MCA, the eighteen-year-old had the goods despite the hype. He'd come up through Austin's roots music scene as a prodigy and had backed up the likes of Bob Dylan, Keith Richards, and Ron Wood.

Surprisingly, the Replacements were receptive to the notion of hiring a "featured" guitarist, but decided not to pursue Sexton for typically capricious reasons. "I think we saw one of his press photos or something and thought, 'Naaaah,'" recalled Westerberg. With his tousled hair, pouty lips, and chiseled looks, "Cheekbone Charlie," as Sexton had been dubbed, was unnervingly handsome. "Christ, he was way too good-lookin'," said Tommy Stinson. "Yikes."

No, a full-fledged band member needed to be able to get the Replacements' sense of humor and tolerate their drinking. And he had to be from Minneapolis. Naturally, they began looking in their local tavern. One night at the CC Club they shanghaied their drinking buddy David Postlethwaite into going to rehearsal with them. Peter Jesperson's close friend and roommate, Postlethwaite had played in a number of Twin Cities bands; Chris and Tommy had recently backed him on a track for a Twin/Tone compilation. But with everyone more than halfway in the bag, the late-night session didn't go well, and Postlethwaite faded as a possibility.

A more serious candidate was Jeff Waryan, who'd been in Fingerprints and Curtiss A's band before launching a solo project called Figures on Twin/Tone. "Paul's dad and my dad played golf together," said Waryan. "They would talk about their rock-and-roll sons, and we would joke about going to caddy for them."

They spent two nights jamming at the band's new downtown rehearsal space. Waryan was a slinky, elegant guitarist in the mold of the Only Ones' John Perry. "Paul left the lead stuff up to me, and we actually had a blast." Waryan's low-key demeanor also offered a welcome change from Bob Stinson's outsized persona. Westerberg offered Waryan the job, but Waryan was deeply committed to Figures, which had just released a new album and had a couple of tours already on the books.

With Waryan out, Tommy Stinson decided to take the initiative. That winter he visited the offices of First Avenue, quizzing the club's booker Chrissie Dunlap about potential candidates. As the conversation wound down, Dunlap grinned and said: "If you *really* want the best guitarist in Minneapolis, I happen to know just the guy."

* * *

Born to a distinguished clan of newsmen, lawyers, and politicians, Bob Dunlap had been expected to follow their path. The Dunlaps were Scots who'd arrived in America in the late nineteenth century and settled in St. Paul, where they became one of the city's influential families. Bob's grandfather, Roy Dunlap Sr., was the managing editor for the *St. Paul Pioneer Press and Dispatch* for thirty-five years; his son, Roy Jr., would become the paper's columnist and managing editor.

Bob's father, Robert Rankin Dunlap, graduated from the University of Minnesota law school in 1941—just as the Japanese attacked Pearl Harbor. He spent the next few years fighting in Europe, eventually in the medical corps. He returned home in 1946 with a new bride, Jane Elizabeth Smith, whom he'd met while stationed in Virginia. Jane was a grade school art teacher, and the couple would have five children together—three girls and two boys—with Robert Bruce Dunlap arriving in the middle of the pack on August 14, 1951.

Plainview, Minnesota, was a town of 1,500, ninety miles southeast of the Twin Cities. There, the elder Dunlap served as a country lawyer to a community of farmers and field hands. There was little money around. "He'd work for a half a hog, or a farmer would pull up and dump a bushel of corn on our doorstep, and that was payment," recalled his son. Eventually, Dunlap was elected to the Minnesota State Senate as a Republican, representing Olmstead and Wabasha Counties for thirteen years, starting in 1953.

Though he made his name in public service, Robert Dunlap was also a gifted piano player who favored the ballads of Hoagy Carmichael. "That's probably why he tolerated my ambitions towards music and would help me along, even though he worried about it," said Bob Dunlap. "It always was and always would be a horrible way to make a living."

As a boy, Bob was highly intelligent, somewhat eccentric, and incredibly skinny. With his mop of curly black hair, big ears, and pipe-cleaner arms, he cut a curious figure among the corn-fed farm kids, who teased him for his brains and lack of brawn. The catcalls were always about his size: Beanpole, Skinny, Slim.

Music was his refuge. He loved rock's greasy-haired rebels—Elvis, Eddie Cochran, Gene Vincent—but his great hero was the bookish Buddy Holly. "It was so fun to hear a new Buddy Holly song on the radio—the utter simplicity of it compared to recordings by Perry Como, with fancy strings and a twenty-seven-piece orchestra."

By his early teens, Dunlap would sneak into his older sister's room to pluck away at her little tenor guitar. Finally, his father bought him his own six-string. "I stayed up all night long for decades working really hard to get good," said Dunlap. "For some people, music comes really easy. Other people have to work really, really hard to simulate that. In my case, no one can really know just how hard."

In 1964, as he was entering high school, Dunlap's father moved the family to neighboring Rochester. "There were two cliques in the town, the rich kids and the poor kids, and I never really made it with any group," he said. Dunlap would frequently skip school to wander the country's byways alone. His father had to pull strings to get his son a diploma.

After graduating, Dunlap would carry a worn copy of Woody Guthrie's *Bound for Glory* as he hitchhiked around the state. In 1969 he enrolled at the University of Minnesota in Minneapolis but dropped out after a couple semesters. He spent most of his time there tracing Bob Dylan's steps through Dinkytown. "To someone my age, there was no touching his importance," said Dunlap.

His first band was a Small Faces–styled mod outfit, Mrs. Frubbs. At one of their shows at a farm outside the cities in 1971, Dunlap met Chrissie Nelson. "Bob was so cool, you'd never know he was from the Midwest," she recalled. "He actually spoke with a bit of a British accent, which was a little odd, but we were all very young."

Born in August 1950, Nelson was raised in the Minneapolis suburb of St. Louis Park; her father was an architect, her mother a pharmacist. She attended her first show at age fourteen: Jimmy Reed at the Marigold Ballroom. Chrissie forged a note from her mother to gain entry. She'd also dropped out of the U of M after a couple of semesters. Chrissie took one look at the lean, frizzy-haired guitarist onstage and fell in love: "Bob and I sat up on a hay bale talking all night, and we've been together ever since."

Dunlap spent the early seventies "in some god-awful bands," he said, as well as working as a cab driver. In 1976 he joined Thumbs Up, a variety band led by a wild white-soul shouter named Curt Almsted, aka Curtiss A. "We all lived this white trash existence in the city, but Slim was a little different," said

Almsted. "He'd had this small-town existence, but he also grew up reading *The New Yorker.* He was smart."

As the city dragged around in flares and a Quaalude haze, Almsted served up the sharkskin-suit soul of Wilson Pickett and the melodic finery of the British Invasion. Thumbs Up helped sow the seeds of Minneapolis's first-wave punk. "We all went to see Curt's band all the time," said Peter Jesperson. "I wanted to start a record label to make Curt Almsted records."

Inspired by Scotty Moore and Chet Atkins, Dunlap had learned to play with a thumb-pick. "I was never into playing fast and fancy anyway," he said. Dunlap would use his thumb and fingers to pull at chords; his colleagues would refer to "Bob's Chinese guitar." "He'd provide these moody, atmospheric, almost keyboard-like sounds," said Almsted.

Thumbs Up toured the five-state ballroom circuit in a rickety school bus, making a nice living on the road. "Those were good years, even though I was left alone most of the time," said Chrissie, who married Dunlap and raised their daughter Bee and twins Delia and Louie. By the late seventies, Thumbs Up switched its name to the Spooks. Though Almsted and Dunlap were old guard, punks and new wavers welcomed them at the Longhorn.

The Spooks signed to the newly minted Twin/Tone, releasing an EP in 1978, while Chrissie got a job at the recently reconstituted Sam's, later First Avenue, in 1979. Though major labels in New York poked around, Almsted quickly soured any potential deals, telling A&R men: "If you guys fuck me over, I'm going to slit your throats."

In 1979 the band changed its name again, to the Personals. During sessions for that band's Twin/Tone album, Almsted got drunk, punched a metal wall, and broke his hand. The rest of the group bailed, including Dunlap, who went on to front his own short-lived group, the Sentimentals.

Driving his cab, Dunlap would see Bob Stinson walking along Lake Street. One winter night he picked him up, and they struck up a deep, almost profound friendship—two sensitive children saved by music. In 1981, when Stinson's band opened for the Sentimentals, "they blew me off the stage," said Dunlap. "When we started playing, you could just feel it: what we were doing was old, and this was the new thing."

By the mid-1980s, Dunlap was working as a janitor at First Avenue and the Uptown Theater and playing local gigs. He was the consummate sideman—in thrall to the music even if it wasn't a career anymore.

* * *

I ronically, the person urging Dunlap to go for the job most was Bob Stinson. As they shined First Avenue's floors each day, Stinson would badger Dunlap to try out for the Replacements, occasionally grabbing a mop to mime the licks Dunlap needed to learn. Referring to Westerberg, Stinson would tell him, "Oh, he's from hell. I don't wish him upon my worst enemy, but *you* . . . you could do it."

Dunlap never quite understood the reasoning. But Carleen Krietler said it was always Bob's firm and faithful belief that Dunlap was the only man *worthy* of taking his place in the band. In fact, when Westerberg fired him, Stinson had suggested Dunlap as his successor: "I heard Bob say," Krietler remembered, "'I sweep floors with someone who's pretty good.'"

Tommy Stinson was coming to the same conclusion. He'd known Dunlap for years. "He sang good backgrounds . . . had cool guitar sounds. And he seemed to be Curt's better half," recalled Tommy. On a personal level, Dunlap was Westerberg's kind of character: a wry, Midwestern intellect, like a cranky, comic uncle who also possessed a calming manner to help stabilize Paul's moods, as he had Almsted's. To High Noon and Warner Bros., Dunlap—thirty-five, married, three kids—was a strange choice, which itself was part of the attraction for the band.

In January 1987, Dunlap was at Nicollet Studios playing pedal steel on a Curtiss A record when Tommy came by and invited him to meet the band for a drink at J. D. Hoyt's, a bar near the 'Mats' rehearsal space. It was an audition of sorts; they wanted to see how he handled his booze.

The Replacements didn't mince words: they wanted Dunlap in the band. He demurred—he was too old, he couldn't tour, he couldn't play Bob Stinson's stuff right, every excuse he could think of. Eventually, they talked him into coming next door to rehearse. "I tried desperately to play 'not the guy'–type guitar," said Dunlap. "But they had a couple new songs that I liked, and it was a good little moment."

Returning to Hoyt's, the band again pressed him to join, but Dunlap was still resistant. They went back and forth for many hours and many rounds. Finally, a cracked compromise was reached: They would all drink until somebody dropped. If one of the 'Mats went down first, they'd leave Dunlap alone; if he fell before them, he would join the band.

The next morning Dunlap rubbed his bleary eyes and reached to steady his pounding head. He looked around and saw that he was at home, in bed, but couldn't remember when or how he'd gotten there. All he was sure of was that he was the Replacements' new guitarist.

Dunlap was an unconventional choice: "Like the Rolling Stones deciding to replace Brian Jones, not with Mick Taylor, but with Carl Perkins," said Westerberg, who later joked that they'd selected Dunlap primarily because he had something none of the rest of the band had: a driver's license. But Westerberg's interest was more serious than that. His songs were changing, and a versatile, sympathetic player like Dunlap would be an asset. "I wanted someone bluesier, who was hip to country music," said Westerberg, "'cause that's where I envisioned the band going."

For Dunlap's sixteen-year-old daughter Bee, it was a surreal turn. "She was a Replacements fanatic," said Chrissie Dunlap. "She *loved* that band. I almost came to hate the *Sorry Ma* record, because that's all she played for a long time.

So when Bob joined the band, it would've been like if my dad had joined the Beatles."

Dunlap had a teenage daughter and two younger children entering grade school. With a solid year of roadwork awaiting the band, he'd be pulled away for months at a time. "Paul always was very aware of that, and concerned," said Chrissie. "He asked me more than once if that was going to be okay." But Chrissie had always championed Bob's music. "It was an answer to my wishes. I couldn't imagine holding him back for a second."

The next order of business was a new handle. "Tommy couldn't deal with calling him Bob," said Daune Earle, "because it was just such a wrenching thing for him to go from one Bob to a [different] Bob." Slim, the schoolyard jibe from Dunlap's childhood, was now his affectionate stage name.

Given Dunlap's fairly prosaic local CV, the band decided to feed the national press a series of whoppers. Chuckled Westerberg: "We figured we would pretend we found a genuine bluesman." They claimed he was "Small Town Slim," an ex-con from the wilds of Wabasha County. Foreign journalists were told the tale of "Blind Boy Slim." "I remember being on tour in the Netherlands," said Dunlap, "and a guy telling me, 'You see pretty well for someone who was blind. It's in the paper that for many years you were blind and just recently recovered your sight.'"

But Dunlap's role with the Replacements was less mythmaking than grounding. He would become a close confidant to Mars, offer emotional encouragement to a still-maturing Tommy, and serve as counsel, musical foil, and amateur psychologist to Westerberg.

Yet like the others, he had an incredibly jaundiced view of the music business. "He was just like them," said Gary Hobbib, laughing. "He didn't trust anybody, didn't like anybody. He was a born Replacement."

CHAPTER 35

In spite of the *Saturday Night Live* debacle, the firings of Peter Jesperson and Bob Stinson, and the canceled tour, High Noon was determined to rally the Replacements' label to their cause. "Warner Brothers would put out so many records a week, and they weren't just any records—it was Van Halen and ZZ Top," said Russ Rieger. "We had to get enough key people on board to mount a serious campaign."

The rough mixes from Memphis made it clear that the album was going to be far more viable commercially than *Tim*. High Noon began badgering Seymour Stein for help. "We said, 'We can't take the record around from office to office,'" said Hobbib.

Under the right circumstances, High Noon figured the Replacements could actually be charming and ingratiating. Rieger suggested that Stein pay for key Warner staff to fly to Memphis for a playback party with the band at Ardent. They would have dinner and drinks, spend a night on the town with the boys, and get everyone excited about the record. Stein agreed and on January 14 sent a memo to more than two dozen Warner and Sire employees:

> The Replacements are truly becoming a household word. Our goal in 1987 is to expand these households from a basic college and grass roots following to the rock 'n' roll world at large. . . . To expand this company's awareness of the Replacements and their increased potential Sire Records would like to host a listening party celebration. . . . Please join us in Memphis. I guarantee no one will be disappointed.

If nothing else, Stein knew how to throw a party. Set for mid-February, the trip would include accommodations at the historic Peabody Hotel and a VIP tour of Graceland. The very fact that the company was shelling out for such a lavish excursion didn't escape anyone's attention. "You didn't pile people from Burbank and New York and fly them to Memphis to listen to records normally," said national sales manager Charlie Springer. "We might've done it for Paul Simon or Madonna, but not for a band like the Replacements."

The 'Mats themselves were oblivious to High Noon's coup. "It went over our heads. It seemed perfectly natural that everyone at the company should be there because we are the Replacements and *we've* made a record," said Westerberg. "We were that arrogant. We had no idea that this was a special privilege."

On the day of the party, the band ventured to a Goodwill near Beale Street and outfitted themselves in deafeningly loud plaid suits, fat ties, and misshapen homburgs. But their label head one-upped them. "Seymour arrived in Memphis off a plane from Paris," said Jim Dickinson. "He was wearing a tuxedo jacket with little Playboy bunnies all embossed over it. . . . I don't think he'd been asleep in a week. The first words out of his mouth were 'Where's the coke?'"

Amid a steady flow of booze and substances, playback commenced. "We were putting our best foot forward, in a way," said Tommy Stinson. "We tried to embrace some of the Warner people, probably the most we did ever. Sitting there in a room with thirty people playing our new record? That was a huge goddamn move for us."

As the band went around the room greeting label execs, many of whom they hadn't met, Tommy began to repeat a little joke: "Pleased to meet me, the pleasure is all yours." The band would use that phrase—"Pleased to Meet Me"—as the album's title. The cover depicted a Faustian handshake between a scruffy rock-and-roller, played by Westerberg, and a bejeweled record executive.

Somehow, Westerberg and Stinson managed to convince the rest of the label that their new guitarist Slim Dunlap—whom the brass were meeting for the first time—actually was a gun-wielding ex-con with a hair-trigger temper. "I think we actually had them going," said Stinson.

One Warner staffer asked Dunlap, with a slight air, what he'd done before joining the band. Dunlap snapped back: "What the fuck do you do for a living?"

The Replacements didn't need any help being ornery. "We probably insulted a couple people during the party," said Westerberg. "The fucker in the leather pants, the guy in charge of getting the record on the radio, Tommy said something rude to him, and one of us might've pissed on his foot in the bathroom."

As the partygoers mingled, the record played repeatedly. It was greeted by universal excitement—though Stein did take Hill and Westerberg aside to tell them the album needed another track, since it was only twenty-eight minutes long, prompting the adding of "Valentine" to the running order.

The party moved to Justine's. Housed in a nineteenth-century Italianate mansion, the French restaurant, a favorite of Stein's, was known for its rich crab and lobster dishes and signature cakes. "I think the main reason Seymour was willing to pay for the whole trip was just so he could eat there," said one Sire employee.

Stein had arranged for a private second-floor dining room. The Warner crew did its best to keep up with the 'Mats' drinking pace. "Later on, a lot of people at the label started going to AA and rehab," said marketing staffer Jo Lenardi. "But Memphis was well before that time, so everyone was acting pretty crazy."

During dinner, Stein proffered a toast to the band, delivering a wildly impassioned speech connecting the Replacements to Memphis's rich legacy and placing them in the continuum of great American music.

Then dessert was served.

As the waitstaff brought out soufflés and elegantly arrayed silver bowls filled with chocolate sauce and crème fraîche, it was obvious where things were headed. "The trouble started with Chris Mars," recalled Dickinson. "I saw him tilt a little sideways, [then] he took off his hat, took this poufed-up pie, put it on his head, and put the hat back on."

"The next thing you know," said Warner's radio promoter Steve Tipp, "the band was making hot fudge sundaes on each other's heads."

Wide-eyed waiters looked on as the Replacements and their label overlords engaged in a massive food fight, chasing each other around the room. "Seymour was the wildest," said video producer Randy Skinner, who watched Stein running around smearing chocolate onto the restaurant's silk damask wallpaper. "I remember Tommy looking at me like, '*This* is the head of the label?'" said Julie Panebianco. Just then, Stein jumped up on a table to belt, off-key, "You Are My Sunshine." The band hopped on and joined in.

Justine's management had seen enough. "They said the chandeliers were about to fall off the ceiling," recalled Stein. "I was keeping the beat on the table. The Replacements were on relatively good behavior for them, and it was me that fucked up. But it was a great, great night."

"After that night," said Michael Hill, "everybody walked away with a commitment to work that record."

* * *

If the Replacements' relationship with Warner Bros. was on an upswing, the band's dealings with Twin/Tone were becoming increasingly contentious.

While Peter Jesperson retained his partnership in the label, he was still licking his wounds from the Replacements experience. Working a day job in a warehouse, he removed himself from Twin/Tone's business for several years.

Though Jesperson was sitting on hours of unreleased Replacements material, there was little concern that he might release or bootleg the material for financial gain. The band didn't share that same faith when it came to Twin/Tone's head, Paul Stark.

The group's enmity toward Stark had only grown over the years. Westerberg's refusal to sign a contract with Twin/Tone meant the first four Replacements records were made on a handshake agreement and an understanding that once the group recouped, they'd be given a 20 percent royalty. By 1987, the 'Mats' back catalog was shifting serious units. The group was far and away the company's top act, representing over half of its overall sales, with the Mekons and Soul Asylum a distant second and third.

Despite that boost, Twin/Tone was in constant financial turmoil, largely owing to a series of crippling distributor bankruptcies; the first, in 1986, was Los Angeles–based Greenworld, which went under owing Twin/Tone over $100,000. "It seemed like one big distributor bankruptcy would happen every year," said Dave Ayers, who remained Twin/Tone's vice president until 1991. "They would always leave a five- or six-figure debt that we'd never be able to reconcile."

Making matters worse was the somewhat precarious manner in which the label's day-to-day operations were handled. "Bless Paul Stark's heart, but he did not know how to run a business," said one former Twin/Tone employee. "Whoever was screaming the loudest would get paid; otherwise, you wouldn't."

In the fall of 1986, Twin/Tone was heavily promoting Soul Asylum's third album, *While You Were Out*, hoping for a breakthrough. At the same time the company began missing its scheduled royalty payments to the Replacements. "The justification became, 'Do we stop putting records out and pay a few people whose royalties are due, or do we keep putting records out, sell them, and then we can pay everybody?'" said Ayers. "That's what it turned into."

By issuing more product, Twin/Tone was incentivizing its remaining distributors to pay on time. To keep the product flow steady, Twin/Tone continued signing bands and hiring employees. At one point its roster included nearly forty acts, including the 'Mats' road pals Agitpop. "I remember telling Westerberg, 'I think we're gonna sign to your old label,'" said Agitpop's John DeVries. "He laughed in my face."

It appeared, from the outside at least, that Twin/Tone was doing well. "It was all a shell game," said Ayers. "There was no money there."

By early 1987, the Replacements claimed they were owed nearly $30,000 in royalties; the label put the figure closer to $5,000. Stark did little to assuage the animus brewing. "He fueled the paranoia," said Ayers. "It would've been very easy for him to dispel a lot of that, but he just wasn't interested."

If Stark wasn't going to respond on his own, the 'Mats would just have to find a way to get his attention.

* * *

In the last week of February, Slim Dunlap rounded up the band for a photo session in a black Dodge van. Driving through Uptown, Westerberg noticed an old rifle wrapped in a blanket in back. Dunlap had been given the gun by a friend who wanted him to test it out. Westerberg encouraged him to use it as a prop, to play up the "Small Town Slim" persona.

After finishing with the photographer, the band was drinking its lunch at the Black Forest Inn, a German biergarten a stone's throw from Twin/Tone's offices, and stewing about the money they were owed. To add further insult,

Twin/Tone had just announced that it was going to release *Sorry Ma*, *Stink*, and *Hootenanny* on cassette for the first time.

As the drinks and anger flowed, the band got an idea: they would steal their master tapes from the label. In fact, they would destroy them. Westerberg advocated a ceremonial end by casting them into the Mississippi River.

"That part never made any sense to me," said Dunlap, who proposed hiding the tapes in his basement. "If you steal 'em, then keep 'em. Why throw them in the river? But it wasn't a logical discussion."

Dunlap pulled up in front of the Twin/Tone complex on Nicollet and left the engine running. The other three entered the building. Tommy chatted up receptionist Roz Ferguson, while Westerberg and Mars headed for the storage area and began rummaging through the tape library. "If it went to court, I don't think anybody could testify that they actually *saw* Chris and I grab any tapes," said Westerberg coyly.

Initially, staffer Chris Osgood and office manager Abbie Kane didn't give the band's presence much thought. "They had this look on their faces like they were up to something," said Osgood. "That wasn't weird in itself—they were always up to something."

After a few minutes, Mars and Westerberg left quietly. Stinson soon followed, carrying a large box. Kane held the door for him. She watched Dunlap's van peel off and walked back inside. "I got maybe ten steps in and Paul Stark came running out saying, 'Where the hell did Tommy go?'" recalled Kane. "'Where are the tapes? *Where are the tapes?*'"

Tearing down Nicollet Avenue, the band looked through their haul. "The stuff wasn't clearly labeled," said Tommy. "Some of it was ours. But we could've gotten other people's records too." (A later inventory revealed that the band had mostly grabbed Replacements album safeties used for promotional cassette dubs. The band's master tapes were actually stored inside Twin/Tone's second-floor suite of offices. "See," said Westerberg, "we were too lazy to even go up a flight of stairs.")

Heading downtown, Dunlap pulled over by a railroad bridge. Westerberg wanted to send the tapes dramatically over the water. "But I said, 'What if you get out onto the middle of the bridge and a fucking train comes along?'" recalled Dunlap. "There was no place to walk. That freaked 'em out. So they decided, 'We better not hike out there.'"

They found a safer spot near the old Pillsbury Mill building. Atop a small embankment, they began bowling down spools of tape into the Big River. "It was fun," recalled Westerberg. "A lot of them we rolled down the hill and the reels came undone. Then we realized we had to go to the edge, down to the lip, to get them into the water. Instead of floating out and then gently plopping down," he said, "they just sunk like a stone."

Initially in high spirits, the 'Mats headed to the CC Club, crowing about the caper. Somewhere between rounds, the realization hit that they'd actually failed in their original mission. The handful of tapes they'd gotten couldn't have been their master reels. If they weren't at the studio, the band figured they must be stored at Stark's home in the nearby suburb of Golden Valley.

"By the time we'd gotten past the part of throwing things in the river, we were even drunker," said Stinson, "and we took it to the next level: 'Let's go to Stark's house; let's go rob him.'"

Despite Dunlap's reluctance, he took the wheel again. Soon the band began creeping through Stark's tony neighborhood. When they arrived at his house, it was obvious that Stark's wife, Julia Bertholf, was home.

Tommy rang the bell. The plan, such as it was, called for another charm diversion. Bertholf, however, was immediately suspicious of her rubber-legged, reeking young visitor. She slammed the door in his face and quickly dialed her husband.

The 'Mats' drunken initiative was dissipating into alcohol fatigue. The legal implications hit them as well: "Stealing from the record company what we thought was ours was one thing, but entering a guy's home . . . that's when it got a little dicey," said Westerberg. The band skittered away empty-handed. "We figured we'd made our point anyway," said Stinson.

By then, word had already gotten back to the Twin/Tone offices that the 'Mats had thrown the stolen tapes in the river. "When we heard that, I do remember some irreverent laughter," said Kane. "It was the Replacements—you really had to just laugh. Unless you were Paul Stark." The next morning, the story of the heist was being wildly exaggerated around town—one version of the tale had Slim and his rifle holding the label's employees at bay while the others grabbed the tapes. "That was no longer funny," said Dunlap.

Unsurprisingly, the cold war between the band and the label grew chillier over the next eighteen months, culminating in a 1988 lawsuit seeking a lien on the unpaid royalties. The parties settled out of court two years later. By then, Twin/Tone was in better financial shape, having signed a pressing and distribution deal with major label A&M (later Soul Asylum's home). Stark agreed to pay off the 'Mats' balance—now unarguably in the $30,000 range—over a year. He also got his wish: the wording of the settlement acknowledged that the label *did* have a binding contract with the band.

In November 1990, Tommy Stinson signed the agreement on behalf of the group, as vice president and partner of the Replacements LLC. Technically speaking, Twin/Tone never did get Westerberg's signature on a contract.

CHAPTER 36

Happy as Warner Bros. was with *Pleased to Meet Me*, there was still no consensus on a first single.

A sixteen-year promo veteran from Cleveland, George Gerrity, Warner's VP of rock promotion, had become a dominant figure in the radio world. In 1986 nearly half the records topping the year-end AOR chart were Warner acts. Gerrity saw *Pleased to Meet Me* as a major step in the Replacements' development. "To my ears, we had a record we could do something with," he said.

On the label's alternative side, staff members like Steve Tipp felt that "Alex Chilton" was the right direction to go: get traction among college and free-form stations and then use the buzz to build the record at mainstream radio. But in other quarters, there was doubt that a track paying tribute to an obscure figure like Chilton would fly. The horns and strings of the album's other standout, "Can't Hardly Wait," seemed too much of a stylistic stretch. Besides, the band itself was adamantly against it. "Down the line maybe," said Westerberg, but as a leadoff, "it would've seemed like false advertising."

Eventually, Gerrity decided on "The Ledge," figuring its driving backbeat and blistering guitar solo would appeal to AOR. By early 1987, aside from a few outliers like U2, the format was a mixture of arena superstars (Van Halen, ZZ Top), seventies holdovers (Heart, Foreigner), younger hair bands (Whitesnake, Bon Jovi), and heartland bores (John Mellencamp).

Most of the 150 or so AOR stations in the United States were tightly playlisted, controlled by national consultants like Burkhart/Abrams and the Pollack Media Group. New bands and songs trying to break into the format were subject to a rigorous audience testing process. "That was *the* era of market research: 'Here, listen to seven seconds of this record: do you like it?'" said Gerrity. "That's how judgments were made."

Moreover, many AOR outlets ramped up the number of classic tracks in rotation to appeal to an older demographic, leaving fewer slots for up-and-coming bands. "No one at AOR was going to take a big risk with the

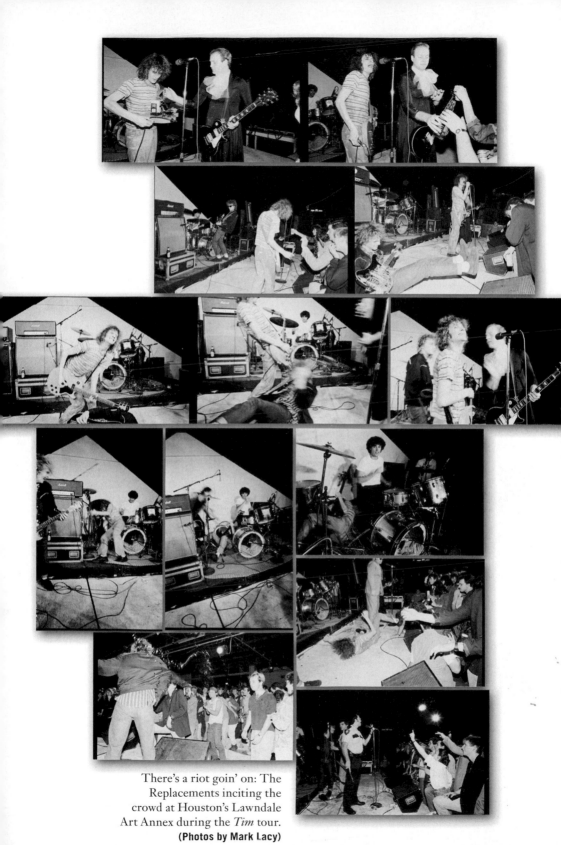

There's a riot goin' on: The Replacements inciting the crowd at Houston's Lawndale Art Annex during the *Tim* tour. **(Photos by Mark Lacy)**

High Noon Management's Gary Hobbib **(left)** and Russ Rieger began steering the Replacements career starting in late-'85. **(Author Collection)**

The brotherhood between Tommy and Paul was fully forged with the decision to kick Bob out of the band in 1986. "We figured: now we're in this thing together," said Tommy, "come hell or high water." **(Photo by David Brewster. From the Minneapolis Star and Tribune News Negative Collection; courtesy of the Minnesota Historical Society)**

Bob Stinson with his future bride Carleen Krietler at the CC Club: "Is being in the [Replacements] healthy for you?" she asked him. "I don't know if he wanted to answer that honestly." **(Photo by Just Loomis)**

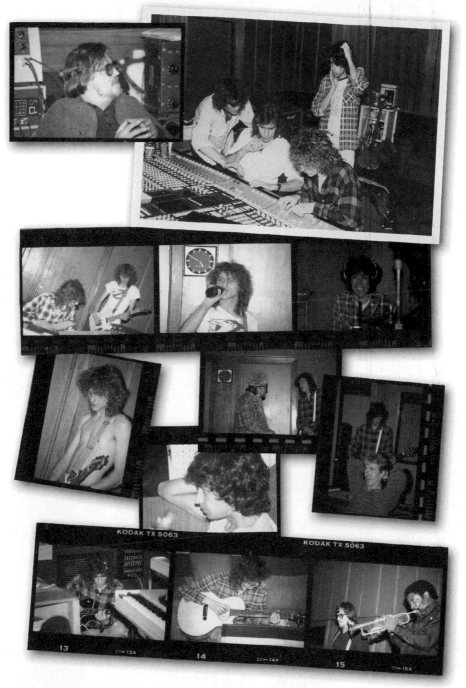

Recording *Pleased to Meet Me* at Ardent Studios in Memphis. Top left, producer Jim Dickinson. Top right, the 'Mats surround engineer Joe Hardy. Third row, far right: Westerberg cuts a guitar track as engineer John Hampton listens. Bottom row, far right: Dickinson supervising the horns on "Can't Hardly Wait," as trumpeter Ben Cauley plays.
(Photos by Jim Lancaster, courtesy of Rhino Entertainment Company, A Warner Music Group)
(Top right photo courtesy Ardent Studios)

Bob "Slim" Dunlap would join the Replacements as a lead guitarist in early 1987. **(Courtesy of Rhino Entertainment Company, a Warner Music Group)**

Slim's wife, First Avenue booker Chrissie Dunlap. **(Photo by Alison Cummings)**

The Replacements, making an art of offending *everyone*. **(Photo by Daniel Corrigan, courtesy of Rhino Entertainment Company, A Warner Music Group)**

Sire's Seymour Stein and Warner Bros.' Michael Hill are all smiles as the Replacements present them with the tape of *Pleased to Meet Me* at the Memphis playback party. **(Courtesy Ardent Studios)**

Outtakes for the *Pleased to Meet Me* album cover. **(Photo by Daniel Corrigan, courtesy of Rhino Entertainment Company, a Warner Music Group)**

On the road in '87: Slim getting into the spirit; Paul mugging; Tommy preening; Chris turning into "Pappy the Clown" as Westerberg and the Georgia Satellites' Dan Baird look on. **(Photos by Julie Panebianco)**

All dressed up: The Replacements and Phil Westerberg **(far right)**, put on tuxes for Paul's wedding to Lori Bizer.

Paul and Lori: "I settled down," said Westerberg, "but only on paper."
(Photos courtesy of Lori Bizer Leighton)

The band in Los Angeles at the end of the difficult, drawn-out recording sessions for *Don't Tell a Soul*. **(Photo by Dewey Nicks)**

Chris Mars and his wife, Sally Schneidkraut. **(Photo by Julie Panebianco)**

The disastrous tour opening for Tom Petty in 1989: Stinson with the Heartbreakers' keyboardist and 'Mats fan Benmont Tench. "I didn't understand why they would just thumb their nose at the whole experience," said Tench. **(Photo by Carl Davino)**

Paul and Slim join the Heart-breakers on stage. **(Photo by Carl Davino)**

Wearing the Heartbreakers' wives dresses and riling up the crowd in Nashville. **(Photo by Carl Davino)**

Mayhem and madness on the road in '89: Westerberg transforming the 'Mats' bus into a "gerbil cage." **(Photo by Jim "Velvet" Sullivan)**

Westerberg, wet and wasted: If the band "couldn't have fun that one hour onstage we'd make sure we had fun the other twenty-three hours of the day." **(Photo by Jim "Velvet" Sullivan)**

Tommy as a crazed clown: "We're not respected anywhere! We don't have respect. We don't want it!" **(Photo by Jim "Velvet" Sullivan)**

Paul struggling to record vocals for *All Shook Down*: "I was drinking myself into a stupor." **(Photo by Donna Ranieri)**

Westerberg in a haze at the Hyatt House in Hollywood: "*Throwin' us trunks as we're starting to drown . . .*" **(Photo by Donna Ranieri)**

Westerberg and Stinson try to salvage the band: "Paul knew that he needed Tommy as much as Tommy needed him," said Daune Earle. "And maybe some of that was alcoholic codependency." **(Photo by Michael Wilson)**

Tommy, with wife Daune and daughter Ruby, in Minneapolis, summer of 1990. **(Photo by Michael Wilson)**

Paul, on his own, at the end of his marriage and his drinking. **(Photo by Michael Wilson)**

Veteran Twin Cities drummer Steve Foley was tapped to take over for Chris Mars on the Replacements final tour.
(Photo by Daniel Corrigan)

The "traveling wake" comes to an end with the 'Mats' farewell show at Chicago's Grant Park.
(Photo by Paul Natkin)

Tommy says goodbye: *"Yeah, you were robbed . . . and I'm stilllllllll being robbed!"*
(Photo by Paul Natkin)

Bob Stinson with his sister Lonnie in the early '90s. "That's how I see him," she said, "still that little boy . . . trying to convince people that he had value; that he had merit." **(Photo courtesy of Lonnie Stinson)**

Bob with his mother Anita. **(Photo by Daniel Corrigan)**

Tommy, Paul, and Chris, together again in the studio, December 2005. **(Photo by Darren Hill)**

Paul and Tommy arrive for the first Replacements reunion show in Toronto in August 2013. **(Photo by Ben Perlstein)**

Laughing on stage in front of 14,000 fans at Midway Stadium in St. Paul, 2014. **(Photo by Steven Cohen)**

A complicated brotherhood, sealed with a kiss. **(Photo by Steven Cohen)**

Replacements at that time," said Gerrity. "A band like that wasn't going to research well. And frankly, Paul's ability to write was a little beyond what average radio audiences were able to comprehend." He figured that if "The Ledge" failed, they could try again with "Alex Chilton" or "Can't Hardly Wait."

Historically speaking, Warner Bros. had no qualms about spending time and money to break in an act slowly. "It wasn't a one-and-done situation," said Gerrity. "I had the latitude and the budget to take a couple runs at it." But High Noon was desperate for immediate results. For a band that tended to lose interest and motivation quickly—that had nearly broken up six months earlier—the first shot was the most crucial.

Nevertheless, enthusiasm ran high at Warner that spring. Following the Memphis party, Sire formally picked up the Replacements' option, committing to an additional four albums, with an option for six in total. The advance and recording budgets for subsequent records would nearly double, from $150,000 to nearly $300,000. "They felt like Paul was writing great songs and the best was still ahead of them," said Rieger.

Westerberg's response to the news was less than sanguine: *"Suckers."*

★ ★ ★

*P*leased to Meet Me was officially slated for late April, and Sire's media department began readying a PR campaign. New York publicist Liz Rosenberg, who represented Madonna, put her assistant Mary Melia in charge of the project. "When you worked in her office, you ended up with the acts she didn't want," said Melia. "But I loved those guys."

Melia's mandate was to reach untapped markets and demographics—not easy, given the band's reluctance to court anyone. Sometimes it made for fine comedy, as when Melia landed a Replacements feature in *Guitar World*, then enjoying a circulation boom among teenage metal fans. "Don't buy those pointy guitars, kids," Westerberg warned the magazine's Ibanez-wielding readership. *"They'll give ya VD."*

On the other end of the spectrum, Melia pitched the band to a variety of upscale publications. "Elegant, international, fun-spirited are *not* the words that come to mind re: The Replacements," wrote back an editor at *Elle*.

Ironically in light of the band's still-fresh *Saturday Night Live* appearance, there was talk of the 'Mats appearing on TV. The most natural place on network television for the Replacements was NBC's *Late Night with David Letterman*, which followed Johnny Carson's *Tonight Show* and had given Devo, Talking Heads, and R.E.M. all airtime. But by 1987, *Late Night* was mandating that its musical guests perform with the show's Paul Shaffer–led house band rather than their own rhythm sections, and the 'Mats passed on Letterman's offer.

★ ★ ★

Not that the Replacements needed TV to remain press darlings. *Musician* editor-in-chief Bill Flanagan traveled to Minneapolis to spend a few days with the band. His feature, along with RJ Smith's *Village Voice* profile, became one of the band's defining portraits. Flanagan led off with a funny retelling of the Twin/Tone tape-tossing story—leaving out the aborted raid on Paul Stark's home.

Flanagan also probed Westerberg on becoming a major-label commodity. "The record company wants us to be big stars, but we're uncomfortable with that. We don't want to give them everything. We don't want to give them a hundred percent," said Westerberg. "As soon as you do that, you've got nothing for yourself."

Challenging him, Flanagan got something close to the truth. "I guess it's the fear of failure," admitted Westerberg. "I don't want to give everything and have it turn out to be shit or have people not like it."

Rolling Stone made *Pleased to Meet Me* its lead review, under the headline "Meet the Misfits." "It's really thought out, and yet there is that wildness to it, that balance of crazy and concentrated," recalled David Fricke, who wrote the *RS* review. "In terms of emotions, in terms of physical dynamics, that record is all over the place. And yet it sounds so much a piece."

Those plaudits fed Westerberg's ego. "I bought into half of it," he said. "Half of me laughed at it, and the other half thought, *Hey, I am the best song-writer in the world.*"

But Westerberg was unable to reconcile the critics' embrace with the industry's resistance. "We've got forty critics across the land who love the band, but forty million people who don't know us from a hole in the wall," noted Westerberg at the time. "So I'd prefer the people hear us now."

CHAPTER 37

Sending the Replacements out to do live radio interviews was a calculated risk, and High Noon knew it. "It could turn very ugly, very quickly," said Russ Rieger. Especially now that they were visiting large-market alternative and independent stations and the more progressive AOR outlets, rather than largely inconsequential college stations.

The first and most significant incident took place during an appearance on KROQ in Los Angeles in May. The band had been booked to appear on the station's *New American Rock* show, a midnight slot hosted by "Swedish" Egil Aalvik.

A pioneer of the alternative/modern rock format, Hollywood club promoter Gary Bookasta launched KROQ in 1972 as a low-rent, free-form progressive station. In 1979 Rick Carroll took over as program director and began playing songs by new wave artists in tight top 40–style rotation until they were hits, helping make stars of Duran Duran, Culture Club, Human League, and Depeche Mode. Infinity Broadcasting purchased KROQ in 1986 for $45 million, the largest cash transaction for a station at the time. The station moved next door to Warner Bros. in Burbank.

KROQ was resistant to play emerging American rock bands like the Replacements anywhere but overnights and the odd specialty show. "We never gave the time of day to 'Mats or Hüsker Dü, even R.E.M. to an extent," said former KROQ music director Lewis Largent. "Rick Carroll was doing a lot of drugs at the time. He was into that electronic new wave-y stuff and wasn't responding to that rockier sound."

Largent, one of the 'Mats' few vocal supporters at the station, hoped to bring the band into the fold starting with the *New American Rock* appearance. Paul and Tommy spent that day drinking with *Creem* writers Bill Holdship and John Kordosh, who'd moved to LA along with the magazine the previous year. The last thing they wanted to do was drive to Burbank for a radio spot.

"Tommy and Paul said they would only do the show if John and I went on with them," recalled Holdship. "Management was fine with that—whatever got them on. In retrospect, it was probably a bad idea."

Largent greeted the red-faced quartet in KROQ's lobby and escorted them to the studio. Aalvik, with his sonorous voice and Scandinavian accent, made a perfect target for the band. "They came on beyond inebriated, totally obnoxious and trying to be funny, and it was a disaster," said Largent. "There was an underlying meanness there."

"Do you have any udder songwriters in de band?" wondered Aalvik.

"Tommy and Chris both write songs, they're just not as good as Paul," croaked Westerberg.

"Paul, why do you write songs?" asked Largent.

"Because I wanna make Tommy and Chris look bad . . . no, I do it because I'm gay."

A pie-eyed Kordosh demanded that Aalvik take calls from listeners ("I want some pussy," one caller requested), while Stinson badgered the accented deejay about his "fake voice."

"Dank you for coming," offered a relieved Aalvik when the thirty-minute segment finally, mercifully ended.

"The pleasure was all yours," said Westerberg.

Repentant drunk that he was, Paul began to wonder if they'd gone too far—in Warner's backyard no less. "Afterwards, I do remember that he looked a little morose," said Holdship.

The response from KROQ was swift and public. The following morning, deejay Richard Blade—an Englishman with little love for boorish American rockers—brought a still-wounded Largent on the air to recount the incident. The segment ended with Blade dramatically breaking a copy of *Pleased to Meet Me* on the air. "The bosses were more than happy to say, 'We'll just drop them. They're not worth it,'" said Largent.

* * *

A few weeks later, the Replacements stopped by Providence's WBRU. Program director Kurt Hirsch, a longtime supporter, interviewed them during drive time, in advance of their show in town that night.

It didn't take long for Hirsch to get nervous. "[Westerberg] wasn't making any eye contact," said Hirsch. "He was looking everywhere but at me."

Hirsch gamely tried to keep the segment moving. "We have some tickets to give away to your show tonight," he said. "What should we make people do to win this?"

"How about a little phone sex," offered Westerberg. "We'll be the judges."

Hirsch continued to serve as a straight man for the band's zingers, while dutifully playing tracks off *Pleased to Meet Me.*

"Damn," said a bemused Stinson, "you're too nice for us. What is this crap?"

"Ooh, that's one of the seven words," said Hirsch, cutting him off. "No one heard that. If you heard that you weren't supposed to . . . "

"The big C-word?" asked Stinson.

"'Cause the FCC doesn't like that—they're getting down on all the . . . "

"*Crap?*" repeated Stinson.

"Don't say it again. This is . . . this is very bad. I gotta get them out of here. . . . The Replacements, thanks for coming by, but you're gonna get me in big trouble with the FCC because you said that word over the air."

"That's not a bad word," muttered Stinson.

"Just forget it—which song are we playing?" said Hirsch. "'Nightclub Jitters.' Anything to say about it?"

Westerberg finally looked Hirsch square in the eye as he leaned into the microphone: "It's a *motherfucker.*"

"Oh gee, good-bye," said Hirsch. "They're gone."

As the song cued up, the deejay was laughing nervously on the air. But the band, and its Warner reps, recalled being tossed onto the street in record time.

By the time the 'Mats arrived in Chicago for an appearance on WXRT, they were coming up with more creative ways to offend. The station had actually been on board as far back as "I Will Dare" and was pledging to support "The Ledge." More importantly, WXRT was a bellwether: if it added a song to the playlist, smaller stations throughout the Midwest frequently followed suit.

Johnny Mars, host of the station's *Big Beat* evening show, was another avowed fan. "I knew they were drinkers, so I bought a six-pack of Heineken and gave it to them," said Mars. "But they came in toting bottles of champagne."

The interview went smoothly until the first commercial break, when Westerberg began riffling through the station's library of blues LPs. His eyes lit up when he came across Sonny Boy Williamson's *Bummer Road*. He excitedly nudged Tommy. Mars asked him if there was anything they wanted to hear. Westerberg requested "Little Village."

On the LP was a big note: "Do not under any circumstances play 'Little Village.'"

Mars tried to distract the band, but Westerberg began answering everything with: "If we can't play 'Little Village,' then I can't answer that." Soon the rest of the band was badgering the deejay to play it.

Finally, he relented: "So tell me about this Sonny Boy Williamson song you want to hear so badly."

"This is the problem we have when we're recording," said Westerberg. "The engineer doesn't understand the artist. And Sonny handles it beautifully, I think."

"Well," said Mars, "I think that's as good an introduction as we'll ever get, so let's hear it."

Recorded in September 1957, "Little Village" was a legendary studio outtake that captured a spirited, half-joking argument between Sonny Boy and engineer Leonard Chess that contained two "motherfuckers," two "son of a bitches," and a "goddamn" in the first few seconds alone. Mars's face flushed, but he played the track to completion.

"That's . . . I guess . . . what could happen in a recording studio . . . is . . . is that how you guys record?" waffled Mars.

"That has more to do with the Replacements than anything I've ever heard in my life," cackled Westerberg.

After the show, Mars and music director Lin Brehmer took the band for drinks at the nearby Bucket O' Suds, where the 'Mats insulted the bartender and embarrassed the WXRT staff. The following day, Brehmer sent a scathing missive to the radio industry newsletter *Friday Morning Quarterback*, lambasting the group for its behavior and for putting the station's license at risk. "I just unloaded," said Brehmer. "I didn't hold back."

A week later, every program director in America knew the Replacements' name. It wasn't the kind of recognition any band would've wished for.

* * *

Those incidents didn't go unnoticed in Burbank. "Let's be honest, anybody that can walk into WXRT or KROQ and get into trouble really had to work at it," said George Gerrity.

Sire label manager Suzanne Emil, Stein's chief liaison with Warner Bros., did her best to control the damage, but few radio field staffers were willing to go all out for the 'Mats. "In those days you needed to go to the radio guys in the markets where you were doing okay and really talk them up," said Emil. "Unless your song was just some unbelievably great, undeniable hit single, that was what you had to do to sell records."

To Westerberg's thinking, radio was all a rigged game anyway: airplay was bought and paid for by the label and its promoters. That may have been true to an extent—a new radio "payola" scandal had broken the previous year. But it was still human beings programming radio stations, and none of them wanted to be the butt of the joke.

* * *

High Noon's first eighteen months with the Replacements had yielded one crisis after another. Rieger and Hobbib had managed the chaos and steadied the band's career. Now, as they coordinated the campaign for *Pleased to Meet Me*, the band was starting to chafe at their handlers.

Westerberg and Stinson always had a better personal relationship with the more grounded Hobbib, who spent time on the road with the band. "They were closer to Gary, who was mellower," said Rieger. "I'm over the top. I could stumble over myself and be an idiot at times when I got very emotional."

A torrent of big talk and crazy schemes, Rieger had an instinct for hype that made the band nervous. For instance, he wanted the band to promote the album by traveling down New York's Fifth Avenue playing live on a flatbed truck. Aside from the fact that the Rolling Stones had done this a decade earlier, and that the 'Mats wouldn't have made it a block without being stopped by police, it reeked of desperation. Rieger also suggested that the band make a promotional appearance riding on the back of an elephant.

"They always had ridiculous promotional angles," said Slim Dunlap. "Even asking the Replacements to visit distributors and record production facilities. . . . What good was ever gonna come of that? Even to do in-stores was pointless. The more the fans met the Replacements, the more the band was rude, the less they liked them. It worked in complete reverse."

For Hobbib, bringing up serious matters with Paul and Tommy was always a fraught process. "They were drunks," he said. "So it was always a strategy: What's the right time to call? What's the right setup? Everything we needed to discuss business-wise was a stretch for them."

"Russ was really rah-rah, and so it made Gary the one to have to deal with things in a realistic way," said Warner's Julie Panebianco. "As time went on and the band was getting frustrated and resentful, they weren't going to pick on each other. They were going to pick on the managers."

High Noon kept the 'Mats on $750-a-month salaries, mostly so they wouldn't burn through band savings. "Maybe it was my conservatism, but we always kept money in the coffers and didn't tell them," said Hobbib. "Rather than, 'Here's a bunch of money, go and blow it all.' Because whatever you gave Tommy, he'd call a week later asking for more."

Westerberg was becoming suspicious that High Noon was ripping the band off, and he was growing equally dubious about Burton Goldstein, the high-powered business manager they'd hired to look after the band's financial affairs. He also felt that attorney George Regis was treading too lightly with Twin/Tone over the issue of royalties because of his relationship with Dave Ayers—though he also knew that Regis wasn't afraid to question Goldstein's accounting. "My feeling was: I don't trust any of these guys," said Westerberg. "But at least I got them watching each other."

"They were based on fear," said Hobbib. "They were afraid to do things because it would ruin them. Or they were afraid because someone was trying to fuck them."

CHAPTER 38

On September 2, 1986, Joe Major, an eighteen-year-old resident of Bergen-field, New Jersey, a blue-collar suburb ten miles north of New York City, went with some friends to a party at the Palisades, the steep line of cliffs overlooking the Hudson. He drank a little too much that night. Messing around perilously close to the cliff's edge, Major lost his footing and fell 200 feet, dying on impact.

After the accident, Joe's girlfriend, sophomore Lisa Burress, and her sister Cheryl would frequent his gravesite in Paramus, leave him notes and presents, and pray for his soul. Major's best friend, Tommy Rizzo, who'd watched Major die, was struck by horrible nightmares. He began hanging out with another troubled teen fresh out of rehab, Thomas Olton. Before long, Olton was dating Lisa Burress.

Most of these kids came from broken homes; there had been suicide in their families and trouble with substances and the law. They were rock-and-rollers—mostly fans of thrash and speed metal.

On the evening of March 10, 1987, Rizzo, Olton, and Lisa and Cheryl Burress decided to go out together. Cheryl told a friend she was going to "go see Joe"—he simply thought she meant a visit to Major's grave.

The four kids spent the night drinking and doing coke and driving around the streets of Bergenfield in Olton's Camaro. At approximately 3:00 AM they stopped at a local Amoco station and bought a few dollars' worth of gas. They asked the attendant if they could take a hose from the station's car vacuum cleaner, but he refused. Later, they drove to an apartment complex where they'd frequently partied with Major, parked the Camaro in a vacant garage, and around 5:00 AM turned on the engine, rolled down the windows, and let their lungs fill with carbon monoxide.

One of the items found among the bodies in the car—along with a pack of razor blades and some AC/DC cassettes—was a brown bag on which a long suicide note, signed by all four, had been written, expressing a desire to be buried together.

The so-called Bergenfield suicide pact shook the region to its core. It also sparked fears of a "suicide cluster." It was a phenomenon that had become increasingly common in the eighties following high-profile teen suicides: other kids would take their own lives in imitation or in some strange form of solidarity. The day after the Bergenfield tragedy, two girls, seventeen and nineteen, killed themselves in the same manner in the Chicago suburb of Alsip. A week later, police stopped a young couple trying to gas themselves in the very same garage where the "Bergenfield Four" had died.

Just as the furor over the issue was beginning to build nationally, the Replacements released "The Ledge"—a single that was unmistakably about teen suicide.

Promoting the album that spring, Westerberg was forced in nearly every interview to defend the motivations behind "The Ledge." "When everybody heard it, they said, 'Oh, man, are you gonna get in trouble! Is this about the kids in New Jersey?' No, no. I'm not trying to glorify that or jump on that bandwagon," he said to *Musician*. He also told *The Gavin Report*: "It's not a phase or fad or anything. It's just happening, and I just wrote about it."

★ ★ ★

In April the Replacements reunited with "Bastards of Young" video director Bill Pope and producer Randy Skinner in Los Angeles to shoot a clip for "The Ledge." The band had consented to be in the video this time, though they wouldn't act or lip-synch.

Improvising a setup at Television Center Studios, Skinner and Pope placed a couch and a couple of chairs in the middle of the soundstage and spent a few hours filming the band essentially doing nothing. The resulting video was a collection of static black-and-white images: Paul smoking, Tommy eating lunch, Chris and Slim casually talking. "Even then, you can see how uncomfortable they are being filmed," said Skinner. "They're twitching."

At least you could see their faces, which possibly meant getting MTV on board. Warner Bros. had already played advances of *Pleased to Meet Me* for several key MTV executives back in February, who'd responded positively to "The Ledge" in particular.

Rick Krim, MTV's music and talent department manager, was a fan, and also part of a small group that decided which videos were played. He worked directly with Michelle Vonfeld, who described herself as the network's "one-person standards and practices department." It was her duty to decide whether a video passed muster.

Krim would sit with Vonfeld and go over each video frame by frame to remove profanity and offensive images: crotch shots, exposed nipples, drug logos on clothes or instruments. MTV claimed that fewer than 5 percent of submitted videos were sent back for editing. Even in the tits-and-ass-heavy hair metal era, videos could be made to conform to standards pretty easily. "Usually it was an edit here or an edit there," said Krim. "It was rare for a video to be flat-out rejected."

The last week of May, "The Ledge" was submitted for review. The biggest quandary for Vonfeld in assessing "The Ledge" wasn't the images in the video but the subject matter of the song. Warner Bros. sent over a copy of the lyrics. Looking over them, Krim and Vonfeld found it hard to see where any meaningful change could be made; there wasn't a single word or line that could be easily excised. "It was really a situation where we thought, 'We can't play this,'" said Krim. MTV decided to reject the video outright owing to lyrical content.

"MTV feels the lyrics are detrimental to the youth of America," said Westerberg after the decision came down. "But for them to play Mötley Crüe and not play our video . . . if it had a bunch of sexist bullshit, they would've played it. But if it's something deeper, if it's emotions, it's taboo."

High Noon was particularly angered by the decision: MTV's rejection attached a stigma to the song. Soon many radio stations already spinning the track began to drop it from their playlists. "It all crumbled from there," said Rieger.

By late June, Warner Bros. quietly moved on to "Alex Chilton." "We had no choice," said Rieger. "But in terms of radio and general perception, you can't just switch to the next single two days later. It would look like there's no commitment to the band. . . . Internally, everyone knew the record was dead."

* * *

While the MTV decision played itself out, the Replacements prepared to play their first shows in nearly a year, and their first ever without Bob Stinson.

Bob would never quite muster much animus toward Westerberg, though others in Minneapolis did. "There was a lot of people that didn't even want Bob coming into their bar," said Stinson's friend Ray Reigstad. "But there was people on the other side of the fence who literally wanted to kick the shit out of Tommy and Paul. Anybody that knew them guys knew there was four fuck-ups in that band."

Bob himself was hurt that the coverage of his dismissal made him the convenient scapegoat for *all* the band's failings. "But Westerberg's still falling off the stage," Bob noted.

Bob and Paul, outwardly at least, seemed to reconcile. Restoring relations with Tommy was more complicated. For the benefit of their mother Anita, they remained cordial. "But it was very uncomfortable for Tommy whenever we had to go for holidays and family things," said Daune Earle. "Tommy likes to make things better for everyone. In that case, he just couldn't."

The press was certainly curious. "He doesn't like me anymore," Tommy would say of Bob, always eager to change the topic. "And that's the end of that story."

Once the Replacements got on the road, there would be ugly, persistent reminders of the split. "There's always that jerk in the front row who yells,

'What'd you do with your brother?'" said Tommy. "Fuck you. We grew up and he didn't."

After his firing, Bob would derisively refer to the band as "the Diet Replacements." Yet, privately, he acknowledged that the 'Mats couldn't have progressed any further with him involved. "The Replacements wanted to get to that next level," said Reigstad. "Bob didn't give a shit about that stuff. He didn't have the discipline, but he didn't have the desire either."

In truth, once he was out of the 'Mats, Bob felt a tremendous relief. By the end, the band had affected his new marriage and exacerbated his drinking even further. "He *was* happier," said Reigstad. "For a while, anyway."

Stinson soon moved on from his janitor job at First Avenue and began washing dishes at Curly's, an all-night café on Lake Street. He also started playing with Sonny Vincent.

A New York City punk refugee, Vincent came to Minneapolis in 1980, after the breakup of his first-wave CBGB band the Testors. The Replacements and Vincent's later outfit, the Extreme, had shared a bill at Goofy's Upper Deck back in 1982. "After the show, Bob came up to me and said, 'I want to join your band,'" recalled Vincent, who thought he was joking.

In early 1987, Bob and Sonny reconnected, forming Model Prisoners, going through a couple different rhythm sections, touring the Midwest, and even recording a handful of tracks. It was an important step for Bob; Twin Cities musicians hadn't exactly beaten a path to his door. "Sonny gave Bob a fair chance when no one else did," said Reigstad. "He dealt with him, even though he knew Bob had problems."

Playing with Vincent restored some of Stinson's creative self-confidence, which had all but vanished amid the 'Mats' ruinous atmosphere. "I'd look at Sonny and say, 'Let's do it this way or that,' and he'd let me go. I didn't have to turn to Paul and ask [permission]."

Seven years Stinson's senior, Vincent tried to act as a big brother to Bob, doing his best to meter his alcohol consumption. "Bob . . . could unlock his immense talent only when he had the right amount of alcohol lubrication," said Vincent. "If he drank too much, it was terrible. If he didn't drink at all, it was worse. But with the right amount of drinks under his belt, he was doing brilliant stuff on the guitar."

But even Bob's gifts couldn't make up for his all faults. After a while, he was up to his old tricks: going directly to the promoters after shows, collecting the band's gig money, and then disappearing for days. "Soon everyone wanted to kick Bob out of the band," said Vincent. When it happened, Bob broke down crying. "I got off the phone and decided I would be a fool to kick out a brother who was crying tears because he loved music so much."

Instead, Vincent took the unusual step of taking the entire band to see a therapist together. "People thought that was pretty funny, a band going to therapy," said Vincent. "But we tried it. It kept us together for a while, but still the crazy shit didn't stop."

Model Prisoners broke up in 1988. Vincent would eventually move to Europe, though he would enlist Bob for various projects in later years, including his band Shotgun Rationale—where Stinson formed a wild two-guitar attack with the Dead Boys' Cheetah Chrome—and some overseas tours in the early nineties.

CHAPTER 39

The Replacements kicked off the *Pleased to Meet Me* tour in late April with a series of warm-up shows in Florida and elsewhere in the Southeast, making up the dates that had been canceled in the wake of Paul Westerberg's hand injury the previous summer.

Slim Dunlap had spent a couple months learning the 'Mats' catalog—listening to live bootlegs and consulting with Bob Stinson on specific parts.

His home debut, May 13 at First Avenue, was a fairly normal affair. The band stayed away from covers and focused on the new album, though on "Can't Hardly Wait" Westerberg did attempt a violin solo—no doubt a cheeky tribute to Jim Dickinson's string additions.

The band's return to First Avenue two weeks later sought to debunk any notion that they'd gone straight. Opening with a sour "Hello Dolly"—the first of multiple versions that night—they plowed through ten ragged covers, with Westerberg having to urge Mars on frequently (*"Plaaaaaay!!!"*) before delivering their first original tune.

"We're shit, we know it . . . *thank you!*" offered Westerberg in between songs.

Westerberg was becoming ill at ease in his own backyard, and Minneapolis gigs often took queer turns as a result. "In other places, you don't have the responsibility of being cordial to people you know," he said. "But if you have to be nice to all your friends, you tend to be overly rude when you play." The 'Mats would only play their hometown a handful more times.

The concerts showcased their new look: clashing plaid-and-stripes suits, like a gang of burlesque comedians. (Paul pilfered much of it from his father's golf outfits.) It was partly homage to Slade, partly an effort to ward off criticism that they'd gotten too serious. Mostly it was a way of violating expectations. They might have been the hippest rock band in America at that moment, but they'd be damned if they were going to look the part.

The tour wound through the Midwest in May, then on to Europe in June. Though Dunlap grasped Westerberg's depression and was sympathetic, living with him on the road yielded even more challenges. "Early in the morning, you'd know the kind of day you were in for," said Dunlap. "Paul's very mercurial. Some days he was funny and fun to be around. But there were horrible days where he would test your patience."

Without Bob around, Dunlap became the focus of Westerberg's ire. "You'd play something he didn't like and he'd glare at you," said Dunlap. "That's part of the deal—I was the foil that took it."

Some of Westerberg's behavior was calculated. Curtiss A had advised him, "Slim can play really good, but ya gotta get him *mad*." At one gig, Paul walked up while Dunlap was in mid-solo and unplugged his guitar. "He was so pissed he wanted to beat me up," laughed Westerberg. "But it was true: to rile him up was to get the fire out of his guitar."

Westerberg might have messed with Dunlap onstage, but he also respected and relied on him. "He more or less said, 'I'll be damned if I'm gonna stand idly by and watch the Replacements go down the toilet,'" said Westerberg.

* * *

On May 29, the Replacements flew into London's Heathrow Airport to start an eighteen-day, fifteen-date tour that would take them from England to Germany, France, Spain, and back.

Unlike their maiden voyage, when they were relative unknowns, the band's 1987 arrival was met with far more interest. WEA international executive Phil Straight, who'd attended the Memphis playback, had laid the groundwork for *Pleased to Meet Me*, and Warner UK publicist Barb Charone had lined up a banquet of interviews.

The band's profile got a boost from a *Melody Maker* cover story timed for their London arrival. Writer Simon Reynolds had been to the United States and traveled with the band. Though more of a postpunk and dance-music aesthete, Reynolds was immediately converted: "The Replacements represent the complete antithesis of all my dreams for the future of pop," he wrote. "And yet, I can't help myself. I love them so much it hurts."

Dubbing the Replacements "America's inebriate counterpart to the Smiths," Reynolds was one of the few European journalists to grasp the peculiar alchemy that fueled the 'Mats: "At the heart of the Replacements lies fatigue, insecurity, a sense of wasted or denied possibilities, but this is a pain that comes out bursting and exuberant, a world weariness that's positively, paradoxically boisterous."

A return feature in the *NME*—which Westerberg had tweaked with pro-Reagan comments during their first Euro tour—was far less flattering. The paper's Michele Kirsch interviewed Paul and Tommy in London. The piece opened with the pair pissing on the roof of the WEA building: "Don't put this part in the article, okay?" Westerberg had asked.

Later, when questioned about Bob Stinson's firing, Westerberg told her: "We loved Bob." Then he shut off Kirsch's tape recorder, adding confidentially, "But Bob is a drug addict." When the story appeared in print, the whole exchange was published in full. "Hollywood tabloids can't hold a candle to them English scumbags," complained Westerberg. "They won't respect a comment off the record."

The European shows themselves were solid and occasionally spectacular— Dunlap found his fire and his place within the songs. But outside of the two fairly riotous London dates bookending the tour, the gigs were pretty much the same as in '86: the audiences weren't very big or especially enthusiastic. "Everyone dressed in black, please leave," bellowed Westerberg, opening a gig at Club Vera in Holland. "There's no reason to be morose."

The 'Mats responded to the audiences' indifference by ratcheting up their drinking. After just a few gigs, Westerberg's voice was shot and remained so throughout the tour. "I like to drink, and I make no excuses for it," Westerberg thundered to a *Q* magazine journo. "My father drinks, my grandfather drank— you look like you like to tip a few yourself!"

Their own excess was acceptable—not so with the crew. In London, soundman Wilkes and crew member Bill Sullivan were supposed to go to the French consulate early one morning to sort out the band's visas. Instead, they stayed up all night partying and blew the assignment. "We behaved like *them*," said Wilkes. "I remember Bill saying, 'They don't like it when you hold up the mirror, man. They don't like it one bit.'"

After the tour, the band would all but abandon the idea of breaking in Europe. In the four years before they set foot on the continent again, a whole new wave of US alternative acts—Dinosaur Jr, the Pixies—managed to become major stars in England as interest in all things American peaked at the end of the eighties. The Replacements had come too late and left too early.

* * *

Being a blood-and-guts American rock-and-roll band on a major label was a lonely proposition in 1987. "There wasn't that many: Tom Petty was still trying to hold the banner up; the Del Fuegos were trying; the Del-Lords, the Scorchers, and we were trying," said Georgia Satellites singer Dan Baird.

The Atlanta-based Satellites were the Replacements' gap-toothed country cousins. They carried on together for a few years, covering each other's songs and turning up at each other's gigs. "We were all fearless, all stubborn, with a core set of beliefs that may not have been obvious to anybody else," said Baird.

Baird wasn't much of a drinker, but Satellites guitarist Rick Richards could party and play at the 'Mats level. "We approached things in the same way and didn't take anything very seriously—plus, we were ready to have a good time at the drop of a hat," said Richards, whose Southern fashion finery included bolo ties and stovepipe hats, leading Westerberg to quip that Richards resembled "Colonel Sanders on crack."

The Satellites had been around for years as the house band at the North Atlanta dive Hedgen's, and in the fall of 1986 a refurbished version of the band featuring bassist Rick Price and drummer Mauro Magellan released a self-titled debut. They played Minneapolis the following winter. A few songs in, a full cup of beer hit Baird square in the chest. "All right, who the *fuck* threw that beer on me?" shouted the angry singer. Westerberg elbowed his way to the front. "I hear this cackling on the right, and it's [Tommy] Stinson in the wings, laughing his ass off," recalled Richards. "I hadn't even met them. Dan's like, 'Get your asses up here,' and gave them the guitars. They ended up playing for, like, thirty minutes."

By *Pleased to Meet Me*, Baird could sense the Replacements were suffering through some serious growing pains. "That was their fight: how to be the band that got in trouble on *Saturday Night Live* and the band that could also write a song like 'Unsatisfied.' That dichotomy was always going to be there and was always the gasoline on the floor waiting for the right match."

The Satellites dealt with that struggle too, but they had a distinct advantage: a radio hit. The Baird-penned "Keep Your Hands to Yourself," a holdover from the band's first EP, was included on the group's Elektra record almost as an afterthought. Surprising everyone, it shot to number two on *Billboard*'s singles chart in the spring of 1987. MTV treated it like a novelty—real rock-and-roll *was* a novelty on the network at the time—but the Satellites' album went platinum and landed them opening gigs for Bob Seger and Tom Petty.

The lack of a hit would become an albatross around Westerberg's neck. "You don't get to choose," said Baird. "There are people who'll tell me: 'Oh, you wrote "Hands" . . . that is such a cute song.' And they'll come up to Paul, and talk about ten different songs: 'That one broke my heart; this other one tore me up; that song hit me where I lived.' Not many people get *that* kind of response."

While the Satellites could appreciate the Replacements' professional conundrum, no band was quite as connected to their skewed sensibility as the Young Fresh Fellows. Westerberg had first been turned on to the eclectic Seattle indie popsters by his girlfriend Lori Bizer. "She's the one who kinda got hip to the Fellows, when our first record came out in '84," said Fellows' leader Scott McCaughey.

The Fellows' McCaughey, bassist Chuck Carroll, and drummer Tad Hutchinson met up with the 'Mats on the road in Providence in 1985, sparking an immediate connection. "They were really good guys—really easy to hang with," said Tommy Stinson. "They were kind of like us, just lost in a cacophony of noise. We were like an island of misfits—the same island."

By '87 the 'Mats were talking up the Fellows in interviews. "If you think we're good, they're the best band in the world," Westerberg told *Creem*. "They're like the new NRBQ, only sloppier." He convinced the Replacements' booking agent Frank Riley to take on the Fellows, who would open a pair of West Coast legs of the *Pleased to Meet Me* tour.

The jaunts were among the most memorable pairings for the 'Mats, as the Fellows matched them in terms of consumption, chaos, and comedy. "I will say the two of us together exacerbated the problem, for sure—or made it more fun, however you want to look at it," said McCaughey. "We spurred each other on to great heights. And neither of us needed any help in that regard."

Like the 'Mats, the influences of the Faces loomed large in the Fellows' presentation. "We tried to make shows like a party," said McCaughey. "We tried to take a party out to the people."

Amid the high jinks and high spirits, the Fellows saw the Replacements locked in an awkward dance with their label and management. "The 'Mats felt like those people were from another world," said McCaughey, who would tag along to Warner Bros.–sponsored dinners and soirées, getting a behind-the-scenes look at the machine that powered things. "To me, it felt like this is what the big-time rock-and-roll is all about, but it also felt like the Replacements didn't belong in that environment. They were crazy, and the way they dealt with all that stuff was by acting even crazier."

CHAPTER 40

In the last week of June, the 'Mats launched a West Coast tour built around a sold-out two-night stand at the Variety Arts Center in downtown Los Angeles. The shows doubled as a Warner Bros. showcase—part of Russ Rieger's plan to keep the company's support for *Pleased to Meet Me* rolling.

The large corporate turnout and High Noon's fussiness about the show's importance all but guaranteed a swan dive. This time the unlikely culprit was Chris Mars, who'd drunk himself nearly paralytic by showtime. After struggling through the first song, he simply retired from the drum kit and left the stage in a stupor. Tad Hutchinson, drummer for the opener, the Young Fresh Fellows, stepped in for a while, even donning a black Beatles wig to simulate Mars's appearance. But Hutchinson wasn't in much better shape than Mars and didn't last long.

In desperation, Westerberg called out into the mic: "Is there a drummer in the house?" The question seemed to pop a cork on the chaos. "Not only was there a drummer in the audience, there was hundreds, I guess," recalled Fellows front man Scott McCaughey. "People kept coming up. It seemed like half the audience was onstage at one point." So many stragglers strapped on the 'Mats' instruments that Slim Dunlap didn't even have a guitar to play. "I don't remember the band actually finishing one song all the way through that night other than 'California Sun,'" said *Creem*'s Bill Holdship.

Among those in the Variety Arts audience watching was boho singer-songwriter Tom Waits, an avowed 'Mats fan. "I like their stance," he noted that fall. "They're question marks." Waits looked on in bemusement as the band went down fighting themselves and the crowd. "There was this guy trying to climb up, and they kept throwing him back, like a carp. No, you can't get in the boat! It was like something out of *Mondo Cane*."

Rieger and Hobbib tried to keep brave faces on as they watched the embarrassed Warner executives leave one by one. "That show was well attended with senior execs who wanted, *wanted*, to like them," said Hobbib. "And they basically gave them the finger."

The events of the past twelve months had begun to stir a quiet disaffection in Mars. He'd stood by as Westerberg and Stinson took control of the group. He saw their egos being fed by the press and a group of fawning acolytes. "Tommy and Paul's heads got too big," said Mars. "They [tended] to think of the Replacements as something much more of a household word than they really were."

Over time Tommy had usurped Mars's role in the group and in Westerberg's affections. "I think in a lot of ways Chris fell back," said Stinson. "Things had changed. It was a whole different band in a way."

The pandering aspects of major-label life had also become a sore spot. "Show business, hobnobbing with [people], it was this glitzy crap that I could do without," said Mars. Westerberg felt Mars had purposely thrown the Variety Arts show, blown the big LA label gig, as a way of letting everyone know he still wielded some power in the band. "He felt he needed to remind us that the Replacements were gonna flop if he wanted us to."

* * *

M ars recovered sufficiently for the following evening's Variety Arts show. True to form, the 'Mats delivered arguably the tour's best performance. Only a smattering of Warner's staff returned to see it.

The next day, at the band's hotel, Rieger got into a heated discussion with Westerberg, telling him: "This car-crash mentality is something you have to move away from. You write these amazing songs. Why are you sabotaging your own songs?"

Rieger's platonic ideal of a performer was Bruce Springsteen: someone who wrung emotion out of every lyric, put himself on the line with each show, and gave 100 percent night after night. That's what he wanted out of the Replacements.

"I'm not giving you a hundred percent," replied Westerberg.

It had become his refrain, practically a mantra, during *Pleased to Meet Me*. When Westerberg said it to Jim Dickinson, it was a question of trust; as he acted it out with the record company, it was a matter of insecurity. But as he spit out the words again to Rieger, it went far deeper. "I can't mean it every night," admitted Westerberg, meeting Rieger's eyes. "I just can't fuckin' mean it every night."

Westerberg viewed performing, as he did everything, in stark black-and-white terms. He could live with drunken insouciance or bored incompetence, so long as it was real. What he couldn't do was fake it. And he wasn't willing to put himself on the line emotionally. "For him there was no middle ground," said Rieger. "That's part of the reason people gravitated to him as an artist. It was all or nothing."

* * *

For their American tour in 1987, the Replacements had a new tour manager: Derek Wilkinson, a foulmouthed British ex-pat from Hartlepool who'd spent a decade with acts like the Average White Band and the Allman Brothers. He came to the 'Mats straight off a gig with Foreigner. When the Replacements picked him up at LAX, Wilkinson was wearing a new $3,000 Armani suit. The band immediately spray-painted it yellow. Wilkinson didn't flinch. "I had no idea who these motherfuckers were," he said. "But I was as crazy as them. So we just hit it off."

Belying his relatively slight build, Wilkinson had a background in boxing; he'd picked up some karate from the Allman Brothers' black-belt guitarist Dickey Betts. Promoters who tried to mess with the 'Mats were threatened with physical violence. "He could have got sued for what he did in a couple places," Stinson said. "But he took care of us."

Unlike most 'Mats road managers, Wilkinson drank and drugged with them and handed out money with little regard for accounting. Yet the whole machine moved along for what would prove to be the band's longest tour.

The Replacements traveled in a small convoy: the band and Wilkinson in one van; roadie Bill Sullivan, soundman Brendan McCabe, and the gear in another. Warner alternative marketing staffers like Julie Panebianco, Mary Hyde, and Jo Lenardi usually followed somewhere behind.

After the shows, Wilkinson would typically be ginned up, so Dunlap—barely any more sober—would insist on handling long-distance drives. Slim was frequently behind the wheel during some hairy situations. "The road manager would be out cold. The plan was to score," Dunlap said. "So the band would reach into [Wilkinson's] case and pull out eight hundred dollars. We'd be creeping down the street in the middle of the night, going up to strangers: 'Hey, dude, ya holdin'?'"

Slim had also quietly taken to carrying a handgun on the road, in case things got ugly. "Paul, especially, would say things to people that pissed them off. I wasn't fearless."

Winding through the East Coast in July and August, it was clear that the band's reputation was producing not just sold-out concerts but a carnival-like atmosphere around the gigs. The Replacements typically played rooms holding between 1,000 and 1,500—roughly half of the demand. "People were completely nuts for them," said Panebianco. "You'd open the side door into the parking lot and see hundreds of people milling around, just listening."

On July 23, they stopped in New York City for a pair of concerts. The first was at the 3,000-seat Beacon Theater, the band's biggest NYC date yet. Naturally, the venue brought out the best, and the worst, in the band.

Relying on the benevolence of a clearly jacked-up audience, Westerberg spent most of the twenty-eight-song set playing around: delivering a giggling scat-jazz "Nightclub Jitters," attempting the final climactic scream from "Nevermind" half a dozen times after the song was over. The bulk of the show was dedicated to light comedy: an a cappella "Hello Dolly" had the audience clapping rhythm; a ferocious "Gary's Got a Boner" threw a dig at High Noon ("Gary's fired . . . and so is Russ!"); and Westerberg sang a version of "If Only You Were Lonely" as he sucked from a helium balloon, which turned his voice into a ridiculous squeak.

By the time the band stumbled out for a belated encore, the house lights were up, the stagehands were tearing down equipment, and half the crowd had filed out. "Whaddya think we are—*fuckin' entertainers?*" asked a slurring Westerberg of the remaining patrons. "There's a fine line between a self-indulgent freak show and rocking pandemonium," wrote *New York Times* critic Jon Pareles, "and the Replacements walked it at the Beacon."

A few days later at the smaller Ritz, fans outside were literally begging for tickets: "Offering fifty dollars and up, all to see a band of drunken punk 'n' roll hooligans who have never even seen the inside of the top 100," David Fricke reported in *Melody Maker*.

By now, the pattern was predictable: the Beacon had been a glorious shit-show; inevitably the Ritz would be a genuine triumph. "For once in their lives the Replacements played their own songs. Correctly! With the power and spirit they deserve," noted Fricke. "No screwing around! They played the covers straight too. . . . What made the Replacements give so much of themselves tonight? Who cares?"

With Dunlap girding things, the *Pleased* dates represented the band's most consistent performances ever. Yet it became clear that proficient playing wasn't what audiences had come to see. "People weren't paying to see guys stand there and play," said Dunlap. "They were paying to see this gigantic drunken caravan." And Westerberg was usually more than willing to give them a sideshow.

* * *

The *Pleased to Meet Me* tour was a banquet of excess. For the first time, there was real money, proper riders, free everything, every night. Nobody ate food, but the liquor was robust. The band mostly seemed to subsist on handfuls of Tums to quell their constantly churning stomachs.

The cycle of abuse, combined with the nature of life on the road, had a roller-coaster effect. "Every day you go up and down. Every morning you wish you were dead, but come five o'clock you're ready for the next [gig]," Westerberg explained to a reporter. "You're not at home, you don't feel at home, and you don't act human. You abuse yourself, not intentionally. But you . . . can never relax in the place you are, so you tend to distract yourself by drinking."

The 'Mats' new member quickly came to realize that drinking was as much a part of the job as playing. "I lived the life of being a hired drunkard," said Dunlap. "I was quite intoxicated in those days. You couldn't be teetotal. You couldn't do it."

Warner Bros. had thrown a series of parties in New York and Los Angeles to celebrate the release of the record. Once the band got on the road, there was hardly a sober moment. When they went to visit a distributor or a radio station or to do an in-store, there was always a bottle and a case waiting. By the time they got to the venue, the buffet of booze was endless. "The label was certainly accommodating us and willing to push that image," noted Westerberg. "That said, they didn't do it to us. We were alcoholics."

Dunlap marveled at and then began to fear Westerberg's consumption. "Before a show he would be carrying around a jug, a pretty heavy-duty thing, of Wild Turkey, and later it'd be empty. You'd think: *If he drank that much he's dead. That would kill a person.*"

There were moments when the band's behavior was tempered, like the rare occasions when their girlfriends and wives were around. "It was fun to see them around their women because they were totally different," recalled Wilkinson. "The girlfriends were backstage one night, and the band was twiddling its thumbs. And I'm winding them up: 'Oh, so you're not drinking tonight, boys?'"

"Finally, the girlfriends left, and Tommy and Paul got a saucer and filled it up with Jack Daniels, put it on the floor, and jumped on it like two dogs lapping it up. I was fucking howling and pouring beer on their heads: '*Do you want a chaser with that?*' By the time they got onstage they'd licked half a bottle of Jack Daniels and were soaking wet with beer. They went right into the first song like nothing happened."

The band's capacity to drink and then deliver onstage was an essential part of their mythos. Before a show, they could barely stand, but then the adrenaline of the stage would kick in and carry them through, their bodies rapidly metabolizing the alcohol while they played, even as they continued to guzzle. "The stories of them being legless and then being able to get up and play a great show," said Dunlap, "that part of the legend was true."

The band's performances and drinking were both being exacerbated by their use of drugs, namely cocaine. "The creeps who had substances, suddenly there were more of them around, there was more of it available, and we indulged," said Westerberg.

"When cocaine comes into the picture, that's another evil that you don't need," observed Mars. "It tends to make you want to drink twice as much, and then you're really screwing up. . . . As our popularity increased, our insecurity pretty much stayed the same. That was part of it too. [All] that helped us perform."

High Noon's Gary Hobbib was out on the road regularly with the 'Mats that summer, partly to connect with Warner Bros.'s field staff and partly to stay bonded with the band. "I was partaking as much as they were," said Hobbib. "It's good because they felt I was with them. But it's hard for me to then stand up and say, 'Guys, cut it out.'"

More distressingly for Hobbib, profits were short of expectations. Much of the outlay for the tour had come from Warner Bros. After seeing the backlash suffered by the Del Fuegos for appearing in a Miller Beer ad, the 'Mats refused any endorsements or sponsorships and decided not to even sell any merch.

Meanwhile, outside the gigs, bootleggers did brisk business in Replacements T-shirts.

Paul and Tommy were unrepentantly profligate and derived a perverse thrill in behaving that way. When they needed drugs, they would bust into the road manager's tour cash. As soon as they got their weekly per diems they would gamble the money away. After a while, the rush of losing cash at cards wasn't enough. Westerberg and Stinson would simply cut to the chase and light their per diem money on fire.

"We'd go and knock on the road manager's door to get an advance for the next week so we could burn it," said Westerberg. "Chris, needless to say, would try and pull away from that the best he could, and Slim would pretend he was a little light. But Tommy and I would burn the damn money." Like so many of their seemingly negative, ritualistic acts, it was also a form of bonding between them. "'The money's gone—what are we gonna do tomorrow?'" said Westerberg. "'I don't know. But we got each other; we'll get by.'"

CHAPTER 41

On October 2, 1987, the tour's debauchery was held at bay for the wedding of Paul Harold Westerberg and Lori Susan Bizer.

The couple had been dating for almost three years, living together for two. Bizer had uprooted her life to come to Minneapolis and be with Westerberg. With him on the road for months on end, she wanted some reassurance. "I don't want to say I pushed him into it. That sounds terrible," said Bizer. "But we were in a domestic situation, and women want to take the next step."

Westerberg would say—perhaps truthfully, if somewhat uncharitably—that the reason he got married was to appease Bizer, to keep her from crying every time he left town. But there was more behind the decision.

Westerberg was still only twenty-six. He was living impossibly hard, enjoying the bounty of feminine attention on the road and still striving—in his own way—to carve out a career. But the more time he spent touring and the more chaotically he lived while traveling, the more desperate he became for some semblance of order when he came home. "He probably needed some reeling in more than anyone really knew," said Tommy Stinson.

Stinson followed down the aisle eleven months later; Chris Mars would tie the knot just weeks after that. In hindsight, the band's rapid-fire marriages were at least partly an attempt to control the chaos of being in the Replacements. "We needed moorings," said Stinson. "We had this *ultra-insane* existence, and there needed to be a break from it."

Bizer was conservative at heart. "There was not a thing out of place in her house; the way she cooked, everything about her was regimented," said Panebianco. For Bizer, who'd grown up with an alcoholic, depressive father, Westerberg's increased drinking and mood swings didn't register as warnings. "Because of my dad, I thought that's what a mate was supposed to be like," she said.

Some 150 guests attended the ceremony at the Antioch Lutheran Church in the Detroit suburb of Farmington Hills. Paul's brother Phil was the best man, and the rest of the Replacements served as ushers. "We *definitely* were the odd men out there," said Tommy. "Her family was not into him marrying their daughter at all, or us being there." Bizer's mother, Louise, in particular "went out of her way to make Tommy feel extremely uncomfortable," said Stinson's girlfriend, Daune Earle. "She almost banned him from the church because of his hair. It was really horrible, and Paul didn't stick up for him."

The Young Fresh Fellows, dressed in powder-blue thrift-store tuxedos, helped usher and served as the wedding band. ("I couldn't afford NRBQ," cracked Westerberg.)

The couple said their vows as part of a traditional Lutheran ceremony, conducted by a Pastor Johnson—whose first name was Gary. "Paul and the band sang 'Gary's Got a Boner' for him at the reception," said Bizer. "The pastor actually went and saw the Replacements on their next show in Detroit. They converted him to a fan." By the end of the night, however, the reception turned into a "classic" Replacements concert complete with drunken, half-finished rock-and-roll covers.

After a brief honeymoon in Maine's Acadia National Park, Paul and Lori purchased a cottage on West Fifty-Fourth Street. Then Westerberg returned to the road. Little changed in his behavior. "I settled down, but only on paper," he said. "Being young rock-and-rollers, we left the wives at home and left the notion of marriage at home too."

Touring could wreak havoc on any marriage, even one as strong as the Dunlaps'. Slim wasn't a womanizer, but after months on the road drinking at a level and rate he'd never experienced, his relationship with Chrissie began to be affected. "He really changed, being in that band," she said. "There were three children who wanted their dad. And he wasn't in dad mode. He was in rock guy Replacements mode.

"After one fight or another, he would say, 'I'll quit if you want me to.' 'That's not what I want. I want you to go play, and I want you to call me every day and tell me you miss me, and I want you to come home and be nice to us.'"

★ ★ ★

The 'Mats headed back on tour in November for the first time in four years without the help of Frank Riley's Venture Booking.

For over a year, High Noon had been bringing bigger agents in for clandestine road meetings. Typical was the face-to-face with Rob Light of CAA, the powerful Los Angeles–based firm run by superagent Michael Ovitz. Light flew to see the band play at Washington University in St. Louis. After the sound check, he recalled, "I walk into this old funky college locker room and it's pitch-black. Taped to the ceiling is a flashlight over a stool. And all you hear is banging on these old metallic lockers, like a drum beat, and the guys are humming that theme from *The Wizard of Oz* where the flying monkeys go 'Oh wee oh . . .' at the top of their lungs."

"Sit down!" commanded a disembodied voice from behind the lockers, which turned out to be Westerberg.

Immediately he began firing all manner of ridiculous questions at Light—"Can we open for Madonna?" "What's your favorite TV show?" "Forget Madonna, can we open for Michael Jackson?"—while the rest of the band snickered their approval.

Light passed the band's initial test, and they agreed to have a drink with him after the show at their hotel. "We're trying to have a serious conversation about touring and what CAA could do, but their focus is in and out," said Light. "And within thirty minutes they've each had three doubles. They're just drinking themselves into a stupor."

The bartender announced last call. Drunk and tired, Westerberg told Light the band would sign with him if he could get CAA head Mike Ovitz on the phone . . . right then. Light looked at his watch and saw that it was well past midnight in LA. He wasn't about to rouse his boss and put Westerberg on the line with him. "I'm not waking up Mike Ovitz, Paul," Light told him.

It took Westerberg a moment. "Okay, then, here's what I want," he said. "I want you to drop your pants and walk around the bar clucking like a chicken. And if you do that, I'll sign with CAA."

Light thought about it for a moment, then shook his head. "I love your music. I love this band. But my pride is worth more to me than representing you," said Light. "I'm gonna pass."

* * *

After flirting with several other agents in similarly ridiculous fashion, the band finally went to the Premiere Talent Agency, run by Frank Barsalona, an intimidating figure who'd helped build the rock concert business in the sixties and seventies with the Who, Cream, Jimi Hendrix, and Led Zeppelin. He'd later work with punk acts, including the Ramones, the Clash, and the Sex Pistols.

Barsalona exuded the air of a mobbed-up tough guy; Westerberg certainly thought he was "connected." That fall Chicago's WXRT was pressing the Replacements to play a free concert for the station, as a way of apologizing for the "Little Village" radio incident months earlier. Westerberg knowingly asked Barsalona to "tell the 'boys' in Chicago to lean on [WXRT] so that we don't have to play this gig. He looked at me like, 'What the hell are you talking about?'"

Westerberg professed ignorance over the Frank Riley decision. "I barely understood the notion of a booking agent and his fee," said Westerberg. But according to First Avenue's Steve McClellan, "they dumped Riley very unprofessionally. He heard he might be losing the band, so he flew to Minneapolis to go to one of their . . . shows that he'd booked. Word is that Tommy threw bologna at him."

McClellan had seen the work Riley had put in with the band over the years. "They were a pain in the ass to deal with, they drank too much, and they didn't make that much money," said McClellan. The timing of Riley's dismissal also stung. "We ignored loyalty," admits Rieger.

A quarter-century on, Riley—now one of the most successful agents in the business—can barely bring himself to talk about the Replacements. "You get kicked in the nuts at some point," he said, "and it's hard to forget."

* * *

By late 1987, *Pleased to Meet Me*'s second single, "Alex Chilton," had steadily gained traction. Warner Bros. simply resubmitted "The Ledge" video, totally unchanged, for "Alex Chilton," and it received a few daytime airings and play on MTV's specialty alternative show *120 Minutes*, helping improve the band's fraught relationship with the network.

Industry tip sheet *The Album Network* even took the rare step of repicking *Pleased to Meet Me* for its best new music section: "The Replacements are touring and according to Sire are very willing to support radio with station-sponsored concerts."

"Very willing" may have been an exaggeration, but the band did play a couple of free promo gigs for radio stations to help push the single. One was for KROQ—a special daytime show at the Country Club in Reseda, California. Lewis Largent was again on hand, this time to emcee.

"As I'm introducing the band, unbeknownst to me, Tommy Stinson kneels down behind my legs and Westerberg walks up and pushes me over him," recalled Largent. "I catch air and you could hear the sound of me hitting the floor on the mic. And Stinson is going, 'Lemme tell you something, we fucking hate KROQ, man.'" Even so, "Alex Chilton" was one of the station's ten most-played songs that year.

* * *

Wherever the Replacements played, sales would typically jump, so the label and management kept the band touring through December. For the final legs, High Noon replaced road manager Derek Wilkinson with Larry Weinles, another seasoned pro.

The 'Mats quickly nicknamed him "Larry Wine-Less," since he was charged with keeping a lid on the band's drinking. Weinles had worked for Alice Cooper and Natalie Cole in their postsobriety stages. "I certainly did turn into the strict babysitter," said Weinles. "But it was pretty much impossible with the Replacements."

On December 1, the band was hanging out at Seattle's Mayflower Hotel bar with Scott McCaughey when Westerberg suggested they all shave their eyebrows. "By the time we actually got done with it," said Stinson, "the feisty stage was over, and it was like, 'Oh . . . *shit*. I'm going to bed. I hope this goes away by the time I wake up.' It didn't."

The following night during a gig at the Moore Theater, McCaughey discovered the value of eyebrows. "I had sweat just pouring into my eyes, blinding me," he remembered. "Plus, they take forever to grow back. I walked around like that for months."

The finale of the tour had the Replacements doubling back up the West Coast, playing the Palladium in LA, the Gift Center in San Francisco, and the Pine Street Theatre in Portland.

Neither the Replacements nor the Young Fresh Fellows slept much after the Gift Center gig. The long haul up Interstate 5 to Oregon made everyone especially cranky. "We walked into the Pine Street Theatre at five o'clock, and Paul was sitting in a chair. He just looked at me and went: 'Drink!' So we commenced," said McCaughey. "I think I was still drunk from the night before. It went downhill from there."

The evening began with the Fellows and the 'Mats tossing a couch out of the theater's second-floor dressing room window. It ended with Westerberg swinging from the theater's chandelier like Tarzan before yanking the entire fixture down on himself. "They always fall," said Westerberg sagely. "But damn, it feels so good for that one split second."

In between, the bands made desperate attempts to play. "We were actually so hapless during our set, they came up and grabbed instruments and started playing for us," recalled McCaughey. Backstage, Westerberg had grabbed McCaughey's tour bag, taken every piece of clothing in it, and put it all on. He and the band then began stripping and tossing the garments out into the crowd. The 'Mats ended the set playing in their underwear. "We flopped like murder," said Westerberg. "I don't think we got paid that night either." Westerberg later memorialized the evening's events in a song called "Portland," an apology to the city.

With the tour concluded, *Pleased to Meet Me* had pushed past 170,000 sales, more than double *Tim*'s total. It was cold comfort for High Noon. "*Pleased to Meet Me* should've gone gold," said Russ Rieger. "But it was crippled because of 'The Ledge.'"

Still, the band made serious retail inroads and, despite themselves, got a foothold in alternative radio. More importantly, Warner Bros. announced it would form a new radio promotions department under its reactivated Reprise banner, ostensibly to focus on hipper, up-and-coming acts like the Replacements. "Everything was lined up for the next record," said Hobbib.

There was just one problem: the band itself was in a state of early decay. "By the end of that tour, we were wasted: morally, physically, and mentally," said Westerberg. And they were still missing their eyebrows.

CHAPTER 42

Reeking of booze and Ben-Gay from the previous night's gig, Paul Wester-berg shifted uncomfortably in his seat. As the Replacements drove back to Minneapolis from the final dates of the *Pleased to Meet Me* tour, he sat staring at the latest issue of *Rolling Stone*.

From its cover, four familiar faces peered back beneath the headline: "R.E.M.—America's Best Rock & Roll Band." Their sixth album, *Document*, had transformed the group from an intriguing college rock band to certified million sellers, thanks to a top-ten hit in "The One I Love." It was a triumph of sonic semantics: Stipe's voice had finally been forced to the front of the mix, Bill Berry's drums had been invested with a new power, and the song was simple and insistent, yet vague enough for mainstream radio.

The man responsible for the shift was Scott Litt, the former Power Station engineer who'd been considered and rejected for *Pleased to Meet Me*. With R.E.M., he'd effectively midwifed alternative rock as a commercially viable genre.

"With 'The One I Love,' I would say to the guys, 'I hear this alongside a Whitney Houston song on a top-forty station,'" said Litt. "I thought that the execution of this type of music could be just as big."

Rather than systematically alienating Warner's field staff and undertaking kamikaze attacks on taste-making stations like KROQ and WXRT, R.E.M. had been busy charming radio brass. "We did make an effort to do all that," said R.E.M.'s Peter Buck. "I don't mind going into a room and shaking people's hands. I don't mind going to a couple radio stations and talking to them so they'll play a record that I think is a hundred times better than the crap they're playing anyway."

Westerberg would view R.E.M.'s success as a matter of maturity rather than music. "Like Sammy [Davis Jr.] says: 'It's show, and it's business.' We knew the show and didn't want to hear about the business. We were bound and determined to fight it."

In April 1988, R.E.M. signed a seven-figure, multi-album pact with Warner Bros. The next few Litt-produced R.E.M. albums would build on *Document*, each becoming bigger than the last, and the band would be catapulted to international stardom and pop-culture celebrity. "When they had the hit, they didn't run away from it, they embraced it and found their way through it," said Rieger.

For Litt, the 'Mats always had the 90 percent that makes a great song but were lacking the 10 percent that makes a hit. "Look, if 'Alex Chilton' was called 'Buddy Holly,' it could've been the Weezer hit," said Litt. "Something that small can be . . . the difference between selling 300,000 records and selling a million."

* * *

R.E.M.'s ascent dramatically altered the landscape for bands like the Replacements. None of this was lost on Westerberg. "He was bothered a lot," said his wife Lori Bizer. "Seeing people become successful and he's still scrapping. I think he started to feel the pressure."

As Westerberg limped home at the end of 1987, after eight months of touring and nightly self-abuse, his new bride was left to deal with the damage. "He didn't want to do anything. Didn't want to go anywhere, didn't want to see anybody," said Bizer. "He needed a recuperating period. But then that would go on for a long time." Westerberg spent the winter of 1988 as a hermit. High Noon had sent along a Tascam four-track cassette recorder so he could cut demos at home. This modest home studio would have a fundamental impact on Westerberg's songwriting—and the Replacements' creative dynamic.

For eight years he'd been writing songs designed to impress—first Peter Jesperson and the band, then the small army of critics who championed his work. By the time Westerberg was in the major-label spotlight, he admitted, "I might have gotten to the point where most of my songs were written for beer-swilling nineteen-year-old males."

Finally able to flesh out arrangements on his own, he began to write as he pleased, presenting the material to the band as a fait accompli. "I knew I was changing," said Westerberg. "I wasn't feeling like the Replacements. I was just feeling like myself for the first time."

He was coming up with far more character-driven pieces, partly after further immersion in Flannery O'Connor and Tennessee Williams. Ultimately, much of the new material played as portraits of the women in Westerberg's life: his sister, his wife, his numerous road dalliances. "I never knew what, or who, his songs were about," said Bizer. "I'd ask him and get a different story every time. So I stopped asking."

Of course, some of Westerberg's female protagonists were merely disguised versions of himself. "It is easier for me to say what's on my mind by using a character. And it's generally a woman," he said. At the same time, many of the

new tunes—raw reflections like "They're Blind" and "Rock 'n' Roll Ghost"—
were more nakedly autobiographical than ever.

In early 1988, Westerberg wrote dozens of songs, the most he'd written in
one spurt since the run-up to *Sorry Ma*. Much of this material, like "Last Thing
in the World" and "Forever's Outlaw," wouldn't make the LP; still more never
even left the basement. "Every time I would ever go to his house, he would play
me a bunch of new songs that killed, none of which ever saw the light of day,"
said Slim Dunlap. "He would just tape over something when the next song idea
came along."

Westerberg wrote most of the new material on his Yamaha acoustic guitar.
Initially, he thought the next album should follow suit and be all acoustic, sans
drums. Instead, his compromise was to stop categorizing the songs: "I decided
to make the ballads more rockin', and the rockers more tuneful," he said.

Still, one question remained: how did the band, Chris Mars in particular,
fit his material? Along with his four-track, Westerberg had also gotten an Ale-
sis HR-16, a rudimentary drum machine. He developed a bizarre attachment
to its rigid programmed beats and, with it, an acute case of "demo-itis" that
would plague him for the rest of his career. "Now he's got this rhythm in his
head of how the song should be played," said Tommy Stinson. "It wasn't just
about Chris. He didn't understand why something that worked on his four-
track didn't work the same with us playing. Well, it's just different. Four guys
in a room are never going to sound the same as your demo. That really changed
things."

★ ★ ★

Chris Mars's 1988 was bookended by two major events. In January his eighty-
one-year-old father, Leroy Mars, died, and in the fall he married his girlfriend Sally Schneidkraut. A brunette pixie with a toothy smile, Schneidkraut
had materialized on the Minneapolis scene the previous year. Born in Queens,
New York, in 1964, she was the youngest of four kids, like Mars. She was Jewish
but had been raised in a blue-collar Catholic neighborhood like the one Mars
had grown up in.

As a teenager, Sally went to live with her older brother Andy in Colorado.
Her parents eventually followed them out, and her father ran a little Italian
restaurant in a tourist town outside Rocky Mountain National Park. In 1981
Schneidkraut enrolled at Colorado State University in Fort Collins, where she
majored in fine art.

Her brother Andy was a massive rock-and-roll fan—he founded Boulder's long-running record store Albums on the Hill—and Sally began doing
production for a local concert company. "I started with stage production for
small clubs and venues and quickly wound up working 18,000-seat arenas," she
said. She moved to Minneapolis and began a career in broadcast production.
There, she met Mars, who, despite his boyish good looks, was painfully shy

and had never really had a girlfriend before. They'd both lost parents in 1988; Sally's mother died not long after Chris's father, and they bonded in their grief.

Schneidkraut gave Mars a confidence he'd always lacked, encouraging his visual art. From the start, the Replacements saw her as an interloper. Paul and Tommy, who tended to view women in simplistic rock-and-roll terms, viewed Schneidkraut as a groupie. She'd glommed on to Chris and was soon meddling in the band's affairs.

Mars had become increasingly passive within the group; after their marriage, Sally began speaking for him. Their coupling may have accelerated the process, but Mars had already been questioning his place within the band. As the *Pleased to Meet Me* circus rolled on, Mars spent more and more time with his pastels and sketchpads. "We'd dump him off at his hotel room, and he'd go in there and draw all night long," said Dunlap. "The rest of us would go out and party and hang around somebody's kitchen until four in the morning."

For Mars, the only remaining joy he took in the band was helping shape the music. But with Westerberg cutting demos on his own, that was being closed off as well. On *Pleased to Meet Me*, Westerberg had given the group four cowrites for their input and inspiration—but writing and arranging songs on his own also meant that the band would share fewer credits and less publishing money.

CHAPTER 43

Sire had budgeted nearly $300,000 for the next Replacements album, but who the hell was going to produce it? Michael Hill racked his brain for a solution that would satisfy everyone. The first impulse was to reunite with Jim Dickinson. Russ Rieger, always the loudest voice in the room, wouldn't have objected, especially if they brought in a hotshot mixer to give the singles an extra polish (as he had on "Can't Hardly Wait," hiring Jimmy Iovine to give the single a radio friendly luster). However, Rieger claimed, there was lingering ill will about the string overdubs and postproduction tinkering on *Pleased*. "There was a lot of bad blood after the fact," said Rieger. "Paul felt Dickinson had done things behind their backs."

Counters Westerberg, "I didn't have a bad feeling towards Dickinson. It was more, 'That producer didn't get us a hit, so we gotta find one that can.'"

Scott Litt's name inevitably came up again, but the last thing the 'Mats wanted at that point was to look like they were riding R.E.M.'s coattails. (Besides, Litt was already booked for Stipe and company's Warner Bros. debut.) Suggestions from Talking Heads' Jerry Harrison to Pat Benatar guitarist Neil Giraldo to Bon Jovi/Aerosmith man Bob Rock went nowhere with the band. Neither did guitarist and Warner artist Ry Cooder. "The feeling was that maybe Westerberg and Cooder could work together—you know, curmudgeon to curmudgeon," said Hill. "But thankfully, we thought better of it."

By April they'd gotten nowhere. Then Warner VP Michael Ostin (Mo's son) called Hill and suggested that he look up someone who hadn't been on anyone's radar: Tony Berg.

★ ★ ★

Born in 1954, Tony Berg had been raised in a house of Hollywood intellectuals. His father, Dick Berg, was a writer and dramatist who'd created the made-for-TV-movie format. Eldest brother Jeff would eventually be the powerful chairman of the International Creative Management talent agency; youngest brother Richard would become a film and TV producer; and middle sibling Scott would write biographies of Charles Lindbergh and Sam Goldwyn, among others, and win a Pulitzer Prize.

A preternaturally talented guitarist, at nineteen Tony became the music director at the Mark Taper Forum, before serving in the band for the original production of *The Rocky Horror Show.* Later he became Bette Midler's musical director. In 1976 Berg began several years as guitarist, arranger, and right hand to madman producer Jack Nitzsche. In the early '80s, he was in the ill-fated major-label acts the Coyote Sisters and Channel. "But what I had always wanted to do was produce records," he said.

Berg began recording demos in his Brentwood garage, leading to major-label deals for Michael Penn and Eric Johnson. In 1987 he got his first proper production job, helming the debut by MCA baby band Broken Homes. MCA A&R man Michael Goldstone was so impressed with Berg's work that he enlisted him as coproducer, with veteran engineer Bob Clearmountain, of Charlie Sexton's sophomore album. Berg was at Bearsville Studios in upstate New York working on the project when Michael Hill called.

Michael Ostin recommended Berg for the Replacements gig largely on the basis that they shared a manager. It was a favor—Berg had hardly any credits. He did, however, have an abundance of charm. "Tony was very erudite about music," said Hill. Berg and Westerberg talked on the phone, and Paul suggested Tony send a postcard listing his ten favorite records. "I said, 'These records mean a lot to me; I hope you respond to them,'" recalled Berg. "I added, 'But if you don't, you can go fuck yourself.' I got a call immediately—he said to come to New York and meet."

Berg sold the production as an effort to find the delicate balance between a great songwriter and a great rock band. "He said everything that you wanted him to say," said Gary Hobbib. "We all went, 'Wow, this guy's really good.'" Eventually Westerberg mentioned that they'd tossed the Replacements' master tapes in the Mississippi: "As if to tell me, 'This is who we are and what we do,'" said Berg.

Suddenly, Westerberg grabbed Berg's leg, pulled off his boot, and poured a beer in it. "He drank out of my shoe, slammed it down, and said, 'You're our man!'"

Hill was relieved, but Rieger wasn't: he'd wanted an established hit-maker. He was also suspicious about the band's reasons for agreeing to the youngest, least experienced candidate. "I think they felt like they could manipulate Berg," said Rieger. "But I wasn't going to win the argument. And the record had to be made."

* * *

B erg, the band, and the label brass—including Seymour Stein—went out for
a celebratory dinner. During the meal, Stein began his usual playful flirtations with Tommy. But soon his attentions took on a belittling edge. Tommy
"was being picked on and picked up on," said one witness to the scene. "It was
very uncomfortable."

Sensing this, Westerberg threw a possessive arm around Stinson and
half-jokingly hissed at Stein: "Fuck off, faggot . . . he's *my* bitch." Berg was
"impressed by how fiercely protective Paul was of Tommy," he said. He would
eventually discover just how protective.

Berg had an unexpected opening in his schedule; the Replacements could
be squeezed into the break. They'd have ten days up in Bearsville to record.
"Management was very aggressive about starting immediately," said Berg. "So
instead of rehearsing or doing any real preproduction, we were thrust into the
recording."

Bearsville had a peculiar setup. A studio complex founded by Bob Dylan's
manager Albert Grossman in 1969, it was nestled in the woods just west of
Woodstock, its bucolic grounds dotted by residences, including a series of small
cabins, for the bands to stay in. Working there wasn't unlike being sent away
to summer camp. Bars were hard enough to find, much less women, drugs,
or excitement. But there was no time to argue. The boys were heading to the
country.

CHAPTER 44

In the months leading up to the Bearsville sessions, Paul Westerberg had evinced an unusual degree of pride, even optimism, about his new songs. But as the session date grew closer, his spirit darkened. "Paul built up this incredible anxiety about making that record," said Slim Dunlap.

Arriving from Minneapolis in early June, the band stopped in New York City en route to Bearsville, meeting Michael Hill, Julie Panebianco, and a group of friends gathered at Paul's Lounge, a West Village bar, for a send-off. Westerberg's mood was anything but celebratory. "He was being so negative about the label, about recording. At one point, I got up from the table crying," said Panebianco. "He was already in the knock-it-down phase, before he'd even created it."

"They started to get really drunk and I got the whole earful: 'Warner Brothers hates us. You don't like us. No one likes us,'" said Hill. "They were at a point in their drinking lives where, after a certain amount, it would really turn ugly."

Tim Perell, a twenty-one-year-old former High Noon intern, was hired to babysit the band. He drove them upstate, doled out per diems, and called Russ Rieger and Gary Hobbib with daily status reports. "I don't think anybody was under the illusion I could keep them out of trouble," said Perell. "I had to bring beer when I picked them up. We got stuck in traffic on the Long Island Expressway, and they were all peeing in the well of the van. That was my inauguration. They'd asked me what I'd done, and I told them I'd just graduated college. So for the first few days they called me 'Einstein.'"

The Replacements arrived at Bearsville with a chip on their shoulders. The studio's Scottish manager, Ian Kimmet, politely informed the band that their producer was in the middle of a catered family dinner. Berg had brought his wife, children, and young sister-in-law for a visit. The 'Mats were undeterred. "They all barged past me up to the private quarters like punks, real yobbo types," said Kimmet. "They spread out round the table and Tony's party. They had it in for him—it was obvious from the very first moments."

* * *

Tony Berg would come to view his brief time with the Replacements philosophically. Today Berg is a respected industry veteran with over 100 productions to his credit. In 1988, however, "I was not prepared for the chaos of the Replacements," he admitted.

For the first couple of days, Berg managed to keep their gang dynamic at bay. He settled in with Westerberg to go over songs, rehearsing in Bearsville's barn studio. "Paul and I would sit down with two acoustic guitars and dig in, and it didn't include the band that much initially," said Berg.

Berg had flown out his new Sony digital multi-track recorder and his trusted engineer Dan Bates. His plan was to track the band live, keeping the spontaneous performances, and later adding a smattering of overdubs. "To produce much beyond that would be false," noted Berg. "I felt the work that needed to be done was mostly arrangemental.

"Paul was responding very well to the dialogue—that there would be real discussion of parts and choices. We talked about guitar parts. And then, more profoundly, we discussed lyrics. That was the strength of the relationship. How it proved the relationship's undoing, in my opinion, is that the band had never witnessed that before. And Tommy in particular—it was profoundly unsettling for him."

In Memphis, Jim Dickinson had encouraged Tommy's songwriting. In Bearsville, Berg relegated Stinson to the role of sideman. "The star is the guy you have to please and court," said Slim Dunlap. "If you're smart, you do it very subtly. If you're not smart, you do it overtly and create tension and alienation. And Tony just played it terribly."

In Berg's mind, Westerberg was seeking to push further in the direction his new songs were headed, even if that meant making something like a solo record. "Tommy was being very careful of the Replacements—more than Paul, in a way," said Berg. But the trust they established was fleeting. "He was a little heavy-handed when it came to changing the songs around, which I wasn't really into," said Westerberg, who also cringed at Berg's "flashy riffs" on guitar: "He was too good a musician."

Berg was also dealing with a group that was simultaneously congealing—this was Dunlap's first time in the studio with them—and falling apart, with Bearsville another step in Chris Mars's growing estrangement from music. "Drumming wasn't the most important thing to him," said Berg. "He had moved on."

At least Mars was docile. Dunlap, on the other hand, held Berg in open contempt; the producer compared the guitarist to *Lil' Abner*'s Pappy Yokum: "It felt like they'd brought their country uncle. He could play. But he was *extremely* ornery."

"Tony had declared that it was his job to 'bring the Replacements into the 1980s,'" recalled Westerberg. "Of course, it was almost 1989."

★ ★ ★

Despite the mistrust, the band recorded for twelve-hour stretches each day, beginning around 11:00 AM with a meal—burgers, typically—then proceeding to drink and play. "We had a regimen," said Stinson. "It wasn't like we were always total raging alcoholic assholes. We'd loosen up and get to the place it's got to be."

The band got even looser after they were involved in a small fender-bender driving to the studio one day. "Some guy pulled out of a driveway and hit us," said Tim Perell. Dunlap immediately began complaining of back pain and after a quick stop at a nearby doctor's office, came back with a large prescription bottle of the muscle relaxer Flexeril. The rest of the band were soon gobbling the pills and chasing them with liquor—with a narcotic effect audible on a number of the Bearsville tracks.

In addition to cutting eleven new Westerberg songs, Dunlap led the band on a languid reading of James Burton's 1965 instrumental "Love's Lost." The group also worked up an untitled rockabilly number and cut a track for a covers compilation of classic Disney songs for A&M Records, including "Cruella de Vil" from *101 Dalmatians*—though the band's initial version was unusable given Westerberg's improvised lyrics ("I'll fuck ya in the face, Cruella de Vil").

The gem was "Portland," an apologia for the Pine Street Theatre debacle the previous winter. A spiritual sequel to 1983's "Treatment Bound," "Portland" finds Westerberg looking around at a gang of fading souls ("Sitting in between a ghost and a walking bowl of punch") as the band's shine starts to dim ("Bring in the next little bunch").

"They were not what I would call a tight band, but they were a spirited band," said Berg. "Paul's talent was clear from his writing, but the surprise to me was Tommy."

Stinson's instincts would elevate "Portland" in particular. Tommy had requested a classical bass for the track and was given a gorgeous German model from a rental company in New York City. Although he'd never played upright before, he proceeded to work the instrument with a cellist's grace—before jumping on and destroying it, at a cost of some $4,000. After hearing the playback, Tommy decided the track also needed bongos. "Which was funny to me, because 'Portland' was essentially a country song," said Berg. "But he was absolutely right."

One of the only full-tilt rockers they recorded was "Wake Up." Berg came up with a countermelody—answering the guitar riff with a flourish of synth strings. It was an incongruous but inspired addition that the band loved.

Yet a cloud still hung over Westerberg. Seymour Stein had paid a lot of money for the record, and Berg was trying to cultivate a crossover hit. For all his conflicts about success, Westerberg still feared failure more. "If this one don't fly," he said, "then it's back to the brooms."

* * *

In the studio, Berg was a taskmaster when it came to tempo and pitch, concepts the Replacements were only loosely familiar with. They reacted as they always did: with passive and not-so-passive aggression.

Stinson spent much of the session unnerving Berg by brandishing a giant blade and playing Five Finger Fillet, jabbing between his digits. One evening, driving with Berg during a break, Stinson was in the backseat when a Bon Jovi song came on the radio. As Berg went to change the station, "Tommy kicked the radio as hard as he could with his boots and got my hand instead," said Berg, who spent the rest of the session with his fingers bandaged.

Berg had also brought a collection of beautiful guitars, including his prized Gibson ES-335, for the band to play. Dunlap had an identical 335, but a beater, way past real use. In the midst of a take, Westerberg began smashing Dunlap's guitar behind a baffle and then hollered to Berg: "Do you wanna see your guitar? Come on in here!" Berg saw the shattered 335 and "went into shock," said Dunlap. "We finally managed to calm him down. But even the thought that Paul would destroy a guitar was just scary to him."

"Tony had such reverence for the instruments, and Paul said, 'It's just a piece of fucking wood,'" recalled Perell. "That illustrated so perfectly the difference between them."

Another night, the band coerced Berg, who was borderline teetotal, into imbibing with them. "We got him dead drunk," said Westerberg, who plied the producer with pain pills. "Somebody held his arms, and we put a bunch in his mouth and made him drink a couple Singapore slings." Berg figured, "I was being initiated. You had to go through it."

The stifling environment at Bearsville only exacerbated the ill will between Berg and the band. Within a week the Replacements had come down with cabin fever, à la *The Shining*. "In each of our cottages there was a little kitchenette with knives," said Stinson. "Every night we'd go to one of the cottages and start playing 'Dodge Knife.' That's like dodgeball but with knives. It got very . . . troubling."

One night Dunlap drunkenly spread cream cheese all over the raw pine walls of his cottage. According to Berg, "They had car accidents. They trashed the studio. They trashed the living quarters. They were on medication that you would normally prescribe for horses and bears. They were just a mess."

* * *

On day seven, the Replacements had been cutting live for a particularly inspired stretch when the producer realized his Sony digital recorder had been using an unformatted reel. The entire section had been lost. Berg made a show of firing engineer Dan Bates for the oversight, but, said Perell, "that *really* infuriated the band."

That night, while recutting his part on "Asking Me Lies," Berg wanted Stinson, the bassist claimed later, to funk-slap the instrument; Berg said he simply wanted a "funkier" part. The discussion ended abruptly when Tommy hurled a half-gallon of gin through a studio window. Then Westerberg lit the remnants of the smashed Gibson guitar on fire in a garbage can on the studio floor. "You didn't want to be around us," said Stinson. "We were gone-crazy-devil-drunk."

The chaos climaxed with a Stinson-Westerberg game of "I Dare Ya." "I believe I was dared to walk across the studio console," recalled Westerberg. Bearsville was home to a truly magnificent Neve 8088 board that had been custom-built for the Who. Westerberg was instantly up on the $250,000 console, Jack Daniels bottle in hand, nimbly tiptoeing around the faders and knobs.

Berg became apoplectic. A screaming argument erupted, a week's worth of frustration spilling out. As things boiled, each man tried to flee the studio in a different direction, but they simply wound up following one another down the hall. "By the end of it, Tony and I were in tears, crying and yelling," said Westerberg.

They arrived at the canteen, where the members of Metallica, in Bearsville to mix *And Justice for All*, sat quietly eating Chinese takeout. As the meltdown passed dramatically before them, their jaws visibly dropped. "They had this look like, 'What the fuck is this? A prank?'" said Westerberg. "I'm sure we looked like a bunch of lunatics."

Before escaping the studio, Berg, remembering the story of the Twin/Tone heist, grabbed the session masters. "They were acting so irrationally, I thought they might do something horrible," he said.

After a few more hours of drinking, the Replacements came back to the studio to hear the day's work and were furious to discover Berg had taken the tapes. Westerberg summoned Berg to his cabin for a showdown. The producer walked to their cabin in the pitch-black night, dreading what awaited.

Suddenly, the ground fell from beneath him. He plunged a dozen feet down a stairwell that led to a basement apartment where the widow of the Band's Richard Manuel lived. "I completely fucked up my knee," said Berg. "I get back up and hobble over to the band's place, in really bad shape, only to be met by these furious renegades."

He managed to placate the band, despite Dunlap hissing: "Are you with us or agin' us?" After a long night's sleep, an uneasy denouement was reached. The sessions carried on without incident for a few more days before the band packed up and headed back to New York City.

"We went up there, hit a fucking tree, threw knives at each other, walked across the board, smashed up some shit, scared Metallica," said Westerberg. "But we felt like, 'That's it, we're done with the fucking woods.'"

* * *

"I walked away from there like a Civil War veteran," said Berg of the Replacements session. Despite everything, he remained eager to finish the record. "I genuinely loved the songs," he said. "I went to bed singing them, I woke up singing them."

Even unmixed, half a dozen of the songs (they'd tracked fifteen, twelve with vocals) seemed like potential keepers. But High Noon was not so optimistic. "There was absolutely no edge to the tracks," said Rieger. "We were a little bit surprised how much Rieger disliked it," said Westerberg. "But there wasn't any real magic there."

With more than $70,000 invested so far and a fall release impending, Michael Hill persuaded everyone it was worth another shot with Berg. The producer would fly to Minneapolis in June and work with the band to recut "Cruella de Vil"—minus the X-rated lyrics—and further discuss the album.

When Berg met the band at the CC Club, he said, "I felt such hostility from [Tommy] immediately." After some increasingly strained conversation over drinks, Stinson got up and went to the bathroom. There, alone, he suddenly broke down crying.

Westerberg walked into the commode and asked Stinson what was wrong. "I can't ever be in a fucking room with that guy again," Stinson replied. He didn't articulate it, but the message to Westerberg was clear: *This guy's best credit is Bette Midler. I play with* you. *This ain't us, man.*

Westerberg knew bailing on Berg would bring serious repercussions. For all his faults, Berg was a songwriter's producer; they *had* connected on the material to some extent. Yet again, Westerberg had to choose: be true to himself or be a Replacement.

Westerberg finally motioned to the door. "Fuck it then, Skunk," he said. "Let's go."

Back at the table, Berg felt the air grow colder. Finally, he demanded: "Look, Tommy, do you have an issue with me producing this record?"

"*Yeah*," Stinson snarled. "I think you're too young to produce our record."

Berg was taken aback: "Are you *purposely* sabotaging this record?"

"Yes," said Stinson. "I am."

Berg looked to Westerberg hopefully. Paul said nothing, leaning into the booth next to Tommy. Berg stood up, marched angrily to a nearby pay phone, called his manager, and told him he was coming home. He was through with the goddamn Replacements.

Shortly afterward, Peter Jesperson walked over to their table to say hello, unaware of the scene that had just been played out. After a long, awkward silence, Westerberg grinned and made introducitons: "Hey, Tony, this is Pete. He was our manager. We fired him," he said. "Pete, this is Tony. He was our producer. We just fired him."

CHAPTER 45

Calls poured into Michael Hill's office. He listened quietly, and when the angry voices relented, he hung up and let out a long, tired sigh. As the events in Minneapolis were relayed back to him, Hill almost had to laugh. They hadn't even made it into the studio; the whole thing had blown up over drinks in a bar.

"I certainly would say the Replacements were more a lifestyle than a normal A&R gig," Hill noted. When something went wrong—and something *always* went wrong—he bore frustration from all sides: label, management, and frequently the band itself. "It was all so ridiculous, but I believed that somehow everything was going to work out," said Hill. "Maybe it's like when you're in an abusive relationship."

Within Warner Bros., Hill was always something of an outsider: East Coast, working-class, and Gentile, as opposed to Californian, affluent, and Jewish, as the label's key A&R figures had historically been. Hill didn't have an appetite for the era's music biz avarice. He didn't rub elbows with attorneys or industry power players, didn't join their boys' clubs or jostle to see who the biggest *macher* was.

"Michael was like the band; he was young and alternative. He didn't have any clout," said Gary Hobbib, who felt Sire's Seymour Stein had largely abdicated his responsibilities as the 'Mats' label head, leaving Hill to fend for himself.

"Someone heavy-handed might've been a help to the Replacements, because they needed a push," said the band's attorney, George Regis. "Michael was not that guy. Michael would not presume in that way."

For his part, Hill saw no benefit in being a hard-ass, acting like some record company hammer. "Maybe some people would've called me an apologist for the Replacements," he said. "But what was the point in yelling or getting mad at the band? Besides, I loved Paul's work. In the end . . . I really carried a torch for that music."

Though his feelings for the work ran deep, he understood Westerberg's tendency to reject those who got too close. Hill had consciously decided not to buddy up to him. Yet to succeed at the level they were playing at now, there needed to be some deeper trust between them. "Paul and the band had strong opinions about everything," said Hill, "but they would express them by acting out in a manner that would force someone's hand."

They'd certainly forced Tony Berg's hand. "We had no plan B for a producer," acknowledged Russ Rieger. "This was a problem." Scott Litt, working on R.E.M.'s *Green* that summer, was hearing apocryphal tales of the band "covering Berg in peanut butter and hanging him on a hook."

There would be no album before 1989's first quarter. If more time passed, Westerberg might decide not to record the current batch of songs at all. "There was a sense of urgency," said Rieger. "I wouldn't say panic . . . well, yeah—*panic*."

* * *

Lenny Waronker's father Si was a classical violinist who'd cofounded Liberty Records and Metric Music Publishing in the midfifties. Lenny Waronker got his start at Liberty before joining Warner Bros. as a producer in 1966. For sixteen years he guided a roster that included Ry Cooder, Paul Simon, and his childhood friend Randy Newman and headed an A&R department that was the envy of the industry. In 1982, he was named president of the label.

Waronker remained more creatively involved than any other label head. "If Lenny gave his stamp of approval, people took it seriously," said Howie Klein, who became Sire's general manager in 1988. That became difficult by the late eighties, said Waronker: "There was so many records, so many artists."

By then, the man with Waronker's ear was his connection to the burgeoning alternative world—Steven Baker, VP of product management. Baker had helped make Talking Heads and the Smiths priorities for the company; now, along with Michael Hill, he began selling Waronker on the Replacements. "I would talk about Westerberg's songcraft—that's something that really interested him, because Lenny's above all a song man," said Hill.

Hill played Waronker the tracks from Bearsville. Once he heard the new material, he was convinced. "As I listened, I realized Paul was a force. I thought, 'Jesus Christ, no wonder,'" said Waronker. "The songs are amazing. The guy . . . he has the gift." Having spent his life with Randy Newman, Waronker could also appreciate Westerberg's stubbornness, dark moods, and mordant wit.

Waronker sensed that Westerberg wanted to move away from the Replacements' chaotic posturing. "If the stance gets in the way, to the point to where it stifles musical growth, that's when you really have to take a hard look," said Waronker, who took it upon himself to solve the Replacements' producer problem.

* * *

Ababy-faced, soft-spoken twenty-eight-year-old, Matt Wallace seemed unassuming—*gentle* even—in every way. But his looks and manner belied a bulldog tenacity that would serve him well in the music business. Born in Tulsa, Oklahoma, on January 10, 1960, his father, Ed Wallace, was a commercial pilot for a series of international airlines. The Wallaces lived throughout the Middle East (Cairo, Beirut, Tehran) and Japan before finally moving back to the United States in 1975. They settled in Moraga, a San Francisco suburb.

Wallace was a singer and a multi-instrumentalist who'd been playing in bands since his preteens. He also had an intuitive understanding of electronics. At fourteen, he'd developed a wireless guitar system out of a pair of GI Joe walkie-talkies, then built a four-track studio, dubbed Dangerous Rhythm, in his parents' garage a few years later, ostensibly to record his own band. "But I got derailed and started making other people's records," he said.

Charging twelve bucks an hour, the teenage Wallace recorded dozens of Bay Area acts—in particular, a group that would eventually become Faith No More—while pursuing an English degree at UC Berkeley. After graduating, he opened a larger operation in Oakland and eventually helmed projects for Faith No More and Sons of Freedom, both on Slash Records.

Slash was distributed by Warner Bros., for which Wallace was tapped to produce the New Monkees. That album stiffed, but it established a relationship among Wallace and Waronker and Baker, who encouraged Slash to hire Wallace full-time as staff producer and A&R man. He'd just moved to Los Angeles when the Replacements were starting their producer search.

Wallace, who had been following the Replacements since *Let It Be*, had called Baker every week to throw his hat in the ring for the 'Mats gig; after Berg's departure, Baker said he might have a shot.

Wallace hadn't produced anything of note—Faith No More had yet to break big—but he had Waronker's support. "He had the right personality to get in there and make it work," said Waronker. "Anytime there was a potential hook, he might be able to embellish that."

Westerberg agreed to a trial session with Wallace after they spoke on the phone. Paul and Slim Dunlap would fly to LA first and work on a couple of songs. If everything seemed all right, they'd come back out with Tommy Stinson and Chris Mars. "By the way," he told Wallace at the end of their conversation, "we drink a bit."

"That's fine, I don't drink at all," replied Wallace. "We'll get along famously."

Paul and Slim arrived in Los Angeles on September 1 and set up in the smaller room at Cherokee Studios in Hollywood. They spent a few days on "They're Blind," with Dunlap playing bass and Wallace programming beats on a drum machine. "From the moment I met Matt," said Westerberg, "I thought, 'This guy is very smart, has a sense of humor, and is gonna roll with it.' I liked him right away."

"The fact that I had so little of a track record actually appealed to Paul," said Wallace. "I think they felt like they could push me around and do what they wanted to do."

Dunlap was immediately dubious of Wallace, but kept his opinions to himself for a while. Stinson wasn't exactly enamored to have Wallace—even younger than Berg—running the show, but for the time being he trusted Westerberg's instincts. "I don't think I ever thought anyone was the right guy for that record," said Stinson. "At that point, we just had to make the fuckin' record."

Rieger also stewed—Warner Bros. was pushing yet another inexperienced, no-name producer on them—but stayed quiet, since he planned to wage war, if necessary, to bring in a top radio mixer.

The months off after Bearsville had given Westerberg time to write new material, including several uptempo numbers such as "Anywhere's Better Than Here" and "Talent Show," to balance out the Berg sessions' dolor. In a way, Bearsville had served as the preproduction rehearsal that the 'Mats had always strenuously avoided. "We were really ready," said Westerberg.

Waronker's interest buoyed them as well. "We got real sick of acting like we didn't care," Stinson said at the time. "We do care—I don't want to push a broom, and that's what I'd be doing if I wasn't in this band."

CHAPTER 46

Michael Hill wasn't taking any chances. He flew to Los Angeles for the start of the Matt Wallace/Replacements sessions with a knot in his stomach. "You started to wonder: are these guys just unrecordable?" said Hill.

His fears seemed legitimate. Sitting with Wallace and the band at a prerecording evening out at Musso & Frank's Restaurant in Hollywood, he watched Tommy Stinson ask, upon meeting Wallace, "You know what I think of you?"—then hock a giant loogie onto the ground. Slim Dunlap was only slightly less subtle. He'd practically crushed the producer's hand while shaking it.

"I was threatened to be beaten up numerous times during the sessions, mostly by Slim," recalled Wallace. "By virtue of the fact that he was the newest guy in the band, he was the enforcer. The only guy who was nice to me was Chris Mars. Paul sat back and watched how it unfolded and decided how to move after that. Once we started recording, Paul was really ornery too."

Wallace started with some rehearsals, a process he likened to "trying to keep marbles from rolling down a hill." He quickly moved the 'Mats to Cherokee's big room to cut rhythm tracks. Cherokee was an expensive, high-tech studio founded by the '60s Midwest bubblegum musicians the Robb Brothers. Knowing he'd have his hands full, Wallace brought in veteran engineer John Beverly Jones, whose credits ran from Olivia Newton John to Camper Van Beethoven.

As at Bearsville, workdays began around 10:00 AM and went for twelve- to fourteen-hour stretches, fortified by little other than grains and hops. "Those guys didn't eat anything," said Wallace. "The caloric ingestion was pretty much all alcohol." Much of Wallace's energy was spent trying to hide the daily afternoon liquor delivery until they'd recorded something usable.

Wallace made all the basic Replacements rookie mistakes. He handed them their weeklong per diems at once; they returned next day with empty pockets. "What happened?" he asked. "Well," they explained, "we went to the bar, and the bartender was such an asshole we tipped him everything we had."

Almost immediately, the same group psychosis that had marred the Bearsville sessions took hold. During a take, Tommy's Gibson Thunderbird bass began to wobble out of tune. Suddenly, Wallace saw him begin to smash the instrument wildly. As Stinson sent shards and splinters flying around the studio, Westerberg pulled out a crisp $100 bill and lit it on fire.

After three difficult days, the tension was unbearable. Extending an olive branch, the 'Mats invited Wallace and Jones to join them for a night out. The six of them headed to the Rainbow Room on Sunset Boulevard. If the band's behavior had been slightly mitigated in the studio, being in the bar removed any remaining reserve.

As Wallace nursed a light beer, Stinson grabbed a black marker and began drawing all over his pants and shirt. Meanwhile, Dunlap was drinking heavily, eventually getting in his face. "You're a young fuck," he hissed. "You don't know shit. *I'll kick your ass.*" Wallace's blood began to boil. "I was like, 'Fuck it—I'm done with this stuff, let's fight,'" said Wallace. "That's not even me. I'm not a fighter." The Rainbow's bartender was forced to break things up.

"If they had been more confident, or more honest, they could've said: 'Look, we're scared shitless. We've run through a bunch of producers; we've already scrapped one version of this record; we're working with you now, this is a big deal for us—what can we do?'" said Wallace. "But they couldn't say that. So they did the best they could do, which was lash out."

The next day Jones arrived at 4:00 PM—six hours late—to tell Wallace he quit. Three studio days and one night out had been more than enough Replacements for him.

Fortunately, the Replacements' old Minneapolis soundman Mike Bosley happened to be a Cherokee staff engineer. He came on board and watched the group gang up on Wallace. "There was a lot of friction between them," said Bosley.

Being in their label's backyard only heightened the Replacements' sense of loathing. Hill and Baker were doing their best to keep the project's momentum going, but the band was turning against them as well. One evening Hill and Baker were hanging with the 'Mats at Barney's Beanery. Leaving the bar, a sozzled Tommy Stinson stumbled and fell in the street. For a moment he lay in the gutter, looking up at his label benefactors.

"This is how you see us anyway, right?!" Stinson bellowed, somewhat theatrically. "This is what you think of us!"

Driving the band back to their digs at the Roosevelt Hotel, Hill got a further earful from Westerberg: "Warner Brothers doesn't respect us. You make us work with the guy from the New Monkees," he slurred angrily. "You fuckin' hate us!"

First thing next morning, Hill got a call: a hungover Westerberg effusively apologized and invited him for coffee. "He'd get really drunk and say all this stuff, then call up and apologize," said Hill. "That was his way."

Wallace was growing desperate. The first two weeks he'd tell his girlfriend each night he was quitting. But he didn't. "Matt and I got really close, being in the foxhole together," Hill said. "He was just trying to stay the course."

* * *

E ven as he thought about throwing in the towel, Wallace began to forge a bond with Westerberg. He would be the only producer to work with Westerberg more than once, and they would develop an enduring personal friendship as well.

"For someone like Paul, it's really difficult to reconcile his need to get the stuff recorded and accommodate some technical allowances too," said Wallace. Often, in the midst of a manic creative spell, Westerberg would be itching to lay down a vocal. By the time Wallace was set up, Westerberg would beg off, saying the moment had passed.

Still, the producer learned how to anticipate his needs as the session wore on. "With the Replacements, there wasn't a lot of latitude," said Wallace. "You had to wing it, but you also had to *nail* it. You might not get a second chance."

Wallace finally won Stinson over by insisting they record one of his original songs, "First Steps." "Even though Paul was the big cheese of the band, Tommy's really the heart and soul of the thing," recalled Wallace. "It wasn't a Paul Westerberg record; it was a Replacements record."

A breakthrough moment came late in the second week of the session, as Wallace packed the band into his 1982 Honda Accord for a midday booze-and-blow run.

The 'Mats were the worst kind of nervous backseat drivers: Julie Panebianco used to call Paul and Tommy "Grandma and Grandpa."

As a prank, Wallace decided to pull a heart-stopping hand-brake turn in the middle of the street. "It frightened the shit out of those guys," he recalled. "They were yelling at me." He'd finally turned the tables. "I decided right then: If all these guys end up dying . . . I am still going to finish this record."

* * *

F or the first time on record, Chris Mars played drums to a click track in his headphones, to ensure his time was tight as possible. Even so, the Replacements constantly bemoaned Mars's lagging behind the beat.

Westerberg had been joking about Mars's skills ever since "I Hate Music" ("Chris needs a watch to keep time!"). While his tempo could veer wildly onstage, he'd seldom had problems in the studio. Wallace heard nothing wrong, so one night after the group had gone home, he compared Mars's playing to the click track. "Chris was bang on it," said Wallace. "He was the most solid guy in the band." It was actually the rest of the group that was off.

Unbeknownst to the band, Wallace went in and tightened the tracks. Using a Publison digital delay, he went through each song meticulously, bar by bar, and set the guitars and bass back by hand. "We're talking about thirty to forty to fifty milliseconds, pretty substantial stuff. I'd take Paul's guitar and run it through a delay. Slim's guitar. And even the bass—all that stuff was leaning forward."

The real unspoken problem was Mars's versatility—the lack of it, truthfully. As Westerberg's songwriting and rhythmic approach began to vary, Mars's limitations were becoming more obvious. It wasn't a coincidence that Westerberg had chosen to record the tricky 6/8-time "They're Blind" while Mars wasn't around. Wallace added live drums to the track himself.

* * *

In the middle of the session, the Replacements met one of their heroes. Paul and Tommy had run into Kim Buie, a longtime 'Mats fan and Island Records A&R rep, at Club Lingerie, and she mentioned she was working with Tom Waits. Westerberg instantly snapped to attention: "I wanna meet Tom."

Waits and the 'Mats had developed a mutual admiration society from afar. Waits had seen and been thoroughly entertained by the group's chaotic Variety Arts concert the previous year. He'd praised the band in interviews with *Musician* and *Playboy*. "The Replacements? They seem broken, y'know?" said Waits. "One leg is missin'. I like that." He was particularly amused by the notion of a teenage Tommy Stinson earning his education on the road rather than in a classroom. "The idea of all his schoolmates stuck there with the fucking history of Minnesota," he said, "and he's on a bus somewhere sipping out of a brandy bottle, going down the road of life."

Westerberg, usually sparing in his praise of other musicians, had also been touting Waits publicly. He noted in interviews that his older brother Phil had turned him on to Waits's boozy boho LPs back in the '70s and that his work had been a direct influence on *Pleased to Meet Me*'s "Nightclub Jitters."

The band got together with Waits and his wife and collaborator Kathleen Brennan at the Formosa Café in West Hollywood. Though Waits and Westerberg could both be shy in such situations, they hit it off grandly. Waits was particularly enamored of Dunlap, who seemed like a character straight out of one of his own songs.

The band invited Waits back to Cherokee to hear their new tracks. "Waits's wife was with him, and he was being really mild-mannered," recalled Matt Wallace. "And the band is drinking a lot, of course." Around midnight, Brennan got tired and taxied home. The moment she left Waits reached for a bottle of Jack Daniels and began chugging. "And he just turned into *Tom Waits*," said Wallace. "It was like Dr. Jekyll to Mr. Hyde."

Before long, they were playing covers as well as each other's songs. "The drunkest men in the world," recalled Westerberg, "me singing 'Ol' 55' and him singing 'If Only You Were Lonely.'"

The 'Mats decided they should get Waits to sing on a new song called "We Know the Night." They began working out a vocal arrangement with him, running down individual parts.

"We'll get those rise and falls," said Waits, "and those retards."

"The re-tards?" asked Westerberg,

"Well, you got two of them," cracked Stinson. "One on each side."

The three of them then delivered a ramshackle, countrified rendition of the song, a howling celebration of nocturnal living.

> *We don't know the pain of a broken day*
> *We don't know what's wrong or what's right*
> *We know the night*

Working up a Jimmy Reed–style original, "Lowdown Monkey Blues," they traded off improvised verses.

"Well, I can jump like a frog, I can fly like a bird," growled Waits. "I can fly through the sky on your gospel word."

"I'm a lowdown, *lowdown* sack of shit," countered Westerberg. "But at least I know what I am, and you have to deal with it." Behind him, Waits audibly cracked up.

Waits then set up behind a B-3 organ and began orchestrating another new tune, the stomping gospel number "Date to Church." After a few passes at the song, things began to really warm up. "Let's give it the fucking gusto," said Westerberg.

With the band on its feet, Waits began playing fat fills and delivering a wild hellfire preacher rap. "There was a whole track of him yakking behind Paul," said Dunlap. "He was going, '*Jesus has the tools! Jesus is the carpenter!*'—all this religious stuff. Oh, man, it was awesome."

The band and Waits spent the rest of the wee hours playing and draining bottles of whiskey until the sun came up. For one night at least, the pressure of making an important record, of hassling with Wallace and with each other, was totally forgotten. The Replacements had found solace with a kindred spirit, a fellow traveler down the road of life.

CHAPTER 47

With most of the Replacements' new material having been written during the physical and spiritual hangover following the *Pleased to Meet Me* tour, the songs were downbeat, if not downright defeated. "Anger is not on the top of my list anymore," Westerberg admitted at the time. "It's been replaced by despair."

That was clear in the first song recorded for the album, "They're Blind." He and Dunlap worked it up as a lilting, doo-wop-tinged ballad, consciously making it as pretty as possible while working the lyrics into a diatribe about the record business: "And the things you hold dearly / Are scoffed at and yearly / Judged once and then left aside."

"Talent Show" explored a similar theme: over a folky acoustic riff, Westerberg placed the 'Mats in the music industry's maelstrom, vying for attention on the big stage ("Got our guitars and we got thumb picks / And we go on after some lip-synch chicks"). The track itself was like a Replacements concert in miniature, the band falling apart and pulling it back together for a triumphant finale.

After Bearsville, Westerberg scrapped the wistful band narrative "Portland" and cannibalized its drawling chorus ("It's too late to turn back, here we go") for the coda to "Talent Show." He insisted that the song lead off the album to signal a different kind of 'Mats record.

"Asking Me Lies," meanwhile, was an attempt at seventies bubblegum R&B à la the Jackson 5. "We heard that just as much as we heard Brownsville Station and the Raspberries," noted Westerberg. Filled with surrealist imagery and non sequiturs ("At a Mexican bat mitzvah for seven hundred years"), it also included some of his sharpest wordplay ("Well, the rich are gettin' richer and the poor are gettin' drunk / In a black and white picture there's a lot of gray bunk"). Along with the jacked-up "I Won't" and the stomping "Anywhere's Better Than Here," the new songs were a respite from the album's funereal atmosphere.

The band also attempted a couple of fairly grandiloquent statements. "We'll Inherit the Earth" was a spiritual sequel to "Bastards of Young" that utilized similar biblical themes, though lacking its lyrical profundity. The band spent many days working up the song, on which Wallace "played" a typewriter (pecking out "we'll inherit the earth" over and over), and Dunlap added Mellotron (including the opening distress-signal hook), while Westerberg delivered two separate spoken-word tracks and then wed them together into a chattering Greek chorus for the bridge. Among the few clearly discernible lines is a whispered "Don't tell a soul," which ultimately became the album's title.

"Darlin' One" was similarly labored over. Westerberg's bird-on-a-wire lyrics had been floating around for several years. The music—martial rhythms and an expansive chorus—was written by the band during the *Pleased* tour (it would be the only group writing credit on *Don't Tell a Soul*) and further honed at Bearsville. As with much of the new album, Dunlap defined the song. "Slim . . . knows really subtle things to put in songs to give it more ambience," said Chris Mars, who also noted that the guitarist "could look at us objectively. He had an outside view."

* * *

Despite his reputation as post–punk rock's preeminent wordsmith, Westerberg never committed his songs to paper and refused to include lyrics on Replacements albums. "He figured if you don't write it down, they have to interpret it mentally," said Stinson. "That way your song can mean anything to anyone."

Westerberg would willfully disguise details—writing in the third person, changing genders and identifying details—on his most revealing songs. "Looking back," said Stinson, "a lot of that stuff was autobiographical"—especially on *Don't Tell a Soul*. For instance, the domestic standoff of "Back to Back" was a reflection of the distance that was already creeping into Westerberg's young marriage.

"Achin' to Be" also provided insight into its author. Westerberg claimed the song's protagonist was a composite of several people, though one clear inspiration was his younger sister Mary. A Minneapolis rock scene habitué and budding radio deejay, Mary was experiencing the same post-adolescent uncertainties Paul had gone through prior to the Replacements. (The parallel between brother and sister was made explicit in the video later shot for the song, which cast Mary as both Paul's shadow and reflection.)

"Achin'" also spoke to Westerberg's confounding personal nature. He craved intimacy but didn't want the risks it entailed. "Thought about, not understood / She's achin' to be" might be his most autobiographical line, despite the gender switch.

For Westerberg, the album's revelatory song was "Rock 'n' Roll Ghost," begun as an ode to his high school hero, John Zika, who'd committed suicide in 1977. "Out of the blue one day, I was thinking about him," Westerberg recalled. "I don't want to get spiritual and shit, but . . . I felt his presence." Written in an unadorned style, the lyrics play like Westerberg's internal monologue as he talks himself through a loss he never really processed ("I was much too young . . . much too cool for words").

The musical track was built around Westerberg's echoing slide guitar—a loving nod to Big Star's "Nighttime"—Dunlap's gauzy keyboards, and Mars's claves and Stinson's sandpaper percussion. Setting up to record the vocal at Cherokee, Westerberg asked the rest of the band to leave the room, then pulled a screen across the sound booth so Wallace couldn't see him either. On his third and final pass at the track, Westerberg became increasingly emotional and added a new ending:

There's no one here to raise a toast
I look into the mirror and I see . . .
A rock 'n' roll ghost

"That wasn't written," said Westerberg. "It was a little bit scary." It finally dawned on him: the song wasn't about John Zika, but about himself. The realization overwhelmed him. "That was my real first breakdown in the studio," recalled Westerberg. "I went running down the hall, and Tommy came after me. Had to go sit in the alley and have a cigarette and wipe my tears away."

★ ★ ★

After nearly a month at Cherokee, the Replacements headed to Capitol Studios to cut more vocals. Westerberg was taken with Capitol's lore and unique echo chambers, where Frank Sinatra had recorded some of his most memorable sides. First, however, the band had some business to attend to.

Westerberg had become increasingly paranoid about bootlegging. He'd visited Bleecker Bob's in Manhattan and found a set of *Pleased to Meet Me* outtakes in stock. He was enraged that illegal recordings of his unreleased songs and drunken caterwaulings were being sold openly. "They didn't want anyone going back through the tapes again and hearing them being drunk or screwing around," recalled Wallace. "They wanted to know how they could get rid of the stuff."

Engineer Mike Bosley let slip that Cherokee was in possession of a bulk eraser, an ominous-looking black metal machine that could wipe multi-track recordings en masse. In a flash, the 'Mats began scurrying around the studio, wildly grabbing reels of two-inch tape and handing them over to be erased. Wallace actually had to fight to keep the band from taking the album masters. "I was literally yanking tapes out of their hands," said Wallace. "I ended up sitting on them. I've never seen a band want to destroy stuff like that." Among the things that were wiped was the full-band twenty-four-track version of "We Know the Night."

With their rhythm tracks complete, Mars and Stinson went home to new lives in Minneapolis. Mars married Sally Schneidkraut in mid-October, in a ceremony that took place in the end zone of the Metrodome. "She's a big sports fan," he reported. Tommy had already quietly tied the knot with Daune Earle just as recording began in early September. The marriage was spontaneous: when Earle was offered a job in San Francisco, the thought of her leaving was too much for Stinson, so he proposed. The couple eloped to the river town of Stillwater for a small ceremony in front of Tommy's sister Lonnie and Julie Panebianco. A couple of days later, said Earle, "we had a big party at our apartment and told everyone."

Not quite everyone. Stinson managed to keep the news of his marriage secret from the label. Certainly, Seymour Stein wasn't going to be thrilled that the 'Mats' twenty-one-year-old heartthrob had settled down. "He knew no one was gonna give him the thumbs-up," said Westerberg.

The fact that Tommy had not invited Paul indicated the growing schism between their band and personal lives. "When they got married, they had trouble adjusting to that," said Julie Panebianco. "The guys didn't talk about stuff, and then they had very prickly wives. It became another complicated thing."

With Stinson in Minneapolis, Westerberg and Dunlap continued to work on the album, arguably overworking certain tracks in the process. "We spent so much time on 'Asking Me Lies' because we thought that was going to be a smash," said Westerberg. "We used our heads too much and forgot to have fun."

* * *

That October, R.E.M.'s Warner debut, *Green*, was formally launched with a companywide satellite presentation from a mansion in the band's Athens, Georgia, home base. Sitting at the band's feet, Lenny Waronker gave an awkward, gushing testimonial. "R.E.M., to me, is a special group . . . who have vision, passion, they're uncompromising," said Waronker as Peter Buck twitched nervously in the background. "To me, this is the epitome of a Warner Brothers record."

The fuss over *Green*—recorded, like the two most recent 'Mats albums, at Ardent and Bearsville—was not lost on the Replacements. "There was always a close comparison to R.E.M.," said Matt Wallace. "In hindsight, that may have been a factor in trying to make more of a pop record than the Replacements had made before."

The Replacements' resentment toward R.E.M. was real. "A lot of it had to do with how we were perceived," said Tommy Stinson. "We didn't hide the fact that we did drugs and drank and were fucked up. We wore our shit on our sleeve, and they hid their shit. Those guys hid it pretty well. And we know that, because we did their drugs and drank with them. I thought they were a bit phony, just playing the game. . . . Though they were nice guys, I guess."

Steven Baker was a presence in both bands' camps. "When we'd had twenty beers and he'd had two, he'd ask us a couple pointed questions," recalled

Westerberg. "Like: 'What do you guys really want?' I looked him in the eye and told him I wanted to be as big as R.E.M., and he looked . . . sad. Because he knew that that would never happen. And I think I knew it too."

It wasn't just R.E.M. zooming past the Replacements. The Sire-signed UK hard rockers the Cult—whom Westerberg disdained—had scored a top-forty hit and sold half a million copies of *Electric*. Even newcomers like LA's Jane's Addiction (whom he liked) had some small chart success with *Nothing's Shocking*—produced by Dave Jerden, another producer the 'Mats had rejected.

Most of the Replacements' early contemporaries were gone now; even Hüsker Dü had called it quits earlier that year. Westerberg was almost thirty, and he felt the sell-by date for the band nearing. Deep in recording, Westerberg was still trying to come up with more songs, hoping to deliver that one hit that could change their fortunes. "When he couldn't, he'd just be utterly depressed," said Dunlap. "Everything was coming to a head. The underlying feeling was that this record has to break, or we're done. This one has to be that record. And everyone was counting on Paul to pull it over."

Late in the process, Lenny Waronker came to the studio to listen to the band's new tracks. Waronker had a dry, biting sense of humor that Westerberg appreciated. "For some reason I just blurted out, 'Boy, I don't ever want to become a famous celebrity,'" he recalled. "Lenny turned down the volume and said: 'With a voice like that, you don't have to worry about it, Paul.' And then he turned it back up."

Waronker suggested that the band change Dunlap's loud, bluesy solo on the otherwise delicate "They're Blind." Dunlap went back and added a more conventional, melodic lead. "We did bow to the powers that be some," admitted Westerberg.

Warner Bros. was looking for a hit. "In some ways, a hit covers up for a lot of errors," said Waronker. The Replacements' most clearly promising new tune was "I'll Be You," which cast Westerberg as a hardheaded protagonist, the proverbial "rebel without a clue," chasing a rock-and-roll dream "too tired to come true." At Bearsville, it had been a pleasant, if slight number. Over time the 'Mats pumped it up, adding piano, a call-and-response chorus, and a vocal jump in the third verse to heighten the song's drama.

Listening back, Waronker agreed that "I'll Be You" had hit potential, but he felt that something was still missing. They didn't know what else to add. At a loss, they began messing with the pitch. Westerberg became enamored with the vari-speed effect and wanted to make it go faster and faster.

In the end, Wallace barely altered the track at all. But when Waronker heard the song again a couple of days later, suddenly he was sold. "Lenny couldn't figure out what we'd done to it, but he loved it," laughed Westerberg. "So we really felt like we'd pulled one over on the old man."

* * *

A long with Wallace, Westerberg and Dunlap headed back to Minnesota in early October to finish overdubs and vocals at Paisley Park Studios, the new $10 million, 65,000-square-foot studio and production facility built by Prince in the Minneapolis suburb of Chanhassen.

When they arrived, the studio had just installed a forty-eight-track API console. The 'Mats would be the first to use it. As they settled in to work, Westerberg accidentally spilled a giant tumbler full of Jack Daniels across the newly refurbished board. Wallace recalled the studio tech's horrified face as he watched the sticky brown liquid dripping into the faders. "We had basically announced our presence," said Wallace.

Westerberg committed another faux pas when he encountered the daughter of R&B icon Ray Charles, Sheila Charles, at the studio. "I told her I had this great song that her dad should sing, and I played it for her," recalled Westerberg. "I was serious. I really thought it would be something he could do. But I get halfway through the song, and she's looking at me real weird."

Westerberg went to the restroom, and there he realized that he'd suggested that Ray Charles sing "They're Blind." "It didn't even occur to me," he said sheepishly. "Not one of my finer moments."

High Noon had long planned on hiring someone else to mix the album, though Wallace was laboring under the impression that the project was his to finish. Russ Rieger had been waging an aggressive campaign to convince a reluctant Michael Hill and an even more reluctant Paul Westerberg that it was the right decision.

Rieger's instinct was good: combining an alternative band and indie producer with a mainstream radio mixer was a formula that would ultimately make Nirvana's *Nevermind* a success a few years later. In fact, a prime candidate for *Don't Tell a Soul* was engineer Andy Wallace, the hard-rock hit-maker who'd give *Nevermind* its sheen.

Under pressure, Westerberg finally acquiesced. "I figured, 'Well, we've already got the stuff down on tape, what bad can happen here?'" To many on the outside, the move was seen as a crass attempt to court airplay. "It was an insurance policy," said Hill. "The radio people, the promo guys, the label, they all felt more comfortable if they knew someone with that kind of track record was involved."

After considering several candidates, High Noon zeroed in on Chris Lord-Alge. The New Jersey–bred son of a jazz-singing mother and the self-described "Lord of the Mix," Lord-Alge had become known for his dynamic range: booming drum sound, effects-laden guitars, and liberal use of compression. He was an aggressive character who spoke in a caricature FM deejay voice and loved to wow his clients—from James Brown to Steve Winwood—by putting their songs, as he put it, "on steroids."

Lord-Alge didn't know anything about the Replacements or the band's history. "What I did care about was the record I was going to make," he said.

Lord-Alge listened to Wallace's tracks and felt confident he could make them "sound less demo-ish and more like an across-the-board record."

In early November, Westerberg and Dunlap headed back to Los Angeles to hang around as Lord-Alge mixed the album at Skip Saylor Recording. From the start, they were suspicious: Westerberg noticed that Lord-Alge had MTV playing in the studio constantly, while Dunlap surveyed his disturbingly large battery of compressors and effects processors. Matt Wallace tried to offer Lord-Alge some direction—but he was rebuffed. "Lord-Alge was like, 'This is what we're going to do.' Basically, get out of here and don't bug me."

Lord-Alge boosted the drums, swathed the vocals in reverb, chorused and harmonized the guitars, and gave the record a three-dimensional, radio-ready sound. Some of the sonic accoutrements were aesthetic choices; others were made to mask the band's flaws. "I remember fixing a bunch of it just instinctively," said Lord-Alge. "Part of the charm is that it's sloppy; it's like a Rolling Stones record. When the stuff is not really loud, or it's just mushed together, you don't notice any problems. But when you really pump the stuff up . . . then you notice the issues."

Lord-Alge made it harder to find the imperfections, but he also made it harder to find the essential sound of the band. Wallace, Westerberg, and Dunlap went over to the studio every couple of days to listen. They had wanted to make something timeless; instead, they got an album doomed to forever sound like 1988.

"You don't hire Chris Lord-Alge and say, 'Make this sound like a garage band.' That's not what he does," said Dunlap. "But it was like, '*Come on.*'" After trying to make a record for nearly a year, Westerberg had little fight left. "I was sick of it," admitted Westerberg. "I thought the little things I'd cut in my basement were closer to what I wanted."

In hindsight, Lord-Alge probably shouldered too much blame for *Don't Tell a Soul*'s poor reputation, not only because Westerberg badmouthed the mix publicly but also because he made a convenient scapegoat. The band's conflicted desire for success and the excessive overdubbing following Stinson's departure were equally culpable.

Moreover, the record documented a Westerberg caught between his allegiance to the Replacements and his emerging singer-songwriter self. *Don't Tell a Soul* is the most bipolar album in the band's catalog, slotting the bonehead rock of "I Won't" alongside the harrowing realization of "Rock 'n' Roll Ghost."

"We were trying to make a bigger, broader, deeper, wider Replacements record," said Wallace. "Anyone who wanted the straight-up-the-middle Replacements was going to be disappointed."

Not everyone was so pessimistic. High Noon was over the moon: they finally had something sonically competitive enough for mainstream radio. The early feedback from the Warner/Reprise radio staff was especially encouraging. "We got the record in, and we loved it," said Rich Fitzgerald, who would direct the campaign for *Don't Tell a Soul*. "It wasn't just 'I'll Be You,' but the whole album."

Tommy Stinson may have been the most relieved when he heard the finished LP. "When I got a tape of the mixes, finally, I quit panicking," he said. "Hearing it song by song, separately, you'd go, 'Man, I dunno about this. This is a little out there.' But after the mix, hearing everything in sequence, it hit you. It turned a scary thing into an [exciting] thing."

CHAPTER 48

While the Replacements were busy trying to craft their breakthrough, Bob Stinson was starting from scratch. Gigging as a sideman with punk veteran Sonny Vincent had been good for him, a needed boost to his ego after the blow of being booted out of the Replacements. But Bob pined for the camaraderie and rewards that came with building a group from the ground up. He would tell anyone who'd listen: "If you wanna be in a band, you gotta sweat, fight, bleed, puke, shit, and laugh . . . together."

"He had this whole list of things that he said made a great band," recalled Ray Reigstad. "Basically, he was saying: you gotta give everything."

Since meeting his young pals Reigstad and John Reipas a couple years earlier, Bob had been casually jamming with them. Though they were relative amateurs on their instruments—Reipas played drums and Reigstad bass—they'd work up Bob's favorite '70s covers by the Guess Who, the Sweet, and Bread. In the summer of '88, they finally decided to get serious and form a band playing original material. Bob told Reigstad he should just sing and not play. "'Cause he didn't want the lineup to look like the Replacements," said Reigstad. "That was really important to him."

They recruited a bassist named Chris Corbett, an eighteen-year-old blond art student from Texas to whom Stinson took an immediate shine. "He was Bob's surrogate Tommy," said his wife, Carleen Krietler. Since their group included a couple of part-time cab drivers, they took the name Static Taxi. The four of them were like peas in a pod: prone to schoolboy high jinks, pranks, and roughhousing, with Bob leading the way.

Woodshedding with the band was like reliving the glorious early days with Dogbreath. "It was going back to his roots," said Carleen. "Bob helped everyone learn their instruments and get up to speed technically. They were willing to work with Bob and catered to him."

After his experience with the Replacements, it felt good to be the undisputed leader of a band once again. "I can get them to go in the direction I want, and they don't already have an opinion," noted Bob as the band was getting started. Stinson wanted to create complex, dynamic songs; he saw Static Taxi as playing a brand of "art-blues, blues twisted around and made pretty."

"The Replacements was my noisy years. I couldn't really play that well, if at all," said Bob. "I finally took the time to learn . . . I want to be taken seriously as a guitar player. It's a conscious thing: either get better or forget it."

In Static Taxi, Bob's playing was just as profound and strikingly enigmatic as it had always been. "The peaks and the valleys of brilliance and absurdity were so extreme," said Reigstad. "He could fluctuate between sounding like a clown then into something that hit you in the heart, within a fraction of a second. That's why it's so hard to put your finger on Bob's playing. That incline was so incredibly steep."

The band spent the summer of '88 rehearsing and coming up with new material under Stinson's direction. "Some songs we wrote note by note," recalled Reigstad. "Bob took it incredibly seriously, yet we had so much fun."

They set up shop, practicing in the office of an old flour mill and warehouse on the edge of Dinkytown. Later the band moved into an abandoned railroad box car nearby; they carpeted and decorated it, ran power to it, and set up their instruments and PA inside.

The area was filled with disenfranchised Vietnam vets, rummies, and drifters who lived in the tunnels beneath the warehouse's grain silos. It was basically a hobo encampment. "There were these bums who always had a fire going in a barrel, and these guys were hardcore alcoholics," said Reigstad. "They were our audience."

The setup was nirvana for Stinson: "As much as Bob loved trains and amps and beer, this was like heaven for him," said Reigstad. "He was just fucking keyed to go to practice."

"Most people would view playing in a box car as rock bottom," said Carleen. "But he embraced it. He saw it as a revelation to be part of this train culture, this homeless culture, and meet all these people from all over the country hanging out."

Although Bob's addictions remained, in their own way the guys in Static Taxi tried to control his drinking and drugging. Bob hated Budweiser—he called it rice beer—because it always gave him a headache. "So we always brought Budweiser to practice 'cause that way he'd only drink eight or ten instead of eighteen," said Reigstad.

The band did its best to keep him off coke too, which only caused him to drink more. Instead, they turned him on to lysergics. "I don't know if this was a good idea or not, but we got him more into acid, clean blotter acid," said Reigstad. "We'd take a half hit each and then we'd play . . . 'Last Train to Clarksville' for five hours straight."

As Static Taxi developed their sound and songs into 1989, Bob tried to get some gigs and label attention, but there was always resistance in the

Minneapolis rock community, usually accompanied by unfavorable comparisons to the Replacements.

Bob brought a batch of Static Taxi demos to Twin/Tone, but the label rejected the group, saying Reigstad sang off-key. "We were hurt about the Twin/Tone thing. But we weren't doing it for any commercial purposes," said Reigstad. "We got the sense that we were never going to be much bigger than we were. We knew Bob wasn't gonna go on tour or anything."

They made just one out-of-town trip, to Las Vegas in the summer of '89. Mostly, they gigged in and around the Twin Cities, playing at the 400 Bar, the Cabooze, the Entry, and a number of warehouse parties.

For Bob, Static Taxi was a success on a personal and creative level. But the band's failure to gain any real traction was also a reminder that the Replacements had been something truly special—the kind of perfect alchemy that might only come along once in a lifetime.

* * *

Though he pursued music with his usual passion, the bigger concern in Bob's life was the impending birth of his first child.

Carleen had gotten pregnant in the spring of 1988, but it wasn't entirely joyous news. "At first, I wanna say the marriage was stabilizing," said Bob's mother Anita. "And then she wanted to have a baby, and that kinda undid him. He came to work one day and said, 'Mom, you know I'm not ready to raise a child.'"

Though he'd had horrible father figures in his own life, Bob did his best to embrace the role of dad. "When I was pregnant, he'd go around wearing a pillow wrapped around his stomach to pretend like he was carrying a child, to see how it would feel," said Carleen. "He got off on feeling the baby kick. But it wasn't something he'd put a lot of thought into, it was more like something that had happened that he had to adjust to."

Bob and Carleen's son, Joseph Aaron Stinson, was born in January 1989, the spitting image of his father. Bob was over the moon. "He loved that child to pieces," said Anita.

But Joey's arrival put an enormous pressure on Bob to provide for his family, to make something of himself. "He said, 'You made me a son. Now I've got to live up to that,'" said Carleen. "He felt that he had to be more successful than ever."

Bob did make some progress in the real world, getting a job as a cook at the downtown Hyatt's Pronto restaurant, where he was written up in the paper for his signature artichoke pizza.

But a part-time cook's salary wasn't enough to support a family. Ever since splitting with the Replacements, Bob had felt he was due some kind of payout or financial settlement. After a while he suspected there were monies owed that he wasn't seeing. He was right: by this point, the 'Mats' Twin/Tone royalties had been frozen in the legal tussle over the band's refusal to sign a contract, though the label's Paul Stark said that he continued to give Bob money personally whenever he asked.

Bob began calling the Replacements' management, ringing High Noon in New York. Office assistant Michelle Picardo was usually the one to field the calls. "Bob and I got to know each other really well, because he was such a good egg on the phone," said Picardo. "He'd tell me fun stories about the band back in the day. But mostly he sounded like a desperate guy. You could tell he was having issues. He's like, 'I gotta talk to Gary or Russ,' and those guys never wanted to get on the phone with him."

"He just always felt like there was money for him. There was royalty money he wasn't seeing and he wanted to find it. And he indicated Tommy wasn't talking to him—nobody was really talking to him. He had nobody to really vent to within the Replacements family except for me. And I was just the one taking the phone calls. It was very sad."

The need for money became more pressing when Joey fell ill in the fall of '89. Though a colicky baby, he'd been given a clean bill of health after his birth. Nine months later, however, he developed a high fever that doctors initially thought was the result of pertussis, or whooping cough. He was rushed to the emergency room and put in the children's intensive care unit with a 106-degree temperature. Bob and Carleen were told that if his temperature didn't come down quickly, the chances of survival were grim—a prolonged fever in an infant could result in serious complications.

Eventually, doctors were able to use a high-powered antibiotic to save Joey's life. But the nearly six days of high fever he suffered through had caused irreparable brain damage. It took a while for the symptoms to fully reveal themselves. "Joey wasn't developing speech and motor skills," said Carleen. "By his second birthday, Anita and I took him to the neurologist, who broke the news to us that Joe was a quadriplegic with cerebral palsy. And that he probably would never talk or walk. The geneticists, the barrage of doctors we saw, no one could ever answer the question: 'Why? Why Joe? Why us?' So I quit asking."

Joey's diagnosis was a shattering moment for Bob. "The stress of Joe's situation was probably enough to break any father. Joe's illness was especially overwhelming and made him feel . . . fatalistic. It's a hopeless feeling when you're out of control."

For Bob Stinson, his son's fate was just another in a long line of inexplicable heartbreaks in his life. He'd long ago quit asking: "Why?"

CHAPTER 49

In the final weeks of 1988, the Replacements prepared for their first concert in a year and their biggest gig to date: an arena show with Keith Richards.

Premiere's Frank Barsalona had landed the group a one-off slot opening for the Rolling Stones guitarist at Brendan Byrne Arena in New Jersey on December 17. Richards had released his first solo album, *Talk Is Cheap*, that fall, and the show would conclude a tour with his band, the X-Pensive Winos.

Meeting the Replacements in New York was Warner Bros. publicist Bill Bentley. A laconic, bespectacled Texan who'd worked with acts like Lou Reed and Elvis Costello, Bentley and East Coast publicist Mary Melia would wage the press campaign for *Don't Tell a Soul*.

Staying at the Mayflower near Central Park, the 'Mats were drinking in the hotel bar when Paul Westerberg got into a contretemps with Richards's longtime press agent, Charlie Comer. "We thought he was a roadie," recalled Westerberg. "The whole talk was 'Could we please have the PA on for the show? We know it's not gonna be at star volume, but could we have it turned up a little bit?'" Their drunken palaver quickly turned nasty. Finally, an angry Comer told Westerberg, "Listen, laddie, you just be sure to show up on time and play."

"Fuck you, man—we'll go on whenever we want to," replied Westerberg.

"It was a silly argument," said Bentley. "But I thought it was gonna turn into a fistfight. I actually had to get the band out of the bar."

The negative vibes carried over as the 'Mats began bar-hopping through Manhattan in a chauffeured limo provided by Warner Bros. At a certain point during the night, Tommy unexpectedly started in on Paul, voicing his festering resentments. Mostly, his anger had been directed at outsiders Tony Berg and Matt Wallace. But inequities over publishing credits, financial recompense, and creative control had become more pronounced.

In the limo, Stinson began hectoring Westerberg: "It's not your band, you know. It's *our* band. . . . You think you're better than us? Why are you getting all the fuckin' money anyway?"

Westerberg finally responded, coldly: "You can't write a song. That's the difference. If you can write a song, let's see the songs. You think it's easy to write a song? It's not fuckin' easy."

A nervous Bentley looked over his shoulder and saw Westerberg and Stinson kicking at each other angrily. "I thought somebody was going to get hurt. I told the driver, 'Keep going—if they tear up the car, we'll pay for it.'" The encounter shook the publicist: "It didn't feel like they were an all-for-one band anymore. It felt like Paul . . . and them."

* * *

The following night, on time, the Replacements sauntered onto the arena stage for their forty-minute slot. Westerberg was slightly agitated: the band's wives had been flown out for the occasion. "Paul was mad at me that night," recalled Lori Bizer. "I came in dressed really crazy. Julie Panebianco and I were hanging out and being nutty. He didn't like me being outgoing."

Contrary to Westerberg's fears, the sound levels were fine, but there was something unusually hesitant about the band's performance. "'What are we doing here?' you might ask yourself—we ask ourselves the same question," said Westerberg, as the 'Mats opened with hard-charging versions of "IOU" and "Bastards of Young," before premiering several songs off the forthcoming album. They even serenaded Richards—who was turning forty-five the next day—with "Happy Birthday" before dedicating "Unsatisfied" to the man who'd written "Satisfaction."

Despite his obvious discomfort, Westerberg was uncharacteristically giddy about sharing a bill with a hero. Backstage, the Replacements mingled with Richards's coterie. Tommy chatted with Stanley Booth, author of the seminal *The True Adventures of the Rolling Stones*; Memphian Booth had heard all about the band from his good friend Jim Dickinson. He had been knocked out by the 'Mats' performance and bantered about maybe writing a book on them. Slim Dunlap, meanwhile, huddled with author and essayist Fran Lebowitz.

Bill Bentley's crucial assignment that night was securing a photo of the 'Mats with Richards for *Billboard*. Keith was in a private room, so Bentley enlisted Richards's official tour photographer, Paul Natkin, to help. "I told the band to just hang out at this table they were at, and when Keith was through cutting his birthday cake, I would ask him," recalled Natkin.

He returned fifteen minutes later, as promised, with Richards in tow. "The only one left was Slim, who was sound asleep at the table," said Natkin. "Keith and I just looked at each other, smiled, shrugged, and went back to the party."

* * *

With *Don't Tell a Soul* complete, the 'Mats offered Slim Dunlap, who'd been essentially a hired hand, full-fledged membership in the group. "I was de facto in the band every night we played. Why do you have to change the LLC to make it legitimate?" said Dunlap. "I told them, 'Don't bother bringing me into the corporation, it's a waste of time and money.'"

Westerberg remembers Dunlap practically laughing at the suggestion. "Slim, smart son of a country lawyer that he was, knew he'd just be incurring a quarter of our debt to the record company. He declined, wisely." Having effectively worked as a session musician on *Don't Tell a Soul*, Dunlap was owed several hundred dollars an hour, for many hundreds of hours. "They remunerated me fine," said Dunlap. "I never really saw the band as a chance to get wealthy, anyway."

Chris Mars was raising more pointed questions about finances. More specifically, his new bride was raising them. Sally began regularly asking High Noon for updates on budgets and earnings. Westerberg regarded her sudden involvement as an annoyance; Stinson considered it a greater breach of band protocol. Tommy's relationship with Chris had already grown distant, and now it began to sour.

Stinson had his own financial concerns: his wife Daune Earle had become pregnant that winter. At the time, the couple was still living in a shoebox apartment on Bryant, and Stinson was unhappy about it. "After ten years in a band," said Stinson, "you want to know you did it for something. Suddenly, your singer has a house and looks pretty happy. And you're fucking living in an apartment. It's like, 'What the fuck? My brother started this goddamn band.'"

High Noon arranged for Stinson to buy a modest place on Thirty-Ninth and Lyndale. "It wasn't like suddenly I could afford to buy a house—because I couldn't," said Stinson. "I borrowed the money from the band, or what ended up turning into band money."

* * *

On the eve of *Don't Tell a Soul*'s release, Stinson's concerns were more about the future than about money. Much of the album's fate was contingent on Paul's cooperation with the label in promoting the record—always a dicey proposition. "Tommy was freaked out," said Earle. "This is all he knew since he was twelve. He always wanted the band to grow, and Paul didn't."

"That was not a subject to talk about," said Lori Bizer, who, having worked for labels and in radio, understood the ramifications of her husband's actions. "He continued to shoot himself in the foot a lot of times—not show up for interviews or blow people off. And they were people who were fans. He let a lot of people down."

Much as Stinson might've wanted to push Westerberg, said Earle, "he couldn't break rank with Paul." Stinson and Westerberg's union had evolved dramatically, but the former began to think there would always be an inequity in their relationship. "Tommy maybe realized that this is all it's ever going to be with Paul," said Earle. "He was never going to take him seriously." During their entire marriage, Earle said, she never heard Stinson utter a single negative word about Westerberg.

The irony was that, in many ways, Stinson was far better suited to being the Replacements' leader—a born performer and bandleader with a gregarious personality suited to the outside demands of stardom. Warner Bros. knew it too and would often seek Tommy out for the duties that Westerberg was too ill-tempered to handle. "They went to Paul for the serious things. And Tommy was the cute one, the happy one, the rock star," said Earle. "That's how he was regarded. Which, to him, was an empty thing to be."

* * *

Part of the great compromise to promote *Don't Tell a Soul* was making a more conventional video. "We would watch [director's] reels for hours and hours with the guys, and they just hated everything," recalled Randy Skinner, once again in charge of producing a Replacements promo clip.

The band finally settled on the team of Doug Freel and Jean Pellerin, who'd done a number of memorable glam-metal videos for the likes of Def Leppard and Poison, as well as Joan Jett and the Georgia Satellites. Filmed on a soundstage in Silverlake, "I'll Be You" was shot in color and featured the band performing the song, though they made little effort to lip-synch to the track. "They did not want to fake that," said Skinner. "It was a huge thing for them."

The video is a catalog of old 'Mats tricks—switching instruments and clothes, destroying gear—as well as a few bits of comedy (including a very real and painful Westerberg fall from atop Chris Mars's drum kit). It wasn't "Thriller," but for the Replacements it was a quantum leap forward.

For the album's package, Warner Bros. went in a more serious direction, hiring fine-art photographer David Seltzer, known for sumptuous black-and-white imagery and ghostly multiple-exposure photos. Seltzer and Warner art director Kim Biggs traveled to Minneapolis to shoot the band at its rehearsal space, which Biggs described as "like a Dumpster. . . . I think the ceiling was actually falling apart. There was urine and feces on the floor."

To top it off, the band began to dress up in drag. "I thought, *Well, this is an interesting group*," recalled Seltzer. "Nobody said anything; we just went about our business." Eventually, after collecting some pictures of them in fishnets and lipstick, Seltzer had all four strip to the waist and then took a series of portraits, merging several into ethereal-looking group shots.

The image that best caught the record's (and title's) mood was a solo shot of Westerberg with his finger to his lips. High Noon was careful not to overlook the rest of the group: the back cover composite featured a massive Stinson in the foreground, with Dunlap and Mars in sharp focus and Westerberg all but blurred out.

High Noon and Warner's publicity department hoped again to broaden their reach with features and items in mainstream publications like *Newsweek* and *People*. In December, Mary Melia sent an internal memo to Bill Bentley and PR vice president Bob Merlis, outlining the potential pitfalls of a broader media campaign: "Usually one-on-one they're great, but when the four of them get together, it's 'wipe carbon paper on the walls' time. So, here's hoping."

Finally armed with a properly playable 'Mats clip to take to the network, the band and High Noon went for a formal dinner that winter with a contingent of MTV executives at New York City's China Grill. "We almost got kicked out 'cause the band was throwing martinis on each other," said MTV's Rick Krim.

As Rieger and Hobbib stood talking up the prospects of a fruitful partnership between MTV and the Replacements, Westerberg turned to Krim and whispered conspiratorially: "They're not really our managers. Don't listen to anything they say."

* * *

When Westerberg first heard R.E.M.'s *Green*, released in November, three months ahead of *Don't Tell a Soul*, he breathed a sigh of relief. "Our record is better than theirs," he told Julie Panebianco, with some hubris.

That competitive streak ran both ways. "I know when I would listen to one of their records," said R.E.M.'s Peter Buck, "if our record kicked their ass, or their record kicked our ass, I could tell—though I'd never tell you which I thought was which." By the time *Don't Tell a Soul* hit stores, *Green* had already gone gold and was nudging toward platinum.

The 'Mats' early album press augured well. Ira Robbins wrote *Rolling Stone*'s three-and-a-half-star lead review, preparing listeners for a downshift: "More than half of the songs on *Don't Tell a Soul* are built on acoustic guitars; layers of harmony vocals, keyboards and modest studio effects are part of the sonic overhaul."

SPIN, however, took an opposing view in a three-fer review (with R.E.M. and Matthew Sweet). "Art is pretty much what kills this Replacements album," wrote the magazine's senior editor Joe Levy. "It's not just the worst Replacements album ever, it completely sucks. And part of the reason is that they're trying for the first time to be craftsmen with a wide range of artistic expression."

Other critics complained about Chris Lord-Alge's high-gloss mix. But "sellout" charges had been leveled at the Replacements as far back as *Hootenanny*. Speaking of old fans who'd felt the group had abandoned them, Westerberg told the hometown alt-weekly *Twin Cities Reader*, "They can go fuck themselves."

* * *

"The Last, Best Band of the '80s," trumpeted the cover of *Musician* magazine's February 1989 issue, over a photo of the smiling Replacements. Inside was a six-page feature penned by Minneapolis writer Steve Perry.

This was no small matter: *Musician* was then at its zenith. "In 1988 we decided, 'Let's see how many magazines we can sell,'" said editor Bill Flanagan. "Every issue of 1988 had a big star on the cover: McCartney, Bono—we had the biggest year we ever had." By contrast, they decided that 1989 would be "the 'hip' year," said Flanagan. "We had the ridiculous vanity of thinking just as many people would buy the magazine."

The *Musician* cover line became a subject of contention at the magazine's office—namely, whether a comma should separate "last" and "best." "I fought very hard against it," said Flanagan, who envisioned it as a semi-joke. "There had already been so many 'Best Bands of the Eighties.' Every two years there was one: it was the Police, then it was U2, then it was R.E.M."

"What have we got—eight, nine months left to be the best band of the eighties?" cracked Westerberg. "They *could* have said 'best band of the nineties.'"

That winter Warner Bros. sponsored a *Don't Tell a Soul* listening party in New York, at Carmelita's Reception House, an East Fourteenth Street bar that had supposedly once been a bordello. The night was chaos: the Replacements drank heavily and hid from the assembled guests for most of the evening. Eventually someone set off stink bombs. "We thought it was someone from the bar because they wanted to get rid of us," recalled Mary Melia. Westerberg had to be practically carried out by Julie Panebianco in the middle of the party, only to return later.

When Flanagan arrived at Carmelita's, Westerberg was sitting alone on the steps, looking glum and wasted. "I said, 'So, Paul, are you happy?'" recalled Flanagan. "And Paul said, 'Well, I'm drunk, anyway.' He didn't really say it as a wisecrack. I thought, *Wow, maybe this isn't going to end well for them.*"

* * *

By early 1989, the Replacements had reached the radar of Warner Bros.'s chairman, Mo Ostin, who visited the Carmelita's party in New York. "I don't think I paid the proper respect to Mo," recalled Westerberg. "We didn't quite understand the significance of him coming all the way for this."

That winter, doing press in California, Westerberg was summoned to Burbank for a visit with Ostin. The band's rebel stance had become a selling point for *Tim* and *Pleased to Meet Me.* But ten years into their career, it was time to change course. Westerberg figured he was capable of doing the dance. He was aware that "if Mo wants to spend fifty million dollars to promote something, he'll do it. It's nothing to him."

With his salt-and-pepper beard and oversized glasses, Ostin had the unassuming air of an accountant—the job he'd trained for at UCLA. After working as comptroller for the jazz imprint Verve, Frank Sinatra tapped him to head his Reprise label in 1960. Seven years later, Ostin took over the newly merged Warner-Reprise operations, turning the company into the jewel of the music business over the next two decades. Having worked closely with Sinatra, Ostin was well versed in the Sicilian culture of favors and fealty.

At his office, Westerberg laid on the charm and laid out his case. "I asked him: 'Mo, can we have a push?' 'Cause it was always the Cult or R.E.M. that got the handful of people to work the records. And Mo, in Mafia-style fashion, had a favor for me."

Changing the subject, Ostin mentioned that he had a friend, Irwin Jacobs, a Minneapolis financier, who was involved in the development of a new megamall that was going to be constructed just outside the city. There would be a groundbreaking ceremony in the summer. Ostin wanted to know if the Replacements would be willing to play the event.

The irony was almost too much for Westerberg. The future Mall of America was being built in Bloomington, the wretched suburb where he'd spent his preband days working as janitor. Westerberg took a deep breath and gave his answer: "No—no, we don't play malls."

"And that was sort of the end of meeting," recalled Westerberg. "It's like, Christ, I was asking for something, and he was asking for something in return. I really should've been smart enough to say, 'Yeah, we'll do it.' But . . . we can't play a mall. Tiffany and [New Kids on the Block] and that kind of person were making headlines at the time playing malls. He was testing my loyalty to the fucking firm. And I didn't have any."

"Certainly, we played worse things than a mall," said Tommy Stinson. "We played a Taco Bell in Indiana at one point. But part of the 'Mats' legacy is, yes, we were too proud to do that stuff. We just didn't know how stupid it was that we turned it down."

In the short term, failing to get Ostin's papal seal didn't automatically doom the 'Mats record. In fact, promotion head Rich Fitzgerald insisted there was an "unlimited budget to spend at radio. There wasn't one faucet that wasn't turned on for the Replacements."

Still, the next time Westerberg saw Ostin, he was in Lenny Waronker's adjoining office playing some new demos. Ostin came from around his desk, and Westerberg rose to meet him. With a wave, Ostin motioned for him to sit down. Then he shut the door.

CHAPTER 50

The *Don't Tell a Soul* tour, slated to begin in Ann Arbor in early March, would encompass four legs and nearly seventy headlining shows, many in the biggest venues the Replacements had played yet.

To make it happen, the Replacements' insular touring party expanded dramatically, from a couple of vans to a pair of buses, one for the band and one for an expanded eleven-man crew, including longtime roadie Bill Sullivan and soundman Brendan McCabe.

High Noon was reluctant to hand road-managing to Sullivan—Rieger and Hobbib viewed him as one of the band. "Any road manager that took the job was completely incompetent next to Bill," said Dunlap. "A lot of the operation was thanks to Bill that it ran as smoothly as it did. He dealt with four people who were just incorrigible."

Nevertheless, High Noon found an established road manager in Roger Vitale. Big and bearded—Westerberg nicknamed him "Crummy Bear"—Vitale had seen his share of rock-and-roll debauchery on Aerosmith's *Rocks* tour; he'd come to the Replacements after a long run with Megadeth, then deep in the throes of heroin addiction.

But the Replacements experience was singular. "They were off the wall," said Vitale. "Everybody was into sex, drugs, and rock-and-roll, but not the way these guys were. They just didn't give a fuck. Which was not the style I was used to working for."

Vitale brought in some of his own people, including monitor man Carl Davino. From Queens, with a pronounced dese-dem-dose accent, Davino had started out playing drums in local bands and wound up doing sound professionally for metal bands like Warlock and White Lion. The Replacements quickly took a shine to him. Westerberg delighted in forcing him to don a purple smoking jacket and plaid pants and man the monitor desk onstage.

Davino gamely battled the band's ridiculous volume. "You always heard that Motörhead was the loudest band ever, and I used to say bullshit. Motörhead was pussies compared to dese guys," said Davino. "I've never been in such a loud situation. Anything could happen; every show was entirely its own entity. And something would happen every night. You knew you were in the midst of something insane."

The most put-upon member of the crew, however, was guitar tech Yuek Wong. A slight, unassuming figure, Wong was an incredibly resourceful road hand who would go on to work with Patti Smith and Bob Dylan. The Replacements gig was a trial by fire, as Westerberg spent much of the tour smashing guitars. As the crew bus hit a new town, Wong would immediately scour vintage guitar stores for new ones.

For the first time, the Replacements had also decided to augment their tour income by selling merchandise. They'd signed an exclusive deal with top merch company Brockum for a $50,000 advance. Jimmy Velvet, aka Jim Sullivan, handled their account. A Rhode Island native, he'd gotten his start hustling merch for his cousin, East Coast rocker John Cafferty, then worked for everyone from Van Halen to the Georgia Satellites.

But only the Replacements had ideas like these. Chris Mars suggested putting their faces in the shirts' armpits, rather than across the front. Stinson wanted to sell a T-shirt that, after a first wash, revealed invisible ink saying: HA! HA! SUCKER!

The band needed every cent it could get. The Replacements were still scrapping and still getting heavy tour support from Warner Bros.—all of which added to their growing label debt. And though they played bigger venues and earned bigger guarantees, the need to step up their payroll meant that, as Hobbib put it, "now you're playing for fifteen thousand dollars and barely breaking even."

He continued: "They'd burn themselves out on the road after three weeks and have to go home for a week or two. Then what do you do with the crew, the busses, and everything then? Everybody was on half-salaries during the time they were off. It was a total waste of money." It did little to curb Paul's and Tommy's profligacy. Velvet's jaw dropped the first time he witnessed one of their stranger road rituals: "They used to rip up their per diem . . . ripped it up and threw it."

* * *

MTV didn't hesitate to support *Don't Tell a Soul*, putting the clip for "I'll Be You" into its "Buzz Bin" rotation. "That was the best video they made," said Rick Krim. "It was done in enough of an edgy way that they didn't feel like they were completely selling out."

Things were equally promising for radio. Rock promotion head Michael Linehan, a committed fan, was particularly heartened by early audience-testing data the company had collected on "I'll Be You." "It called out well, in terms of research, which surprised me," said Linehan, who headed Warner's Reprise field staff, an up-and-coming division filled with regional reps who were more in tune with the band's spirit—and unlike the earlier promo team, hadn't yet been put off by them.

The only spanner in the works was the band itself. At the outset, they promised High Noon and themselves they'd cooperate. "I guess I don't want to give the record company an excuse for not getting behind this record," said Westerberg at the time.

Still, it was obvious there were limits to what they could or would do. Early on, Linehan booked studio time with the 'Mats to record a stack of radio liners—station IDs and commercial copy—to be read by the band. In radio, this was the coin of the realm. "When you're a programmer and you're thinning out your playlist," said Linehan, "an enthusiastic liner is the kind of thing that can make a decision."

This was the exact sort of pandering drudgery the band hated most—audibly so. Stinson would read in a deadpan monotone, or in the midst of a take Westerberg would blanch: "I'm not going to say this bullshit."

Early in the tour, *Rolling Stone* dispatched writer Steve Pond to meet up with the band in Rochester, New York. The resulting feature story focused heavily on the 'Mats' efforts to sell themselves and the album. Pond witnessed an awkward postconcert encounter between Westerberg and a pair of deejays from the local rock station:

> "Sorry we missed the show," says one. "He was on the air til ten."
>
> "Too bad," says Westerberg, good naturedly. "We were actually good tonight."
>
> "That's what I hear, man," says the other. "That's what I hear."
>
> "So, are you playing us a little bit?" asks Westerberg.
>
> "Not yet, we're not playing you *yet*," says the first guy, pointing to his pal. "It's up to him, he's the music director."
>
> The music director laughs nervously. "Yeah, we gonna—," he begins and then stops.
>
> "We gotta . . . check out, and . . . "
>
> "Well," says his colleague, interrupting. "Good luck on the tour."
>
> "Thanks a lot guys," says Westerberg, as they retreat. "See you again, I guess." Then he turns away and under his breath, he mutters, "Kiss my fuckin' ass *sideways*."

Reading the piece a couple months later, the Reprise promo staff winced. "Radio guys hang together as a group," said Linehan. "It's like: 'Why should we help these guys? There's a million bands that would love me to play their record, and they're cooperative.'"

* * *

I n spite of the Replacements' conflicted promotional efforts, "I'll Be You" began to gain serious momentum; that spring it was on top of both the modern rock and AOR charts—a number-one song in two different formats. With that, Warner Bros.'s radio chieftain Russ Thyret green-lit the single's promotion to pop radio.

Soon after, Russ Rieger got the call from Linehan: *"Breaker! Breaker!"*— the trade magazine *Radio & Records* had given the song "Breaker" status: it was making significant chart movement, quickly moving into the "Hot 100," it apparently was headed for the top 40. "That was the first time I really allowed myself to buy in: 'This could go all the way,'" said Rieger.

The developing hit yielded immediate results: the Replacements watched as their fan base got bigger and younger almost overnight. "I remember being in some store and the song was playing and a group of little girls were singing along," said Gary Hobbib. Yet the band took little enjoyment in their sudden new popularity—and on some level they resented it.

"We were noticing the audience was doubling at our shows, and all of them came because they heard 'I'll Be You.' And a couple of nights, in our own fashion, we forgot to even play the damn thing," said Westerberg. "Once we started to get hip to it, we would play it right off the bat and half the people would leave." Dunlap watched as Westerberg began to chafe against this new fan base: "It was: 'Here's your fucking hit—fuck you.'"

More problematic than Westerberg's attitude was that "I'll Be You" sounded little like the rest of the Replacements' music. "People heard this nice poppy little song, and then 'The Ledge' comes on next," said Dunlap. "It was such a downturn."

* * *

D espite his occasional protestations, Westerberg enjoyed making his way through life aboard a Silver Eagle. Touring was confirmation that he'd beaten the system. Once, returning to the Twin Cities from a run of dates, the band's bus arrived in the morning just as a crush of commuters was heading to work. Westerberg looked out the window and surveyed the rush-hour nine-to-fivers. "Ha!" he laughed. *"Suckers!"*

The Replacements' bus was always blasting music at ungodly volume, with Westerberg as resident deejay. That spring Gladys Knight and the Pips' "Midnight Train to Georgia" seemed to be on a constant loop. "No matter what day it was, no matter what time, when that song came on and it got to the chorus where they do the 'whoo-hoo!' train whistle part—Paul would always get up and do that," said Jimmy Velvet. "He could be in the middle of a conversation."

Much of the downtime on the long drives was filled with drinking. Bored to tears on a long Sunday drive to a show in Virginia, the band loaded up on muscle relaxers and Mad Dog wine and transformed the bus into a "gerbil cage," ripping to shreds newspapers and magazines, methodically slicing open every pillow and removing the stuffing; then unspooling cassettes, spreading the tape around like tinsel.

"Tommy got his makeup case out, and everyone started painting up, pouring beer over their heads," said Velvet. "They were just entertaining themselves. It was funny, but you sorta looked at them and also thought, *Boy, there's issues here.*"

Increasingly, the Gutter Twins Westerberg and Stinson, like the Glitter Twins Mick Jagger and Keith Richards, lived an intertwined existence. "There's a period where Mick and Keith start to look like each other and dress like each other," said Westerberg. "Me and Tommy were like that. 'I'm not gonna wear this tonight, you wanna wear it?' We were sort of . . . *girlfriends.*"

Drink, drugs, and women were never in short supply. On one occasion, they were both engaged with girls in the back of the bus when they decided they wanted to switch dates, but somehow do it tactfully. "We were like, 'Let's you and I start making out, then we'll swap.' I think it worked, if I recall," said Stinson. "He's the only dude I've ever made out with."

Back home with their wives, that sort of licentiousness wasn't appreciated. "Tommy compartmentalizes things extremely well," said Daune Earle. "So when he was gone, that was his life, and this didn't exist. And when he was home, the other didn't exist. As mature as he was, as self-aware as he could be, this was not an area where he was that way. There was a mix of things going on, and I was not okay with it."

Lori Bizer, too, understood the split nature of her husband's existence. Westerberg would still call her dutifully each night, before or after the gig, as much for his benefit as hers. "I think he just wanted me to be able to sleep, thinking everything was all right," said Bizer. "I think that was so he could go on and do his other things, feeling that he'd checked in with me."

* * *

When the *Don't Tell a Soul* tour reached New York for a pair of shows at the Beacon Theater in March 1989, the 'Mats asked Johnny Thunders to open them. He'd been tickled by "Johnny's Gonna Die," though he was gruff about it: "I hear you wrote dis song about me, huh?" he asked Westerberg backstage after the record came out.

Though still on junk, Thunders had been trying to reinvent himself professionally. A couple of years earlier, his erstwhile New York Dolls partner David Johansen had created a cartoon lounge singer character called Buster Poindexter and scored a novelty hit with "Hot! Hot! Hot!" Thunders, meanwhile, had hired buxom diva Patti Palladin and a horn section, creating a slick show-band version of his old punk act.

After watching Thunders's set the first night, Tommy Stinson threw a purist's fit. When Thunders stuck his head into the dressing room to say hello,

Stinson gave him both barrels. "Hey, fucker—*what the hell are you doing?*" he said. "You need to play all the hits, and don't suck. This is a good gig and I know you ain't getting many like this anymore. And lose Jessica Rabbit," he added, meaning Palladin, before slamming the door on Thunders.

The 'Mats' own set at the Beacon didn't exactly set the crowd on fire. "It was a miserable night for them—they were very average which, to them, was misery," said Georgia Satellite Dan Baird, who got up to sing "Waitress in the Sky" and a truncated "Battleship Chains."

In the middle of "I Will Dare," Westerberg called out for Thunders, and someone in the audience shouted, "Johnny's gonna die!!!!"

Westerberg snapped, genuinely pissed: "Oh, fuck off, will ya? Have a little respect." Later the band brought out Thunders for a blues version of the 'Mats rarity "Never Been to College."

The energy onstage was already tense. "At one point, Tommy Stinson threw his bass at Chris Mars's drum kit, saying something like, 'Stay awake,'" the *New York Times* noted. "Mr. Mars, who had been putting real muscle into the music throughout the set, responded by flinging a drumstick at the bassist."

"Is it my imagination," Westerberg asked, "or are we flopping?"

A long night of partying at the China Club followed. Next day, come showtime, Westerberg could barely speak, much less sing. The band panicked at the prospect of blowing the two most anticipated shows of the tour.

They went out and opened with an oldie, "I'm in Trouble," keeping their fingers crossed. Westerberg sang the first couple of lines in a barely audible croak. It seemed a lost cause. In the middle of the song, as he began screaming *"Trouble!"* his body quivered and he began to cough. Suddenly a ball of tissue and phlegm (among other residue) erupted in a mass from the back of his throat.

"He had a hundred percent of his voice from that moment on," said Baird. "The band was so happy that they might've played the best show they ever played. They burned for ninety minutes. Absolutely fucking burned. Seriously, I saw them about fifteen, twenty times, and it was head and shoulders above any of them."

Thunders joined them for a cover of Chuck Berry's "Around and Around" and a ragged "Born to Lose" to close the show.

"I'd like to thank da lads," Thunders said, getting the last word in. "And I'm sure they'd like to thank me very much."

* * *

A few days later, midshow, Westerberg was playing his favorite guitar, another beautiful-sounding Gibson 335. Suddenly, he grabbed it by the body and slammed the neck down on the amplifier and splintered it completely. Afterwards, soundman Brendan McCabe approached him in shock: "Paul, what the hell did you do that for? How could you wreck that guitar? You loved that thing."

"Well, that's the difference between me and you, Brendan," he told him. "You cherish things that you love. Me? I destroy 'em."

During two sold-out shows at Hollywood's Palladium, Westerberg's drained mood and mental health was obvious. "Westerberg appeared cranky at times, muttering sarcastic things about people's expectations of the band," observed the *Los Angeles Times*.

The LA gigs were packed with industry players and celebrities, people pestering the band with opportunities: to record for soundtracks, to appear in movies. "It was happening for us. We were sensing it. And it was absolutely no big whoop whatsoever," said Westerberg.

After the shows, even among old friends, Westerberg was sullen and angry. He'd sit on the bus and crank "Midnight Train to Georgia." "You know that line in the song 'LA proved too much for the man'?" said writer Bill Holdship. "He was giving us a message, I thought."

CHAPTER 51

Steven Baker had been trying for some time to get the Replacements on board with Hollywood. In 1988 Westerberg, Stinson, and Michael Hill watched a rough cut of Jonathan Demme's *Married to the Mob* in New York; the director wanted the 'Mats on the soundtrack. That was scotched when Westerberg piped up about halfway through: *"This is shit!"*

Westerberg finally consented to a movie placement a year later, when Cameron Crowe used *Hootenanny*'s "Within Your Reach" in the high school romance *Say Anything*. Crowe, a former *Rolling Stone* writer making his directorial debut, had a particularly keen ear for music choices, though it was the film's star, John Cusack, who had pushed for the song.

That spring another teen film was announced: the sequel to 1979's *Rock 'n' Roll High School*. The original, directed by Alan Arkush and starring the Ramones, had become a cult classic. *Rock 'n' Roll High School Forever* was set to begin shooting in August, with Sire signed on for the soundtrack and the Ramones lined up to do a cameo. Producer Jed Horowitz told the press he favored one band for the starring role: "The Replacements are leading the pack," he said. Seymour Stein also thought it was a great opportunity, and the 'Mats were actually considering it. But Michael Hill queered the deal, taking the band aside privately and advising them against participating—wisely, as the released film turned out to be a major embarrassment. "Michael was very good for us," said Westerberg. "We dodged a bullet there."

Ironically, the era's best teen film would be heavily influenced by the Replacements but wouldn't actually feature their music. Daniel Waters began writing the script for *Heathers* while working as a clerk at a video store in Los Angeles. "I wasn't actually listening to the Replacements in high school," said Waters. "But by listening to their music, I got back to that kind of place."

Waters's story was a black satire of John Hughes's sanitized Midwestern high school fantasias, as well as a comic dissection of the recent national teen-suicide panic. Just as Westerberg had tried to demystify suicide's romance with "The Ledge," so Waters did by mocking society's response to it.

Waters peppered his script with Replacements allusions—from the school being Westerburg High (the spelling of Paul's surname was changed at the urging of a film exec who felt that the name Westerberg seemed "a little too Jewish" for a Midwestern high school) to male lead J.D. (Christian Slater) and one of the titular Heathers saying, "Color me impressed."

Waters wanted *Tim*'s "Swingin Party" to play over the closing credits, but New World Cinema's $2.9 million budget wouldn't allow for it. "I'm pretty sure we didn't even bother asking, given our paltry resources," said Waters. The film's 'Mats connection was strengthened when female lead Winona Ryder bonded with the scenarist over their mutual love of the band.

Heathers did modest box office upon its March 1989 release, but it won serious attention from critics and developed a fervent cult following. In *Rolling Stone*'s 1989 "Hot Issue," *Heathers* was named hot movie, and Ryder and Slater hot actress and hot actor. The film's timing coincided with *Don't Tell a Soul*'s release. Westerberg would later claim to have never seen the movie. He would become familiar, however, with the film's female star.

* * *

Born just a couple hours outside the Twin Cities, Winona Laura Horowitz was the daughter of a hippie-beatnik family. She was raised on a farm located in the bluff country along the Mississippi; her godfathers were Timothy Leary and Lawrence Ferlinghetti. The family left Minnesota for South America, then moved on to a commune in Northern California before settling in nearby Petaluma, where she began acting. She took her stage name, Ryder, from one of her father's Mitch Ryder LPs.

An older cousin exposed her to '80s American indie rock when she was twelve, and she went to her first Replacements show, also in the Bay Area, when Bob Stinson was still in the band. "They were very drunk, and pissing the audience off," she recalled. "I had never seen anything like it. There was a sense of wanting to root for them."

On set, Ryder blasted the 'Mats on her Walkman to prepare for scenes—ballads for the emotional stuff, rockers for the arguments. "Paul's music was so important to me, so critical and seminal to my work," she said. "It was this Salinger-esque thing: you feel like he's singing directly to you and these songs are about your life."

The Replacements played LA's Palladium in the spring of 1989. That day Ryder bumped into Westerberg at the Mondrian Hotel. "I was completely starstruck," she said. Westerberg thought she was "cute as hell" and invited her to the Mondrian bar. He drank; she didn't. After an awkward silence, Ryder finally worked up the nerve to ask Westerberg about his songs, quizzing him about "Here Comes a Regular." Their conversation ended abruptly when Paul headed to sound check.

Ryder and her boyfriend, Johnny Depp—then starring on Fox's hit *21 Jump Street*—saw the show that night. "I was dancing and jumping up and down, and he was sitting back," she said. Ryder allowed that her fascination with Westerberg became a mild annoyance to Depp after a while.

Later that year, Ryder went to a 'Mats show in New York on her own. Afterwards, Westerberg walked her back home. "It was the first time we ever had a real conversation," she recalled. "It was very, very sweet."

Their socializing made at least one gossip column at the time. (The paper noted, falsely, that Westerberg was separated from his wife.) "He was married and I was with Johnny," said Ryder. "It always felt like there was this secret-type feeling, like not wanting anyone to know. I guess it was because . . . he didn't want rumors."

The press would eventually begin asking Westerberg about her. "Wait 'til they hear about me and Phyllis Diller," he told *SPIN*, annoyed. Nevertheless, the hearsay was torrid. "For years I felt I got this really bad rap, when in reality it was a handful of times of hanging out with him," said Ryder. "It was not this love affair at all."

There were glimmers of something more. "I definitely own up to having romantic feelings at certain points, but the timing just didn't happen," said Ryder. "Later on, Paul would joke and say, 'Everyone thinks we had this thing. Why didn't we just have it?'"

CHAPTER 52

In the last week of May, the Replacements headed to New York for their first American network television appearance since *Saturday Night Live* three years earlier. They'd been booked to play the inaugural International Rock Awards, a "tribute to the world's foremost rock 'n' roll artists," to air on ABC in the United States and in forty other countries. Keith Richards, Eric Clapton, Tina Turner, the Bangles, and Robert Palmer were also confirmed to appear.

The band was joined in New York by their wives, who weren't particularly friendly with one other. Lori Bizer was viewed as cool and aloof by the other women, while Chrissie Dunlap was older and had her own social set. Daune Earle was the most outgoing—she even liked Chris Mars's wife Sally Schneidkraut, but Tommy Stinson's negative feelings toward Sally roadblocked their friendship. "Nobody socialized or had dinner together," said Earle.

"There's nothing worse than riding in the van or bus," said Westerberg, "and the first thing out of somebody's mouth is, 'My wife thinks that . . .'" Already annoyed with Schneidkraut for meddling in band business, Westerberg would say of the couple: "It's as if Yoko married Ringo."

"It wasn't the liquor that tore the band apart; it was the women," Westerberg would claim. "They crack the little gang, three or four guys who have a brotherhood. When you have someone who's in your ear, who you love in a different way . . . that tends to be the beginning of the end."

Others saw the situation differently. "Chris was enough of an individual that it was going to happen anyway," said Slim Dunlap. "You get into your thirties and you're in a rock band that has such a horrible, fatalistic view of the world, which could implode at any moment. . . . Chris was inevitably going to grow apart from them."

Mars had come to see the emptiness of his relationships with Paul and Tommy and the ugliness of the gang mentality. "You had to be a Replacement when you were with the band," said Mars. "We were like bar mates and not really close friends. . . . I don't really know them as people."

Chris was also dissatisfied with how the 'Mats' affairs were being handled. The youngest of seven children, raised blue-collar, Mars knew the value of a dollar. "He was a tight-ass," chuckled Dunlap. "And he saw all this money being thrown around. Chris saw it as, 'Nobody's in command here who has any practicality or sense.'"

The others responded in kind. In Los Angeles, hanging out with Bill Holdship, Stinson and Westerberg began badmouthing Mars's playing. "That was the first time I heard that kind of dissension," said Holdship. "They'd say smart-ass things to each other, but that was the first time I felt like there was any problems going on."

* * *

By mid-May, "I'll Be You" had reached number fifty-one on the Hot 100. But it would go no higher. Warner Bros. had come to the conclusion that the record wasn't going to break into the top 40, no matter how much more money or promotional muscle they put behind it. The 'Mats' first—and probably best—shot had missed the mark.

Though Westerberg passed it off publicly—"It's not like 'I'll Be You' is number one and I'll have to play it for the rest of my life," he told an interviewer—privately both he and Stinson were crestfallen. Publicist Mary Melia recalled an evening at the band's hotel when they let their guard down. "They were plastered and kept talking to me about trying to get famous—they didn't say it in those words exactly. I never thought they cared."

That night, Paul and Tommy called Maxwell's owner Steve Fallon in Hoboken and arranged to do a last-minute, unannounced show there the following evening. They hadn't played a small club in a while, and they were itching to have some fun in a familiar room.

There was a hitch: Chris and Sally Mars already had dinner plans. "Everyone else, including me, was like, 'Well, cancel them,'" said Chrissie Dunlap. "Her response was, 'No, we're going to dinner.' I was like, 'You don't get it.' I can only imagine Paul and Tommy's reaction."

Years later Westerberg would look back on Mars's decision to skip out on the band and the show that night as justified. "To defend him in hindsight, he had made plans previously," said Westerberg. "I don't hold it against him now. But back then, it was someone else's spouse getting in the way of what the band wanted to do. Us three wanted to play."

Undaunted, the rest of the Replacements played Maxwell's, taking the stage for the first time ever without Chris Mars. Monitor man Carl Davino was behind the kit. "Tommy just said, 'You wanna play tonight?' I said, 'Play what?'" recalled Davino. "At that point, it'd been ten years since I'd played the drums."

Word about the secret appearance spread quickly, and by showtime Maxwell's was teeming with excited fans.

"Well, Chris couldn't make it," announced Tommy Stinson from the stage. "His mommy wouldn't let him."

Finding his place behind the drums, Davino stuck out among the 'Mats with his hair-metal roadie style. "Here's Carl Bon Jovi," joked Stinson.

"I'm thinking to myself, *God I'm rusty as shit*," recalled Davino. Though he had become familiar with the songs mixing them night after night, "knowing the material and playing it are two different things. I managed to make it through the whole show anyway."

Remarkably, Davino not only held his own but actually played with real confidence. The band was at its loose-limbed best, working up covers alongside originals as the audience sang along giddily. Maybe it was the crowd or the confines, but it was one of the best nights of the whole tour—and certainly the most enjoyable.

Westerberg and Stinson walked off the stage with their eyes having been opened. "Realizing the roadie could actually play his kick drum and had a little swing to his beat was really sorta fun," said Westerberg. "It makes you play different. And we held that against Chris a little. He had his two beats that he played really good."

Later that week, Westerberg and Stinson taped an on-camera interview for MTV. Asked what their future plans included, Paul's answer even caught Tommy off guard. "We might fire the drummer," he said with a laugh, before backpedaling and changing the subject.

★ ★ ★

Naturally, ABC wanted the Replacements to play "I'll Be You" at the International Rock Awards. But Westerberg wanted to plug the likely next single, "Talent Show." The network found a red flag: the second verse's line about "feeling good from the pills we took."

Recalled Dunlap, "They said, 'That can't go on the air in any way, shape, or form. If you sing it that way, we'll have to censor it.'" Westerberg was unusually—suspiciously—obsequious about the matter. "If ya gotta bleep out the line, that's fine," he told the producers.

Show day began, Stinson recalled, with "an eight ball and limousine" depositing the Replacements at Greenwich Village's National Guard Armory, the ramshackle venue where the awards were being held. Instead of dressing rooms, the Armory had a communal area to get ready in. "So we basically shared the dressing room with Keith Richards and Eric Clapton and Alice Cooper, all these people," recalled Westerberg. "We're huddled in the corner looking at each other, and looking at them, and thinking. 'What are we doing here?'"

Richards was the first to arrive. Westerberg made a beeline and introduced himself: "We opened for you a few months ago." Richards responded warmly: "He lit my cigarette, and I looked to the band, like *C'mon*, and everybody whipped over there. He was so charming and nice. The flip side was Dave Edmunds, who wanted to kill us."

It was especially ironic given that Edmunds's *Tracks on Wax 4* had been one of the first records Westerberg played for Dogbreath a decade earlier. Edmunds was "looking at us like, *I'm gonna get out of this chair and murder you, you fucking cunts*—for no reason. I guess we didn't look like we belonged there. We *didn't* belong there."

Stinson and Bill Sullivan commiserated with Alice Cooper as he pulled on his leather pants. The 'Mats listened respectfully as Eric Clapton laid out his Armani duds and espoused the best methods for ironing clothes. When David Bowie walked in, he spotted Stinson's polka-dot suspenders and teased hair and cooed, "My, aren't you the bright young things."

The show was a lively mess. The award itself was in the shape of a golden hip-swiveling Elvis Presley ("And the Elvis goes home with . . . "). The Traveling Wilburys won album of the year, Guns N' Roses picked up artist of the year, and Bono and Madonna were best male and female vocalists. Most of the big winners were no-shows.

The Replacements appeared toward the end of the broadcast, just as they were soaring from a day of liquid and powder refreshment. One of the production assistants, aided by John Oates of Hall & Oates, managed to distract Westerberg long enough to get the flask out of his hands and push him onstage.

The band's reputation preceded them. "We apologize," came the group's introduction, "Here they are: the Replacements."

"What the hell are we doooin' here?" bleated a pallid Westerberg into the microphone in his Minneapolis honk, a camera crane swooping in. Then he stuck his tongue out at a cameraman who got too close. The 'Mats' wives watched from a table out in front of the stage. Nearby, Tina Turner covered her ears from the volume.

Sure enough, the line about "pills" was muted from the broadcast. The rest of their performance was loose and euphoric. Stinson got on the mic and poked fun at the Elvis award. They all seemed to be laughing at some private joke.

For the song's closing "It's too late to turn back" coda, Westerberg began to sing "It's too late to take pills" instead—several times. The censors missed it completely and let it go out live on the air.

"The reaction afterward was nightmarish," said Dunlap. By the closing all-star jam, led by Richards and featuring most of the evening's performers, the 'Mats had already been ushered out of the building. The next morning at the hotel coffee shop, Russ Rieger sat with his head in his hands. The band waited three years to return to network TV, only to spit in ABC's eye as well.

CHAPTER 53

Touring was scheduled to resume at the University of Wisconsin, a show Warner Bros. was set to record for live promotional radio release. The drive from Minneapolis to Madison turned into a rowdy early morning episode that Westerberg would later immortalize in the song "Someone Take the Wheel."

Merch man Jimmy Velvet and tour manager Roger Vitale were both asleep in their bunks when they were shocked awake by *Never Mind the Bollocks, It's the Sex Pistols* blasting at window-rattling volume. A raging party was under way in the front lounge. Velvet turned on his video camera. Paul was making screwdrivers, then throwing the glass against the wall and chugging vodka straight from the bottle. Not to be outdone, Tommy leapt around miming to Johnny Rotten in his tighty-whiteys. Even Chris was mugging for the camera. Slim was near the front, nursing a beer, keeping one eye on the road.

As "Bodies" kicked in, Paul and Tommy began ripping out the bus's tables and fixtures, methodically uprooting everything nailed, screwed, or glued down. The driver, a Georgia good ol' boy who worked for the bus's owner, glanced over his shoulder with increasing concern as the band lay waste to the lounge. Finally, he jerked the bus over to the shoulder of the interstate and became apoplectic once he realized how much structural damage they'd done.

"Guys, this is fucking ridiculous. I mean fuckin' reee-diculous," ranted the driver. "I wouldn't take my friends and come to yer house and turn the fucking furniture out."

"This ain't your house—is it?" replied Westerberg. "This is more our house."

"I'm responsible."

"You're responsible? We pay for it, don't we?"

"You want to pay for a whole interior to be rebuilt? It's only about sixty grand."

"We might just do that," nodded Westerberg cockily.

The driver still couldn't believe the wreck all around him. "If you want to rebuild the whole bus, fine," he said. "You need to buy a bus that you can destruct twice weekly and rebuild."

Paul suddenly flushed with anger: "*Don't* . . . don't mommy me now."

"I don't wanna be out here to be your momma. I'm not gonna stand around here and have my fuckin' bus tore up, man."

"It comes with the territory," sniffed Westerberg.

Tommy tried to defuse the situation, promising to take care of everything.

"You've never built a bus, have you?" asked the driver.

"Not recently, no," sneered Westerberg. "I've broken a few. And I've paid for a lot of them."

"Paul—look, man . . . don't tear up the fucking bus."

"*We're makin' a video!*" Westerberg shouted emphatically pointing to Velvet's camera, though he couldn't even keep a straight face.

Roger Vitale had finally roused himself from bed. He took one look at the bus, then sat and hung his head.

The driver was getting even more worked up about what his boss was going to say: "I mean, tearing the fucking furniture out, that's carrying it too far."

By this point, Westerberg's buzz had started to fade and he was getting grumpy.

"We ain't done nothin'. *Christ almighty*. It's some wood . . . it's wood with screws. What did we do? We pulled some screws out."

"If you pull it out, you take a screwdriver and you take it out—you don't rip it out of the wall."

"I would've, but I don't have the tools," said Westerberg. Now it had become absurdist comedy.

The driver begged for a bit of sanity: "Can you turn it down a little bit and be a little less destructive?"

"We'll turn it up," said Westerberg defiantly. "That'll make us normal."

"Just a little mutual respect on the bus, that's all I'm asking."

Finally, Tommy had heard enough and began yelling theatrically. "*We're not respected anywhere! We don't have respect. We don't want it!* Now, let us turn it up and do what we want." End of argument.

Arriving in Madison, Vitale—shocked silent the whole time—was first off the bus. As Tommy and Paul trooped down its steps, he was waiting for them. "Guys," he said, shaking his head and mustering all the disapproval he could. "I am *not* impressed." Paul and Tommy practically fell down laughing. For the rest of the tour, Vitale's line—"I am *not* impressed"—became a running joke. The bus driver, meanwhile, quit the business and became a born-again Christian.

★ ★ ★

At U-Wisconsin there were more new faces in the crowd than ever, which suddenly seemed to gall the band. "Paul was saying: 'Did you see us on that stupid TV show? Is that why you came? Did you hear "I'll Be You"—is that why you're here? Are you the new regime?'" said Velvet.

Warner Bros. had told the band it was making a live recording, thereby guaranteeing mischief or a dud show. As a joke, or perhaps in an effort to mar the results, Westerberg asked the crowd to boo after all the songs rather than applaud. Later, when Steven Baker got the tapes in California, he discovered that Westerberg's between-song patter included such gems as, "Here's another one for that asshole, Mr. Moneybags Steve Baker, back in Burbank."

"They knew I'd be listening to it, so they'd say something horrible," said Baker. "But it was kind of endearing too—a long-distance jibe."

Winding through Missouri, Iowa, and Illinois, Westerberg was burning out. Nearly seventy shows in four months of hard road living had caught up to him. By the time of their final date a couple of days later at Chicago's Aragon, Westerberg was openly talking about giving up the road and rock-and-roll. As he admitted to the *Tribune*, "It's the first time I've felt old on a tour."

* * *

Don't Tell a Soul's flattening sales figures were worrying the band's label and management. Although the Replacements hadn't warmed up for anyone—aside from the one-off Keith Richards gig—since opening for the R.E.M. tour six years earlier, Frank Barsalona dangled the prospect of a tour with another of his clients, Tom Petty and the Heartbreakers. Encouragingly, 'Mats pals the Georgia Satellites and Del Fuegos had been part of a successful package tour with Petty a couple of years earlier.

In April '89, Petty had released his first solo album, *Full Moon Fever*, which became his biggest seller. He and the Heartbreakers would be touring in July. The Replacements were offered a slot opening almost forty shows, mostly at outdoor amphitheaters and sheds, along with a handful of arenas. The 'Mats would make only a couple thousand bucks a night, the standard pittance for an opener. The trade-off was that the venues ranged in capacity from 12,000 to 20,000.

Lenny Waronker and Steven Baker both made it clear to Westerberg that playing with Petty would be good for him personally: "They put it to me like, 'Petty's a singer–songwriter–front-man. He's a professional, and you can learn a thing or two,'" said Westerberg. The underlying message was that Westerberg's career was likely to carry on beyond the 'Mats, and he needed to prepare. It helped that Westerberg liked *Full Moon Fever*.

Dunlap was dubious about the tour. "Paul was already reaching a point where he was complaining to me that he . . . didn't want to do this for the rest of his life," Dunlap said. But they'd already gone all in with *Don't Tell a Soul*; what did they have to lose?

CHAPTER 54

Appropriately named, the Strange Behavior Tour kicked off in early July with a half-dozen shows throughout Tom Petty's native Florida. Heartbreakers keyboardist Benmont Tench was already a Replacements fan. "I'd been reading all the hype about them," said Tench. "I'm always leery of that. But a friend of mine played me their stuff, and I got into the records."

Tench would often join them for "Nightclub Jitters" and "I'll Be You." "To play with them was an education," said Tench. "With somebody like Paul, it's deceptive. The chord voicings he uses when he writes and the way those guys play them, it's not as clear-cut as you might think."

Rolling Stone had dispatched a reporter to follow the Petty tour, and he captured the two bands' initial meeting. Guitarist Mike Campbell went and introduced himself and came out of the Replacements' dressing room laughing at the band's cheek. "You gotta meet these guys," Campbell told Petty. "They're great. They were telling me how much they like your new song 'Running Down the Drain.'"

Bonding over mutual opening-night nerves, Stinson tried to loosen Petty up with some drinks. "Nah, you're opening Pandora's box there," said Petty.

Stinson asked an amused Petty if he still played "Breakdown."

"That was the first song I ever sang with these guys," chimed in Westerberg, fibbing to flatter him. "But I couldn't really get the high parts. My voice won't do that."

"Why don't you do the song and then we won't have to?" said Petty.

Petty was enthused by the group's presence, inviting Westerberg and Dunlap onstage to jam. "Tom liked having the spark of this upstart new band on the road," said Dunlap. "He watched Paul intently every night. I don't think Paul realized how much." As a gesture, Petty even gave Westerberg the hat he wore in the "I Won't Back Down" video. "I was like, 'Oh man, thank you,'" said Westerberg. "Then I turned around and gave it to a guy for some drugs the next night."

At Miami Arena, the Replacements struggled to adjust to the bigger stage's sound and dimensions. Dunlap had already left the Keith Richards gig at the Meadowlands thinking, *None of our songs work in this environment.*

To tepid applause, the 'Mats brought the opening night set to a close with a car-crash rendition of "Achin' to Be." "Thanks," said Westerberg. "We'll be better by next week, but by then we'll be in Memphis."

Westerberg would later admit that the band didn't go out with a positive attitude. "We played brilliantly at least twice and got no reaction," he said. "Middle American Petty fans don't want it, unless they've seen it on TV first or heard it on the radio."

"Petty's audience at that time just wanted to sing along to 'Free Fallin','" said Dan Baird of the Georgia Satellites. "They were indifferent to the Replacements, and that's the last thing Paul and those guys wanted."

The response delivered a deep psychological blow to Westerberg. "We paid our dues, went to a moderately big level, then went to a huge level on that Petty opening slot," he observed. "But it was like playing a tiny club where no one cared—except there was 20,000 of them every night. I mean, the rejection of a small club is one thing. But the rejection of a small city was tough."

Things got worse once the tour hit the outdoor sheds. "There'd be nobody in the stands—like, twenty, thirty people sometimes," recalled soundman Carl Davino. "Every once in a while there may have been three or four hundred people." In the daylight, the band watched ushers showing people to their seats and looked into the faces of disinterested Petty fans.

Many nights Westerberg would stand in the wings and listen to Petty play the "The Waiting." As the sound of thousands of fans shouting back the song's "yeah-yeah-yeah" refrain washed over the stage, his heart sank. "That's when it really hit me," he said, "that maybe we just weren't made of the stuff that makes popular music."

* * *

The Replacements were not going down without a fight. After playing it straight to no response, they decided to go out and give Petty's audience a taste of vintage 'Mats chaos. "We just had this attitude: 'Well, they don't like our music, let's just let them remember us,'" said Westerberg.

This "anarchist" approach, as Heartbreakers drummer Stan Lynch described it, was partly a reaction to watching the headliners. "I love Tom Petty and his band. But they're boring," said Slim Dunlap. "The first show was impressive. The second and third gig, it's less impressive; a month into it, it's agony." Said Westerberg, "They did the same thing note for note, word for word, every night. It was the opposite of what we were."

Tommy was especially galled when Petty would play a few notes of a familiar hit, then coyly ask, "You don't really want to hear that, do you?" "It was Rock

101," said Stinson. Occasionally, the 'Mats would poke fun at Petty's shtick. In Bristol, Connecticut, Westerberg told the crowd, "Tom Petty's teaching us all this groovy rapport with the audience. I think I've got . . . it down. Whaddya think of this?" he said, striking a typical Petty pose as the audience sat silently. "They roar for him, I dunno."

"You'll love it when he does it," laughed Stinson.

The 'Mats would pull out their most caustic punk covers, they'd trade instruments in the middle of songs, and Westerberg would suck on helium and sing like Mickey Mouse. The band turned their only recognizable number, "I'll Be You," into a tortuous two-beat crawl and even played a mocking version of "Breakdown."

The Petty camp was starting to wonder about the Replacements. More often than not, the band was coming onstage drunk, belligerent, and playing almost ineptly on purpose. "The Heartbreakers never understood that—a guy going up there and being deliberately bad," said Dunlap. "It was unheard of in their world."

Their attitude was, said Benmont Tench, "too cool for school. But it doesn't have to be fake unless you make it fake. I didn't understand why they would just thumb their nose at the whole experience."

One night Westerberg caught Mike Campbell and couple of other Heartbreakers watching from the wings. "So I decided, let's just show them what we can really do," he said. "And we sorta blew them away . . . and confused them. The next day their roadie said to me, 'I don't get it, man. You guys are, like, *brilliant* if you want to be. Why don't you want to be?' I didn't have an answer for him."

On August 5 at Nashville's Starwood Amphitheatre, the 'Mats felt especially feisty. Before the show, the band went to the Heartbreakers' wardrobe mistress, Linda Burcher, and began rummaging through the Heartbreakers' wives' things, even getting help from Petty's wife, Jane. They arrived onstage looking like down-and-out drag queens: Westerberg in a denim skirt and white string top, Dunlap in a blue silk dress and violet sweater, Stinson shirtless in pink pants. Swigging from a quart of Jack Daniels, Westerberg started giving the crowd his heel routine.

"Last night Tom Petty told us if we fuck up again we're fired," he said. "Well, fuck you, Tom Petty . . . and fuck you, Nashville."

As the baffled, then infuriated, audience looked on, the group played a few of their own songs before working up a meandering, seemingly endless version of "Walk on the Wild Side." Later, Westerberg asked for a drum solo from Chris Mars, who responded by throwing his sticks into the crowd.

Westerberg ended the show abruptly after thirty minutes. "Boo if you have the guts," he said, leaving the stage. The crowd happily obliged him.

When the Heartbreakers arrived onstage, Petty quipped, "The opener played a short set, so we're going to play extra long, because we care." The crowd cheered. "See, we're a little different."

* * *

The only way out of the tour, the Replacements decided, was to get fired. "That started the real behavior," said Dunlap. "Deliberately being grating, trying to really piss these fuckers off."

The "fuckers" in question were Petty's veteran road crew, who had little time for the 'Mats' attitude. "When you're the support act, the headliner's crew take the approach that you guys are beneath us; here's our rules, play by them," said Premiere Talent's Steve Davis. "That's the last thing you ever wanted to say to Tommy or Paul."

A cold war commenced. If Petty's stage manager told them they had three songs left in the set, the band might cut things short and walk off right then, or continue way past their allotted time, leaving the crew fuming either way.

The band also engaged in a running feud with Alan "Bugs" Weidel, Petty's longtime guitar tech. Weidel would spend much of the 'Mats' sets tuning instruments and smoking joints, blowing huge plumes of pot smoke onstage, aggravating Westerberg.

Finally, Tommy called him out on the mic: "Don't you ever be smoking pot while I'm onstage. I don't want to be smelling that shit when I'm playing."

Weidel's attitude was simple: *Tough shit, kid.* He'd go into the 'Mats' dressing room just before they arrived and toke up. "I always got the impression the Heartbreakers were amused by how we would wind them up," said Weidel.

At one point Petty's crew "accidentally" wrecked one of Dunlap's guitars. In retaliation, the 'Mats spread word that that they'd sprayed Weidel's pot stash with Raid. "It got uglier and uglier," said Dunlap. "For a jaded road crew, that's their fun, mashing the opening band. They came up against a band they couldn't mash."

"I actually thought they were a brilliant band," said Weidel. "They squandered that by not caring. I remember telling one of them: 'All I'm doing is showing you the same amount of respect you're giving your audience.' It went over their heads."

Before long, the group was taking to more basic forms of bad behavior, such as destroying dressing rooms. One such episode in Phoenix left Petty with a $5,000 bill for damages. For a while after that, the 'Mats had their dressing room privileges revoked and had to get ready on their bus.

When asked about touring with the 'Mats, Petty would later joke that he'd "never paid for more broken furniture in my life, but it was worth it." The Replacements didn't think so. They also weren't going to get fired. They'd have to see it to the bitter end.

* * *

Before leaving for the Petty tour, the 'Mats had shot a plaintive black-and-white video for "Achin' to Be" in Minneapolis, directed by Doug Freel. MTV gave the clip some early play but didn't give it their full weight. In August, after just four weeks, "Achin' to Be" peaked at a disappointing number twenty-two on the modern rock chart; it did worse on rock radio, topping out at number thirty-seven. *Don't Tell a Soul* had already exited the *Billboard* 200 for good in July.

The failure of "Achin' to Be" to galvanize the band's alternative fan base was particularly damaging. "If you've got a second song that's breaking out at your core, that keeps your base solid, it keeps driving sales. It helps build, or at least hold, that foundation," said Reprise promotion head Rich Fitzgerald. "But we didn't have that song."

"It never seemed to me like they were going to make it in a mainstream way," said Dunlap. "When I really like something, then I know it's going nowhere. It's the thing no one wanted to accept: certain kinds of music aren't for all ears. I was not defeatist about it; I was realistic about it."

* * *

The 'Mats only had to play forty-five minutes a night. If the band "couldn't have fun that one hour onstage," Westerberg figured, "we'd make sure we had fun the other twenty-three hours of the day."

"It pushed us further into drugs and alcohol—not so much more, but in a way that was dark," said Stinson. "From there it was irretrievable."

Not for everyone, however: months earlier, Chris Mars had finally decided to stop drinking. "It was hard to keep up that pace for me," said Mars. "So I just started slowing down. I found that I could play a lot better. I moderated myself. Everybody else went on and didn't."

It further isolated the drummer from the band. "I felt very alone," said Mars. "There was no one I could relate to. The road crew and the band and everybody was drinking all the time."

By the Petty tour he saw the group as "all circus and no cohesive depth, chemistry-wise," said Mars. "Ironically, [booze] was something that was part of the act, but ultimately destroyed it, as did cocaine. Nobody ever talked to anybody when they were sober, or when they were hungover, in their own little world. Then the booze and the coke would start floating around, then [we were] buddies again. It became this really stupid circle."

The band's drug use reached a point where Mars was "scared someone was going to die." Dunlap, too, was concerned about Westerberg and Stinson: "Guys would hand Paul a handful of pills, and he would just be the cocky rock star and down them all. And Paul would be downing it all with a bottle of whiskey," he said. "That isn't smart."

In Philadelphia, Stinson had gone on an all-night bender and failed to show up for the next day's hotel lobby call. Fearing the worst, the rest of the band charged up to his room. "We were thinking, 'Oh my God,'" said Mars. "We're pounding on the door, and there's no answer. It turned out he was just asleep, but it was spooky. It was to the point to where it was a realistic thing that that could happen. That was creepy."

* * *

The band struggled through the second leg of the Petty tour. The *Chicago Tribune* reported that at Poplar Creek, Westerberg ended the set "lying on his back, howling at the moon while the crowd, largely made up of Petty fans, howled at him."

At Pine Knob in Michigan, Lori Bizer turned up to see her husband play. "Where are you, raise your hand?" said Westerberg, scanning the crowd for his wife. "I think she got a date," chided Stinson. Westerberg eventually spotted Bizer and went into the audience to slow-dance with her as the band played "Love's Lost."

Perhaps it was Bizer's presence, but Pine Knob would be one of the tour's better shows. Benmont Tench joined for an exquisite lounge rendition of "Nightclub Jitters" and a pounding version of the Rolling Stones' "Happy." The 'Mats seemed to come alive whenever Tench sat in. "It's nice to have a real musician onstage once in a while," said Stinson—though the band was still getting their little digs in at Tench's boss.

"We're gonna play one more tune," said Westerberg, "and then Johnny Thunders and the Heartbreakers will be up next."

"We'll be back again after Johnny," chuckled Stinson.

With the tour winding down, road manager Roger Vitale finally made his escape. After six torturous months with the Replacements, he jumped ship to go work for Cyndi Lauper. "God, it was such a relief," said Vitale.

In Syracuse, the 'Mats crossed paths with Guns N' Roses singer Axl Rose, who joined Petty for a couple of songs during the Heartbreakers' encore. It was a warm-up for a Petty-Rose duet scheduled for the MTV Video Awards the following week. Rose had seen the 'Mats play on the *Pleased to Meet Me* tour and come away unimpressed. The feeling was fairly mutual. Westerberg had admitted to liking Guns N' Roses "up to a certain point. When they don't try and use their heads," he said. "They're a great band from the neck down . . . maybe the waist down."

Before a late August show at Great Woods outside Boston, the 'Mats' merch man Jimmy Velvet had a gift for Tommy: one of Michael Jackson's old Jackson 5 stage outfits. Stinson promptly donned the garish ensemble—a yellow flower–pattern polyester top and red bejeweled bell-bottoms—and played the gig in costume. Westerberg could hardly get through the set without cracking up.

Laughs, however, were generally few and far between. Backstage, before a date at a state fair in Allentown, Pennsylvania, Tommy Stinson was bitching to

Petty about the indignity of having to do a gig where the hogs and cows were being judged. "We'd never be playing a fuckin' fair if we weren't on this tour," groused Stinson.

"Really?" said Petty. "Well, I'm making a quarter of a million dollars tonight. That's why I'm playing here." Stinson was stunned into silence. His take-home that night would be a few hundred.

* * *

By tour's end, Westerberg's increasingly negative feelings toward the band were unmistakable.

For Stinson—twenty-two, married, and expecting a child—the 'Mats' future had become paramount. "Tommy was still young, and this thing was dying," said Slim Dunlap. "He looked at Paul like, 'You're not doing anything about it; you don't care if it dies.' Paul was a successful songwriter. Tommy felt like: 'What do I have? And now you're just going to dump me on my ass?'"

Heading to Canada for the final show on September 2, Westerberg discussed the possibility of making another album. If and when the group recorded, however, he wanted to have more control of the production and to bring in outside musicians. That was fine with Stinson—he knew, sooner or later, Westerberg would need him. Dunlap had little ego invested in the band, but also felt that Paul trusted him too much to cast him aside.

In effect, the idea of opening things up to other musicians simply meant that Chris Mars was likely to be shut out. "It was a little uncomfortable," said Stinson. "I don't think Chris was into that."

The Replacements' last show of 1989, at Toronto's Kingswood Music Theatre, was unlike any of the other 140 gigs they'd played that year. After starting with an incendiary "Color Me Impressed," the set quickly shifted into a songwriting experiment. With Benmont Tench sitting in, the band worked through several new numbers, including the elegant ballad "Sadly Beautiful." They even composed a couple songs—"Susan" and "All Is Gone"—onstage, with Westerberg coming up with lyrics and calling out chord changes, the band filling in gaps.

"The final night in Toronto was terrible," said Westerberg. "We sang lyrics to one song while playing the music to another. It just sounded really bad; it sucked. We couldn't even muster a rousing boo. And that's the death of any rock band—when nobody cares."

By fall, *Don't Tell a Soul* had sold a disappointing 319,344 copies. In the Replacements' Warner Bros. label file, someone scrawled and underlined: "Not enough."

PART IV The Last

I could say we ran out of picks, we ran out of strings, ran
out of time, ran out of patience. They're all true. We all
smelled smoke, and I was the first one to say that the thing
is on fire, boys, let's exit the building quietly.

PAUL WESTERBERG

CHAPTER 55

As Paul Westerberg descended the steps of the large black tour bus, Lori Bizer could see the defeat on his face. "If [the tour] was four months, we'd drink for four months," said Westerberg. "We would never reach that level of giddy drunkenness, we were always in a depressed fog—at least I was."

Back home in South Minneapolis, he'd usually dry out and readjust to a more tempered domestic life. This time he didn't stop. "Drinking was a way to not think, to hide," he said.

The only place Westerberg confronted his problems was in his work. In his basement he wrote some twenty songs whose titles told the story: "Torture," "Someone Take the Wheel," "Bent Out of Shape," "All Shook Down," and "The Last." As Bill Flanagan would note, this material had "all the optimism of a suicide note." "Rather than talk it over with someone or keep a diary," recalled Westerberg, "I sat down and wrote songs."

It provided little relief. Instead, the songs forced Westerberg to own up to the fact that he was fed up with nearly everything in his life. It had started with "Rock 'n' Roll Ghost." "That song was the beginning of me starting to think, *What am I doing? I still don't know. Am I happy?*" More and more the answer was no. He was unsatisfied with himself, the band, and his marriage: "It frightened me to think that this was my lot in life."

As with so much else, Bizer was not privy to the depths of his doubts—or his alcoholism. "He did most of his drinking away from me," she said. "Maybe it was selective on my part. . . . I didn't want to see a lot of stuff." But she couldn't miss the growing distance between them. Paul constantly held Lori at bay; any efforts to discuss his problems were rebuffed. "To keep the peace, or to keep the relationship, I stayed away from a lot of that stuff," she said.

Westerberg felt that to save his health and salvage his marriage, he might have to abandon his career. "The drinking and the drugs had become so wrapped up with the music that I thought I'd have to give up the music to survive," he said.

He thought about trying to farm his songs out to other artists. "Sadly Beautiful" had been written with Marianne Faithfull in mind; he'd heard that country star George Jones was planning on doing "Here Comes a Regular" and bluesman Stevie Ray Vaughan wanted to record "Bastards of Young." Maybe he could just become a professional songwriter.

For Russ Rieger and Gary Hobbib, Westerberg's crisis of faith was cause for concern. By the end of 1989, High Noon's business was in a precarious position. Their other big band, the Del Fuegos, was also on the verge of imploding. Following the departures of guitarist Warren Zanes and drummer Woody Giessmann, the Fuegos had rebooted with a new lineup on 1989's slickly produced *Smoking in the Fields.* But the album's poor reception led front man Dan Zanes to a solo career the following year. The Replacements remained the High Noon act with the most commercial potential.

Rieger and Hobbib consulted with manager Tim Collins, who'd helped revive Aerosmith's career by getting them into rehab; they discussed doing the same for Westerberg. "I knew Paul was *not* the kind of guy to do an intervention with," said Hobbib. "He didn't have a ton of friends. Who are you going to bring around to an intervention? All the people he's getting screwed up with?"

* * *

As fall turned to winter, Westerberg had a moment of clarity. He was about to turn thirty. The eighties were nearly over. He decided to quit the Replacements.

Westerberg had already fleshed out and demo-ed his new songs at home with his four-track and drum machine. Listening back, he simply couldn't conceive of the rest of the 'Mats playing the material; moreover, he didn't want them to. "The most valuable thing that the band ever had . . . is their attitude and spirit," he said. "But I just saw no place for that on these songs. To me, that would have rung hollow."

These weren't really Replacements songs at all. "I felt sort of empty with the fast-rockin' shit," said Westerberg. In January, Westerberg called High Noon and told them he was going solo. He saw "no future" in the Replacements.

Rieger and Hobbib quickly traveled to Minneapolis to try to change his mind. "We told him, 'You want a solo career? Then you want it off the biggest band record possible. You gotta do another Replacements album,'" said Rieger. "It wasn't a creative or emotional argument; it was a business argument."

For the label, the difference was semantics. "My feeling always was, 'We all thought you were the Replacements anyway'—with no disrespect to Tommy," said Michael Hill. "'You're the singer, the songwriter, and the focal point. Why change it now?'"

High Noon strongly intimated that the budget for the next album and Warner Bros.'s interest in promoting it would significantly lessen for a solo record, as opposed to a Replacements one. Strictly speaking, the label hadn't actually taken such a position, but High Noon was happy to leave Westerberg with that impression. "I wanted it to be a solo record," he later told *Rolling Stone*, "and the heads of the label didn't."

This drama played out unbeknownst to the rest of the band. Tommy and Daune's daughter, Ruby, had been born in October, and he was enjoying his first months as a father. By this time, direct contact between the band members was almost nonexistent anyway. "Management became go-betweens," said Chris Mars. "We wouldn't even talk to each other."

Finally, Westerberg agreed to hold off on his solo career, albeit grudgingly. The Replacements were still a band, if only in name.

✶ ✶ ✶

C hoosing a producer would not involve the usual mischief this time around. Matt Wallace lobbied for the gig early, visiting Westerberg in Minneapolis. Immediately after *Don't Tell a Soul*, Wallace produced Faith No More's *The Real Thing*, which spawned a top 10 pop hit with "Epic" and sold 1.5 million copies worldwide. Wallace also felt he'd learned how to work with the 'Mats and could make a better record.

To Westerberg, familiarity wasn't an especially good thing; besides, he genuinely liked Wallace and didn't want to throw him back into another tense recording situation. He told Wallace they'd work together another time. (They did: Westerberg tapped him to make his official solo debut, 1993's *14 Songs*.)

One or two other candidates were briefly considered, including X-Pensive Winos drummer Steve Jordan. A musical polymath, Jordan was appealing as he could both produce and play drums. Whatever Westerberg envisioned for the rest of the band, it was clear that Chris Mars's role would be minimal at best.

Jordan was in the midst of producing Soul Asylum's *And the Horse They Rode In On* at New York City's The Electric Lady when Westerberg dropped by the studio. Waiting until Dave Pirner and Dan Murphy were out of the room, he sidled up to Jordan. "So, man," Westerberg said pointedly, "when are you gonna come work with the 'A Team'?" "And I look at this cat, like, you gotta be kidding me, man," laughed Jordan. "That was his way of asking me to produce the Replacements." Westerberg had thrown down the gauntlet, but Jordan never heard from him again.

Scott Litt soon became the clear favorite, a major turnaround for Westerberg. By 1990, in addition to back-to-back platinum R.E.M. records, Litt had also overseen a gold record for the Indigo Girls and polished up Patti Smith's comeback LP *Dream of Life*.

Litt had the added advantage of being close friends with Replacements attorney George Regis and Westerberg confidante Julie Panebianco; both touted him for the job. Hill was supportive of the choice as well—though he groused that the label would now have to shell out six figures for Litt's services, far more than four years earlier.

By his own admission, Litt had never been a big Replacements fan. But he liked the idea of being the one to finally realize their elusive potential. "I saw it as a feather in my cap," said Litt. "I looked at the Replacements as the Rolling Stones to R.E.M.'s Beatles. They'd had a lot of critical acclaim, but they hadn't sold records. I was driven to make a record with them that was going to be successful."

Litt's undeniable pop nous was an attraction. He'd produced "Walking on Sunshine" for Katrina and the Waves, a record Westerberg had always liked. Litt's pedigree also included tutelage under Chic's Nile Rodgers at the Power Station, a connection Paul also viewed as "kinda hip." The major lure, however, was that Westerberg wanted to capture the essence of his home demos. Litt proposed a setup where they would record to analog tape, but use a Macintosh computer, a sequencing program called Performer, and an Akai sampler for the drum parts. They could then cut studio demos that would serve as templates to build finished tracks around. "It was like combining preproduction and production," said Litt. "Paul was excited about that possibility."

Westerberg and Litt would start work alone, and the group would join in later. "But Paul, in a way, orchestrated how much interaction he wanted with the rest of the band," said Litt. "That whole working situation with the Replacements at the time was very, *very* messy."

CHAPTER 56

The recording of the album that would become *All Shook Down* took place at four studios in three cities over two months and involved over a dozen musicians. But the project began rather simply that March, with Westerberg creating sketches of the songs at Platinum Island Studios in New York's Greenwich Village.

Westerberg would start by playing a twelve-string acoustic guitar—and sometimes piano—to drum beats and loops Litt created on his sampler. They worked backward, in a sense: "We wanted to get inside the songs and build them that way," said Litt, "so we didn't want a [live] drummer bashing around."

Notably, this was the first time Westerberg committed his lyrics to paper rather than keeping them in his head. He was listening a lot to singer-songwriter Nanci Griffith and Celtic combo Mike Scott and the Waterboys—hence the folksier melodies. His narratives also reflected the John Updike, O. Henry, and Dorothy Parker he'd been devouring.

The album's key song was also Westerberg's departure point: "Sadly Beautiful," written for Marianne Faithfull, was more direct and delicate than anything he'd done before. "Coming from a female standpoint," said Westerberg, "allowed me to do things that might be harder to write as a man." It was hard to believe that the author of "Gary's Got a Boner" also wrote this lyric: "From the very last time you waved and honked your horn / To a face that turned away pale and worn / Had no chance at all to let you know, you left me sadly, beautiful."

"Merry Go Round" offered a reworking of "Achin' to Be" and once again traced the intertwined lives of Westerberg and his sister Mary ("They ignored me with a smile, you as a child"). Like "Sadly Beautiful," the song featured an "O. Henry ending": concluding the song with a shift in the narrative's perspective, a device Westerberg had come to master.

If Westerberg had largely shied away from writing about the Replacements on the previous album, he couldn't help but let the band's troubles seep into the songs this time. "Someone Take the Wheel" recounted the bus-dismantling episode and the destruction of the group's morale: "Rip out the table, we need room to move / In a life unstable you're so easily amused."

"Happy Town" played on his fear of rehab culture and borrowed liberally from the Dorothy Parker poem "Bohemia"; it also included a warning to his bandmates regarding their post-'Mats careers ("I'm willing to bet you don't last a year").

The songs were filled with similar personal messages. "There are lyrics directed at people who are close to me," admitted Westerberg. What he could not express directly—to the 'Mats, to his wife—he would inevitably put into his work. "If writers had a little more guts, maybe they wouldn't be writers. They wouldn't need to put their feelings in a song."

But "The Last" was a note to self, a Sinatra-style piano ballad summing up Westerberg's confused relationship with the bottle. "It's a drunken man writing about love, who doesn't know love from drinking," he said.

Westerberg spent much of his downtime in a bar next to the studio, and its impact was audible in the performances: his voice was unusually weak, as if his lungs couldn't generate wind, and his enunciation was slurred, overly sibilant. "I was drinking myself into a stupor," he said.

Michael Hill dropped by the sessions frequently and was alarmed by how Westerberg had changed—from feisty and pugnacious to a sad booze-sodden figure. "He would get really morose," said Hill. "He went past giddy, past animated, past mean even, and straight to depressed."

* * *

The more troubling Westerberg's reality, the more quickly he fell head over heels. During the recording of *All Shook Down*, as his marriage unraveled, Westerberg was in love "with at least two other girls . . . one on the West Coast, one on the East."

Donna Ranieri was a bright, beautiful, doe-eyed brunette who'd caught Westerberg's attention at a concert in New York the year before. A Philadelphia native, Ranieri was a photographer who'd worked for *Tim* cover artist Robert Longo before being hired by Warner Bros. She'd recently lost her mother to cancer; her father was fighting the same disease. Her relationship with Westerberg started as friendship ("Nobody was wearing their heart on their sleeve immediately," she said), a union of mutual need: "Like two people in the middle of an ocean holding on to the same life preserver."

Ranieri would photograph the *All Shook Down* sessions. Her camera caught Westerberg at his most unguarded: laying vocals while holding a bottle of Jack Daniels; lost in a narcotic haze atop his hotel room bed. In Ranieri, Westerberg saw a glimmer of better days and perhaps even a chance at a new life together.

When the sessions moved to the West Coast, Westerberg spent time with writer and poet Emily Woods. Raised in Tampa, Woods had moved to Los Angeles after college. She was a redhead who looked a little like Ann-Margret, save for some puffiness in her face, the result of the medicine she took for severe asthma. A dedicated 'Mats fan, she'd traveled all over to see them. "She and I were friends, lovers—but very connected," said Westerberg. "You have that person you don't think about for six months and you get on the phone to call them and you pick up the phone and they're calling you."

Pieces of their conversations, drawn from their drives around LA together, would turn up as lines in *All Shook Down*'s title track. Their relationship was deep, though undefined. "One of the last times I saw her, she'd come to my hotel and some other girl was just leaving my room," recalled Westerberg. "And she said, 'Oh dammit, and I was going to tell you I loved you.' But she got me, and knew things about me that no one else did." Woods would die from an asthma attack in 1995, age twenty-nine.

There were also several women coming in and out of the sessions as well, a rarity for the Replacements' typically boys-only atmosphere. Westerberg had been looking for a female partner for the rocking duet "My Little Problem."

After trying a singer-songwriter from Wisconsin named Loey Nelson ("Paul just chewed her up and spit her out," said Litt) and a stripper who'd been sent to the studio as a bawdy birthday present for Litt by R.E.M. manager Jefferson Holt ("She was a good hang, so she stayed a while," said Litt), they brought on Johnette Napolitano, frontwoman for the Los Angeles rockers Concrete Blonde. Napolitano had moved to London and flew to New York for the session.

"He gave me all this shit about how I was the only woman to be on a Replacements album," said Napolitano. "Like, 'Wow, lucky me!' We knocked it out in the studio, basically. And Paul wanted to do it again, again, again, and I ended up saying, 'I'm going to get some cigarettes.'" Napolitano never came back; after a few hours, Westerberg called her hotel and was told she'd flown back to England.

* * *

It took about a week for word to filter back to Minneapolis: Westerberg wasn't just cutting demos but making an album. "Paul had started recording it without telling anybody," said Chris Mars. "It felt like another sneaky passive-aggressive thing," said Daune Earle.

Tommy Stinson finally got Westerberg on the phone. Paul admitted that he and Litt had called in British session bassist Sara Lee (Gang of Four, the B-52s), but the results hadn't felt right. "I might've pushed my weight and said, 'Dude, fuck that. I'm coming out,'" said Stinson.

Tommy's arrival instantly changed the recording's tenor. Hearing Westerberg's rough version of "Sadly Beautiful," he immediately asked for an upright bass, then played a supple part that gave the song a new melodic and emotional depth. (Westerberg later added dulcimer, with guitarist Dave Schramm overdubbing lachrymose pedal steel.)

Though Stinson was not enamored of Scott Litt's manicured style, he understood and wanted to support Westerberg's new direction. "I liked every one of the songs, even the ones I didn't play on," said Stinson. "What was important was that the songs be represented the right way."

It didn't take long before the Gutter Twins were back in sync, musically and personally. "Whatever crap there was between us and the band, we still ran together really well when it was just the two of us," said Westerberg. "In New York, it was really the first time it was me and Tommy. We had a goddamn blast for a while."

"Paul knew that he needed Tommy as much as Tommy needed him," said Daune Earle. "And maybe some of that was alcoholic codependency."

Ever since Chris Mars had gone AWOL from the Maxwell's gig the previous spring, Westerberg and Stinson had eyed other drummers—in particular, Charley Drayton, the twenty-four-year-old scion of a noted Brooklyn jazz family. A protégé of Steve Jordan and a fellow member of the X-Pensive Winos, Drayton was a multi-instrumentalist who'd done sessions with the Rolling Stones and Iggy Pop and had backed Neil Young during his epochal *Saturday Night Live* performance in the fall of 1989.

Westerberg and Stinson had tried to shanghai Drayton into the 'Mats for months. "If I was in LA at a hotel, I would get a phone call, and all they would want to talk about was how I could join the band," recalled Drayton. "It's beautiful to be sought after like that. But when the phone would ring anywhere from two AM to four AM, I would almost be afraid to answer it."

The *All Shook Down* sessions finally gave them the opportunity to work together. Drayton was fine-tuning his kit when Westerberg's voice boomed over the talkback mic: "Hey, Charley, are ya holdin'?" "That's how the session started off, and it wasn't even noon yet," said Drayton. "Paul and Tommy were toasted, but they were really excited."

They had good reason to be. Drayton quickly cut his parts for a handful of songs, including "Merry Go Round" and "Someone Take the Wheel." With his shotgun snare and rolling swing, Drayton infused the tracks with a swagger the Replacements had been missing for a long time. "I thought, *Jesus, if we had that kind of thing going on, we would be big*," said Stinson. But Drayton politely declined the offer to join the Replacements.

Despite the drummer's rejection, rekindling his relationship with Tommy and developing the new songs got Westerberg enthused about being in a band again. It was decided that he and Stinson would head out to Los Angeles with Scott Litt to finish the record. Mars and Dunlap would join them there.

CHAPTER 57

As soon as the Replacements arrived at Hollywood's Ocean Way Studio in mid-April, the air was thick with tension.

It had never really escaped Mars's attention that before Westerberg came along *he* had been Dogbreath's songwriter. By 1990, "I got a four-track machine, started writing in the basement," said Mars. "I wasn't content anymore in just being a drummer."

As the sessions started, Mars gave Westerberg and Litt a tape of his songs— he wanted them considered for the album. As his later solo career would prove, Mars was a more than competent songwriter, with a cerebral pop touch. But the order of the band had been firmly established for a decade. At a time when Westerberg was looking for more control over the music, not less, the idea was folly. "And quite frankly," said Westerberg, "the label didn't want Tom and Chris singing three songs apiece [on an album]."

If not getting his songs on the album felt like a slight, hearing someone else playing drums on a Replacements record was a slap in Mars's face. Litt had the unenviable task of explaining why they'd used Charley Drayton on some of the New York tracks and would keep programmed beats on several others. "Obviously, there was a lot of history there," said Litt. "I was naive about it. And I didn't mind being naive about it."

Lenny Waronker stopped by Ocean Way early on to hear the new songs. Mars sat in the back of the room, listening to Drayton's playing, tapping his foot angrily and muttering: "I could fucking do that better." Mars knew what this meant: he wasn't so much a Replacement as he was replaceable.

The singer-songwriter-oriented Waronker was impressed: what he was hearing was right up his alley. He felt that the 'Mats' evolution might even result in more commercial success—they "could go further as they grew up." But he wasn't kidding himself either: "My gut feeling was that the band was folding," said Waronker.

The heavy air lifted briefly when Benmont Tench spent a day overdubbing piano and organ, notably on the magisterial ballad "Who Knows." Despite being a bit overwrought musically, that song contained some of Westerberg's better lyrics ("When the fire in his eyes has turned to ashes, and the heat that it gave no longer glows / Who will be the next to dry your lashes . . . maybe one who knows").

As they worked, there was a pall over the session. "We weren't sure what to do," said Stinson. "Chris didn't like us anymore, and it had gotten weird." Though Westerberg and Stinson had been angling to replace Mars for months, they'd done so on the sly. But at Ocean Way, they got careless. One afternoon Mars arrived to find Paul and Tommy happily jamming with roadie Carl Davino, who'd come out to LA. Already on edge, Mars saw Davino sitting behind his kit and blew up. "That's it! I've had it with you fuckers," he shouted, storming out. Mars would return, but the mood had turned permanently sour.

* * *

The Replacements' time in Hollywood was largely split between Ocean Way, the nearby bar Small's, and the infamous Hyatt House Hotel—the "Riot House"—where they flopped.

Westerberg and Stinson were exhibiting stranger behavior than usual. One day while the whole band was in the middle of a take, Paul and Tommy looked at one another, threw their instruments on the ground, and disappeared out the back door of the studio without a word, leaving everyone puzzled. After a few hours, the pair returned completely wasted, wearing orange street cones on their heads, with grease all over their faces, laughing and hugging one another.

Another evening, Paul and Tommy commandeered a taxi near the Hyatt and offered the cabbie $100 to drive to Small's—nearly three miles away—*backwards.* Hurtling down Gower and over to Melrose, the pair was cackling, shouting out the window, as the cab zoomed dangerously past confused drivers and alarmed onlookers.

Such amusements disguised a darker reality. In Hollywood, Westerberg and Stinson had begun smoking speedballs—a combination of heroin and cocaine—to blot out the shattered state of their band and their lives. "You could feel it unraveling," said Stinson. "There was a lot of disappointment. We were at the peak of drugging and drinking, and our personal lives were falling apart because of it in a way. We just took it further."

Occasionally their raw emotions peeked out. The 'Mats had been trying to rent some high-quality guitars for overdubbing. One of the studio techs told them he had an "old mate" who lived nearby with some decent instruments he was willing to loan out. The friend turned out to be British singer-songwriter Terry Reid, whose self-titled 1969 LP had been a staple of Peter Jesperson's late-night listening parties.

When Reid arrived at Ocean Way with his guitars, Westerberg immediately started peppering him with questions. To Reid's surprise, the band blew off the day's session and spent several hours jamming with him. "I told the lads, 'You're bloody nuts, this is costing you two thousand dollars a day!'" said Reid. "But we sat and played for the longest time. I loved that bunch: they were rough, loose, and ready." Westerberg corralled Reid to sing on the album, getting him to hit the vaulting high-note tag on "Someone Take the Wheel."

Later that night, Westerberg and Stinson sat with Reid in the Ocean Way canteen. They prodded him to play the melancholy "May Fly." He grabbed an acoustic guitar, cleared his throat, and began to sing.

As Reid's spine-chilling vibrato filled the room, a wave of nostalgia washed over them. For a moment it was 1980. They were back at Jesperson's apartment, their future in front of them. Then the feeling turned to sadness, because it was 1990, and Paul and Tommy both knew the band's run was coming to a bitter end.

When Reid finished singing, Paul and Tommy were both in tears. "It was unnerving," said Stinson. "At that moment, we died a little death. Then we went on to get completely hammered with him."

★ ★ ★

The 'Mats would encounter another musical hero while in Hollywood. At Ocean Way's front studio, Bob Dylan was doing overdubs for his new album, *Under the Red Sky*. Looking like the Unibomber, he walked the halls in sunglasses and a hooded sweatshirt pulled tight around his head.

On the first day of the session, as the group was setting up, Dylan suddenly materialized on the studio floor. "He just walked in and started talking to the band," recalled engineer Clif Norrell. "He was saying, 'My kid loves you; my son's really into your band.' You could see their eyes light up, and then Dylan goes: 'You're R.E.M., right?'"

Dylan soon figured it out and was eager to engage his fellow North Country natives. One night Dylan, lying on a studio couch, flagged Tommy down: "He started talking to me about Minneapolis, asking questions about the West Bank for, like, forty-five minutes," said Stinson.

A few nights later, at the end of a rough day, with Westerberg's voice a gnarled croak ("He sounded like Lemmy," recalled Stinson), they decided to serenade their studio neighbor with an epically loud rendition of Dylan's "Like a Rolling Stone," which they retitled "Like a Rolling Pin."

The band was playing in a circle, with Westerberg facing them, his back to the studio glass. At the start of the take, a slurring Stinson jokingly called out to Dylan: "Heya, Bob, come on in here and play guit-ar." They began playing a shambling, out-of-tune version of the song, with Westerberg ad-libbing lyrics as he went ("Once upon a time / You threw the 'Mats a dime").

A minute later, Dylan appeared behind the glass. "We see Bob walk in with the hoodie and everything," said Stinson, "and we're looking at Paul like: *Cut it out*." Stinson pulled his finger across his throat, but Paul paid him no mind. Tommy finally gave up. "I led them through the whole thing having no idea he's standing behind me," said Westerberg. "Those guys hung me out to dry. Let me go through the whole damn thing with Bob watching." When he opened the control room door and saw Dylan, "I dropped to my fucking knees: 'God, man, I am *so* sorry!'" recalled Westerberg. "Nah, man," Dylan mumbled. "It was *cool*—it sounded like Hendrix."

It turned out Dylan's kids Jakob and Anna really were Replacements fans, and he brought them down to meet the band. Dylan would routinely return to the 'Mats' studio to hang out. At one point, he reached into their well-stocked mini-fridge to help himself to a beer. "Hey, fucker," shouted Stinson, catching him, "that's two bucks!" Dylan awkwardly fished around in his pockets before Tommy grinned: "I'm kiddin' ya, man."

Once, Westerberg and Dylan were alone and made small talk. Dylan nodded toward the studio floor: "I like the way you're setting it up there," said Dylan—the Replacements recorded live in the round, as he'd done in the midsixties.

"Thanks," replied Westerberg. "The fucked-up thing is, they don't want us to play like this."

Dylan cocked his head: "Who's *they?*"

"You know," said Westerberg, waving a hand in the air, indicating an army of oppressors real and imagined. *"Them."*

All of a sudden, Dylan became animated, almost angry: "Who's 'they'? Who's 'them'? Who are you talking about?" Then he stepped forward and told Westerberg: *"There isn't any 'them.'* You're the artist: you do what you want. No one tells you what to do."

* * *

After about ten days of work at Ocean Way, Stinson and Mars went home. Westerberg was worried that the record had become hopelessly mired and asked Dunlap to stay behind to help with overdubs and vocals.

Dunlap felt Litt was editing too much, flying in pieces from alternate takes rather than getting single solid versions of the songs. One reason for Litt's editing, however, was that Westerberg wasn't in any physical shape to deliver a sustained performance.

Slim was deeply alarmed by Westerberg's state. "You wanted to call mental health facilities and get some advice: 'What should we do here?'" he said. "It was getting scary. You didn't know what was happening. And no one seemed to care."

Westerberg would channel some of his desperation into the recording of the album's title track. "All Shook Down" was a spare, ghostly song built around a loop of Westerberg breathing; its lyrics were a haunting swirl of biography and surreal wordplay. He rolled into the studio early one morning, bleary-eyed and hungover, to cut the vocal. Lying on his back halfway under a piano, he paged through a notebook of snippets, whispering into the microphone:

Tinkertown liquors, emperor's checkers
Some shit on the needle, like your record . . .
The fifth gripping week, an absolute must
"One of the year's best" ain't sayin' much
Throwin' us trunks as we're starting to drown
All . . . shook . . . down

"That song seemed pretty insubstantial until it had that vocal attached to it," said Dunlap. "Then it was like, 'Whoa, man, that's a heavy little moment.'"

Dunlap eventually went back to Minneapolis too—fearing for his friend, but unable to do much. "I just figured, finish the record, rest up, and see how you're doing after that," he said.

By the end of the sessions, Westerberg seemed like a wraith. When Litt brought Los Lobos' Steve Berlin to add woodwinds to the album (he'd play sax on "One Wink at a Time" and "Too Much" and ocarina on the title track), Paul sat silently in the farthest corner of the room. "It felt like he was so unbelievably alone," said Berlin.

The speedballs didn't help. "Heroin is the evilest stuff in the world," said Westerberg. "I can count the times on one hand that I did it, and I still think about it almost every other day. It's the peace that some of us seek." Westerberg thought about buying some more dope and taking it back home, but stopped himself: "I could make the horror of losing myself in that shit brilliant enough in my mind to say no."

Westerberg rallied himself to join Stinson for the final touches at New York's Skyline Studios. A number of songs still needed live drums. At Michael Hill's suggestion, they called in Michael Blair. A classically trained percussionist who'd worked with Tom Waits and Elvis Costello, Blair was versatile and ideally suited for the task. "When a band who has a drummer hires another drummer to come in, one can guess things are a little shaky," said Blair.

After a night drinking with Paul and Tommy, Blair got in the right mindset, channeling the spirit of Charlie Watts on "My Little Problem," serving up Keith Moon–style rolls at the end of "Happy Town," and shading songs like "The Last" with elegant brushwork.

"We got a little jazzed there for a second," said Westerberg of playing with Blair. He and Stinson asked the drummer to join the band. Blair was living in Sweden at the time (his wife was a native of the country), but he agreed to tour with the 'Mats after the album came out.

To fill out "Sadly Beautiful," Litt suggested calling the Velvet Underground's John Cale to play viola. Westerberg figured he was joking, but a couple hours later the imposing Welshman showed up at the studio, instrument in hand. "We couldn't find [Cale] a pillow for his fiddle, so he had to get some beer rag that we had wiped the floor up with the day before, so you kinda see him holding his nose while he's playing it," said Westerberg. "I was absolutely floored watching John play it . . . and having him ask me about the words and saying it reminded him of Nico."

Cale's fellow ex-Velvet Lou Reed stopped by as well; he was thinking of hiring Blair and wanted to hear him work. The notoriously cranky Reed listened to a rough mix of the 'Mats record and raved. "I was like, 'Really?'" recalled Litt. "He loved it. That got me excited."

It was obvious the album wasn't going to be a radio-friendly step up from *Don't Tell a Soul*. Russ Rieger, as usual, wanted to bolster the tracks with more guitars. "But I didn't want to hear big loud guitars," said Westerberg. "I wanted to make an eclectic, spooky little farewell record that wasn't a pretend rock record."

Still, Westerberg worried that the album might be too light, so in Minneapolis he cut an additional rocker at Metro Studios. "Bent Out of Shape" was a diary of desire ("I smell your hair on the clothes I wear / I miss your face") that felt the most like a "classic" 'Mats track. Despite this, Chris Mars did not play on it; instead, Westerberg went to Georgia Satellites drummer Mauro Magellan. Only a couple of the album's tracks (most notably "Attitude") featured all four Replacements playing.

Within the band, *All Shook Down* was the most divisive Replacements album. Mars was not a fan; Dunlap liked the material, but found Litt's production "too zigged and zagged." Stinson, however, loved the record. He played his advance over and over at home with his infant daughter and felt it was arguably the band's best record. "That record was a masterpiece," he said. Masterpiece or not, it was going to be a hard sell. But for once, Westerberg and the Replacements had bigger worries than how well their new album was going to do.

CHAPTER 58

Looking for a cover to match *All Shook Down*'s somber tone, Warner Bros. had Westerberg go through portfolios of art photographers, including Michael Wilson, a Cincinnati native who specialized in moody black-and-white street scenes.

Wilson gave the label a packet of images he'd shot as a student at Northern Kentucky University in the late seventies. One particular photo stood out. During a Sunday in 1979, a bitter winter morning perched between rain and snow, Wilson was tooling around the college town of Newport when he came upon a pair of wet wandering dogs in the middle of the road. Their expressions—at once sad and defiant—caught Wilson's eye as he stopped and clicked.

Westerberg chuckled when he saw the image: "That's the one," he said. The picture seemed a perfect metaphor for him and Tommy. "The dogs look like they've seen it all before and are a little bit disillusioned," noted Westerberg. "They might be stray, they might be lost, but don't go try and pet them, 'cause you'll probably lose an arm."

Like the animals in the photo, Westerberg and Stinson huddled together, trying to figure out what to do next. By this point, they were running the band like a tight conspiracy. After the sessions at Ocean Way, Chris Mars's future in the band was tenuous, at best. Even Slim seemed to be drifting away, tired of the chaos and eager to return to his family. "Honestly, I was ready for things to be over," admitted Dunlap.

When Michael Wilson arrived in the Twin Cities to shoot photos of the band, he was told he would just be taking pictures of Paul and Tommy. "They hadn't told Slim or Chris that there was a photo session going on," recalled Wilson. "We spent the day in St. Paul, going to bars where they thought they wouldn't be recognized or run into anyone they knew."

Wilson couldn't help but notice Westerberg struggling with alcohol. "That was very much a topic. I didn't know his personal history, but he was making a strong effort not to drink—or at least not drink liquor. 'Cause there was lots of beer drinking going on."

For Westerberg, there was no denying it any longer. After a decade of herculean abuse, his body was suddenly rejecting alcohol, his legendary tolerance reduced to nothing. At his peak, he could down a quart and a case, then play a gig. Now he'd be legless after a couple rounds. Following one daytime barhop in Minneapolis, he found himself disoriented and on the verge of a blackout. He called his wife on a pay phone to come pick him up, then passed out on the sidewalk.

By textbook standards, Westerberg had reached the final stage of chronic alcoholism. "I got to the point where I was practically poisoned. All drunks will tell you they reach that point," he said. "Half a beer would knock me on my ass. One half of one beer would make me so drunk I couldn't stand. Suddenly my tolerance was gone. And I could not sober up. I would sip a beer and wouldn't know my middle name. I was damaging my brain."

He confided to Tommy. "I remember him and I sitting down and having drinks when it was all dark and him saying, 'I gotta quit, dude, or my marriage is going to end,'" recalled Stinson. It might've benefited them both to quit right then. But Stinson wasn't ready to change.

Still, Tommy knew he was not far behind his friend in terms of abuse and the damage he was doing to his own young marriage. "We were living the same circumstances," admitted Stinson. "My life didn't get to where his life was until later. But I knew my shit was fucked up and on par with him."

Warner Bros. sales head Charlie Springer, once a serious drinker, had recently gotten clean. "I told Paul I'd stopped drinking," he said. "I wasn't trying to convert him or anything. But I had one of those conversations with him where I said, 'You know, the stuff was just killing me.' He was like, 'Yeah, but what a way to go.'"

Manager Gary Hobbib might've confronted Westerberg about his drinking, but he too was emotionally walled off. "We never talked through his problems," said Hobbib. "I didn't say, 'You're fucked up every day of the week. What's really going on?' We never had that."

By his own design—not to mention his Catholic-Scandinavian-Midwestern repression—Westerberg had become an island. At one point, Slim Dunlap came to him, concerned about his drinking, almost in tears. "Paul is not the kind of person you can confess your fears to, 'cause he would just laugh it off," said Dunlap. "But I was really scared for him."

*　*　*

In his alcoholic fugue state, Westerberg's relationship with Lori Bizer was clearly slipping out of his grasp, compounded by his involvements with others. "I was feeling like there might be a fresh beginning with her," said Westerberg. "And with *her*, and with *her*, and with *her*."

For all the distance that had grown between him and Bizer, he was scared to end the marriage. "I already felt like I'd lost the band. Now am I gonna lose my marriage? Am I gonna lose everything else? The drinking fueled all of the wrong things, whatever dumb choices I made then."

Westerberg began looking to other writers for guidance, devouring the novels of John Updike, especially 1975's *A Month of Sundays*. Westerberg saw himself in the book's protagonist and narrator Tom Marshfield, the exiled minister stuck in an unhappy marriage, ringing up multiple affairs, and dealing with a diminishing faith in his convictions.

That spring Bizer had returned to the world of radio, taking a job as a deejay on the local modern-rock station KJJO. At first she was working late nights—10:00 PM to 2:00 AM—"which was terrible" for their relationship. Even so, Bizer didn't quite perceive how bad things had gotten with Westerberg. "So much flew right over my head," she said.

Whether it was an act of conscience or a calculated attempt to bring things to a head, Westerberg decided to confess his sins to Bizer. "The shit hit the fan at home one day, where, as a fool, I fessed up to a little liaison," he said.

Paul would ultimately reveal not just his romantic indiscretions, but the full extent of his drinking problem, even his flirtations with hard drugs. "I didn't know about the [heroin]. That was one of the things he let slip, which totally disturbed me," said Bizer. "I didn't expect that at all. I felt it was extreme and dangerous. That wasn't why we split up. But it didn't bode well."

At first, Bizer was furious: "Well then, we have to get divorced," she told him. But they made an attempt to reconcile and went into couples counseling.

In therapy, Westerberg was detached, clearly going through the motions, or worse, getting caught in further deceptions. "I discovered he was lying in counseling, which I thought was the worst thing ever. You're obviously not working on it," said Bizer. "My problem was more his attitude about trying to heal, which he wasn't willing to do."

Bizer felt that her husband was lost to her. The couple decided to separate. That summer Westerberg moved back into his parents' house on Garfield Avenue.

* * *

Hal Westerberg had been retired a few years, after a lifetime of service in the auto business. In his golden years, there would be no vacation-home golf dreams in Arizona, or even a chance to take the demonstrator sign off and finally have his own Cadillac. "That's the sad part," said Westerberg. "He got a broken watch and a plaque and ended up with a used Buick."

Looking back, Paul realized Hal's drinking had been a reverse mirror image of his own. His father would struggle through the days at work, come home and take a couple quick belts to steady his nerves, then drink himself to sleep, waking up chipper each morning. Paul would rise in an uncertain mood, drink until he was roaring, and then take the stage. Both had used the bottle as a crutch.

"He got worse, of course," said Paul. "It was only later on, once he retired, that I'd find him on the floor. When you take the job away, the bottle comes out at eleven in the morning. I remember one Father's Day going and picking him off the floor. That was a bad scene."

Now they sat at home, father and son, whiling away the hours. "It had its nice angle at first," said Paul. "It was good for me to get in touch with him again."

They spent warm afternoons together moving between small talk and silence. "He and I used to sit on the back porch, drinking beer, looking at the birds," recalled Paul. "It just became so obvious that this was my destiny—to just sit around and do nothing. He was a great doer of nothing. But that didn't seem like much fun."

All season Westerberg drank and devolved physically, refusing to heed the warning signs. "The guy was on his deathbed, just about," said Gary Hobbib. "Which usually is the case. Something drastic has to happen before you do anything."

Westerberg had also reconnected with his younger sister Mary, hitching rides with her, hanging out and going to shows—anything to distract himself.

Westerberg's moment of clarity came when he found out that Mary had been going to Al-Anon, the support group for families of alcoholics. "That was the catalyst," said Westerberg. "Because I knew she was going just as much for me as she was for my dad. The reality was that my dad was a fall-down drunk . . . and so was I. That's when I decided: *I gotta fix this.*"

In the middle of August, after a long night out on the town—he couldn't even remember where or what—Westerberg stumbled home and in a moment of booze-fueled bravado decided to climb the trellis up to his second-story bedroom. "I got about two rungs up and came crashing down flat on my back." He lay in the cool dirt for a good long while, just thinking.

The next afternoon when he awoke, sore and hungover, Paul Westerberg took a long, deep breath and decided he was going into rehab.

"I grabbed a phone book and looked up the numbers and everything. But I chickened out," he said. "It was a Friday, and I said, 'I'm not gonna have a drink tonight. I'll go tomorrow.' And the next day came and I got scared again. I said, 'Well, I won't have a drink today then either. But if I do have one, then I gotta go to treatment.' Going to treatment scared me so much I stopped drinking.

"I'd known lots of guys—Bob, everybody—who'd come and gone to rehab. I knew it meant sitting around with a bunch of people where everyone's shouting and crying. Let's see if I can buck up and put this shit down by myself. And I did. I could."

It would not be easy. He shook and retched and cursed and feared every day, but he did not drink. In lieu of liquor, he flooded his body with cup after cup of hot tea. He drank so much tea that, in later years, the mere whiff of chamomile would send him into nauseous flashbacks.

A few days of not drinking became a week; a week became a month, then two.

"I don't think he even told me he had stopped," said Hobbib. "If you know his personality, he'd never go out and proclaim that. It was only when I got together with him—I came out to Minneapolis and I met him at a place for tea—that's when I realized."

CHAPTER 59

Walking through the streets of Uptown, Paul Westerberg stopped at some freshly paved sidewalk. The concrete was soft enough to mark. His finger scrawled: REPLACEMENTS, RIP. *All Shook Down* was coming out in just a few weeks, and Westerberg was with a reporter, promoting it.

The record's September release occasioned the music press support: *Rolling Stone, SPIN*, and *Musician* all ran 'Mats features, though after the disappointment of *Don't Tell a Soul* the stories were shorter, the placements less prominent.

The interviews were conducted in Minneapolis. Just a couple of weeks removed from his last drink, Westerberg wasn't quite ready for New York or Los Angeles yet.

Struggling with his newfound sobriety, and still stinging from not being allowed by the label to go solo, Westerberg sounded rueful about the past, pessimistic about the future, unsure of his own desires, and generally miserable. The new-album fanfare read more like a requiem.

At Warner Bros., executives on both coasts had attended solitary, uncomfortable listening sessions. "Paul was there and no one else was," recalled Warner publicist Mary Melia of one such event in New York. "We were all sitting there, and he was by himself at the board. He was looking at me like: 'Why am I here?' It was embarrassing."

Though everyone acted sufficiently gung-ho about the tracks, Warner and Sire had been hoping for a slickly produced, radio-ready redux of *Don't Tell a Soul*. Instead, they got a spare singer-songwriter LP. "I would've much rather seen them do a real band album," said Seymour Stein. "The meetings about the Replacements weren't as exciting," said publicist Bill Bentley. "There wasn't the same feeling for this album."

Even longtime stalwarts like Charlie Springer had lost enthusiasm. "I wasn't as emotionally involved," he said, "because in the end they didn't want that emotion."

* * *

"In my mind, right now, there is no band," Westerberg told *SPIN*. "It got to the point where just flipping through the paper and seeing the word *replacement*, even if it's replacement windows, I would get a tight knot in my stomach. . . . I've always felt that they were dependent on me, and it's just recently that I've realized that I'm dependent on them."

Westerberg had come to realize that it would be easier to make himself into a star than to do the same for the Replacements. He'd been the architect of the band's intractable with-us-or-against-us ethos, but now he viewed his creation as a millstone. "The Replacements do have an attitude of we are what we are and we won't be anything else," he told the fanzine *The Bob*. "I'd like to break out of that attitude."

The reviews of *All Shook Down* had only reinforced his desire to free himself from the group. The LP's only real raves came from *Rolling Stone* and, of all places, *People*. For many, the softer tone of Westerberg's songs and voice undercut the album's impact. Some strident observers took to mocking the group's so-called "adult" direction.

Minneapolis alt-weekly *City Pages*—which had championed the band from their earliest days—delivered the most serious pummeling, from critic Burl Gilyard: "*All Shook Down* is the Replacements' ghostwritten suicide note that should have been slugged *The Cheese Stands Alone*."

* * *

Nearly every Replacements story that fall found Westerberg making pointed barbs about his bandmates, but his most incendiary comments were reserved for *Musician*. Having put the band on its cover the previous year, the magazine had planned only on running a brief front section story on the new album. "But Paul and I got talking, and everything he said was really interesting," recalled editor Bill Flanagan, who expanded it to a six-page Q&A.

In "The Replacements' Little Problem," Westerberg further revealed his conflicted feelings about breaking up the group. "This thing runs deep and dark," he noted of the band. "It's not so easy."

The subject of Chris Mars's drumming came up. Flanagan had privately been critical of Mars's playing after the Beacon Theater show the previous year. Now, in a very public forum with Westerberg, he threw out a loaded question on the topic:

Musician: From the outside it seems like Chris is not as versatile a drummer as the kinds of songs you're writing now require.

Westerberg: Yeah, exactly. Chris is the perfect drummer for the Replacements circa 1985. And it's 1990. There are those songs I know

Chris can smoke on, and then there's other things that, honestly, he doesn't have a clue. That's why on the credits for this album you see four drummers. I mean, we didn't bring in any guitar players. Chris is a great guy, but he doesn't practice, he doesn't rehearse. I don't rehearse playing guitar or singing, but I'm constantly writing so I feel at least that I'm doing what I do all the time. He won't pick up his drumsticks until two days before a tour. We do miss having a funkier drummer on certain things.

Westerberg's scathing assessment was, in fact, a calculated move to shock Mars—to "light a fire under his ass." The term had come from *All Shook Down* session drummer Charley Drayton: "He used to say that him and Steve Jordan had 'lit a fire under Neil Young's white ass' when they played *Saturday Night Live*," recalled Westerberg. "That became me and Tommy's thing: let's light a fire under Chris. All of his time, he was painting and drawing, and that's where his creative energy was going."

Daune Earle had watched as Stinson and Mars's relationship turned particularly cold. "Tommy held a lot of anger that Chris just didn't care. But he was treated like shit, so why should he? He had his art. And Sally pointed out to him: 'What the hell is going on and why are you putting up with it?' Tommy got really angry at Chris for listening to her."

Later in the *Musician* story, Westerberg rejected the notion of actually firing Mars and expanded his criticisms to the rest of the band, including himself. "Slim is no better than Chris and Tommy's no better than Slim. Together when we click is what works," he said, adding: "We've kept Chris around for that many years not to expose *us!*" Despite the attempt to lighten the tone of his criticisms, Westerberg had crossed a line.

Some in the Replacements camp viewed Westerberg's cutting remarks as a by-product of his uneasy sobriety. If he was at times a nasty drunk, he would prove to be an even nastier "dry drunk." The rub was that Mars had quit booze first and hadn't struggled quite as much to get clean. "Chris was the first to lose his appetite for that Budweiser performance," said George Regis. "That's when Westerberg's public shots at him started."

* * *

It had been five months since the Ocean Way sessions, the last time the Replacements had functioned in any way resembling a working band. In September the group returned to Los Angeles to make a video for *All Shook Down*'s first single, "Merry Go Round." With Westerberg's okay, Warner Bros. hired Bob Dylan's twenty-three-year-old son Jesse Dylan, who was just starting to direct.

Filmed on a soundstage in Hollywood, it was a straight performance piece, shot in black and white and later edited to include some colorful conceptual inserts. From the opening moments, with a stone-faced Westerberg staring blankly into the camera, the video felt like a chore, lacking any of the chaotic energy or playful spark that had marked their other clips. Paul and Tommy managed a few smiles, and Slim played along gamely. Chris, miming to Charley Drayton's drum track, was understandably less than enthused.

The one bright moment that month came as the band went into Prince's Paisley Park Studios to record. Warner Bros. wanted to put together a promo EP to send to radio stations. *Don't Buy or Sell, It's Crap* would feature the *All Shook Down* single "When It Began" and a mishmash of album cast-offs and covers, including "Kissin' in Action" and the Dylan nod "Like a Rolling Pin." Short a song, the band decided to cut one of Tommy Stinson's tunes, a spiritual cousin to "Left of the Dial" called "Satellite."

"Satellite" was the final fleeting glimpse of hope for the band's future. Stinson played bass and guitar and sang lead on the track, while Dunlap and Mars added their parts. Westerberg, meanwhile, acted as arranger and producer, helping Stinson flesh out the song's chorus hook, adding backing vocals, and suggesting a couple of embellishments. It was the kind of collaboration that Stinson had long clamored for and that, surprisingly, reenthused and reenergized Westerberg as well.

Though he'd been sounding the 'Mats' death knell for months, Paul was still looking for ways to keep the group going. "I saw the recording of 'Satellite' as possibly being a new beginning for the band," he said. "I really thought maybe we could continue on like this, taking on different roles. It would've been nice to do a Replacements record that way." But, he also admitted, *All Shook Down* would really have to hit big to justify another 'Mats album.

Those chances quickly grew dim. Westerberg had gone on the road with Gary Hobbib stopping at radio stations that fall, pressing the flesh and promoting the single "Merry Go Round," which went into heavy alternative-radio rotation. But the track didn't gain crossover momentum, and the LP got no higher than number sixty-nine, well below *Don't Tell a Soul*'s peak. *All Shook Down* sold barely a third as well as its predecessor.

"Merry Go Round" did reach number one on the alternative chart, but it was an illusory achievement. By the end of 1990, the landscape of rock radio was in major flux. The 'Mats had gotten caught in the slipstream between the demise of the AOR as the dominant format and the rise of alternative radio as a viable commercial entity. "They were stuck in between these worlds—they didn't really have a base," said Sire's Howie Klein.

In contrast to Warner's current crop of fast-rising bands—Faith No More, Jane's Addiction, the Red Hot Chili Peppers—the Replacements of *All Shook Down* were suddenly out of step with the burgeoning trend toward the loud, raw, and rude. The irony was not lost on A&R man Michael Hill: his rock-and-roll "Wild Bunch," once so edgy, were now considered too tame for the alternative world they'd helped create.

"Back in '85, there was a guy who worked at Warner Brothers in artist development," recalled Hill. "I asked what he thought of *Tim*. He said, 'Michael, those are really great songs, but it's just too raw for radio.'"

Fast-forward five years later to the release of *All Shook Down*: "I swear to God, this same guy comes into my office, and I ask him what he thought of that record, and he replied: 'Michael, those are really great songs, but it's just too polished for radio.' That epitomized the Replacements. You couldn't win for losing."

* * *

After a couple of months of drying out, Paul Westerberg was feeling strong enough to consider touring again. Besides, the Replacements hadn't played a concert in over a year, and they all needed the money.

The 'Mats had already agreed to appear at a special First Avenue anniversary gig at the end of December. High Noon and Premiere began booking a national tour to start in January 1991. Westerberg was apprehensive about going onstage straight even for one gig. The idea of white-knuckling through a six-month tour was terrifying. "I'll be more ready than I am now," he admitted that fall, "but I'll still be very scared. I hope I can do it, but I don't guarantee anything."

In November, the band began practicing regularly again. Chris Mars had come in with a renewed commitment. With no other real options, he decided to put the slights of the past year behind him and try to make things work. "I was ready to give it hell," said Mars.

Then Mars got his hands on a copy of *Musician*. Reading Westerberg's words, his ears burned. *He doesn't have a clue. We didn't bring in any guitar players. He doesn't practice, he doesn't rehearse.* "Paul would say stuff when he would be drunk, and I let it slide: 'Oh, that's Paul just being drunk,'" said Mars. "But then things started being said after Paul had been sober for a couple months. And I thought, *Well, this isn't the alcohol, this is* him."

Mars had held his tongue for years, but no more. "It was the first time I stood up and said, 'I'm not gonna take any more of this shit.'"

In mid-November, after a rehearsal, Mars—gripping a rolled-up copy of *Musician*—finally called out Westerberg about the article. Recalled Stinson, "He's like, 'I want you to call Bill Flanagan and I want you to [make] a written apology to me.'" Westerberg, who hated this kind of direct confrontation, hemmed and hawed, then grudgingly agreed: "If that'll make ya feel better," he told Mars. But he soon changed his mind and decided he wasn't going to bother.

The plan to motivate Mars had backfired. "I felt horrible about making him feel bad," said Westerberg. "But I didn't think a public apology was required. We wanted him to have the same enthusiasm as when we started, and it wasn't there, obviously."

Stinson, for his part, was tired of Mars's complaining, sick of his wife Sally's meddling, and bored with his playing. "When he first started spewing, we were already thinking, 'We've got to get rid of this fucker, he's bumming us out, he's a drag,'" said Stinson. He and Paul had gone to see the Go-Gos play at the Orpheum and talked about hiring the band's drummer Gina Shock; failing that, they had session man Michael Blair in their back pocket. They figured Mars wouldn't be hard to replace.

The 'Mats continued to rehearse, or at least tried to, for a couple of weeks. But much as had happened during the Ocean Way sessions, Mars's presence was becoming a black cloud hanging over the band. "We wanted him to quit, because we didn't have the guts to fire him at first," said Stinson.

Finally, Mars forced the issue by effectively giving Westerberg an ultimatum. "If you're not going to write that apology, I just don't see how I can do this anymore," he told him. "I feel really mistreated."

For a long time the others had assumed that any complaint Mars lodged was actually coming from Sally. But by this point Chris had been kicked around long enough. He even called *Musician*'s Bill Flanagan—in England on assignment—and informed him "that if Paul didn't write an apology, he was leaving the band. And he wanted me to know that," said Flanagan.

Finally, said Paul, "we decided to call his threat."

The first week of December, Westerberg, Stinson, and Dunlap took an informal vote: "It was sorta like, 'Chris is threatening to leave; I say we move on without him,'" said Westerberg. "'All in favor? Aye.' 'Aye.' 'Aye.'"

Both Westerberg and Stinson spoke to Mars on the phone and said, point-blank, that they didn't want to play with him anymore. The brotherhood had shattered.

Management quickly made things official: a leaving member agreement was drawn up, freeing Mars of his obligation to the band and also insuring that he would never be permitted to perform under the Replacements moniker. Once the legalities were settled, little else was said. "It was almost like, 'Chris is out, let's not talk about him again,'" said Russ Rieger.

Mars went through a dizzying array of feelings: shock, relief, anger, but most of all, uncertainty. He had devoted his entire adult life to the Replacements. With a pen and paintbrush in hand, he began picking up small illustrating jobs, hoping to eke out a living until he figured out his future. "I'll do whatever I have to do," he told a reporter a couple of weeks after his firing. "It got to the point where, hell, a janitor job sounds more exciting than being in this band."

CHAPTER 60

Paul Westerberg had barely hung up the phone with Chris Mars when he dialed Michael Blair and asked him to tour with the 'Mats. But Blair already had blocked off the first part of 1991 to record with Lou Reed and was forced to decline.

The following day Paul and Tommy adjourned to the CC Club to ponder their options. As the pair sipped Cokes, Stinson pored through his contacts, calling Blondie's Clem Burke, among other candidates, without any luck.

Making his way back and forth to the pay phone, Stinson spied a familiar face across the bar. It was mere chance, but Steve Foley was in the right place at the right time.

Born June 4, 1959, Stephen Brian Foley was the fourth of seven kids in a big boozing Irish-Catholic family from Hopkins, Minnesota—the musically fertile Twin Cities community that had spawned the Suicide Commandos, the Suburbs, and Peter Jesperson.

From earliest childhood, Foley was always banging on tabletops. He got his first drum kit as a teenager and after graduating high school moved to South Minneapolis and fell into the city's late seventies music scene, joining the surf-punks the Overtones.

After a stint in New York with the R&B big band the Neighborhood, Foley returned to Minneapolis. He joined a succession of groups—Things That Fall Down, the Suprees, Routine 11—and was also mentored by Curtiss A, with whom he played off and on for a decade. By 1990, Foley—a handsome, affable figure who wore Buddy Holly horn-rims—was playing in a group called Wheelo and working as a courier driver for DHL. Though he'd seen little success from it, he was a determined musical lifer.

That first Saturday in December, he decided to grab brunch with his bassist brother Kevin and a couple of friends at the Uptown. The place was packed, so they'd ventured over to the CC instead. That's when they ran into the Replacements.

Westerberg didn't know Foley, but Tommy did and began whispering in Paul's ear.

Foley's brother nudged him: "God, Steve, your ears are burnin', man. They keep looking over here."

Foley got up to go to the bathroom and in passing told Westerberg he loved the 'Mats' new CD.

"Really?" said Paul, arching an eyebrow. "Ya wanna join the band?"

Foley thought he was being put on. Westerberg told him: "Tommy's got his black book out, and he's trying to find us a new drummer—you wanna do it?"

"Fuck yeah! Are you kidding?"

They called Slim Dunlap to meet them at the rehearsal space, and Stinson and Westerberg hopped into Foley's van to head downtown and audition him. As he turned the ignition, his stereo happened to be blasting "Bent Out of Shape."

"You're already in!" cackled Stinson.

Foley surprised everyone by playing the songs like he'd known them for years. Stinson loved the tight sound of his snare and the feel of his backbeat: "He had the right groove. He grew up listening to [Stax Records house drummer] Al Jackson Jr. He was very much about that same feel as Steve Jordan or Charley Drayton, the guys we were into then."

Westerberg liked Foley's playing; mostly, he relished the thought of being able to say they'd picked the first guy they saw in the bar to replace Chris Mars.

"So—tomorrow night?" Westerberg asked Foley, whose face flushed. "You wanna rehearse?"

★ ★ ★

Steve Foley's first show was a baptism of fire at First Avenue. Club owner Steve McClellan was celebrating the twentieth anniversary of the venue with a series of year-end concerts, and the 'Mats were slated as special "secret" guests on December 30. By showtime, the club was heaving with bodies.

As soon as the band kicked off the chords to the opener, "IOU," spit, bottles, quarters, and trash began pelting the band, Westerberg especially. The old guard punk scenesters and the younger kids who'd been weaned on the band's legend were letting them have it.

"I see glass still breaks," said Westerberg, surveying a handful of broken bottles littering the stage. He looked haggard, his eyes sunken, his face drawn. It wasn't the first time he'd been onstage sober, but it would be the first time without the crutch of a drink if he needed it.

In the middle of the second song, "Bastards of Young," the crowd doused Westerberg with beer, a cruelly symbolic act. He went back to the drum riser, grabbed a giant water bottle, and proceeded to spray the audience in front. It wasn't a playful moment. "You could feel we'd reached our expiration date by then," said Westerberg. "God forbid that we would not be drunk. And God forbid if we were wearing white shirts instead of plaid shirts. The backlash had begun."

Though he strained to hit the high notes and the band was still working out the kinks ("Two demerits," Westerberg kidded Foley after a flubbed fill), there was still a kind of joy to their performance by the end of the set. After fifteen months' layoff, the Replacements at least felt like a band again.

By the start of 1991, *All Shook Down*'s prospects were nil. Warner Bros. had moved on to a second single, "Someone Take the Wheel," with a halfhearted promotion. The song never got past number fifteen alternative, nor did it gain any crossover momentum.

Promoting the tour, Westerberg seemed resigned to the fact that the album wouldn't be breaking. "The fans who have stuck with us for all these years are the people we're playing for. We're not out there to sell anything to them. We're just going to play and have everybody enjoy themselves. . . . I would say this is definitely our farewell comeback tour."

Bill Sullivan was gone—he'd taken over the road operation for Soul Asylum, just signed to Columbia. "I think Bill hopped in when it was fun and he hopped off when it wasn't," said Westerberg. "I don't blame him. But I was captain of the ship; I had to go down with the fucker."

To keep Westerberg on the straight and narrow, High Noon hired Robert Bennett, a veteran tour manager who had handled a fresh-out-of-rehab John Hiatt and survived tough nuts like Miles Davis. "Tommy Stinson's first words to me were: 'Oh, you're the guy they've sent out to get us to stop drinking,'" recalled Bennett. "I said, 'Not at all—what are you having?' Tommy made it clear he wasn't gonna be slowed down by anybody."

The rest of the crew, handpicked by Bennett, were Hiatt veterans and included soundman Steve Folsom. Early in rehearsals at Paisley Park, said Folsom, "Paul asked me where the guitar channels were on the mixer, and then he just pushed them all the way up as loud as they could possibly go: 'Don't touch those for the rest of the tour.'"

The crew included several holdovers from the 1989 tour, including Carl Davino as production manager, guitar tech Yuek Wong, and merch man Jimmy Velvet. One T-shirt design of Velvet's said it all: an image of a woman leaning against a sign that read WELCOME FUNERAL DIRECTORS and underneath it, THE REPLACEMENTS.

* * *

The "traveling wake," as Westerberg dubbed the tour, began in California. The 'Mats tapped the Seattle power-pop combo the Posies, newly signed to Geffen Records and Premiere Booking, to open the first month of shows.

Led by singer-songwriters Ken Stringfellow and Jon Auer, the pair had grown up witnessing the 'Mats in all the band's glory. "The two shows they did with Young Fresh Fellows at the beginning and end of the *Pleased to Meet Me* tour were mind-blowing, life-changing, the greatest rock shows I've ever seen," said Stringfellow. A couple of years later, the Posies opened for the

Replacements at Vancouver's Commodore Ballroom and Stringfellow made an ill-advised attempt to drink with them that ended with them vomiting in the alley behind the venue: "Slim patted me on the back: 'Don't worry, kid. Someday you'll learn how to drink.'"

The clean and sober Replacements took the stage of Freedom Hall on January 15, 1991. Ironically, the venue—on the campus of UC Davis—had been the scene of some of the Replacements' most debauched, drunken antics. "Good evening, suckers," said Westerberg.

The band blasted through its set with a power that seemed to surprise even them. After the ravages of the past year, Westerberg's voice was finally back, stronger and more commanding than ever.

For the first time the band was working with a proper set list: "I Don't Know" into "I Will Dare" into "Achin' to Be," usually followed by several *All Shook Down* songs before Westerberg ceded the spotlight to Tommy singing "Satellite." The rest of the show mixed "hits," a few ballads (including an "Unsatisfied"/"Sadly Beautiful" mash-up), and a few covers (often T-Rex's "Raw Ramp") near the end, before the final encore.

The second show, at San Francisco's Warfield Theatre, came on the evening the United States launched airstrikes against Iraq, marking the start of the Gulf War. President George Bush was scheduled to address the nation from the Oval Office. As the band sat in their dressing room watching the speech on television, antiwar protests raged outside on Market Street.

The weird vibe spilled into the show. From the back of the room, someone kept shouting for Chris Mars.

"Chris Mars died, I'm sorry to inform you," said Westerberg. "Was he ever living?"

Though they played brilliantly at the Warfield, the crowd was strangely unmoved. Midway through the gig, Stinson chuckled to Foley: "Welcome to your first flop, Steve."

★ ★ ★

By the time the tour reached Southern California, highlighted by a gig at the Palladium in Hollywood, Paul decided to start tending to his fans. "I do remember Paul having more of an aura of a rock star at that point," said Bill Holdship. "I remember seeing him signing autographs, doing stuff that he always seemed to hate in the past."

Finally clear-eyed, Westerberg could accept what had always unnerved him: the intensity of people's connection to his songs. "I used to not be able to deal with some of the fans," he said. "The ones who come up with tears in their eyes, saying, 'You changed my life.' At one time, I didn't want the responsibility. I couldn't even take care of my own life."

After the show, a handful of VIPs were led up into the Palladium's balcony to hang out with the 'Mats. Another writer chum, Chris Morris, walked up to

Westerberg, who was sitting alone. "He looked like all the air had been let out of him—just completely bummed out," said Morris.

Barely two weeks on the road, Westerberg had lost his enthusiasm for the tour. By the time the caravan reached Texas in late January, he was sniping at Foley, struggling to face down rowdy crowds with his new, more delicate songs, forcing himself through the gigs. "It came thundering down on me that, sober, I could face my feeling, which was 'This is not any fucking fun,'" said Westerberg. "It wasn't so much that I needed the alcohol to face the audience; I needed the alcohol to mask the disillusionment."

There were five more months of shows to go.

* * *

At the tour's outset, Tommy had given the impression, publicly at least, that the Replacements would show solidarity with Westerberg. "I'm looking forward to the sober thing," Stinson told *Rolling Stone*. "Hell if I know what or how I'll do it, but if Mötley Crüe and Aerosmith can do it, why not us?"

Dunlap was only too happy to swear off the sauce after years of rough living and started pounding non-alcoholic O'Douls instead. But Stinson was soon boozing full tilt, perhaps more than ever before. "Let's give him the benefit of the doubt: he was drinking for me now as well," said Westerberg, who wouldn't even drink orange juice—if it sat too long it could ferment into alcohol.

Though Paul didn't let on, Tommy's heedlessness did bother him. "He would crack the bottle right before we'd hit the stage, and say, 'We're on.' I'd be thinking, *Well, we're not on until I'm on.*" Stinson enlisted Steve Foley as his new running buddy. "Steve was the new guy, but he was also my pal," said Stinson. "We found ourselves in some pretty goofy situations."

There seemed to be an underlying edge to Stinson's behavior. "Sometimes it felt like he was doing it to jab Paul," said soundman Steve Folsom. "Especially dragging Steve Foley into it—hard. Steve was in over his head trying to party with Tommy."

Downtime between gigs had once been a playground of mischief and excess; now the preshow lulls took on a heavy air. "Paul would stay away from Tommy as far as I remember," said Davino. Inevitably, things turned frosty between Paul and Tommy. In Canada, a drunken crowd member lurched onto the stage. "Hey, dude," drawled Westerberg, "you know how to play the bass?"

It was a joke, but a pointed one—after all, the bass player was the only one Westerberg hadn't replaced.

* * *

The first week of February brought a not entirely triumphant two-night stand at downtown Minneapolis's Orpheum Theatre. In Jon Bream's *Star-Tribune* cover story, Westerberg sounded the usual pessimistic notes about the 'Mats tour and future—and its history. "I don't take a view anymore that this band is special, unique and we're going to change this and that," said Westerberg. "I think I may have fooled myself earlier thinking the band was more important than we actually were. We're just a rock 'n' roll band; we have songs and as long as people want to hear us, we're going to go out and give it a try."

Naturally, Chris Mars's split came up. Mars had played a couple of times with local cover band, Golden Smog, and toyed with the idea of forming a new group with Bob Stinson: the Replaced. It was a nonstarter: Bob, said Mars at the time, was "a little heavy on the sauce these days."

To the *Star-Tribune*, Westerberg claimed that the drummer had left on his own accord. Mars noted that he planned on attending one of the Orpheum gigs: "It'll be kind of fun to see what we look like."

Chris and Sally did come for the first show. He immediately walked to the merch booth, where he scanned the tour T-shirts that now featured Steve Foley as the fourth member. "Look," said Mars, somewhat incredulously, "I'm not on the shirts."

Chris and Sally's seats were ten rows from the stage. It was strange being in the crowd, seeing a decade of his life from the other side. He soon got bored and left. "But then, I got bored onstage when I was playing too," said Mars. "I think we all got bored."

For longtime friends and fans, Mars's absence was a shock they couldn't get over. "Steve Foley was a great dude and a great drummer, but you can't replicate that thing they had with Chris," said local musician turned rock critic Jim Walsh. "It was like seeing your mom go out with someone else." The Magnolias' John Freeman kept thinking: "Is this really the same band I saw at the Walker Art Center?"

Listening to recordings of the shows, it's hard to understand such complaints. The Orpheum gigs were among the best performances of the 1991 tour—arguably the best shows the band had played in Minneapolis in half a decade. But for the true believers, the memories had come to overwhelm reality.

Like Mars, Bob Stinson had also turned up at the Orpheum. He spent much of the show trying to muscle his way onstage, only to be dragged down the aisle by security and kicked out of the venue several times. "All the cops there at the Orpheum knew him—they were on a first-name basis," recalled Stinson's friend Mike Leonard. "They kept letting him back in, but were telling him, 'You can't keep trying to get onstage, Bob.'"

If he had, there wouldn't have been much for him to do. Of the roughly thirty songs the 'Mats performed, only a couple were associated with the elder Stinson. Even the few Twin/Tone-era tunes were essentially solo Westerberg pieces, such as "Within Your Reach." Pockets of the crowd chanted for old punk favorites like "Fuck School"—pleas Westerberg strenuously ignored.

CHAPTER 61

Watching the Replacements every night for a month, the Posies' Ken Stringfellow came away feeling that the danger of their unpredictability was lost, much to the band's detriment. "In 1987 they were the best thing I've ever seen, and that's incontestable. In 1989, I recall the shows being really great. In 1991, the shows were sometimes a little tired. The peaks weren't really coming; neither were the valleys."

"That doesn't ring true to me," said Slim Dunlap. "I thought Paul was a better singer; he certainly remembered the words better."

Even sober, Westerberg felt the need to defend his past drinking and the band's checkered reputation. "You guys wouldn't let it lie," he railed to a reporter for the *Washington Times* that spring. "It was the band without an image, who just so happened to take a drink all the time. . . . To us, it was a stumbling block."

Around the Midwest and South into February and March, the tour played out like a final act of penance. "I wasn't savvy enough to pick up on that at the time, but it seemed like they were making a lot of amends," said Stringfellow. "They would go to Tipitina's in New Orleans, and as soon as they walked into the venue they would start apologizing to people. Like, 'We're really sorry for last time.' Slim had mentioned that he had actually vomited on the statue of Professor Longhair in the entrance."

Still, the band remained partly unrepentant. As always on the road, the 'Mats would be deluged with cassettes from fans and local bands; these ended up in a special box. "They'd dance on the box, jump on it, stomp on it, do all this stuff," recalled tour manager Robert Bennett. "Then they'd start pulling out the tapes and see if any of them still played. And if one of them played, they'd play it as loud as they could."

There were darker behaviors too. For all his attempts at reaching out to his fans, sometimes Westerberg couldn't keep his nastier impulses at bay. "There were the typical stories you heard—some kid coming up and saying, 'I've always loved your music,' and Paul lifting his straw out of his iced tea and blowing it in the kid's face," said Bennett.

Nor was Tommy immune to such petulance. Before a show at George Washington University, a fan gave Stinson a custom bass guitar he'd made for him. "The guy probably built five guitars a year and had built one for his hero," recalled Steve Folsom. "The guy's sitting down front, and Tommy came out and played it during the first song on the show. Then he smashed it and threw it in the guy's lap."

Eventually new drummer Steve Foley became Westerberg's chief target onstage. One night, vamping on "Hey, Good Lookin'," Foley missed a cue for a turnaround.

"Oh, Chris would've got that," muttered Westerberg into the mic.

"This gig does not come with instructions," said Stinson, jumping in to defend his friend. "He's doin' all right."

In Atlanta, Westerberg, feeling that Foley was running out of gas, stepped to the drum riser and started smashing his Les Paul Jr., sending chunks and splinters of guitar flying everywhere. Foley simply bit his tongue each time.

"I was tempted to tell him to fuck off," said Foley. "But I let it go. Being a new guy, it was like, 'What the fuck have I gotten myself into?'"

By the middle of the tour, Foley was feeling overwhelmed. Besides suffering Westerberg's onstage abuse and trying to keep up with Tommy after the shows, he was having a hard time with the 'Mats' deafening stage volume.

"I remember him sitting in a bar one night just saying, 'Is it supposed to sound like paper is tearing when people are talking to me?'" said Bennett. "His drum monitor was so loud, and he was suddenly thrown into a situation where he was destroying himself." Dunlap felt for Foley—though he was also relieved not to be in Westerberg's crosshairs anymore.

★ ★ ★

For much of the tour, Westerberg flew between gigs. After years of flinging himself around, he'd developed chronic, persistent back pain—though it was clear to everyone that he didn't want to be trapped on the bus with the band anymore either.

He'd also met someone. Kim Chapman was a black-haired, green-eyed beauty who resembled a young Elizabeth Taylor. Raised in the South, her parents divorced when she was a kid. After her mother remarried and settled in Texas, she grew up in a combined "Brady Bunch" family. Chapman had studied philosophy and psychology in Dallas at the University of Texas and planned to pursue a law degree. Then, after a bad breakup, she fell hard into the city's wild eighties party culture—a scene fueled by music, dancing, and drugs (coke and ecstasy in particular) at places like the Starck Club.

In 1987 Chapman was popped on a felony possessions charge. She caught a lucky break from a sympathetic judge, receiving deferred probation rather than a life-crippling conviction. She stopped drugs cold; by 1990 the twenty-nine-year-old had decided to pursue acting and art. "I was intent on not letting anything I'd done in those few years mar my future," said Chapman. "I wasn't really dating or doing anything."

Out one night at Trees, a club in Deep Ellum, to see the band Hagfish, her friend nudged her: "Oh my God, that's Paul Westerberg!" He was in town with Gary Hobbib visiting radio stations to promote *All Shook Down*.

Chapman didn't know the Replacements, but she went up and introduced herself. "He told me he was recently separated and had recently gotten sober," she recalled. "We talked about everything—it ran the gamut. It was very little in terms of music or his public persona." Westerberg asked her to join him on his promo tour that night. She refused and left without giving him her number.

A few months later, when the 'Mats passed through Dallas, they hooked up again. He spent the night at her house after the show. The next morning she walked into the kitchen and found Westerberg wearing one of her summer dresses, cooking breakfast. Things quickly grew serious. "It's the only relationship that either one of us had to that point where alcohol or drugs hadn't played a part—which was significant," said Chapman. "We'd both quit the same way—decided, 'I'm changing my life.'"

Chapman was an unrepentant new ager: she meditated every day, attended a progressive Unity church, and generally had a pure, positive light about her. "How did a guy like me end up with someone who's so 'Up with People'?" Westerberg asked her one night.

They talked constantly on the phone, and Westerberg soon began flying her out to gigs. They met in Austin and Cincinnati and frequently, between dates, in Chicago. "If he was in a city for more than a couple days, I'd join him and we'd hang out," she said.

They would share afternoon tea or watch TV downing Caramello bars and Barq's root beer ("We were on a sugar high," she said). Chapman could sense Westerberg's uncomfortable vigilance about his sobriety. He'd scan labels to make sure nothing he ate had even a trace of alcohol. "I wouldn't have a drink because if he kissed me, that was enough for him," she said.

The relationship became an oasis: Kim reinforced Paul's decision to get sober and provided a respite from the band's turgid final days. As he became less optimistic about the 'Mats, he became more open about the other parts of his life and future. "He wasn't sharing who he was becoming with the band," said Chapman. "He felt: 'I gotta keep up that gruff facade.'"

In the Twin Cities, Westerberg was still living at his parents' house or staying in hotels. Between tour legs, he would decamp to Dallas with Chapman instead of going home. "That was probably the best time we ever had," she said. "I know he enjoyed the freedom of just being able to be himself there. That was where we started planning our life together."

After Chapman visited him during a gig in Missouri that spring, Westerberg told her, "I know what I have to do now." When he returned to Minneapolis, he asked Lori Bizer for a divorce.

* * *

It was perversely fitting that the third and final single from *All Shook Down* was "When It Began"—a nostalgic song about the early, happy days of the band. In Los Angeles, the group shot footage for a video that combined live performance with a narrative featuring the 'Mats as Claymation characters. It went to number four on alternative radio that March, then fell out of the top 20—the Replacements' last gasp on the charts.

That winter, *All Shook Down* was nominated for a Grammy Award in the newly established category of Best Alternative Music Album. The 'Mats already had a gig scheduled in Montreal on February 20 and couldn't attend the ceremony at Radio City Music Hall. The band and High Noon soon began hearing rumors that Chris Mars—who'd technically played on the album and received a formal nomination—was attending the ceremony and, if *All Shook Down* won, planned on accepting the award and badmouthing the band on live television. "It could've been Chris spreading the word around Minneapolis just to be antagonistic," said Russ Rieger.

Though Mars and his wife Sally did attend the Grammys, the award was presented as part of the pre-telecast, and Sinead O'Connor ended up taking home the trophy.

* * *

In late March, the Replacements went abroad for the first time in four years, spending a month in Europe and Scandinavia, their longest-ever tour overseas. Few, if any, of the 1,000-plus-capacity rooms and smaller clubs would be filled; some were practically empty.

Most of the European press focused heavily on Westerberg. *Melody Maker*'s feature included a full-page image of him, but no pictures and hardly any mention of the rest of the band. Westerberg would recall a gig in Germany where the promoter came in carrying a poster trumpeting an appearance by "Paul Westerberg" and, in smaller print, "the Replacements." Tommy Stinson tore it in half: "That's fucking it," he said, storming out.

At Den Bosch in the Netherlands on April 12, Westerberg walked off before the encore. "It was a shitty show, the wrong vibe," recalled Stinson. "Things were very depressed." Tommy, bombed, stumbled back onstage by himself, strapped on Westerberg's guitar and began playing a song he'd recently been working on, half-improvising the lyrics. Foley joined in, playing a martial beat as the chorus kicked in: "Friday night is killing me . . . It's killing me again."

Standing there buzzing in the spotlight, Tommy started to believe that he could do this himself—write songs, front a band. He'd spent the last few years clinging to a romantic idea of him and Paul together against the world. It was all he'd known since he was thirteen. He'd never wanted to let it die. But in that moment he finally decided to let go.

Late in the European tour, Warner Bros. forwarded the band some back-logged fan mail. The correspondence included an anonymous letter addressed to Tommy—a nasty diatribe castigating him for his continued drinking. Stinson was pissed at first, but then began to think perhaps he'd been acting callously. "It really hit home," he said.

For the first time in a long while, he and Westerberg sat down and talked.

"Does it bother you that I still like to drink?" Tommy asked him.

"No—fuck no," Paul assured him. "You do your thing. I do mine."

Privately, however, Westerberg was struggling with his addiction. He'd been calling Chapman from all over Europe, leaving worrying messages: "Paul [was] sounding really distressed and said something to the effect of 'needing mental assistance,'" she recalled.

Near the end of the tour in London, the 'Mats set up for a couple of gigs at the Marquee. In town to promote her new film *Mermaids*, Winona Ryder showed up. Afterwards, hanging out with Westerberg at the Central Park Hotel, she noticed scores of empty NyQuil bottles strewn about the room. It was the dry drunk's end-run play: desperate, Westerberg had downed loads of the cold medicine, getting high off the alcohol in it. Afterward, as the nasty blue-green residue covered his mouth, he felt sick and guilty.

A few nights later, during the final European show at the Olympia in Dublin, Michael Hill showed up to see the band. The gig was a riotous affair. "It was their first time over there, and the Irish kids were just going nuts for them, the crowd was just getting loaded and loving it," said Hill. "Here's the ultimate Irish drinking band, in a sense—probably next to the Pogues—and there was Paul in the middle of it, sober and miserable."

★ ★ ★

After they returned to the States, a May–June run through the Southern and Western states was next. Though a late summer Australia-Japan jaunt was discussed, Westerberg shot it down. He was running on empty already; he also wanted to preserve those opportunities for his inevitable solo career.

Tommy, meanwhile, started working up demos of his own songs. He'd gotten positive intimations from Michael Hill and Seymour Stein that Sire might be willing to pick up the solo option in his contract. He'd even started thinking about putting a new band together; Steve Foley was already in.

The band weren't the only ones planning for a post-Replacements future. Unbeknownst to Gary Hobbib, Russ Rieger had begun talking with London Records about becoming the label's president.

By now, the Replacements were crossing out dates on the calendar, grabbing a few final laughs where they could. In Athens, they arrived at the Georgia Theater and found that someone had spray-painted the wall behind the venue:

Paul Westerberg Is God (à la the famous sixties London graffiti: Clapton Is God). Tommy posed for pictures in front of it, kneeling in mock prayer.

In Cincinnati, the band's old pal Dan Baird, who'd quit the Georgia Satellites a few months earlier for a solo career amid a farrago of bad feelings, jumped onstage for "My Little Problem." He nailed Johnette Napolitano's part. "It was as high as I could possibly sing," said Baird. "I think I made Slim and Tommy nearly throw up laughing."

Backstage, Baird sensed a resignation among the 'Mats. "They weren't screaming at each other, they weren't crying. Slim was going, 'I don't know how much longer any of us can carry on with this.'"

★ ★ ★

Earlier in the year, while hanging out in the lobby of New York's Mayflower Hotel, Westerberg almost didn't recognize the man who complimented him on *All Shook Down*—he spoke with a British accent and looked like a disheveled rabbi. Soon Paul was chasing him down: Elvis Costello, then in his hirsute *Mighty Like a Rose* phase.

A few months later, Costello offered the 'Mats a run of summer arena and shed dates opening for him—eight shows in mid-June, from Cleveland's Nautica Stage to New York's Madison Square Garden. Though the Heartbreakers disaster still lingered, there was less risk in Costello's offer—only two weeks, and a hipper crowd. The concerts with Costello were memorable mainly for how unremarkable they were. At Toronto's Kingswood Music Theatre—the site of their last date with Petty—it was hard to know who was more apathetic, the audience or the band.

With the end in sight—the band's calendar was filled only through early July—it was a challenge to muster any enthusiasm. The Madison Square Garden date began with an indignity. "To go to the gig, they brought us in some crappy van," recalled Westerberg. "And they wouldn't let us in. We went to the artist entrance, and it took us twenty minutes to convince security we were the opening act."

Things didn't get lively until the end: in a mini-encore of "Hootenanny," Stinson hollered the title refrain repeatedly while the band sped up and slowed down the groove several times as a goof.

Costello watched from the wings. He could appreciate Westerberg's current situation. Having been the archetypal "angry young man" with a taste for alcohol himself, Costello had moved away from his much-beloved band, the Attractions, after a decade as his creative desires evolved. "There's something about the daredevil nature of certain kinds of groups like the Replacements that can't really be sustained or revived," he said. "You have to move forward."

CHAPTER 62

After being jettisoned by the 'Mats, Peter Jesperson stepped back from the music business for a time. Though he remained a partner in Twin/Tone, he had little to do with the label during the latter half of the eighties. Mostly, Jesperson spent those years numbing himself with drugs and booze. Eventually his money ran out, and so did the drugs, but he continued to drink more viciously than ever.

Much as the pain of being booted out of the 'Mats' inner circle lingered, Jesperson had been hard-pressed to totally avoid the band. By the time of *Don't Tell a Soul*, he'd built back up a tentative friendship with Paul Westerberg. However, he remained estranged from his former "little brother" Tommy Stinson. He simply couldn't shake the image of Stinson's smirking face that day at the Uptown when they'd dumped him. "I held a grudge against Tommy for a long time because of that," said Jesperson.

Jesperson eventually returned to helping advise the Minneapolis groups A Single Love and Bad Thing, then managing Toronto's 13 Engines, led by singer-songwriter John Critchley. The band signed with EMI label SBK Records and would record at Los Angeles's Sound City with producer David Briggs.

While waiting at the airport with Critchley to head to the session, Jesperson began to get the shakes. He lied and told Critchley he was going to the bathroom. Instead, he found a bar in the terminal and quickly downed a beer and several shots. Then the feeling dissipated. "That was the first time I knew that I had a real problem," said Jesperson.

After the 13 Engines sessions, Jesperson crumbled further and became unable to handle dealing with labels and attorneys and business matters. It felt like a replay of the Replacements. Rather than wait to be fired again, he called Critchley and said, "I just can't do this anymore."

Jesperson soon found a new project, the Leatherwoods, led by Kansas-to-Minneapolis transplants and longtime Replacements fans Todd Newman and

Tim O'Reagan. Jesperson made them his "comeback" Twin/Tone signing in 1990.

Jesperson played the band's demos for Westerberg, who was taken with the combination of Newman's songs and O'Reagan's voice. Westerberg (under the pseudonym "Pablo Louserama") wound up playing on the record, *Topeka Oratorio*, and cowriting a couple of songs, including the album's standout, the bubblegum jangler "Jamboree."

By the fall of 1990, Jesperson had become bloated and would wake up shaking worse than ever. In November, he decided to check into a rehab facility in suburban Brooklyn Park. Once he stepped inside and saw the white walls and rows of metal beds—the place was set up like some archaic sanitarium—he decided to leave immediately, but the hospital forced him to stay for the state-mandated seventy-two hours. When he got out, he had the DTs again and headed to the nearest convenience store, shotgunning beers to keep steady.

The first weekend in March 1991, Jesperson's body finally forced him to stop. After a long Saturday night partying with friends and a Sunday spent in a hungover fog, he suffered a seizure at his apartment. He couldn't remember exactly what had happened, but he must have fallen flat on his face, which became purple and swollen. Though he didn't know it yet, he'd come down with an acute case of pancreatitis—his organs had turned toxic from years of abuse.

As his roommate Peter Bystol headed to work that morning, Jesperson asked him to grab a pint of Jim Beam on his way home. Bystol, haunted by Jesperson's appearance, rang up Peter's best friend, Dave Postlethwaite. Together they went over and demanded that he go to the hospital immediately. Jesperson didn't fight.

As they were about to admit him to the Hennepin County Medical Center, Peter suffered a second seizure. The medics strapped him to a gurney, cut off his clothes, and wheeled him into the ER, where he had yet another seizure—his third in under twelve hours.

Jesperson came to eight days later in intensive care. A doctor stood over his bed, staring. "I want to tell you two things," he said. "First, it's a miracle you're alive at all. And second, it's an even bigger miracle that your brain isn't completely damaged after what you've been through."

"I remember thinking: *I am done*," said Jesperson. "*Absolutely done. Whatever I need to do—I am never gonna have another drink as long as I live.*"

As a precaution, Jesperson entered the treatment program at St. Mary's Rehabilitation Center—the same rehab center Bob Stinson had attended years earlier. Jesperson devoted three weeks to getting clean and exploring the reasons for his descent. Chris Mars and Slim Dunlap came by and visited as Jesperson began to take stock of his life.

"One of the things I realized was that there were a whole lot of people in rehab that had it really bad, who didn't have anything to get out for, anything 'to live for.' I wasn't like that. I knew exactly what I was gonna do when I was done with that place."

Upon release, Paul Stark welcomed him back to Twin/Tone full-time. Jesperson set up his own imprint at the company called Medium Cool and began signing new bands again. The label would release albums by the Leatherwoods, Athens's Dashboard Saviors, and singer-songwriter Jack Logan. It would mark the start of a successful return to the music business, and a second act for Jesperson. The Replacements were behind him at last.

CHAPTER 63

By summer, everyone in the Replacements knew it was all over. The last item on the 'Mats' docket was a concert in Chicago—a free July 4 show sponsored and broadcast by radio station WXRT, part of the city-staged "Taste of Chicago" festival, for thousands of sun-baked drunks in Grant Park. By the start of their late afternoon set, the crowd had swelled to nearly 25,000, the biggest audience they'd ever played for.

It was as good a place as any to bring the curtain down. Westerberg dreaded the thought of a big "farewell" concert in Minneapolis. In fact, the 'Mats didn't want any formal announcement or fanfare about their swan song.

About a week earlier, Slim Dunlap had told Peter Jesperson, "We got this thing in Chicago and nothing booked after that. You might want to think about coming." Though he was just a couple months out of treatment and still somewhat fragile, Peter decided to go.

Jesperson, his girlfriend, Uptown Bar booker Maggie Macpherson, and Chrissie Dunlap all flew down to Chicago. Passing the airport newsstand, Jesperson spied the latest issue of *SPIN*. On its cover, crouching in shades and gripping a guitar, was Paul Westerberg. "In Search of the Soul of Rock 'n' Roll" was the story's headline; the magazine had chosen Westerberg as the music's living embodiment. Asked if he envisioned making another record with the Replacements, he was direct: "No. The way I'm thinking right now, no."

Arriving at the band's downtown hotel, the group walked into Slim Dunlap's room as he ironed his stage clothes. He seemed almost chipper. "It was not a dark day for me," said Dunlap.

Paul was holed up with Kim Chapman. She remembered Westerberg feeling antsy, eager for the end. It seemed he had something special planned for the final gig. "He not only wanted to draw a line in the sand, but demarcate it with piss," said Chapman.

* * *

WXRT's Johnny Mars, the victim of the on-air "Little Village" prank four years earlier, introduced the group. "Speaking of institutions . . . our third band and headliner, some people have said belong in one," said the deejay.

The band was greeted with a roar. They looked odd in the daylight—naked somehow. Dunlap and Foley gleamed in their crisp white outfits, while Paul and Tommy wore loud print shirts and looked bedraggled.

Westerberg grabbed the mic. "We've had quite enough out of you, *Marrrs*," he said in mock approbation.

The show would not turn out to be a Viking funeral; it was more a muted bon voyage. The sense of closure was obvious from the opening jangle of "I Will Dare." "Meet me anyplace, anywhere, anytime—I don't care, meet me tonight, if you would dare . . . *one last time*," sang Westerberg.

Most of his ad-libs that day centered on the finality of the occasion. During "Achin to Be," he closed his eyes and cooed: "I been achin' eleven years now." On "Happy Town," he cracked Tommy up by singing: "Who knew . . . First Avenue was bound for Happy Town." Knowing the concert was being broadcast live, Westerberg unleashed a torrent of "fucks" between verses on "Bent Out of Shape."

Despite a strong opening salvo, the show quickly devolved into a sloppy and occasionally perfunctory performance. "Now you can see why we're hanging it up," joked Dunlap after a messy pass at "When It Began." Next up was "Someone Take the Wheel." "Here's another one you don't wanna hear," said Westerberg. "Frankly, neither do I."

As the breakdown for "Talent Show" approached, Westerberg paused. For most of the tour he'd been playing a fast Chuck Berry riff to kick the song back into the chorus. On this day, though, he stepped back and started up a mournful refrain on his Stratocaster. Soon the melody came clear: Stephen Sondheim's "Send in the Clowns."

In the crowd, Peter Jesperson felt a lump in his throat. "That was the moment where I went, 'Wow, this really is it,'" he said. "When Paul played that I went, 'Okay, I get it. This is the end.'" Jesperson clapped hard and fast—a solitary, hopeful sound that had rattled around the Longhorn eleven years earlier now washed away among 25,000 others.

The 'Mats turned out one last perverse coupling of covers: the Only Ones' "Another Girl, Another Planet" and Hank Williams's "Hey, Good Lookin'," with Dunlap on vocals. The set's penultimate song was a momentous "Can't Hardly Wait"; the "'Til it's o-ver" refrain had never sounded quite so cathartic.

During the last half of the gig, Westerberg kept asking stage manager Jeff Ousley and guitar tech Scott Esbeck how long they'd been playing—"Every ten minutes or so," said Ousley. "He had something planned out."

The last time Westerberg asked, Esbeck read his watch incorrectly. He told Paul they'd been playing for seventy minutes; they'd barely played fifty.

With that, Westerberg signaled the closing number. They did their old musical-chairs act, switching instruments for the two-chord shuffle of

"Hootenanny": Paul moved to the drums, Tommy strapped on his guitar, and Slim grabbed the bass, handing Foley his guitar.

"Well, it's a hootenanny!" sang Stinson, "for the fucking last time you'll ever hear it."

Westerberg, cigarette dangling and limbs flying, played double-time as Foley soloed giddily.

"Well, it's a hootenanny!" bellowed Stinson. "Twenty minutes of this!"

Tommy was riffing now on the Sex Pistols' adieu, which Johnny Rotten had capped with: "Ever get the feeling you've been cheated?"

"*Yeah, you were robbed,*" Stinson bellowed at the audience. "*And I was robbed at birth. And I'm stilllllll being robbed!*"

Pounding the kit, Paul motioned Ousley over to the riser, then thrust a drumstick in his face: "Get up here and *play.*" They made an awkward exchange, but Ousley took his place on the stool and managed to keep the beat.

Westerberg then walked to the side stage and directed the other roadies to grab the instruments, one by one. Foley handed his guitar to Esbeck. Slim gave the bass to Jimmy Velvet.

Tommy, in the center, was still going, the only actual Replacement left onstage. From the wings he could hear Westerberg cackling. "There was this look of 'Oh, that bastard,'" said Esbeck.

As the roadies played on, Stinson unstrapped the guitar, set it against the amps, then ran all of its knobs up. Feedback erupted.

Exiting, Tommy slowed and gave a shy little wave on his way to the wings. It might have been the first shy thing he'd ever done onstage.

The "replacement Replacements" jammed for another minute longer. Velvet strutted around the stage, while Esbeck and Ousley tried to keep a groove. The song finally fell apart, as Stinson's guitar continued echoing like a siren.

Backstage, WXRT deejays Frank E. Lee and Tom Marker provided a play-by-play on the air. "What a wild conclusion," said Lee. "The crowd is still hungry out there." For a moment it looked like the band might oblige the audience with an encore. But just as quickly, they disappeared.

After a short while, Lee told the audience, "I believe . . . they're not going to be back."

As Ousley and the others transitioned out of momentary rock stardom, the event's staff accosted them. "We started packing up the gear, and some city officials came running up at me: 'Hey, they're supposed to be onstage for ninety minutes!' I'm going, 'Dude, they're not coming back.' Backstage, all you see is a cloud of dust and the band's bus leaving."

The 'Mats' career had ended with a final middle finger: *one last chance to get it all wrong.*

* * *

Dunlap's first post-Replacements act was to find his wife Chrissie and put her on the coach. "I thought I'd be flying home with Peter and Maggie," she recalled. "But Slim said, 'No, you're coming home with me on the bus.' I was like, 'Really? I'm allowed on the bus?' He said, 'It's the last show—what are they gonna do?'"

Dunlap was once again where he belonged: with his wife, headed back to his kids, no regrets. "I knew I'd never be at that level again," he said. "But I did everything I could do to make that band as good as I could. And then I was done."

Steve Foley climbed aboard the bus with a deep sense of loss. On the ride home he blasted a cassette of *All Shook Down* over and over again. It provided the sad soundtrack as he knocked back endless Heinekens and tried to process what he'd just been through. In the morning, he'd wake up back in his small South Minneapolis apartment and start collecting unemployment. In a way, Foley would spend the rest of his life trying to recover from his seven months as a Replacement.

As Tommy hurried to board the bus, he saw Paul headed toward a waiting limo. "See ya around, huh?" hollered Stinson.

Westerberg looked back. He lingered for a second, thinking of that moment a dozen summers ago when he'd first laid eyes on the little boy playing bass, and of all the years and miles and heartbreak since.

Westerberg nodded. "Yeah, dude . . . see ya around."

Westerberg got into the car with Kim Chapman and headed for the hotel. They spent the night in a suite surrounded by windows with sweeping city views and watched fireworks explode all over Chicago. The next day Westerberg did something unusual: he took in a museum, visited the zoo, and enjoyed the city. His mantra had always been "We're on tour, we're not tourists." The tour was finally over.

Tommy rode back to Minneapolis lost in thought. He had sacrificed more than anyone for the Replacements. He'd given up his adolescence, his relationship with his brother, and much of his sanity. The band—his identity—was gone now.

When he got home, his little daughter Ruby and wife Daune were waiting. "He was lost for a long time, just so super-depressed," she said.

The Silver Eagle pulled away from the Stinsons' house. On the tour bus's destination board, bands proudly displayed their names as a marker of their renown.

On this bus, the sign in the window read simply: NO ONE YOU KNOW.

EPILOGUE

We were pioneers and the pioneers don't get it. Somebody's got to start it and somebody's got to pick it up, and maybe water it down, crank it up, do something to it and make it work. We were five years ahead of our time, we were ten years behind.

PAUL WESTERBERG

Part I

Bob Stinson wasn't exactly devastated about the breakup of the Replacements. "Actually, he couldn't hide his glee," said Slim Dunlap. "It would be hard if you were Bob not to gloat a little. He had no hatred, but you could tell he enjoyed the fact that the band didn't quite pop without him."

But Bob had little opportunity for schadenfreude, as his own life was coming apart. In late 1990, his wife Carleen Krietler took their two-year-old son Joey and filed for divorce. Bob was still prone to periodic mental snaps, sometimes violent—like the incident with Carleen that had landed him in jail in '85. "It was a self-protective impulse on my part with the baby," she said. "I loved Bob, but I couldn't live around the threat of some freak-out incident, worried about him hurting me or hurting the baby. Or killing himself."

Sadly, Bob was doing just that with his increased drinking and drug use. Though he'd managed to play with Static Taxi for the better part of three years, by the summer of '91 the group was collapsing under the weight of Bob's new addiction to heroin.

Throughout 1991 and 1992, Bob's weight fluctuated wildly and his appearance worsened. His family tried to help, but Bob was petrified they would force him into rehab, and ultimately their concern did little to influence his behavior. "He really wouldn't listen to anybody," said Static Taxi's Ray Reigstad. "I look at what he was doing as self-medicating and trying to feel normal. At the time, he was talking a lot, reviewing all the things that had happened to him in his life."

Two decades after their flight from Florida, the specter of Nick Griffin still cast a dark shadow over the Stinson family. "I didn't find out until I was thirteen what a rotten, fucked-up guy he was," said Tommy Stinson. "I didn't want to have anything to do with him once I knew what he'd done to my brother and sister." As she hit her teen years, Tommy's younger sister, Lisa Stinson, became curious about the father she'd never known. Griffin was still living in Florida, and there was some contact between them—a couple of calls and a letter—just prior to his death in 1989. "I was glad when he died," said Tommy, "as you would be for someone horrible as that. It wasn't no skin off my back."

In later years, when the subject of Griffin's abuse would come up, Bob would say he'd forgiven him, that he was unaffected by what had happened in his childhood. "He'd tell you it was no big deal," said Krietler. "It was someplace he didn't want to go."

After thirty years of estrangement, Bob and his sister Lonnie did make an effort to establish a relationship with their birth father, Neil Stinson. A taciturn figure, he had remained a roofer in Mound. Bob would make occasional trips to visit the man who'd rejected him as an infant. "It was tough, because Neil was very pensive and aloof, it was hard to get words out of him," said Carleen. "But he always had a big bear hug for his son. You could see Bob just fill with gratitude when his dad would hug him. It was good for him to have that, finally. But, by then, it wasn't enough to fix everything, you know?"

* * *

Chris Mars had been licking his wounds since being fired from the Replacements at the end of 1990. Collecting unemployment, taking freelance illustrating gigs, and getting his fine art career off the ground, Mars also was making music. He briefly played drums with the Twin Cities cover band Golden Smog, an all-star collective featuring members of Soul Asylum, the Jayhawks, and Run Westy Run.

In the meantime, Mars's wife Sally—now acting as his manager—began shopping demos of his solo material to labels. To their surprise, they found a taker in Smash Records, a subsidiary of the major label Polygram.

Recorded at Paisley Park in Minneapolis, with Mars handling most of the instruments, his debut, *Horseshoes and Handgrenades,* was greeted with pleasantly surprised reviews upon its release in April of '92. There had been little expectation for his post- 'Mats career, and critics were generous, overlooking his limitations as a vocalist and seizing on his knack for shaggy alt-pop hooks instead.

The lyrics on the album read like an open letter to his former mates in the Replacements. "Monkey Sees" was a direct shot at Tommy Stinson, casting him as Paul Westerberg's obedient pet: "Like a bent disciple, carbon clone . . . always within reach, on the keeper's leash." (Asked by a reporter that fall if he'd heard Chris's album, Tommy replied tartly, "Chris *who?*") Tracks like "Ego Maniac" and "Popular Creeps" took aim at Westerberg and Stinson for their cliquishness and mistreatment of Mars and his wife Sally. "Talking bad about us when our backs are turned," sang Mars. "Riding high until the day they get burned / Who's gonna love them when they're unknown?"

Uncharacteristically, Westerberg refrained from blasting back at Mars. "I tried to take the high ground," he said. Still, asked where his relationship with Mars stood, he didn't mince words. "I don't talk to Chris," said Westerberg. "Don't miss him. We don't miss each other."

* * *

Following the Replacements' Grant Park finale, Slim Dunlap was ready to get off the road for good. But an offer to play with Dan Baird of the Georgia Satellites kept him out for a couple more tours in late '91 and early '92. After that, he came home and took a job delivering sandwiches.

Dunlap's old friend Peter Jesperson had been urging him to make a solo record for a couple of decades. "It took him about that long to get the confidence," said Dunlap's wife Chrissie. "He was so used to being the sideman, deferring to Curt [Almsted] and then Paul."

Jesperson signed him to Twin/Tone's Medium Cool imprint, coproducing Dunlap's *The Old New Me*—a loose and lovable Americana LP, a grab bag of Slim songs, stories, and styles. Westerberg guested on the album, and the lyrics were rife with references to Dunlap's 'Mats experience. The wistful "Ballad of the Opening Band" was inspired by the vagaries of the Tom Petty tour: "Now the dream world of every little opening band, it soon gets shattered when the headliner takes command." He would romanticize the alliance between Paul and Tommy on the lilting "Partners in Crime" ("We're on a fast cruise headed to the bottom . . . having one hell of a time"). Dunlap would also fire back at Chris Mars on the cutting Dylan-esque boogie of "Ain't Exactly Good": "I got your new CD and, man, what a cover / As for the rest of it, I wish I hadn't bothered."

Released in 1993, it would be the first of two solo records for Dunlap. (*Times Like These* would follow three years later.) He toured in support of the discs, playing clubs and dives on both coasts, and would spend hours before and after shows regaling fans with tales, sometimes very tall, about the Replacements.

His solo career might've been small stakes compared to what he'd experienced during the 'Mats' height, but Dunlap relished it all. "Every time I get done playing, and I go to settle with the club owner, I ask, 'How much do I owe you?'" he said. "I feel like I have no business being paid, no matter how meager it is. It's too much fun to call that work."

* * *

As the lesser-known Replacements stepped into the spotlight, Paul Westerberg pulled back from the world.

Back in Minneapolis, he broke things off with girlfriend Kim Chapman. "He'd never been on his own," said Chapman. "Never bought his own furniture. Never cooked for himself. So he retreated from the relationship to try that. It was what he needed to do."

Free from booze, the band, and any personal attachments (his divorce from Lori Bizer would also become final), Westerberg sought solitude instead. He rented a little bungalow in South Minneapolis and lived a simple, ascetic existence. "I was alone for the first time ever, and I enjoyed it," he recalled. "I had a piano, a rug, a rocking chair, and a couple good books. I learned how to play saxophone. I started gardening. Soon after that, I began writing and the stuff just poured out."

Producer Matt Wallace had come to Minneapolis and set up a simple home studio for him to use and demo songs. A new positivity emerged in Westerberg's writing—the brooding spirit that had marked the material on *Don't Tell a Soul* and *All Shook Down* lifted. "I finally brought my guitar and equipment up to the first floor," said Westerberg. "I've always recorded and written in the basement. This [was] the first batch of songs that were written actually looking out the window."

Over time, solitary living would lose its appeal and Westerberg would settle into a new significant relationship. "Oddly enough," he said, "I ended up with a girl I had known for a long time."

Laurie Lindeen was the front woman for the Twin/Tone-signed pop-punk trio Zuzu's Petals. She was a Wisconsin native—a dishwater blonde with sparkling eyes and dimpled cheeks—and a self-described "high school over-achiever" who had moved to the Twin Cities to play music and pursue rock-and-roll stardom.

Those plans had been complicated when, at age twenty-four, she was diagnosed with multiple sclerosis—which she discovered after suffering paralysis en route to a Replacements concert. She and Paul had first met when the 'Mats played Madison back in the old days, and they ran into each other again in Minneapolis in 1991 at a Soul Asylum show. The Westerberg she encountered seemed far removed from the hell-raising figure of legend. "He retires around 10 p.m. and wakes up bright and early to either walk or bike," Lindeen would write in her memoir, *Petal Pusher*. "He grocery shops and cooks . . . he meditates and reads. He quit drinking and drugging and yet is still fun."

Lindeen thought it might just be a passing "rock star" fling, but it soon became something more, despite her reservations. "I'm falling in love with you," she told Westerberg, "but, you know, you have a terrible reputation. . . . I can't set myself up like this." Westerberg pointed to his sobriety. "I am living proof that people can change," he said. "I've changed."

"I surrendered," wrote Lindeen. "This might be . . . where I make a deal with the devil, but who cares—there are thousands of girls out there who would love to have such a dilemma."

Their relationship—marked by myriad joys and dilemmas—would last for the next two decades.

* * *

The end of the Replacements left Tommy Stinson bewildered. Back home with his wife Daune and daughter Ruby, he tried to make some sense of the experience, what the last dozen years had meant, but couldn't find easy answers. "Tommy went into a deep funk that neither of us recognized at the time," said Daune. "Not that the band was stable, but there was a certain security to it. When it was over, he drank heavily and just kinda checked out. And then there was problems with us too."

Tommy pondered his options, even briefly considered going back to school to get his GED, before deciding to move forward with a new band for Warner Bros. With Steve Foley on drums, his brother Kevin Foley on bass, and ex-Phones/Figures guitarist Steve Brantseg, Tommy formed Bash & Pop. In the fall of '92, the group headed to Southern California to record an album, with the trusted Tom Petty and Keith Richards collaborator Don Smith producing.

Though it started as a band project—and would feature a roll call of noteworthy guests, including the Heartbreakers' Mike Campbell and Benmont Tench—Stinson ended up cutting most of *Friday Night Is Killing Me* on his own, singing, playing guitar and bass.

An uncredited contributor to the project was Paul Westerberg. After about six months of silence between them following the 'Mats' finale, Paul and Tommy had resumed talking and rekindled their friendship. Westerberg joined him in the studio in LA to add backing vocals to a couple of tracks. Despite vague insinuations in the press, Westerberg had nothing to do with writing the material—though Stinson would allow that his influence was inevitable: "When you hang with someone for so many years, you pick up a lot."

Friday Night would prove the best of the Replacements members' solo records. It's an album without polish or pretense, but full of Stinson's heart, soul, and spirit. "It's just me and my guitar and my guts basically, and you can hear that," said Stinson, who basically learned how to sing during the sessions, even taking vocal lessons to improve. "I don't mind growing up in public. I've been doing it all my life."

By the time the record came out in the spring of 1993, Tommy's marriage to Daune Earle had reached an end. He'd become seriously involved with indie label A&R woman Kelly Spencer and followed her out west. "I moved to LA 'cause I was in love," he said.

"He left for California, left me with a three-year-old. There was a lot of anger and hatred on my part," admitted Earle. "He didn't have a lot to do with Ruby, was kind of in and out of our lives. That affected us, and him, greatly for a long, long time." (Stinson would express regret for leaving his young family—"I hurt people I wish I hadn't," he lamented in 2008—and would do his best to make it up to Earle and his daughter in later years.)

Beyond his new relationship, Stinson's move to LA was also motivated by concerns for his career, a desire to place himself in view of Burbank-based Warner Bros. "I wanted to be closer to the record company—to keep an eye on them," he said. "It didn't really help."

The album's singles "Loose Ends" and "Never Aim to Please" struggled on radio, and the record quickly slipped from the buzz bin to the cutout bin. "It was partially the label, and partially the timing," said Stinson. "I made a real rock-and-roll-y record, and it wasn't the time for that. Grunge was exploding."

* * *

While Tommy labored over his album and Westerberg tended to his garden, Nirvana had conquered the world. The Seattle band, led by singer-songwriter Kurt Cobain, had released its major-label debut for Geffen in the fall of 1991, just a few months after the Replacements called it quits. The 'Mats' biggest album had sold 300,000 copies total. By early 1992, *Nevermind* was selling 300,000 copies *a week*. In a blink, Nirvana had minted grunge as a genre, launched alt-rock into the commercial mainstream, and effected a sea change in popular music.

Pundits would suggest Nirvana had picked up the proverbial torch that the Replacements had fumbled away. "Cobain sings and writes about romantic complexities and youthful apathy with much of the intensity and insight of . . . Paul Westerberg," wrote Robert Hilburn of the *Los Angeles Times*. "Cobain, indeed, could be the Paul Westerberg of the '90s." But Westerberg thought they had little in common: "I guess I wore a plaid shirt, and yes, I played real loud," he said, "but Nirvana sounds to me like Boston with a hair up its ass."

Cobain and Westerberg would cross paths just once, in late 1992, in San Francisco. Westerberg was in town recording, Cobain was there producing an album for the Melvins, and they were both staying at the Triton Hotel. One evening they rode up an elevator together in awkward silence, exited on the same floor, walked to neighboring rooms, then shut their doors without acknowledging one another.

Days later, Westerberg would dash out a song called "World Class Fad" ("You wax poetic about things pathetic, as long as you look so cute / Don't be sad, you're a world class fad") that many, including Cobain, interpreted as a diss. "I never respected Kurt Cobain enough to write something about him," said Westerberg. "Maybe he felt he was a world class fad."

Ultimately, if indirectly, Westerberg would benefit from the success of Nirvana when he was asked to contribute to the soundtrack of director Cameron Crowe's *Singles*, a grunge-centric rom-com set in Seattle. Westerberg had been in Warner Bros. president Lenny Waronker's office playing him some new demos, including a song called "Dyslexic Heart." Waronker thought the tune had potential for Crowe's Warners-distributed movie and quickly got on the phone with his film people. "Lenny told them, 'I got a song here that's hit-ish'—that was his term, 'hit-*ish*,'" chuckled Westerberg. "I think that's Yiddish for shit."

With Scott Litt producing, Westerberg cut "Dyslexic Heart" and "Waiting for Somebody"—tracks that would anchor the otherwise exclusively Seattle-oriented *Singles* soundtrack. Crowe also asked Westerberg to score the picture; he spent a couple of weeks at a studio in LA screening the film and composing a selection of instrumentals for it.

Released in the summer of 1992, *Singles* was a modest success at the box office (earning $18 million on a budget roughly half that). But the soundtrack was a monster. Riding the grunge explosion, it sold over 2 million copies. Westerberg—whose "Dyslexic Heart" became a number-four hit on the alternative chart—earned his first and only platinum album. "I didn't feel one bit of pride over that," he said, noting that "there's ten [other] bands on the thing."

* * *

A twenty-one-year-old native of Edina, Minnesota, Mike Leonard was the guitarist and front man for a fledgling Twin Cities band called the Bleeding Hearts. "We were admittedly influenced by the Replacements," said Leonard. "So I figured, why not get Bob Stinson to play guitar?" Stinson and Leonard had become friendly hanging out, drinking at the Uptown Bar. They'd jammed a bit around 1991, but Bob had begged off the project and recommended another guitarist. The following year, with Static Taxi over and his reputation in local circles further damaged, Stinson was eager for an opportunity to play with the band.

Leonard invited Stinson to join the Bleeding Hearts and come live with him. "The only way I'd be able to keep him in check, and keep some of the unseemlier people away, was if he moved in with me," said Leonard. "He still had problems with substances, for sure, but he was happy to be in the band and playing around again."

In the fall of 1992—just as the Bleeding Hearts were prepping their first album for California-based indie Fiasco Records—Bob's health took a strange, nearly grave turn. At the end of October, he'd been complaining to his mother about an extremely painful toothache. He went into Hennepin County Medical Center for what he figured might be an abscess but turned out to be a severe bacterial infection.

The staff, noting the track marks on his arms, thought he might have AIDS or hepatitis. He was held overnight for tests, but the bacteria quickly spread to his head, neck, and, critically, his brain. "He had a golf ball–size swelling protruding from both temples," recalled Carleen Krietler. "His neck was like a funnel cloud shape." Bob was rushed into surgery to relieve the pressure and was told that the swelling had to go down within forty-eight hours or he would die.

After a difficult waiting period, the infection finally began to clear. Bob spent ten days in the hospital recuperating.

"Bob shouldn't have lived through that," said his sister Lonnie. "I remember thinking, *Well, maybe this will be the thing that changes him.*" But even the near-death experience didn't curb his habits. "Pretty soon," said Ray Reigstad, "he slid back with the beer and coke and then the heroin again."

★ ★ ★

R euniting with producer Matt Wallace, Paul Westerberg began work on his solo debut in the fall of '92. Despite his relief at being free of the Replacements, the record mostly found Westerberg in search of a band. He cut with various combinations of musicians—including members of the Georgia Satellites and Wire Train, Ian McLagan from the Faces, even Alex Chilton—as the project carried on in fits and starts for four months at studios in New York, San Francisco, Los Angeles, and Minneapolis.

Released in the summer of 1993, the resulting disc, *14 Songs*—named in homage to J. D. Salinger's *Nine Stories*—saw Warner Bros. create an elaborate promotional campaign and fund a high-dollar video for the eventual first single, "World Class Fad" (directed by future *Superman* helmer Zack Snyder). "They dumped a lot of money into the setup of that record," said Westerberg manager Gary Hobbib.

Industry confidence in Westerberg was high, and he also signed a lucrative publishing pact with Warner-Chappell, reportedly worth seven figures. "I was a millionaire for one whole day," he said, "and then came the manager, the taxman, and I bought a house. The money was gone in an afternoon, literally."

To promote *14 Songs*, Westerberg would put together a solo band (his "paid companions," as he called them): Boston-based guitarist Dave Minehan of the Neighborhoods and Raindogs/Red Rockers bassist Darren Hill. On drums was twenty-year-old Josh Freese, a member of the SoCal pop punks the Vandals and a Replacements die-hard who'd played on a couple of *14 Songs* tracks.

For once, Westerberg was determined to play the shows straight and serious. The '93 tour was his most focused and consistent ever. "I definitely felt like I owed it to people," he said. "For every time I'd gone out there before and sucked, this time I was going out there with a band that knows the songs . . . [they're] gonna get them as best as I can play them."

Though he'd been offered opening spots with U2 and Peter Gabriel, Westerberg started out headlining a US club and college tour instead. It was a strategic underplay, to sell out the shows and build a buzz, with plans to jump to theaters on the next leg as "World Class Fad" rose up the charts. The problem was that it never really did. While the song did spend a couple of months in rotation on alternative radio, peaking at number four, and *14 Songs* managed to get up to number forty-four on the album charts, neither developed real legs. "Once again, I was curiously disappointed that it didn't fly," said Westerberg. "But at that point, who could I blame but myself?"

Taping an appearance on MTV's flagship alternative music show *120 Minutes*, Westerberg played just one of several planned songs, said he was going out for a pack of smokes, and then didn't return. Gary Hobbib found him several hours later back at his hotel room, looking deeply distressed. "I think I'd been in the closet praying," said Westerberg. "I definitely had some sort of breakdown there, like a severe anxiety attack or something."

Although he'd stopped drinking, Westerberg had not dealt with his alcoholism or depression issues. Back on the road, he was white-knuckling his way through his promotional obligations, through concerts, through his life. "He's not drinking. He's trying to behave in a new relationship. And at the end of the day he was all alone," said Hobbib. "There was no Tommy anymore. He didn't have Tommy to bounce his discontent off of. Now it's all on him, and it started to eat him up."

With *14 Songs* increasingly looking like a bust—it would cap out at 150,000 copies sold—Westerberg began searching for scapegoats and seized on Hobbib. After eight years together, the relationship was growing stale and becoming strained.

On the road, Westerberg was being seen to by Warner Bros. artist relations rep Larry White. He began asking White about other managers. White knew Lindy Goetz, a former musician and MCA promo man, who'd gone on to success managing the career of the multi-platinum Warners act the Red Hot Chili Peppers. Goetz was halfway toward retiring, but said he'd take on Westerberg if White quit the label and joined his firm as part of the package.

In mid-August, Westerberg decided to make a change and go with Goetz and White. The following day he rang up Hobbib and fired him. "That call was actually more of an intimate moment than any other we had," said Hobbib, "where we kinda got into expressing some feelings for each other."

White would take over day-to-day management of what was proving to be an increasingly fraying situation with Westerberg on tour. In Columbia, Missouri, Westerberg played to barely 150 people in the 1,800-capacity Jesse Auditorium. In the middle of the set, he went down on the ground, singing flat on his back. The band thought he was fooling around until bassist Darren Hill walked by and Westerberg grabbed his ankle and began groaning for help. The show was halted, and Westerberg, who'd thrown his back out severely, was carried off by the band to the dressing room. "It was like the moment in Spinal Tap when Nigel Tufnel can't get off the floor and the roadies come out to pick him up," recalled Josh Freese.

Westerberg was insisting on scrapping the remaining dates on the tour—though everyone knew that would be the death knell for Warner Bros.'s promotion of the record. "I'm not saying the back injury was psychosomatic, but his mental state played a part," said White. "He definitely wanted that tour canceled." (White soon became another casualty himself—fired after just a few months, as his relationship with Westerberg quickly soured.)

Westerberg did return to the road begrudgingly in December to play out a few remaining obligations, including an appearance on *Saturday Night Live*.

During rehearsals, A&R man Michael Hill told Westerberg's band members to keep quiet about the fact that he'd been in the Replacements; no one wanted to risk *SNL* producer Lorne Michaels's wrath if he realized Paul's involvement with the 'Mats' '86 fiasco.

The show, hosted by actor Charlton Heston, was relatively uneventful as Westerberg did "Knockin on Mine" and a version of the Replacements' "Can't Hardly Wait" with a full horn section. After the credits had rolled, a stern-looking Michaels made a beeline for Westerberg, who held his breath. "But Lorne was nice to me," said Westerberg. "I told him, 'See, I didn't break anything, I didn't swear.' And he patted me on the shoulder and said, 'You grew up, you learned.' I guess I did. But it sure wasn't as much fun as the first time."

★ ★ ★

Given the indifference to Bash & Pop's debut, keeping a band together proved a challenge. Tommy Stinson's main partner in the project, Steve Foley, decided to leave. Soon after, Tommy asked for a release from his Warner Bros. contract.

Before Stinson could put together a new lineup or look for a new record deal, however, financial reality intervened. "I was fucking dead broke," said Tommy, whose girlfriend Kelly Spencer had been supporting him for months. "I was in arrears for child support." Aside from his one-day stint as a dishwasher during high school, his only job had been playing in a rock-and-roll band. Now, at twenty-seven, he had "no other options" but to look for work.

Reading the back page of the *LA Weekly*, he spotted an ad for a telemarketing job. It paid seven bucks an hour and didn't require any of the things he was lacking: experience or a high school diploma. With no car—he still hadn't learned to drive—Stinson would rise at dawn and catch a series of buses across town to his new job: selling printer toner over the phone.

Though he'd sworn himself to rock-and-roll as a kid, Tommy's greatest triumph wouldn't come playing onstage or in a studio, but rather in a drab cubicle making cold calls to sell office supplies. "In the process, I learned how to sell myself. And I got out of the Replacements mind-set—that self-sabotage, self-defeating shit," he said. "I got to a point where I got more confident as a person. What I found out was that people are attracted to confidence, rather than guys who are sitting with a tear in their beer all bummed out. That's when I finally fuckin' grew up."

Part II

To those outside of the Twin Cities, Bob Stinson had become a mystery. After being booted from the Replacements in 1986, he'd all but vanished as far as the rock public was concerned. There would be the occasional mention of his activities in 'Mats articles—that he was playing with some local group or that he'd started a family—but few knew where life had really taken him in the seven years since leaving the band.

Charles Aaron was a thirty-year-old writer from North Carolina, working freelance for *SPIN* magazine in New York City. He'd been a Replacements fan in college, seen the band play with Bob, and wondered what had become of him. In early 1993, Aaron's editor at *SPIN* encouraged him to go to Minneapolis, find out, and come back with the story.

A hungry but still relatively inexperienced reporter, Aaron took on the task. Through some Minneapolis contacts, he got Bob's number and rang him up with a pitch for the piece. Stinson was playing with the Bleeding Hearts, and the band was readying its debut LP, so a story in *SPIN* was a major opportunity. On the phone at least, Bob seemed relatively together. "People think, 'Oh, you found the guy, the saddest man in music, and hopped a plane to go suck his blood,'" said Aaron. "But honestly, I had no idea. I talked to him and he sounded like good old goofy Bob."

When Aaron arrived, it was clear that this would not be a redemption story. Stinson had aged dramatically, clearly abusing himself with drugs and alcohol, and his mental state was confused. "It was really kind of overwhelming to meet Bob," said Aaron. "He was one of those force-of-nature people that no matter how much he was weakened or not thinking clearly, he swept you up in this bear hug of activity, stage-managing everything, and being honest in a disarming way."

Aaron would drink and hang out with Stinson all around Minneapolis. He would talk to Bob's old friends like Terry Katzman and Chris Mars and his ex-wife Carleen Krietler. The article would tell the story of Bob's firing from the Replacements and his subsequent travails, including his son Joey Stinson's medical condition and his own issues with addiction. What came out was a bleak picture that still only hinted at the entire truth:

[Stinson] is offhandedly brutal about his risks and disappointments. "You know, I'd really like to meet myself sometime. I'd probably beat the shit out of myself for letting opportunities go by," he says, adding, "I guess you could say I'm never pleased, or in Paul's words, I'm unsatisfied." More problematically, he rambles on about his life's almost-clownish misery. "It's like trying to commit suicide. The bigger the gun, the less likely you are to make it happen. I mean, I put a gun to my head, but I'm still alive. I don't have a problem with that."

"If I walked into that situation now, I wouldn't continue with the story," said Aaron. "I would've said, this person needs some help. The last thing he needs is somebody writing a magazine story about how much trouble his life has been. But at the time I didn't know any better, and I just kept going with it."

Aaron witnessed a reunion between Bob and Tommy Stinson and their mother Anita as the Bleeding Hearts opened for Bash & Pop at the 7th St Entry. "Playing that show and having me there I guess must have brought up a lot of stuff," said Aaron. "He was trying to figure out his place in the world, and in music, and even in his family."

"He started opening up about all of the regrets about his whole life. He said stuff about his [childhood] that I didn't even feel comfortable printing. He was trying to make sense of a situation that there was no sense to it. And there was a lot of reminiscing about the Replacements. He had never gotten over leaving the band."

After a week in Minneapolis, Aaron was drained, ready to go home. "I felt like this is one of the saddest experiences I've ever had. But I really admired the guy; he was such a completely original figure."

Before Aaron left, he and Stinson were trooping around a frozen Lake Harriet.

"Have you ever done heroin?" Bob asked him suddenly. "Ever use a needle?" Aaron shook his head no. "You can really get some good, cheap stuff around here. I don't really do it, but if you wanted to, we could get some and do it, you know, later, if you wanted." The exchange ended up as part of the disturbing conclusion to Aaron's published piece.

"The moment where he asked me about doing drugs, the tragic thing is that he trusted me," said Aaron. "We were hanging out, becoming buddies a little bit. He wanted to share what, at that point, his life was. As I wrote more features I learned that's the stuff that you really don't put in. But that's the part that people still remember."

When the *SPIN* story, titled "Hold My Life," finally hit newsstands in June 1993, its 3,500 words weren't as shocking as the photos of Stinson that accompanied the piece. The extreme close-up image of his face that opened the spread showed a man who appeared twenty years older than he was, with a lost, unsettled look in his eye. "I had no idea that photo was gonna be the way it was," said Aaron. "That was horrifying to me. I was furious and completely melted down about it. But it's like, who am I to blame anybody for anything? What I did was just as bad."

Slim Dunlap would remember Bob privately feeling "devastated and betrayed" by Aaron's piece. Chris Mars felt the article was "a bunch of bullshit. Bob is the kind of guy who wears his heart on his sleeve. He'll just blurt out anything, ya know?" said Mars. But Stinson never disputed the quotes or contents of the story: "It's all true," he told the *Pioneer Press.*

In the aftermath of the piece, the Bleeding Hearts finished their record, but Bob's relationship with Mike Leonard became strained by his drug use. Bob eventually moved out of their apartment. "It got harder to keep track of him and get him to practice," recalled Leonard.

In the end, Bob was fired from the Bleeding Hearts too. "We opened for the Magnolias at the Entry, and he collected the money and took off," said

Leonard. "It was such a minor thing, a few bucks, but for whatever reason that was the final straw." The band would play the CMJ Music Festival that fall with Magnolias' guitarist John Freeman standing in for Stinson. Caught up in label limbo and then legal tussles, the Bleeding Hearts album with Bob would never be released.

* * *

Without a band to ground him, without music to tether him to the world, Stinson became even more lost. He would spend the last year-plus of his life drifting between homes and friends, old habits and new hopes—and evincing deeper symptoms of mental illness.

By early 1994, even Bob acknowledged he needed help. His mood swings were more extreme, his thinking had become disconnected and delusional. He'd become fixated on Kurt Cobain. He saw himself and the Nirvana front man as kindred spirits somehow. Cobain would commit suicide that spring.

In June, Bob finally checked himself into the Hennepin County Medical Center. He'd been there before and met with a psychiatrist, who somewhat cursorily diagnosed him as bipolar. For the first time in his life, Stinson began taking prescription medications for his condition.

Bob was also spending time with a couple he'd met, Ed and Lori Hoover, and eventually moved into their basement. One night Ed Hoover rented *Mr. Jones*, the 1992 Richard Gere film about a man battling bipolar depression. Bob watched, nodding along in recognition. "He kept saying, 'Yup, yup. That's what it's like. That's what I'm like,'" recalled Hoover. "He'd say, 'I've been like this my whole life.'" Despite recognizing his problems, Stinson would only take his prescriptions for a while, then give up and return to self-medicating with alcohol and drugs.

As the months wore on his old friends began to get a sad premonition of his fate. In late '94, Paul Westerberg ran into Bob on the street. "I was returning a video and he was on his way to the liquor store, and we stopped and talked for a second," recalled Westerberg. "He sorta gave me that look like, 'You wanna come? Gonna go get some beer, go back and get high, up in this girl's apartment.' I hesitated for a millisecond. Almost like, 'Sure, I'll do it.' Then I said, 'No, I guess I'll go back home.' It was so sad then. He was the kind of guy, you knew it was coming. We all knew it was coming."

In January of 1995, Bob moved out of the Hoovers' basement. Floating between friends' couches, he soon found a new girlfriend, a woman known around town as Anna Nimmity. Bob took up residence in her apartment at 815 West Lake Street.

Claiming he'd fallen in love, Bob decided to dry out and straighten up. He seemed to be on the relative straight and narrow ("Drinking beer—and nothing else," said Carleen Krietler) as February arrived. Slim Dunlap remembered encountering Bob carrying a bag of vitamins, saying he was going to lose weight and get healthy. "He was desperately trying to find health, because he didn't feel good," said Dunlap. "But when you abuse yourself for so long, there's no instantaneous way to go back to zero and start all over."

Whatever stability Bob found with his new girlfriend was short-lived. By mid-February, his mental issues had once again become acute. The final week of his life was a familiar replay of previous breakdowns—of his teenage troubles and the dark days before being dismissed by the Replacements.

Starting on February 9, Bob became violent toward his girlfriend, who was threatening to leave. A couple of days later he overdosed on sleeping pills and ended up at the Hennepin County Medical Center. After getting out, he began drinking again and threatened suicide with a knife during a delusional episode. On Monday, February 13, after another incident, Stinson was charged with a fifth-degree domestic assault against his girlfriend. He was booked on the misdemeanor and then released.

On Wednesday, February 15, after all the drama had faded somewhat, Bob walked down to his ex-wife Carleen's place. He wanted to see his son Joey. Carleen remembered that he didn't look well. "His skin was jaundiced. He was having dizzy spells," she said. "He couldn't maintain his body temperature—hot flashes, then cold flashes. It was scary."

Carleen offered to drop him off at the Hennepin County Medical Center, so he could check in with his doctors. But Bob didn't want to go. He told Carleen he was going to ask his girlfriend, Anna, to marry him. "We talked about Anna. We talked about our marriage and how not to repeat the same mistakes with her," she said. "We talked about his recovery, life, his goals and plans. We talked about Joey."

That afternoon Bob paid a visit to his mother Anita at the Uptown Bar. "He was in to see me at work. He told me about his psychiatrist he'd been seeing. He said, 'I'm really gonna work on it this time, Ma.' And I said, 'Good for you, Bobby.' Then he walked out the door. That's the last time I saw him."

On Thursday, Bob headed over to the Twin/Tone Records office on Nicollet. He wanted to get an advance on his next Replacements royalty check. Peter Jesperson was out of the office, but another employee gave him some cash, and he went on his way.

Bob ended up back at home in the Lake Street apartment that evening. Sometime in the night he put on a favorite old Yes record. He lay on the couch, listening blissfully to a Steve Howe solo, and then fell sleep.

On Saturday evening, Anna Nimmity passed the apartment and noticed that the same lights had been on for a couple of days. She decided to check in on Bob.

A little while later, Anita Stinson was home crocheting when the phone rang. "Anita, this is Anna," said a voice on the other end of the line. "I just came from Bobby's. I think he's dead."

Anita was in shock: "Can you imagine getting a call like that?" she said. Unsure what to do, she waited for her husband Tom Kurth to get home. She eventually called the local police precinct and asked them if they had any news on her son. They would only confirm that there had been an emergency call at the Lake Street address where Bob was staying. She waited and then finally rang the city morgue. They told her Bob's body was there, that he'd been identified by his fingerprints—on file from one of his arrests. Anita went down to confirm it herself. "Until I saw him, I really didn't believe it," she said. In her panic, Anita had called Lonnie Stinson, paging her at a nightclub where she was out dancing with friends. "I came and got the call and I lost it," said Lonnie. "Just screaming and screaming. I couldn't believe it."

Then Anita dialed up Tommy in California and told him what had happened. Despite the presence of a syringe on a table near Bob's body, Tommy refused to believe his brother's death was an overdose—unintentional or not. "My mom told me Bob had sobered up, 'cause he wanted to get his life together," said Tommy. "He didn't OD."

The autopsy would ultimately prove him right. Though the medical examiner's report listed Bob's various conditions ("chemical dependency with acute and chronic alcoholism; hepatic cirrhosis; intravenous narcotism with recent opiate use; bipolar affective disorder"), he would also determine that Robert Neil Stinson had died of "natural causes."

"He'd been so beat up—from the [infection] a couple years earlier, and everything else, that his body just gave out," said Tommy. "Did he die because he abused drugs or alcohol over the years? Possibly. Who knows how much the body can take? Did he die because my dad crushed his spirit as a fucking kid? Maybe. Who knows how much the heart can take? I think his heart gave up because he was tired. He was just . . . *tired*."

As the news sank in, Tommy sat for a time. Then he picked up the phone and called Paul Westerberg.

"He didn't have to say anything," recalled Westerberg. "When I heard his trembling voice, I knew what it was."

"Did ya hear?" Tommy asked him.

"Oh . . . *no*," Westerberg said, sputtering.

"Yeah . . . Bob."

"*No, no, no, no, no, no.*"

"I sat down and fucking cried my eyes out," recalled Westerberg.

He spent the night at the piano in his grief, putting words to a song he'd been unable to finish for months.

In the dreams you tell me
Tell them only you were tired
Sing along, hold my life
A good day is any day that you're alive
Hold my life, one last time

* * *

Amid the media attention and local gossip that followed there were some who tried to point fingers, to place blame for Bob's death on the Replacements for firing him, to paint Paul and Tommy as "Mick and Keith leading Brian to the swimming pool," said Westerberg. "But I'm comfortable with mine and Bob's relationship. The little shit that we shared together. We were close. Even though there was jealousy and petty crap. I loved him. We loved each other. Far as what other people said . . . I learned that it can be hard to survive and take shit for it. It's hard to stay alive and be accused of something. I think Tommy and I both learned that."

No one in Bob's family wanted to pin his fate on how things had ended with the 'Mats. "I don't place responsibility on them," said Lonnie Stinson. "I place it on Nick in a big way. I place it on all of us, his family, for not doing more to help. But it wasn't any one thing that did him in. It was an accumulation of his whole life. From the time he was three years old and my dad told him he couldn't come out and change the tire . . . it was always, 'You're never good enough; you're wrong.' It went on that way his whole life. That's kind of sad, but that's how I see him: still that little boy and yet a grown man, trying to convince people that he had value; that he had merit."

* * *

A year or so before he died, Bob Stinson gave an interview to a Minneapolis journalist and author named Neal Karlen. Karlen was researching the subject of drugs and rock-and-roll for a book. He was having a hard time getting people to speak honestly and on the record. Someone suggested he look Bob up.

Karlen found him at the Uptown Bar, cadging drinks off strangers who knew him by his fading, once-famous reputation. "So I bought him a drink, and we started talking," said Karlen. "We had a long conversation. He was very frank and insightful, and I got what I wanted. And then some other people bought him drinks, and I started to feel like it was turning into a geek show. I wanted to go."

Before Karlen left, Stinson said one other thing: "I was a Replacement," Bob told him.

"There was a kind of pride in the way he said it," recalled Karlen. "Like that was *who* he was. That it was his life's work. That he would be satisfied with that as an epitaph."

"I was a Replacement," repeated Stinson, almost to himself. "I was *always* a Replacement."

"It's true: we were all Replacements," said Westerberg. "To a man, we felt that way. We lived that way. Bob died that way. It's a burden to be a Replacement."

Part III

In the summer of 1995, Paul Westerberg began work on his second solo album and the final record of his contract with Warner Bros.

The label paired him with the Pearl Jam/Stone Temple Pilots producer Brendan O'Brien. A jocular Georgian, O'Brien was a skilled record maker whose aesthetic appealed to rock radio. (He'd previously been tasked with mixing "World Class Fad" off *14 Songs*.) Westerberg decamped to his Atlanta studio with drummer Josh Freese in tow and began recording.

Everyone around the sessions was excited by the results O'Brien was getting, but Westerberg quietly chafed against the producer, creatively and personally. After a couple of weeks, he bailed on the sessions without a word. A&R man Michael Hill tried unsuccessfully to get Westerberg to reconsider. "Probably my firing Brendan was the last straw in the label's mind," said Westerberg. "Like, 'This guy has shot himself in the foot too many times.'"

Westerberg would finish the record, coproducing it himself with Lou Giordano and backed by studio pros like drummer Michael Urbano and bassist Davey Farragher. Though the album, *Eventually*, included some gorgeous tunes in "Love Untold" and "Good Day," as with *14 Songs*, something was missing. "I think his material flourished in the band construct, in a way it never did when he went solo," said rock critic Chris Morris. "It was like he needed the other guys, Tommy in particular." In the Replacements, Stinson had always been the built-in bullshit detector, an instinctive editor, who kept Westerberg's questionable songs and musical impulses at bay. On his own, Paul sometimes failed to understand where his strengths lay—"To this day, I can't tell my best songs from my crap," he would admit—and he often relegated his most effective material to B-sides or the trash heap.

After so many years of trying, Warner executives seemed unsure if they could ever connect Westerberg with a wider audience. "Paul has written some great songs and if we can get those songs out to the people that *should* happen," the label's Howie Klein told *Billboard* magazine rather unconvincingly.

If Warner Bros. had little to give Westerberg, it was because the company itself was coming apart. After twenty-five years as the head of Warner Bros., Mo Ostin had been forced out at the end of 1994 in a corporate power struggle. Label president Lenny Waronker would soon follow him out the door, and both men would set up shop at the David Geffen/Steven Spielberg/Jeffrey Katzenberg start-up DreamWorks Records.

Ironically, it was the Replacements' longtime product manager and ally Steven Baker who would take over the presidency of Warner Bros. In light of Ostin's and Warnonker's departures, Baker was desperately trying to steady a wobbly ship and keep the company's credibility intact. That meant giving a new contract to R.E.M.—then at their commercial peak, they were about to become free agents and threatening to walk from Warners.

That summer Warner Bros. signed R.E.M. to an unprecedented $80 million deal—the largest recording contract in history. Westerberg would be asked to comment on R.E.M.'s financial windfall and ascension to the ranks of megastars. "I've had to mention them in every interview I've done since 1981," he said wearily. "The problem is, they don't have to mention [the Replacements]. They simply don't have to acknowledge us anymore. They won."

* * *

As Westerberg prepared to hit the road in support of *Eventually* in the summer of 1996, he began affecting a new look and manner. He was dressing up, wearing tailored suits, and donning tinted prescription glasses—the specs he'd ditched in high school because they didn't look sufficiently rock-and-roll. He'd even quit smoking.

In interviews, he consciously punctured holes in his youthful punk image, playing up his love for John Coltrane and Joni Mitchell, suggesting that as he'd grown older he'd lost his appreciation for the Sex Pistols. He tried to put as much space between his old band and himself as possible. "I've distanced myself from the Replacements," he said, "what they represent, what they are, so much that I barely know they exist."

Westerberg put together a new solo band, with a rhythm section that couldn't have been more removed from the 'Mats. Michael Bland was a prodigiously gifted Twin Cities drummer who'd been a member of Prince's New Power Generation. Westerberg had met him during the *Eventually* sessions and become smitten with his playing. Bland convinced Westerberg to bring in conservatory-educated polymath Ken Chastain to play bass. Unable to stomach any of Bland's muso guitarist pals, Westerberg enlisted an indie rock ringer, calling up his old friend the singer-songwriter Tommy Keene to do the gig.

When Keene got to the rehearsals in Minneapolis, he blanched at how slick and manicured the songs, particularly the old 'Mats' numbers, sounded. Westerberg, meanwhile, was a surprising taskmaster. "I'm thinking this is gonna be like playing with the Replacements," he said. "But it was like joining the Buddy Rich Band. I'm getting yelled at. I could do the parts, but I had a roughness coming from indie bands. Paul was like, 'I don't want any of this amateur shit'—which is what he came out of." Keene felt Westerberg was trying to change the whole way he was perceived. "He wanted to be seen as a real cat—a professional, moneymaking, on-top-of-his-game musician . . . and not as some drunken kid playing Kiss covers."

Westerberg had signed on with Gold Mountain Management. The LA-based firm had guided the careers of Nirvana and the Beastie Boys and was known for running a tight touring operation. The first leg of the *Eventually* dates went well enough—crowds were enthusiastic, and reviews were good—"but then Paul began to have second thoughts," recalled Keene. "He started to throw shows on purpose. He was reacting to this world he'd created—like, 'This is too slick. What was I thinking?'"

Westerberg had responded to the uncertainty of his career by trying to go pro, but what he really craved was the instinctual quality of the Replacements. "I'd had a band who used to be able to read my mind, read my left foot. And now I had high-priced guys, who could only do what they were supposed to do each night," he said. "You don't know what you've got till it's gone."

A frustrated Westerberg soon began turning over the whole crew. "He fired the lighting guy onstage. Fired the monitor guy onstage. He went through five bus drivers," said Keene. "He fired the T-shirt guy because he didn't know who else to fire. That was the joke: 'Who's getting the ax today?' It was a circus."

In early June, *Eventually*'s first single, "Love Untold," peaked at number twenty-one on the alternative chart, then slipped off entirely a few weeks later. In an effort to keep the album's flagging momentum going, Westerberg consented to play a series of industry events.

He appeared at a gathering of radio execs in Boulder, going on before the headliner, punk poetess Patti Smith. In the middle of the show, the soundman asked Westerberg to cut his set short; Smith was demanding to start her show early. Paul flipped him the bird and kept playing until they cut the power off. Afterward, in their shared dressing room, Smith went on a star trip and laid into Westerberg. He looked to her guitarist Lenny Kaye, a 'Mats fan, for help. But Kaye just stared at the floor. Finally fed up with Smith's diva act, Westerberg cut her off—"Why don't you go write another one of yer fuckin' limericks"—and slammed the door behind him. "The sad part," said Westerberg, "is I never got a chance to tell her we shared a birthday."

One of the final dates of the tour saw Westerberg and the band playing the "Big Day Off," a massive outdoor radio festival at a speedway in western Massachusetts. The bill was filled with flavor-of-the-moment alternative bands like Poe and Goldfinger, and the audience comprised teenagers who were skipping school and had never heard of the Replacements.

With his pressed suit and slower songs, Westerberg became an object of scorn for the young crowd, who'd learned rock concert comportment by watching the mud-slinging at Woodstock '94. "These kids were just yelling shit and throwing stuff," said Keene, who got hit with an orange, while Westerberg was pelted with a water bottle. "It was almost surreal."

Westerberg reverted to old instincts, instructing the band to serve up a Replacements-style "pussy set." Confused at first, they went along, playing "Kiss Me on the Bus" and "Color Me Impressed" as slow as possible before Westerberg cut the show and stormed off. "At that point," he said, "it was pretty clear my fifteen minutes of fame was up. I was an absolute nothing."

* * *

As painful as Bob Stinson's passing had been, in a sense it freed Tommy Stinson. "From the time my brother died, everything negative died with him. And there was a lot of stuff. A lot of bad stuff early on, and stuff with the Replacements—just the fucked-up drugs and arguments and bullshit. It all went away. And all I could remember was how awesome my brother was. I think my mind just had to do that."

After his brother's loss, Tommy would find comfort in familiar faces from his past as well as new friends.

Out of the ashes of the latter-day lineup of Bash & Pop he formed a new group called Perfect, with drummer Gersh Gershunoff, guitarist Marc Solomon, and bassist Robert Cooper (and later, guitarist Dave Philips). They gelled quickly, becoming a real band in a way that Bash & Pop had never been—and there was none of the brooding or passive-aggressive behavior that had marked the Replacements.

For Stinson, who'd been living a kind of arrested rock-and-roll adolescence for so long, his adult life really began once he finally shed the baggage of his old band. "It's a real weird thing, but the Replacements were very antisocial people. Except when we were with ourselves—then it was a gang mentality," said Stinson. "In LA with Perfect, I learned what it was like to be a friend, and I started having friends. It's nice to have people you can call and talk to and hang out with—other than Paul. Not that he was a bad thing, but we'd gone our separate ways." At thirty years old, Tommy Stinson had "finally started figuring all that regular life stuff out."

At Bob's funeral, Tommy had reconnected with his long-estranged friend Peter Jesperson. He'd moved out to Los Angles to run his Medium Cool imprint, under the umbrella of Restless Records, which had signed a pact with Twin/Tone. "Peter turned up at [a Perfect] show, and much to my surprise, he liked us," said Tommy. "That was sort of the catalyst for our relationship starting over again. And my brother's death had something to do with it as well. I felt sort of an urgency to keep track of friends who really meant something to me."

Jesperson would eventually sign Perfect to Medium Cool, which released their debut EP, *When Squirrels Play Chicken*, in the summer of 1996. Though it had been shattered a decade earlier, Peter and Tommy would restore the deep bond that had existed between them. Stinson would stand as the best man at Jesperson's wedding the following year and remain family from then on.

In late 1997, Perfect traveled to Ardent Studios in Memphis to record, and Stinson would reunite with the paternal producer Jim Dickinson. "This whole thing is a return in a way," said Stinson about the sessions, which began almost eleven years to the day after the Replacements started tracking *Pleased to Meet Me*. "Tommy has blossomed," noted Dickinson. "He is a different person. He's managed to learn an awful lot about what he does . . . and in a way, he's still the nineteen-year-old punk that I knew years ago."

★ ★ ★

Returning to the Twin Cities from tour, Paul Westerberg found himself followed by a black cloud. "I've flirted with depression all my life," he noted. "I stopped flirting and had a full-blown romance with it." Faced with such feelings, he did what he always did: wrote songs. "I had a good two months, almost like a hermit at home," said Westerberg, who turned out a batch of strange, disquieting material during this spell.

He thought work might provide relief, but when the songs stopped, the darkness remained. The few friends he talked to during this period were getting disturbing signals about his mental state. Tommy Keene remembered Westerberg calling him up, sounding suicidal. By the time Paul's old friend Julie Panebianco came to Minneapolis to visit, Westerberg was in a near-catatonic state. "We went to dinner and I didn't say a word," he recalled. "I didn't talk for a couple months. It was scary."

Bob Stinson's passing and the culmination of his Warner Bros. contract represented the end of something bigger in Westerberg's mind. "I started playing guitar in bands when I was fifteen. I had a dream, and for twenty years I'd pursued it," he said. "It dawned on me that my dream came true. Maybe it didn't play out like I thought it would, but I'd lived my dream. At that point I realized I didn't have another one. And that was somehow terrifying."

After avoiding it for much of his life, Westerberg finally decided to seriously seek professional help. "I went to a couple bohunk psychiatrists until I found the right guy," he said. His therapist would listen to Westerberg explain his professional neuroses, how he'd watched as his avowed musical disciples, like Johnny Rzeznik of the Goo Goo Dolls and Billie Joe Armstrong of Green Day, had taken his influence and outstripped him, selling millions of records.

"There was a point when . . . I did think that everyone on the radio sounded like me," he said. "Not in a crazed way, but I could hear me in a lot of other artists. So I was telling this to the guy I was seeing, and he thought I was paranoid and out of my mind," laughed Westerberg. "He's sitting there taking notes. I think he was just writing the word *loon* on his pad."

His doctor did some poking around and realized Westerberg wasn't delusional; he *had* influenced a younger generation of artists, but felt somehow shut out of that success, alienated by the very thing he'd created. "Just having him understand that was validating," said Westerberg.

Beyond the talk therapy, Westerberg also got on prescription medication for his depression and anxiety. "After a lifetime of self-medicating, doing it on my own with alcohol and street drugs and prayer and self-help and whatever else, the [doctor] told me . . . 'There are things that are made to help people like you.' That kinda saved [me]."

Westerberg would still struggle, having to alternate between antidepressants and anti-anxiety meds. "There's no cure for either together. 'Cause one offsets the other. That would be a whole other journey for me." He would document that journey on an indie EP he released under the pseudonym Grandpaboy that year. Among the tracks was "Psychopharmacology," a song that spelled out his new dilemma: "I need somethin' to calm me down / I need somethin' to keep me focused / Narcoleptic and paranoid, borderline hopeless . . . ADD, PCP, F-U-C-K-E-D, that's me."

* * *

With Westerberg's time at Warner Bros. officially at an end, A&R man Michael Hill would produce a beautiful farewell to the Replacements in the form of a two-disc, "best of" and rarities compilation of the Sire years, titled *All for Nothing/Nothing for All.*

When the comp came out in the fall of 1997, it felt like a tombstone for the band. Westerberg declined to promote it, leaving an annoyed Tommy Stinson holding the bag. "Paul won't speak—which is very hypocritical," Stinson told an interviewer, dodging questions about the Replacements' legacy and the prospects of a reunion. Tommy's message on the 'Mats was clear. "We're over," he said. "Forget about it. Get a life."

A few months later, as part of department downsizing, Michael Hill would be laid off after fourteen years at Warner Bros.

* * *

In early 1998, Tommy Stinson's band Perfect had finished recording its debut with Jim Dickinson, and they were waiting for Restless Records to come up with a marketing plan and release date. Though the company had sunk a small fortune into recording and mixing—upward of $200,000—Restless president Joe Regis suddenly lost his enthusiasm for the project. "He decided he wasn't going to put it out 'cause they didn't hear a radio hit," said Stinson. Peter Jesperson, who was handling A&R for Perfect under the Restless umbrella, was so incensed by the decision that he severed ties with the label in protest.

In spite of his personal triumphs, Tommy was feeling beaten down after another failed experience trying to lead his own group. "You work and you work and you work . . . and nothing," he said. "By the time the Perfect thing was falling to pieces, I was so fed up. I just wanted to go play bass with some band and hang out." That opportunity would soon present itself.

After becoming the behemoth of the rock world in the late '80s and early '90s, Guns N' Roses was starting over. By 1998, singer/leader Axl Rose had decided to reboot the multi-platinum band. Several members of the group—including guitarist Slash and drummer Matt Sorum—had left or been dismissed, so Rose enlisted a new lineup to begin work on the album that would become the long-gestating epic, *Chinese Democracy.*

This new version of Guns included Paul Westerberg's band drummer Josh Freese. As Guns was working on new material, founding bassist Duff McKagan decided to leave the group. "We needed a bass player, and I thought of Tommy," said Freese. Stinson tried out at GNR's rehearsal space. "They actually filmed me doing the audition," Tommy recalled. "I didn't pretend like I was playing a show. I just played."

Whatever he did impressed Axl Rose—no one else was auditioned. Despite their different musical backgrounds, Rose and Stinson found common ground. "He knew about the Replacements. He told me that he and [GNR tour manager] Del James had come to see us in some club back in the day, and they were not impressed," said Stinson, laughing. "He and I both had a chuckle about the fact he wasn't a 'Mats fan and I wasn't a Guns fan." A couple days later, Stinson got a formal contract offer to join Guns N' Roses as its new bassist.

For Stinson, the job meant much-needed financial stability—he could finally take care of his daughter Ruby properly. As good as he'd proven to be during his stint as a telemarketer, Stinson was best suited for only one job. "I never got much of a formal education. But playing bass in a loud rock-and-roll band?" he said. "I got a fucking doctorate in that shit."

* * *

Paul Westerberg felt his life needed a bigger purpose than music. His therapist encouraged him to start a family. Despite coming from a big Catholic brood, none of his siblings had any children. Westerberg was reluctant to start a family, recalling how his own parents had been preoccupied and ignored him during his troubled teen years. He'd articulated that ambivalence on an *Eventually* track called "Mamma-Daddy Did": "Decided not to raise some mixed-up kid, just like mamma daddy did."

His first wife, Lori Bizer, had wanted children during their marriage, "but I would not have been ready," he said. "I always felt like while you're still on the road it's not right to have a family," he said. "If you got a little one you should be there for 'em."

After *Eventually*, Westerberg decided his days on the road were over. "I always said I'd quit if it was no fun, and it was no longer fun—touring at least," he noted. "I was at the point where it was like one more tour and I wouldn't be returning—in a pine box maybe."

In the fall of '97, Laurie Lindeen got pregnant. Their son, John Paul Westerberg, came into the world the following May.

Westerberg would become a devoted stay-at-home dad to his little boy. Once a nocturnal rock-and-roller, now he was "fine with staying up all night to give him a bottle. I used to put him in this little backpack and play the guitar and walk around." The birth of his son, he said, "brought me back to life."

* * *

The material Westerberg had written during his post-*Eventually* malaise was striking, unlike anything he'd created before. "A different kind of song [had] started coming out," he said. Westerberg continued creating spare, mostly piano-based pieces that were closer to Stephen Sondheim than the Rolling Stones.

Capitol Records president Gary Gersh—the industry veteran who'd worked with David Bowie and signed Nirvana—heard these demos and signed Westerberg to the label in 1998. Gersh, who would personally serve as his A&R man, encouraged Westerberg to leave the rock-and-roll ghost of the Replacements behind for good. "Don't just be another guy with a guitar," Gersh told him, throwing in a new Steinway concert grand as part of the Capitol contract.

Gersh suggested that Don Was coproduce the album with Paul. Was had become an ardent fan of Westerberg's *14 Songs* while sharing a flat with Keith Richards as they worked on the Rolling Stones' *Voodoo Lounge* in Ireland. Westerberg immediately hit it off with the jazzy, low-key Was, who recognized his creative dilemma. "Paul's got a difficult lot in life coming out of the Replacements," he said. "The thing that's a blessing is, his music means a lot to people. The curse is, you feel like you can't veer too much from the path that people expect you to be on. I've seen it happen with Iggy Pop and even with the Stones. You continue to grow as an artist and as a human being, but people wanna freeze you in a moment from your past."

Westerberg's new album—with the multiple portmanteau title *Suicaine Gratification*—would be a radical departure: light on guitars, heavy on trenchant self-examination, lyrics painted with impressionistic strokes. Was felt that Westerberg had written an autobiographical concept album. "But a guy like Paul will purposely make that trail disappear," said Was. "He reveals something deep inside and then turns his back." Westerberg would admit as much in the album's opening track, "It's a Wonderful Lie": "I've been accused of never opening up / You get too close, then I keep my mouth shut."

Westerberg had sabotaged his own career plenty, but this time it was bad luck that doomed *Suicaine Gratification*. The day the album was being mastered, Gary Gersh resigned from Capitol, forced out over philosophical differences with parent company EMI. Westerberg was suddenly left without his biggest ally. Capitol's new regime didn't understand or embrace his strange new record—they wanted to know where the rock guitars were, where the single was.

When *Suicaine Gratification* was released in February 1999, Westerberg did his best to promote it in the press—he'd made it clear at the outset that he wouldn't be touring in support of the LP. Largely misunderstood by fans and critics, and effectively orphaned by the label, it sold a major-label career-worst 52,000 copies for Westerberg. The reaction to the album, he said, "felt like the last straw."

He would quickly escape from Capitol; the label actually paid him off *not* to record the second record guaranteed in his contract. "Best deal I ever made," he said. Soon after, Westerberg shed himself of all his professional ties, leaving his management company and eventually letting go of longtime lawyer George Regis.

He was ready to leave the major labels and the music industry behind and disappear from public view. "I figured," he said, "that nobody can really miss you unless you go away."

* * *

With the '90s ending and a new millennium about to begin, the Replacements' lives were as far removed from one another as could be.

Chris Mars's fine art career, his real dream since childhood, had finally become a reality. His surreal Hieronymus Bosch–inspired paintings would soon be displayed in museums and galleries, selling for tens of thousands of dollars apiece.

Slim Dunlap remained a proud journeyman, working a tough shipping job at a warehouse and playing little local gigs for handfuls of fans on the side. He and his wife Chrissie were mostly counting down their days to retirement, golden years they planned to spend together playing golf, taking boat rides, and enjoying their grandchildren.

Tommy Stinson was mired in the morass of making *Chinese Democracy*—a project that grew more strange and byzantine as the years wore on. While a succession of record producers and band members came and went (and sometimes fled), Stinson remained GNR's bedrock. He would become Axl Rose's trusted musical lieutenant and right-hand man. It was a role he was accustomed to playing.

On New Year's Eve of 2000, Paul Westerberg marked his fortieth birthday, ensconced in a quiet domestic life with his family, his backaches, and his mood pills. He would once again retreat to the basement to make music alone, amid memories of what was gone and thoughts of what still could be.

Part IV

More than a decade of flirting and fighting, of distance and death, of half-starts and false-starts, would pass before the Replacements could be reborn.

Following three years of professional seclusion, Paul Westerberg would finally reemerge in 2002. The seeds of his comeback were sown with the purchase of a guitar—a cherry red Gibson ES-330. Like a fifteen-year-old with his first six-string, the fortysomething Westerberg took to the instrument like a favorite, forgotten foil and began playing rock-and-roll in the basement, an activity that reignited his passion for music and helped him rediscover his muse. "I'd made my I'm-gonna-kill-myself record, that was the end of that phase," said Westerberg. "I felt like rockin'."

Westerberg would release a pair of albums, *Stereo* and *Mono*, for Los Angeles indie label Vagrant, a company started by Replacements fanatic Rich Egan.

That winter Westerberg had an idea for a bit of guerrilla promotion. He called up Tommy Stinson to see if he wanted to join him on a Midwest tour that February, one that would visit the cities Buddy Holly was scheduled to play before his 1959 plane crash. Stinson thought it sounded like fun; he was game. "Unfortunately, he called me back two days later and said he couldn't do it because his cohort [Axl Rose] needed him," said Westerberg. "So the idea lasted about half a minute."

Paul then roused Slim Dunlap and asked him to come on the road and to make an appearance together on *The Late Show with David Letterman.* Slim agreed, and they began rehearsing. Then, suddenly, Westerberg stopped calling, stopped coming over. Something Dunlap had supposedly said—allegedly disparaging of Paul's new songs—had gotten back to Westerberg. The tour never happened. Paul and Slim began an estrangement that would last nearly a decade.

Promoting *Stereo/Mono* (the records would be packaged as one set), Westerberg seemed eager to wipe away the memory of his softened solo years and remind people of his role as the architect of the Replacements' sound. "I'm not trying to say it was all me all along, but when Tommy was twelve and Bob didn't know a major chord from a minor and Chris didn't know what beat to play, I would suggest this beat, and this chord and that. And they were my band. It belonged to them too," he said. "But they didn't sound like the Replacements before I started playing with them."

* * *

The cycles of life had begun to intersect for Westerberg, as he found himself simultaneously caring for his infant son Johnny and his ailing septuagenarian father Hal. "Not to get too gruesome," Westerberg said, "but when you're wiping your little boy's ass and then having to do the same to your father, that changes you. It turns you into an adult."

Even during the final years of his life, when Paul was playing nice sit-down theaters in Minneapolis, Hal Westerberg hadn't gone to see his son perform. "I'm perfectly fine that he never came to my office and watched me work, you know. It kept it pure that I was his son, that I was no more than the little boy he played catch with, who now plays catch with his son. I was never looking for his applause. I never needed it, never wanted it, and never got it," laughed Westerberg.

Hal's final years were difficult ones. "He had emphysema, he broke his back, had facial cancer," recalled Paul. They gave Hal last rites on Halloween 2003. "And he lived eight or nine days more. I was with him at the end."

Paul sat there as his father gasped his final breaths and held his mother Mary Lou as they watched the hearse drive off with his body. "Maybe I should've worked with dying people," mused Westerberg. "'Cause everyone was coming unglued and I managed to stay levelheaded. I think I took the whole thing too easy. Then again, I started smoking cigarettes after that. He dies of emphysema and the first thing you know I'm smoking again. That's one for Freud."

* * *

Westerberg would remain busy after the comeback of *Stereo/Mono*. In 2003 he released the concert documentary DVD and soundtrack *Come Feel Me Tremble* and put out *Dead Man Shake*, a blues album credited to his alter ego Grandpaboy, for the Mississippi label Fat Possum. (As part of the deal with the company, Westerberg requested that his payment include a switchblade, a revolver, and a bottle of whiskey.) He followed up with his fifth album in two years, *Folker*, in the fall of 2004.

He would make a series of in-store appearances, then do a solo tour in 2002, before heading back out on the road with a full band (drummer Michael Bland, his neighbor and the onetime Dads' guitarist Kevin Bowe, and his new pal, Jim Boquist, formerly of Son Volt, on bass). Touring brought back familiar boredom and temptations. Dealing with chronic back pain and the drudgery of the road, Westerberg had begun abusing prescription pills—he'd tellingly dubbed his band the Painkillers. After more than a decade on the wagon, he started drinking again in 2003. "I drank for seventeen years and was sober for thirteen and then have started to casually drink again," he admitted. "I have no solid answer other than the fact that every article on me would usually start with 'The former hard-drinking front man. . . . And it's like, I might as well do what I want to do 'cause I'm never gonna live that down."

But the booze fueled his old insecurities. By the middle 2000s, a new generation of ersatz Westerbergs had emerged in the music world. Watching TV or flipping through magazines, Paul would see the latest rock singer-songwriter rage, some kid wearing his old haircut and bad attitude. "How can you like him better than me?" sang Westerberg in a track off *Folker*. "How can you like him? After all, it's me."

He would confide his confusion to his friend, the writer, Bill Flanagan. "Paul said what upset him when he saw people imitating him was that first his ego would say, 'That guy is imitating me,'" said Flanagan. "And then the other side of him, his insecurity, would go, 'No, that guy never heard of you. *Nobody ever heard of you*. You never had a hit record. You're just some guy sitting in his basement in Minneapolis.' The whole thing kinda made him question reality."

* * *

A one-off Replacements reunion nearly happened in October 2004, at a benefit for Soul Asylum bassist Karl Mueller, who was battling cancer. The Twin Cities music community had rallied around the much-loved Mueller, and Westerberg tried to get the 'Mats to perform. "A couple of them were unavailable," reported Westerberg, who played the benefit with Jim Boquist instead. "I was . . . disappointed that we didn't. We never did anything good in our life for anybody. It would've been a nice thing to do for Karl." (When Mueller died the following year, Tommy Stinson would honor his widow Mary Beth Mueller's request and join Soul Asylum on bass, recording and touring with the band over the next several years in between his Guns N' Roses commitments.)

By 2005, the festering ill will between Westerberg and Stinson became public as Tommy promoted his first solo album, *Village Gorilla Head*. Westerberg had made disparaging comments in the press about Stinson joining GNR, and Stinson was still smarting. "Westerberg's gone out on a limb to say a bunch of nonsense that's made me look bad, that's made Axl look bad, that's made [Rose] feel bad. . . . It's just lame."

Tommy would tell reporters he found it far easier to work with his current bandmate in Guns N' Roses than his old Replacements partner. "He keeps pulling out the 'Paul Westerberg's more difficult to deal with than Axl Rose' line," said Westerberg. "And I think, 'Yeah, of course. Wouldn't Van Gogh be more difficult than Norman Rockwell?'"

When he wasn't serving up one-liners, Westerberg was busy coaching his son Johnny's youth sports teams or serving as his school's playground monitor. After a while the kids knew him well enough that he stopped wearing the orange vest that came with the gig. Though he was living out his Mr. Mom years, reminders of his former life were never far away. "I was helping coach my son's basketball team," recalled Westerberg. "I had this SpongeBob [Squarepants] hat on, and this kid came up to me and said, 'Why are you wearing that? That's not cool. You're supposed to be cool. You're a rock star.' And I was like, 'I'm the coach, dude. Go do a lap.' If I'm here, I'm not Steven fucking Tyler, y'know?"

* * *

At the end of 2005, through a series of labyrinthine label acquisitions, the Warner Music Group ended up with rights to the Replacements' Twin/ Tone albums, and their entire catalog was finally placed under one roof. Warner's reissue division, Rhino Records, hatched plans for a career-spanning retrospective and wanted new 'Mats songs as an enticement for fans. They offered Westerberg and Stinson a deal for the band to reunite and record.

Westerberg and Stinson ended their feud and agreed to do it. They did not invite Slim Dunlap to participate. ("He acted like he didn't care," said his wife Chrissie, "but he was hurt.") Westerberg would, however, extend an olive branch to Chris Mars. The two former friends had finally patched things up, after running into one another in the street in Minneapolis. "He's doing great with his art, and he's quite a nice guy now," said Westerberg.

Though he'd made it clear he didn't want to play, Mars would turn up for the Replacements' reunion session at Minneapolis's Flowers Studio in

December of 2005 to lend his support. Josh Freese had flown out to play drums. "And Chris, he was still a Replacement," said Westerberg. "The first thing out of his mouth to Josh was something like, 'Man, you *almost* played that really good.' That's what we missed. You don't have to play the drums. You can just bring the attitude." The band would record a pair of nostalgic rockers, "Message to the Boys" and "Pool and Dive," for the comp, titled *Don't You Know Who I Think I Was?*

The following year, when Westerberg was in Hollywood recording the soundtrack to the animated feature *Open Season*, he invited Tommy to the sessions to play bass on a few songs. Westerberg and Stinson would appear onstage together for the first time in fifteen years that September at the premiere of the film, held at LA's Greek Theater.

Tommy, Paul, and Josh Freese were scheduled to play a couple of songs from the soundtrack before a screening for studio brass, VIPs, and their children. "It was totally bizarre," recalled Freese of the gig. "Right before we were gonna play, Tommy pulled out a flask of something, and Paul lit up a smoke. We're smoking and drinking. Meanwhile, four feet on the other side of the curtain are all these kids with cotton candy waiting to see us."

After the second number was over, Westerberg kicked into a raucous unplanned version of the Replacements' "IOU," panicking the event's organizers, who'd planned and timed the program down to the second. The three of them blasted away in front of a visibly flummoxed audience. "You could see people in the front row plugging their ears and covering their kids' ears," said Freese. "Everyone was confused and kinda pissed off."

If it was to be their only reunion, said Westerberg, "then it was a perfect way to go out."

* * *

Tommy Stinson continued to balance his many professional obligations with Guns N' Roses (whose *Chinese Democracy* was finally released in 2008 after a decade of labor), Soul Asylum, and his own solo career. Amid all that, he would find stability in his family life. His daughter Ruby had grown up well, thanks to her mother Daune. Ruby would be the first Stinson to go to college, graduating from the Parsons School of Design and getting a job working for rock-and-roll fashion designer John Varvatos. She would also launch her own pop singing career on the side, with Tommy helping to produce some tracks for her.

Stinson also started a new family, siring another daughter, Tallulah, with Philadelphia musician Emily Roberts in 2008. The couple would eventually marry and leave LA for Pennsylvania, before settling in Hudson, New York. The artsy, bucolic community was the place that Tommy hoped to finally plant roots in. "I want to have a real home," said Stinson wistfully. "It's kind of weird to be transient your whole fucking life."

* * *

In 2008 Rhino Records finally reissued all eight Replacements albums in expanded editions, produced by Peter Jesperson. As they listened and approved bonus tracks for the project, Westerberg and Stinson began spending time together in Minneapolis. Out of those visits came the first serious discussions about a 'Mats reunion. Rock festivals like Coachella and Lollapalooza were making big six-figure offers for the band to re-form.

After dismissing the idea for years, Stinson had come around to a reunion. "We've got unfinished business, if we want," he said. "And if Paul and I can hang out and play together and enjoy each other's company, why not do it? At least until I hate him again."

Stinson was understandably wary. Westerberg had stung him privately and in the press over the years. "Paul tends to make jabs without meaning to make jabs or hurt anyone's feelings or be an asshole, but it comes off like that," said Stinson. "We all have to be accountable for the shit we say and how it affects people. If you want to go down that road, you lose friends."

Westerberg felt there was something else standing between their reunion: the ghost of Bob Stinson. "The answer to the million-dollar question is yes, when Bob died, something died in me and Tommy, and we've never been the same since," said Westerberg. "And it's always been awkward, and it's always been unsaid and unsayable and strange and weird between us."

Regardless, in late 2008 they tried rehearsing in Minneapolis with Michael Bland on drums and Jim Boquist rounding out the lineup on guitar. Westerberg was once again sober. "Every time I feel like having a drink, I just take a deep breath," he said. "I might overdose on oxygen soon." Stinson felt that Westerberg was unfocused, almost bouncing off the walls. "It wasn't booze, or lack of it, it was just that he hadn't played with anyone else in a few years," said Tommy.

"I've run out of confidants—and confidence," said Westerberg of a 'Mats reunion. "There's no one I can really turn to and ask, 'What do you think I should do here?' I've gone each and every way with it, and I really don't know anymore."

* * *

Each year, like clockwork, the reunion offers came, the money got bigger. But as he turned fifty, Paul Westerberg worried whether he could measure up to his younger, more inchoate self. "When I listen to those first few Replacements records, I hear myself, and that guy is closer to being born than I am to his age right now," he said. "And I think, *Could I go out and do that again?*"

The Replacements myth had become daunting, even to Westerberg. The band had become a hip touchstone for successive generations of music fans. They developed a romance as beautiful losers—"a band that could, but didn't," as a 2006 *New York Times* headline described them. "The fact that we came up short is the thing that's kept us interesting. That is part of the attraction. We've retained this mystique," said Westerberg, who would demur, again and again, refusing reunion offers.

He would go eight years without playing a show, almost as long without releasing a real record (though he would put out a spate of smaller digital releases online). He almost never went out to socialize, hardly ever left Minneapolis. "I've kind of removed myself from humanity," Westerberg would say.

"It's a sad thing for me to see him not doing anything," said Tommy. "He's a very talented guy. I fucking admire him, he's my brother. He's been my brother my whole life, you know? My brother was my brother, but so was Paul. And it's like watching your brother just fading away, alone in his basement."

* * *

Over the next few years, death would brush up against the Replacements repeatedly.

In August 2008, the band's latter-day drummer Steve Foley died. After the 'Mats and Bash & Pop, Foley had stepped away from music and gotten a job selling cars. Following a rough personal patch, when he'd gone through a marriage and rehab, he seemed to be doing better, but somewhere along the way he got lost again. He was felled by an "accidental drug overdose"—a mix of prescription pills and methadone—at the age of forty-nine. Before the end, he would reflect fondly on his brief, memorable membership in the Replacements: "Some days I walk down the street and go, 'God, I was in that fucking band?' Unbelievable."

In August 2009, after months in failing health, producer Jim Dickinson died in Memphis. He had continued talking to Tommy Stinson, encouraging him from his hospital bed, until the very end. Six months later, Alex Chilton died from a heart attack in New Orleans. Having made him myth in song, Westerberg would eulogize him in print in the *New York Times*. "The great Alex Chilton is gone—folk troubadour, blues shouter, master singer, songwriter and guitarist," he wrote. "Someone should write a tune about him. Then again, nah, that would be impossible. Or just plain stupid."

Others who'd been part of the 'Mats' circle—Suburbs guitarist and album designer Bruce Allen, the band's early roadie Tom Carlson, longtime soundman Brendan McCabe—all passed on as well.

Amid the funerals and farewells, the Westerberg-Stinson relationship would continue to run hot and cold. There would be periods filled with calls and intense contact, and then nothing. "We can go years without seeing each other or talking, but there's a closeness I have with him that I have with no one else," said Westerberg.

"Sometimes the phone rings and I'll hear that so-and-so just croaked, like the call came with [Chilton]. But the call I always fear is the one telling me that

Tommy is gone. I guess in my own macabre way . . . if you ask, 'Who do I love the most?' well, if something were to happen with him, I don't know that I'd recover from that."

* * *

Bob Stinson's son Joey had not been expected to live past the age of four. Somehow he had persevered through his myriad health conditions, including a bout with cancer.

Even with the aid of home nurses, caring for Joey eventually became too much for his mother Carleen Krietler, who'd remarried and given birth to a daughter. She would be forced to give up her son. "Carleen reached a point where she couldn't handle Joey anymore," said Anita Stinson. "Everyone faulted her for that . . . but with Joey it was a twenty-four-hour-a-day thing. It would've been overwhelming for anyone."

Joey was placed in the foster system. At eighteen, he became a ward of the state, and Anita Stinson was named his legal guardian. She and her husband Tom Kurth would care for Joey tenderly until the end of his life, which came on December 1, 2010. Joey Stinson had lived to be twenty-one. His funeral service was held in the same chapel as his father's.

"Until you have the opportunity to love someone the way I loved Joey, you don't know what love is about," said Anita, teary-eyed. "And yes, caring for him, it's what I missed with Bobby. I miss them both every minute. I miss Joey, and I miss Bobby more because I miss Joey, if that makes any sense. But you remember them, and they go on in your heart."

* * *

Slim Dunlap was barely sixty, but for several years he'd shown dramatic signs of slowing and aging. He shuffled his feet around the house, seemed almost disengaged from his own life. His wife Chrissie pushed him to go to the doctor, but he refused. Later it would come out that he'd suffered a pair of strokes, in 2007 and 2011. He'd fallen at work and knew there was something wrong, but stayed silent. He didn't want his wife and family to worry.

In February 2012, Chrissie and her grandkids were getting ready to leave the house to go ice skating when they heard a thud from the bathroom. The littlest child, Audrey, ran in to see what the sound was and found her grandfather lying on the bathroom floor.

Chrissie and the kids somehow managed to drag Slim down the hall and into bed. "As I tried to get him up, I realized he couldn't stand, couldn't move his leg. I knew something bad had happened," said Chrissie, who ran to call an ambulance.

Dunlap had finally suffered a major stroke; he was hemorrhaging from the left side of his brain. "He didn't open his eyes for three weeks," said his wife. "We didn't know if he was going to live."

Paul Westerberg was among the first to visit Dunlap at the Hennepin County Medical Center. Paul and Slim hadn't spoken in years, having fallen out over something that seemed so stupid and pointless now. When Westerberg saw the stricken Dunlap lying there, hooked up to a phalanx of tubes and machines, his heart sank. "Then he crawled into bed with Slim and held him close and kissed him," said Chrissie.

Slim would spend nine months in and out of hospitals and rehab facilities and nursing homes. Chrissie finally quit her job and brought him home to look after him full-time. Slim was paralyzed on his left side, his speech and motor function dramatically affected. Unable to swallow and fed via IV, he was prone to infections and pneumonia and would return to the hospital a staggering forty times over the next few years. The medical bills were piling up, tens of thousands of dollars' worth, and tens of thousands more would be needed to continue care.

A friend of the Dunlaps, Brian Balleria, emailed Peter Jesperson suggesting the idea of a tribute record to help defray Slim's medical costs. That led Jesperson to develop the "Songs for Slim" benefit, a singles series featuring various artists covering Dunlap's songs; it would result in a double album. An array of Slim's old friends and admirers would contribute, including Soul Asylum, Lucinda Williams, the Wallflowers' Jakob Dylan, the Pixies' Frank Black, X's John Doe, and Wilco's Jeff Tweedy. All the artwork would be done by Chris Mars.

The project would kick off with an EP of Dunlap's songs and covers done by Paul Westerberg and Tommy Stinson, billed as the Replacements. They started with a limited vinyl pressing of the record, auctioning the copies off before a general release. All told, "Songs for Slim" helped raise over $200,000 for Dunlap's medical fund. "What they did putting the band back together . . ." said Chrissie, "there's no words for how grateful we are to Paul and Tommy."

* * *

Inevitably, Paul and Tommy's work on the "Songs for Slim" benefit began to stir thoughts of a full-scale Replacements reunion. Perhaps it was a clear sense of their own mortality, but this time there seemed to be real momentum.

For years, Westerberg had quietly nursed a hope that Chris Mars would change his mind and be part of a reunion in some way. Chris had contributed his own solo track to the Replacements' "Songs for Slim" EP, but he was clearly done with the band. "In a way, Chris puts the Replacements on a level with his paper route as a kid," said Westerberg. "He had a paper route, then he played drums in a rock band, and then went on to become an artist, which is what he always dreamt of. But I can't quite dispose of it that easily."

Even so, Westerberg was leery of taking the Replacements back out on the road, of possibly spoiling the legend that had built up around the band. Slim Dunlap would be the one to finally convince him.

"We were talking to Slim when he was in the hospital," said Westerberg. "And I was like, 'Should we play?'" Back in 1987, Slim had given the Replacements new life, had made them whole again with his loyalty and tenacity. Now he would do it again.

"Yes," Dunlap told Westerberg, his slurred words suddenly crystal clear. *"Go play."*

* * *

It wasn't just Slim's encouragement that compelled them to re-form.

After twenty years together, ten of them married, Paul Westerberg's relationship with Laurie Lindeen was over. Meantime, Tommy Stinson's young marriage to Emily Roberts had come to an end as well. Both men were separated, headed for divorce.

Once again Paul and Tommy found themselves together, their lives at loose ends—just as they'd been when they first met, a nineteen-year-old dropout janitor and a thirteen-year-old juvenile delinquent. "Paul pointed out that we've kinda always been in this situation," said Tommy. "When we started talking about playing together this time, I really got the feeling that we needed each other in a way that hadn't been there in the other years when they were offering us [reunion] shows. I know I needed to come do this; we both felt like we needed to hang out."

The Replacements would reunite with a trio of concerts in late summer 2013 as part of the traveling punk-rock-rooted Riot Fest, headlining dates in Toronto, Chicago, and Denver. Paul and Tommy would be joined by their mutual friend Josh Freese on drums and Boston guitarist Dave Minehan—it would be a quasi-reunion of Westerberg's 1993 solo band: the group's bassist, Darren Hill, was also behind the scenes helping manage things.

Predictably, there were those who questioned the validity of the band's return. How did only two original members, Paul and Tommy, constitute a "real" Replacements reunion? The math made it clear: only six people had ever played with the 'Mats; two were dead, one was incapacitated, and another had left the band behind emotionally. Paul and Tommy were in the group from beginning to end, the ones still playing when the ship went down. Now they were back to raise it. They *were* the Replacements.

With the first concert in Canada, on August 25, drawing closer, some questioned if Westerberg would really go through with it. But as showtime approached, Paul "was unnaturally calm. I can't explain it. We weren't drinking, we weren't worrying. We didn't have any wardrobe, we just ripped up a few things before we went on," he said. It helped that the 'Mats would be forced to follow Iggy Pop and the Stooges. "You watch Iggy and you realize you better not get up and suck."

Toronto would set the tone for their return. While the band occasionally sounded rough, they were so adrenalized by the moment and the affection of the audience that they carried through triumphantly. "The crowd for that show was really forgiving and beautiful," recalled Stinson. "It was touching."

In the midst of their reunion, the Replacements would be named among the finalists for induction into the Rock and Roll Hall of Fame—though they ultimately would fall short of election.

"I think we happened to coincidentally like all of the funky quirks of the classic rock bands—the Who, the Rolling Stones, the Ramones—to a certain extent," mused Westerberg. "We didn't have the things that made those bands huge; we had the thing that made them infamous and decadent and, perhaps, great."

* * *

Two decades after handing their instruments off to the roadies in Grant Park, the Replacements returned to Chicago, this time to Humboldt Park, where a crowd of 20,000-plus would be gathered to witness their comeback.

Among the backstage contingent was Tommy's ex-wife Daune and their daughter Ruby, as well as the members of his old band Perfect. Westerberg, too, would come with a retinue of his own. "My son was watching from the side of the stage with his buddies," said Westerberg. His boy Johnny was fifteen years old now. A good-looking kid, an athlete, he'd come with a gang of his high school pals to finally see his pop's famous band. "He immediately pointed out the stuff that sucked in the show. He thought 'Swingin Party' sucked," laughed Paul. "I don't know where he gets that negative shit from."

Paul's and Tommy's kids were with them when the Replacements played NBC's *Tonight Show with Jimmy Fallon* the following summer. Their appearance was trumpeted as a triumphant return to Rockefeller Center, the 'Mats' first time back since being banned following their *Saturday Night Live* performance in '86.

Among the other guests that night was Keith Richards. Twenty-five years after they'd opened for him, the Replacements would reunite with the Stones guitarist, posing for pictures, a beaming Paul and Tommy looking like his long-lost sons.

Hanging around the studio hall with his daughter Ruby, Tommy did a double take as Barbara Streisand—rehearsing for a special next door—passed by them.

"That's Barbara *fuckin'* Streisand!" Tommy exclaimed.

Without breaking stride, Streisand exclaimed: "At least someone gets my name right."

While Richards was taping his segment, Westerberg and his boy poked their heads into his empty dressing room. Keith had left behind a burning spliff and the remnants of a whiskey. Paul pointed to the glass, then to Johnny. "There," he said. "That's your first drink."

The kid grinned, but shook his head. "Nah, I don't think so."

* * *

The Replacements would spend 2014 on the festival circuit, playing a slate of multi-band bills from Boston to Seattle. The only dud was the first of two weekends at the Coachella Festival in the California desert. It was a big payday, but a bad gig—Coachella had largely turned into a dance festival, and the Replacements were out of place. "There's four thousand people in the front who are stoked and fifteen thousand kids with glowsticks, scratching their heads," said Josh Freese.

Before the second Coachella date, Westerberg's back troubles returned. He enlisted Green Day's Billie Joe Armstrong to sub on guitar, help sing, and save the day. The experience would be a rock-and-roll fantasy camp for Armstrong, who continued to turn up and play with the 'Mats at several more shows—until Westerberg decided the extra help was no longer needed. "Billie, I'm firing the whole band," he told Armstrong, "but we're going in alphabetical order."

As the fall of 2014 arrived, the Replacements staged the first shows on their own, playing sold-out dates at St. Paul's Midway Stadium and in New York City's Forest Hills Stadium. The band's two biggest champions, Peter Jesperson and Michael Hill, were there. They watched the 'Mats perform as tens of thousands celebrated their return. The songs once considered radio flops had become anthems for multiple generations. When they played "Can't Hardly Wait," the sound of the crowd singing along nearly drowned out the band. At long last, Jesperson and Hill had proof: their faith had not been blind.

The offers came pouring in to do more shows—a US theater tour, dates overseas. The band even made a couple of attempts to record new material at studios in Boston and Minneapolis. "Once you open this Pandora's Box, it's open for a while," said Stinson of the reunion. "The amount of fun we have doing this . . . you gotta keep it [going]. We'd have to kill each other to break it up again."

By the end of their spring 2015 tour, Westerberg and Stinson seemed ready to at least maim one another. The same issues that had marked their first breakup—control, respect, and money—cropped up again. Westerberg griped that the reunion had become a money grab for others, that he could be making more playing solo gigs. He didn't like the studio tracks the reunited Replacements had cut, preferring his own home demos of the songs. The 'Mats' entire life cycle had played out in twenty months instead of twelve years.

During the final show of the tour in Portugal, in June, Westerberg announced that the gig would be their final performance ever. The comments caused a major stir online. Fans and pundits lamented that the 'Mats, finally enjoying their long-overdue success, had snatched defeat from the jaws of victory once again.

But despite Westerberg's words, despite all the speculation, the band was not done.

The Replacements had become bigger than their personal squabbles, bigger than Paul's power to banish the music they created. The emotional connection that people found in the 'Mats, the legacy they'd forged—along with the myths, realities, and deaths—couldn't be dismissed so easily. The band had transcended Paul and Tommy—yet it wasn't enough to raise them above the history and flaws and failings that made them who they were.

The essence of the Replacements remains immutable: it's the unmistakable air of juvenile halls, Catholic schools, and basement keggers; the smell of mop buckets, filthy tour vans, and burning money; the sound of drunken laughter, of overdriven amps, and rock-and-roll.

In the end, the pain and desperation, the chaos and the noise, it had meant something.

"However finite and small," observed Tommy Stinson, "we left a mark."

"We did leave a mark," said Paul Westerberg. "And no one can take that away. We were a great little band."

NOTES

This book is based on interviews conducted with some 230 people between 2009 and 2015. Additionally, I was given access to the Replacements' archives at Twin/Tone Records and the Warner Music Group. My research also draws on an array of published pieces, transcripts, documents, and audio/video material from the band's career and subsequent solo endeavors. Interview sourcing is provided in the notes for each chapter, followed by a selected bibliography.

INTRODUCTION
Author interviews with Tommy Stinson, Paul Westerberg, Lori Barbero, Ray Reigstad, Mike Leonard, Anita Stinson, Lonnie Stinson, and Carleen Krietler.

Other Sources
Bream, Jon. "Replacements' Ex-Guitarist Found Dead." *Minneapolis Star-Tribune*, February 20, 1995.
Channen, David, and Neal Justin. "Guitarist Stinson's Friends Recount Full, but Tragic, Life." *Minneapolis Star-Tribune*, February 23, 1995.
Walsh, Jim. "Replacements' 'Lunatic Guitarist,' Bob Stinson, Dies." *Saint Paul Pioneer Press*, February 20, 1995.
Wilonsky, Robert. "No Mere Replacement." *Dallas Observer*, May 11, 1995.

CHAPTER 1
Author interviews with Anita Stinson, Lonnie Stinson, and Tommy Stinson.

Other Sources
Birmingham, Steve. Interview with Bob Stinson, April 3–4, 1994 (transcript).
Hennepin County Welfare Department. Case file: "Robert Stinson," March 13, 1975.

CHAPTER 2
Author interviews with Paul Westerberg.

Other Sources

Valania, Jonathan. Interview with Paul Westerberg, April 30, 2002 (transcript).

Walsh, Jim. *The Replacements: All Over but the Shouting: An Oral History.* Minneapolis: Voyageur Press, 2007.

CHAPTER 3

Author interviews with Lonnie Stinson, Tommy Stinson, Anita Stinson, and Robert Flemal.

Other Sources

Minnesota, State of, Department of Corrections. Uniform case report: "Robert Neil Stinson," June, 30, 1975.

———. Monthly progress report: "Robert Neil Stinson," October 3, 1975.

———. Transfer summary: "Robert Stinson," June 15, 1976.

———. Uniform case report: "Robert Neil Stinson," May 4, 1977.

———. Uniform case report: "Robert Neil Stinson," December 5, 1977.

Vorrath, Harry H., and Larry K. Brendtro. *Positive Peer Culture*, 2nd ed. New Brunswick, NJ: Transaction, 1985.

Zellar, Brad. "The Walls of Red Wing." *City Pages*, December 3, 2003.

CHAPTER 4

Author interviews with Paul Westerberg, Ben Welter, Dave Zilka, Mary Rose Zika, Maggie Gray, Bruno Pellagalli, Jeff Johnson, Jef Jodell, Jack Jodell, and Paul Bolin.

Other Sources

Bream, Jon. "The Faces Had Smiles at Concert." *Minneapolis Star*, November 3, 1975.

Schmickle, Sharon. "Holy Angels: No More Eyebrow Pencil Seams, but Educational Traditions Persist." *Minneapolis Star*, October 8, 1981.

Valania, Jonathan. Interview with Paul Westerberg, April 30, 2002 (transcript).

CHAPTER 5

Author interviews with Tommy Stinson, Curtis Olson, Andrea Olson, Lonnie Stinson, Anita Stinson, and Robert Flemal.

CHAPTER 6

Author interviews with Chris Mars, Paul Westerberg, Andrea Olson, Robert Flemal, Tom Byrne, and Jeff Johnson.

Other Sources

Bahn, Christopher. "Interview: Chris Mars." The A.V. Club Blog, February 28, 2006. http://www.avclub.com/article/interview-chris-mars-16470.

Calderone, Tom. Chris Mars, "Modern Rock Live" interview, April 6, 1992 (transcript).

Gentry, Lana. "Interview with Chris Mars." *beinArt*, January 30, 2010.

George-Warren, Holly. Interview with Chris Mars, 1992 (transcript).

Hallett, Tom. "Chris Mars: An Intimate Portrait of the Artist." *Round the Dial*, January 2010.

Mars, Chris. KROQ "Lovelines" interview, June 11, 1992 (transcript).
———. "MN Original" video segment, January 11, 2015 (transcript).
Walsh, Jim. *The Replacements: All Over but the Shouting: An Oral History.* Minneapolis: Voyageur Press, 2007.
———. "On Art(s) and Artists: A Conversation with Chris Mars." *Minnesota Post*, November 13, 2008. https://www.minnpost.com/arts-culture/2008/11/arts-and -artists-conversation-chris-mars.
Wilonsky, Robert. "No Mere Replacement." *Dallas Observer*, May 11, 1995.

CHAPTER 7

Author interviews with Paul Westerberg, Anita Stinson, Robert Flemal, Tommy Stinson, and Tom Byrne.

Other Sources

Birmingham, Steve. Interview with Bob Stinson, April 3–4, 1994 (transcript).
Ross, R. E. "Bob Stinson: Displacement." *Cake*, November–December 1990.

CHAPTER 8

Author interviews with Anita Stinson, Paul Westerberg, Tommy Stinson, Jef Jodell, Peter Jesperson, Paul Stark, Mike Lasley, Steve Skibbe, Mike Burns, and Kevin Bowe.

Other Sources

Azerrad, Michael. *Our Band Could Be Your Life: Scenes from the American Indie Underground 1981–1991.* New York: Little, Brown & Co., 2001.
Bream, Jon. "Mars Takes His 75% Less Act to Radio." *Minneapolis Star-Tribune*, May 6, 1993.
George-Warren, Holly. Interview with Chris Mars, 1992 (transcript).
Ross, R. E. "Bob Stinson: Displacement." *Cake*, November–December 1990.

CHAPTER 9

Author interviews with Peter Jesperson, Andy Schwartz, Terry Katzman, Bob Dunlap, Curtis Almsted, Chris Osgood, Paul Stark, Chan Poling, Jay Berine, Steve McClellan, P. D. Larson, Paul Westerberg, Tommy Stinson, Jef Jodell, Danny Amis, and Steve Skibbe.

Other Sources

Bream, Jon. "Rock's Rudder Works at the 'Oar.'" *Minneapolis Star*, September 11, 1979.
Holmes, Tim. "Twin Town Tones." *Trouser Press*, August 1980.
Magnet Magazine. Interview with Kevin Cole, 2005 (transcript).

CHAPTER 10

Author interviews with Peter Jesperson, Terry Katzman, Mike Hoeger, Lori Barbero, Tommy Stinson, Bob Dunlap, Lou Santacroce, Chris Osgood, Chan Poling, Steve Skibbe, Bob Mould, Paul Stark, Curt Almsted, Martin Keller, P. D. Larson, Dave Ayers, Wayne Kramer, and Steve Fjelstad.

Other Sources
Bourdaghs, Michael. Interview with the Replacements, January 30, 1981 (transcript).
Farrell, Christopher, "Accept No Replacements." *Trax Magazine*, August 1980.
Hoeger, Mike. "The Dads, the Ben Day Dots, the Replacements." *Minnesota Daily*, October 17, 1980.
Larson, P. D. "POW! Go the Replacements." *Sweet Potato*, February 18, 1981.
Orshoski, Wes. "The Billboard Q&A: The Replacements' Paul Westerberg." *Billboard*, April 22, 2008.

CHAPTER 11

Author interviews with Peter Jesperson, Paul Westerberg, P. D. Larson, Lou Santacroce, Tommy Stinson, Steve Fjelstad, and Greg Helgeson.

Other Sources
Birmingham, Steve. Interview with Bob Stinson, April 3–4, 1994 (transcript).
Bourdaghs, Michael. Interview with the Replacements, January 30, 1981 (transcript).
Orshoski, Wes. "The Billboard Q&A: The Replacements' Paul Westerberg." *Billboard*, April 22, 2008.

CHAPTER 12

Author interviews with Peter Jesperson, Paul Westerberg, Lori Barbero, Lucinda Teasley, Lou Santacroce, Tommy Stinson, Daune Earle, David Roth, Casey Macpherson, Chris Johnson, Dave Ayers, Bob Mould, Terry Katzman, P. D. Larson, Paul Stark, Chan Poling, and Dave Pirner.

Other Sources
Carslon, Angela. "Change of Replacementality." *Minnesota Daily*, September 21, 1984.
Davis, Phil. "Sorry Ma, Forgot to Take Out the Trash." *New York Rocker*, February 1982.

CHAPTER 13

Author interviews with Peter Jesperson, Paul Westerberg, Tommy Stinson, Dave Pirner, Dan Murphy, David Roth, Dave Ayers, Blake Gumprecht, Chris Osgood, Kevin Bowe, and Paul Stark.

Other Sources
Ayers, David. "Replacement Part." *Minnesota Daily*, June 30, 1982.
Birmingham, Steve. Interview with Bob Stinson, April 3–4, 1994 (transcript).
Mars, Chris. "Eight Really Dumb Things the Replacements Did." In *Rolling Stone's Alt-Rock-A-Rama*, edited by Scott Schinder, 269–274. New York: Delta, 1996.
McGowan, David. Interview with Paul Westerberg, KFAI Radio, May 1983 (transcript).

CHAPTER 14

Author interviews with Tommy Stinson, Peter Jesperson, Paul Westerberg, Michael Hill, Glenn Morrow, Mike Hoeger, Julie Farman, Lilli Dennison, Warren Zanes, and Julie Panebianco.

Other Sources

Casey, Vickie Gilmer. "The Sullivan Show; Veteran Roadie and 400 Bar Co-owner Bill Sullivan Takes a Break from the Club Wars to Indulge a First Love: Rock 'n' Roll." *Minneapolis Star-Tribune*, October 29, 1999.

Goldberg, Emily. Interview with Bill Sullivan, November 1987 (transcript).

Hoeger, Mike. "Native Sons Rise in the East." *Minnesota Daily*, April 22, 1983.

Riley, Frank. Email to author, December 6, 2010.

CHAPTER 15

Author interviews with John Doe, Exene Cervenka, Chris Morris, Peter Buck, Brian Baker, Casey Macpherson, Paul Westerberg, Tommy Stinson, Peter Jesperson, and Tommy Keene.

Other Sources

Amorim, Kevin. "Another Soul Saved by Rock and Roll." *New York Newsday*, August 16, 2002.

CHAPTER 16

Author interviews with Peter Jesperson, Paul Westerberg, Peter Buck, Tommy Stinson, Dave Ayers, Daniel Corrigan, John Freeman, Mary Beth Gordon, Lori Bizer, Paul Stark, and Blake Gumprecht.

Other Sources

Heibutzki, Ralph. "Brats in Babylon." *Goldmine*, October 29, 1993.

Morrow, Glenn. Interview with Paul Westerberg, January 10, 1985 (transcript).

CHAPTER 17

Author interviews with Paul Westerberg, Tommy Stinson, Bill Mack, Peter Jesperson, Mike Bosley, John Freeman, Ross Shoemaker, and Ward Dotson.

Other Sources

George-Warren, Holly. Interview with Chris Mars, 1992 (transcript).

CHAPTER 18

Author interviews with Paul Westerberg, P. D. Larson, Frank Black, Wayne Coyne, Ward Dotson, George Lewis, Peter Jesperson, Steve Ralbovsky, Steve Albini, Peter Buck, Warren Zanes, Tommy Stinson, Lori Bizer, Julie Farman, and Lilli Dennison.

Other Sources

Goldberg, Emily. Interview with Bill Sullivan, November 1987 (transcript).

Mundy, Chris. "The Rolling Stone Interview: Paul Westerberg." *Rolling Stone*, June 24, 1993.

Paul, Alan. "A (Pretty Damn Good) Interview with Paul Westerberg, 1996."

CHAPTER 19

Author interviews with Dave Ayers, George Regis, Peter Jesperson, Joanna Spock Dean, Steve Ralbovsky, Michael Hill, and Paul Westerberg.

CHAPTER 20
Author interviews with RJ Smith, Blake Gumprecht, Peter Jesperson, Paul Westerberg, George Regis, Dave Ayers, and Seymour Stein.

CHAPTER 21
Author interviews with Seymour Stein, Michael Hill, Sandy Alouette, Howie Klein, Steve Ralbovsky, and Paul Westerberg.

Other Sources
Cornyn, Stan. *Exploding: The Highs, Hits, Hype, Heroes, and Hustlers of the Warner Music Group.* New York: It Books, 2002.

Herbers, Tom. "Three Tracks, Echo, and a Bunch of Hungry Teenagers." *City Pages,* June 8, 2005.

Katznelson, David. Interview with Seymour Stein, SXSW, March 13, 2008 (transcript).

CHAPTER 22
Author interviews with Carleen Krietler, Ray Reigstad, Tommy Erdelyi, Michael Hill, Peter Jesperson, Tommy Stinson, and Paul Westerberg.

CHAPTER 23
Author interviews with Peter Jesperson, Tommy Stinson, Paul Westerberg, Tommy Erdelyi, Lynn Blakey, Michael Hill, and Peter Buck.

Other Sources
Birmingham, Steve. Interview with Bob Stinson, April 3–4, 1994 (transcript).

Ross, R. E. "Bob Stinson: Displacement." *Cake,* November–December 1990.

CHAPTER 24
Author interviews with Carleen Krietler, Lonnie Stinson, Ray Reigstad, Paul Westerberg, Tommy Stinson, Robert Longo, Peter Jesperson, and Monty Lee Wilkes.

Other Sources
Aaron, Charles. "Hold My Life: Bob Stinson's Regrets." *SPIN,* June 1993.

Azerrad, Michael. *Our Band Could Be Your Life: Scenes from the American Indie Underground 1981–1991.* New York: Little, Brown & Co., 2001.

Goldberg, Emily. Interview with Bill Sullivan, November 1987 (transcript).

Magnet Magazine. Interview with Kevin Cole, 2005 (transcript).

CHAPTER 25
Author interviews with Larry Butler, Michael Hill, Sandy Alouette, Steven Baker, Adam Sommers, Cathy Lincoln, Jo Lenardi, Julie Panebianco, Tommy Stinson, Charlie Springer, Casey Macpherson, Monty Lee Wilkes, Peter Jesperson, Wayne Coyne, John DeVries, Tom Bunch, and Marty Racine.

CHAPTER 26

Author interviews with Peter Jesperson, George Regis, Mike Lembo, Russ Rieger, Gary Hobbib, Warren Zanes, Sandy Alouette, Seymour Stein, Michael Hill, Paul Westerberg, and Tommy Stinson.

CHAPTER 27

Author interviews with Michele Galfas, Steven Baker, Jeff Ayeroff, Peter Jesperson, Paul Westerberg, Daune Earle, Carleen Krietler, Russ Rieger, Gary Hobbib, Monty Lee Wilkes, Tommy Stinson, Mary Melia, Julie Panebianco, and Michael Hill.

Other Sources

Bennetts, Leslie. "Struggles at the New 'Saturday Night.'" *New York Times*, December 12, 1985.

Heibutzki, Ralph. "Brats in Babylon." *Goldmine*, October 29, 1993.

Shales, Tom, and James Andrew Miller. *Live from New York: An Uncensored History of Saturday Night Live, as Told by Its Stars, Writers, and Guests.* New York: Little, Brown, & Co., 2002.

Sharbutt, Jay. "NBC's Grant Tinker Looks Ahead with Optimism for 1986." *Los Angeles Times*, January 7, 1986.

CHAPTER 28

Author interviews with Jeff Ayeroff, Carleen Krietler, Ray Reigstad, Peter Jesperson, Paul Westerberg, Tommy Stinson, Bob Dunlap, Ward Dotson, Anita Stinson, Russ Rieger, Gary Hobbib, George Regis, and David Ayers.

CHAPTER 29

Author interviews with Randy Skinner, Steven Baker, Paul Westerberg, Andy Proudfoot, Monty Lee Wilkes, Gary Hobbib, Carleen Krietler, Anita Stinson, and Russ Rieger.

Other Sources

Pouncey, Edward. "The Replacements Drink and Drive." *Sounds*, November 9, 1985.

Snow, Mat. "The Replacements: Hits from the Sticks." *New Musical Express*, January 11, 1986.

CHAPTER 30

Author interviews with Andy Proudfoot, Julie Panebianco, Paul Westerberg, Robert Longo, Seymour Stein, Sandy Alouette, Gary Hobbib, Carleen Krietler, Bob Dunlap, Ray Reigstad, Tommy Stinson, Mike Owens, and Russ Rieger.

Other Sources

Azerrad, Michael. *Our Band Could Be Your Life: Scenes from the American Indie Underground 1981–1991.* New York: Little, Brown & Co., 2001.

Heibutzki, Ralph. "Brats in Babylon." *Goldmine*, October 29, 1993.

Valania, Jonathan. Interview with Paul Westerberg, April 30, 2002 (transcript).

CHAPTER 31
Author interviews with Russ Rieger, Steven Baker, Dave Jerden, Michael Hill, Scott Litt, and Paul Westerberg.

CHAPTER 32
Author interviews with Jim Dickinson, Michael Hill, Russ Rieger, Jim Lancaster, Tommy Stinson, Paul Westerberg, Joe Hardy, and John Hampton.

Other Sources
Dickinson, Jim. "True Story Pictures Presents: The Music Interviews," 2009 (transcript).
Smith, RJ. "Dixie Fried: Jim Dickinson's Memphis Productions." *Village Voice Rock & Roll Quarterly*, Summer 1992.

CHAPTER 33
Author interviews with Paul Westerberg, John Hampton, Jim Lancaster, Rick Raburn, Lori Bizer, Tommy Stinson, Michael Hill, Russ Rieger, and Joe Hardy.

Other Sources
Aaron, Charles. "Hold My Life: Bob Stinson's Regrets." *SPIN*, June 1993.
DeMuir, Harold. "Minneapolis Dropouts Go Digital." *BAM*, September 11, 1987.
Drozdowski, Ted. Interview with Jim Dickinson, 2006 (transcript).
George-Warren, Holly. *A Man Called Destruction: The Life and Music of Alex Chilton, from Box Tops to Big Star to Backdoor Man*. New York: Viking, 2014.
Hall, Russell. Interview with Jim Dickinson, 2005 (transcript).
Herrington, Chris. Interview with Jim Dickinson, 2008 (transcript).
Holdship, Bill. Interview with Jim Dickinson, 2005 (transcript).
Iorio, Paul. "The Replacements' 'Pleased to Meet Me': This Year's Masterpiece." *Cashbox*, March 2, 1987.
Panebianco, Julie. Interview with Paul Westerberg, 1987 (transcript).
Standish, Peter. "The Other Guy from Minneapolis: Paul Westerberg and the Replacements." *The Gavin Report*, June 19, 1987.
Trakin, Roy. Interview with Paul Westerberg, August 1987 (transcript).
Walsh, Jim. Interview with Paul Westerberg, March 1987 (transcript).

CHAPTER 34
Author interviews with Paul Westerberg, Tommy Stinson, Peter Jesperson, Jeff Waryan, Chrissie Dunlap, Bob Dunlap, Curt Almsted, Carleen Krietler, Daune Earle, and Gary Hobbib.

CHAPTER 35
Author interviews with Russ Rieger, Gary Hobbib, Seymour Stein, Charlie Springer, Paul Westerberg, Tommy Stinson, Bob Dunlap, Michael Hill, Jo Lenardi, Steve Tipp, Randy Skinner, Julie Panebianco, Peter Jesperson, Dave Ayers, John DeVries, Chris Osgood, Abbie Kane, and Paul Stark.

CHAPTER 36

Author interviews with George Gerrity, Steve Tipp, Paul Westerberg, Russ Rieger, Mary Melia, Bill Flanagan, and David Fricke.

Other Sources

Flanagan, Bill. "Replacements: Paul Westerberg's Band May Ascend to the Stars or Splatter All over the Road." *Musician*, September 1987.

Fricke, David. "Pleased to Meet Me." *Rolling Stone*, July 2, 1987.

CHAPTER 37

Author interviews with Russ Rieger, Lewis Largent, Bill Holdship, Kurt Hirsch, Johnny Mars, Paul Westerberg, Lin Brehmer, George Gerrity, Suzanne Emil, Bob Dunlap, Gary Hobbib, and Julie Panebianco.

Other Sources

KROQ. Interview with the Replacements, *New American Rock*, May 1987 (transcript).

WBRU. Interview with the Replacements, July 1987 (transcript).

WXRT. Interview with the Replacements, *Big Beat*, August 1987 (transcript).

CHAPTER 38

Author interviews with Randy Skinner, Rick Krim, Paul Westerberg, Russ Rieger, Ray Reigstad, and Daune Earle.

Other Sources

Fein, Esther B. "Tracing the Tragic Path to Four Teen-Age Suicides." *New York Times*, March 23, 1987.

Gaines, Donna. *Teenage Wasteland: Suburbia's Dead End Kids*. New York: Pantheon Books, 1991.

Marks, Craig, and Rob Tannenbaum. *I Want My MTV: The Uncensored Story of the Music Video Revolution*. New York: Dutton, 2011.

Morrison, John F. "Teen Suicides a 'Tribute to Joe'?" *Philadelphia Daily News*, March 12, 1987.

Partain, Jack. "Sonny Vincent Interview (Part 1 and 2)." *Perfect Sound Forever*, August 2011. http://www.furious.com/perfect/sonnyvincent.html.

Wilentz, Amy. "Teen Suicide: Two Death Pacts Shake the Country." *Time*, March 23, 1987.

CHAPTER 39

Author interviews with Paul Westerberg, Bob Dunlap, Tommy Stinson, Monty Lee Wilkes, Dan Baird, and Rick Richards.

Other Sources

Gill, Andy. "Husker Du and the Replacements: Euphoric . . . Urgent . . . Raucous . . . Drunk." *Q*, August 1987.

Kirsch, Michele. "Taking Out the Trash." *New Musical Express*, June 13, 1987.

Reynolds, Simon. "The Replacements: Rebel Yell." *Melody Maker*, May 16, 1987.

CHAPTER 40

Author interviews with Scott McCaughey, Bill Holdship, Russ Rieger, Paul Westerberg, Gary Hobbib, Charlie Springer, Derek Wilkinson, Tommy Stinson, Bob Dunlap, and Julie Panebianco.

Other Sources

Davis, Bruce. Interview with Chris Mars, December 18, 1990 (transcript).
Fricke, David. "Spirit in the Sky." *Melody Maker*, August 8, 1987.
George-Warren, Holly. Interview with Chris Mars, 1992 (transcript).
Pareles, Jon. "Rock: The Replacements in Songs from 3 Decades." *New York Times*, July 26, 1987.
Rowland, Mark. "Tom Waits Is Flying Upside Down (on Purpose)." *Musician*, October 1987.
Trakin, Roy. Interview with Paul Westerberg, August 1987 (transcript).

CHAPTER 41

Author interviews with Lori Bizer, Paul Westerberg, Tommy Stinson, Scott McCaughey, Daune Earle, Chrissie Dunlap, Rob Light, Steve Davis, Steve McClellan, Lewis Largent, Larry Weinles, and Russ Rieger.

Other Sources

Keller, Martin. "Mythunderstanding the Replacements." *Twin Cities Reader*, April 29, 1987.
Pareles, Jon. "This Band Speaks for Lowbrows and Underdogs." *New York Times*, July 19, 1987.
Riley, Frank. "Venture Bookings: Industry Hotwire." *Pollstar*, October 12, 1987.
———. Email to author, December 6, 2010.

CHAPTER 42

Author interviews with Paul Westerberg, Scott Litt, Peter Buck, Lori Bizer, Gary Hobbib, and Tommy Stinson.

Other Sources

Elder, Heather. "From Rock 'n' Roll to Advertising: Getting to Know Minneapolis Art Producer Sally Mars." Notes from a Rep's Journal, January 29, 2013. http://notesfromarepsjournal.com/2013/01/29/from-rocknroll-to-advertising-getting-to-know-minneapolis-art-producer-sally-mars/.

CHAPTER 43

Author interviews with Michael Hill, Russ Rieger, Paul Westerberg, Tony Berg, and Gary Hobbib.

Other Sources

Chmielewski, Dawn C. "Dick Berg Dies at 87; Television and Film Writer and Producer." *Los Angeles Times*, September 3, 2009.

CHAPTER 44
Author interviews with Bob Dunlap, Julie Panebianco, Michael Hill, Tim Perell, Ian Kimmet, Tony Berg, Dan Bates, Paul Westerberg, and Tommy Stinson.

CHAPTER 45
Author interviews with Michael Hill, Gary Hobbib, George Regis, Russ Rieger, Howie Klein, Steven Baker, Lenny Waronker, Matt Wallace, Paul Westerberg, Bob Dunlap, and Tommy Stinson.

CHAPTER 46
Author interviews with Michael Hill, Matt Wallace, Steven Baker, Paul Westerberg, Tommy Stinson, Bob Dunlap, Mike Bosley, and Kim Buie.

Other Sources
O'Hagan, Sean. "I Just Tell Stories for Money." *New Musical Express*, November 14, 1987.
Oney, Steve. "Tom Waits: 20 Questions." *Playboy*, March 1988.
Rowland, Mark. "Tom Waits Is Flying Upside Down (on Purpose)." *Musician*, October 1987.

CHAPTER 47
Author interviews with Paul Westerberg, Matt Wallace, Mike Bosley, Tommy Stinson, Bob Dunlap, Steven Baker, Lenny Waronker, Russ Rieger, Michael Hill, Chris Lord-Alge, and Rich Fitzgerald.

Other Sources
Gilyard, Burl. "Kinda Like an Artist." *Minnesota Daily A&E*, February 3, 1989.
Holdship, Bill. Interview with Paul Westerberg, 2005 (transcript).
R.E.M./WEA. Satellite presentation, October 13, 1988 (transcript).
Saccone, Teri. "Portraits: Chris Mars." *Modern Drummer*, March 1990.

CHAPTER 48
Author interviews with Ray Reigstad, Carleen Krietler, Anita Stinson, and Michelle Picardo.

Other Sources
Heibutzki, Ralph. "There Goes a Regular: Bob Stinson's Secret Life After the Replacements." *Vintage Guitar*, January 2005.
Ross, R. E. "Bob Stinson: Displacement." *Cake*, November–December 1990.

CHAPTER 49
Author interviews with Bill Bentley, Paul Westerberg, Tommy Stinson, Lori Bizer, Stanley Booth, Paul Natkin, Bob Dunlap, Debbie Rose, George Regis, Daune Earle, Randy Skinner, David Seltzer, Gary Hobbib, Mary Melia, Rick Krim, Julie Panebianco, and Bill Flanagan.

Other Sources

Goetzman, Keith. "Don't Sell Your Soul." *Twin Cities Reader*, January 25, 1989.

Levy, Joe, and Christian Logan. "Spins: Don't Tell a Soul." *SPIN*, March 1989.

Perry, Steve. "Achin' to Be Understood." *Musician*, February 1989.

Robbins, Ira. "Don't Tell a Soul." *Rolling Stone*, February 9, 1989.

CHAPTER 50

Author interviews with Brendan McCabe, Bob Dunlap, Roger Vitale, Carl Davino, Jim "Velvet" Sullivan, Gary Hobbib, Rick Krim, Michael Linehan, Russ Rieger, Gary Hobbib, Paul Westerberg, Tommy Stinson, Daune Earle, Lori Bizer, Dan Baird, and Bill Holdship.

Other Sources

Cromelin, Richard. "Replacements Aren't Replaceable at Palladium." *Los Angeles Times*, May 8, 1989.

Pareles, Jon. "On a Wild Joyride with the Replacements." *New York Times*, April 4, 1989.

Pond, Steve. "The Growing Pains and Pleasures of the Replacements." *Rolling Stone*, June 1, 1989.

CHAPTER 51

Author interviews with Steven Baker, Michael Hill, Paul Westerberg, Daniel Waters, and Winona Ryder.

Other Sources

Britt, Bruce. "Replacements Have Inside Track to Star in 'Rock High' Sequel." *Los Angeles Daily News*, May 18, 1989.

CHAPTER 52

Author interviews with Daune Earle, Paul Westerberg, Bob Dunlap, Bill Holdship, Mary Melia, Chrissie Dunlap, Carl Davino, and Tommy Stinson.

Other Sources

Davis, Bruce. Interview with Chris Mars, December 18, 1990 (transcript).

George-Warren, Holly. Interview with Chris Mars, 1992 (transcript).

Valania, Jonathan. Interview with Paul Westerberg, April 30, 2002 (transcript).

CHAPTER 53

Author interviews with Roger Vitale, Jim "Velvet" Sullivan, Paul Westerberg, Tommy Stinson, Steven Baker, Steve Davis, and Bob Dunlap.

Other Sources

Kot, Greg. "A No-Strings Band: Replacements Want Popularity—On Their Terms." *Chicago Tribune*, June 7, 1989.

CHAPTER 54

Author interviews with Benmont Tench, Bob Dunlap, Dan Baird, Paul Westerberg, Tommy Stinson, Carl Davino, Steve Davis, Alan "Bugs" Weidel, Jim "Velvet" Sullivan, Rich Fitzgerald, and Roger Vitale.

Other Sources

George-Warren, Holly. Interview with Chris Mars, 1992 (transcript).
Kot, Greg. "Replacement Parts." *Chicago Tribune*, January 31, 1991.
Petty, Tom, and Steve Hochman. "On the Road with Tom Petty and the Heartbreakers: If It's Monday, This Must Be Miami." *Rolling Stone*, October 5, 1989.

CHAPTER 55

Author interviews with Paul Westerberg, Bill Flanagan, Lori Bizer, Gary Hobbib, Russ Rieger, Matt Wallace, Steve Jordan, Scott Litt, and Julie Panebianco.

Other Sources

Davis, Bruce. Interview with Chris Mars, December 18, 1990 (transcript).

CHAPTER 56

Author interviews with Scott Litt, Paul Westerberg, Michael Hill, Donna Ranieri, Fred Woods, Tommy Stinson, Daune Earle, and Charley Drayton.

Other Sources

Conner, Shawn. "Interview—Johnette Napolitano." *The Snipe*, January 18, 2012.
Davis, Bruce. Interview with Chris Mars, December 18, 1990 (transcript).
Fazed.com. "Interview with Johnette Napolitano." Fazed.com, 2011.

CHAPTER 57

Author interviews with Paul Westerberg, Scott Litt, Lenny Waronker, Tommy Stinson, Terry Reid, Clif Norrell, Bob Dunlap, Steve Berlin, Michael Hill, Michael Blair, Russ Rieger, and Mauro Magellan.

CHAPTER 58

Author interviews with Michael Wilson, Donna Ranieri, Paul Westerberg, Bob Dunlap, Tommy Stinson, Charlie Springer, Gary Hobbib, and Lori Bizer.

Other Sources

Valania, Jonathan. Interview with Paul Westerberg, April 30, 2002 (transcript).

CHAPTER 59

Author interviews with Paul Westerberg, Mary Melia, Seymour Stein, Charlie Springer, Bill Flanagan, Daune Earle, Tommy Stinson, George Regis, Randy Skinner, Jay Healy, Howie Klein, Michael Hill, and Russ Rieger.

Other Sources
Davis, Bruce. Interview with Chris Mars, December 18, 1990 (transcript).
Flanagan, Bill. "The Replacements' Little Problem." *Musician*, December 1990.
Holdship, Bill. Interview with Tommy Stinson, 1992 (transcript).
Linden, Amy. "Replacements R.I.P." *SPIN*, December, 1990.

CHAPTER 60
Author interviews with Michael Blair, Tommy Stinson, Paul Westerberg, Robert Bennett, Steve Folsom, Jim "Velvet" Sullivan, Ken Stringfellow, Bill Holdship, Chris Morris, Jim Walsh, John Freeman, and Mike Leonard.

Other Sources
Davis, Bruce. Interview with Chris Mars, December 18, 1990 (transcript).
Holdship, Bill. Interview with Tommy Stinson, 1992 (transcript).
Walsh, Jim. *The Replacements: All Over but the Shouting: An Oral History.* Minneapolis: Voyageur Press, 2007.
Wilonsky, Robert. "No Mere Replacement." *Dallas Observer*, May 11, 1995.

CHAPTER 61
Author interviews with Ken Stringfellow, Bob Dunlap, Robert Bennett, Steve Folsom, Kim Chapman, Russ Rieger, Paul Westerberg, Winona Ryder, Michael Hill, Dan Baird, Julie Panebianco, and Elvis Costello.

Other Sources
Gowen, Anne. "Sobriety Fuels Rumors of Drinking Band's Split." *Washington Times*, March 4, 1991.
Holdship, Bill. Interview with Tommy Stinson, 1992 (transcript).
Walsh, Jim. *The Replacements: All Over but the Shouting: An Oral History.* Minneapolis: Voyageur Press, 2007.

CHAPTER 62
Author interviews with Peter Jesperson, Paul Westerberg, and Paul Stark.

Other Sources
Walsh, Jim. "Peter's Passion." *City Pages*, July 14, 1993.

CHAPTER 63
Author interviews with Peter Jesperson, Bob Dunlap, Chrissie Dunlap, Kim Chapman, Johnny Mars, Paul Westerberg, Scott Esbeck, Jeff Ousley, Jim "Velvet" Sullivan, and Daune Earle.

Other Sources
Blackwell, Mark. "Keeping the Faith—Is the Replacements' Paul Westerberg the Soul of Rock 'n' Roll, or Just the Heel?" *SPIN*, August 1991.

EPILOGUE

Author interviews with Slim Dunlap, Ray Reigstad, Carleen Krietler, Anita Stinson, Tommy Stinson, Lisa Stinson, Lonnie Stinson, Marvin Gleicher, Chrissie Dunlap, Peter Jesperson, Daune Stinson, Kim Chapman, Winona Ryder, Paul Westerberg, Mike Leonard, Matt Wallace, Russ Rieger, Gary Hobbib, Josh Freese, Larry White, Jim "Velvet" Sullivan, Charles Aaron, Lori Barbero, Neal Karlen, Johnny Rzeznik, Lou Giordano, Jeff Tweedy, Jakob Dylan, Michael Hill, Bill Bentley, Chris Morris, Tommy Keene, Gary Gersh, George Regis, Don Was, Bill Flanagan, and Marc Solomon.

Other Sources

Appleford, Steve. "Tommy Boy." *Dallas Observer*, May 21, 1998.

Associated Press. "Q&A with Paul Westerberg." September 28, 2004.

Boehm, Mike. "Finding a Good Replacement: With His Band Bash & Pop, Tommy Stinson Tones Down Defiance and Aims for Longevity." *Los Angeles Times*, June 12, 1993.

Dolan, Jon. "The Replacements: The Greatest Band That Never Was." *Rolling Stone*, September 22, 2014.

Gill, Andy. "Paul Westerberg: The Agony Aunt of Grunge." *Q*, June 1993.

Gilmer, Vickie. "Lonesome Stranger." *Minneapolis Star-Tribune*, February 21, 1999.

Hart, Joseph. "Into the Black: The Final Days of Bob Stinson." *City Pages*, March, 1 1995.

Hilburn, Robert. "Irreplaceable Experience." *Los Angeles Times*, February 14, 1999.

Hirschberg, Lynn. "Strange Love." *Vanity Fair*, September 1992.

Holdship, Bill. "Off the 'Mats." *Los Angeles New Times*, April 25, 2002.

———. Interview with Paul Westerberg and Tommy Stinson, October 11, 2014 (transcript).

Jones, Bill. "Josh Freese of Devo and the Vandals Is the Blue Collar Freelance Drummer to the Stars." *Noisey*, August 21, 2014.

Kandell, Steve. "Billie Joe Armstrong Meets Paul Westerberg." *SPIN*, April 2010.

Kaufman, Gil. "Legendary Producer Joins Perfect's Tommy Stinson." MTV.com, November 11, 1997.

Kuipers, Dean. "Oh the Angst. Oh the Sales." *Los Angeles Times*, July 7, 2002.

Liebrock, Rachel. "Paul Westerberg." *Pop Culture Press*, Fall 2002.

Lindeen, Laurie. *Petal Pusher: A Rock and Roll Cinderella Story*. New York: Atria, 2007.

Masley, Ed. "The Replacements' Tommy Stinson Talks Reunion." *Arizona Republic*, September 26, 2014.

Moon, Tom. "A Different Drummer Now Marches to His Own Tunes." *Philadelphia Inquirer*, May, 24, 1992.

Nelson, Chris. "'Perfect' Direction for Ex-Replacement Tommy Stinson." *MTV.com*, March 20, 1998.

Nicholson, Kris. "Replacements: We're Over. Forget About It. Get a Life." *yeah, yeah, yeah*, issue 10, 1997.

Philips, Chuck. "R.E.M., Warner Records Sign $80-Million Deal." *Los Angeles Times*, August 25, 1996.

Riemenschneider, Chris. "Westerberg Goes from 'Folker' Back to Rocker." *Minneapolis Star-Tribune*, November 5, 2004.

Robbins, Ira. Interview with Paul Westerberg, May 1, 1993 (transcript).

Rosen, Craig. "Paul Westerberg's 'Eventually' Is Now." *Billboard*, March 16, 1996.

Royston, Reggie. "Replacements Reunion? Stinson Says Westerberg Blew It." *Saint Paul Pioneer Press*, November 14, 2002.

Sullivan, Andy. "Song Sung Slim: In His Own Words, Slim Dunlap Tells It Like It Is." *The Squealer*, June–July 1997.

Valania, Jonathan. Interview with Paul Westerberg, April 30, 2002 (transcript).

Vaziri, Aidin. "Q&A with Paul Westerberg." *San Francisco Chronicle*, February 28, 1999.

Walsh, Jim. "Bob Stinson's an Ex-'Mat but He's Nobody's Doormat." *Saint Paul Pioneer Press*, September 19, 1993.

Westerberg, Paul. "Beyond the Box Tops." *New York Times*, March 20, 2010.

Wilding, Philip. "Interview: Paul Westerberg." *Classic Rock*, November 2004.

Wilonsky, Robert. "No Mere Replacement." *Dallas Observer*, May 11, 1995.

———. "Bastard of Middle Age." *Dallas Observer*, February 11, 1999.

ACKNOWLEDGMENTS

Trouble Boys is the result of nearly a decade of planning, research, and work. One doesn't reach the end of a labor like that without a very long list of people to thank.

First and foremost, to Paul Westerberg and Tommy Stinson: I am indebted to you, for the music, the trust, and everything else you've given me. I sincerely hope your story together will continue well past these pages.

It cannot be emphasized enough: this book simply would not exist but for the dedicated efforts of Peter Jesperson and Darren Hill.

Peter made crucial introductions, shared his personal archives, and submitted to years of often difficult questions. He and his wife, Jennifer, took me into their home and hearts. Peter is the ultimate believer, and I hope he feels his faith in me was not misplaced.

From my first conversation with him in 2006, Darren saw the value in this project and, crucially, helped Paul Westerberg see it as well. It's worth noting that in addition to managing Paul and helping bring about the Replacements reunion, Darren also supervised the return of the New York Dolls and the resurrection of Roky Erickson. Put simply: Darren is a friend to rock-and-roll and all who love it. But more than that, he's someone I call friend, which is a privilege.

Michael Hill served as the Replacements' A&R man at Warner Bros. for the better part of seven years. As if that weren't penance enough for one lifetime, he had to endure my questioning presence for a further seven years. Through it all he showed incredible kindness, patience, and understanding for which I will be eternally grateful.

To my agent Erin Hosier, I owe so much. For taking me on, for guiding a first-time author through an unfamiliar process, and for keeping me from the proverbial ledge on the many occasions I was ready to jump—mere thanks don't seem enough.

Ben Schafer at Da Capo was the first to express interest in this project and was steadfast through the many twists, turns, and years of delays it took to bring it to fruition. He fought for me and for this book at so many critical junctures that I can't even remember. But his editorial stewardship and personal support will never be forgotten.

To the Stinson family: I am humbled that you allowed me to tell this story as it needed to be. I owe deep thanks to Anita Stinson-Kurth, Lonnie Stinson, and Daune (Earle) Stinson for sharing what they had every right to keep private. I'm also indebted to Anita's husband, Tom Kurth, as well as to Lisa Stinson and Ruby Stinson. For hospitality in Hudson, I am grateful to Emily Jane Roberts and Tallulah Stinson. In Arizona, Carleen (Krietler) Stinson shared intimate memories that allowed me a better understanding of Bob Stinson.

Everyone has Slim stories, so here's mine: When I contacted Bob Dunlap about this book and told him I was coming to Minneapolis, his first question was to ask me—a total stranger and likely nuisance—if I needed a ride from the airport. In the wake of his stroke and the subsequent public tributes, it became clear that my experience was not unique, that he had demonstrated a lifetime of similar kindness to all he encountered. Watching his wife Chrissie care for him these last few years has shown me the true meaning of love. They are an inspiration.

Mary Lucia is a broadcaster of the highest order and someone who intuitively understands the beautiful drama of rock-and-roll. She provided tea and sympathy and valued friendship when it was most needed. Thanks, Looch, I owe ya.

My conversations with Jim "Spike" Boquist were always informal, but also invaluable in helping shape this work. An artist, a philosopher, and a man of the road, Jim is the sort of fella I'd like to be when I grow up.

I must thank Lori Bizer Leighton for taking the time to recall her life with Paul Westerberg. I am also appreciative of Laurie Lindeen, who was always gracious in welcoming me into her home.

Though Chris Mars did not wish to participate in this project, I am thankful to him and his wife Sally for the courtesies they did extend. I hope I have represented them fairly in this story. The same holds true for Bill Sullivan, who I came to know only a little, but appreciated greatly.

Paul Stark was instrumental in this project, not just in sharing memories but in helping digitize the Twin/Tone and Replacements archives. A hearty thanks to the other Twin/Tone alumni who offered help: David Ayers, Blake Gumprecht, Chris Osgood, and especially Abbie Kane.

Russ Rieger and Gary Hobbib spent many hours on the phone and in person discussing their experiences with the Replacements. This book would not be what it is without their time and contributions. So too George Regis, who recalled his eighteen years of service to the band and Paul with a candor and humor that was deeply appreciated.

The key to the world of Warner Bros. was given to me by my friend, the estimable Bob Merlis. Special thanks are due also to Seymour Stein, Lenny Waronker, Howie Klein, Steven Baker, Charlie Springer, Bill Bentley, Mary

Melia, Sandy Alouette, and Cathy Lincoln. Jo Lenardi and Randy Skinner started out as interview subjects but have become dear friends. I can happily say the same about Julie Panebianco, who shared files, photos, contacts, and insights into the band that helped me along the path tremendously.

I managed to speak with nearly everyone who ever served as part of a Replacements crew. I owe them all a debt, but particularly Monty Lee Wilkes, Carl Davino, Rick Marino, Jim Runge, Andy Proudfoot, Lou Santacroce, Casey Macpherson, Jeff Ousley, Mike Bosley, and Scott Esbeck. In Jim "Velvet" Sullivan, whose support extends far beyond this book, I have found a true pal.

I had the pleasure of making the acquaintance of Tommy Stinson's manager Ben Perlstein midway through this project. Since that moment, Benny has been an indispensable ally and a swell guy to boot.

I was privileged to have so many of my journalistic colleagues volunteer tapes, transcripts, and information that added depth to this work. My sincerest thanks to Jonathan Valania, Matthew Fritch, and Eric Miller at *Magnet* magazine, RJ Smith, Bruce Davis, Holly George-Warren, John Lightfoot, Emily Goldberg, Chris Morris, David Fricke, Jim DeRogatis, Andrew Earles, Russell Hall, Ted Drozdowski, Fred Mills, Rob Tannenbaum and Craig Marks, Caryn Rose, Mike Hoeger, Tony Lonetree, Barney Hoskyns, Bill Flanagan, Greg Kot, Charles Cross, Tony Fletcher, Patrick Berkery, Robert Wilonsky, Jack Partain, Jason Gross, Brett Milano, Roy Trakin, Ira Robbins, David N. Meyer, Charles Aaron, and Steve Birmingham.

I must single out Bill Holdship here. Though telling the Replacements' story ultimately became my charge, in many ways this was Bill's book to write. Under such circumstances, few would've been as generous in sharing their materials and memories. But Bill is a rare sort. For the better part of two decades he's been in my life as a mentor, colleague, and most of all friend.

No band has greater champions in the online world than Kathy Shine, of the Man Without Ties website, and Matt Tomich of The Skyway Internet Mailing List. Replacements fans, myself included, owe Kathy and Matt for their selfless efforts over the years in helping foster a sense of community. Also, a tip of the hat to John Davidson for compiling The Replacements Bible, Brett Hale for creating the "We Love the 'Mats" Facebook page, and Jim Clarke for his work with the "Bob Stinson's Ghost" YouTube page.

My ability to research the collected live recordings of the Replacements was made possible by the kindness of Ralph Bryant and the MatsTapes Collective and Preservation Society: Rob Earp, Remi Williams, Trace Hull, Rene Greblo, Charles Ford, Craig "C9" Cholette, Dana Nordaune, Dustin Henderson, Max Warden, and Bill Reuf.

At Rhino Records and the Warner Music Group, I must thank Mike Wilson, Mike Johnson, Steve Lang, Dave May, Mason Williams, Kent Liu, Brian Hay, Mark Pinkus, Jason Reynolds, and Kate Haffenden for all their help.

Rick Fuller has worked tirelessly for a decade to help create a comprehensive visual archive for the Replacements. I owe him and his wife, Anniken, a great deal professionally and personally. So, too, the crew of filmmakers, editors, and researchers who helped document the 'Mats story on celluloid: Bob Medcraft, Andy Gund, David Richardson, Todd Johnson, Dan Jagunich, Hart Perry and Diana Heinz Perry, Sunday Stevens, and the estate of Peter Nydrle.

Along those lines, I should recognize the many photographers who provided images for this project. The Replacements were fortunate to have two fine artists and even finer gentlemen in Greg Helgeson and Daniel Corrigan chronicling their early career. Also thanks to Michael Wilson, Dewey Nicks, Ted Barron, Kevin Scanlon, Wayne Viens, Steven Cohen, Paul Natkin, Marty Perez, Jason Sands, Ebet Roberts, David Seltzer, Steve Linsenmayer, Lisan Sieroty Lema, Deborah Feingold, Mark Lacy, and Just Loomis. An extra special thanks to Donna Ranieri for going above and beyond in all ways.

For insights, encouragement, and assistance, I would like to thank Matt Wallace, Tony Berg, Lou Giordano, Don Was, Andrea Olson Lorimer, Steve Davis, Frank Riley, Gary Gersh, David Browne, Bob Mould, Kim Buie, Tony Philputt, Dan Baird, Rick Richards, Warner Hodges, Benmont Tench, Alan "Bugs" Weidel, Mary Klauzer and East End Management, Andy Schwartz, Lynn Blakey, Morgan Neville, Ken Feinleib, Michelle Picardo, Angie Carlson, Steven Hyden, Daniel Waters, Danny Bramson, Jeff Tweedy, Jakob Dylan, Glenn Dicker, Mike LaMaistre and Andy Cirzan at Jam Productions, Marty Lennertz, Johnny Mars and Lin Brehmer at WXRT, Rick Krim, Chris Coleman, Audrey Bilger, Cheryl Pawelski, Greg Allen and all at Omnivore Recordings, Steve Wynn and Linda Pitmon, Ken Weinstein, Greg and Esther Cartwright, Josh Freese, George Lewis, Glenn Morrow, Fred Woods, Brad Quinn, Stephen Siegel, Tom Scharpling, Winona Ryder, Chuck Prophet and Stephanie Finch, Amy Salit, Henry Owings, Gena Rositano, Dave and Kathleen Philips, Neko Case, Ryan Adams, Scott Giampino, Chad Quierolo, Luther Dickinson, and Dr. Warren Zanes.

During my many trips to the Twin Cities, I came to understand that "Minnesota Nice" is not just lip service. For their help and hospitality, I thank Curt Almsted, Terry Katzman, Ray Reigstad, Lori Barbero, Kevin Bowe, Chris Riemenschneider, John Wareham, Jon Bream, Jim Walsh, Martin Keller, John Freeman, Mike Leonard, Sonia Grover, Neal Karlen, P. D. Larson, Jack Jodell, Maggie Grey, Mary Rose Zika, and the family of John Zika.

In Memphis, my efforts were aided by Dan Russo, Jody Stephens, and Elizabeth Montgomery Brown of Ardent Studios. Eric Plumley of Burch, Porter & Johnson was crucial in navigating legal issues and acted as counsel and conscience whenever needed. Ross Johnson offered sage advice and many laughs. I'm indebted to Sara Kaye Larson for her years of support. Nor could I have made it through without Winston, Elizabeth and May Eggleston, Dan Holloway, Dr. John Whitmore, Sherman Willmott, David Dunlap Jr., John Paul Keith, Steve and Joann Selvidge, Jack Yarber, Eric Freidl, Zac Ives, John Hoppe, Madison Farmer, Bruce Watson, Justin Bailey, and all my guys at Rhodes hoops.

Thanks in memoriam: Jef Jodell, Tom Carlson, Steve Foley, Kevin Foley, Jim Dickinson, Brendan McCabe, Don Smith, John Hampton, John Fry, Alex Chilton, Ian McLagan, Tommy Erdelyi, Ross Shoemaker, and Rich Fitzgerald.

As I worked on the manuscript, I benefited from the feedback of several trusted readers. Few people know rock-and-roll better than Tommy Keene and Jon Wurster. Their suggestions, critiques, and queries were crucial in the completion of this book. For editing guidance, musical advice, and unbridled enthusiasm (as well as occasional ball-busting), Ari Surdoval proved an invaluable ally time and again.

Michaelangelo Matos cut and shaped an unwieldy manuscript into a proper book without losing its essence. I was fortunate to have his help. Also a special thanks to Da Capo's design and production team: Fred Francis, Jack Lenzo, Amber Morris, and Cindy Buck.

When it comes to literary pursuits, Eric Waggoner has been in my corner—the Mickey to my Rocky—for fifteen years. If this book is worthwhile or moving at all, it's because I strove to reach the bar that he's set for me. Thank you, Brother E, for everything.

In addition, I must pay respects to a group of authors who are inspirations as well as friends: Robert Gordon, Jimmy McDonough, Stanley Booth, Nick Tosches, and Peter Guralnick.

For two decades I've been fortunate to work for and with several fine publications. I've been a proud contributor to *MOJO* magazine in the United Kingdom since 2003; though we operate at a remove, the following folks are always close to my heart: Jenny Bulley, Andrew Male, Phil Alexander, Ian Harrison, Lois Wilson, Keith Cameron, Danny Eccleston, and Piper Ferguson. While he was at *SPIN*, Steve Kandell assigned me a Replacements feature that was instrumental in making this book a reality. Steve remains my editor at BuzzFeed and a voice to whom I always listen. From my years at the *Phoenix New Times*, I need to thank the man who gave me a career, Gilbert Garcia, as well as Dewey Webb, Brian Smith, Dominic Salerno, and Jeremy Voas. At the *Chicago Reader:* Kiki Yablon, Alison True, Mark Athitakis, Jim Shapiro, Philip Montoro, Kate Schmidt, Sheila Sachs, and Elizabeth Tamny. In Memphis, at the *Commercial Appeal:* Louis Graham, Peggy Burch, John Beifuss, Chris Herrington, Richard Robbins, Peggy McKenzie, Mark Richens, Rosemary Nelms, and Jan Smith.

I was sustained throughout all my work on this book by the friendship of Ali Borghei, my ace Zac Crain (who always has my *dough-nuts*), and Charles A. Levy IV, who helped in untold ways. My life would not be complete without Sara Cina, Mark Zubia, Patrick Sedillo, John Fogarty, Jeff Pettit, Lawrence Zubia, Amy Lombardi, Sally Timms, Jon Langford, Adam Weiner, Derek Erdman, Jim Newberry, Alec Pappas, Scotti Moore, Katie Parker, Josh and Connie Venable, Jim Swafford, Robert Shipp, Bill Leen, Scott Johnson, Michael Lundsgaard, Amy and Jim Adkins, Brent Babb, Curtis Grippe, Steve Larson, G. Brian Scott, Sandra Quijas, and, especially, the late Doug Hopkins, without whose inspiration I'd still be writing articles on supply chain management.

In the end, I owe everything to my family, both extended and immediate, especially my baby sister Bebe, my Uncle Sam, and my Uncle Shirzad, who instilled in me a passion for music and writing from an early age. To my parents, Ted and Cima—who never made demands, loved unconditionally, and supported me in ways big and small—I hope to someday be worthy of all you've given me.

And last, a special thanks to my darlin' one, Lindsay "Coco" Hames, whose love made all the difference.

INDEX